Ventura Publisher®
for Windows™

INSIDE WINDOWS™ GUIDES

Ventura Publisher® for Windows™

Jesse Berst ▪ Byron Canfield ▪ Paul Henry

PUBLISHED BY
Microsoft Press
A Division of Microsoft Corporation
One Microsoft Way, Redmond, Washington 98052-6399

Copyright © 1991 by CompuThink, Incorporated

All rights reserved. No part of the contents of this book may be reproduced or transmitted in any form or by any means without the written permission of the publisher.

Library of Congress Cataloging-in-Publication Data
Berst, Jesse.
Ventura Publisher for Windows / Jesse Berst, Byron Canfield, Paul Henry.
     p.   cm.
  Includes index.
  ISBN 1-55615-335-X
   1. Desktop publishing. 2. Ventura Publisher (Computer program)
3. Microsoft Windows (Computer program) I. Canfield, Byron, 1953- .
II. Henry, Paul, 1948- . III. Title.
Z286.D47B49 1991
686.2'2544536—dc20   91-14103
                                               CIP

Printed and bound in the United States of America.

1 2 3 4 5 6 7 8 9 AGAG 6 5 4 3 2 1

Distributed to the book trade in Canada by Macmillan of Canada, a division of Canada publishing Corporation.

Distributed to the book trade outside the United States and Canada by Penguin Books Ltd.

Penguin Books Ltd., Harmondsworth, Middlesex, England
Penguin Books Australia Ltd., Ringwood, Victoria, Australia
Penguin Books N.Z. Ltd., 182-190 Wairau Road, Auckland 10, New Zealand
British Cataloging-in-Publication Data available.

Acquisitions Editor: Dean Holmes
Project Editors: Sally Brunsman and Eric Stroo
Copy Editor: Tim Toyoshima

Contents

Trademarks xii

Acknowledgments xiii

Part One: Orientation

1 Introduction 3
How to use this book

- What Ventura can do for you 4
- What this book can do for you 5
- What you need to get started 6
- How this book is organized 6
- How to use this book 8
- What the Easy Access system offers 10

2 Starting Out Smart 13
A hands-on introduction to Ventura for Windows

- The guided tour 13
- The road to success 32
- Continuing on 36

Part Two: Chapters and Style Sheets

3 Building Basic Styles 41
How to set up and use a simple format

- How Ventura creates documents 41
- Basic style sheet skills 43
- Basic style sheet strategies 49
- Setting the font 50
- Aligning and indenting text 54

Controlling spacing 60

Controlling breaks 66

Creating ruling lines and boxes 76

Continuing on 84

4 Building the Underlying Page 87
How to create master page formats

What is the underlying page? 87

Setting the size and layout of the page 89

Setting margins and columns 94

Creating headers and footers 99

Creating vertical rules 108

Continuing on 114

5 Building Advanced Styles 117
How to unleash Ventura's full formatting power

Creating bullets 118

Creating big first characters 124

Creating tabs and leader dots 132

Numbering automatically 138

Vertical justification 154

Fine-tuning text formats 161

Controlling hyphenation 178

Continuing on 182

Part Three: Text

6 Handling Text in Ventura 187
How to load, create, and edit Text in Ventura

- Getting text in and out of Ventura 188
- Creating text in Ventura 193
- Editing text in Ventura 198
- Continuing on 206

7 Creating Text with Other Programs 209
How to create and preformat text files for Ventura

- Choosing a file format 209
- Creating the text 214
- Using databases and spreadsheets 216
- Pretagging text 220
- Preformatting text with bracket codes 223
- Continuing on 238

8 Creating Tables 241
How to enhance your documents with attractive tables

- Inserting a table 242
- Adding table text 250
- Formatting a table 250
- Creating tables in a word processor 261
- Creating tables with a spreadsheet 264
- Continuing on 266

Part Four: Pictures

9 Creating Pictures in Ventura 271
How to create pictures with Ventura's Graphic tools

- Creating simple shapes 273
- Advanced tips and tricks 285
- Continuing on 289

10 Creating Pictures with Other Programs 291
How to create Ventura-compatible pictures with outside programs

- Images versus line art 291
- Choosing the file format 298
- Continuing on 308

11 Loading and Placing Pictures 311
How to import picture files into a Ventura document

- Creating frames 311
- Loading pictures into frames 324
- Adding margins inside frames 328
- Anchoring frames 331
- Continuing on 338

12 Enhancing and Editing Pictures 341
How to edit pictures in Ventura

- Adding captions 341
- Adding ruling boxes and lines 351
- Padding pictures 357
- Scaling pictures 358
- Cropping pictures 363
- Continuing on 366

Part Five: Printing and Advanced Features

13 Printing Ventura Documents 371
How to print documents and work with fonts

- Understanding printing 371
- Preparing to print 378
- Printing a single chapter 391
- Printing multiple chapters 397
- Printing special jobs 400
- Continuing on 415

14 Creating Indexes and Tables of Contents 417
How to automate indexing and contents listings

- Creating an index 418
- Creating a table of contents 440
- Continuing on 452

15 Creating Footnotes and Equations 455
How to add footnotes and equations to Ventura documents

- Creating footnotes 455
- Creating and editing equations 471
- Continuing on 478

16 Managing Ventura Files 481
How to take control of your document files

- Working with chapter files 481
- Working with publication files 486
- Continuing on 492

17 Power and Speedup Techniques 495
How to use power techniques to save production time

    Automating functions with macros 495

    Using third-party utilities 501

    Creating chapter templates 506

    Production tricks and tips 510

    Tips for filenames 513

    Customizing Ventura 525

    Editing the chapter file 530

    Continuing on 535

Part Six: Hands-On

18 Building a Business Proposal 541
How to build a single-column report or proposal

    Planning the proposal 542

    Loading the files 544

    Setting up the underlying page 547

    Applying and refining the style sheet 549

    Adding pictures 557

    Printing the proposal 559

    Continuing on 560

19 Building a Newsletter 563
How to build a three-column newsletter

Planning the newsletter 564

Loading the base document 565

Setting up the underlying page and text frames 567

Loading text 577

Refining the style sheet 578

Loading and adjusting pictures 587

Copyfitting and final touch-ups 593

Continuing on 598

Part Seven: Resources

20 Portfolio 603
A sampler of design ideas

Continuing on 620

21 Rapid Reference 623
Job aids and reference materials to speed up production

22 Glossary 659

Index 664

Trademarks

This book contains product names for computer hardware, software, utilities, and equipment. Many of the designations used by manufacturers and sellers are claimed as trademarks. Microsoft Press and CompuThink have made every effort to print these designations with the capitalization and punctuation used by the trademark holder. Microsoft Press and CompuThink attest that they have used these designations only for editorial purposes and to benefit the trademark holder with no intent to infringe on the trademarks.

Adobe®, Adobe Type Manager®, and PostScript® are registered trademarks of Adobe Systems, Inc. PageMaker® is a registered trademark of Aldus Corporation. Macintosh® and LaserWriter® are registered trademarks of Apple Computer, Inc. dBase® is a registered trademark of Ashton-Tate Corporation. AutoCad® is a registered trademark of Autodesk, Inc. Bitstream® is a registered trademark and Fontware™ is a trademark of Bitstream, Inc. Borland® and Reflex® are registered trademarks of Borland International, Inc. MacPaint® is a registered trademark of Claris Corporation. CompuServe® is a registered trademark of CompuServe, Inc. Arts&Letters™ is a trademark of Computer Support Corporation. Gem™ is a trademark of Digital Research, Inc. Epson® is a registered trademark of Epson America, Inc. FoxBase™ is a trademark of Fox Software, Inc. VideoShow™ is a trademark of General Parametrics. Hewlett-Packard® is a registered trademark and NewWave™ is a trademark of Hewlett-Packard Company. Intel® is a registered trademark of Intel Corporation. IBM® and PS/2® are registered trademarks of International Business Machines, Inc. ITC Avant Garde Gothic®, ITC Bookman®, ITC Zapf Chancery®, and ITC Zapf Dingbats® are registered trademarks of International Typeface Corporation. Helvetica®, Linotronic®, and Palatino® are registered trademarks of Linotype AG and its subsidiaries. 1-2-3®, Freelance®, and Lotus® are registered trademarks of Lotus Development Corporation. Micrografx® is a registered trademark of Micrografx, Inc. Microsoft® and MS-DOS® are registered trademarks and Windows™ is a trademark of Microsoft Corporation. Nantucket® is a registered trademark and Clipper™ is a trademark of Nantucket Corporation. NEC® is a registered trademark of NEC Corporation. Bridge™ is a trademark of Softbridge Microsystems Corporation. Ventura Publisher® is a registered trademark of Ventura Software, Inc. WordPerfect® is a registered trademark of WordPerfect Corporation. WordStar® is a registered trademark of WordStar Corporation. XyWrite™ is a trademark of XYQUEST, Inc. PC Paintbrush® is a registered trademark of ZSoft Corporation.

Acknowledgments

The authors extend their thanks to the cast and crew at Microsoft, including Jim Brown, Sally Brunsman, Dean Holmes, Mike Morrow, David Rygmyr, Eric Stroo, and Lori Walker.

Our thanks as well to Ventura Software, and especially to Cindy Howard, who reviewed the manuscript for technical accuracy.

Our appreciation to our field testers Martha Lubow and Stuart Trippel.

Many thanks to David Perrell for his sleepless nights working on **PS✤x**, his file extractor utility, which saved many hours in the final production. Single pages were extracted from chapter print files using **PS✤x**™, GEM/Ventura and Windows PostScript File Page Extractor. This utility extracts single pages and/or ranges of pages from print files created either with the GEM version of Ventura or any multi-page Windows application that creates PostScript files that adhere to the Adobe PostScript 3.0 specification. Unfortunately, it was completed just a little to late to include in chapter 13, Printing Ventura Documents. **PS✤x**™ is available from Hearn/Perrell, 23022 Hatteras St., Woodland Hills, CA 91367, (213) 394-8373.

And heartfelt thanks to our patient, long-suffering editors, Tim Toyoshima and Scott Dunn.

Part One:
■ Orientation

1 Introduction

How to use this book

- **What Ventura can do for you** 4
- **What this book can do for you** 5
- **What you need to get started** 6
- **How this book is organized** 6
- **How to use this book** 8
- **What the Easy Access system offers** 10

We're going to make your life easier. That's a pretty big promise. But if you work with Ventura Publisher for Windows, we think it's a promise we can keep. We, the three coauthors of this book, have been using Ventura for years. We have trained hundreds of users. We have created thousands of pages, from flyers to newsletters to prize-winning books.

Among the three of us, we've probably made every mistake there is to make (some of them more than once). Now, we're going to steer you around the pitfalls. More than that, we're going to show you the shortcuts, the tricks, the secrets, and the turbo-charged, pedal-to-the-metal power techniques we've developed to push Ventura to the max.

That makes it sound like we'll be spending much of the book on show-off stunts and glitzy graphic effects. Not so. Like you, we spend the bulk of our time with routine documents—reports, proposals, newsletters, manuals, and books. So we spend most of our time figuring out ways to make these everyday documents easier and faster to produce. Yes, our techniques often depend on inside information and undocumented capabilities. But no, these methods are not hard to use or understand.

So this book is ideally suited for beginning and intermediate users. It steps you through all facets of Ventura with a practical, real-world, let's-get-some-work-done approach. Still, it doesn't ignore advanced users. You'll find a wealth of power techniques, design samples, and high-octane effects, especially in the later chapters.

Are you ready to put Ventura's power on your side? The first step is to skim this chapter. It explains what you can expect from Ventura and from this book. And it shows you several different ways to use this book, depending on your needs, your skill level, and your interests.

What Ventura can do for you

With Ventura Publisher, you can generate advertisements, books, brochures, directories, forms, labels, letters, manuals, memos, newsletters, overhead transparencies, parts lists, press releases, reports—the list is almost endless. From its inception, Ventura has been the best desktop publishing program available on IBM PC-compatible personal computers. Now, with the Windows version, Ventura gives you even more possibilities:

- *Switch back and forth between programs.* Now you can jump from Ventura to another program without reloading and restarting each time. When you return to Ventura, you are at the exact spot where you left off.
- *Use Windows' accessories to bolster Ventura.* For instance, you can use Windows' built-in File Manager to copy, move, and rename files; or Windows Paintbrush to edit a picture; or Terminal to send a file to a typesetting service bureau.
- *Use any display or printer available to Windows.* If it works with Windows, it works with Ventura.
- *Print in the background while you go back to work.* Windows' built-in Print Manager handles the printing of long documents while you go back to work on the screen.

At the same time, the Windows version of Ventura continues to offer the same features and advantages that made the GEM version a bestseller:

- *Work with your favorite software.* Ventura lets you import pictures and text from your favorite graphics and word processing programs.
- *Save disk space.* Some page layout programs copy text and graphics into separate files, more than doubling the disk space required. Ventura merely "borrows" these files without duplicating them. The result is more storage space for you.
- *Make changes easily and quickly.* Ventura stores formats in style sheets. Thanks to this versatile feature, you can change a design in seconds. Best of all, the changes apply instantly to every page in the document. That spares you the pain of having to make corrections page by page.

■ *Format long documents efficiently.* Ventura lets you create tables of contents, generate indexes, number lists automatically, label figures and tables, cross reference other pages, use footnotes, and print hundreds of pages in one pass. You can't find a better program for producing books, catalogs, reports, technical manuals, or lengthy documents (Figure 1-1).

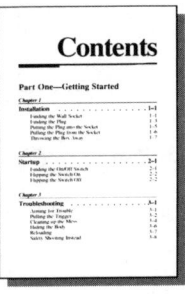

Figure 1-1. Ventura has the advanced features needed to produce directories, manuals, handbooks, and other long documents.

What this book can do for you

This volume is more than a book. It's a collection of tools designed to help you get the most out of Ventura in the least amount of time. These include:

- A clear and concise instructional course in Ventura Publisher
- Clearly marked hands-on examples to try out what you've learned
- A reference resource you can return to again and again for guidance on difficult functions
- Sample documents to show you what Ventura can do in the hands of the pros
- A visual guide called Easy Access at the end of each chapter that shows you where to turn for more help and information
- Keyboard shortcuts, typefaces, character sets, and other quick-reference charts you can photocopy and keep next to your computer (Figure 1-2)

Tip: Be sure to explore Chapter 21, "Rapid Reference," a summary of commands, codes, keyboard shortcuts, and other helpful guides. This chapter is marked by a thumb tab along the edge, so that you can flip to it quickly.

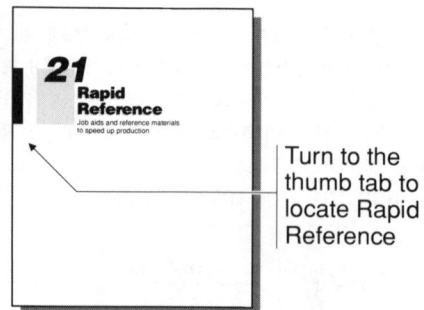

Figure 1-2.
The Rapid Reference chapter at the back of the book puts the tools you need into one convenient spot.

Turn to the thumb tab to locate Rapid Reference

What you need to get started

You'll need the following three things to use this book:

1. A personal computer with an Intel 80286 (or more powerful) processor, 2MB of RAM, a hard disk, and a mouse or pointing device. (Although it's theoretically possible to run Ventura from the keyboard, you'll find it much faster if you have a mouse, trackball, or other pointing device.)
2. Windows 3. You'll need to install Windows before you can install and use Ventura.
3. Ventura Publisher Windows version. You must install Ventura before you can use this book.

How this book is organized

Okay, your computer is set to go, you've got the software installed—but you don't know how to use Ventura. You've come to the right place. This book follows a common-sense strategy for developing Ventura skills. This strategy has four parts:

- Instructions
- Practice
- Samples
- References and tools

Almost every section of this book includes these elements. First, you get guidance and a general overview. Then you get an example, so that you see how the theory works in real life. Next, you see some inspiring samples (when appropriate). Finally, at the end of each chapter, we show you where to go for details on related topics or for job aids and reference materials.

To make it easier to find your way around, we've signaled notes, tips, warnings, and examples with a special format. For instance:

Note: Here's an example of a note. Look for a similar format for tips, warnings, and examples.

We've also divided the book into seven sections. Let's look at these in a little more detail.

Part One: Orientation
You're reading the orientation section right now. It helps you get your bearings with Ventura by providing a road map and some experiences so you'll feel more at home. Part One also gives you some basic skills to help you find your way around Ventura and this book.

Part Two: Chapters and Style Sheets
In this section, you'll build the foundation for your entire Ventura experience. In just three chapters, you'll learn the structure of Ventura files—and its style sheets, which are the key to designing and creating attractive publications.

Part Three: Text
As you might guess, Part Three is about words: how to create, format, edit, and import text into Ventura. You'll even learn how to create great-looking tables with minimal effort.

Part Four: Pictures
Here you'll get the skills to become a pro at creating, loading, cropping, and editing artwork for your publications.

Part Five: Printing and Advanced Features
In this section, you'll learn how to print pages with a maximum of quality and a minimum of pain. We'll also give you the lowdown on the use and abuse of fonts. And here's where we shift into high gear using Ventura's special features. You'll find out how to create great-looking tables of contents, indexes, footnotes, and equations. You'll also learn our favorite techniques for streamlining the Ventura process and managing your files.

Part Six: Hands-On
This is our cookbook section. We'll walk you through a couple of typical documents so you can see how they're done and then try them on your own (Figure 1-3).

Figure 1-3. Part Six gives you step-by-step instructions for creating these two documents.

 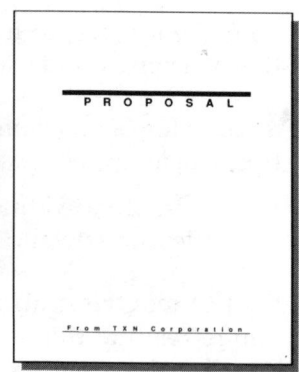

Part Seven: Resources
This section shows you examples of Ventura's work from experienced pros and throws in a few of their special hints. It also includes "Rapid Reference," a collection of reference tools and job aids.

How to use this book

You may be wondering, "Where do I begin?" We've organized this book so no matter what your background, you can get the information you need quickly and easily. Just find the best description of your experience level in Table 1-1, on page 9. Then use its suggestions to map out the learning strategy that's best for you.

Table 1-1. *Learning strategies*

If you are...	Read this	For this reason
Brand new to Windows	*Microsoft Windows User's Guide*	Provides familiarity with Windows' basic functions before you tackle Ventura
New to Ventura and have enough time	The entire book start to finish	Ensures a thorough command of Ventura's many features
New to Ventura and have to learn it in intermittent sessions	Chapter 2	Gives you a feel for Ventura and an understanding of basic terms and approaches
	Chapters 3, 4, and 13	Give you a basic foundation in core concepts
	Chapters 21	Includes a valuable collection of tools you'll use every day
	Chapters 5, 7, 11, and others as needed	Provide additional coverage of core topics; read as needed
	Index, Glossary, Easy Access system	Help you find what you need, understand new material, and spot related topics
Upgrading from the GEM version	Chapter 2	Summarizes new features found in Windows version; glance through to see what it looks like
An occasional user	Chapters 2, 3, 4, 5, 7, 11, 13	Provide must-know essentials for using Ventura
	Chapter 21	Includes command summaries
A full-time user	Entire book	Ensures complete mastery; if short on time, follow the strategy for beginners above but come back and learn everything as soon as possible
A power user	Index	Helps you chase down topics you need now
	Chapters 16 and 17	Give you file management strategies and power techniques
	Chapters 20 and 21	Provide design ideas and job aids

What the Easy Access system offers

To make it as easy as possible to find your way around this book, each chapter ends with an Easy Access table. The Easy Access system presents a visual road map to related topics so you can customize your learning course. You get exactly what you want when you want it. Later, when you need to learn other skills, you can follow the Easy Access map down a different path. You decide what you want to learn and how you want to learn it.

Want to see how Easy Access works? Following is an Easy Access table for this first chapter. Use it to help you decide where you should go next as you take your first steps toward mastering Ventura.

Happy desktop publishing.

Easy Access

For more info on...	See chapter...
Taking a hands-on guided tour of Ventura plus using a road map for successful document-building	**2** Starting Out Smart
Building a business report step by step	**18** Building a Business Proposal
Building a newsletter step by step	**19** Building a Newsletter
Studying samples of real-life Ventura documents	**20** Portfolio
Locating job aids that make working with Ventura easier	**21** Rapid Reference

2 Starting Out Smart

A hands-on introduction to Ventura for Windows

- **The guided tour** 13
- **The road to success** 32
- **Continuing on** 36

The best way to get to any destination is to know where you're going and how you're going to get there. Reading this chapter will do both for you. To start off, we're going to hop right into Ventura and go for a test drive. In this hands-on tour, you'll load and format a simple document using text, style sheets, and pictures supplied with the program. You'll also grasp the basic terms and concepts of Ventura that are used throughout this book.

Now that you've revved up your engine, the second part of this chapter will give you a road map to your destination: the creation of any document using Ventura Publisher. Use this map each time you build a document, and you'll avoid the dead ends and meandering byways that can slow down your publishing project.

The guided tour

What's the best way to use the guided tour? Just enjoy it. Don't try to memorize what you're seeing or doing. Don't worry if there are slight discrepancies between your screen and the pictures in this chapter. And don't think you have to understand everything that's happening before you go on to the next step. We'll explain each concept in detail in later chapters. Feel free to stop and explore on your own; when you're ready, come back and finish the rest of the steps.

And what are those steps? Our guided tour involves four simple procedures:

1. Starting the program.
2. Exploring the screen and the interface.
3. Adding text, style, and pictures to a document.
4. Saving the document.

Note: If you haven't already installed Ventura and its sample files, do so now. Start Windows and open the Program Manager before beginning the guided tour. (Unless you have changed the original settings, Windows automatically starts with the Program Manager window open.)

Starting Ventura

You start Ventura the way you start any Windows application. The easiest way is to open Program Manager and double-click on the Ventura icon. The Ventura install program placed this icon in a program group called Windows Applications. To start the tour:

1. To start Ventura double-click on the icon (Figure 2-1).

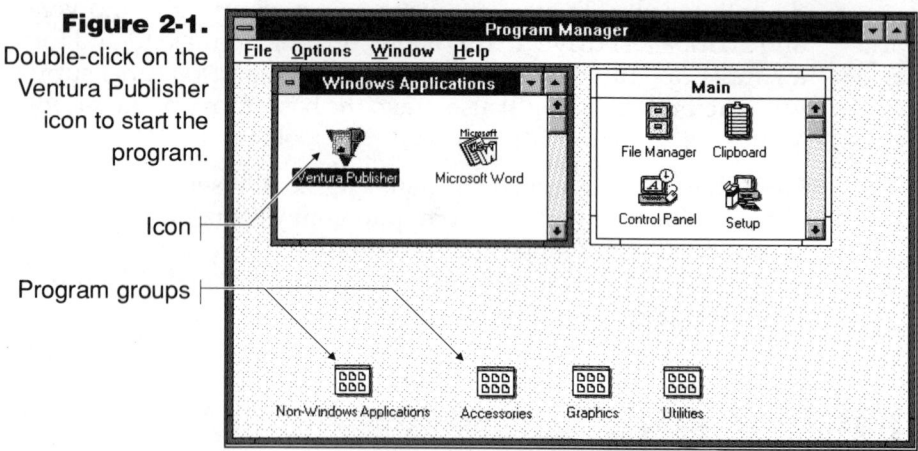

Figure 2-1. Double-click on the Ventura Publisher icon to start the program.

After starting Ventura, you're ready to start exploring its screen.

Exploring the Ventura screen

Before you start building the document, take a minute to explore the elements on the screen and in the dialog boxes. Let's examine the Ventura screen. Locate the elements shown in Figure 2-2.

Note: If your screen doesn't look similar to the one shown in Figure 2-2, choose Set Preferences from the Edit menu. In the Set Preferences dialog box, click on the arrow next to the Text To Greek list box to see the available options. Click on None. Then click on OK. Next, click on the View menu and be sure a check mark appears next to the items listed below. If no check mark is showing, choose the item by clicking on its name.

- Reduced View
- Show Column Guides
- Column Snap
- Toolbox Window
- Tag List Window
- File List Window

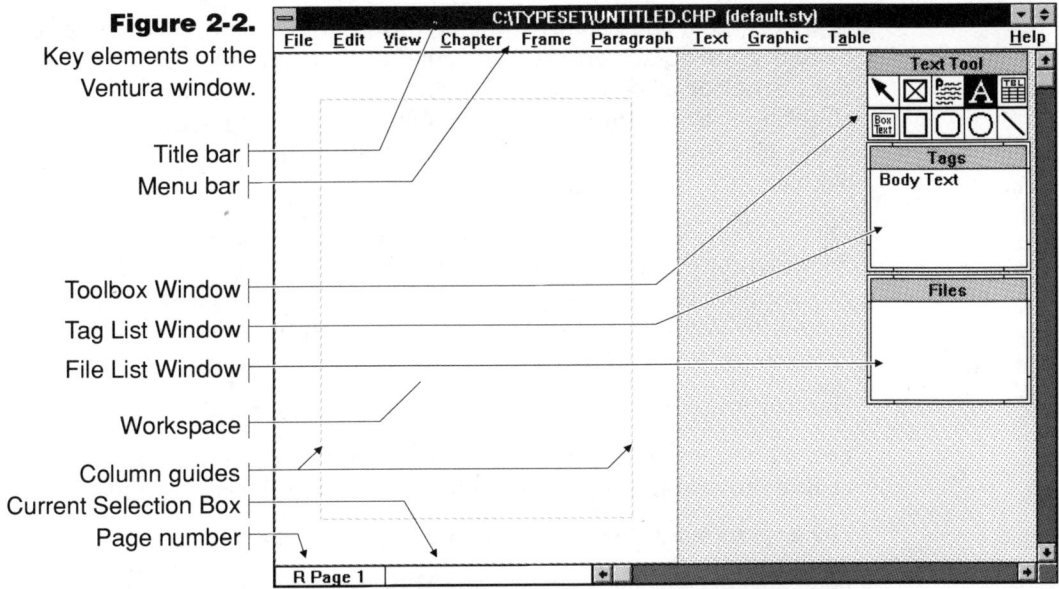

Figure 2-2. Key elements of the Ventura window.

Note: Don't panic if your screen display doesn't exactly match Figure 2-2. For example, it doesn't matter if your View menu shows other items checked in addition to those mentioned above. Also, don't be concerned if the fonts (alphabet characters) on your screen differ from the pictures in this chapter; you'll learn how to adjust those in Chapter 13, "Printing Ventura Documents." Finally, don't worry if your screen shows a different style sheet name on the title bar. You'll be loading a new style sheet in a few moments anyway.

The *title bar* shows the name of the current document. If you haven't given the document a name yet, you see the word "UNTITLED.CHP." The title bar also shows the name of the current style sheet in parentheses. A *style sheet* is a computer file that contains the tags (the formatting instructions) for a document.

The *menu bar* contains the names of the menus. The menus, in turn, contain the *commands* you use to operate Ventura. To choose a command, click on the menu name in the menu bar, which drops down the menu, and then click again on the name of the command.

The *Toolbox* displays icons representing Ventura's key functions. On the top line are the Frame Tool, the Add Frame tool, the Paragraph Tool, the Text Tool, and the Table Tool. On the bottom line are five drawing tools. To select a tool, click on its icon. The title above the Toolbox shows which tool is currently selected.

The *Tag List Window* shows the tags that are currently available to format your document. A *tag* is a set of instructions that describes the format or appearance of a paragraph: typeface, size, spacing, alignment, and other attributes. After you create a tag, you can apply it to any paragraph for instant formatting. In Figure 2-2, the list has only one tag, called Body Text.

The *File List Window* is empty in Figure 2-2. However, as you build documents, you can bring in text files from word processors and picture files from graphics programs. After you load text or pictures into Ventura, their filenames appear in the File List Window. From there, you can place them into your document.

The *workspace* is the area where you actually create the document.

The *column guides* represent the document's boundaries. They are visible only on the screen, not when you print the document.

The *page number* shows which page you are on at the moment.

The *Current Selection Box* gives additional information. When you click on something, a brief description appears inside the box.

Exploring dialog boxes

Much of Ventura's power lurks behind the scenes in bite-sized, digestible chunks known as dialog boxes. Dialog boxes appear after you choose a command from a menu. Dialog boxes include a number of different features to let you specify your choices:

- Text boxes
- List boxes
- Command buttons
- Option buttons
- Check boxes

If you do not already understand the distinctions between these various buttons and boxes, turn to your *Microsoft Windows User's Guide* and see Chapter 2, "Basic Skills," for a review. After you learn these differences, you'll know how to take control of Ventura.

The elements we've described so far form the key parts of Ventura. Let's use those elements to build a simple business report.

Note: If you are brand new to Ventura and to desktop publishing, skim the nearby sidebar "Ventura Terminology" before you start working on the report.

Trying some text

When you started Ventura, you began with an untitled document. That document looks a little bleak with nothing in it. Let's fix that by adding some text. Bringing text onto the page consists of two steps, *loading* and *placing*. Like most Windows tasks, these tasks involve nothing more complicated than pointing and clicking.

Loading a text file
To load a text file into your untitled document:

2. Choose Load Text/Picture from the File menu (Figure 2-3).

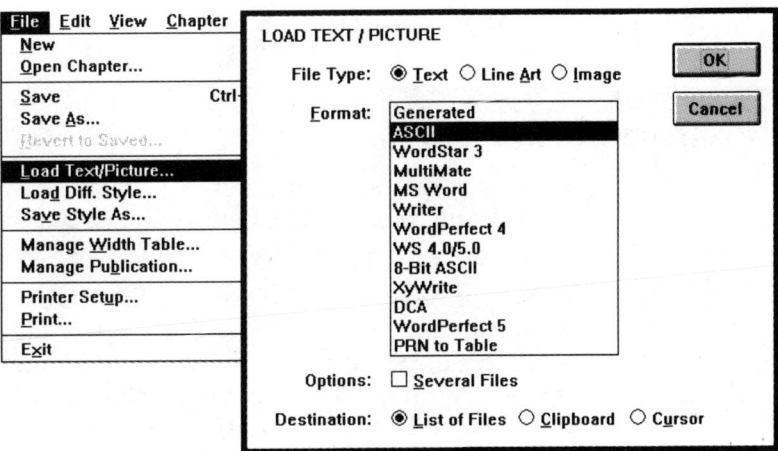

Figure 2-3. You use Load Text/Picture from the File menu to tell Ventura what type of file you want to load.

3. Take a moment to explore the different parts of this dialog box before you use it to load a file. Click on the Text option button from the File Type buttons (the Text button may already be selected). Now click on the Image button and notice how the items in the list box below the buttons change. Now click on Text again.

4. In the Format list box, click on ASCII. From the Destination buttons, click on the List Of Files button. (Note that these options may already be selected.) Finally, be sure the Options check box called Several Files is *not* checked. Click on OK. As soon as you click on OK, the Open File dialog box appears.

Note: If you installed Ventura on a drive other than C:, substitute that drive letter in place of C: throughout this chapter.

You have at least two ways to select the text file that you want to load into Ventura. You can simply type the full path and name into the text box. Or you can use the mouse to navigate to the directory where the file is stored. Using the Directory list box (labeled Path Is), you can double-click your way to your desired directory. To open a directory, double-click on the directory name, which appears in brackets. To move back to the parent directory, double-click on the [..] symbol. In each directory, you'll see a list of files in that directory with the TXT extension. You use the scroll bars to move down the list until you see your file and click on the filename. Try it:

5. Select the file SAMPLE.TXT from the \TYPESET directory and click on Open. Or double-click on the filename (Figure 2-4). After you select the file, Ventura returns you to the workspace.

Ventura terminology

If you are new to Ventura, one of the first things you should do is study the terms listed below. This is important because Ventura often uses ordinary words in new ways.

Document refers to any piece or publication created by Ventura. A document can be a business card, a 700-page manual, or anything in between. In Ventura, a document is composed of many electronic files, including a chapter file and a style sheet, plus optional text files and picture files.

A *chapter file* is the central piece of a Ventura document. Think of it as a supervisor that controls and refers to all the other files—text, graphics, style sheets. Because the chapter file is the most important part, many people use the shortened term *chapter* as a synonym for document, as in "Let's create a new chapter."

A *style sheet* controls the appearance of a document. It contains formatting rules for the various elements on the page. For instance, a style sheet stores the information that tells Ventura how big to make the headlines in a newsletter, what typeface to use, how much space to leave below the headlines, and so on.

A *text file* (also called a *word-processing file*) contains the words in your document. Generally, the easiest way to get text into Ventura is to type a file with your word processor and load it into Ventura. A Ventura chapter can contain more than one text file.

A *picture file* (also called a *graphics file*) contains electronic pictures. Ventura includes some primitive drawing tools, but for

Placing a text file

Notice anything different after loading the text file? Some of you may see the text file already placed onto the page (we'll tell you why in a moment). (If so, you can skip doing steps 6 through 8—but read them anyway.) Others may see a blank page. In either case, the File List Window shows the name of the SAMPLE.TXT file you just loaded.

After a filename appears in the File List Window, you can place it in your document. All you have to do is tell Ventura where to put the file on the page. Here's how:

6. Select the Frame Tool (the arrow at the top left of the Toolbox).

---

sophisticated pictures you will want to create picture files with an outside program and then load them into the Ventura document.

A *publication* is a collection of several chapters. By linking chapters together, you can perform certain tasks with them all at once. For instance, you can print the chapters with one command, or create a table of contents, or build an index, or copy all the chapters to a different disk.

A *frame* is a container that can hold either text files or picture files. You draw frames onto the page, then you place files inside the frames. This sidebar, for instance, is a text file that was placed inside a gray frame.

Loading a file into Ventura means making it available for use in the document. When you load a file—whether text or picture—Ventura converts it to a format it can understand. Then it makes a record of the file's location on your disk. From then on, it knows where to find that file for use in constructing the final document.

Placing a file means telling Ventura where you want the file to go. For example, if you load a picture, Ventura still doesn't know where it should appear on the page or how big it should be. To tell Ventura what to do, you draw a frame on the page to act as a container. Then you place the picture file inside the frame. You can't place a file until you've loaded it.

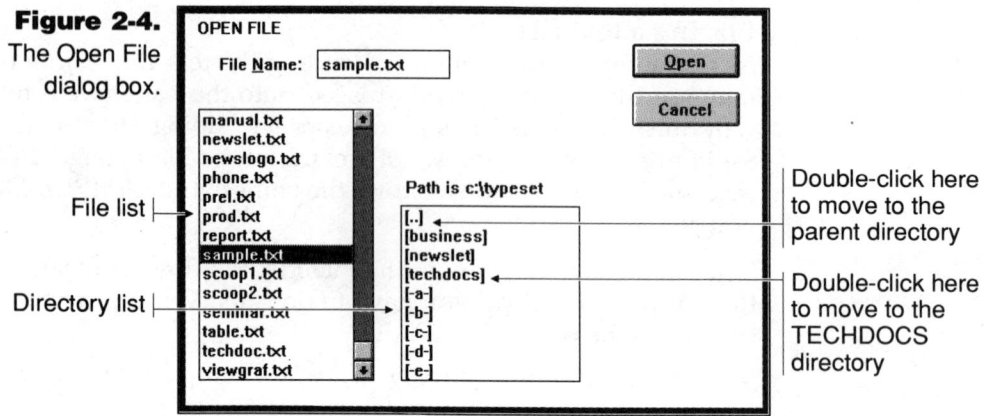

Figure 2-4. The Open File dialog box.

7. Click once on the workspace so that the eight black boxes called *sizing handles* appear around the edges (Figure 2-5).

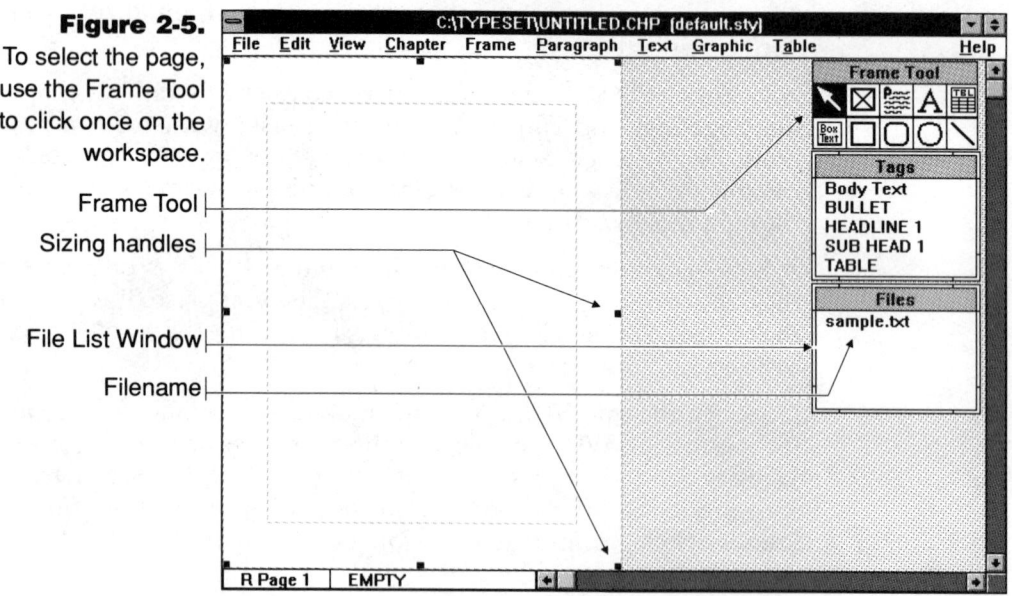

Figure 2-5. To select the page, use the Frame Tool to click once on the workspace.

8. Click once on SAMPLE.TXT in the File List Window.

The text flows onto the page (Figure 2-6). (Again, don't be concerned if yours looks slightly different.) Your next step is to load a style sheet that makes your document resemble this example.

As we noted before, some of you may not need to place the text file. After you load the file and return to the workspace, the text file may be on the page already. This occurs if you select a page or a

Figure 2-6.
The text file flows onto the page after you click on its name in the File List Window.

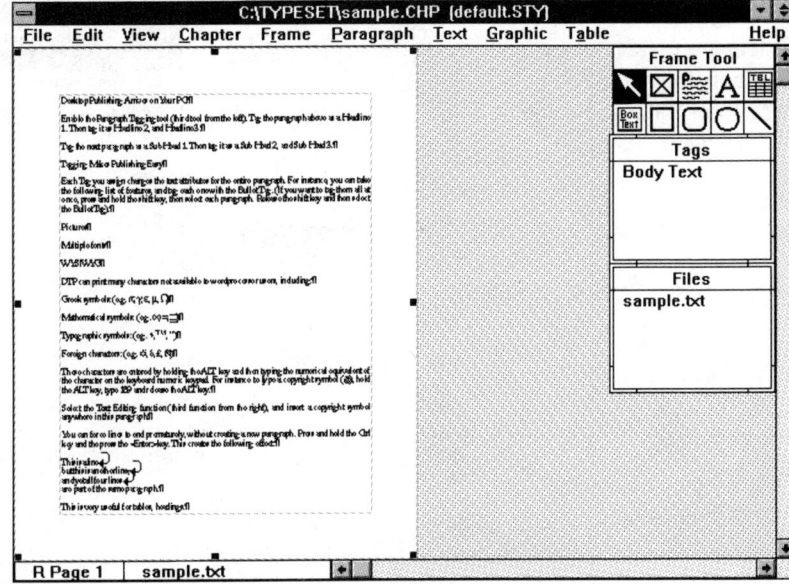

frame *before* you load a file. Ventura assumes that you want to put the file onto that page or frame and flows it inside automatically.

That's all there is to placing text in a document. Now, let's practice some editing techniques.

Editing text

You can add, delete, or copy text, or change its attributes. To work with text, you use the Text Tool:

9. Select the Text Tool from the Toolbox (the letter *A*).

When you move the cursor back to the workspace, you'll see that it has changed from an arrow to an I-beam shape to remind you that the Text Tool is active. Now let's try selecting some text and giving it an attribute such as boldface. Here's how:

10. Choose Normal View from the View menu.

11. Select the phrase "Paragraph Tagging" from the first paragraph by placing the cursor in front of the word *Paragraph* and dragging the mouse to the right until the phrase is highlighted.

12. Choose Bold from the Text menu to make the selected text boldface (Figure 2-7).

Now that you've sampled the basics of loading text and using the Text Tool, let's dress up that text a little.

Figure 2-7.
Select the phrase "Paragraph Tagging" and then choose Bold from the Text menu.

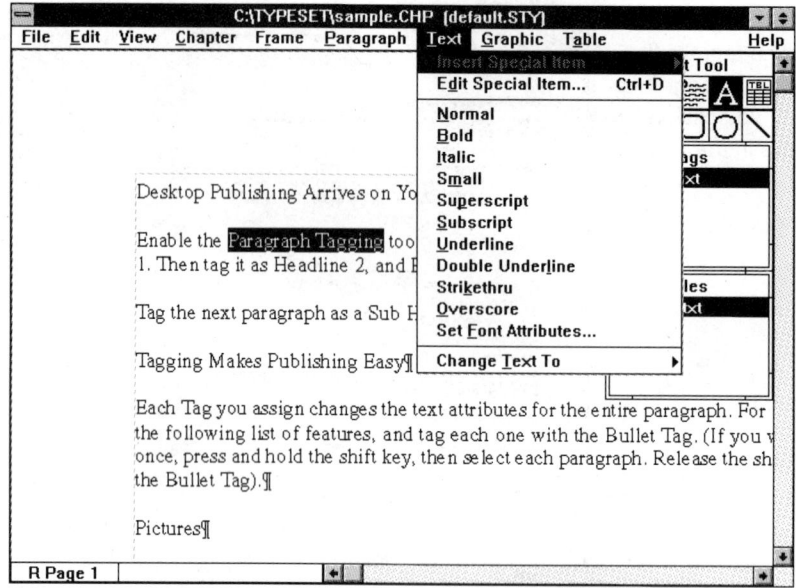

Adding some style

It's time to add some panache to your page with Ventura's powerful formatting tools. The heart of these tools is the style sheet, which consists of a collection of tags. Tags are an extremely powerful yet simple method of applying formatting information—such as typeface, line spacing, indents, ruling lines, and more—to a paragraph. The process of applying these formats is called *tagging* (Figure 2-8).

Figure 2-8.
To change the appearance of text, you attach a tag, which contains formatting instructions.

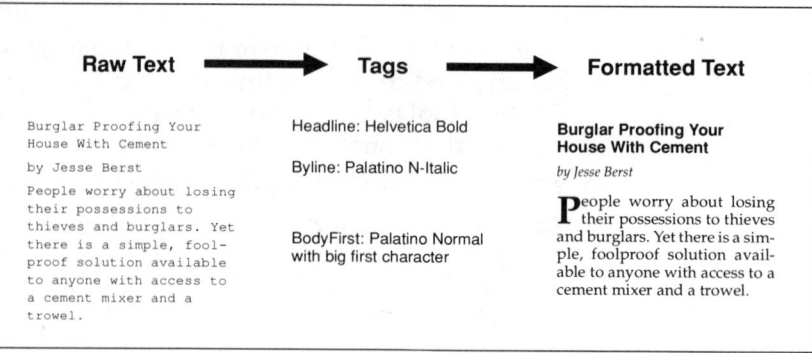

Loading a style sheet

To use a style sheet, you must first load it into the document. Then you use the mouse to tag individual paragraphs, thereby changing their appearance.

Here's how you load a style sheet:

13. Choose Load Diff. Style from the File menu. The Open File dialog box appears (Figure 2-9).

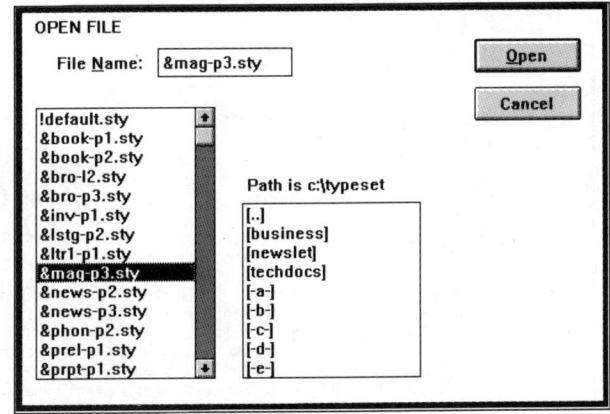

Figure 2-9. Use the Load Diff. Style command to select the style sheet called &MAG-P3.STY from the \TYPESET directory.

14. Select the style sheet &MAG-P3.STY from the \TYPESET directory.

15. Click on Open to return to the workspace.

When you return to the workspace, look at the title bar. You'll see the style sheet name in parentheses following the name of the document (When you place a text file on the page of a document that hasn't been saved, Ventura gives that document a temporary name that matches the text file—in this case, SAMPLE.CHP). You'll also notice that the SAMPLE.TXT text is now formatted with three columns. Now you can apply individual tags from this new style sheet to the text you loaded earlier.

Applying tags

Applying a tag is a simple two-step process. First, you tell Ventura which paragraph you want to work on. Then you tell Ventura which tag to apply. You can perform both steps easily with the mouse.

16. Use the scroll bars to move to the top of the document so the first paragraph is visible.

17. Select the Paragraph Tool from the Toolbox (the one with the *P* and several wavy lines).

When you move the cursor back to the workspace, you'll see that it resembles a tiny paragraph to denote the Paragraph Tool.

18. Click on the first paragraph on the page ("Desktop Publishing Arrives on Your PC!"), to select it (Figure 2-10).

Figure 2-10. Select the Paragraph Tool, then click on the first paragraph.

Paragraph Tool
Tag List Window

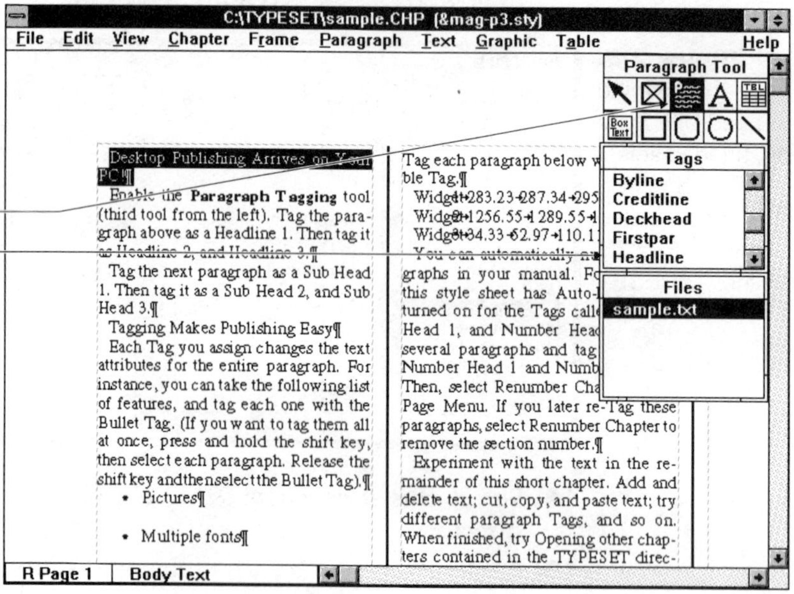

19. Scroll down the Tag List Window until you see the tag called "Headline." Now click once on Headline. As soon as you click on the tag name, the text changes appearance.

20. Choose Reduced View from the View menu to see how the paragraph's format has changed (Figure 2-11).

Now, you're about to experience the true power of style sheets. By loading a new style sheet, you can completely change the look of a document. Try it for yourself.

21. Choose Load Diff. Style from the File menu to load the style sheet SAMPLE1.STY from the \TYPESET directory. As before, click on Open to return to the workspace. (Hint: If you don't see SAMPLE1.STY in the dialog box list, use the scroll bars to scroll the list until it's visible).

As soon as you load the new style sheet, the document changes from three columns to two (Figure 2-12). The formatting of your

Figure 2-11.
The selected paragraph after applying the Headline tag.

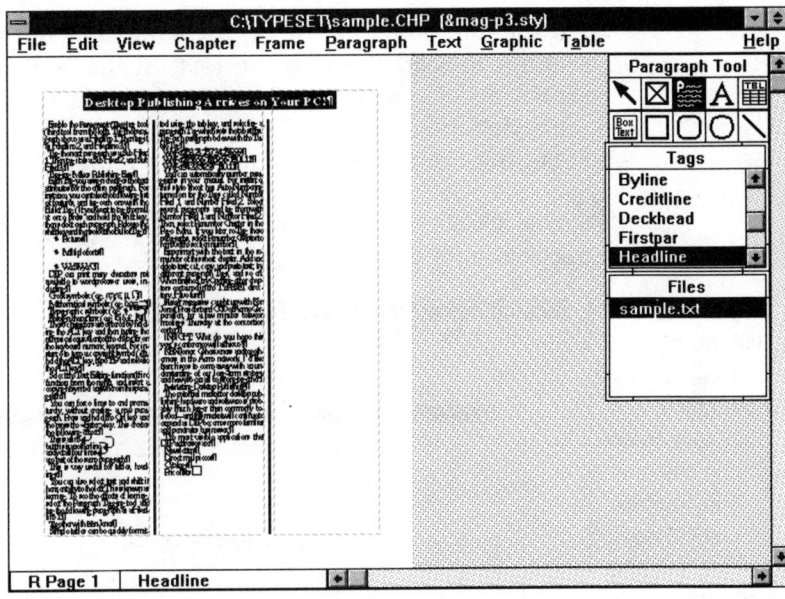

headline has changed. And the list of tags in the Tag List Window is different, representing your new formatting options.

Figure 2-12.
The new style sheet SAMPLE1.STY has two columns instead of three.

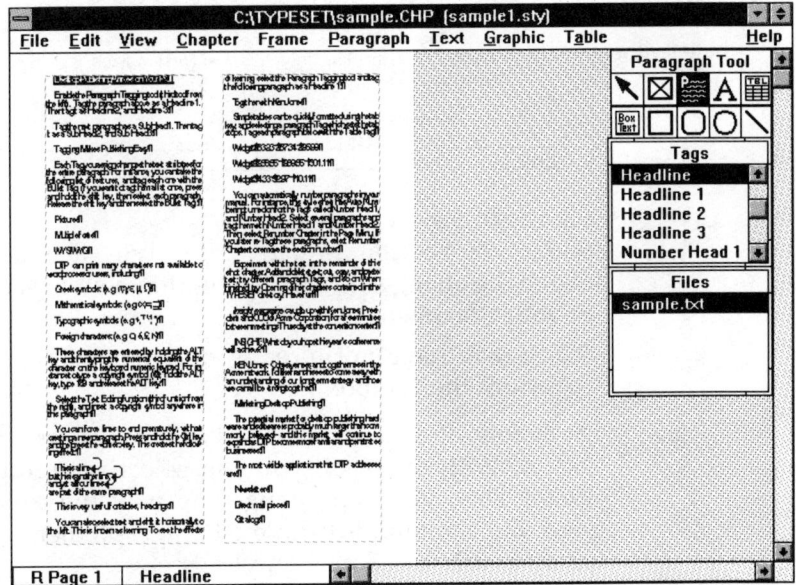

22. Choose Normal View from the View menu to return to a closer view of the page.

Now, explore tagging on your own. Pause in the guided tour long enough to read through the text on the screen and follow its instructions. Then, using what you've learned so far, try to make your document resemble Figure 2-13. (Hint: Use the tags called Headline 1, Sub Head 1, Bullet, and Table).

Note: Don't worry about accuracy for this guided tour. Just try to approximate what you see here.

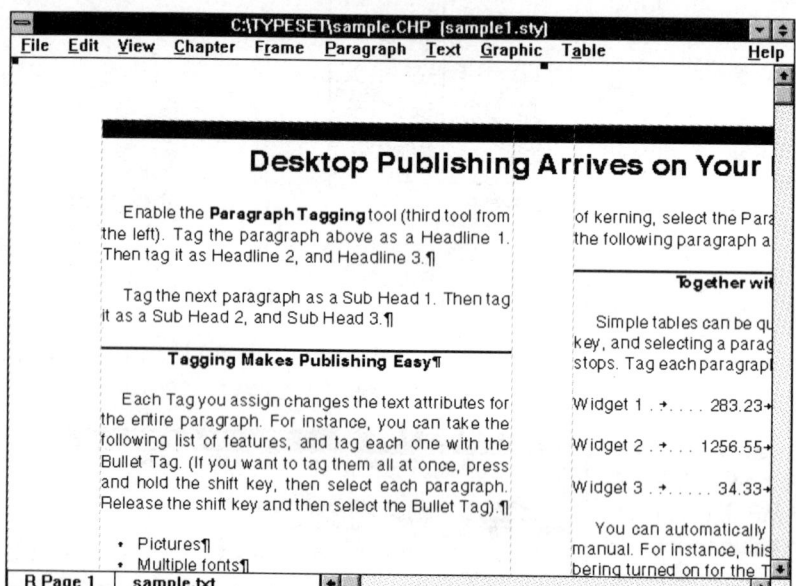

Figure 2-13.
Use the tagging procedure you just learned to make your screen resemble this one. The Toolbox, Tag List Window, and File List Window have been hidden (using the View menu) to give you a better view.

Changing a style sheet

So far, you've seen how to load a style sheet and apply a tag. You can make changes to the tags within a style sheet to alter the look of your document.

23. If you have not already done so, select the Paragraph Tool from the Toolbox.

As before, the cursor changes to a shape resembling a tiny paragraph. With this tool, you can select paragraphs by clicking on them. Then you can change the way these paragraphs look by selecting commands from the Paragraph menu. The results of your changes are stored in the style sheet.

24. Click on the third paragraph, "Tagging Makes Publishing Easy," to select it. The paragraph is highlighted to show it has been selected. Now let's change its alignment.

25. Choose Alignment from the Paragraph menu (or try the shortcut: Alt-P-A) to bring up the Alignment dialog box (Figure 2-14). Right now the text cursor is in the text box labeled In/Outdent Width.

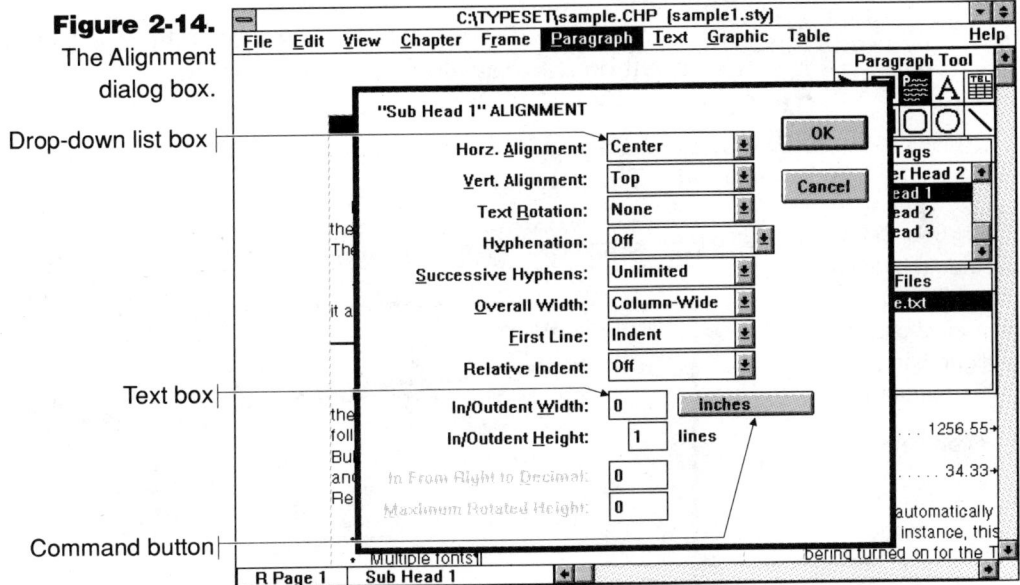

Figure 2-14. The Alignment dialog box.

Drop-down list box

Text box

Command button

26. Press the Delete key to get rid of any text currently in the In/Outdent Width box. Then type 1 into the box.

27. Now move to the next option by pressing the Tab key.

Can you see the dark line that surrounds the command button immediately to the right of the In/Outdent Width text box? You'll see this measurements button over and over again in Ventura's dialog boxes. It cycles through four different measurement options: Inches, Centimeters, Picas & Points, and Fractional Points. The button shows the units of measurement for the nearby numbers.

28. Click on the measurements button and cycle through the different units until you return to Inches.

When you click on the measurements button, it changes to a different unit. The "1" that you typed into the In/Outdent Width text box also changes. Ventura automatically converts measurements from one system to another, so that you don't have to do the math.

29. Use the mouse to place the cursor in the In/Outdent Width text box. Delete the 1 that you just typed. Then type a 0 (zero) to return In/Outdent Width to its original setting.

Now, let's go to the Horz. Alignment list box to adjust the horizontal alignment. You can move to the Horz. Alignment box by pressing the Tab key a few times (or move backward to it with Shift-Tab). Or you can use the Alt key shortcut: Alt-A. For now, let's just use the mouse.

30. Click once on the downward arrow to the right of the Horz. Alignment box. A drop-down list appears (Figure 2-15).

31. Click once on the word "Left" in the list.

32. Click on OK to close the dialog box and implement the changes. The paragraph is now aligned to the left.

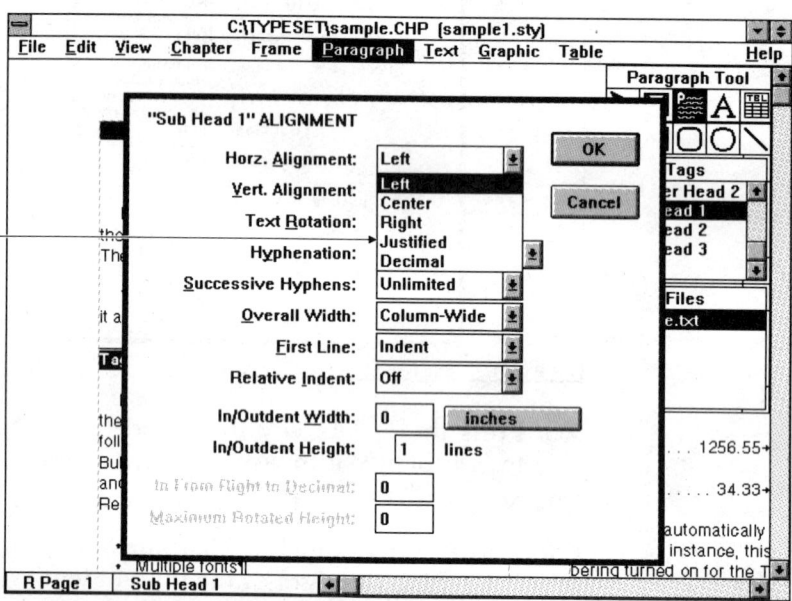

Figure 2-15. Use the drop-down list box next to Horz. Alignment to change the alignment of the paragraph.

Drop-down list

Note: When you use the Paragraph Tool to change the appearance of text, you are really changing its tag. Not only will the original paragraph look different, but so will all other paragraphs that use that same tag. For instance, if you change the the Sub Head 1 tag, all other Sub Head 1 paragraphs will also change. If you want to change only selected words or characters, Ventura permits that too. But we'll save that for Chapter 6, "Handling Text in Ventura."

Placing a picture

Let's add some final visual touches to the document by adding a picture. Placing a picture is a simple, three-step process: (1) draw a frame to hold the picture, (2) load the picture file, and (3) place the picture inside the frame.

Drawing a frame

You draw a frame by dragging the mouse with the Add Frame tool. Here's how it works:

33. Choose Reduced View from the View menu.

34. Select the Add Frame tool (second from the upper left in the Toolbox).

You can tell that Add Frame is active because the cursor shape changes to a frame corner with the letters *Fr* when you move the cursor over the workspace.

35. Position the Add Frame cursor where you want the upper left corner of the frame. In this case, position it in the second column just beneath the paragraph that begins with *"Insight magazine."*

36. Drag the mouse down and to the right, until you have created a rectangle that stretches from one side of the column to the other and down to the bottom of the column (Figure 2-16). The sizing doesn't have to be exact. Then release the mouse button. When you release the mouse button, your cursor reverts to the Frame Tool.

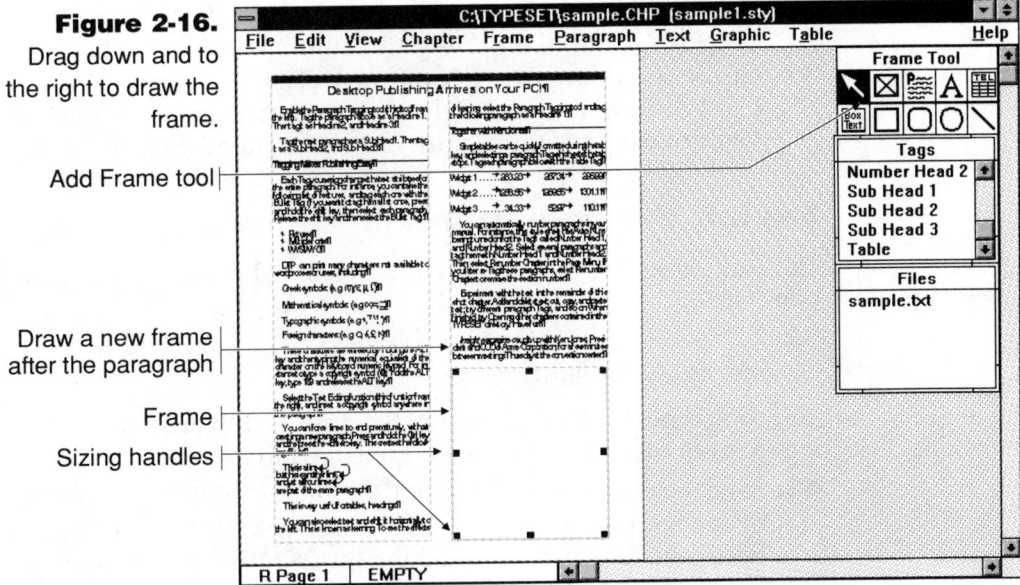

Figure 2-16.
Drag down and to the right to draw the frame.

Add Frame tool

Draw a new frame after the paragraph

Frame

Sizing handles

Loading a picture

To load a picture file, use the Load Text/Picture dialog box—the same one you used to load a text file. Here's how:

37. Choose Load Text/Picture from the File menu. The Load Text/Picture dialog box appears.

38. Select File Type: Image, and Format: TIFF. Be sure the Options check box called Several Files is *not* checked. Click on OK. The Open File dialog box appears.

39. Load the POT4.TIF from the \TYPESET directory: select the filename and click on Open. Upon returning to the workspace, you'll see the name POT4.TIF in the File List Window.

Note: Don't worry if nothing happens for a few moments. It takes extra time to load, convert, and display this type of image. With slower computers, you may experience a lag of several seconds.

Placing a picture

You recall that placing a text file means telling Ventura where to put it by pointing and clicking with the mouse. The same technique holds true for picture files.

Note: If an empty frame is selected when you load a file, Ventura places it in the frame automatically (skip the next two steps).

40. If it's not already active, select the Frame Tool (Toolbox) and select the frame. (Hint: Click once anywhere inside the frame.)

41. Click once on the filename POT4.TIF from the File List Window. After a brief delay for necessary computations, Ventura displays the picture inside the frame (Figure 2-17).

Saving the document

Our tour wouldn't be complete if we didn't show you how to save your work.

42. Choose Save As from the File menu. The Save File As dialog box appears (Figure 2-18).

You could choose Save instead of Save As, but that risks overwriting existing files. Use Save As to give the document a new name.

43. Save the document as TOUR.CHP in the \TYPESET directory by navigating to the \TYPESET directory, typing TOUR in the File Name text box, and clicking on OK. Ventura will automatically add the CHP extension for you.

Figure 2-17.
Click once on the frame and once on the filename to put the picture file into the frame.

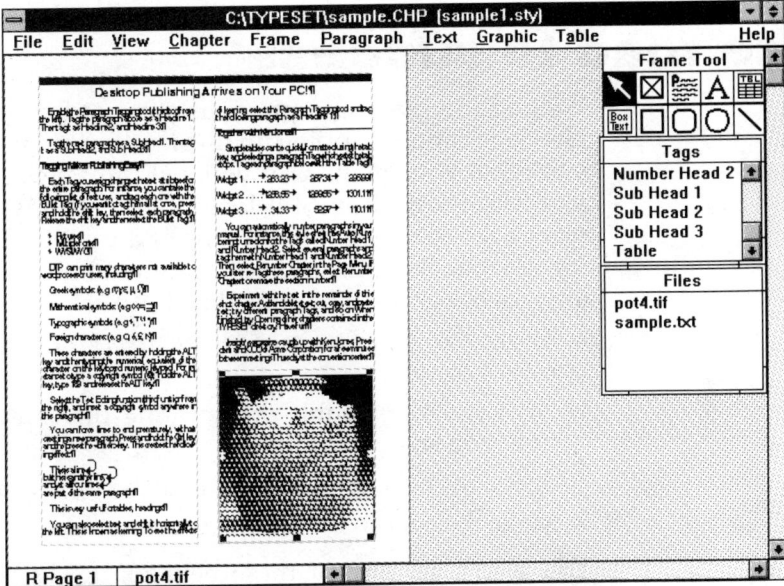

Figure 2-18.
The Save File As dialog box.

Type the filename here

Double-click here to move to the parent directory

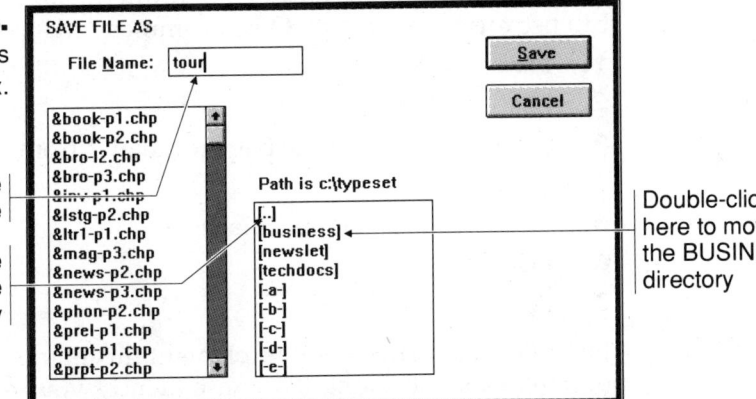

Double-click here to move to the BUSINESS directory

This isn't the only way to save a document. You can also type the full path and filename in the File Name text box, or you can move to another directory and the type a filename in the File Name text box. Ventura calls documents *chapters*. That's why it automatically adds the chapter extension (CHP) to any filename you type.

Congratulations, you've created your first Ventura document. Now that you've taken a general tour of Ventura, we'll give you a strategy for creating successful Ventura documents.

The road to success

We had fun loading a previously created style sheet, adjusting a few tags, and dropping in a picture. But what happens when you're on your own? Can you just throw everything on the page and tinker with it until it looks okay? Well, yes—but only if you want to spend a lot of extra time and trouble. To get the best-looking documents in the shortest amount of time, you need a different approach. You need to plan ahead. An established procedure will:

- Spare you the *what do I do first?* confusion that plagues most beginners
- Save you the trouble of repeating the same set-up tasks each time you start a project
- Speed up projects as work habits become routine
- Make it easier to monitor progress in workgroup situations

You won't get any of these benefits unless you have a plan of attack, a road map for building Ventura documents, a strategy you can use for every project. Our recommended strategy is as follows:

1. Plan and sketch
2. Load the files
3. Set up the underlying page (or load it from a template)
4. Place text
5. Apply and refine the style sheet
6. Place pictures
7. Print

Before you can effectively implement this plan, you'll need a foundation in some basic skills. Consequently, you may not follow this exact order the first time you create a style sheet or build a document template. But after you have these basics down, this plan will guide you to the lap of layout luxury. In later chapters, we'll concentrate on each subject. But first, we want to give you an overview of the whole process so you can see how everything fits together. Let's take a look at how you might put a typical document together.

Note: Don't worry if you don't understand new concepts such as the *underlying page* and *templates*. We'll give you brief definitions in this chapter and then cover them in detail in later chapters.

1. Plan and sketch

It's tempting to jump into Ventura with only a vague idea of what you want, but if you spend a few minutes to sketch your document on paper first, you'll save time and headaches (Figure 2-19).

Figure 2-19. Begin your layout by making a rough sketch of your document on paper.

2. Load the files

When a contractor builds a house, he or she starts by collecting the raw materials. Ventura pros take the same approach. They start a new document by loading the files they need: the text files, picture files, and style sheet file (Figure 2-20).

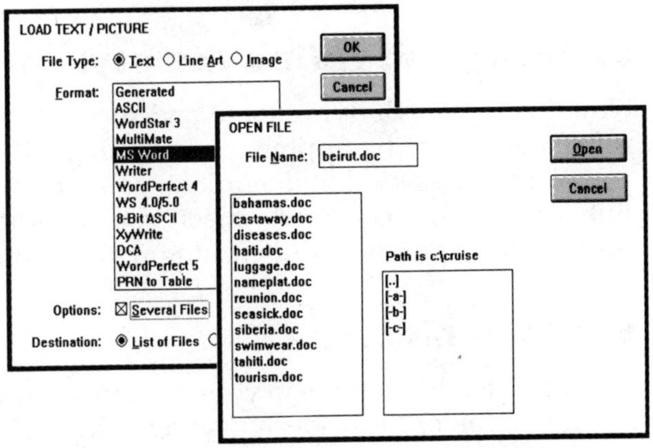

Figure 2-20. Load all the text and picture files you need.

3. Set up the underlying page

The underlying page is the foundation for a document. It's such an important concept that it's the subject of its own chapter (Chapter 4, "Building the Underlying Page"). Smart users set up this master format first. You can build it from scratch, or you can load a *template*. A template is a previously created document that contains only text and pictures you plan to use repeatedly (Figure 2-21). Each time you create a similar document (such as a monthly report, newsletter, or letter on letterhead stationery), you open the template, save it as a new chapter, and load text and picture files.

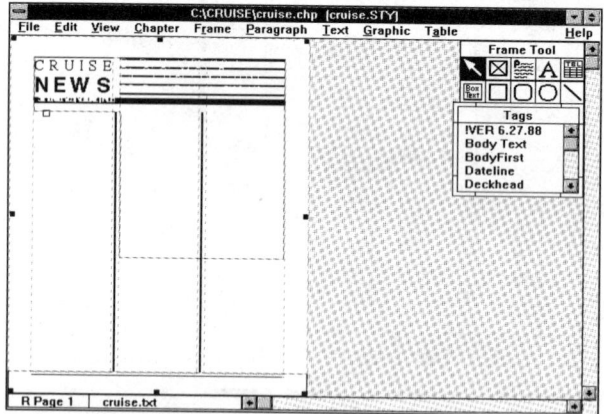

Figure 2-21. For multiple documents with a common design, use a template containing the repeated elements.

4. Place text

In a long document, you usually put the text right onto the underlying page. In shorter documents, such as newsletters, you create frames on top of the underlying page. Then you flow text and pictures into those containers (Figure 2-22).

5. Apply and refine the style sheet

Now that the underlying page and the text are in place, you can refine the format by applying a style sheet. If this is the first time you've built this kind of document, you'll have a lot of work to do. But after you perfect a style sheet, you can apply it to other documents just by pointing and clicking with the mouse (Figure 2-23).

6. Place pictures

Next, you'll add pictures to your document by placing them inside frames on top of the underlying page (Figure 2-24).

Figure 2-22.
Place text on the page or into frames.

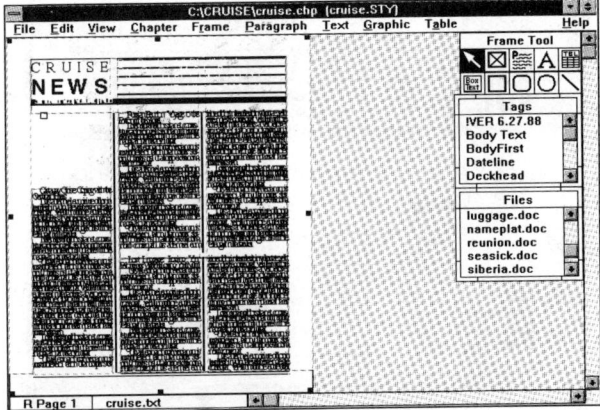

Figure 2-23.
Apply tags to the text.

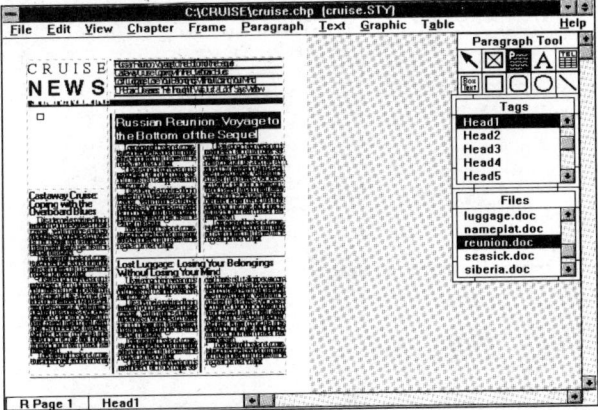

Figure 2-24.
Place pictures inside frames.

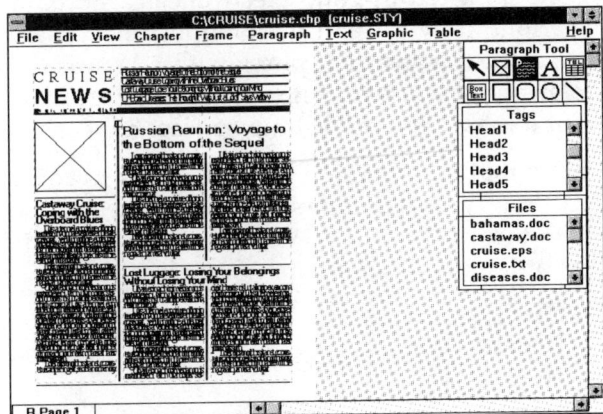

7. Print

Then you're ready to save and print your document (Figure 2-25).

Figure 2-25.
Print your finished document.

Continuing on

Within minutes of starting to use Ventura, you have laid out, edited, pasted up, and electronically stored a document. And by learning how to plan your publishing projects, you've taken the first step toward a happier life with Ventura Publisher. Stopping to plan and prepare may not be as fun as spontaneous experimenting, but it makes the publishing process a lot easier in the long run.

Now that you've got a taste of things to come, let's charge ahead. In Part Two, "Chapters and Style Sheets," you'll get your hands into the nitty gritty of Ventura, creating the basic components for great-looking documents.

Easy Access

For more info on...	See chapter...
Creating a basic style sheet	3 — Building Basic Styles
Building an underlying page for the entire document	4 — Building the Underlying Page
Importing and editing text	6 — Handling Text in Ventura
Loading and placing pictures	11 — Loading and Placing Pictures
Printing	13 — Printing Ventura Documents

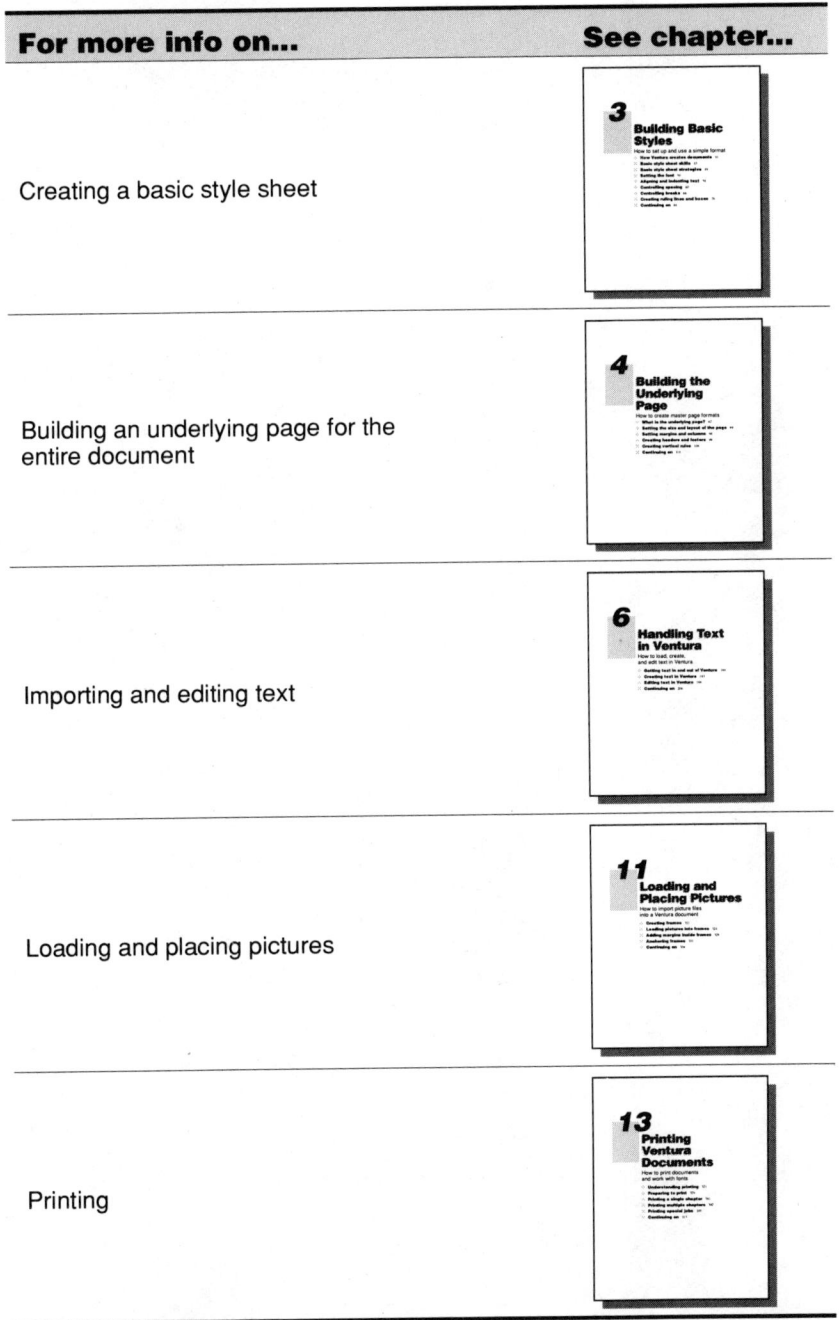

Part Two:
Chapters and Style Sheets

3
Building Basic Styles

How to set up and use a simple format

- **How Ventura creates documents** 41
- **Basic style sheet skills** 43
- **Basic style sheet strategies** 49
- **Setting the font** 50
- **Aligning and indenting text** 54
- **Controlling spacing** 60
- **Controlling breaks** 66
- **Creating ruling lines and boxes** 76
- **Continuing on** 84

inety percent of all Ventura formatting consists of modifying your document's *style sheet*. In this chapter, you'll begin learning how to create, modify, and apply style sheets.

Style sheets contain *tags* that give the formatting commands for each paragraph in your document. You control the *attributes* of tags with the Paragraph menu. Attributes are simply the typographical traits of a paragraph such as font, alignment, spacing, and so on. We'll cover the essentials of tagging here and then teach you advanced techniques in Chapter 5, "Building Advanced Styles."

Most of your work with style sheets will involve performing five basic functions, all of them on the Paragraph menu. These core skills consist of modifying:

- Fonts
- Alignment
- Spacing
- Breaks (where lines, columns, and pages start and stop)
- Ruling lines and boxes

We'll step through these essential functions in a moment. First, let's talk about how Ventura uses style sheets and the basic skills you need to work with them.

How Ventura creates documents

As you recall, Ventura calls its documents *chapters*. Unlike other page layout programs that copy all text, graphics, and formatting information into a single file on your computer, Ventura stores the various parts of your document in a number of files—including one for style sheets, another for captions, and as many text and graphics files as you need. The chapter file (recognized by the CHP extension of its filename) is at the hub, connecting the files together (Figure 3-1). Think of it this way: If your Ventura document is an office building where one office is a text file and another office is a graphics file, the chapter file is the directory in the lobby. It tells Ventura where to find all the other files in your document.

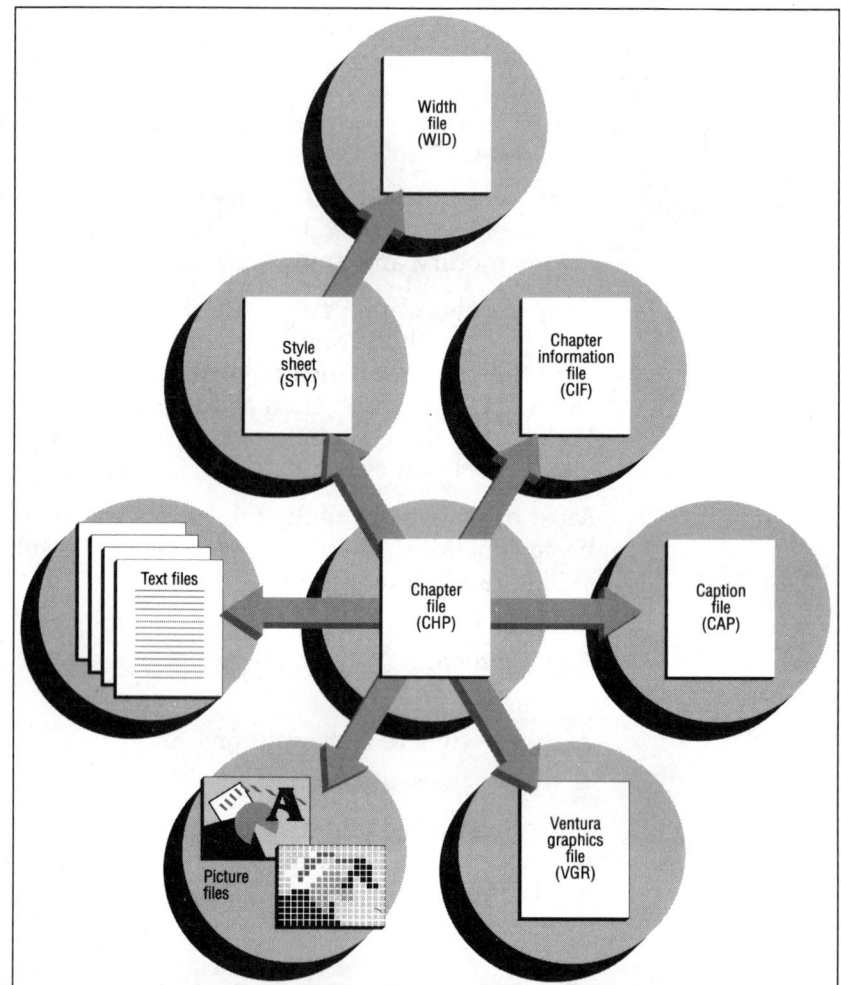

Figure 3-1.
The chapter file tells Ventura where to find all the other files that make up your document.

When you import a text or picture file into Ventura, that file is *not copied* into the chapter file but only *linked* to it. For example, if you change the text with your word processor, those changes show up in Ventura. Conversely, when you change text in Ventura, those changes show up in your word-processing file as well. Likewise, if you change a picture file with a graphics program, the new version will appear in Ventura the next time you open the document.

Note: If you're using Windows' multitasking abilities to jump back and forth between Ventura and a graphics or word-processing program, don't expect to see changes updated immediately. For changes to be visible in Ventura, you must save the file and then reopen it in Ventura.

Most of the formatting that affects the typography of your document is stored in a file called a *style sheet*—recognized by the STY extension. This approach lets you define the appearance for one document and copy that same format to any other document with a minimum of effort. And it lets you change the look of dozens of paragraphs in a single step, instead of changing them one at a time.

Now that you have the big picture, it's time to learn some basic style sheet skills. For more information on how Ventura handles files, see Chapter 16, "Managing Ventura Files."

Basic style sheet skills

Before you can format with style sheets, you have to know how to load them, apply them, and add new tags to them.

Loading a style sheet

You loaded a style sheet in the guided tour in Chapter 2,"Starting Out Smart," but let's review the steps.

You never start from absolute zero. Ventura always has a style sheet and at least one page in the workspace. The style sheet's tag names are displayed in the Tag List Window. When you start Ventura, it automatically loads the style sheet used during the previous session.

To load a style sheet:

1. Choose Load Diff. Style from the File menu.
2. Navigate to the directory containing the style sheet, if it is not in your current directory.
3. Double-click on the style sheet that you want to load.

Example: For those of you who want to follow along on your computers, be sure you have prepared the proper files as explained on the following pages. If you have trouble with these steps, review the guided tour in Chapter 2, "Starting Out Smart."

1. Start Ventura. If Ventura is already running, choose New from the File menu.

2. Choose Load Diff. Style from the File menu. From the \TYPESET directory, select DEFAULT.STY and click on Open (or just double-click on DEFAULT.STY).

3. Choose Save Style As from the File menu. In the File Name text box, type MYSTYLE and click on Save. (Don't type the extension—Ventura will automatically add the STY extension, saving your file as MYSTYLE.STY.)

4. Choose Load Text/Picture from the File menu. Select File Type: Text and Format: ASCII. Click on OK. From the \TYPESET directory, select BOOK.TXT and click on Open (or just double-click on BOOK.TXT). If the text appears on your page, go to the next step. If not, select theFrame Tool and click on the page. Then click on BOOK.TXT in your File List Window. (If your File List Window is not showing, choose File List Window from the View menu.)

5. With the page still selected, choose File Type/Rename from the Frame menu. In the New Name text box, type \TYPESET\MYBOOK.TXT. Click on OK.

6. Choose Save As from the File menu. In the File Name text box, type MYCHAP and click on Save. Ventura adds the CHP extension, saving your file as MYCHAP.CHP. Now you have a chapter that you can use to follow along with our examples.

Note: If you wish to view all your text, choose Reduced View from the View menu. If you cannot read your text in Reduced View, choose Set Preferences from the Edit menu. From the Text To Greek list box, select None. Then click on OK.

Applying a style sheet

A style sheet and its associated chapter file contains two sets of formatting instructions: one set for the *underlying page* (where elements are repeated on every page throughout the document) and one set for *paragraph tags* (which control the appearance and position of each paragraph of text). When you load a style sheet, it immediately affects the formatting of the underlying page; however, it may not affect the text.

When Ventura applies formatting to text, it tries to match every paragraph's tag with a tag from the new style sheet's Tag List, which is displayed in the Tag List Window. If Ventura can't find a paragraph's tag, it can't apply the tag's formatting commands. When that happens, Ventura applies the format for its default tag, Body Text.

Tagging with the mouse
You can tag paragraphs quickly and easily with the mouse. Here's how:
1. Select the Paragraph Tool from the Toolbox.
2. Click on any block of text ending with a paragraph symbol. (These symbols can be seen on your screen when you choose View Tabs & Returns from View menu.) The whole paragraph is highlighted.
3. Click on a tag name in the Tag List Window. You may need to scroll down the list to see all the tag names.

Presto. You've applied that tag to that paragraph. The highlighted text immediately assumes the attributes of the tag.

Tip: To apply a single tag to a group of paragraphs, click on the first paragraph, and then hold down the Shift key as you click on each of the others. All of the paragraphs you select will be highlighted. If you select one by mistake, you can remove the highlighting by clicking on it again while still holding down the Shift key. Next, select a tag from the Tag List Window. The tag is now applied to all the highlighted paragraphs.

Tagging with function keys
Looking for a shortcut? You can assign up to ten tags to the function keys, so that you can tag a paragraph by pressing a function key. You can use these function keys to tag paragraphs while in Text mode or in Paragraph mode. In Text mode, the function keys save you the time it takes to select the Paragraph Tool, select the paragraph, apply the tag, and return to Text mode again.

To set up the function keys for tagging:
1. Choose Update Tag List from the Paragraph menu.
2. Unless you just saved your file, a VP Alert box appears. If you want to save your current style sheet before you update your tags, click on Save. Otherwise, click on Abandon.
3. Click on the Assign Func Keys button.
4. Click on a function key button in the box on the left and then click on one of the tag names in the list box on the right. The function key's tag changes to the one you selected.

5. Click on OK when you've made all your function key assignments. Then click on OK again to exit the Update Tag List dialog box. Another VP Alert box appears.

6. Click on Save to update the Tag List under the current style sheet; click on Save As to save the changes under another name; or click on Abandon to discard any changes.

After assigning function keys, you apply tags to paragraphs by pressing a defined function key while using the Text or Paragraph Tools. In addition, any document that uses the same style sheet can use those function keys—you don't have to reassign them.

Tip: When using the Text Tool, you can modify the Tag List and reassign function keys using the keyboard shortcut Ctrl-K. This opens the Update Tag List dialog box. Then you can click on the Assign Func Keys button to bring up a dialog box that lets you assign and check on the status of assigned keys (Figure 3-2).

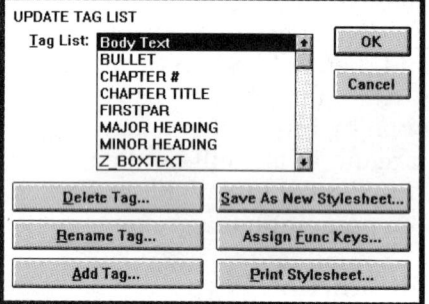

Figure 3-2. These dialog boxes let you assign tags to function keys for one-key speed tagging.

Adding a new tag

Adding a new tag is easy. Basically, you copy an existing tag under a new name and then you change it until it suits you. The key decision is which tag to copy. If you have a tag that already looks similar to the new one you have in mind, then you should use it as the starting point. Otherwise, use Body Text as the starting point.

To add a new tag:

1. Using the Paragraph Tool, select a paragraph with the tag that you want to use for a starting point.
2. Choose Add New Tag from the Paragraph menu.
3. Type a new tag name in the Name To Add text box. You can type up to 13 characters (including spaces).
4. Click on OK.

Example: If you're following along with our example chapter, try creating a tag of your own. Select any paragraph of Body Text. Then choose Add New Tag from the Paragraph menu. When the dialog box appears, type "My Tag" into the New Name text box (Figure 3-3).

When you return to the workspace, the tag name My Tag appears in the Tag List Window. The new tag will already be attached to the paragraph you highlighted.

Figure 3-3.
Adding a new tag.

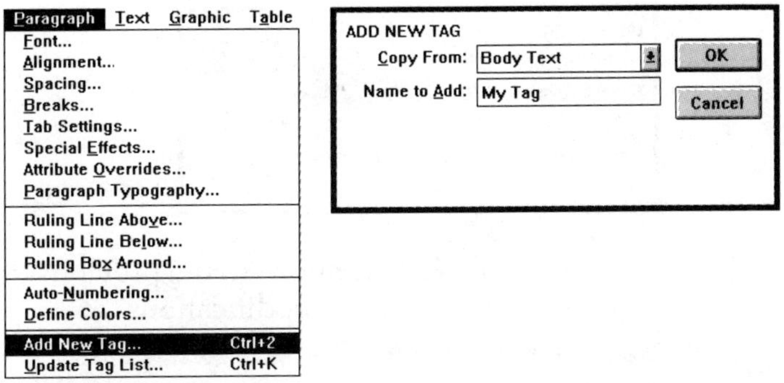

Deleting and renaming tags

Because you build a style sheet by revising an old one, you won't need all the tags from the original. Therefore, you'll want to delete unneeded tags. You'll also want to rename some tags to fit new purposes or match your company's tag-naming system. You delete and rename tags with the Update Tag List command from the Paragraph menu.

***E*xample:** If you're following along with our example chapter, try deleting our newly added tag:

1. Choose Update Tag List from the Paragraph menu (or press Ctrl-K). If the VP Alert box appears, click on Abandon. The list of current tags appears in the Update Tag List dialog box.
2. Select the tag that you want to delete—in this case, it's My Tag.
3. Click on the Delete Tag button. The Delete Tag dialog box appears with two list boxes (Figure 3-4). The Name To Delete list box already has the chosen tag name, My Tag. The Name To Convert To list box contains Body Text. Clicking on the arrow for either name will allow you to select any other name from the current style sheet. Let's stick with these names.

Figure 3-4.
Removing a tag.

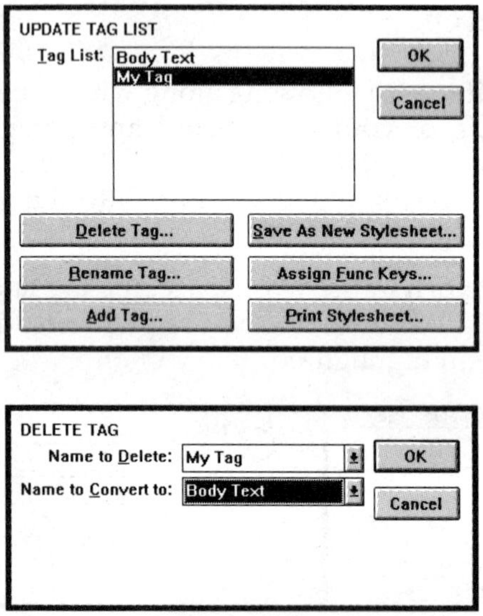

4. Click on OK. You return to the previous dialog box where you can make more tag modifications.
5. Click on OK. A VP Alert box appears.
6. Click on Save to save changes to the current style sheet. You can also use Save As or Abandon.

***N*ote:** Ventura's Law of Conservation of Matter. Like style sheets, tags are always present, must be created from other tags, and must be converted to other tags before you delete them.

Renaming tags is even easier. Just click on the Rename Tag button in the Update Tag List dialog box, select the tag to rename from the

Tag List list box, type the new name in the New Tag Name text box, and click on OK. Exit from the Update Tag List dialog box as usual.

Understanding Ventura's generated tags
You don't have to do all the tagging. When you create items such as headers, footers, and tables, Ventura automatically generates paragraphs and tags them for you.

Ventura begins these generated tags with the Z_ prefix. Z_Footer, for example, is the tag Ventura creates when you tell it to generate a footer for your document. Because the Tag List Window lists tags in alphabetic order, generated tags are grouped together at the bottom of the list. But you won't see them unless you select Generated Tags: Shown in the Set Preferences dialog box (Edit menu). If your style sheet doesn't have a format for a generated tag, Ventura automatically gives that tag the attributes of Body Text. You modify a generated tag's format just as you would any other tag.

Don't worry about using generated tags for now. We'll teach you how later in the book. But we wanted you to know what those mysterious Z_ tags were that appear at the bottom of the Tag List Window. For a table that lists all of Ventura's generated tags, see Chapter 21, "Rapid Reference."

Basic style sheet strategies

You'll have an easier time building style sheets if you understand when to start from Ventura's default style sheet and when to start with an existing style sheet as your base. In this section, you'll learn some important style sheet strategies.

Starting from an available style sheet

Your first—and easiest—option is to load a style sheet that's close to the format you want. There are lots of places to find style sheets. You can buy style sheets from computer stores (some come with a book explaining how to use them). Or you can get them for almost nothing from on-line information services such as CompuServe and private bulletin boards (you'll need a modem). But before you spend any money, start looking right under your own roof—Ventura's sample chapters. They might be all you need.

After you've loaded your model style sheet, rename it to create a new one, or keep the name and make small revisions. You'll want to modify existing tags, delete unneeded tags, and add new ones.

Starting from Ventura's default

Intermediate or advanced users may want a different strategy: starting with Ventura's default style sheet, called DEFAULT.STY. Building everything from the default style sheet may be easier and faster than keeping track of numerous changes to an existing style sheet. Using the default style sheet also provides complete control over all the elements of your style sheet. DEFAULT.STY is Ventura's most basic style sheet: single-sided, letter size, and only one tag. It's as close as you can come to starting from scratch.

Warning: To avoid overwriting your blank slate style sheet, choose Save Style As from the File menu and rename DEFAULT.STY as !DEFAULT.STY.

Setting the font

With the basic style sheet skills and strategies under your belt, you're ready to learn how to set the font, align the text, control the spacing, control the breaks, and create ruling lines. In this section, you'll learn the first step: setting the font.

A *font* is all the characters, numbers, and symbols in a single *typeface* and size (such as 12-point Dutch Bold). A typeface is a single style (such as italic, bold, etc.) within a single type *family* (such as Helvetica, Times, etc.). Ventura calls families *faces*. You determine your font by opening the Font dialog box and adjusting face, size, style, color, and other attributes (overscore, underline, etc.).

Note: Most of the commands on the Paragraph menu are only available when the Paragraph Tool is selected and a paragraph is highlighted. To use these commands, you'll need to select the Paragraph Tool from the Toolbox first, and then highlight a paragraph of text.

Selecting the typeface, size, style, and color

When you choose Font from the Paragraph menu, you'll see three list boxes at the top of the dialog box: Face, Size, and Style. The contents of these list boxes depends on the printer that you use (Figures 3-5 and 3-6).

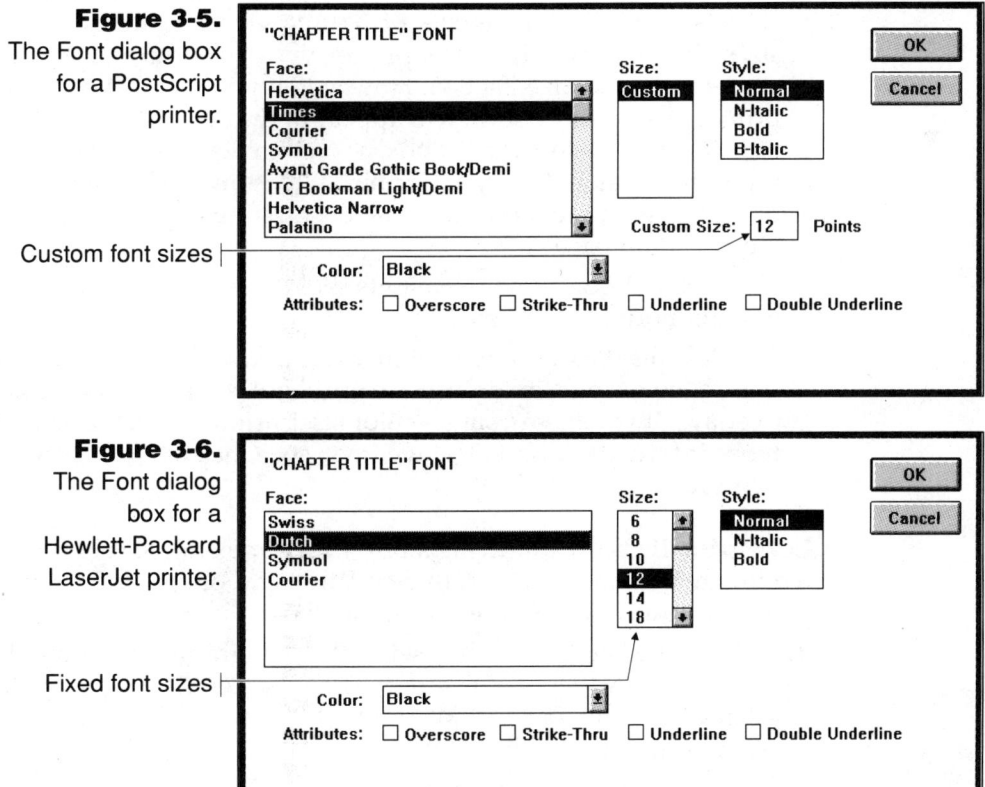

Figure 3-5.
The Font dialog box for a PostScript printer.

Custom font sizes

Figure 3-6.
The Font dialog box for a Hewlett-Packard LaserJet printer.

Fixed font sizes

For example, a PostScript printer will offer a family of built-in fonts whose names differ from those typically offered for a Hewlett-Packard LaserJet printer. Although most PostScript printers have the same built-in fonts, their respective driver files may cause the order and naming of the fonts in the Face list box to differ slightly. The range of point sizes and styles can differ widely as well. You can add fonts from other vendors. When you install new fonts, they will appear in these list boxes as well. For more information on fonts, see Chapter 13, "Printing Ventura Documents."

Here's how the four main list boxes in the Font dialog box work:

- The *Face* list box lists the type families for the current printer. By using a sans-serif face to contrast with the 12-point serif body text, you can make your title stand out and attract your reader's attention.
- The *Size* list box lists the size of the type. It also varies with the printer. For example, a LaserJet may have a fixed series of sizes—usually in increments of 2 (unless you add other point sizes). If you have this type of printer, you click on point size that you want in the Size list box. However, if you have a PostScript printer, the word Custom will appear in the Size list box instead of point sizes. Below the list box, a Custom Size text box lets you type a new value. Change the point size from by clicking inside the Custom Size text box, deleting the existing value, and typing the new point size (14).
- The *Style* list box lists the weights (bold, normal, etc.) and slant of type (normal, italic, etc.).
- The *Color* list box gives you eight color options that you can use with a color printer or use to print out separate spot color overlays. If you have a single-color laser printer, select Black. For more information on color overlays, see Chapter 13, "Printing Ventura Documents."

Example: If you're following along with our example chapter, try redefining the font for the Chapter Title tag. Follow along—we'll give you a quick tour of the Font dialog box:

1. Using the Paragraph Tool, select the paragraph containing the text "The Adventure Begins." The Chapter Title tag is highlighted in the Tag List Window, indicating that the selected paragraph has this tag.
2. Choose the Font command from the Paragraph menu. The Font dialog box appears.
3. Select Face: Swiss (Helvetica if you are using a PostScript printer).
4. Select Size: 14.
5. Select Style: Bold.
6. Select Color: Black (if it is not already selected).
7. Click on OK and check your new chapter title in the workspace (Figure 3-7).
8. When you're finished, choose Save from the File menu.

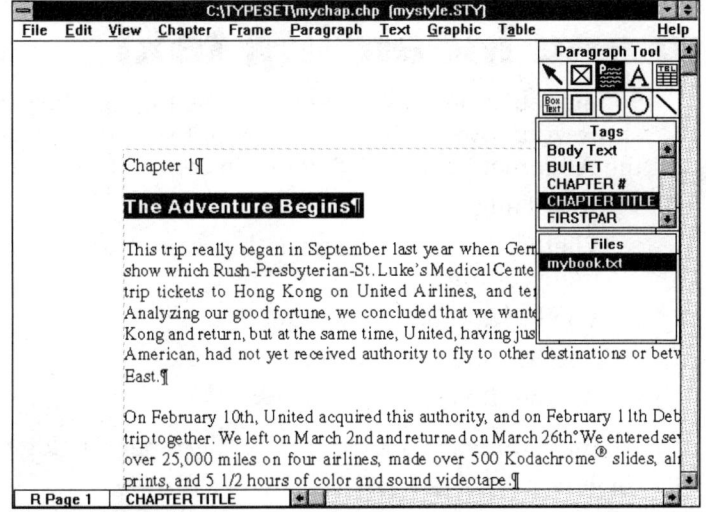

Figure 3-7.
After you make your font adjustments, your example chapter should look similar to this.

Changing other attributes

With the Font dialog box, you can control other attributes:

- Overscore
- Strike-Thru
- Underline
- Double Underline

Remember, the attributes assigned here are applied to every word in the paragraph. A tag with the Strike-Thru attribute, for example, can be useful for marking whole blocks of text (for legal and other purposes) in one quick click.

But if you want to use the Strike-Thru effect for a word or a phrase within an otherwise normal paragraph, then you must use the Text Tool. To format only selected words without changing the whole tag, select the Text Tool from the Toolbox and drag the text cursor over the text to select it. Then choose the attribute you want from the Text menu. For more on formatting text, see Chapter 6, "Handling Text in Ventura."

Aligning and indenting text

So far, you've learned how to choose the font for a tag. Now, we'll show you how to align the lines of text within a paragraph. With the Alignment command, you can control the position of text:

- How it aligns horizontally and vertically
- Whether it stretches across the entire frame or is restricted to a single column
- Whether and how it is indented
- Whether it is hyphenated
- Whether it is rotated

All these things take place in the Alignment dialog box. In this next section, we'll step you through its options.

Getting to the Alignment dialog box is simple:

1. Using the Paragraph Tool, select the paragraph you want to change.
2. Choose Alignment from the Paragraph menu. The Alignment dialog box appears (Figure 3-8).

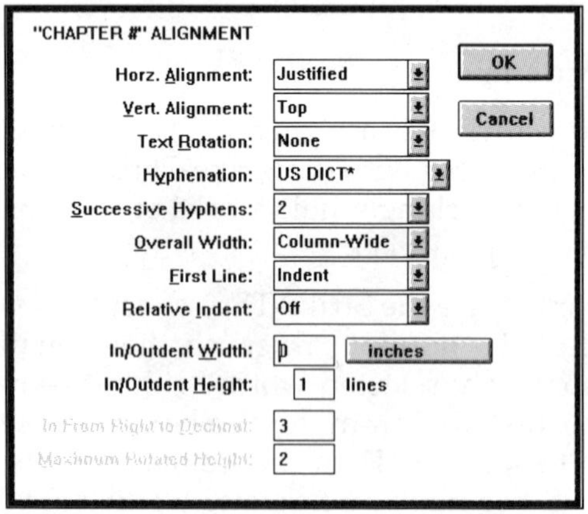

Figure 3-8. The Alignment dialog box.

Aligning text horizontally

To affect how text is positioned in relation to the left and right margins, you select an option from the Horz. Alignment list box. You have five choices:

- *Left* aligns each line of text flush against the left margin, whereas the right side is "ragged"—that is, the right end of the line may be slightly longer or shorter than the one that came before. You may hear people refer to this option as *left alignment*, *flush left*, or *ragged right*. This option is considered the most readable of all the alignment possibilities. Its uneven right margin gives the eye "landmarks," and it keeps the space between words at a standard value.

- *Right* is virtually identical to Left, except that the text is positioned flush against the right margin, while the left edge is uneven (ragged). Graphics arts professionals often call this effect *right alignment*, *flush right*, or *ragged left*. Right alignment is not appropriate for long blocks of text, but you'll often find yourself using it for titles, headings, tables, and labels.

- *Justify* positions text flush against the margins on both the left and the right sides. It is referred to as *justification*. Justification creates an attractive, formal look. However, to make the text fit exactly between the margins, Ventura must shrink or stretch the spaces between the words (and sometimes the spaces between the letters). These variations make justified text slightly harder to read, especially in narrow columns. In addition, you cannot use tab stops with justified text.

- *Center* positions the text at the exact middle point between the left and right margins. It comes in handy for such things as titles and tables.

- *Decimal* is used to align numbers around a decimal point without using tab stops. It's a useful option for tables and financial exhibits. If you select the Decimal option, Ventura also lets you control just how far the decimal point should appear from the right margin by activating a text box at the bottom of the Alignment dialog box (In From Right To Decimal).

Example: If you'd like to see the effects of the different Horz. Alignment options, use the Paragraph Tool to select the chapter number in the example chapter we opened earlier. The chapter number is currently tagged Chapter #. Try Left, Center, and Right. With right alignment, the chapter number is near the edge of a right-facing page (where chapters usually start). This position makes it easy to spot the number when readers thumb through the pages. When you're through experimenting, revert to the previous version of the chapter—because we want to keep a "clean slate" to use with future examples. Simply choose Revert To Saved from the File menu, and then click on OK in the VP Alert box.

Aligning text vertically

As you just saw, horizontal alignment affects the position of text between the left and right margins. Vertical alignment is almost identical except that it affects the position between the top and bottom margins.

To align text vertically, you select an option from the Vert. Alignment list box. You have three alignment options (Figure 3-9):

- *Top* is the default selection, and the one you'll use most of the time. When you select Top, Ventura does not put the top of the text against the top margin. Rather, it counts down enough space so that the tallest letters will still have room (otherwise, capital letters would extend over the margin). (Advanced users: in the Chapter Typography dialog box, you can control whether Ventura counts down by the size of the capital letters or by the amount of inter-line spacing.)
- *Middle* centers the text between the top and bottom margins. This is a useful option for title pages and column titles in tables.
- *Bottom* aligns the baseline of the text against the bottom margin. This option is not used as often as the other two, but it can be useful for title pages and tables.

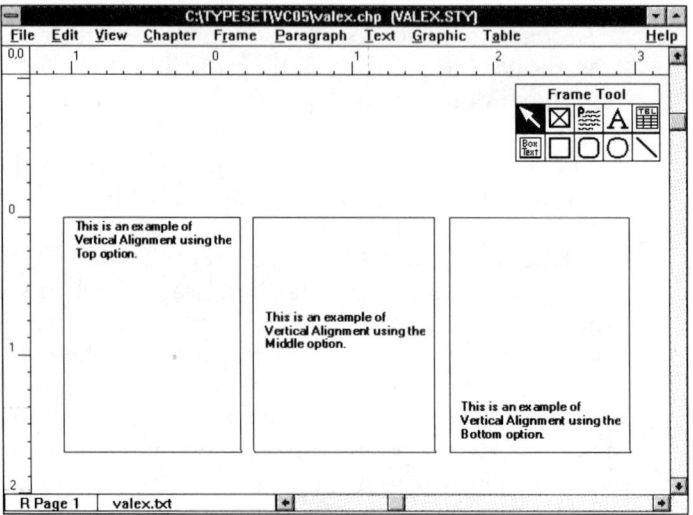

Figure 3-9. Your three vertical alignment options.

Selecting the overall width

To control how text appears in multi-column documents, you select one of two options from the Overall Width list box. *Column-*

Wide restricts the text to the width of the current column. *Frame-Wide* extends the paragraph across the full width of the margins, even if there are many columns.

Imagine, for instance, a heading in a three column document. If you select Column-Wide, the heading will be only as wide as a column. You'd select this option if you were creating a subheading. But if you pick Frame-Wide instead, the heading will extend across all three columns. You'd select this option if you were creating a headline (Figure 3-10).

Note: If a frame-wide paragraph does not begin in the leftmost column, you must select Column Balance: On from the Chapter Typography and Frame Typography dialog boxes (Chapter and Frame menus); otherwise, that paragraph will overwrite any text in the left column.

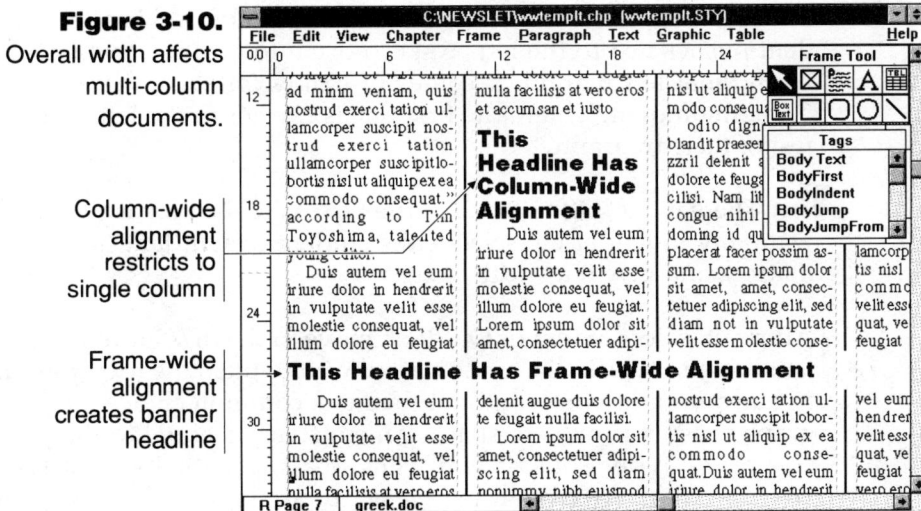

Figure 3-10.
Overall width affects multi-column documents.

Column-wide alignment restricts to single column

Frame-wide alignment creates banner headline

Indenting and outdenting text

Ventura lets you push one or more lines in a paragraph further inside (indent) or outside (outdent) the normal left margin. You can control how far to push the text and how many lines should get this treatment.

Note: Attention word processing users: Ventura doesn't use tabs or spaces to indent the first line of a paragraph, so don't type them into your word processing files. Simply type the text flush left. Then use the procedures below to add an automatic indent to each paragraph.

Indenting and outdenting involve three options in the Alignment dialog box. The First Line list box determines whether you are pushing the text to the right (an indent) or to the left (an outdent). The In/Outdent Width text box controls how far to push the text. And the In/Outdent Height text box controls how many lines will be affected. (A fourth option controls a special kind of indent called a *relative indent*, which we'll explain in a moment.)

You start by selecting either Indent or Outdent from the First Line list box. Indent pushes text to the right. This is the most common choice, and it's the way you create the indented first line that is seen in many books and manuals (although not in this one). Outdent pushes text to the left. You can use it to position text outside the normal left margin. It comes in handy for the effect called a "hanging indent," where the first line is further to the left than the rest of the paragraph.

Tip: There is no "Off" setting in the First Line list box. If you don't want any indent at all, select either Indent or Outdent (it doesn't matter), and give it a width of zero.

After you select Indent or Outdent, move to the In/Outdent Width text box and type in the amount you want to push the text. You can use any amount you want, but the most common choice for paragraph indents is one em space. An em space is equal to the point size of the type. Thus, if you were working with 10-point type, you'd normally apply an indent of 10 points. If you were using 14-point type, you'd indent it 14 points.

Finally, go to the In/Outdent Height text box and type in the number of lines you want to affect. By far the most common choice is to indent (or outdent) only the first line. But Ventura lets you affect up to 99 lines. For instance, you can create an unusual and appealing look for brochures and annual reports by indenting the first two or three lines of each paragraph instead of just the first one.

Note: If you are switching to Ventura from another page layout program or from an advanced word processor, you may have used outdents to create bullet lists and indents for drop caps (a drop cap is an enlarged first character). You don't have to do this work on your own in Ventura. Ventura has built-in formats for bullets and big first characters, which are found in the Special Effects command in the Paragraph menu. These built-in formats do the indenting and outdenting automatically, so you don't have to bother. For more information on bullets and big first characters, see Chapter 5, "Building Advanced Styles."

Example: If you are following along with our example chapter, try indenting Body Text one em space using the three Alignment dialog box options discussed above. (Hint: an em space is equal to the point size of Body Text.) Now, go back to the Alignment dialog box and change First Line from Indent to Outdent. You've just created a hanging indent. Experiment with some other options. For instance, try indenting the first three lines instead of just the first line. (Hint: Make the In/Outdent Height equal to three.) When you're through experimenting, use Revert To Saved from the File menu to return to the previous version of the chapter.

Indenting the first line a relative amount

So far, we've shown you how to indent text a fixed amount. Ventura also has a useful function called a *relative indent*. To create a relative indent, you select Relative Indent: On from the Alignment dialog box. That's all there is to it.

After you make that choice, the first line is indented an amount equal to the last line of the previous paragraph. In other words, each paragraph starts where the last one left off (Figure 3-11).

Figure 3-11. Combining First Line and Relative Indent options will indent a paragraph's first line a distance equal to the last line of the previous paragraph.

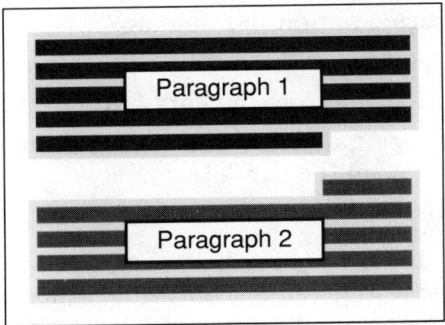

What's the value of a relative indent? It can be extremely useful when you want to combine two separate paragraphs seamlessly (Figure 3-12).

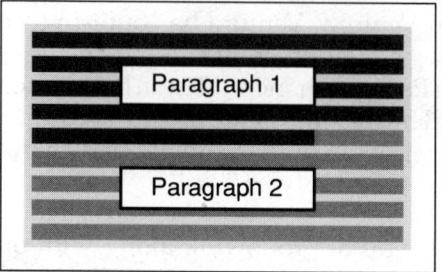

Figure 3-12. Combining alignment options with break options lets two paragraphs share a line.

Note: To combine two paragraphs on the same line, you must also change the break options, which you'll learn about later in this chapter.

Here's an important point: *You can combine a relative indent with a normal, fixed indent.* In fact, when you use a relative indent you'll probably want to use a fixed indent as well, to keep the text from the second paragraph from touching. If you look back at Figure 3-12, you'll notice that the text from the two paragraphs (represented by gray lines) butts up flush. Normally, you would want to create a first line indent of three points or so to separate one paragraph from the other.

Controlling spacing

This chapter is dedicated to the five basic style sheet functions. Up to this point, we've covered fonts and alignment. Now we're going to teach you how to control spacing.

To set the spacing options for any tag:

1. Using the Paragraph Tool, select the paragraph.
2. Choose Spacing from the Paragraph menu.
3. In the Spacing dialog box, type the values and select the options you want (Figure 3-13).
4. Click on OK.

Opening Ventura's Spacing dialog box is easy. But knowing how to use it for best results can be confusing, especially if you are brand new to graphic arts and typesetting. It may help to realize that this dialog box controls three things: (1) the spacing between lines in a

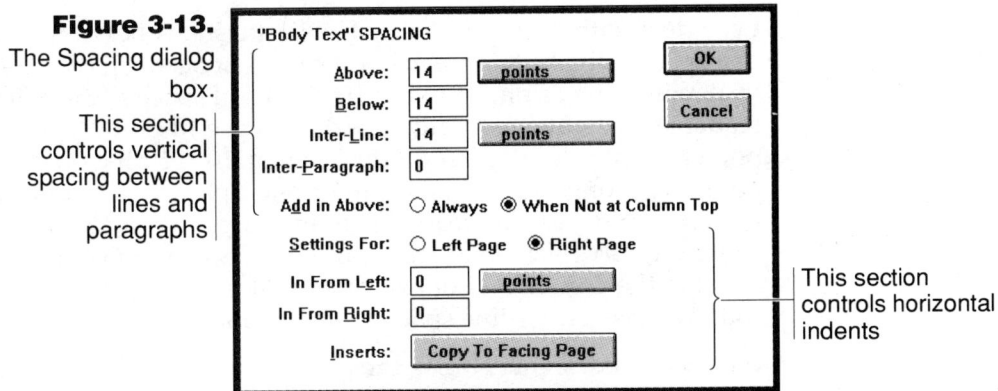

Figure 3-13.
The Spacing dialog box.
This section controls vertical spacing between lines and paragraphs

This section controls horizontal indents

paragraph, (2) the spacing above and below a paragraph, and (3) the space between the sides of the paragraph and the normal margins. Let's look at all three aspects in turn. Then we'll finish this section with a hands-on example.

Controlling inter-line spacing

We'll start our discussion of the Spacing dialog box with inter-line spacing, because it is the most important of the options.

Inter-line spacing is the distance between lines within a paragraph. Designers and typesetters often refer to it as *leading* (pronounced *ledding*). To set inter-line spacing, you simply type the amount you want into the Inter-Line text box, which is the third line down from the top of the dialog box.

Inter-line spacing is closely related to the font size. Font sizes must always be specified in points (Ventura's Font dialog box doesn't give you any alternative). Because of this close relationship, experienced users specify inter-line spacing in points. You should too. Even if you're a beginner, it won't take you long to catch on. To use points, click on the measurements button that appears next to the Inter-Line text box until the button shows Points.

The process of setting inter-line spacing is quite simple. But using this option in real life can be tricky, for two reasons. First, it takes some experience to know how much inter-line spacing to use for pleasing, readable results. Second, Ventura has a feature called Auto-Adjustments (in the Set Preferences dialog box from the Edit menu). Unless you turn this feature off, Ventura may change the inter-line spacing on its own, with unpredictable results.

Let's deal with both problems. The first issue is how much inter-line spacing to allow. As a general rule, text between the sizes of 6 to 18 points needs one to two extra points of space to make it more readable. For instance, many newsletters use 10-point type with 12 points of inter-line spacing (abbreviated 10/12). If you gave 10-point type only 10 points of inter-line spacing, it would seem crowded and hard to read. Anything larger than 18 points can usually be *set solid*—that is, it can be given an inter-line spacing equal to the point size. For example, a 30-point headline that is set solid will have inter-line spacing of 30 points.

Professional designers break these rules every day. You can too, as soon as you've amassed enough experience. In the meantime, these simple guidelines will stand you in good stead for most documents.

Now for the second problem. The Set Preferences dialog box, in the Edit menu, has an option called Auto-Adjustments. This list box has four choices: None, Styles, " And —, and Both. If you have Auto-Adjustments set to Styles or to Both, Ventura will automatically change Inter-Line spacing every time you change the font size. For instance, if you increase the size of the font by 20 percent, Ventura will increase the Inter-Line spacing by 20 percent, too. (It also changes the Above and Below spacing).

We can't think of any time when you would want Ventura to change the spacing for you. If you change the size of the font, it is *always* better to manually change the spacing, so that you can pick the best possible values. Therefore, you should always set Auto-Adjustments to either None or " And —.

Note: The option None does away with all automatic adjustments. The option " And — tells Ventura to filter text files when they are loaded into Ventura. This filter converts typewriter quotes to true typographic quotes and double hyphens to true typographic em dashes.

Fortunately, once you set this preference, it will stay that way in all your chapters until and unless you change it again.

Controlling the space above and below paragraphs

The Above and Below options in the Spacing dialog box control extra space above or below the entire paragraph. They do not affect the lines within the paragraph. You'll find yourself using these options quite often, especially the Above option. For instance, you'll probably want your headings to have extra space above.

As with all the spacing options, the trick is not how to do it (just type the amount of extra space you want into the Above and Below text boxes) but what to put in to make the page look right. For more pleasing page designs, give Above and Below spacing a relationship with the inter-line spacing of the tag. For instance, if the tag has 12 points of inter-line spacing, you should consider Above and Below Spacings such as 6, 12, 18, 24, and so on.

Tip: *Advanced users*: Your page designs will look better if you can work out a scheme so that every tag in the style sheet uses the same basic "unit" of space. That unit should be the inter-line spacing of the Body Text tag. For instance, if Body Text has 12 points of inter-line spacing, then ideally all your tags should have spacing values of 12, 24, 36, 48, and other increments of 12. This applies to both their inter-line spacing and their Above and Below spacing. Such a spacing scheme takes extra time and planning, but it results in consistent, good-looking pages.

Because you can add space both above and below, you may wonder what happens if the two values conflict. For instance, what happens if paragraph #1 has 10 points of space below and paragraph #2 has 20 points above. Will Ventura place 10, 20, or 30 points between the two paragraphs?

In general, Ventura does not add spacing values together when tags conflict. Rather, it looks at both values and uses the one that is larger. In the example mentioned above, Ventura would *not* put 30 points between the paragraphs. It would compare the two tags and then use the larger of the spacing values (20 points in this case).

The fact that above or below spacing from one tag can be overridden by an adjacent tag gives rise to an important rule for beginning desktop publishers. *Whenever possible, use above spacing by itself to add extra space.* You should avoid using below spacing unless there is no other way to get the effect you want. There are at least three reasons for this guideline:

- *Consistency*. You'll always know where to look for spacing effects—there's no guessing whether it's from above spacing, below spacing, or some combination of the two.

- *Fewer conflicts*. If all your tags use only above spacing, there's almost no chance that they'll "bump into" each other. Conflicts arise when one tag has below spacing and the following one has above spacing. That's when Ventura has to decide which value to use. If you mix and match above and below spacing, you find it hard to predict the results. The more tags you have and the longer the document, the greater the likelihood of problems.

- *Greater control.* As we'll discuss in a moment, Ventura gives you extra control over above spacing. You don't have that same control with below spacing.

When you use above spacing you have a decision to make: whether to apply it all the time, or everywhere *except* the top of a page or column. Some text elements (such as headings) need extra space above to set them off from the text. However, they do not need extra space above when they occur at the top of a column, which already has considerable white space already (Figure 3-14).

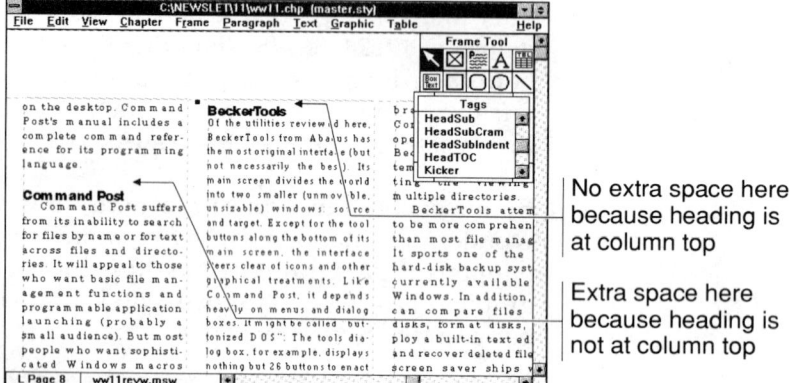

Figure 3-14. Be sure headings have Add In Above: When Not At Column Top to avoid unwanted space at the top of a column.

If you want the space above to appear at all times, select Add In Above: Always. If you want it to show up everywhere except when the paragraph is the first thing in a column or page, select Add In Above: When Not At Column Top. In most cases, you do *not* want extra space at the top of a column or page; therefore, When Not At Column Top is usually the better choice.

We've discussed three spacing options: Inter-Line, Above, and Below. If you looked carefully at the top of the Spacing dialog box back in Figure 3-13, then you noticed that there is a fourth option called Inter-Paragraph. This option applies *only* when there are two adjacent paragraphs with the same Inter-Paragraph spacing value. Otherwise, Ventura ignores the settings.

Note: We recommend that you do not use the Inter-Paragraph options. Set its value to zero for all tags.

Controlling horizontal spacing

To this point, we've discussed the top half of the Spacing dialog box, which controls vertical spacing. The lower half controls horizontal spacing. It lets you put additional space between a paragraph and the normal margins. It even lets you add different amounts of space on left and right pages, to create mirrored pages.

Earlier in this chapter, we showed you how to indent the first line (or first few lines) of a paragraph with the Alignment command. The In From Left and In From Right options in the Spacing dialog box have a similar purpose, with two key differences. First, these options apply to every line in the paragraph. Second, they can be used to indent the paragraph from the right, not just the left.

Many people use these Spacing options together with the Alignment command to create hanging indents. First, they push the entire paragraph to the right with In From Left. Then, they push the first line back to the left with First Line: Outdent from the Alignment dialog box. Another common use for these options is to set a paragraph off from the rest of the text. For example, long quotations are usually indented, so that readers can easily distinguish them from regular text.

To add extra space between the normal margins and the text, type the amount you want into the In From Left and In From Right text boxes. For instance, if you wanted quotations to start 12 points in from the normal body text, you would type 12 points into the In From Left text box and 12 points into the In From Right text box.

You can vary the horizontal spacing on left and right pages using the Settings For buttons. When you open the Spacing dialog box, the Right Page and Left Page buttons correspond to the page you are on. For instance, if you are on a right page when you choose the Spacing command, the Right Page button will be darkened.

You can use these buttons to create different spacing values for left and right pages. One common use for this feature is to create mirrored page designs. On a two-page spread in a mirrored page design, the left and right pages are mirror images of each other. That is, everything is the same, except that it's on the opposite side.

For instance, notice how the main headings in this book appear to the left of the body text. This is true whether you are on a left page or a right page. If we had used a mirrored page design instead, the main headings would have been to the left on left-hand pages and to the right on right-hand pages.

To create a mirrored page design, you first type the spacing values for one page. Then you click on the other Settings For button and type the values for the second page. The values for the second page should be the mirror opposites of the first page. For instance, if your body text is seven picas In From Left on left-hand pages, it will be seven picas In From Right on right-hand pages.

In most cases, you want the same values to apply to both pages. If you do nothing, Ventura assumes that you want the same values on both left and right pages and will set things up that way automatically. All you have to do is type the values for one page, and Ventura will copy them to the other page when you click on OK. However, if you have put different values on the opposite page and you now want to make the pages identical, you can click on Inserts: Copy To Facing Page, which will make the pages match again.

Example: We've spent some time looking at the three aspects of the Spacing dialog box. Let's try them out with our example chapter by creating a special tag for quotations. For the sake of practice, we'll give this new tag extra space between lines, above and below the paragraph. We'll also indent both the left and right sides from the normal margins.

You can get started by selecting any Body Text paragraph with the Paragraph Tool. Choose Add New Tag from the Paragraph menu to create a new tag called Body Quote. Now choose Spacing from the Paragraph menu and give the new tag settings of Above: 28 points, Below: 28 points, Inter-Line: 21 points, Inter-Paragraph: 0 points. Move to the lower half of the dialog box and make In From Left: 28 points and In From Right: 28 points.

After you've looked at the results of your changes, feel free to try out some other spacing options. When you're done experimenting, use Revert To Saved from the File menu to return the chapter to its previous condition.

Controlling breaks

You're almost done. So far, you've learned some essential skills for making a tag: choosing the font, the alignment, and the line spacing. Now, we're going to show you how to break things up.

You can control where a paragraph begins and ends, using the Breaks command from the Paragraph menu (Figure 3-15). A *break* is the point where a line, column, or page begins or ends. There are three types of breaks:

- Page breaks
- Column breaks
- Line breaks

Figure 3-15.
The Breaks dialog box.

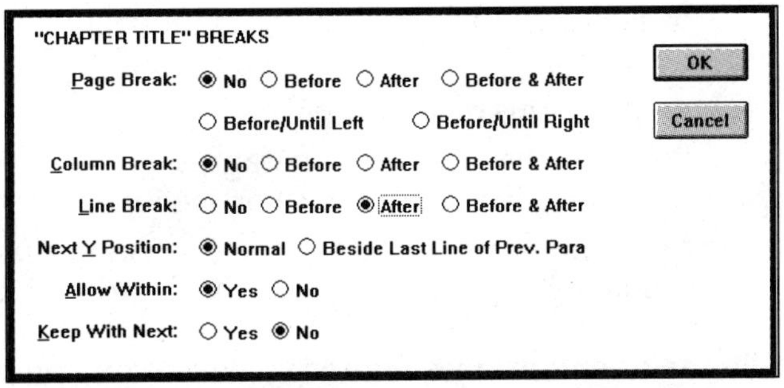

```
"CHAPTER TITLE" BREAKS

Page Break:      ● No  ○ Before  ○ After  ○ Before & After      [ OK ]
                 ○ Before/Until Left    ○ Before/Until Right    [ Cancel ]
Column Break:    ● No  ○ Before  ○ After  ○ Before & After
Line Break:      ○ No  ○ Before  ● After  ○ Before & After
Next Y Position: ● Normal  ○ Beside Last Line of Prev. Para
Allow Within:    ● Yes  ○ No
Keep With Next:  ○ Yes  ● No
```

The Breaks dialog box allows you to apply these breaks to a paragraph tag. A paragraph can have breaks before, after, both before and after, or none at all. The position of the break determines a paragraph's position relative to the paragraphs that precede and follow it. For example, a paragraph that has a Page Break: Before setting will always be at the beginning of a page.

The Breaks dialog box has six groups of buttons. By combining these options in different ways, you can control what parts of your document stay together and where others break apart.

Look scary? Don't worry. In this section, we'll show you how to set the three kinds of breaks (page, column, and line) to get the effects that you want.

For more information on using the Breaks command for advanced formatting tricks such as custom bullets, see Chapter 5, "Building Advanced Styles."

Controlling how pages break

A page break is where a new page begins. The Page Break options let you determine when and where a paragraph has a page break. You have six options:

- *Before* makes the paragraph begin on a new page no matter what proceeds it. Use this option to force major headings to appear at the top of a page.

- *Before/Until Left* makes the paragraph begin on a new left page, creating a blank right page if necessary. Use this option when you want a paragraph to begin a double-page spread.
- *Before/Until Right* makes the paragraph begin on a new right page, creating a blank left page if necessary. Use this option for the first paragraph of a section or chapter in a book—the first page of a chapter is usually a right page.
- *After* makes the paragraph end on a page so that the next paragraph begins on a new page.
- *Before & After* places the paragraph on a page by itself. Use this option to place a document or sectional title on a page by itself.
- *No* gives the paragraph no page breaks. This acts as your "Off" switch when you don't need the page break function.

Note: Ventura does not recognize a word processor's page break codes in text files. Therefore, you must use the Page Break options to manually control page breaks.

Controlling how columns break

A column break is the place where a new column begins. With the Column Break options, you determine where a paragraph has a column break. You have four options:

- *Before* makes the paragraph begin at the top of a new column. Use this option for headings or any paragraph that should always appear at the top of a column.
- *After* forces the next paragraph to a new column.
- *Before & After* places the paragraph in a column by itself. Use this option for headlines in a multi-column layout, such as a newsletter (Figure 3-16).
- *No* turns off this function.

The most common—and usually the best—option is to select Column Break: No. This lets Ventura decide where to break columns. Use this option first. Then use the other Page Break, Column Break, and Line Break options to fine tune the look of your document.

Controlling how lines break

Designers often use the term *line break* to mean beginning text on a new line without creating a new paragraph. (To do this in Ventura,

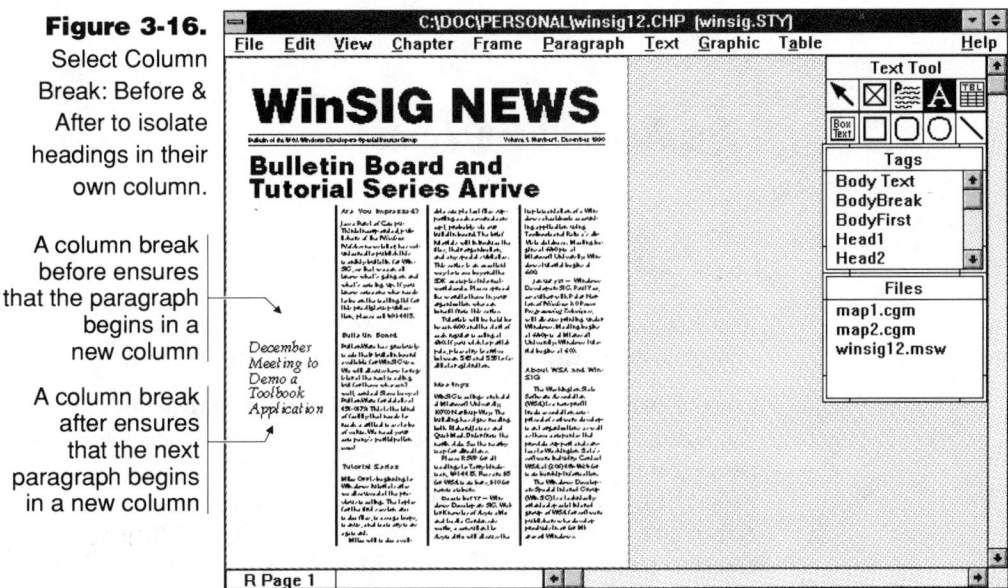

Figure 3-16.
Select Column Break: Before & After to isolate headings in their own column.

A column break before ensures that the paragraph begins in a new column

A column break after ensures that the next paragraph begins in a new column

select the Text Tool, place the text cursor where you want to break the line, and press Ctrl-Enter—the next line will begin at the left on a new line and will still be part of the original paragraph.) However, Ventura's Line Break buttons in the Breaks dialog box control only the line breaks *between* paragraphs, not the lines within them. Most paragraph tags have a line break to separate them from other paragraphs. You have four options:

- *Before* makes the paragraph begin on a new line no matter what precedes it.
- *After* makes the paragraph end with a line break, beginning the next paragraph on a new line.
- *Before & After* gives the paragraph line breaks both above and below it.
- *No* gives the paragraph no line breaks.

Usually, you'll want to keep your paragraphs separated by line breaks—that is you won't want paragraphs to have overlapping lines (Figure 3-17).

To make paragraphs start on a new line, be sure that each paragraph has either a Line Break: Before or Line Break: After setting. Overlapping paragraphs usually occur when a paragraph with Line Break: Before is followed by a paragraph with Line Break: After. To separate a paragraph from surrounding paragraphs using

Figure 3-17.
These two paragraphs don't have a line break to separate them—so the text overlaps.

line breaks, you select Before & After. With this setting, you can ensure that paragraphs don't overlap each other.

On the other hand, you may want certain paragraphs to reside on the same line. To make a paragraph reside on the same line as the preceding paragraph, you select Line Break: No. However, the preceding paragraph must not have a tag with an After or Before & After line break; otherwise, there will still be a line break between the two paragraphs. An After line break overrides a No line break.

With the No line break option, you can create special purpose tags that can work in combination with other tags. See the nearby sidebar, "Creating a special break tag."

Creating special effects with the Breaks command

The No line break option isn't the only way to force paragraphs to reside on the same line. You can use a combination of paragraphs that do not have a line break between them. For example, if you precede a paragraph with a Line Break: After setting with a paragraph with a Line Break: Before setting, you'll get the same effect as the Line Break: No.

By using a combination of paragraphs that have different line break settings, you can create special effects such as blended paragraphs (a paragraph that begins on the last line of the previous paragraph) and side-by-side paragraphs (two paragraphs that begin on the same line, beside each other). However, to get these effects, you'll have to use the other options in the Breaks dialog box—and adjust other paragraph settings as well. First, we'll explain the Next Y Position, Allow Within, and Keep With Next options. Then we'll show you how to use them to create blended and side-by-side paragraphs.

Fine-tuning vertical position

You can force a paragraph to begin on the first or last line of the previous paragraph. You just use the Next Y Position option.

To begin a paragraph on the first line of the previous paragraph, tag the first paragraph with Line Break: Before (or No). Then tag the second paragraph with Line Break: No (or After) and select Next Y Position: Normal. To begin a paragraph on the last line, select Next Y Position: Beside Last Line Of Prev. Para.

Note: If the first paragraph is only one line, the results will be the same for both Normal and Beside Last Line Of Prev. Para.

Creating a special break tag

Using the Page Break option, you can create a special tag to force the next paragraph onto the next page. This technique works best when you apply this tag to a paragraph symbol on a line with no text. This paragraph is called the "null" paragraph.

You can use the Line Break option to place it on the same line as the previous tag and align it horizontally to the right, so it is always out of the way on the right side and is easily visible and selectable. Here's how to make this tag.

1. Using the Text Tool, press Enter at the end of any paragraph to create a paragraph with no words in it. If you can't see the paragraph symbol on your page, choose Show Tabs & Returns from the View menu (or press Ctrl-T).
2. Using the Paragraph Tool, select the null paragraph.
3. Choose Add New Tag from the Paragraph menu (or press Ctrl-2). In the dialog box, be sure Body Text is showing in the Copy From list box. In the Name To Add text box, type the name of your new tag, such as PageBreak. Click on OK.
4. Choose Alignment from the Paragraph menu. Select Horz. Alignment: Right. Click on OK.
5. Choose Breaks from the Paragraph menu. Select Page Break: After, Line Break: No, and Next Y Position: Beside Last Line Of Prev. Para. Click on OK.

That's all there is to it. Now when you want to insert a page break, just use the Text Tool to create a null paragraph and then use the Paragraph Tool to tag the paragraph as PageBreak.

Allowing page breaks within a paragraph

By selecting Allow Within: Yes, Ventura will do some copyfitting for you. If a paragraph occurs at the bottom of a page or column and the whole paragraph won't fit, Ventura automatically splits the paragraph and puts the second part on the next page (that is, Ventura places a line and page break within the paragraph).

However, if you want the entire paragraph to stay together on one page, you simply select Allow Within: No. If the whole paragraph can't fit at the bottom, all of it moves to the top of the next page.

Here are three situations where you should select the Allow Within: No option so that a paragraph can stay together:

- Paragraphs that have ruling boxes
- Headings with multiple lines
- Special notes and warnings like the ones in this book

Keeping paragraphs together

To keep a group of paragraphs together on the same page or column, you select Keep With Next: Yes from the Breaks dialog box. This option keeps the current paragraph with the next paragraph. If there isn't enough space to place the two paragraphs on the same page, Ventura will begin a new page with those two paragraphs (if you also select Allow Within: No). This is useful for keeping headings with their text. That way headings don't wind up at the bottom of the page by themselves (Figure 3-18).

Tip: You can group a series of paragraphs, so that they appear together on the same page. Select Keep With Next: Yes for all the paragraphs in the group except the last one. Be sure that all the paragraphs in the group have Allow Within: No selected—otherwise, Ventura may put a page break within one of the paragraphs to make it fit, placing the last part of your group on the next page. Be sure that all the paragraphs will fit on one page.

Creating blended paragraphs

Now that you know how to use the Keep With Next, Allow Within, and Next Y Position options, you can put your all your new breaks skills to use. We'll start by showing you how to create blended paragraphs.

Blended paragraphs are two paragraphs that are placed together and look like a single paragraph. Why not just combine the two into a single paragraph? Usually that's the best solution. However,

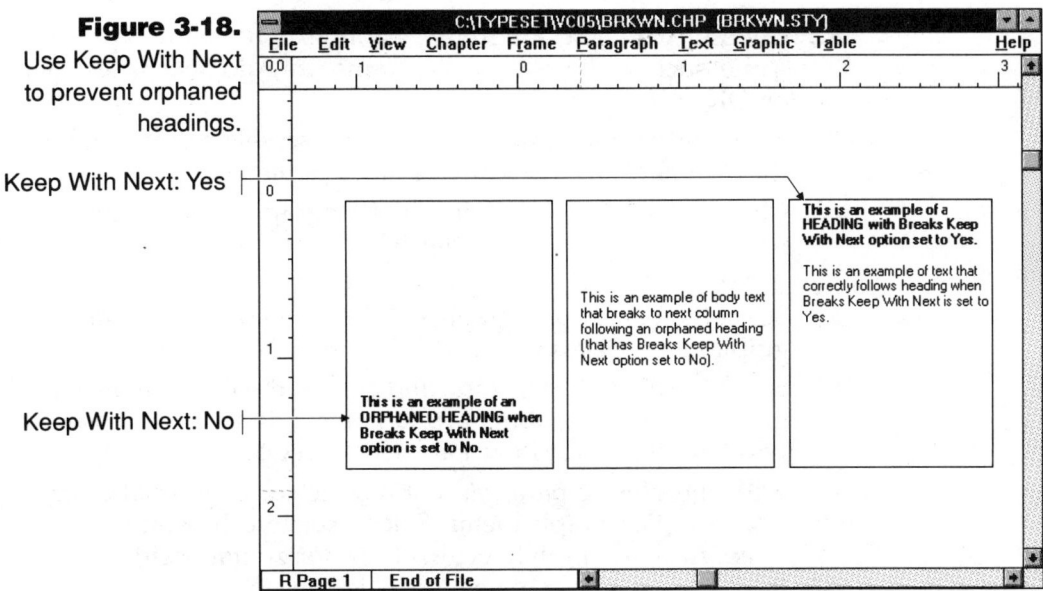

Figure 3-18. Use Keep With Next to prevent orphaned headings.

you may want to keep certain paragraphs distinct from each other, yet appear as though they are part of the same paragraph. For example, we used blended paragraphs for the numbered lists in this book—one paragraph for the number followed by another for the text. This allowed us to apply different formatting for each paragraph easily.

There are three parts to creating blended paragraphs. First, you create new tags for the two paragraphs you want to blend, so that the special paragraph settings won't affect other paragraphs. Second, you use the Breaks dialog box to be sure that the two paragraphs do *not* have a line break between them. Finally, you make the second paragraph begin on the last line of the first paragraph (select Next Y Position: Beside Last Line Of Prev. Para) and give the second paragraph a relative indent (Alignment dialog box) to make it begin where the text of the previous paragraph ends.

***E*xample:** Blending paragraphs isn't something you do every day. If you are following along with our example chapter, try this example to get the hang of it. Let's create a heading that resides on the same line as the main text that follows it. Here's how:

1. Using the Paragraph Tool, select the first paragraph that you want to blend. In this case, select the paragraph that contains the heading "The Adventure Begins."

2. Choose Add New Tag from the Paragraph menu. Type a tag name such as Blend1 in the Name To Add text box. Click on OK.

3. Select the second paragraph. In this case, select the paragraph that begins "This trip really began in September...."

4. Choose Add New Tag from the Paragraph menu. Type a tag name such as Blend2 in the Name To Add text box. Click on OK.

5. Select the Blend1 paragraph and choose Breaks from the Paragraph menu. Select Line Break: Before. Click on OK.

6. Select the Blend2 paragraph and choose Breaks from the Paragraph menu. Select Line Break: After. Select Next Y Position: Beside Last Line Of Prev. Para. Click on OK.

7. With the Blend2 paragraph still selected, choose Alignment from the Paragraph menu. Select Relative Indent: On. This forces the paragraph to begin at the horizontal position where the previous paragraph ended. Click on OK.

Now, you have two paragraphs (with different formats) that have been blended together to look like one paragraph (Figure 3-19).

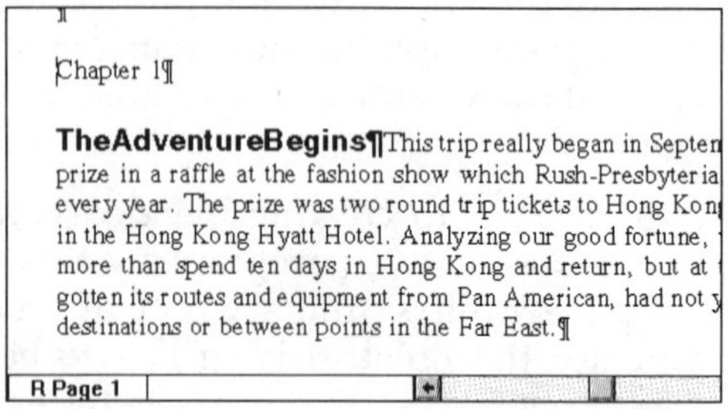

Figure 3-19.
With the Breaks and Alignment commands, you can make two paragraphs look like one.

Chapter 1¶

TheAdventureBegins¶This trip really began in Septen prize in a raffle at the fashion show which Rush-Presbyteria every year. The prize was two round trip tickets to Hong Kon in the Hong Kong Hyatt Hotel. Analyzing our good fortune, more than spend ten days in Hong Kong and return, but at gotten its routes and equipment from Pan American, had not y destinations or between points in the Far East.¶

R Page 1

8. When you're done looking over your handiwork, use Revert To Saved to return the chapter to its previous condition.

Creating side-by-side paragraphs

Side-by-side paragraphs are two paragraphs that reside on the same line. Even though both paragraphs share the same line, you can use In From Left and In From Right spacing (Spacing dialog box) to keep the two paragraphs from overlapping. Side-by-side paragraphs are handy for creating headings beside the main text instead of directly above it.

There are three parts to creating side-by-side paragraphs. First, you create new tags for the two paragraphs you want to place side-by-side, so that the special paragraph settings won't affect other paragraphs. Second, you use the Breaks dialog box to make sure that the two paragraphs do *not* have a line break between them. Finally, you adjust the In From Left for the left-hand paragraph and In From Right spacing for the right-hand paragraph, so that the two paragraphs don't overlap.

Example: Creating side-by-side paragraphs can be confusing the first few times. The best way to get the hang of it is to follow through an example. If you've been following along with our example chapter, try creating a heading that appears beside the main text. Here's how:

1. Using the Paragraph Tool, select the paragraph that you want to place on the left. In this case, select the paragraph that contains the heading "The Adventure Begins."
2. Choose Add New Tag (Paragraph menu). Type the tag name SideHeadLeft in the Name To Add text box. Click on OK.
3. Select the second paragraph. In this case, select the paragraph that begins "This trip really began in September...."
4. Choose Add New Tag (Paragraph menu). Type the tag name SideBodyRight in the Name To Add text box. Click on OK.
5. Select the SideHeadLeft paragraph and choose Breaks from the Paragraph menu. Select Line Break: Before, Next Y Position: Normal, and Keep With Next: Yes. Click on OK.

At this point, you need to decide how much horizontal space to leave for each of the two paragraphs. You make these settings in the Spacing dialog box.

For instance, our example chapter has a 39-pica column width. To set the width of the SideHeadLeft paragraph, subtract the desired width from the column width and type this value into the In From Right text box. To leave 9 picas for the SideHeadLeft paragraph, you subtract 9 picas (the paragraph width we want) from 39 (the column width) and type 30 into the In From Right text box.

To set the width of the SideBodyRight paragraph, you add the width of the SideHeadLeft paragraph to the width of the gutter that you want between the paragraphs and type this value into the In From Left text box. For instance, we've decided to give the SideHeadLeft paragraph a width of 9 picas. To make the SideBodyRight paragraph occupy the rest of the column with a 1-pica gutter between the two paragraphs, add 9 picas (the width of the SideHeadLeft paragraph) to 1 pica (the gutter width). To see how the In

From Left and In From Right option can affect the placement of paragraphs, see Figure 3-20.

Let's continue our example using these calculations for In From Left and In From Right:

6. Be sure that the measurements button next to the In From Left text box reads Picas & Points.

7. With the SideHeadLeft paragraph still selected, choose Spacing from the Paragraph menu. In the In From Right text box, type 30,00. Click on OK.

8. Select the SideBodyRight paragraph and choose Breaks (Paragraph menu). Select Line Break: After, Next Y Position: Normal, and Keep With Next: No. The Normal setting for Next Y Position makes the SideBodyRight paragraph begin on the same first line as the SideHeadLeft paragraph. Click on OK.

9. With the SideBodyRight paragraph still selected, choose Spacing from the Paragraph menu. In the In From Left text box, type 10,00. Click on OK. Now you have two side-by-side paragraphs (Figure 3-20).

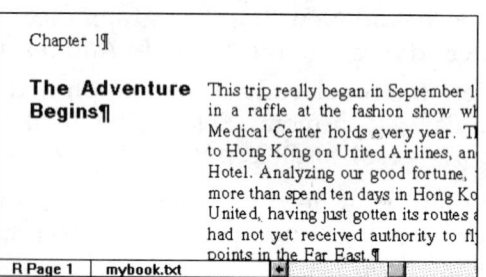

Figure 3-20. With the Breaks and Spacing commands, you can create side-by-side paragraphs.

10. When you've reviewed your work, use Revert To Saved from the File menu to return the chapter to its previous condition.

Creating ruling lines and boxes

You're about to learn the last of the five essential style sheet functions: ruling lines and boxes. You can create ruling lines above, below, or around a paragraph with these three commands on the Paragraph menu:

- Ruling Line Above
- Ruling Line Below
- Ruling Box Around

Each of these commands invokes a dialog box. Three times the number of dialog boxes, three times the trouble? Not at all. All three dialog boxes serve essentially the same function—to draw a line near a paragraph. So they are virtually the same. Things are already getting easier.

Ventura also gives you a preview of your creation. While you select the specifications of your line or box, you can watch a sample of it appear in a Preview Box within the dialog box (Figure 3-21).

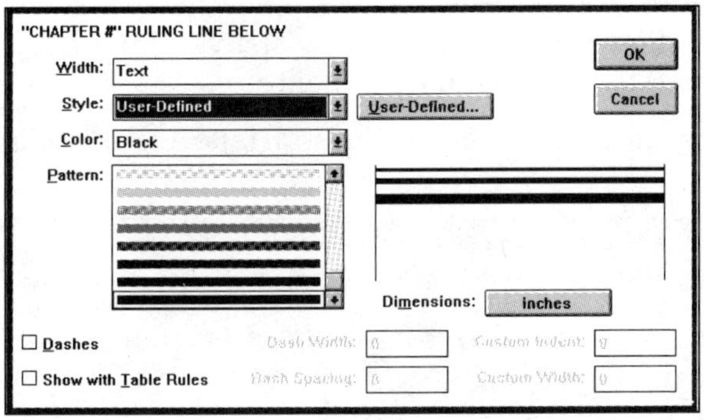

Figure 3-21.
The interactive display and flexible options of the ruling lines dialog box.

We'll guide you through the basic steps of creating ruling:
- Setting the width of the ruling lines
- Creating dashed lines
- Setting the thickness of the ruling lines
- Setting the pattern and color of the ruling lines

Although the number of lines and the overall width have limits, you still have more than enough control over the available options to create unique and striking effects—without ever having to lift your hand to (re)align your lines.

But wait. There's more than one way to draw ruling lines. See the nearby sidebar, "More than one way to draw the line."

Controlling the width of ruling lines

With the Width list box, you control how far a ruling line extends across the page. A ruling line can span the width of four page elements or can be a custom width. Let's take a look at the options:

- The *Frame* setting creates lines that fill the width of the frame containing the paragraph, when the tag's Overall Width is set to Frame-Wide in the Alignment dialog box (Paragraph menu).

- The *Text* setting creates lines that conform to the width of the first line of the paragraph.
- The *Column* setting creates lines that fill the width of the column containing the paragraph, provided the tag's Overall Width is set to Column-Wide in the Alignment dialog box.
- The *Margin* setting creates lines that fill the space between the frame's margins *minus* any In From Left or In From Right spacing applied in the Spacing dialog box (Paragraph menu).
- The *Custom* setting creates lines that start at any horizontal position on the page and can span any width. You'll learn more about this option in a moment.

To see an example of each option, take a look at Figure 3-22.

More than one way to draw the line

Ventura gives you three ways to place lines and boxes around paragraphs:

- Graphic tools
- Box Text
- Ruling lines (Ruling Line Above and Ruling Line Below) and Ruling Box Around commands from the Paragraph menu

Graphic tools. Beginners may be tempted to use this first way, but don't. Boxes made with Ventura's Graphic tools don't move with the text as it changes (through editing or formatting). So consider this a warning, and avoid this method. For more information on creating lines with Ventura's Graphic tools, see Chapter 9, "Creating Pictures in Ventura."

Box Text. This second method is good for text associated with frames (usually pictures). In this case, the boxes you create will stay with the associated text. But Box Text acts like a separate graphic, and not part of the main body of your text. Consequently, you may have difficulty keeping the Box Text positioned just where you want it in the flow of your writing. For more about frames and Box Text, see Part Four, "Pictures."

Ruling Lines and Boxes. Ruling Line and Ruling Box commands give you the most flexibility for adding ruling lines to selected paragraphs within your document. These ruling lines follow the paragraph for which they are defined—wherever it goes.

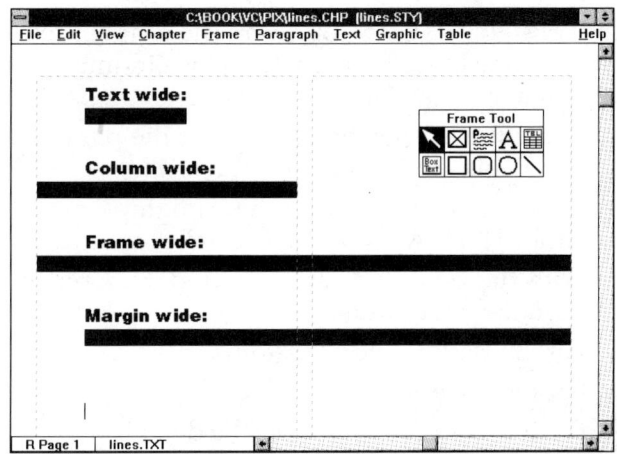

Figure 3-22.
Ventura's predefined line widths. You can also create custom widths.

There is really no difference between the Frame and Column ruling line widths. In either case, the width of the line conforms to the width of the paragraph as specified in the Overall Width list box in the Alignment dialog box.

Like many formatting options, there is no "Off" setting in the ruling line dialog boxes. If you don't want any lines at all, choose the appropriate ruling line command from the Paragraph menu, and set Width to None. This is the default setting.

*E*xample: Now try this command to enhance our example chapter. Using the Paragraph Tool, select the paragraph with the text "Chapter 1" (tagged as Chapter #). Then choose Ruling Line Below from the Paragraph menu. In the dialog box, create a ruling line with a Width of Text and a Style of 4 Point. Click on OK. When you finish, use Revert To Saved from the File menu to return to chapter to its previous condition.

Creating custom widths

Not satisfied with the preset rule widths? Try setting your own. When you select Custom from the Width list box, you activate the Custom Indent (starting position) and Custom Width (length) text boxes in the lower right corner of the dialog box. The Indent can be a positive number (to the right of the left margin) or a negative number (to the left of the left margin). The Width can be any length up to the page width. Naturally, you must type some number greater than zero in this box to see a custom rule.

Example: Try it. Using our example chapter, set a rule starting at 1 inch outside the left margin (into the binding) that will extend out to the right margin. Here's how:

1. Using the Paragraph Tool, select the paragraph "The Adventure Begins" (tagged as Chapter Title).
2. Choose Alignment from the Paragraph menu and select Center for Horz. Alignment. Then click on OK.
3. With the paragraph still selected, choose Ruling Line Below from the Paragraph menu.
4. For the Width, select Custom.
5. For the Style, select 18 Point.
6. For the Color, select Black (the default).
7. For the Pattern, select the third pattern from the top.
8. Click on the Dimensions button until it reads Inches.
9. In the Custom Indent text box, type -1.
10. In the Custom Width text box, type 7.5.
11. Click on OK. Your line should appear on your page.
12. When you've reviewed your work, use Revert To Saved from the File menu to return the chapter to its previous condition.

Controlling the pattern and color of ruling lines

How about something less formal than black and white? You can select from a variety of colors (to use on a color printer or to create spot color masters) and patterns (different tints created by dot patterns). You simply use the Color and Pattern list boxes.

Note: You can set the spacing and height options individually with User-Defined Style. However, the color and pattern of all ruling lines created with a single Ruling Line command must be the same. Of course, you can use different colors and patterns if you use both Ruling Line Above and Ruling Line Below.

Example: If you're following along with our example chapter, use this option to add an 18-point gray ruling line above the paragraph "Chapter 1" (tagged as Chapter #). Make the rule Text wide. Your dialog box should have the same settings as Figure 3-23. Then click on OK. When you're finished, use Revert To Saved from the File menu to return the chapter to its previous condition.

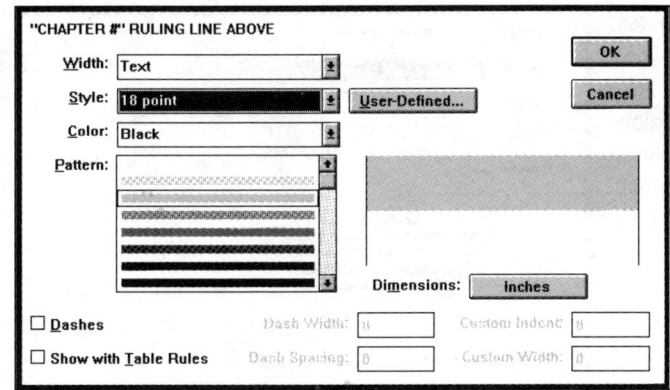

Figure 3-23.
Choosing color and pattern in a Ruling Lines dialog box.

Creating dashed lines

In addition to controlling color and pattern, the ruling line and ruling box dialog boxes allow you to create custom dashed lines. Just set up a line the way you normally would; then click on the Dashes check box near the bottom of the dialog box. This activates the Dash Width and Dash Spacing text boxes, where you specify the size of the dashes and the space between them. The Preview Box in the dialog box shows you what your creation will look like.

Tip: When typing values into the Dash Width and Dash Spacing dialog boxes, the Preview Box isn't always instantly updated. To update the preview, click on some other option in the dialog box, such as reselecting your chosen pattern.

Example: If you're following along with our example chapter, select the paragraph "Chapter 1" (tagged as Chapter #) and create an 18-point gray Ruling Line Above just as you did in the last section. This time, however, click on the Dashes check box, and choose Inches for your Dimensions. Give your dashes a width of .25 inches and a spacing of .1 inches. If you like, also give it a custom width (Figure 3-24). When you're finished, use Revert To Saved (File menu) to return the chapter to its previous condition.

Controlling the thickness of ruling lines

As you've probably guessed, the Style list box lets you control the thickness of ruling lines. Again, Ventura gives you a wide selection of styles, ranging from a single Hairline to Triple 1/2 Point lines (Figure 3-25).

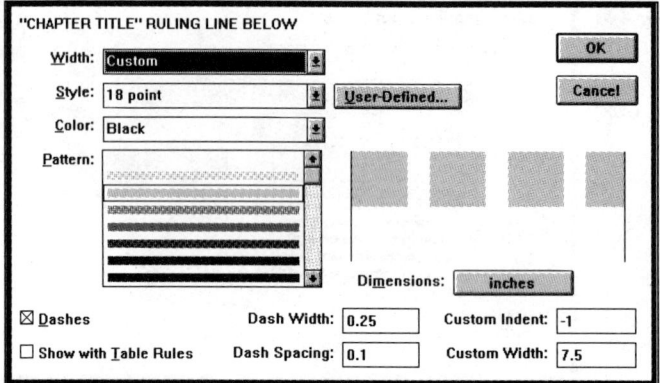

Figure 3-24. Setting a custom indent and width for a Ruling Line Below, with user-defined dashes.

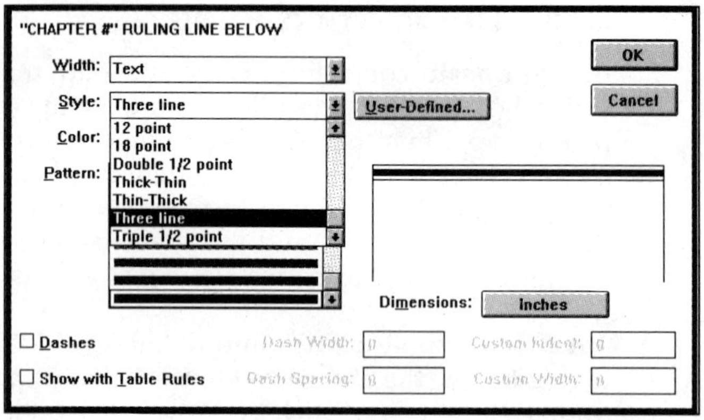

Figure 3-25. Style options in the Ruling Line dialog box.

Although Ventura automatically calculates the spacing between the text and the line when you select predefined styles, you may need to make adjustments to its settings. If you don't like the spacing or if you want to create unequal spacing between the text and each ruling line, you can click on the User-Defined button to create custom spacing and thickness for up to three ruling lines (Figure 3-26).

Note: In the User-Defined Ruling Style dialog box, Ventura refers to the thickness of horizontal lines and boxes as Height. In the next chapter, you'll see that Ventura refers to the thickness of vertical lines as Width.

The text boxes in the User-Defined Ruling Style dialog box are self-explanatory. The Height Of Rule options let you specify the thickness of each of the lines. The Space Above options let you type the exact amount of space you want to appear above the top edge of each line. To add space below the bottom edge of a ruling line,

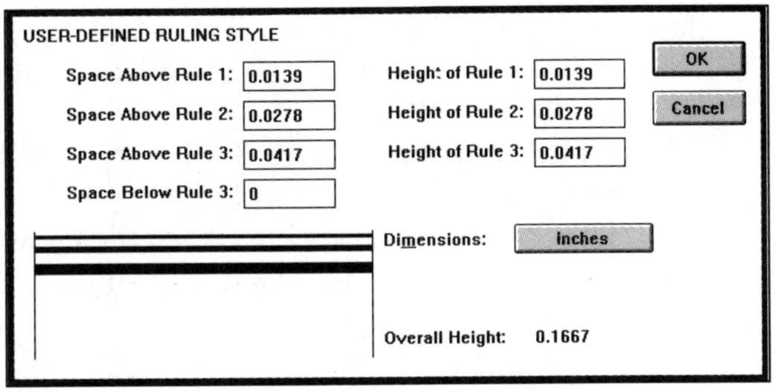

Figure 3-26.
Ventura's User-Defined Ruling Style dialog box lets you create your own styles.

use the Space Below Rule 3 box, even if you only have one or two rules. (For a ruling box, Space Above adds space outside the box; Space Below adds space inside the box.) As usual, there is a Dimensions button, and below that you see the words "Overall Height." Here Ventura reports the total spacing and height of the currently chosen ruling lines. Finally, a Preview Box shows what the settings will look like (just like the previous dialog box).

Note: Though Ventura can only display (actual size) Heights of up to ½ inch in the Preview Box, you can specify larger widths, which you will be able to see in the workspace and on the printed page.

Note: The resolution on your screen differs from the resolution of what is printed on your laser printer and what is printed by a commercial typesetter. This especially affects thin rules. See Chapter 13, "Printing Ventura Documents," for details.

Example: If you're following along with our example chapter, try creating a graduated, triple-line pattern below a paragraph, where each line (and space) gets thinner as it moves away from the text. Select the heading "Chicago to Tokyo" (tagged as Major Heading) and use the Ruling Line Below command. (Hint: Make the height and space above the first rule 1 point, the height and space above the second rule 2 points, and the height and space above the third rule 3 points.) When you're finished, use Revert To Saved from the File menu to return the chapter to its previous condition.

Using negative spacing

Like many commands chosen from the Paragraph menu, the User-Defined Ruling Style dialog box accepts negative number values for spacing. By using a negative value for Spacing Below Rule 3, you can lower a Ruling Line Above, so that it covers the text.

Example: If you're following along with our example chapter, try lowering a gray ruling line so that it covers the "Chapter 1" paragraph. Here's how:

1. Using the Paragraph Tool, select "Chapter 1" (tagged as Chapter #).
2. Choose Ruling Line Above from the Paragraph menu.
3. Select Text for Width, the third pattern from the top (gray) for Pattern, and 18 Point for Style.
4. Click on User-Defined.
5. In the dialog box, set the Dimensions to Points and type -22 in the Space Below Rule 3 text box.

Your dialog box should resemble the one in Figure 3-27.

6. Click on OK in this dialog box and the previous one. Check your results in the workspace.

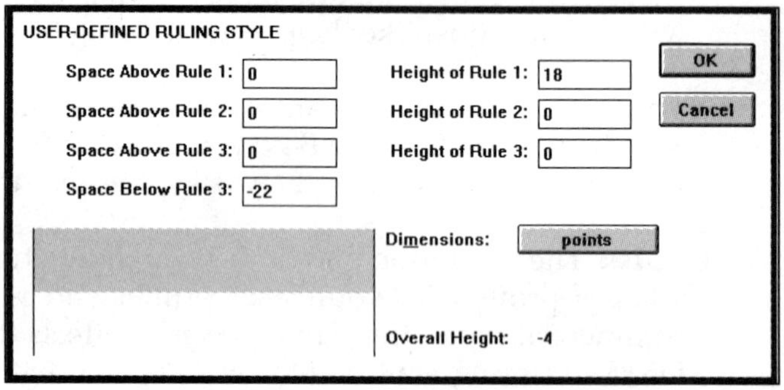

Figure 3-27.
Negative space: plumbing the depths with ruling lines.

USER-DEFINED RULING STYLE			
Space Above Rule 1: 0	Height of Rule 1: 18		OK
Space Above Rule 2: 0	Height of Rule 2: 0		Cancel
Space Above Rule 3: 0	Height of Rule 3: 0		
Space Below Rule 3: -22			
	Dimensions:	points	
	Overall Height: -4		

Tip: This same technique can be used with a darker (or solid black) color as a background behind text with a font color of white for a "reverse" effect. This will only work on certain printers. Print the CAPABILI.CHP as a test for your printer. (Of course, you can choose a color/pattern combination other than black if you are printing in color.)

Continuing on

In this chapter, you've mastered the basic skills that you need to build a style sheet and its constituent tags:

- Loading and applying style sheets
- Using efficient strategies to starting a style sheet

Chapter 3: Building Basic Styles

- Using the five essential style sheet commands: Font, Alignment, Spacing, Breaks, and Ruling Lines

By combining these tools with what you'll learn in the next chapter, you can build almost any basic document—with almost any format—from the ground up.

Easy Access

For more information on...	See chapter...
Building the underlying page	4
Building advanced styles	5
Creating a business report step by step	18
Creating a newsletter step by step	19

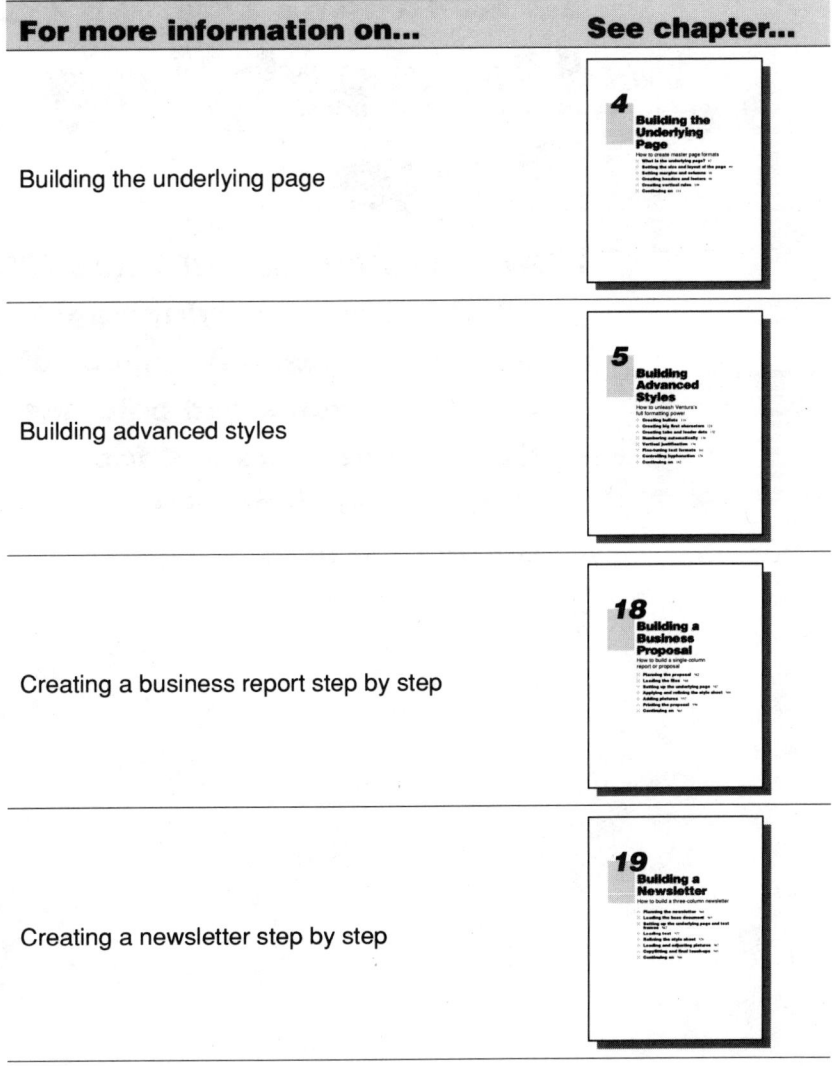

4

Building the Underlying Page

How to create master page formats

- **What is the underlying page?** 87
- **Setting the size and layout of the page** 89
- **Setting margins and columns** 94
- **Creating headers and footers** 99
- **Creating vertical rules** 108
- **Continuing on** 114

 document and its design consist of more than just attractive type or pretty pictures. As important as those elements are, the basic structure—the columns, the margins, the page orientation, the headers and footers—is crucial to the success of a document.

In the previous chapter, we introduced you to the fundamental techniques of style sheets. Those techniques relate mostly to the text—the fonts, the spacing between the lines, and so on. By contrast, this chapter deals with the foundation on which you place that text (and on which you can also place pictures, as you'll learn in later chapters).

In Ventura, the foundation for every page in a document is the *underlying page*. Ventura uses the underlying page to generate the pages in a chapter and to control the basic format.

To set up an underlying page, you simply modify its original settings to suit your needs. You can adjust these five settings:

- Page size and orientation
- Margins
- Columns
- Headers and footers
- Vertical rules

We'll show you how to modify these settings with the Chapter and Frame menus. But first, we'll explain what an underlying page is.

What is the underlying page?

The underlying page is a frame that is exactly the size of a single page in a chapter. To select the underlying page, you use the Frame Tool and click on the page at a place where there are no other frames. Sizing handles then appear around the edge of the page, showing that the underlying page is selected (Figure 4-1).

The underlying page contains the five main settings listed at the beginning of this chapter. These settings apply to every single page in a Ventura document. In short, changing the underlying page changes every page in the current document.

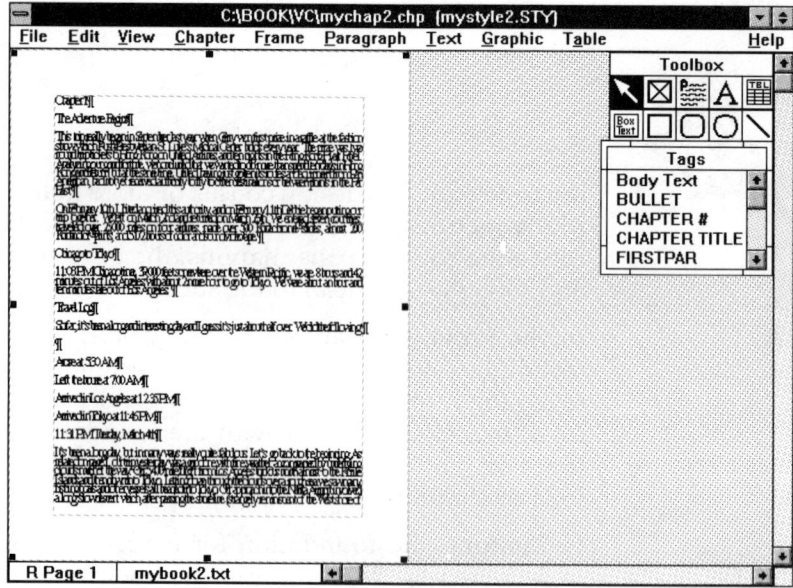

Figure 4-1.
To select the underlying page, use the Frame Tool and click on the page. When selected, sizing handles appear on the edges of the whole page.

In this respect, the underlying page is not like a regular frame. Furthermore, unlike a frame that you create on the page, the underlying page and its settings can never be deleted. Wherever there's a page, there's an underlying page. For more information on the differences between the underlying page and other frames, see the sidebar, "A word about frames," on page 90.

Note: When you load a text file onto the underlying page, Ventura automatically creates as many new pages as are necessary to hold the file. If (before loading text) you change the settings for the underlying page (such as margins and columns), you affect all pages that Ventura creates to accommodate incoming text. The only way to create different settings for individual pages is to choose Insert/Remove Page from the Chapter menu. Select whether the new page should appear before or after the current page and click on OK. Changes to the new page's settings will affect it and any pages that Ventura needs to add to accommodate a text file loaded onto that page.

Example: You'll get more from this discussion if you follow along at your computer. Using an example chapter, we'll lead you through the five main steps for building an underlying page. But first, you'll need to make the following preparations. If you have any trouble, you'll find detailed instructions in Chapter 2, "Starting Out Smart," and Chapter 3, "Building Basic Styles."

1. Start Ventura. As always, it opens to a new file and the last style sheet you used. If you already have Ventura running, choose New from the File menu.
2. Use Load Diff. Style from the File menu to load DEFAULT.STY from the \TYPESET directory.
3. Use Save Style As from the File menu to save the style sheet under the new name MYSTYLE2.STY.
4. Using the Frame Tool, select the underlying page.
5. Use Load Text/Picture from the File menu to load the ASCII text file BOOK.TXT from the \TYPESET directory.
6. Use File Type/Rename from the File menu to rename BOOK.TXT as MYBOOK2.TXT.
7. Use Save As from the File menu to save the chapter as MYCHAP2.CHP.
8. To see the whole page at once at any time during your practice, choose Reduced View from the View menu (or press Ctrl-R).
9. Be sure that all of the remaining commands below Show Rulers in the View menu have a check mark. Activating these commands will help you see how the design of the underlying page affects text and pictures.

Setting the size and layout of the page

Your first step in building an underlying page is to set up the basic size and orientation of your document. To do this, choose Page Size & Layout from the Chapter menu. This produces the Page Layout dialog box (Figure 4-2). The options here control your most basic page formats:

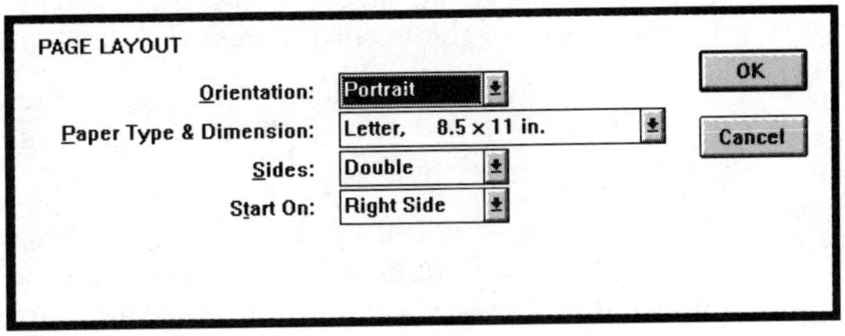

Figure 4-2. The Page Layout dialog box.

```
PAGE LAYOUT
         Orientation:   Portrait                    OK
Paper Type & Dimension: Letter,  8.5 x 11 in.       Cancel
               Sides:   Double
            Start On:   Right Side
```

- *Orientation.* Select Portrait to make the page taller than it is wide or Landscape to make the page wider than it is tall. Portrait is the most common for traditional text-intensive documents. The Landscape option is useful for making signs, overhead transparencies, and two-sided documents folded to form booklets, greeting cards, or brochures.
- *Paper Type & Dimension.* Select one of several standard paper sizes used in the United States and Europe. Ventura lets you select any option in the list box, even if your printer can't handle your chosen paper size. You'll learn how to work around this incompatibility in Chapter 13, "Printing Ventura Documents."
- *Sides.* Select Single or Double depending on the *final* appearance of your document. For example, select Double if you plan to have a commercial printer reproduce the document using both sides of each page—even if your drafts come out of a printer that can only print on one side. The Double option lets you set certain formats (such as margins and certain tags) differently for left

A word about frames

We have said that the underlying page is a frame but is different from other frames. You may be wondering which is which? And what is a frame anyway?

Frames are box-shaped containers that can be individually sized to hold graphics or text. To see some examples of frames, open the file SCOOP.CHP that comes with Ventura (it should be in your \TYPESET directory). Using the Frame Tool, click on the picture of the shuttle. See the eight black squares that appear on the sides and corners? These are the frame's sizing handles. Now click on the story under the picture. Again, you see the sizing handles, indicating the story has been placed in a frame. Click around some more and you'll see that almost everything on the page is inside a frame (except some of the vertical rules). These are regular frames.

Now click in the margins near the edge of the page. Sizing handles appear around the edges of the entire page. This frame is the underlying page.

There are times you'll want to load text into regular frames—for instance, when you have a lot of stories on one page, like the Scoop newsletter. Other times, you'll want to pour text right onto the underlying page—when creating a book, report, or manual.

and right pages. This is a useful option for books and periodicals. The Single option, on the other hand, requires identical formats for each page and is useful for letters and single-sided fliers and reports. The Double option also lets you choose Facing Pages View from the View menu so that you can see a spread that shows both a left and a right page.

- *Start on.* Select Left Side or Right Side depending on whether your document begins on a left-hand or right-hand page. For example, if you create a book using a separate Ventura file for each chapter, this option lets you decide whether your chapter will start on a left-hand or a right-hand page. (If your document is single-sided, it doesn't matter what you specify here.)

Tip: If your document requires a page size not specified in the Page Layout dialog box, don't worry. You can specify a custom page size in Ventura, print it on a standard paper size, and then trim to fit (see the sidebar, "Creating a Custom Page Size," on page 92).

Many of the skills you'll learn in this chapter can be applied both to frames as well as the underlying page: You can set the margins and columns, create ruling lines, and adjust the size of both. Sometimes, Ventura even calls the underlying page a frame (like in the Margins & Columns dialog box).

But there are differences as well. Only the underlying page can (1) automatically create additional pages to hold the text that is loaded onto it, and (2) enable a "magnetic" grid to snap frames into place.

On the other hand, frames have some advantages over the underlying page. You can move and resize frames quickly with the mouse. And you can copy frames (including their contents and attributes). Frames also have a special function that you'll learn in this chapter: They hold headers and footers in a special frame that shows on every page (except pages where you specify otherwise).

You'll learn more about using frames to hold pictures in Chapter 11, "Loading and Placing Pictures." For more on using frames to hold text, see Chapter 6, "Handling Text in Ventura."

Example: That's the theory. Now it's time to get some practice. We'll use our example file throughout this chapter to experiment with different settings just to give you a feel for how they work. Because our goal is experimentation rather than creating a specific document, feel free to play around with the options. For this exercise, let's create an underlying page that is 8.5 x 11 portrait with double sides and begins on the right side. Here's how:

1. Open the MYCHAP2.CHP file you created in the previous example.
2. Choose Page Size & Layout from the Chapter menu.

Creating a custom page size

The Page Size & Layout command lets you select the actual paper size, but not necessarily the final *trim size* (actual size of the page after a commercial printer has printed, bound, and then cut pages for your document). To use a smaller trim size than the physical size of the paper, adjust the settings in the Sizing & Scaling dialog box. For example, here's how to create a document with 7 x 9-inch trim size on 8.5 x 11-inch paper:

1. With the Frame Tool, click on the underlying page to select it.
2. Choose Sizing & Scaling from the Frame menu. This opens the Sizing & Scaling dialog box.
3. Click on the measurements button until it reads Inches.
4. In the Frame Width text box, type 7. In the Frame Height text box, type 9.

To center our custom page on the paper, we'll have to enter values in the Left Side and Top Side text boxes. (If you don't care about centering your page, skip this step.) This will take some simple arithmetic.

5. Subtract the page width from the paper width and then divide by 2:

$$\frac{(8.5 - 7)}{2} = .75$$

Do the same for height:

$$\frac{(11 - 9)}{2} = 1.$$

3. Select Portrait from the the Orientation list box (if it isn't already selected).
4. Select Letter 8.5 x 11 In. from the Paper Type & Dimension list box (if it isn't already selected).
5. Select Double from the Sides list box (if it isn't already selected).
6. Select Right Side from the Start On list box (if it isn't already selected).
7. Click on OK.

Thus, for a 7 x 9-inch page (the size of many books), type .75 in the Left Side text box and 1.0 in the Top Side text box. Your dialog box should resemble the one in Figure 4-3.

6. When you are finished, click on OK.

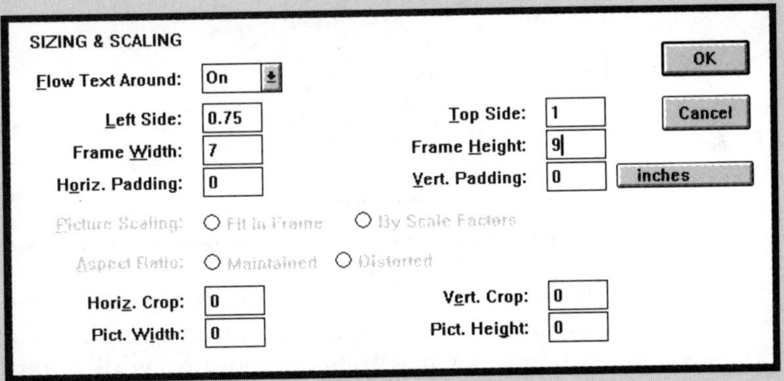

Figure 4-3.
Creating a trim size with the Sizing & Scaling command for a 7 x 9-inch book.

SIZING & SCALING				
Flow Text Around:	On			OK
Left Side:	0.75	Top Side:	1	Cancel
Frame Width:	7	Frame Height:	9	
Horiz. Padding:	0	Vert. Padding:	0	inches
Picture Scaling:	○ Fit In Frame	○ By Scale Factors		
Aspect Ratio:	○ Maintained	○ Distorted		
Horiz. Crop:	0	Vert. Crop:	0	
Pict. Width:	0	Pict. Height:	0	

Note: When it's time to print your pages, Ventura can automatically add crop marks to guide the commercial printer in trimming your pages. Just check the Crop Marks option in the Print dialog box. You'll learn more about this feature in Chapter 13, "Printing Ventura Documents."

Note: The choices we've made for our example chapter are the normal Ventura defaults. Feel free to experiment with other options if you like; then return the settings to those suggested above.

Setting margins and columns

Now that you have your basic page set up, let's define the area where you want your text and graphics to appear. That means setting the margins and columns. To do so, click on the underlying page to select it and choose Margins & Columns from the Frame menu (Figure 4-4).

Figure 4-4. Use the Margins & Columns dialog box to set up the margins and columns of the underlying page.

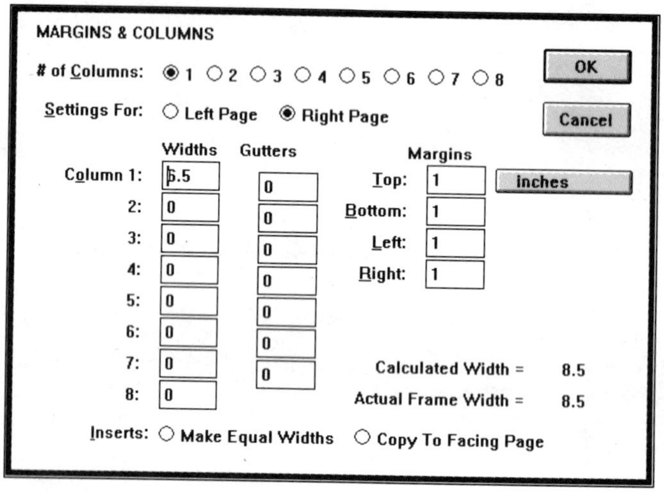

MARGINS & COLUMNS				
# of Columns:	●1 ○2 ○3 ○4 ○5 ○6 ○7 ○8			OK
Settings For:	○ Left Page ● Right Page			Cancel
	Widths	Gutters	Margins	
Column 1:	6.5	0	Top: 1	inches
2:	0	0	Bottom: 1	
3:	0	0	Left: 1	
4:	0	0	Right: 1	
5:	0	0		
6:	0	0		
7:	0	0	Calculated Width =	8.5
8:	0		Actual Frame Width =	8.5
Inserts:	○ Make Equal Widths ○ Copy To Facing Page			

This dialog box is a real number cruncher. Here, you can choose up to eight columns and four margins (for both left and right pages) with individual settings for column widths and gutters (the spaces between the columns). As you select the number of columns and plug in numbers for margins, Ventura automatically recalculates columns and gutter widths.

Note: Ventura uses the term *gutter* to define inter-column space. This term is also used by commercial printers to describe the extra "inside" margin created to adjust for binding (also referred to as a *binding margin*).

This section will show you how to:

■ Set margins

■ Set columns

- Work with unequal columns
- Work with two-sided documents

Setting the margins

Margins are the spaces between the edges of the page (or frame) and the "image area" where text or other elements can appear. Think of it this way—you tell Ventura where *not* to put text (margins, gutters, etc.) and Ventura figures out what remains (columns and image area).

The Margins section is found on the right side of the Margins & Columns dialog box. As you can see, Ventura lets you enter values for margins along the top, bottom, left, and right sides of the page.

*E*xample: Using our example chapter, plug in some new values for the margins on the underlying page. The default values are 1 inch for each of the four margins. Let's change that. Click on the measurements button until it reads Picas & Points. Type 4,00 in the Top, Bottom, and Right text boxes. In the Left text box, type 6,00 (if it isn't already there). This will leave a little extra space (or binding margin) where the pages will be bound together. When you click on OK, you'll see a slight change in your document. Finish by choosing Save from the File menu.

Setting columns

You've probably already guessed how to use this dialog box to create columns on your underlying page or frame. But we'll give you a quick run down of the options. You'll use the following options in the Margins & Columns dialog box:

- *# Of Columns*. Click on the button corresponding to the number of columns you want on your page, from one to eight. When you select a button, Ventura assumes you want all columns the same width. It calculates the values for column widths and displays them in the dialog box's Widths text boxes.
- *Widths*. You can type values in these text boxes to customize the width of each column. The number of boxes you can edit is controlled by the # Of Columns buttons.
- *Gutters*. In these text boxes, you tell Ventura how much space you want between each pair of columns.
- *Make Equal Widths*. If you want uniform column widths and uniform gutter widths, click on this button. When you do, Ven-

tura will calculate new column widths based on the choices you made for margins, number of columns, and the first Gutters text box. If you change your mind and want custom column widths, just click in the appropriate Widths or Gutters text boxes and type new values.

Tip: Ventura does not always instantly recalculate column widths after each change you make. To update the Widths display without closing the dialog box, click on the Right Page button (if you're working on settings for the right page) or the Left Page button (if you're working on settings for the left page), even though the button is already selected. This forces Ventura to redo the calculations. (If you're using equal column widths, clicking on the Make Equal Widths button also does the trick.)

Tip: How wide should you make the gutters between columns? The answer will depend on the purpose and feel of your document (casual, formal, etc.) as well as your own sense of creativity. But if you're new to design, here's a general rule: Make gutters between 1 and 2 picas. Any less is too narrow. Any more can create an unsightly gap.

Example: Using our example chapter, select the underlying page and choose Margins & Columns from the Frame menu. Give your page 3 columns, and type 1,06 picas & points in the first (top) Gutters text box. Then click on Make Equal Widths and watch as the column widths are calculated automatically. Click on OK. Your screen should resemble Figure 4-5. Finish this exercise by saving your chapter (press Ctrl-S).

Note: When you view the results of your choices for number of columns on the page, you may notice something that you didn't select in this dialog box: thin vertical rules are placed between each column. These inter-column rules are part of the settings for this sample style sheet. They only appear when you select more than one column. You'll learn more about these later in this chapter.

Monitoring calculated width

Near the lower right-hand corner of the Margins & Columns dialog box, you see Calculated Width and Actual Frame Width followed by some numbers. What's going on?

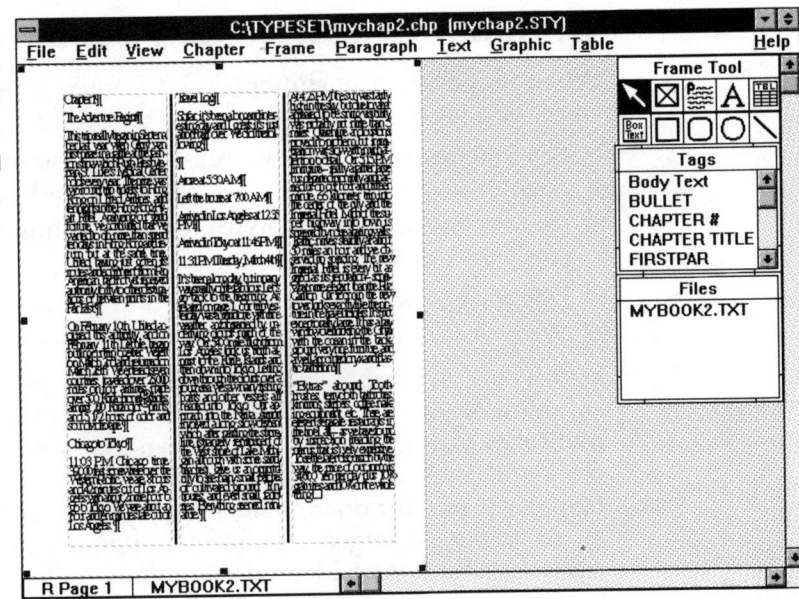

Figure 4-5.
Create this three-column layout with the Margins & Columns command (Frame menu).

Actual Frame Width is the width of your underlying page as specified in the Page Layout dialog box (discussed earlier) if you have selected the underlying page. If you are using this dialog box to format a frame, this shows the current width of the selected frame.

Calculated Frame Width represents the total width of margins, columns, and gutters. If you have used the Make Equal Widths button to generate automatic column widths, this number should be the same as the Actual Frame Width. (Don't worry if it's off a point or two; that's normal.)

If you have entered custom (unequal) widths and gutters, the Calculated Frame Width may differ from the Actual Frame Width. This can have one of two results:

- You will see a VP Alert box stating that the values you're setting for margins and columns exceed the width or height of the frame.
- Ventura will try to implement your changes anyway. When you click on OK, you may have too much or too little space in your margins or gutters.

To avoid these situations, take care to make your Calculated Frame Width add up to the same number as your Actual Frame Width.

Working with two-sided documents

When preparing a document to be printed on both sides of each sheet, you need to make some design decisions. Your options are:

- Documents where the margins and columns of the left-hand page exactly match those on the right-hand page
- Documents where the margins and columns of the left-hand page are a mirror image of those on the right-hand page
- Documents where the margins and columns of the left-hand page are different from those on the right-hand page

With Ventura, you can take your pick. Because *mirrored spacing* is a common design scheme, Ventura lets you create this format automatically. Just set up the margins and columns you want on one page and click on the Copy To Facing Page button. This is particularly useful for documents that require a binding margin (extra space on the left edge for right-hand pages and extra space on the right edge for left-hand pages).

If your document design calls for completely different or completely identical margins and columns on all pages, you'll have to do a bit more work. First, select the page from Settings For near the top of the dialog box. Type your margin and column values. Then choose the other page from Settings For and type in the same values. When you're done, click on OK.

Tip: If you want identical margins and columns on all pages and are using a perfectly symmetrical page design (equal left and right margins and equal column and gutter widths), you won't have as much work. Just use Settings For to set up one page. Then click on Copy To Facing Page to format the opposite or facing page.

Example: Using our example chapter, try creating mirrored margins and columns. Select the underlying page and open the Margins & Columns dialog box (Frame menu). Click on Copy To Facing Page. Then click on Left Page under Settings For. Notice that the wider margin we set earlier (6,00 picas & points) is now the right margin instead of the left margin. This will serve as the binding margin for our document. When you're finished, click on OK and save your work.

Creating headers and footers

A *header* (also called a *running head*) is text (or other graphic elements such as ruling lines) that is repeated at the top of each page in a document. Headers usually contain information such as the name of the whole publication, chapter titles and numbers, section titles, and page numbers. *Footers* are essentially the same as headers—except they occur at the bottom of each page.

It would be a tedious job to create headers and footers manually for every single page. But don't worry. By using the Headers & Footers dialog box from the Chapter menu, you can let Ventura generate headers and footers for every page (Figure 4-6). All you need to do is specify what you want to include in your headers and footers. In this section, we'll show you how to handle headers. Don't panic. We haven't forgotten footers—what we'll teach you about headers applies equally to footers.

Figure 4-6.
Use the Headers & Footers dialog box to type in the text you want to appear at the top or bottom of the page.

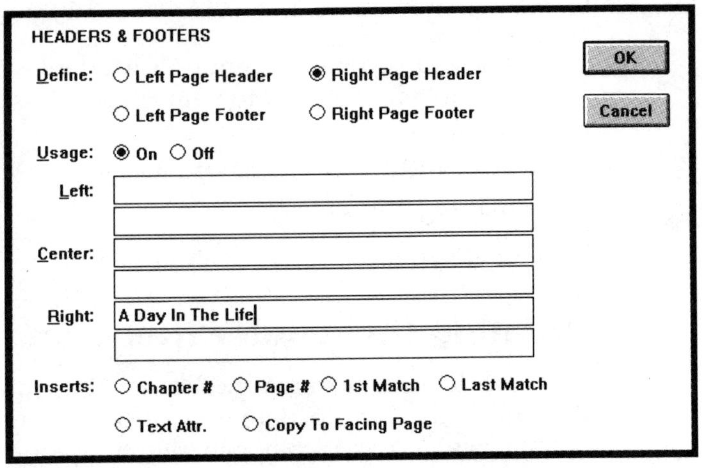

But before you dive headlong into the Headers & Footers dialog box, you'll save yourself some headaches if you know some of the theory behind Ventura's headers and footers. After you've set up the headers (we'll show you how in a moment), Ventura creates a frame for the header text on every page (Figure 4-7). Ventura gives the header frame the same left and right margins as the underlying page and centers the header text between the top of the page and the top margin. You can have up to three groups of text in the header frame: left-aligned, centered, and right-aligned. Each group can be up to two lines long. You can also specify different headers: one for left pages and one for right.

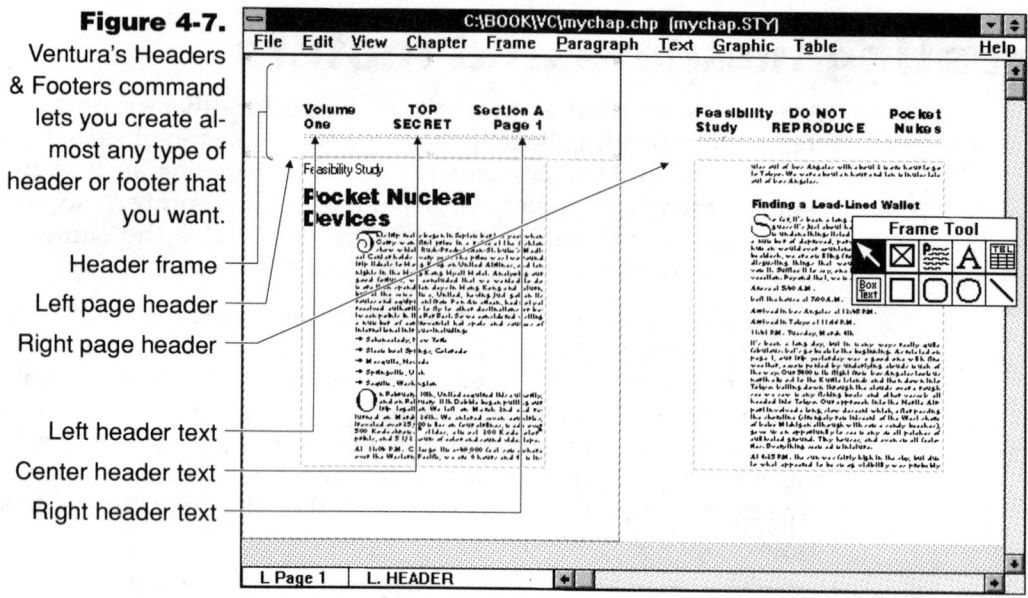

Figure 4-7.
Ventura's Headers & Footers command lets you create almost any type of header or footer that you want.

Header frame
Left page header
Right page header

Left header text
Center header text
Right header text

Now that you know how Ventura's headers work, you're ready to learn how to add a header to your underlying page. There are two main steps:

- Creating the header frame and its text
- Formatting the header

We'll guide you through each step.

Creating the header frame and its text

To create the header frame and header text, you use the Headers & Footers dialog box to define the header (Figure 4-8), and then Ventura will automatically generate the header frame and header text on every page. You can have a different header (as well as footer) for each page (left and right). If you want different headers, you must define the left page header and right page header separately. Otherwise, you can define one page and then create a mirrored copy of it on the facing page by selecting Inserts: Copy To Facing Page (Figure 4-9).

Note: If you selected Sides: Single in the Page Size & Layout dialog box, you can only specify one header—the header for the side you selected in the Start On list box in the Page Size & Layout dialog box. To create left and right page headers, you must select the Sides: Double.

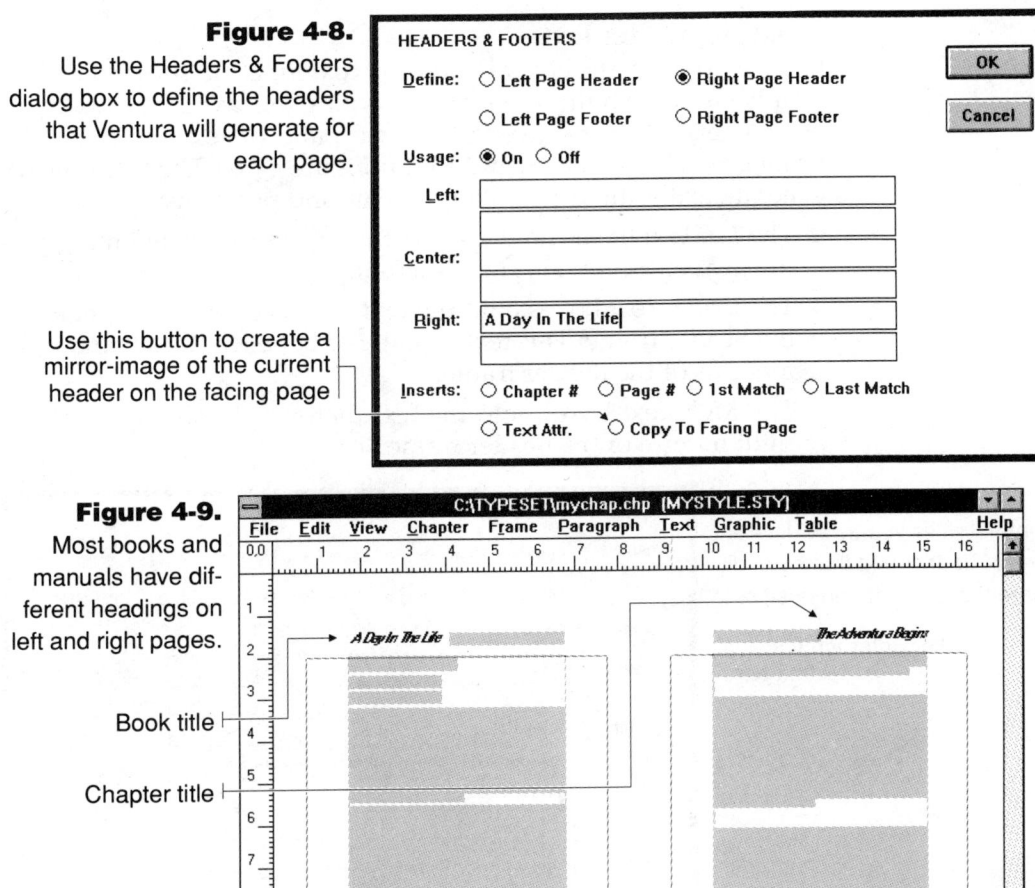

Figure 4-8.
Use the Headers & Footers dialog box to define the headers that Ventura will generate for each page.

Use this button to create a mirror-image of the current header on the facing page

Figure 4-9.
Most books and manuals have different headings on left and right pages.

Book title

Chapter title

To define a header: First, you use the Define buttons to select the header or footer that you want to use. Then you select Usage: On to turn on that header. Next you type the text (in the Left, Center, and/or Right text boxes). Use the Inserts buttons to add special codes for chapter numbers, page numbers, *live* text (text that depends on the contents of specifically tagged paragraphs), and text attributes. We'll discuss these special codes later. After you've defined all the headers that you want, you click on OK. The headers you defined then appear on every page of your chapter.

Creating header text

It's easy to select the header you want to define and turn it on—you simply click two buttons. However, typing the text can be tricky for newcomers. Ventura gives you three pairs of text boxes for the header text: Left, Center, and Right (Figure 4-10). These text boxes generate text with different alignments and positions:

- The *Left* text boxes hold the text that begins at the left margin of the header frame. This text is left-aligned.
- The *Center* text boxes hold the text that appears at the center of the header frame. This text is centered between the left and right margins of the header frame.
- The *Right* text boxes hold the text that is right-aligned with the right margin of the header frame.

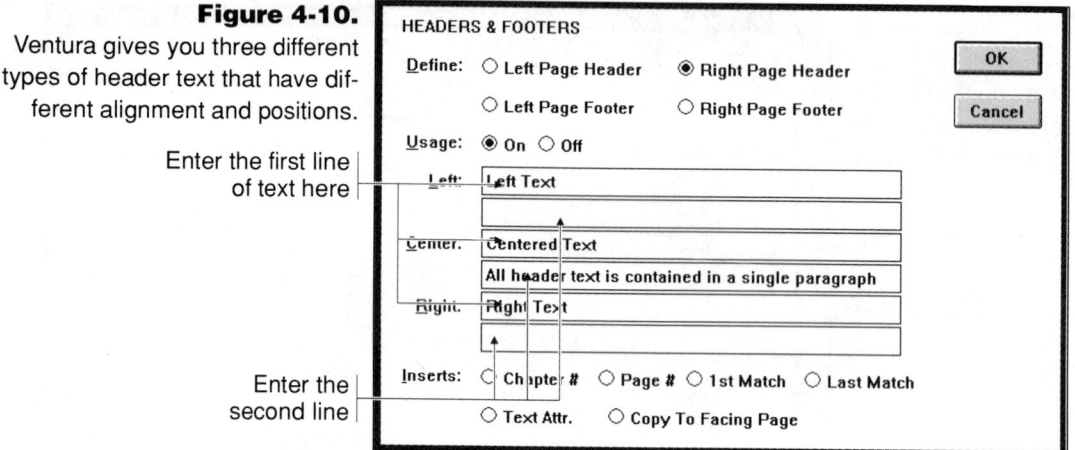

Figure 4-10. Ventura gives you three different types of header text that have different alignment and positions.

Enter the first line of text here

Enter the second line

You can have up to two lines of text for each of these types of header text. That's why there are two text boxes per type: create text for the first line in the text box next to the text box name; create text for the second in the text box below (Figure 4-10).

Note: You can create and type header text *only* in the Headers & Footers dialog box. You cannot type header text with the Text Tool. If you try to do so, a VP Alert box will appear.

Warning: Don't try to create an extra line by using a line break (Ctrl-Enter)—Ventura will think you're selecting OK (pressing Enter) and accept your current settings. But don't worry. You can go back to Headers & Footers dialog box and continue. But this time, use the text box for the second line to create a new line of text.

Example: If you've been following along with our example chapter, try creating a header with the words "Limp Left" on the left side, "Mediocre Moderate" in the center, and "Rabid Right" on the right side. Open the example chapter and choose Headers & Footers from the Chapter menu. Select Define: Right Page Header and Usage: On. Type "Limp Left" in the Left text box, "Mediocre Moderate" in the Center text box, and "Rabid Right" in the Right text box. Click on OK. Press Ctrl-S to save your work. Your chapter should now have a header similar to Figure 4-11.

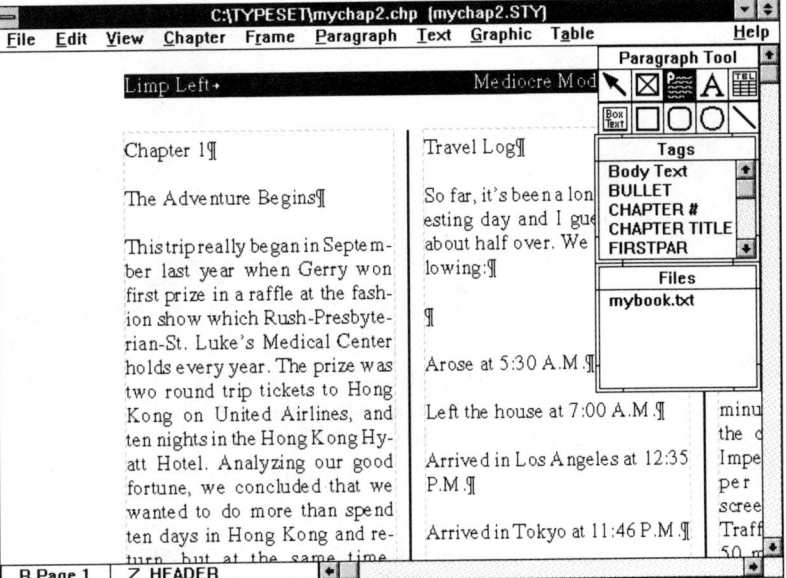

Figure 4-11. Your example chapter should look similar to this. We've selected the header paragraph with the Paragraph Tool.

In Figure 4-12, you can see that all the header text is a single paragraph—we've selected it with the Paragraph Tool. The header paragraph has Ventura's generated Z_HEADER tag (footers have the Z_FOOTER tag). The header paragraph has the attributes of Body Text. You cannot retag the header paragraph. But you can modify it with the Paragraph Tool and Paragraph menu—just as you would with any other paragraph. We'll give you some formatting tips for the Z_HEADER tag later. But first, we'll show you how to add live text and text attributes to the header text.

Note: If Z_FOOTER and Z_HEADER tags do not appear in the Tag List Window, choose Set Preferences from the Edit menu and be sure that Shown is selected in the Generated Tags list box.

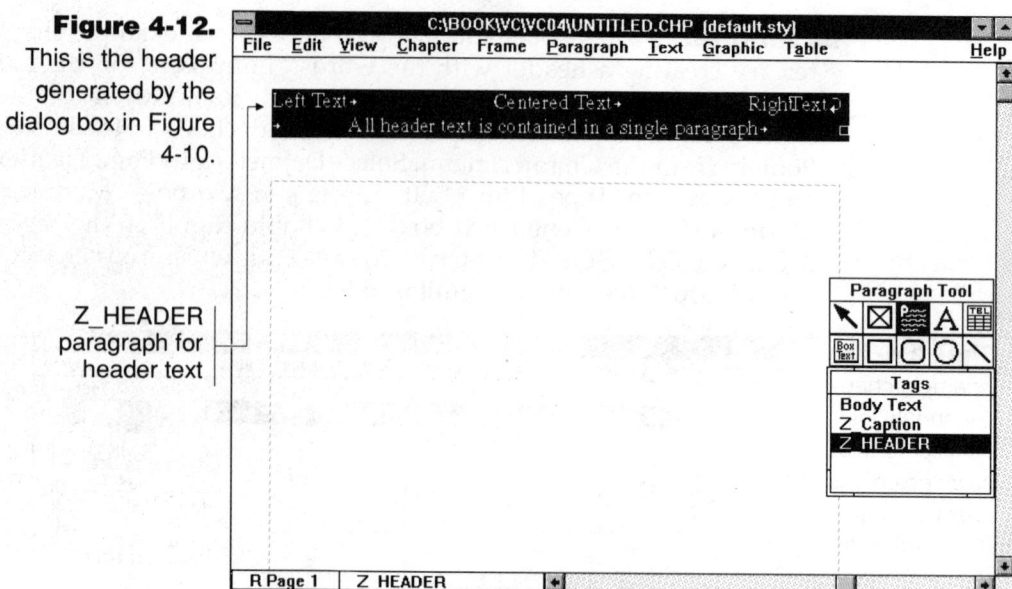

Figure 4-12. This is the header generated by the dialog box in Figure 4-10.

Z_HEADER paragraph for header text

Special codes for live text and text attributes

Typing text into the Left, Center, and Right text boxes is very similar to typing text in a word processor file. You can use bracket codes to give groups of characters an attribute such as italics or give them a different font. (You'll learn about these bracket codes in Chapter Seven, "Creating Text with Other Programs.")

However, unlike a word processor, Ventura gives you some shortcuts and has some unique codes of its own. For example, in the Headers & Footers dialog box, you use the Inserts buttons to add the codes for attributes (which are the same as bracket codes), for chapter and page numbers, and for *live text*. Live text is text that depends on the contents of specifically tagged paragraphs (Figure 4-13).

To apply text attributes, you place the text cursor where you want to begin the attribute, and select Inserts: Text Attr. The code <D> appears at the text cursor. This is the code to turn off the basic text attributes such as bold, italic, and so on. You delete the letter D and type the code that you want between the brackets. For example, <B> is the code for bold. Remember to place the <D> code (or other special return to normal code) where you want the attribute to end. For more information on using bracket codes, see Chapter 7, "Creating Text with Other Programs." For tables listing bracket codes, see Chapter 21, "Rapid Reference."

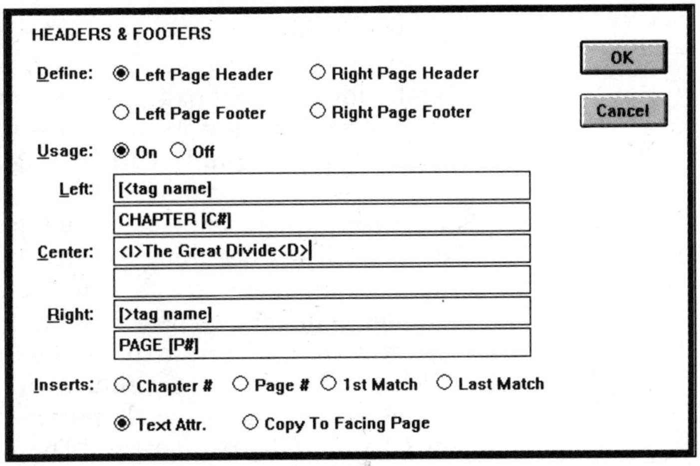

Figure 4-13.
Use the Inserts buttons to add codes for text attributes, cross references, and live text.

```
HEADERS & FOOTERS
Define:   ● Left Page Header    ○ Right Page Header
          ○ Left Page Footer    ○ Right Page Footer
Usage:    ● On   ○ Off
Left:     [<tag name]
          CHAPTER [C#]
Center:   <I>The Great Divide<D>|

Right:    [>tag name]
          PAGE [P#]
Inserts:  ○ Chapter #   ○ Page #   ○ 1st Match   ○ Last Match
          ● Text Attr.  ○ Copy To Facing Page
```

To add chapter or page numbers, you place the text cursor where you want the chapter or page number to appear, and select Inserts: Chapter # for the current chapter number or Inserts: Page # for the current page number. The code [C#] appears for the chapter number; the code [P#] appears for the page number. In the header for an actual page, the number of the current chapter appears for [C#] and the number of the current page appears for [P#].

To add live text, you use the 1st Match and Last Match buttons in the Headers & Footers dialog box. These buttons allow you to place text from paragraphs that have specified tags. However, adding live text is a little more complex because you need to decide how you want Ventura to look for these tagged paragraphs:

- The *1st Match* button tells Ventura to look for the first occurrence of the specified tag on the current page. If it finds the tag, it places the text of that tag into the header. If Ventura can't find the specified tag on the current page, it uses the text from the most recent previous paragraph with that tag.

- The *Last Match* button uses the last occurrence of a tag on the current page. Otherwise, it works the same as 1st Match.

To add the first occurrence of a tagged paragraph on the current page, place the text cursor where you want the live text to appear, and select Inserts: 1st Match. The code [<tag name] appears. Delete the words "tag name", and then type the exact name of the tag that you want to use. In the header for an actual page, the first paragraph with the specified tag on the current page appears for the 1st Match code; otherwise, the most recent paragraph with that tag appears.

To add the last occurrence of a tagged paragraph on the current page, follow the same procedure—except select Last Match. In the header for an actual page, the last paragraph with the specified tag on the current page appears for the Last Match code; otherwise, the most recent paragraph with that tag appears.

Example: If you've been following along with our example chapter, try adding a few things to the header: Add a chapter number on the left and a page number on the right. Make the page number bold italic. Insert a 1st Match in the center for first occurrence of the Chapter Title tag. Your dialog box should look like Figure 4-14. Click on OK. When you return to the workspace, your example chapter should have the chapter number on the left, the text from the Chapter Title paragraph ("The Adventure Begins") in the center, and the page number in bold italic on the right.

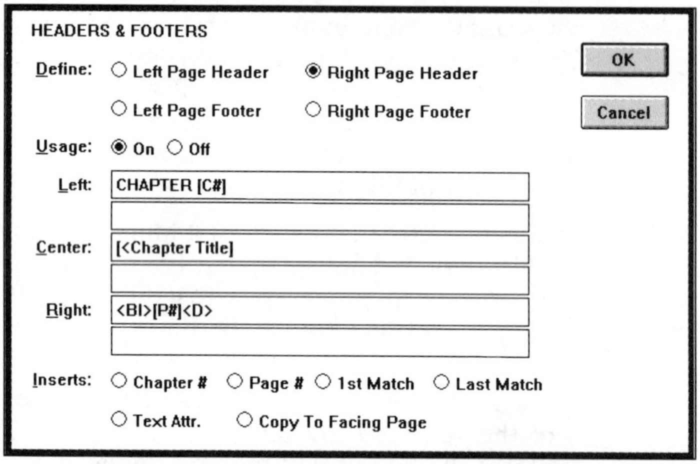

Figure 4-14. Your dialog box settings for our example chapter should look like this.

```
HEADERS & FOOTERS

Define:   ○ Left Page Header    ● Right Page Header      [ OK ]
          ○ Left Page Footer    ○ Right Page Footer      [ Cancel ]

Usage:    ● On   ○ Off

Left:     [ CHAPTER [C#]                    ]
          [                                 ]

Center:   [ [<Chapter Title]                ]
          [                                 ]

Right:    [ <BI>[P#]<D>                     ]
          [                                 ]

Inserts:  ○ Chapter #   ○ Page #   ○ 1st Match   ○ Last Match
          ○ Text Attr.  ○ Copy To Facing Page
```

Formatting headers and footers

You don't have to settle for Ventura's default header formats. You can modify the header frame and the Z_HEADER tag to suit your needs. The details about working with frames and modifying tags are covered in other chapters. We'll just touch on a few points here.

For more information on frames, see Chapter 11, "Loading and Placing Pictures." For more information on creating ruling lines and boxes for frames, see Chapter 14, "Enhancing and Editing Pictures." For more information on modifying tags, see Chapter 7, "Creating Text with Other Programs."

Modifying the header frame

You can do most things with the header frame that you can with any frame. Ventura creates the header frame based on margins you set in the Margins & Columns dialog box. That's why it's important to set margins first. If you've set them properly, you may not need to change the header frame. But if you need to, here's how:

- Change the header/footer margins using Margins & Columns from the Frame menu. For details on how to set margins for a frame, see the section "Setting Margins" in this chapter.

- Add ruling lines or boxes using Vertical Rules, Ruling Line Above, Ruling Line Below, and Ruling Box Around from the Frame menu. You can also add ruling lines and boxes using the Paragraph menu. For details on how to add Vertical Rules to a frame, see the section, "Setting Vertical Rules" in this chapter. For details on how to add ruling lines and boxes for frames, see Chapter 12, "Enhancing and Editing Pictures." For details on how to add ruling lines and boxes to paragraphs, see Chapter 3, "Building Basic Styles."

- Add colors and patterns using Frame Background from the Frame menu. To select a background color, you select the frame with the Frame Tool, choose Frame Background from the Frame menu, select the color from the Color list box and the pattern from the Pattern list box, and click on OK.

However, you cannot delete, resize, or reposition the header frame for a single page. There are ways to get around these limitations:

- To delete a header for a single page, you go to that page and choose Show Page Header so there is *no* check mark next to it. This "turns off" the header for that particular page. You can turn off a header for the whole chapter by selecting its Define button and selecting Usage: Off in the Headers & Footers dialog box.

- To resize or reposition a header frame (or at least get the same effect), you select the header frame, choose Margins & Columns from the Frame menu, and adjust the margins to move the position of the text within the frame. In short, you can't save or move the frame but you can move the text inside.

Why would you want to move the text within the frame? The header text is often positioned too high above the main text and the footer text is too low. For headers, select the header frame with the Frame Tool, then decrease the bottom margin and increase the top margin (Margins & Columns, Frame menu). For footers, increase the bottom margin and decrease the top margin.

Tip: You can also move the text within the header frame by using Spacing from the Paragraph menu. For headers, select the header paragraph with the Paragraph Tool and adjust its tag to increase the space above (Spacing, Paragraph menu). When doing this, be sure to select Add In Above: Always. For footers, select the footer paragraph and increase the space below.

Warning: Often, header or footer text is placed beyond the printable area for laser printers (which only extends up to a 1/4 inch from the edge of the page), especially when your paper and underlying page are letter size.

Formatting the header tag

After you create a header with the Headers & Footers dialog box, Ventura automatically creates a tag for the header paragraph called Z_HEADER. The tag attributes are the same as those for Body Text. To make your header stand out from the rest of the text, you should make the header tag's attributes distinct from Body Text.

You modify the Z_HEADER tag just as you would for any other paragraph. You simply use the Paragraph Tool to select the Z_HEADER paragraph and use the Paragraph menu to change the attributes of the paragraph.

For more information on modifying tags, see Chapter 3, "Building Basic Styles."

Creating vertical rules

Rules, rules, and more rules. You can add vertical ruling lines to your underlying page so that they will appear on every page.

What are vertical rules? They are ruling lines that begin at the top margin and end at the bottom margin. Vertical rules are often used to separate the columns of text in a multi-column document. However, you can also add them to single-column documents to add a decisive border between the main text and a wide margin known as a *companion column* or *scholar's margin* (Figure 4-15).

You can create two types of vertical rules:
- Vertical rules between columns (inter-column rules)
- Vertical rules at specified positions on the page

To create both types of vertical rules, you use the Vertical Rules command from the Frame menu (Figure 4-16).

Figure 4-15.
This report by Herbert Young uses a vertical rule to separate the main text from the scholar's margin.

Water Rights & Conflicts

INTRODUCTION

The use of water in Colorado can be separated into three basic areas: physical supply, legal availability and multiple use. Physical supply is the amount of water provided physically in the form of rainfall, and snowpack (precipitation), and as such is available for use in the rivers and lakes of the state. Legal availability is that amount of water that an entity is legally entitled to take out of the existing physical supply. Multiple Use is the concept of using water for many and often conflicting uses such as drinking and boating.

The State of Colorado (Figure 1) is divided into two distinctly separate regions: the "East Slope" or eastern 1/3 of Colorado and the "West Slope" or western 2/3 of Colorado. West of the Continental Divide (west slope) all water flows to the Pacific Ocean or Gulf of California. East of the Continental Divide (east slope) all water flows to the Mississippi River System. Mean sea level (MSL) elevations in Colorado vary from above 3,500 feet along the eastern Colorado-Kansas border to 14,000 feet along the Continental Divide with Denver, the State capitol, being about 5,280 feet. The second step of the state capitol building in Denver is in fact exactly 5,280 feet.

The precipitation in the state varies from about eight inches annually in the more arid regions of the state to more than fifty inches in the higher mountain ranges. The mean annual precipitation in the Denver meropolitan (metro) area is 14 to 16". Many water

v

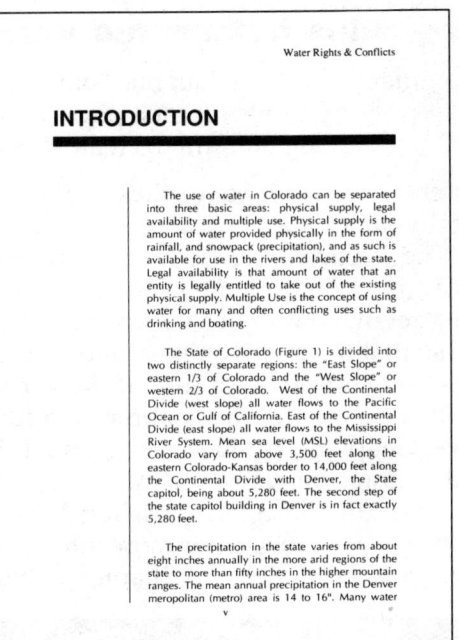

Figure 4-16.
The Vertical Rules dialog box.

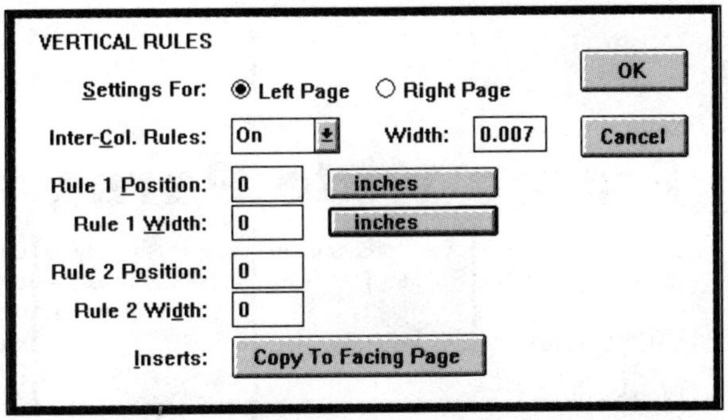

Because you make the settings for both types of vertical rules independently, you can also have both types on the underlying page simultaneously. In this section, we'll show you how to create both types of vertical ruling lines.

Note: You can also add vertical rules to frames—not just the underlying page. Just follow the same steps you'll learn in this section, except you must select the frame to which you want to add the vertical rules instead of the underlying page.

Creating rules between columns

If your document has more than one column, you can add vertical rules between the columns on each page. Using the Vertical Rules dialog box, you can tell Ventura to create those rules for you.

After you enter the settings for these inter-column rules, Ventura automatically centers a vertical rule in each gutter between the columns. The vertical rules extend from the top margin to the bottom margin. When elements such as frames or frame-wide paragraphs get in the way of a vertical rule, Ventura makes a break in the rule so that the rule won't overlap that element (Figure 4-17). For frames, the vertical rules stop at the vertical padding settings for the frame. For more information on adding padding around frames, see Chapter 12, "Enhancing and Editing Pictures." For frame-wide paragraphs, the vertical rules stop at the Above and Below settings (in the Spacing dialog box from the Paragraph menu) of the paragraph tag. For more information on adjusting the spacing for paragraph tags, see Chapter 3, "Building Basic Styles."

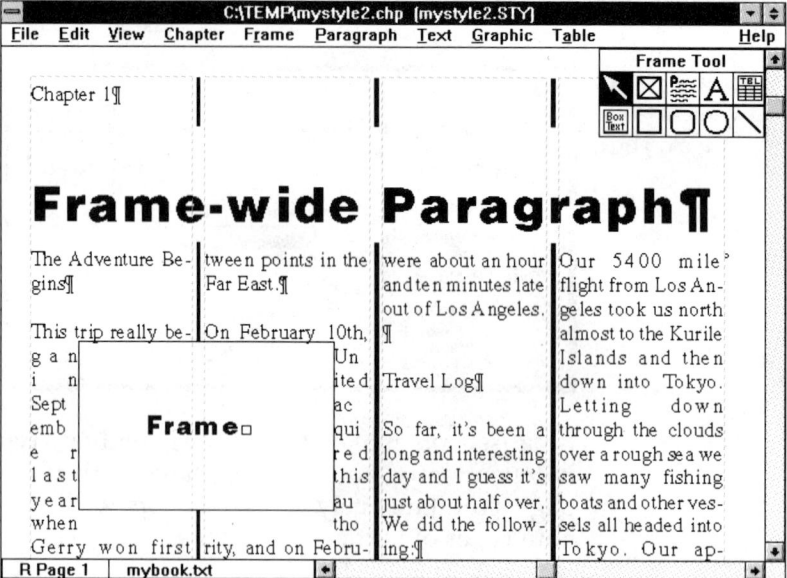

Figure 4-17. Ventura courteously breaks its vertical rules for frames and frame-wide paragraphs that cross its path—so these elements won't get run over.

Ventura also allows you to make different vertical rule settings for left and right pages—you just use the Settings For buttons to select the page for which you want to make settings. By selecting the Inserts: Copy To Facing Page, you can copy the same settings for one page (Left Page or Right Page) to the facing page.

Here's how. To create vertical rules between columns:

1. Using the Frame Tool, select the underlying page.
2. Choose Vertical Rules from the Frame menu. The Vertical Rules dialog box appears.
3. Select the page (left or right) for which you want to create vertical rules by clicking on one of the Settings For buttons.
4. Select On from the Inter-Col. Rules list box to turn the inter-column rule function on.
5. Click on the measurements button next to the Rule 1 Width text box until you see the measurement units that you want for the thickness of the ruling lines (we suggest Points).
6. Type a value for the thickness of the ruling lines in the Width text box (next to the Inter-Col. Rules list box).
7. Click on OK.

Tip: Generally, you should keep inter-column rules unobtrusive—usually less than 1 point. Better still, use inter-column rules that are ½ point or even less.

If you have a document with multiple columns, vertical rules should appear in the gutters between the columns. If you have a single column document, no vertical rules will appear (because there are no gutters). In the next section, we'll show you how to create standalone vertical rules that you can use to make vertical rules in single column documents.

Example: If you're following along with our example chapter, try adding inter-column vertical rules. Choose Margins & Columns from the Chapter menu. Be sure the measurements button reads Picas & Points. Then create four columns with gutters of 0,09 picas & points. Then choose Vertical Rules (Frame menu), select Inter-Col. Rules: On, click on the measurements button next to Rule 1 Width until it reads Points, and type 2 in the Width text box (next to the Inter-Col. Rules list box). Click on OK. Check your changes in Reduced View. Your chapter should look similar to Figure 4-18). When you're done admiring your handiwork, choose Revert To Saved (File menu) to return to the previous version of your chapter.

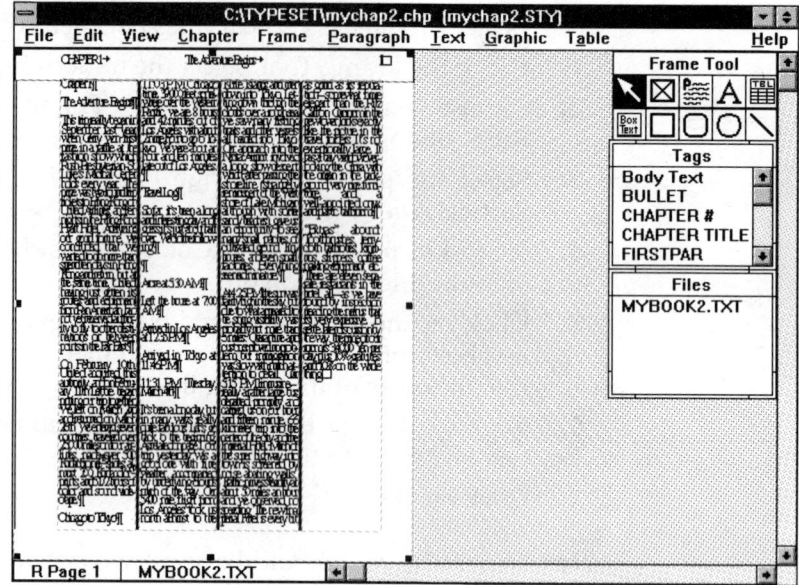

Figure 4-18. After you've completed your changes, your example chapter should look similar to this.

Creating standalone rules

The Vertical Rules dialog box also allows you to create two standalone vertical rules that are completely independent of the Inter-Col. Rules setting. With these standalone rules, you don't need more than one column for the rules to appear—you set the position and thickness of the rules for each page (left and right) manually.

Standalone rules are controlled by the Rule 1 (and 2) Position and Rule 1 (and 2) Width options in the Vertical Rules dialog box. The positions of both rules are measured from the left edge of the physical page (not the frame or margin) and will automatically extend from the top margin to the bottom margin. You use the measurement buttons to select the units for the position (the button next to the Rule 1 Position text box) and width (the lower button) of both vertical rules.

As with inter-column vertical rules, Ventura will interrupt these vertical rules for frames and frame-wide paragraphs. You can also make different vertical rule settings for left and right pages—you just use the Settings For buttons to select the page for which you want to make settings. By selecting the Inserts: Copy To Facing Page, you can copy the same settings for one page (Left Page or Right Page) to the facing page.

Example: If you're following along with our example chapter, try combining some of the other underlying page skills you've learned in this chapter with your new vertical rule skills. Create a scholar's margin (3 inch wide outer margins on each page) and add a standalone vertical rule (5 points thick and .5 inches from the text) to set off the scholar's margin from the main text. Here's how:

1. Using the Frame Tool, select the underlying page.
2. Choose Margins & Columns from the Frame menu.
3. Select # Of Columns: 1.
4. Click on the measurements button until it reads Inches.
5. Select Setting For: Right Page
6. Type 3 in the Margins Left text box to create a wide scholar's margin on the left margin of right pages.
7. Type 1 in the Margins Right text box to keep the right margin from looking too cramped.
8. Click on the Copy To Facing Page so that left pages also have a scholar's margin on the left side.
9. Click on OK.
10. With the underlying page still selected, choose Vertical Rules from the Frame menu.
11. Click on the measurements button next to the Rule 1 Position text box until it reads Inches and click on the measurements button below until it reads Points.
12. Type 5 in the Rule 1 Width text box to give the vertical rule a thickness of 5 points.
13. Type 2.75 in the Rule 1 Position text box to place the vertical rule 2.75 inches in from the left edge of the page and .25 inches from the text (left margin).
14. Click on Copy To Facing Page so that left pages also have the same vertical rule settings.
15. Click on OK.

After making these settings, your example chapter should look similar to Figure 4-19.

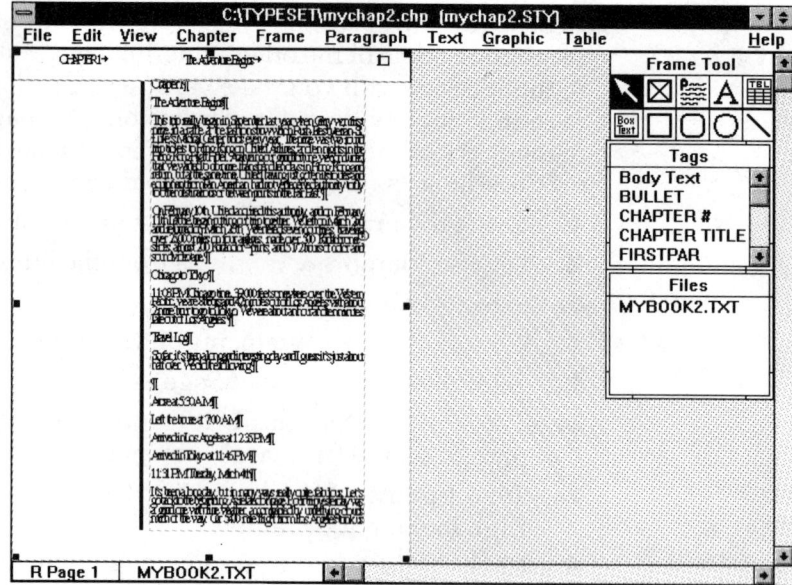

Figure 4-19.
After making your changes, your example chapter should look similar to this.

Continuing on

In this chapter, you learned how a document starts with an underlying page, which defines repeating elements such as margins and columns. You created your first underlying page, specifying the margins, columns, headers, footers, and vertical rules. You're well on your way to constructing the document of your dreams. Now you're ready to delve a little deeper. The next step: building advanced styles.

Easy Access

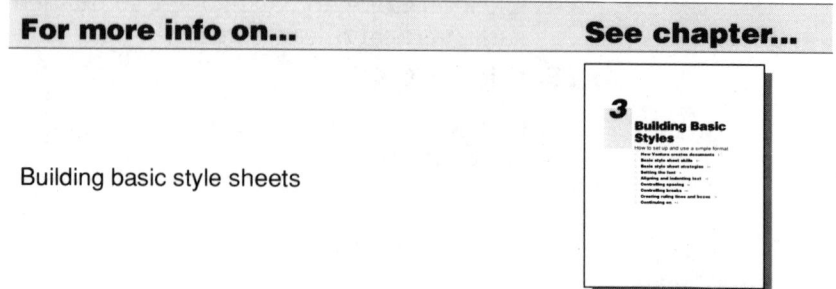

For more info on...	See chapter...
Building advanced style sheets and complex headers and footers	5 — Building Advanced Styles
Putting text onto the underlying page	8 — Creating Tables
Putting frames and pictures onto the underlying page	12 — Enhancing and Editing Pictures
Repeating frames	13 — Printing Ventura Documents
Looking inside chapter files and style sheets	19 — Building a Newsletter

5
Building Advanced Styles

How to unleash Ventura's full formatting power

- **Creating bullets** 118
- **Creating big first characters** 124
- **Creating tabs and leader dots** 132
- **Numbering automatically** 138
- **Vertical justification** 154
- **Fine-tuning text formats** 161
- **Controlling hyphenation** 178
- **Continuing on** 182

entura has a variety of industrial-strength formatting tools. This chapter will put their full power at your disposal.

You don't have to know these functions to build basic reports and other straightforward documents. And you won't use them as often as the basic skills we taught you in previous chapters. But you may appreciate them more. Some of them add flash and special effects to your documents. Others automate key tasks, so you can work more efficiently.

After you learn these advanced style techniques, you'll have the skills to build just about any kind of format. The exceptions are indexing, tables of contents, footnoting, and equations, all of which we cover in Part 5, "Printing and Advanced Features."

If you're just learning Ventura, skim this chapter to get an appreciation for the program's power. You might also keep an eye out for solutions to your own specific design problems. Then come back for in-depth advice when and as you need the individual functions. If you're already comfortable with Ventura, you can use this chapter as a learning guide to take your skills to the next stage. Or you can browse it for new formatting ideas to spice up your documents.

Either way, this chapter is your key to unlocking the advanced functions of Ventura's style sheets.

Note: Because we include advanced effects in this chapter, we sometimes mention text and frame functions that are taught in later chapters. If you are reading this book in order, simply skim these sections to get an idea of what Ventura can do. You can return to them later. We've referenced the other chapters so you can turn to them immediately if you are trying to get work done on a deadline.

Creating bullets

Bullets are used to add emphasis to items in a list. In conventional typesetting, bullets are filled black circles. With the advent of desktop publishing, a bullet can be any character used at the beginning of a paragraph. It might be an arrow, a box , a musical note, or the wretched and overused pointing finger. Figure 5-1 shows a few samples.

Figure 5-1. In Ventura, you can use any character or symbol as a bullet. You can even use small frames with pictures inside.

Standard bullets:	Common bullets:	Less common bullets:	Outlandish bullets:
• Filled circle	■ Solid ballot box	▶ Rotated filled triangle	● .38 caliber
• Simple	■ Available from main Special Effects dialog box or as a Zapf Dingbats character	▶ Zapf Dingbats character	● Brass shell/copper sheath
• Straightforward		▶ Alignment set to rotate 90 degrees	● Fits well in most police issue handguns and Saturday Night Specials
• Is smaller than some so requires less indent value		▶ Takes up more space than either circle or box	● Available at many sporting goods stores, pawn shops and stolen goods vendors
• Is highly readable and not overbearing	■ Can be set as a tint value to reduce impact		

Notice how the paragraphs in the sample are indented from the bullet. And notice that all the lines of text align properly beneath the first one. All that is done automatically by Ventura. You tell it how much space you want between the bullet and the text, and it takes care of formatting the rest of the paragraph to match.

In this section, we'll show you how to:

■ Choose a bullet character (is there a bullet with your name on it?)

■ Create bullets with the Special Effects dialog box so you can add bullets quickly by just tagging paragraphs

■ Create bullets with pictures

■ Create bullets with your word processor

Choosing the bullet character

What characters can you use as bullets? Just about anything you can imagine. The Special Effects dialog box, which you'll encounter in a moment, lists 15 popular choices, including filled circles, filled boxes, and hollow boxes (called *ballot boxes*).

In addition, this dialog box includes a button labeled Other. If you click on that button, you can type in the ASCII number for any character—the same numbers used in bracket codes. (For more information about bracket codes, see Chapter 7, "Creating Text with Other Programs.") That character doesn't have to be in the same font as the rest of the paragraph. Because changing the font is quick and easy, you can use any character, number, or symbol from any font as a bullet. And if that's not enough selection, you can use a picture as a bullet, using the advanced technique we teach you later in this chapter.

Which bullet characters *should* you use? That's a matter of taste. The safest options are the filled circle and the filled box.

Creating bullets with the Special Effects dialog box

The easiest way to create a bulleted paragraph is with the Special Effects dialog box from the Paragraph menu.

As with any other Paragraph function, you must first select a paragraph before you can activate the dialog box. In most cases, you'll want to apply the effect to a new tag, which you create first with Add New Tag from the Paragraph menu. To apply a bullet to a paragraph:

1. Using the Paragraph Tool, select the paragraph and choose Special Effects from the Paragraph menu.
2. Click on Special Effect: Bullet.
3. Click on the button for the bullet character you want.
4. In the Indent After Bullet text box, type the amount of space you want between the left margin and the text.
5. Click on Set Font Properties. When the Font Setting For Bullet Character dialog box appears, select the font and size for the bullet.
6. Click on OK twice (once to close the Font Setting For Bullet Character dialog box and once to close the Special Effects dialog box).

Example: Suppose that your body text is 11-point Palatino. You want to create a new bullet paragraph for lists. The bullets themselves will align with the left margin. The text will be spaced 18 points from the left margin. Here's how you'd build the tag:

1. Using the Paragraph Tool, select a Body Text paragraph. Choose Add New Tag from the Paragraph menu and create a tag called Bullet.
2. With the new Bullet paragraph still selected, choose Special Effects from the Paragraph menu.
3. Click on Special Effect: Bullet and Show Bullet As: Filled Circle (the filled circle is the first button).

Notice that when you click on the filled circle, Ventura puts the ASCII equivalent number into the Bullet Char box. In this case, the ASCII equivalent is 195 (Figure 5-2).

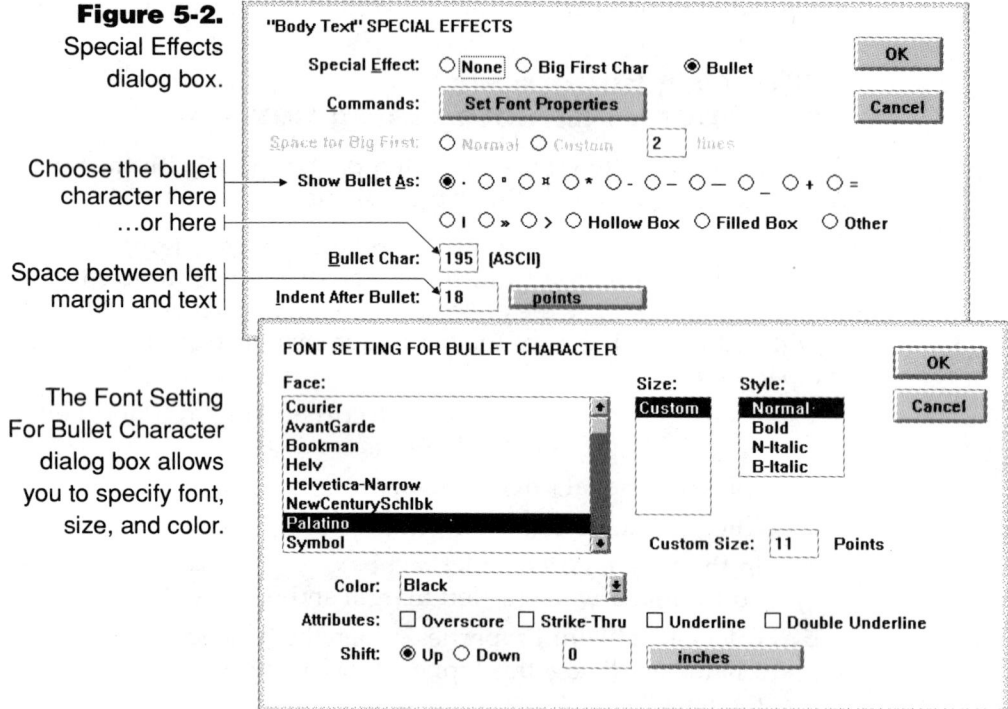

Figure 5-2. Special Effects dialog box.

Choose the bullet character here …or here

Space between left margin and text

The Font Setting For Bullet Character dialog box allows you to specify font, size, and color.

4. Change the measurements to points and type 18 into the Indent After Bullet text box.
5. Click on Set Font Properties. The Font Setting dialog box appears. Make the bullet 11-point Palatino Normal.
6. Click twice on OK to return to the workspace and view your completed Bullet tag.

Note: Chapter 21, "Rapid Reference," contains a table listing useful bullet symbols.

Using pictures as bullets

Beginning and intermediate Ventura users should skip this advanced technique for now. You can use any character from any font as a bullet, so you've already got a wide selection. But you may want to create a more dramatic effect. In such cases, you can use a picture as a bullet character. This advanced procedure involves five steps:

1. Create the picture and put it into a frame. You only need one copy of the picture in the chapter. Ventura will clone it as many times as necessary.
2. Give the frame an anchor name.
3. Create a new tag for a null paragraph, whose only purpose will be to contain the text anchor for the picture.
4. Create a bullet paragraph with an indent wide enough to leave space for the bullet (picture). Put it on the same line as the null paragraph.
5. Put the text cursor in the null paragraph and use Insert Special Item to anchor the frame at that location, using the Relative, Automatically at Anchor option.

Example: Let's step through an example. Try using a picture as a bullet character—in this case a picture of a bullet. Here's how:

1. Create the bullet in your drawing program and save it in a format Ventura can import. (If you don't feel like drawing the bullet, you can still follow along using another picture.)

In our example, we drew the picture in Corel Draw and saved it as an EPS file called BULLET.EPS.

2. Use Load Text/Picture from the File menu to load the BULLET.EPS file.
3. Create a small frame, the size of the desired bullet, anywhere on the page. Select the frame and click on BULLET.EPS in the File List to load the picture into the frame (Figure 5-3).
4. With the frame still selected, choose Anchors & Captions from the Frame menu. Give the frame an anchor name such as Bullet.

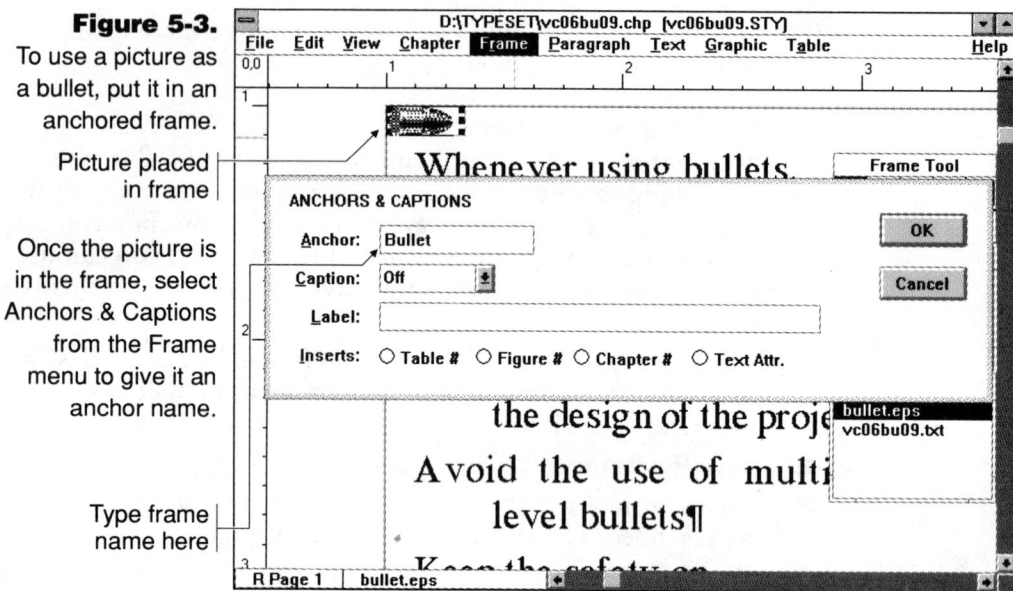

Figure 5-3.
To use a picture as a bullet, put it in an anchored frame.

Picture placed in frame

Once the picture is in the frame, select Anchors & Captions from the Frame menu to give it an anchor name.

Type frame name here

With these first steps, you have created the picture and prepared it for use as a bullet character. Now you must make space for the picture.

5. Create two new tags. The first, called Null, should be identical to Body Text except that it is flush left and has a line break *before*. The second, called Bullet, should have 18 points of In From Left spacing and a line break *after* (Figure 5-4).

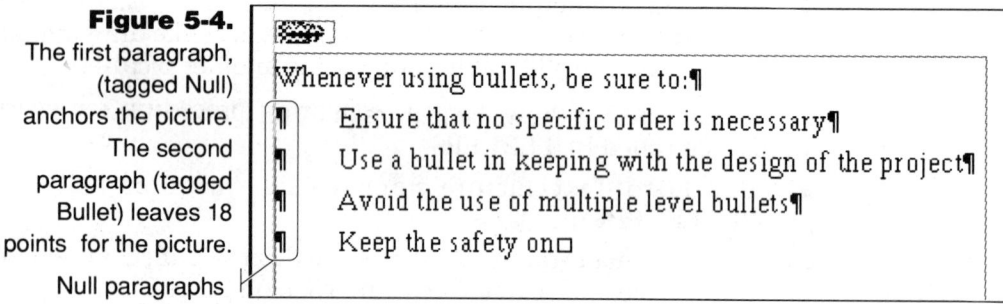

Figure 5-4.
The first paragraph, (tagged Null) anchors the picture. The second paragraph (tagged Bullet) leaves 18 points for the picture.

Null paragraphs

Because the two paragraphs do not have a line break between them, they can reside on the same line. The 18-point indent of the Bullet tag keeps them from overlapping.

Note: Strictly speaking, you don't need a null paragraph. You can put the text anchor at the front of the bullet paragraph, space the paragraph in from the left margin, then outdent the first line to push the picture to the correct position. However, many people find it easier to create a separate null paragraph to contain the text anchor.

Now you've got a picture and a place to put it. The only remaining task is to anchor the picture so it will move along with the text.

6. Using the Text Tool, place the text cursor in the null paragraph.

7. Choose Insert Special Item from the Text menu and select Frame Anchor from the flyout menu. The Insert/Edit Anchor dialog box appears.

8. Select Frame's New Location: Relative, Automatically at Anchor (Figure 5-5).

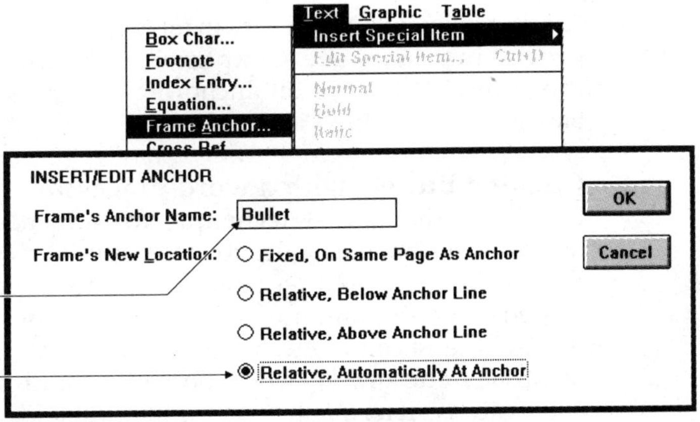

Figure 5-5.
After placing the text cursor, choose Insert Special Item from the Text menu, and choose Frame Anchor.

Last anchor name automatically appears here

Click here for type of anchor

In theory, you could repeat the anchoring procedure for every paragraph that needs this special bullet. In practice, you'll want to find a faster method. The best way is to save and close the chapter, then return to your word processor. Go to the paragraphs you just created. You'll find the new Null paragraph and the bracket codes for frame anchors. Copy these codes, put them into a word processor macro, and use the word processor to insert them in front of each paragraph.

When you return to Ventura and reopen the chapter, you'll find that all the paragraphs now have the bullet picture in front of them (Figure 5-6). You do not have to make multiple copies of the picture. Ventura clones the picture as many times as necessary and inserts it at the anchor points you specified.

Figure 5-6.
Finished typeset result.

For more information on inserting bracket codes into word processing files, see Chapter 7, "Creating Text with Other Programs." For more on anchoring frames, see Chapter 12, "Enhancing and Editing Pictures."

Creating bullets with a word processor
Here's another bullet technique for advanced users only. This method uses bracket codes to insert special characters directly into the text file. As you'll see from our example, you can even overlap symbols to create unique bullets. You simply kern the two characters so the second one appears on top of the first. Figure 5-7 illustrates one bracket code possibility and its effect. Advanced users can use it as inspiration for their own ideas. Figure 5-8 shows more bullet characters that combine the bracket code and anchored picture frame techniques.

For more information on using bracket codes, see Chapter 7, "Creating Text with Other Programs."

Creating big first characters

Ventura calls this formatting effect Big First Character, which we'll abbreviate as *BFC*. The rest of the desktop publishing world usually calls it *drop cap* or *ornamental cap*. Actually, the term should probably be *ornamental first character*, because it may not drop and it may not be a capital letter.

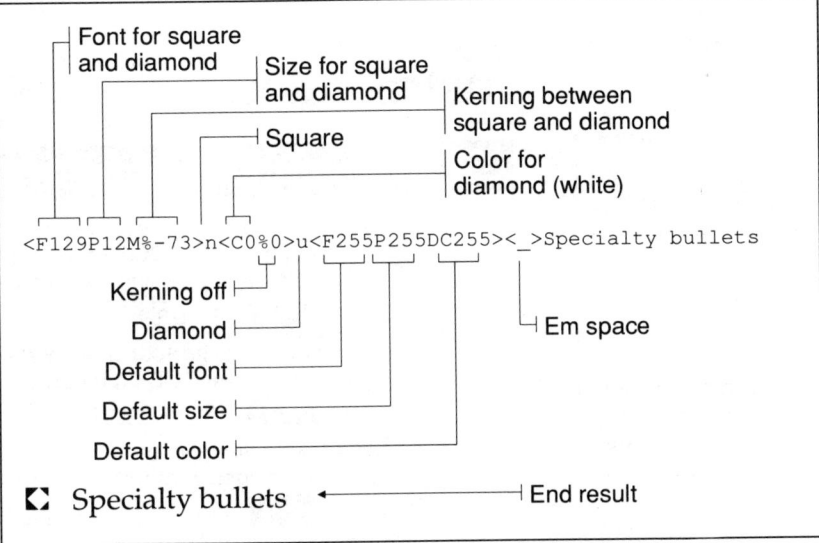

Figure 5-7. Text attributes within a word processor can create bullets when loaded into Ventura.

In this section, you'll learn how to use Ventura's built-in BFC function from the Special Effects dialog box. You'll also learn some alternate methods. We'll cover the ins and outs (as well as the ups and downs) of placing the BFC just where you want it. We'll also show you how to create reverse and shaded (gray tint screen) BFCs.

When Ventura builds a BFC, it enlarges the first character of the paragraph (you control how big it is). Then it indents the first few lines of the paragraph to create space for this enlarged character. You can let Ventura calculate the number of lines to indent, or you can specify the number of lines yourself.

Creating a BFC involves five steps:

1. Add a new tag.
2. With the new tag still selected, choose Special Effects from the Paragraph menu.
3. Click on Special Effect: Big First Char.
4. Click on Space For Big First: Normal to let Ventura calculate how many lines to indent (to make space for the BFC). Click on Custom to manually enter the number of lines.
5. Click on Set Font Properties. The Font Setting dialog box appears. Select the font, size, style, and color of the BFC. You can also shift the character up or down from its normal baseline.

Figure 5-9 shows both the Special Effects and the Font dialog boxes.

Figure 5-8.
For software installation: bulleting alternate instructions for floppy disk versus hard disk installation.

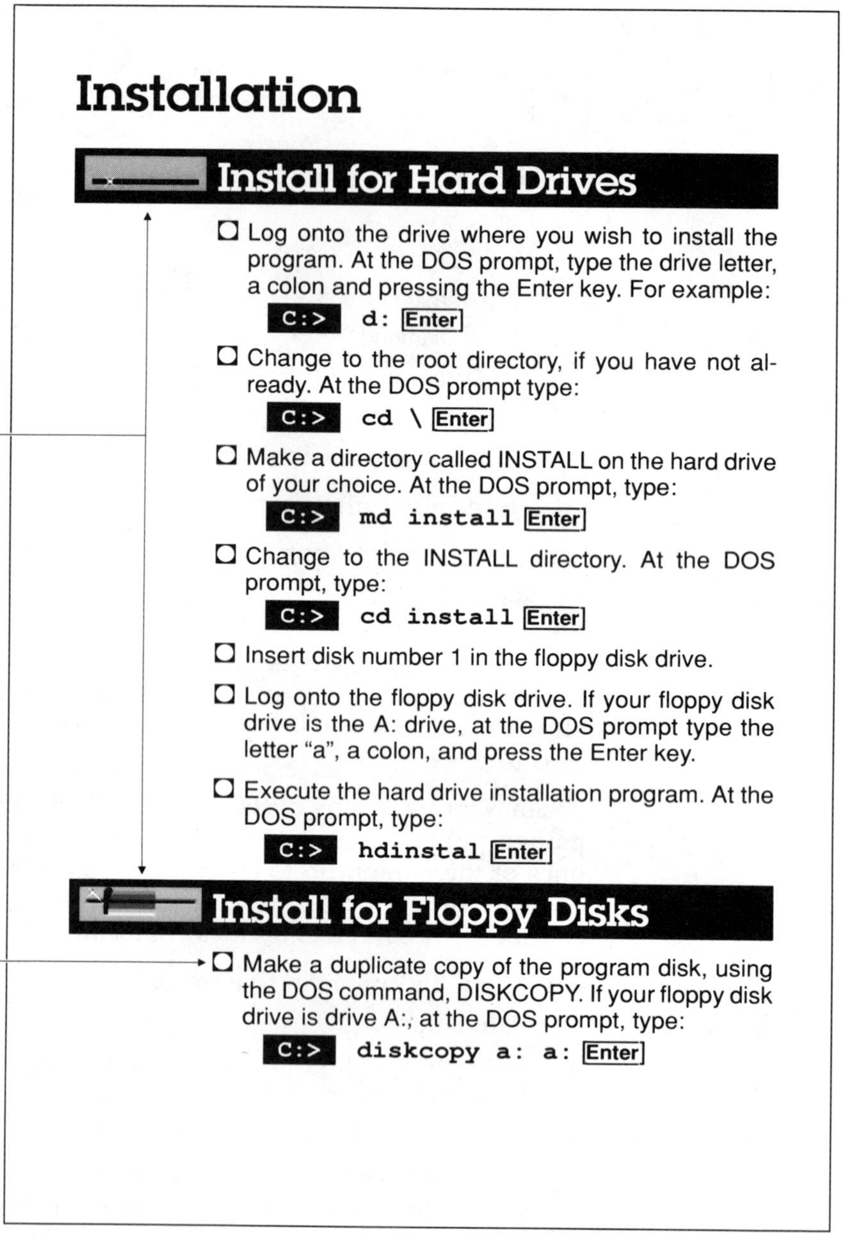

The pictures of hard and floppy disks are anchored frames

This bullet character is formed by putting a white circle on top of a black square with bracket codes in the word processor

Installation

Install for Hard Drives

- ❏ Log onto the drive where you wish to install the program. At the DOS prompt, type the drive letter, a colon and pressing the Enter key. For example:
  `C:>  d: [Enter]`
- ❏ Change to the root directory, if you have not already. At the DOS prompt type:
  `C:>  cd \ [Enter]`
- ❏ Make a directory called INSTALL on the hard drive of your choice. At the DOS prompt, type:
  `C:>  md install [Enter]`
- ❏ Change to the INSTALL directory. At the DOS prompt, type:
  `C:>  cd install [Enter]`
- ❏ Insert disk number 1 in the floppy disk drive.
- ❏ Log onto the floppy disk drive. If your floppy disk drive is the A: drive, at the DOS prompt type the letter "a", a colon, and press the Enter key.
- ❏ Execute the hard drive installation program. At the DOS prompt, type:
  `C:>  hdinstal [Enter]`

Install for Floppy Disks

- ❏ Make a duplicate copy of the program disk, using the DOS command, DISKCOPY. If your floppy disk drive is drive A:, at the DOS prompt, type:
  `C:>  diskcopy a: a: [Enter]`

In this example, we've created a BFC in 72-point University Roman type with a Normal space setting. Let's see how these choices affect the positioning of the BFC.

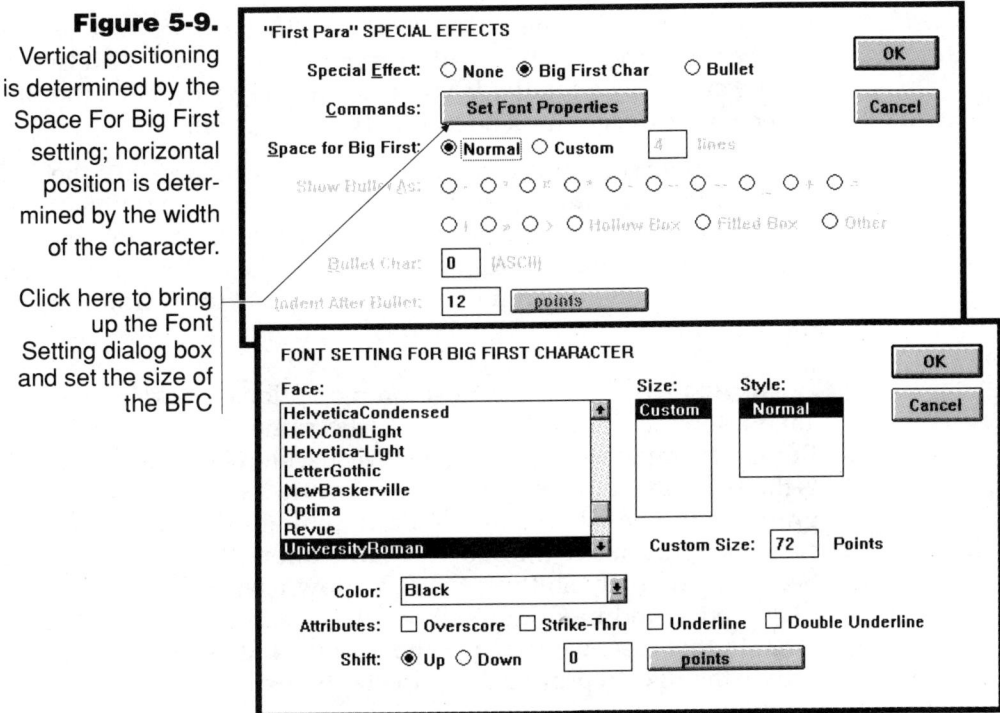

Figure 5-9.
Vertical positioning is determined by the Space For Big First setting; horizontal position is determined by the width of the character.

Click here to bring up the Font Setting dialog box and set the size of the BFC

Positioning big first characters

It doesn't take long to get the hang of building a BFC. But it's harder to learn how to position it exactly where you want. Positioning is determined in part by the size of the character. As you just saw, you set the size with the Font Setting dialog box.

Horizontal positioning is straightforward. Ventura places the BFC at the left edge of the paragraph, just as it would place any other character. Ventura uses the width of the character to decide how much to indent the rest of the paragraph.

Vertical positioning is determined by the Space For Big First setting in the Special Effects dialog box. If you click on Normal, Ventura uses the height of the BFC to calculate how many lines to indent to allow enough space for the BFC. This calculation drops the BFC so it is approximately the same height as the first line of the text that follows.

If you don't like the Normal setting, you can change it. Click on the Custom button. The text box to the right darkens to tell you it is now active. The number you see is the number of lines Ventura would indent with the Normal setting. If you type in a *smaller* number, the top of the BFC will stick up above the body text (which can be an attractive look). If you type in a *larger* number, the BFC will be more deeply imbedded into the paragraph.

So far, you've seen that you can change the positioning of the BFC by changing the number of lines the paragraph is indented. You can also shift the baseline position of the letter itself. Look again at the Font Setting dialog box in Figure 5-9. At the bottom are the Shift buttons, where you can move the BFC up or down from its normal baseline.

Example: How do these positioning options work in practice? Take a look at Figure 5-10. This is the same 72-point University Roman example whose dialog box we just showed you. Option (A) is the standard settings. Notice that Ventura has indented the paragraph four lines, but that standard setting still leaves the BFC sitting slightly above the body text. In Option (B), this problem has been remedied by shifting the BFC down with the Font Setting dialog box. And in Option (C), we show a custom Space For Big First. In this case, we changed the normal 4 lines to 3 lines, which causes the BFC to project above the body text.

Customizing the Big First Character

Advanced users can go beyond the standard BFC effects. In this section, we'll mention several possibilities, and give you enough information to experiment on your own.

Reversed and shaded big first characters

One option is a reversed (white text on a black background) or shaded (black text on a gray background) big first character. Both variations use the same method. Figure 5-11 shows a reversed example.

You don't use the Special Effects dialog box for this BFC variation. Instead, you create the big first character as a paragraph of its own, and use a ruling line above to give it a shaded background. Then you indent the following paragraph to leave room for the BFC. Finally, you put both the BFC and the paragraph on the same line. Here's how:

1. Type a one-letter paragraph containing the character that you want to transform into a BFC.

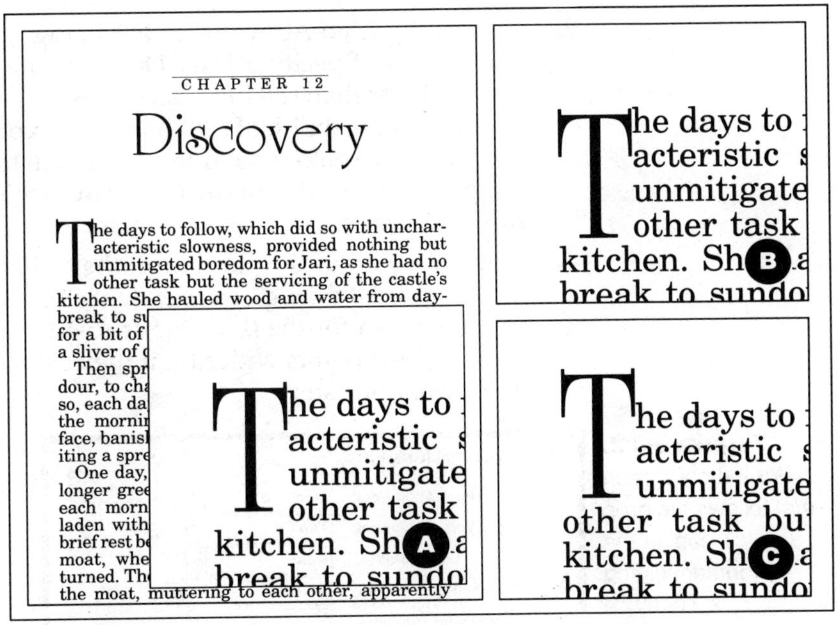

Figure 5-10.
The Normal setting drops the cap to approximately the same height as the first line. The Custom setting lets you specify how many lines to drop the cap.

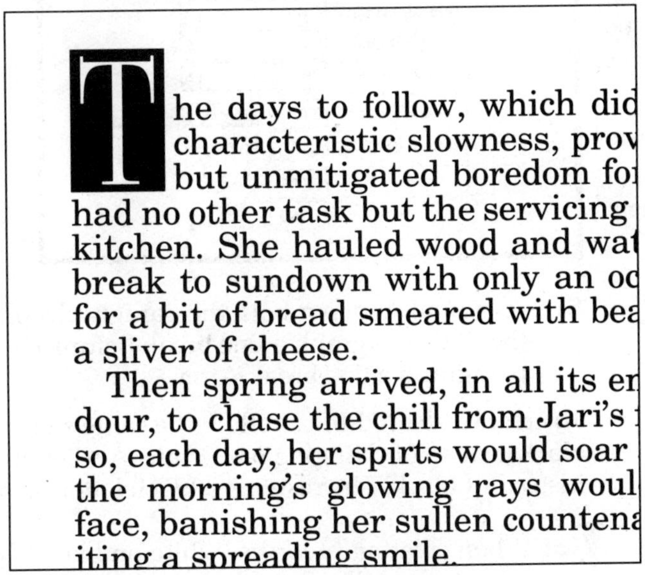

Figure 5-11.
Reversed (white on black) drop cap uses a separate paragraph for the white character and a Ruling Line Above with a Custom width for the black box.

2. Create a new tag for this one-letter paragraph. Set the font to the size you want for the BFC, and make the color white so it will show up against the black box you will create in the next step. Give it an inter-line spacing that matches the font size.

3. Use Ruling Line Above from the Paragraph menu to create a background. Specify a User-Defined rule that is at least four points larger than the BFC. Use a custom width that is slightly wider than the width of the character (experiment). Then enter *negative* space below the third rule equal to the inter-line spacing plus the font size of the BFC. This negative space shifts the rule down so it covers the character.

4. Now move on to the paragraph that will follow the BFC. Use the Alignment dialog box to indent as many lines as necessary to leave room for the BFC (Figure 5-12). The indent should be three or four points wider than the custom rule width you set in the previous step.

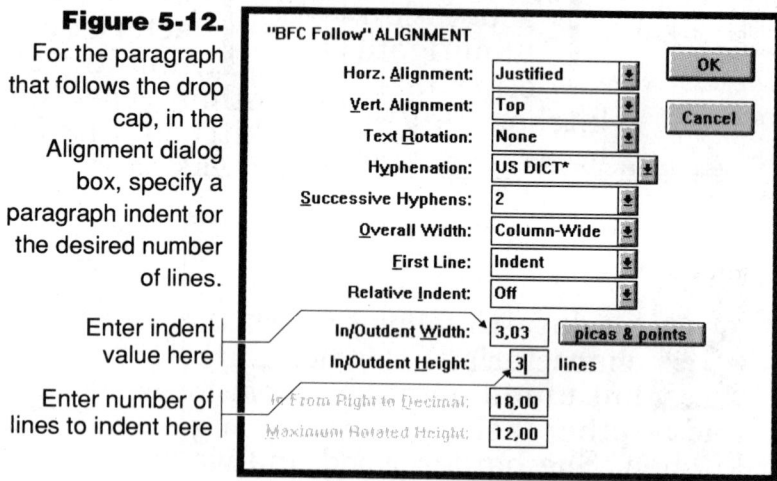

Figure 5-12. For the paragraph that follows the drop cap, in the Alignment dialog box, specify a paragraph indent for the desired number of lines.

Enter indent value here

Enter number of lines to indent here

5. As a final step, put both the paragraphs on the same line. Give the BFC paragraph a line break Before. Give the following text paragraph a line break After.

To create a shaded BFC, follow the same steps. Leave the BFC font black instead of changing it to white. And make the ruling line gray instead of black. The result is a black letter on a gray background.

Tip: When creating reverses (white on black), set the ruling line to a gray pattern until everything else is correct. Change it to black as the final step. This lets you see things that are beneath the black area while you are finishing the formatting.

For more information on ruling lines and on positioning two paragraphs on the same line, see Chapter 3, "Building Basic Styles."

Using pictures as big first characters

Advanced users who aren't satisfied with the standard, reversed, and shaded BFCs can also use pictures as big first characters. Draw the letter with your favorite graphics program and save it in a format Ventura can import (Encapsulated PostScript is a good choice). Create a small frame and load the picture.

Now anchor the frame to the text, using the Relative, Automatically at Anchor option. This option (which was explained earlier in this chapter in the section titled, "Using pictures as bullets") causes the frame to move along with the text. For more information on frame anchoring, see Chapter 11, "Loading and Placing Pictures." Figure 5-13 shows some ornate examples of BFCs created as pictures.

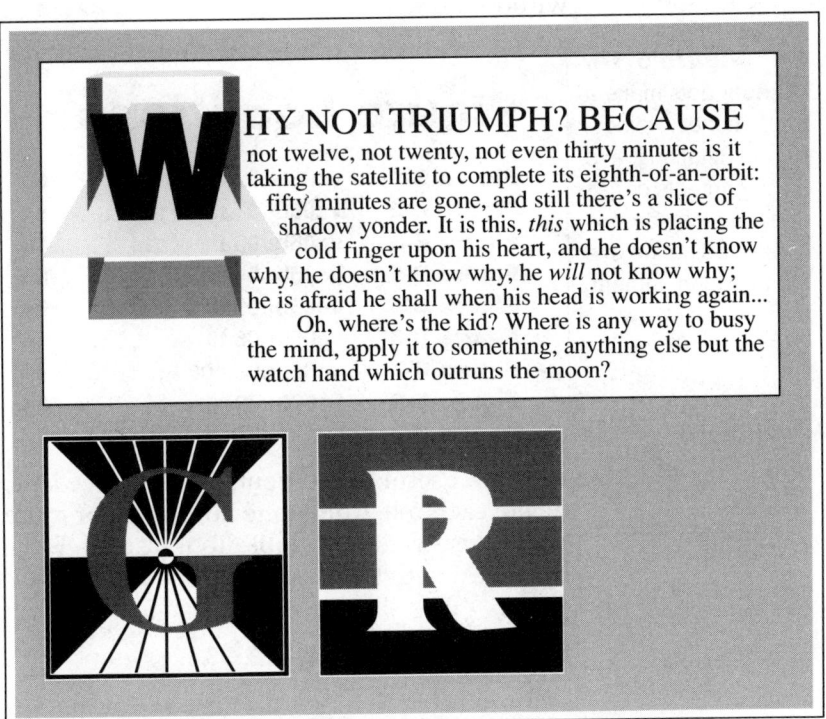

Figure 5-13.
You can import line-art graphics into frames for drop caps, as well.

Creating tabs and leader dots

A tab stop is a special character that skips or jumps a certain amount of space. With Ventura's tab settings function, you can set up to 16 tabs on one line, defining:

- where you want each tab stop
- how you want the text to align
- whether or not to fill the space with leader characters.

Leader characters such as dots are used in reference materials to guide the eye across the page (Figure 5-14). In this section, you'll learn how to get the look you want with Tab Settings. You'll also find out how to apply leader characters, either with or without tabs.

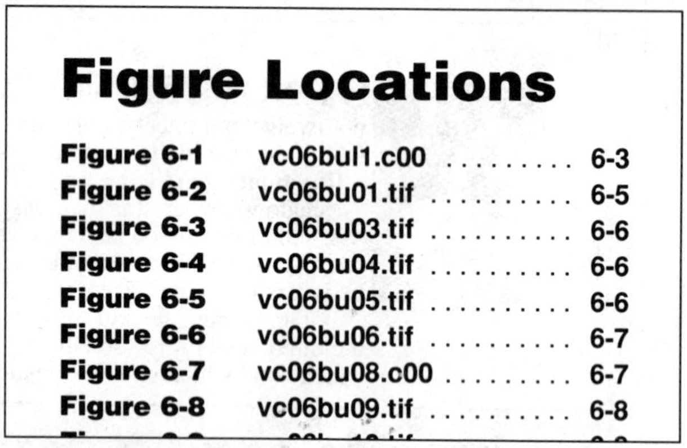

Figure 5-14. Leader dots make a tables, listings, citations, and contents pages easier to reference by leading the eye to the page number.

Figure Locations

Figure 6-1	vc06bul1.c00	6-3
Figure 6-2	vc06bu01.tif	6-5
Figure 6-3	vc06bu03.tif	6-6
Figure 6-4	vc06bu04.tif	6-6
Figure 6-5	vc06bu05.tif	6-6
Figure 6-6	vc06bu06.tif	6-7
Figure 6-7	vc06bu08.c00	6-7
Figure 6-8	vc06bu09.tif	6-8

Tabs are useful for contents pages, price lists, or any simple table where each cell is only one line long. For more complex tables, you should use Ventura's Table Tool instead. For information on creating tables with the Table Tool, see Chapter 8, "Creating Tables."

Understanding tabs

Ventura's Tab Settings dialog box confuses most people, so we'll start this section by explaining a few key points:

Ventura's tabs are measured from the left margin, not the left edge of the page. This sometimes throws users off when they use the ruler to figure out where to put the tabs. The default ruler starts at the left edge of the page. You must subtract the amount of the margin to get the correct tab positions.

Tip: To make it easier to measure and set tabs, temporarily change the zero point of the ruler so it starts at the left margin. Use Set Ruler from the View menu. Type the left margin setting in the Horizontal Zero Point text box. For instance, if your left margin is 1 inch, use 1 inch as the Horizontal Zero Point. After setting the zero point, you can read accurate tab settings directly from the ruler.

You can't set a tab past the left margin. But you *can* set a tab past the right margin. Some users mistakenly push their text off the live area and then can't figure out what happened to it.

Harken back to ancient technology: typewriters. Remember mechanical tab stops? Remember what happened if you typed too far and went past the first stop? If you then hit the tab key, the carriage moved ahead to the next tab stop. Ventura works the same way. If the cursor is already to the right of the first stop, a tab character moves it on to the second stop.

Ventura's default style sheet has typewriter-style tabs set every half inch. Because many people build their style sheets using DEFAULT.STY as the starting point, they end up cloning those same tab stops for every tag they create. These existing built-in tabs can interfere if you don't realize they are active. Solution: clear *all* tab stops and start over again.

Tab settings do not take effect in justified paragraphs. You will receive a warning message from Ventura. To make them appear, select the paragraph with the Paragraph Tool, choose Alignment from the Paragraph menu, and set the Horz. Alignment to Left.

You can set all your tab stops for each tag at one time in the Tab Settings dialog box. You need not open and close it separately for each tab.

Setting tabs

Setting tabs involves four decisions:

- Which tab stop to set
- Where you want it to appear (the position)
- How you want the text to align at the tab stop
- Whether or not to use leader characters

To set one or more tabs:

1. Using the Paragraph Tool, select a paragraph with the tag you want to work on.

2. Choose Tab Settings from the Paragraph menu.

The Tab Settings dialog box appears (Figure 5-15).

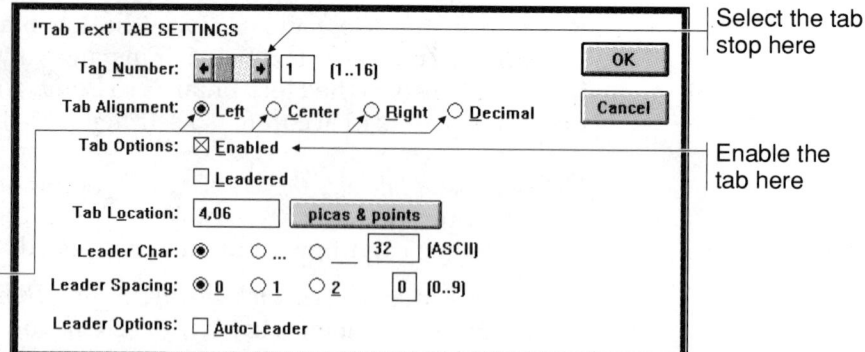

Figure 5-15.
The Tab Settings dialog box tells Ventura what to do when it encounters tab characters in the text.

Select the tab stop here

Enable the tab here

Select the alignment here

3. Click on the scroll arrows for Tab Number to select the tab stop you want to set.

If the paragraph doesn't have any other tabs yet, you will almost always want to work with tab stop 1. It is also good practice to clear all the other tab stops by disabling them and setting each location to zero.

4. Click on the Tab Alignment button that you want to use: Left, Center, Right, or Decimal.

Your tab alignment options work like the text alignment options in Ventura's Alignment dialog box (Figure 5-16).

Figure 5-16.
Ventura's tab alignment options.

	Left: 04,06	Center: 12,00	Right: 18,00	Decimal: 24,00

Table of Meaningless Statistics

Item 1	Left	Center	Right	100.00
Item 2	Arrived	Askew	Wrong	70.00-
Item 3	Status	Balance	Debate	1,256.14

5. Click on the Tab Options: Enabled checkbox to make the tab stop active.

6. In the Tab Location text box, type the position of the tab stop as measured from the left margin. Click on the units of measurement button to select to the units.

7. Click on the leader character you want (if any) as explained in the next section.

8. If you want to set other tab stops now, return to the first step, choose another tab, and repeat the procedure. When you've set all the tabs, click on OK to close the dialog box.

Clearing tab stops

Clearing tab stops is simple: Return to the Tab Settings dialog box, click on the scroll bar to select the tab you want to clear, and then click on the Enabled box to remove the check. It's also a good idea to change the Tab Location to zero.

Using leader characters

Leader characters are an option in the Tab Settings dialog box. In this section, we'll show you how to create leaders both with and without tabs. We'll also show you a technique professional typographers use to make leaders more attractive.

Creating leaders with tab stops

As you know from the previous section, a tab stop is a special character that causes Ventura to jump to a new position horizontally, skipping over the intervening space. Usually, you leave that space blank. But you can also fill it with leader characters. These characters help guide the reader's eye from the left side of the page to the right.

Ventura lets you choose the character you want to use and control how much space is between each pair. To use leaders with tab stops:

1. Using the Paragraph Tool, select the paragraph and use the Tab Settings dialog box to create a tab stop (see the previous section).
2. On the line labeled Leader Char, click on the button for the character you want.

You have four options. The first button uses blanks—no leader character. The second puts dots in the space. The third uses the underline character. And the fourth lets you use any character as a leader—just type in its ASCII code.

For more information on using ASCII codes to create characters, see Chapter 7, "Creating Text with Other Programs." For a list of the ASCII codes for the standard character sets, see Chapter 21, "Rapid Reference."

3. On the line labeled Leader Spacing, click on the button for the spacing you want.

Clicking on the first button, labeled 0 (zero), puts no space between the characters. Clicking on the 1 or 2 buttons puts one or two spaces between each leader character. If you want even wider spacing, you can type a number between 0 and 9 in the text box at the far right.

4. Be sure there is no check mark in the Leader Options: Auto-Leader box. Then click on OK.

With this method, leader characters will appear when you press the tab key. They will fill the space from the point where you pressed the key to the position of the tab stop.

Tip: For a solid line, choose the underline character (the third button) with a leader spacing of zero. This is an excellent way to create fill-in-the-blanks lines for forms and signature lines for contracts.

Creating leaders without tab stops

You can also create leaders without the need to type in a tab stop. In this case, the leader character will fill the space between the last character in the paragraph and the right margin.

Using the Paragraph Tool, select the paragraph, then choose Tab Settings from the Paragraph menu. You do *not* enable any tab stops, but you *do* select a leader character and leader spacing as described above. Now click on the Auto-Leader checkbox at the bottom of the dialog box (Figure 5-17).

Figure 5-17. Another way create leaders is to use the Auto-Leader function in the Tab Settings dialog box.

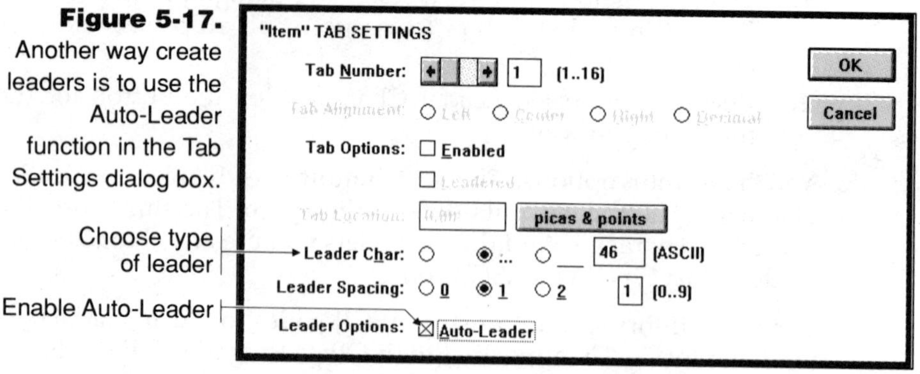

Choose type of leader

Enable Auto-Leader

This method saves you the trouble of typing a tab character to get a leader. But it gives you less control. Every paragraph with this tag will have a leader character on the last line. And the leaders will always stretch all the way to the right margin. With the tab stop method, leaders appear only when and where you insert a tab stop.

Building better-looking leaders

You can follow the instructions above for leader characters. but they won't look as good as professionally typeset materials. You need to create a small amount of space between the last leader and the text that follows it.

Look at Figure 5-18. In this example, the leader characters go all the way over to the numbers. Notice that because the size of the numbers varies, the table appears somewhat ragged on the right side.

Figure 5-18. The first tab in this table of contents has a leader that runs right into the page numbers.

Introduction	ix
How to Use This Book	1-1
Getting Started	1-11
Rearranging Your Desk	3-23
The Big Box Method	3-101
Error Messages	4-103
Index	4-1033

To solve this problem, end the leaders a short space before the longest line of text that follows it. Then use a second tab stop to put the text where you want it, leaving a small blank space between the leaders and the numbers.

Example: Figure 5-19 shows a menu. In this example, both tab stops are aligned right. The first tab stop contains the leaders. The second tab stop has no leaders—it creates the space between the leaders and the numbers.

You can also create this space if you use auto-leaders (leaders without tabs). But you must use two paragraphs. The first paragraph contains the auto-leader. Use In From Right spacing from the Spacing dialog box to force the leaders to stop before they get to the right margin. Then put the numbers into a second paragraph. Align the paragraph with the right margin, and use the Breaks dialog box to put the numbers on the same line as the leader line (Figure 5-20).

Figure 5-19.
This menu uses a tab setting to end all leaders at the same point; a separate tab is used for the prices.

Tab 1 aligns right, with leader

Tab 2 aligns right, without leader

Tab characters here

Figure 5-20.
The Auto-Leader automatically creates a leader from the end of a paragraph to the right margin.

Add In-From-Right to this paragraph tag…

…so that the Auto-Leader stops here

Then, with Breaks, move price up to same line as leader.

Numbering automatically

Ventura's auto-numbering function is worth the price of admission all by itself. The Auto-Numbering dialog box is probably Ventura's least understood, most underused feature. In this section, we'll show you four ways to put it to work:

- Numbering simple lists
- Creating outlines and military-style section numbering
- Generating text automatically, such as placing the word "Caution" at the beginning of every warning note in a manual.

■ Applying special formats, such as creating unusual double ruling lines

Numbering simple lists

Numbering a simple, one-level list involves two steps. First, you use the Auto-Numbering dialog box to specify what you want to number. Second step, you format the resulting numbers.

How do you specify what to number? You have to tell Ventura the name of a tag (or tags) to look for, then it scans the chapter for every instance of that tag. Every time it finds a match, it numbers that paragraph. If you told it to look for Body Text, for example, it would number every single Body Text paragraph in the document. Of course, you'd rarely want to number Body Text. More likely, you'd create a new tag (something like List or ListNum). Then you'd use that tag whenever you wanted automatic numbering.

Setting up the Auto-Numbering dialog box

In the Auto-Numbering dialog box, you tell Ventura which tags to count. To number a simple list:

1. Choose Auto-Numbering from the Paragraph menu. The Auto-Numbering dialog box appears (Figure 5-21).

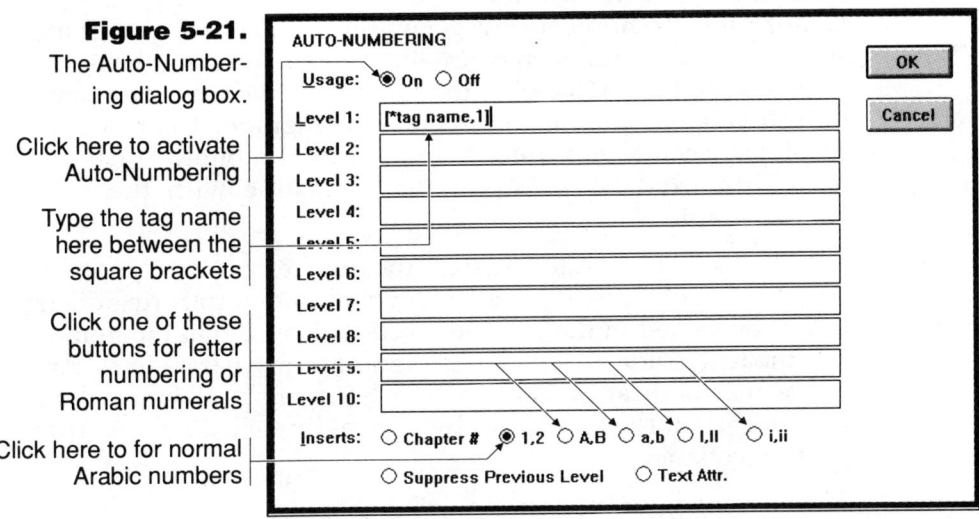

Figure 5-21. The Auto-Numbering dialog box.

Click here to activate Auto-Numbering

Type the tag name here between the square brackets

Click one of these buttons for letter numbering or Roman numerals

Click here to for normal Arabic numbers

2. Click on Usage: On to activate auto-numbering.
3. Place the cursor in the Level 1 text box. Then click on the 1,2 button at the bottom of the dialog box.

Clicking on the 1,2 button inserts the code "[*tag name, 1]" into the Level 1 text box. This is the auto-numbering code for Arabic numerals. If you had chosen the button for uppercase letters instead, the code would be "[*tag name, A]".

4. Delete the words "tag name" and type the real name of the tag.
5. Type the punctuation you want to appear after the number, such as a period. Type it at the end of the line *outside* the square brackets. Then click on OK.

Example: Suppose you want to number a tag called List. First you open the dialog box and click on the Usage: On button. Then you move to the Level 1 text box. You click on the 1,2 button to add the auto-numbering code for Arabic numerals. You delete the words "tag name" and type in the word List. Then you move outside the brackets, type a period and click on OK.

Note: If you're experimenting with the above example and are not getting the results you expected, choose Renumber Chapter from the Edit menu (or press Ctrl-B). This causes Ventura to update any auto-numbering tags in the file. You'll learn more about this feature later in this chapter.

Formatting the numbers

Ventura inserts numbers by generating a separate paragraph. When you see a numbered list like the ones in this book, the numbers and the text look like they are part of the same paragraph. In reality, the number is in a separate paragraph. The text paragraph has been set up to leave room for the number. It has also been formatted to reside on the same line with the number paragraph.

Your first job is to create space for the number. Figure 5-22 shows how a list might look after setting up the Auto-Numbering dialog box as explained in the previous section. Notice that the number and the text reside in separate paragraphs on separate lines. And notice that both are flush with the left margin. If you put the number and the text on the same line right now, they would overlap.

To create space for the number:

1. Using the Paragraph Tool, select the paragraph.
2. Use Alignment from the Paragraph menu to turn on the Relative Indent and to add a first line indent (Figure 5-23).

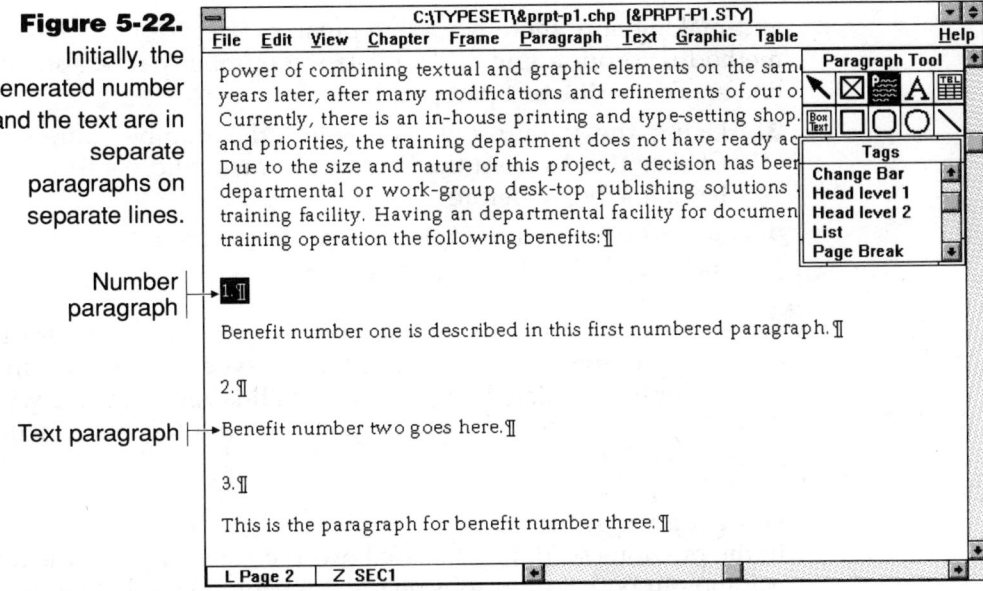

Figure 5-22. Initially, the generated number and the text are in separate paragraphs on separate lines.

Number paragraph

Text paragraph

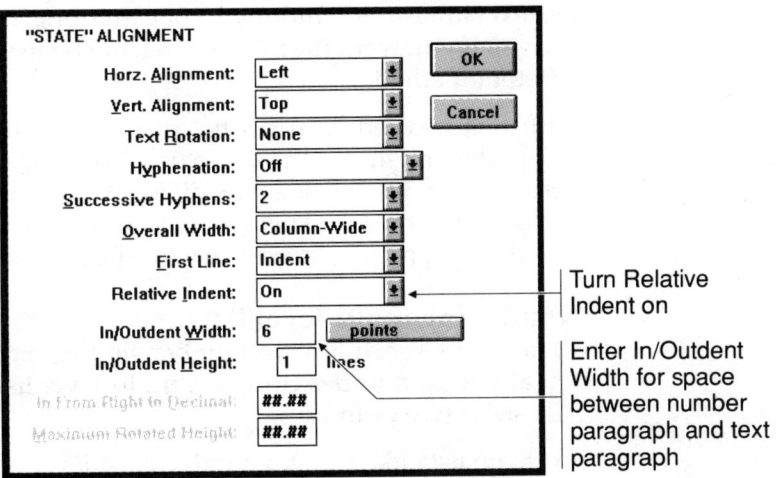

Figure 5-23. To keep the two tags from overlapping, use the Alignment dialog box to give the text paragraph a Relative Indent: On and a small In/Outdent Width.

Turn Relative Indent on

Enter In/Outdent Width for space between number paragraph and text paragraph

A relative indent tells Ventura to start the paragraph exactly where the previous one ended. But that's not good enough. With only a relative indent, the numbers and the text would touch. You also need to specify a small amount of first line indent *in addition* to the relative indent. This creates a small gap between the number and the text. The relative indent should usually be one en space (equal to half the point size of the text).

Now that you've created space for the number, you're ready to put both paragraphs on the same line. This involves checking both tags and making sure there is no line break between them. The safest method is to put a line break *before* the number paragraph and a line break *after* the text paragraph.

3. Using the Paragraph Tool, select the number paragraph. Choose Breaks from the Paragraph menu and confirm that it has a line break Before.

4. Select the text paragraph. Choose Breaks from the Paragraph menu and give it a line break After.

Note: When Ventura inserts the number paragraphs, it also tags them. If you typed your commands into the Level 1 text box in the Auto-Numbering dialog box, the name of this generated tag will be Z_SEC1. If you use the Level 2 text box, the tag name will be Z_SEC2, and so on.

Hanging the number

In the previous section, you saw how to create space for the number and put both paragraphs on the same line. With that method, if the text paragraph is more than one line long, it will wrap to the left margin. If you want the number to hang by itself, you use a slightly different method.

With this method, you do *not* use the Alignment dialog box to indent the first line of the text paragraph. Instead, you use In From Left spacing in the Spacing dialog box to push the entire text paragraph to the left. This prevents it from returning all the way to the left margin and leaves space for the number (Figure 5-24).

Numbering multi-level lists

So far you've seen how to number simple, one-level lists. Ventura can also auto-number complex, multi-level lists. Figures 5-25 and 5-26 show two examples.

To create lists like these, you give each level of the list its own tag name. Then you type these tag names onto separate levels of the Auto-Numbering dialog box. You can choose whether to show the previous numbering levels (military outline), or whether to suppress the previous level's numbering (traditional outline).

Example: Let's walk through the creation of the traditional outline shown in Figure 5-25.

Figure 5-24.
To hang the number, use In From Left spacing to restrict the text paragraph.

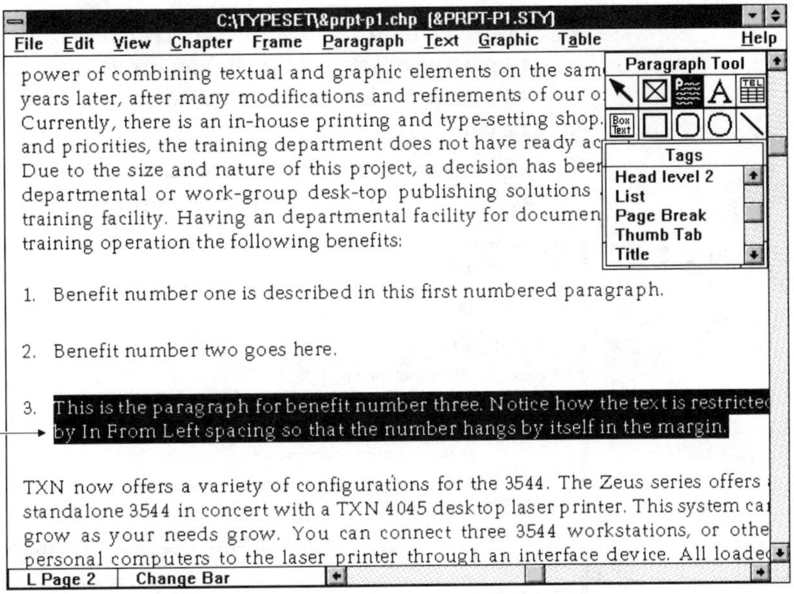

In From Left spacing of 1,06 picas keeps text from wrapping all the way to the left margin

```
C:\TYPESET\&prpt-p1.chp  [&PRPT-P1.STY]
File  Edit  View  Chapter  Frame  Paragraph  Text  Graphic  Table         Help
```

power of combining textual and graphic elements on the sam
years later, after many modifications and refinements of our o
Currently, there is an in-house printing and type-setting shop,
and priorities, the training department does not have ready ac
Due to the size and nature of this project, a decision has been
departmental or work-group desk-top publishing solutions
training facility. Having an departmental facility for documen
training operation the following benefits:

Paragraph Tool

Tags
Head level 2
List
Page Break
Thumb Tab
Title

1. Benefit number one is described in this first numbered paragraph.

2. Benefit number two goes here.

3. **This is the paragraph for benefit number three. Notice how the text is restricted by In From Left spacing so that the number hangs by itself in the margin.**

TXN now offers a variety of configurations for the 3544. The Zeus series offers
standalone 3544 in concert with a TXN 4045 desktop laser printer. This system ca
grow as your needs grow. You can connect three 3544 workstations, or othe
personal computers to the laser printer through an interface device. All loade

L Page 2 | Change Bar

Figure 5-25.
Sample of multi-level numbered list.

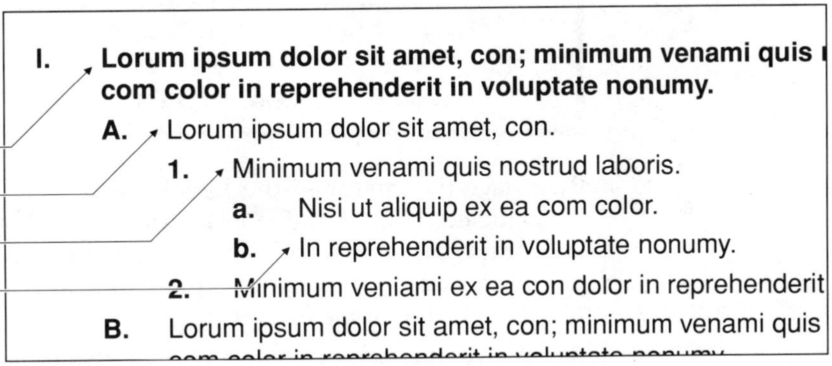

LIST LEVEL 1
LIST LEVEL 2
LIST LEVEL 3
LIST LEVEL 4

I.   Lorum ipsum dolor sit amet, con; minimum venami quis com color in reprehenderit in voluptate nonumy.

   A.   Lorum ipsum dolor sit amet, con.

      1.   Minimum venami quis nostrud laboris.

         a.   Nisi ut aliquip ex ea com color.

         b.   In reprehenderit in voluptate nonumy.

      2.   Minimum veniami ex ea con dolor in reprehenderit

   B.   Lorum ipsum dolor sit amet, con; minimum venami quis

Figure 5-26.
A military-style outline.

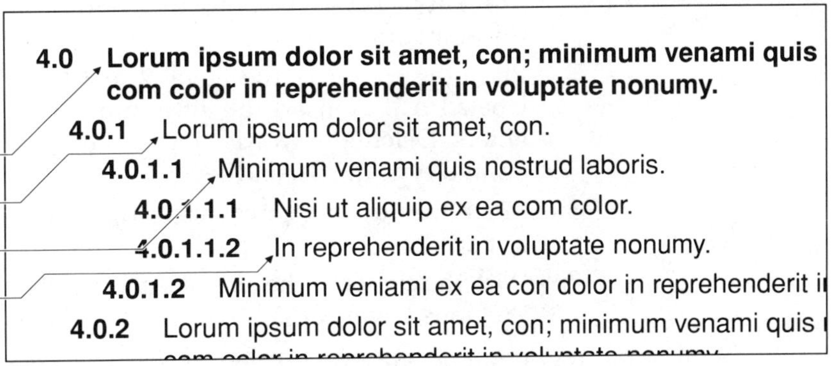

LIST LEVEL 1
LIST LEVEL 2
LIST LEVEL 3
LIST LEVEL 4

4.0   Lorum ipsum dolor sit amet, con; minimum venami quis com color in reprehenderit in voluptate nonumy.

   4.0.1   Lorum ipsum dolor sit amet, con.

      4.0.1.1   Minimum venami quis nostrud laboris.

         4.0.1.1.1   Nisi ut aliquip ex ea com color.

         4.0.1.1.2   In reprehenderit in voluptate nonumy.

      4.0.1.2   Minimum veniami ex ea con dolor in reprehenderit i

   4.0.2   Lorum ipsum dolor sit amet, con; minimum venami quis

1. Start by tagging the text correctly. Tag the first level (the uppercase Roman numerals) as FirstLevel. Tag the second, third, and fourth levels as SecondLevel, ThirdLevel, and FourthLevel.
2. Open the Auto-Numbering dialog box (Figure 5-27). Click on Usage: On to activate auto-numbering.

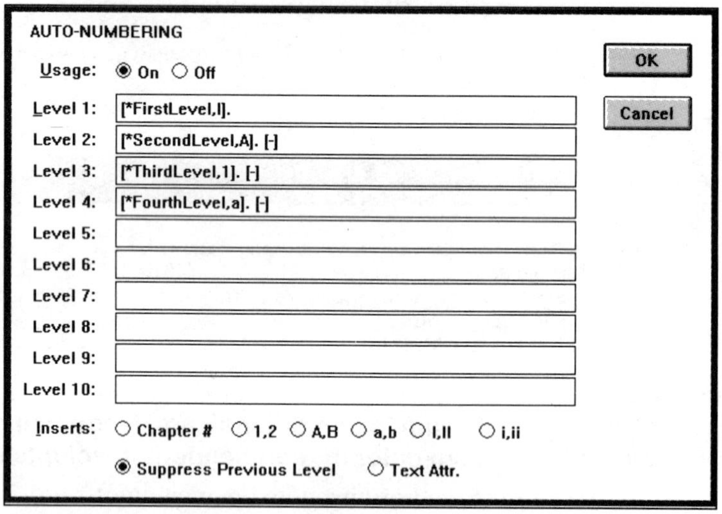

Figure 5-27.
The Auto-Numbering dialog box for a four-level traditional outline.

```
AUTO-NUMBERING
Usage:    ● On   ○ Off                                    [ OK ]
Level 1:  [*FirstLevel,I].                                [Cancel]
Level 2:  [*SecondLevel,A]. [-]
Level 3:  [*ThirdLevel,1]. [-]
Level 4:  [*FourthLevel,a]. [-]
Level 5:
Level 6:
Level 7:
Level 8:
Level 9:
Level 10:
Inserts:  ○ Chapter #   ○ 1,2   ○ A,B   ○ a,b   ○ I,II   ○ i,ii
          ● Suppress Previous Level        ○ Text Attr.
```

3. Place the cursor in the Level 1 text box. Click on the button labeled I, II at the bottom of the dialog box to insert the auto-numbering code for roman numerals. Delete the words "tag name" inside the square brackets and type in "FirstLevel," the name of your tag.
4. Move the cursor to the end of the line outside the square brackets. Type in a period and a space to punctuate the numbers.
5. Place the cursor in the Level 2 text box. Click on the button labeled A,B to insert the auto-numbering code for uppercase letters. Delete the words "tag name" inside the square brackets and type in "SecondLevel."
6. Move the cursor to the end of the line. Type in a period and a space.
7. With the cursor at the end of the Level 2 line, click on Suppress Previous Level at the bottom of the dialog box.

If you did not suppress the previous level's numbering, the outline would look like this:

> I.
>> I. A.
>>> I. A. 1.
>>>> I. A. 1. a.
>> I. B.

By suppressing the previous numbering, you get a traditional outline:

> I.
>> A.
>>> 1.
>>>> a.
>> B.

8. Repeat the previous steps for the third level. Use the 1,2 button for Arabic numerals. Use ThirdLevel as the tag name.

9. Repeat the previous steps for the fourth level. Use the a,b button for lowercase letters. Use FourthLevel as the tag name.

To create a military style outline, you would use similar procedures except that you would *not* suppress the previous level.

Using your numbering options

Up to this point we've laid out the basic auto-numbering procedures. Ventura also has several other numbering options, including:

- Renumbering lists when items have been rearranged
- Deleting numbered paragraphs
- Adding chapter numbers
- Starting the counting at a number other than one
- Starting the numbering over again at one (for multiple lists within the same chapter)

Renumbering

If you delete, add, or rearrange items from a list, you must tell Ventura to recount or *renumber* the chapter. Until you take this step, the numbering will be inaccurate. To renumber, choose Renumber Chapter from the Edit menu, or press the keyboard shortcut Ctrl-B. There will be a short pause as Ventura looks at each page of the chapter and renumbers the list in its new, correct order.

Deleting numbered paragraphs

Ventura will not let you delete the paragraphs it generates for the page numbers. To get rid of them, follow this procedure:

1. Using the Paragraph Tool, select the text paragraph next to the number and retag it as Body Text (or any tag that does not get numbered).
2. Choose Renumber Chapter (Edit menu; or press Ctrl-B).
3. Using the Text Tool, select all the text in the paragraph. (Do not select the paragraph symbol, just the text.) Then press Delete to cut the text.
4. Press Backspace to delete the paragraph symbol (carriage return) *preceding* the now destroyed text paragraph.

Adding chapter numbers

Numbering schemes such as military-style outlines require you to include the chapter number as well as the sequence number. For instance, here's the beginning of a military-style list for the fourth chapter of a manual:

4.1.
   4.1.1.
   4.1.2.

You can add chapter numbers in the Auto-Numbering dialog box. Simply insert the chapter number code wherever you want the chapter numbers to appear. You can type in the code, which is [C#]. Or you can place your cursor at the spot and click on the Chapter # button and Ventura will type it in for you.

Example: For instance, here's the code that asks Ventura to number the tag called List and put a period after the number:

    [*List, 1].

Now here's the code that asks Ventura to put the chapter number before the sequential number, with a period and a space in between:

    [C#]. [*List, 1].

For a list of codes for other advanced cross-referencing commands, see Chapter 21, "Rapid Reference."

Starting with numbers other than one

Normally you want to start numbering with the number one (or the letter *A* or with the Roman numeral *I*). But sometimes you want to start at another number. For instance, if you are working with military-style outlines, you may want to start the first section at zero (as in 4.0, 4.0.1, and so on). Or you may have numbering that crosses chapter boundaries. In that case, you want each successive chapter to start where the last chapter left off.

To start at a number other than one, use the Auto-Numbering dialog box to set up the numbering as usual. Then put the cursor just inside the right square bracket. Type a comma and the number you want to start with (no space).

For instance, here's the standard code for a tag called List as it would appear in the Auto-Numbering dialog box:

```
[*List, 1]
```

And here's the code to start the numbering at zero:

```
[*List, 1,0]
```

Restarting the numbering

Unless you tell it otherwise, Ventura starts with the number one and continues in sequence to the end of the chapter. Often, however, you want to start counting over again within that chapter. For instance, if you are writing numbered procedures like those in this book, you want to start over from one (1) each time you start a new procedure.

You can trick Ventura into starting over with a simple technique. To understand how it works, look at the following multi-level list:

1.
    1.1.
    1.2.

2.
    2.1.
    2.2.
    2.3.

3.
    3.1.
    3.2.

Look at the second level numbering. Notice that it starts over again at one (1) each time there is a new first level. Every time Ventura moves to a new first level number, it automatically restarts all levels below.

You can use this capability to create a special tag for restarting the numbering. You put this tag on Level 1 of the Auto-Numbering dialog box. Anytime you want to restart the numbering, you will tag the *preceding* paragraph with this special restart tag.

But wait a minute—if you put this tag name into the Auto-Numbering dialog box, won't Ventura generate a number for it? Not necessarily. You can instruct Ventura to count a paragraph without showing the number. To do so, you simply delete the comma and the number inside the square brackets.

For instance, here's the code that counts and numbers a tag called Restart:

```
[*Restart,1]
```

And here's the code that counts it without generating a number:

```
[*Restart]
```

Example: Let's review how you'd put this capability to work. Suppose you want to count and number a tag called List. If you wanted the list to be numbered sequentially throughout the chapter, your Auto-Numbering dialog box might look like this:

```
Level 1: [*List,1].
```

This entry counts the tag called List, numbers it with Arabic numerals, and puts a period after the number. Now let's say that you want the capability of starting your lists over again at one within the same chapter. In that case, the Auto-Numbering dialog box might look like this:

```
Level 1: [*Restart]
Level 2: [*List,1].
```

The Level 1 entry uses a tag called Restart to begin the numbering over again at one. As you can see, the tag is counted (thereby restarting the numbering of anything on lower levels), but no number is generated. The Level 2 entry counts and numbers the List tag. Any time you want a List tag to start over at one, you simply precede it with the Restart tag.

Many users tag a null (empty) paragraph with the Restart tag. They format it with 0 line spacing, align it to the right, and let it reside on the same line as the preceding paragraph. In this fashion, it does not affect any of the other formatting and it is invisible on the printed page. It does, however, have the effect of restarting the numbering at one.

Generating text with Auto-Numbering

If you've read the first parts of this section, you already know the techniques needed to generate text with Auto-Numbering.

We've already shown you how to "count" something without actually producing any numbers (you erase the comma and the number inside the square brackets). And we've already demonstrated how to generate text by showing you how to punctuate numbers (you type the punctuation outside the square brackets).

By combining these two techniques, you can use Auto-Numbering to generate text. For instance, let's say you have a special tag called Caution for the warnings in your repair manual. You could instruct Ventura to automatically "count" every instance of that tag. But instead of generating a number, Ventura could generate the word "Warning!"

Here's how the Auto-Numbering code would look to number the Caution tag and put a period after the number:

    [*Caution,1].

Here's how it would look if you wanted the word "Warning!" instead of numbers:

    [*Caution]Warning!

Why use Auto-Numbering instead of simply typing in "Warning!" at the front of every cautionary statement? For one thing, you don't have to worry about consistency between multiple authors. There's no danger that one author will type it as "Warning" and the other as "WARNING." All they have to do is tag the paragraph with the Caution tag. You can decide later what text phrase to associate with that tag.

For another thing, global changes become much easier. If you decide to use "DANGER!" instead, you only need to make one change in the Auto-Numbering dialog box to change every cautionary statement throughout the chapter.

In addition, the Auto-Numbering method can save time, effort, and file space when working with databases. In many cases, you want to label the fields in the database. If you were producing a catalog for instance, you might want to label one field "Product Name" and another "Price" and so on.

One way to create those text labels is to generate a report from the database. You can insert the text in front of each field in the report.

But this method can be difficult to accomplish with certain database programs. And the resulting files are much larger because each and every record contains extra text. It may save time and file space to simply output the data from the database, and let Ventura's Auto-Numbering handle the text labels.

Example: Suppose you are creating a phone directory with the help of a database. You want to label the fields with "Name," "Address," and so on. Figure 5-28 shows how you might set up the Auto-Numbering dialog box to insert this text for you.

Figure 5-28. To generate text with Auto-Numbering, delete the comma and number inside the braces, and type in the text you want outside the braces.

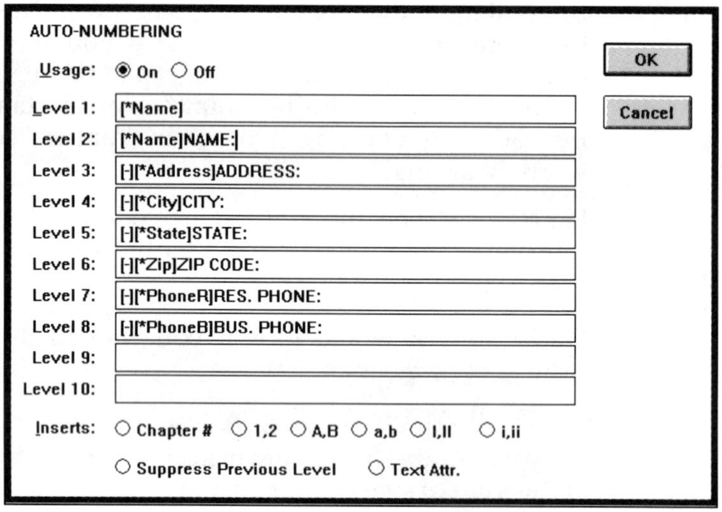

AUTO-NUMBERING	
Usage: ● On ○ Off	OK
Level 1: [*Name]	Cancel
Level 2: [*Name]NAME:	
Level 3: [H][*Address]ADDRESS:	
Level 4: [H][*City]CITY:	
Level 5: [H][*State]STATE:	
Level 6: [H][*Zip]ZIP CODE:	
Level 7: [H][*PhoneR]RES. PHONE:	
Level 8: [H][*PhoneB]BUS. PHONE:	
Level 9:	
Level 10:	
Inserts: ○ Chapter # ○ 1,2 ○ A,B ○ a,b ○ I,II ○ i,ii	
○ Suppress Previous Level ○ Text Attr.	

Look at Level 8. This line instructs Ventura to search for tags called PhoneB. Every time it finds one, Ventura will insert the text "BUS. PHONE:" into a new paragraph. The other levels work just the same. Figure 5-29 shows one way you might format the resulting directory.

Figure 5-29. Sample of Auto-Numbering text and rules.

Short rules associated with paragraph created by Auto-Numbering

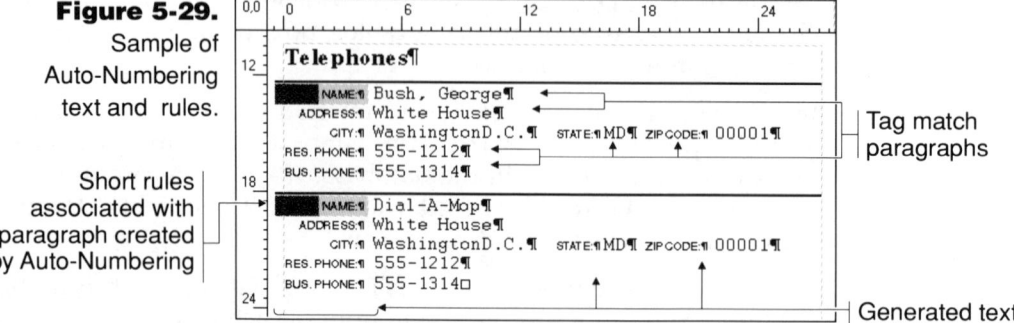

For more information about creating text files with databases, see Chapter 7, "Creating Text with Other Programs."

Formatting auto-numbered paragraphs

You already know that Ventura's Auto-Numbering dialog box works by generating new paragraphs. And you've already seen that those new paragraphs—which we'll call auto-numbered paragraphs—can contain either numbers or text.

As long as you want all of an auto-numbered paragraph to look the same, you can control its formatting with the Paragraph Tool. Select the auto-numbered paragraph and format it with the commands from the Paragraph menu.

But what if you want to format part of the paragraph differently from the rest? You'll quickly discover that you can't use the Text menu while typing in a dialog box. You can't, for instance, select just the first character and change it to a different font. To achieve that kind of text formatting, you have to type bracket codes into the dialog box. Bracket codes are used to create special text effects in word processing files. For more information on bracket codes, see Chapter 7, "Creating Text with Other Programs." For a list of Ventura's bracket codes, see Chapter 21, "Rapid Reference."

Figure 5-30 shows one way to use this capability. In this example, the word "Note" and the preceding heart-shaped character are generated by the Auto-Numbering dialog box. The auto-numbered paragraph is in Helvetica. The heart symbol, however, is in the Zapf Dingbats font. It is also larger than the rest of the paragraph, and it has been shifted down.

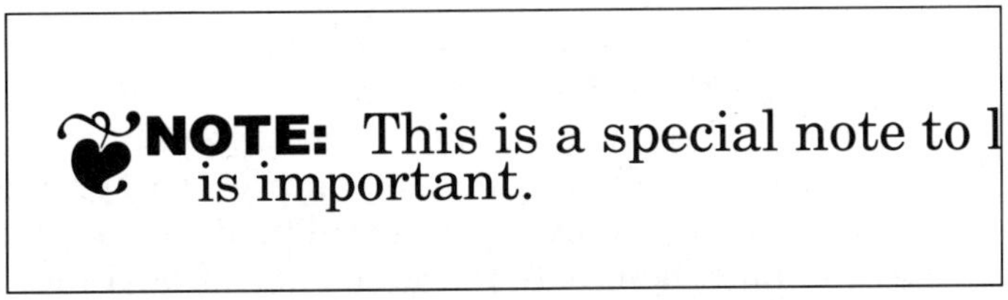

Figure 5-30.
The result of the text attributes applied in the dialog box in the next Figure 5-31.

❤**NOTE:** This is a special note to l is important.

Figure 5-31 shows how these effects were accomplished within the Auto-Numbering dialog box. For other examples of this same technique, glance at the Note, Example, Tip, and Warning paragraphs scattered throughout this book. These special formats were generated with the Auto-Numbering dialog box. As you will see, the first character was enlarged, shifted, and kerned (to move it closer to the rest of the text). All of these changes were accomplished with bracket codes within the Auto-Numbering dialog box.

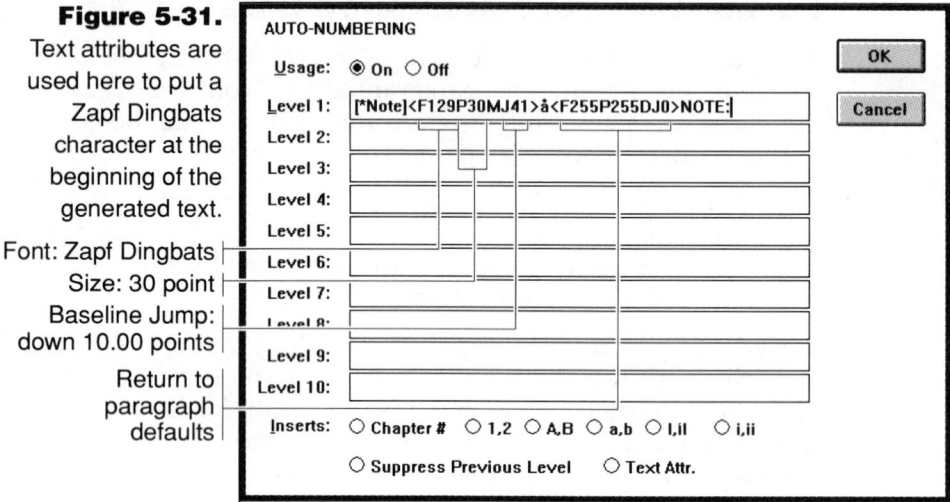

Figure 5-31. Text attributes are used here to put a Zapf Dingbats character at the beginning of the generated text.

Font: Zapf Dingbats
Size: 30 point
Baseline Jump: down 10.00 points
Return to paragraph defaults

Creating unusual ruling lines with Auto-Numbering

Earlier we recommended that you look at the Note, Tip, Warning, and Example formats of this book. The first word of each of these paragraphs (the word "Note" for instance") was created with Auto-Numbering. Did you also notice the gray box behind the big first letter? This box is actually a custom-width ruling line associated with the paragraph. (Ruling lines are explained in Chapter 3, "Building Basic Styles.")

Because the Auto-Numbering dialog box can generate paragraphs, it's no surprise that you can associate ruling lines with those paragraphs. Some users apply this capability to create unusual ruling line styles. They generate "empty" paragraphs with Auto-Numbering. Then they associate ruling lines with those paragraphs and combine them with the ruling lines from other text paragraphs.

Strictly speaking, the Auto-Numbering dialog box won't let you generate a true null paragraph (one that contains only a return, without any text). You have to put something into the paragraph—a number, a text character—before the paragraph will appear. Because they don't actually want anything to appear on the page, many users simply insert a space. The figure space is a popular choice. The bracket code for a figure space is <+> (the plus sign between two angle brackets).

If you type this figure space bracket code into the Auto-Numbering dialog box, Ventura will generate a figure space and put it into a separate paragraph. Then you can use that paragraph for your ruling line effects.

To create an unusual ruling line format, then, you first decide which text paragraph is going to receive the ruling line effect. Then you take these steps:

1. Use the Auto-Numbering dialog box to "count" that text paragraph. Instead of generating a number or a word, however, you generate a figure space.

Now you have two paragraphs, the new auto-numbered paragraph (that has nothing but a figure space), and the text paragraph.

2. Put both paragraphs on the same line by changing the Breaks settings so there is no line break between them (explained earlier in this section). You can push the auto-numbered paragraph out into the left margin, or otherwise format it so it doesn't get in your way and is easy to find.

3. Attach one ruling line to the auto-numbered paragraph and the other to the text paragraph.

Example: Assume that you want your first-level subheads to have a special ruling line style. You want a thin rule that stretches across the entire column, combined with a thicker rule that is only as wide as the text of the subhead. Figure 5-32 shows how you could accomplish this effect.

Figure 5-32.
Double ruling lines of different widths can be created with Auto-Numbering.

Generated paragraph with column-wide rule

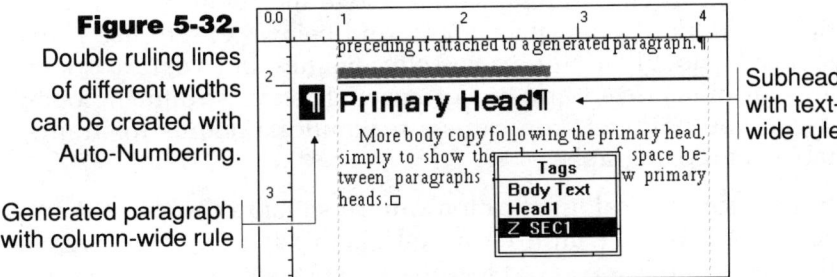

Subhead with text-wide rule

To make it easier to see what's going on, we made one of the ruling lines black and the other one gray. We also separated the lines with a small amount of space. In practice, you would probably make both lines black. You would also change the spacing so they touched. The result would be a unique and attractive ruling line effect that looked like a single unit even though it was actually created with two separate paragraphs.

Vertical justification

Horizontal justification makes text fit flush to the left and right margins. Vertical justification makes it fit flush to the top and bottom margins (Figure 5-33).

Figure 5-33. A three-column page with (left) and without (right) vertical justification.

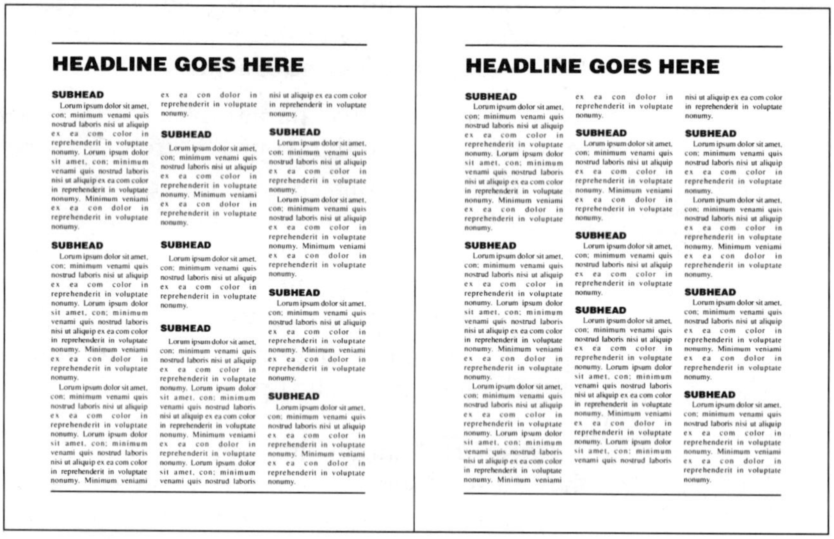

When you tell Ventura to justify vertically, it makes its calculations in a certain order. First it puts space above and below frames. If that doesn't work, it puts space above and below paragraphs. If that still isn't enough, it puts space between lines. But Ventura doesn't add an unrestricted amount of space. It stays within the boundaries you have set. You can set maximum amounts for frames, tables, and paragraphs.

In practice, vertical justification can cause more problems than it solves, unless you handle it carefully. In this section, we'll give you the basics of this advanced feature. To work with vertical justification, you need to understand:

- The difference between carding and feathering
- How to turn on vertical justification for a chapter or a frame

- How to adjust the default settings for individual frames, tables, and paragraphs

Carding versus feathering

To justify vertically, Ventura adds space between paragraphs or between lines to force text to go all the way to the bottom margin. Ventura gives you two ways to add that space, *carding* and *feathering*.

Carding adds space in one-line increments. Thus, if your Body Text has an inter-line spacing of 12 points, the carding adds space in units of 12—12, 24, 48, 64, and so on. Carding limits Ventura's options and often gives bad results. We don't recommend it unless it is vital to align text across columns (Figure 5-34). In such a case, you might want to experiment with carding, because it will always adhere to the same spacing as your Body Text.

Figure 5-34.
The two kinds of vertical justification: carding (left) and feathering (right).

Feathering is the second of Ventura's options, and the one with the most practical application. It adds exactly the amount of space you need, without restricting itself to any special units. For pages with multiple columns, feathering will align the tops and the bottoms of columns, but not necessarily all the lines in between. But it does have the advantage of producing more predictable and attractive results.

Enabling vertical justification for a chapter

You can turn on vertical justification for the entire chapter, or for individual frames. To turn it on for the chapter:

1. Choose Chapter Typography from the Chapter menu.
2. Set the vertical justification options you want, using the last five text boxes of the dialog box (Figure 5-35) and click on OK.

Figure 5-35. You can specify Vertical Justification at the chapter level.

```
CHAPTER (DEFAULT) TYPOGRAPHY SETTINGS
        Widows (Min Lines at Top):  3          [OK]
     Orphans (Min Lines at Bottom): 3          [Cancel]
              Column Balance:       Off
       Move Down To 1st Baseline By: Cap Height
                Pair Kerning:       On
         Vert. Just. Within Frame:  Feathering
         Vert. Just. Around Frame:  Moveable
             Vert. Just. Allowed:   100   %
               At Top of Frame:    0    [points]
            At Bottom of Frame:    0
```

Vertical justification settings

Let's examine each option to see how it affects the chapter:

Vert. Just. Within Frame is misleading, because the frame it refers to is actually the entire chapter. Click on the list box and select the vertical justification method you prefer, Carding or Feathering.

Vert. Just. Around Frame lets you decide whether or not frames can float on the page. If you don't mind if Ventura moves frames slightly, choose Moveable (usually the best choice). If you want to be sure frames do not move, choose Fixed.

Vert. Just. Allowed is a convenient way to change your mind. As you'll see in a moment, you can individually set the vertical justification maximums for every frame, table, and paragraph in the document. But what if you change your mind? Luckily, you don't have to make the modifications individually. You can use this line to specify a different percentage. For instance, by typing 200%, you would be telling Ventura to double the maximums you set previously. By typing 50%, you'd be telling Ventura it could only use half the maximum amounts.

At Top Of Frame and *At Bottom Of Frame* set the defaults for the frames in this chapter. You can override these defaults with the Frame Typography. A typical entry would be 1,00 or 2,00 picas.

Note: If you enable vertical justification in Chapter Typography and nothing happens, check the individual frames, tables, and paragraphs. As you will learn in a moment, they can override the default settings. If the individual settings specify no vertical justification, the Chapter Typography settings will have no effect.

Enabling vertical justification for a frame

It often happens that you don't want vertical justification throughout the chapter, but you do want it for one or two frames, such as the title page (Figure 5-36). Conversely, you may want vertical justification in the rest of the chapter but *not* inside one of your frames. In either case, you can override the default settings with the Frame Typography dialog box.

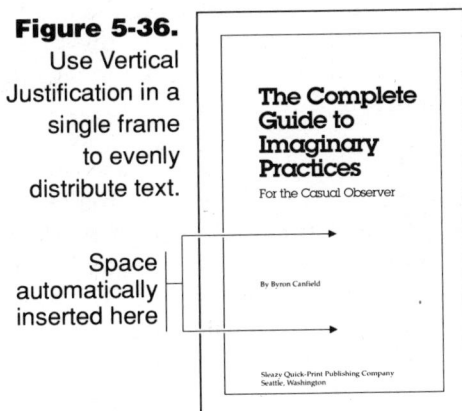

Figure 5-36.
Use Vertical Justification in a single frame to evenly distribute text.

Space automatically inserted here

To set a frame differently from the rest of the chapter:

1. Using the Frame Tool, select the frame.
2. Choose Frame Typography from the Frame menu (Figure 5-37).
3. Change the settings and click on OK.

You can override any of the default settings, including the treatment of the text within the frame, whether or not the frame can be moved for vertical justification, and the maximum amounts of space that can be added above or below the frame.

Figure 5-37.
You can also control Vertical Justification for individual frames using the Frame Typography dialog box.

Vertical justification settings

FRAME TYPOGRAPHY SETTINGS	
Widows (Min Lines at Top):	Default
Orphans (Min Lines at Bottom):	Default
Column Balance:	Default
Move Down To 1st Baseline By:	Default
Pair Kerning:	Default
Vert. Just. Within Frame:	Feathering
Vert. Just. Around Frame:	Moveable
Vert. Just. Allowed:	100 %
At Top of Frame:	0 points
At Bottom of Frame:	0

Note: If you want to change the treatment of the text within the frame, be sure that the tags and tables you use inside the frame also have the vertical justification settings you want. In the title page example from Figure 5-36, you would need to check the tags for the title, subtitle, byline, and publishing company.

Example: It seems to be an unwritten law. As soon as you acquire desktop publishing skills, someone will ask you to make them a business card—possibly the least appropriate use of the technology. Vertical Justification, however, can make the task simpler. Notice the lower right card in Figure 5-38. Even though it has more lines below the name, we did not have to recalculate the spacing of the tags. Vertical justification forced the text to the bottom automatically.

Figure 5-38.
Business cards, four-up, with each frame vertically justified.

Controlling vertical justification above and below tables

If your vertically justified text includes tables, you must set the maximum amounts of space Ventura can insert above or below the tables. To set these amounts:

1. Using the Table Tool, select the table.
2. Choose Insert Table from the Table menu if you are creating a new table. Choose Change Settings from the Table menu if you are modifying an existing table.
3. When the Insert/Edit Table dialog box appears (Figure 5-39), type the maximum space amounts into the vertical justification text boxes at the lower right.

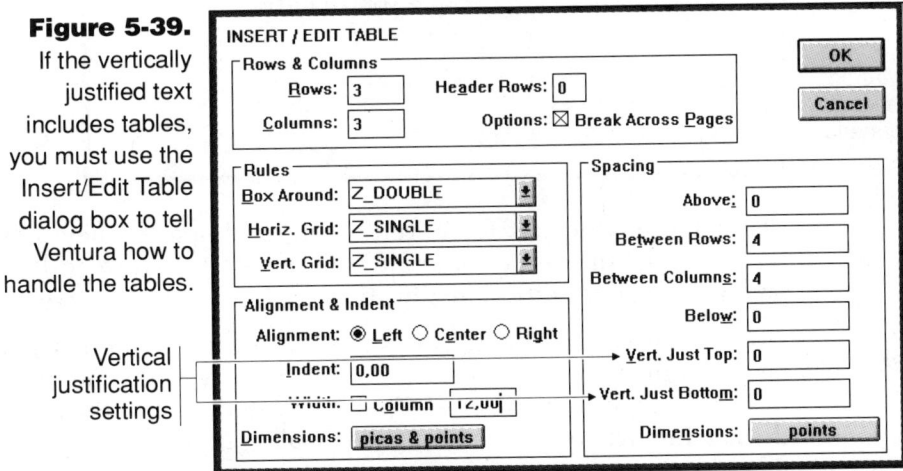

Figure 5-39. If the vertically justified text includes tables, you must use the Insert/Edit Table dialog box to tell Ventura how to handle the tables.

Vertical justification settings

As with frames and paragraphs, typical amounts would be 1,00 to 2,00 picas above and below the frames. That gives Ventura some room to work with, but doesn't permit it to add so much space that it distorts the look of the page.

Controlling vertical justification for paragraphs

It's not enough to turn on vertical justification in the Chapter Typography dialog box. You must also adjust if for each of your paragraph tags. If you get unacceptable, unpredictable results from vertical justification, it's usually because you haven't adjusted the paragraph tags correctly. Remember that the settings you make for the paragraphs override the settings from the Chapter Typography dialog box.

To control vertical justification for a paragraph:

1. Using the Paragraph Tool, select the paragraph.
2. Choose Paragraph Typography from the Paragraph menu.
3. Use the bottom three lines of the dialog box to type the vertical justification settings you want (Figure 5-40).

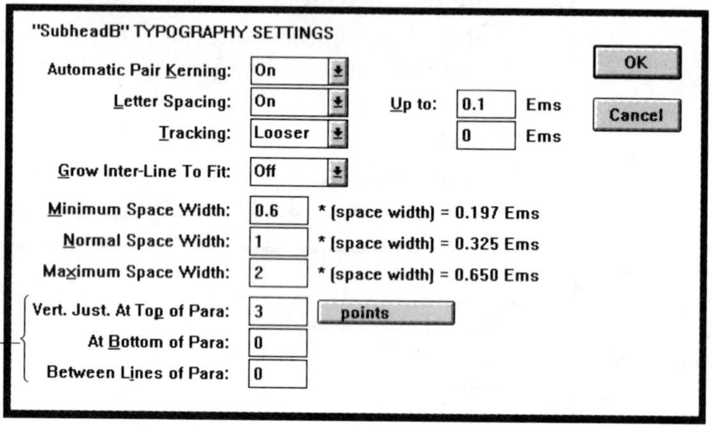

Figure 5-40. For ultimate control over vertical justification, turn to the Paragraph Typography dialog box.

"SubheadB" TYPOGRAPHY SETTINGS

Automatic Pair Kerning:	On	
Letter Spacing:	On	Up to: 0.1 Ems
Tracking:	Looser	0 Ems
Grow Inter-Line To Fit:	Off	
Minimum Space Width:	0.6	* (space width) = 0.197 Ems
Normal Space Width:	1	* (space width) = 0.325 Ems
Maximum Space Width:	2	* (space width) = 0.650 Ems
Vert. Just. At Top of Para:	3	points
At Bottom of Para:	0	
Between Lines of Para:	0	

Vertical justification information

These settings do not force Ventura to add space. They simply represent the maximum amount Ventura is allowed to add when trying to achieve vertical justification.

How much space should you allow? That depends on personal taste and the type of paragraph. For headings, you'd want to allow more space above than below. That way you don't run the risk that the heading will be pushed up and visually separated from the text it belongs to.

You should also allow more space for headings than for Body Text. It is less disturbing to see extra space above a heading—which represents an interruption of thought anyway—than between lines of text. Likewise, it is more acceptable to see extra space above and below paragraphs than between the lines. Don't allow space between the lines of Body Text paragraphs—a point or two at most, if you must, to achieve vertical justification.

A typical hierarchy, then, might look like this:

- Frames and tables: 2,00 picas above and below
- Headings and subheadings: 2,00 picas above and 1,00 pica below
- Body Text: 0,06 picas (six points) above and below (one point between lines only if necessaary).

Fine-tuning text formats

Ventura has a variety of specialized controls for typography. Many users never bother to learn these functions; they are content to work with the default settings. But if you take the time to master these controls you can create useful formats and improve the look of your documents. For instance, you can:

- Create default typography settings for the entire document, and override them individually if necessary
- Run a photo credit sideways up the side of a photograph
- Customize the position and size of underlines, overscores, strike-throughs, superscripts, subscripts, and small caps
- Create professional looking logos right in Ventura
- Tighten up display type to make it look more professional
- Enlarge line spacing automatically for equations and other over-size text

You'll learn these techniques and more in this section, which explains default versus local typography, rotating text, adjusting text attributes, and adjusting the space between letters and words.

Setting default typography

You want documents to be consistent, so Ventura provides a Chapter Typography dialog box where you can define default settings for the entire chapter. On the other hand, you don't want to be forced to use these standard settings all the time. So Ventura provides two more dialog boxes, Frame Typography and Paragraph Typography. These two dialog boxes let you override the defaults if necessary.

In the previous section, you learned how to use Frame Typography and Paragraph Typography to override the default settings for vertical justification for Chapter Typography. In this section, we'll give you more details on how the Chapter Typography dialog box interacts with Frame Typography and Paragraph Typography.

Let's start by explaining how Chapter Typography relates to Frame Typography. The Chapter Typography dialog box sets the defaults for the document (Figure 5-41).

There may be occasions when you want to override the default settings. For instance, perhaps you're creating a newsletter with frames on top of the underlying page. You want most of the

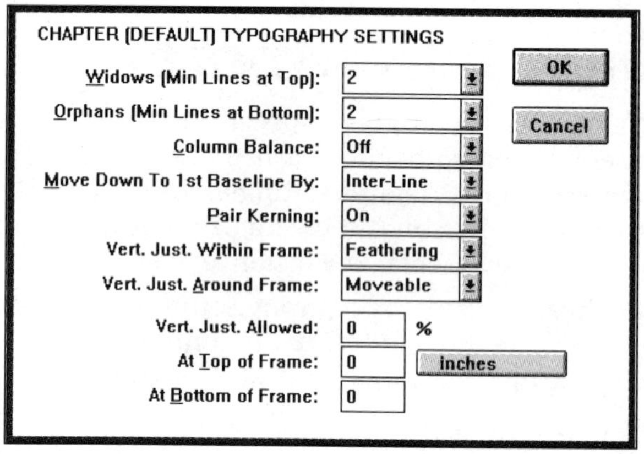

Figure 5-41.
The Chapter Typography dialog box controls global settings for the entire document. You can override these settings.

chapter to have column balance on, but you want column balance off for that one frame.

Open the Frame Typography dialog box. Select the frame with the Frame Tool, then use the Frame Typography dialog box to select a different setting (Figure 5-42).

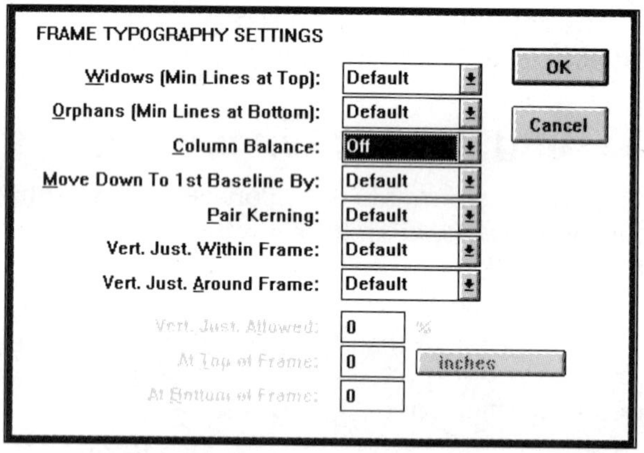

Figure 5-42.
You can use the Frame Typography dialog box to override the default settings.

The Paragraph Typography dialog box does not have the same direct connection to Chapter Typography. However, you can use Paragraph Typography to override your default pair kerning decisions, as you'll see later.

Controlling widows and orphans

Widows and orphans are lines that have become isolated from the rest of the paragraph. A widow comes at the top of a column or page, an orphan at the bottom. Ventura's Chapter Typography dialog box lets you instruct Ventura not to allow widows or orphans. You specify the minimum number of lines that must appear together. If Ventura finds less than this number, it moves the text so it will not be isolated.

For instance, by selecting a setting of Widows: 3, you are telling Ventura to look at the top of every column and page. If it finds less than three lines together, it must move some text onto the page until it has three lines. Likewise, if you set Orphans: 3, you are telling Ventura to look at the bottom of every column and page. If it finds less than three lines in a row, it must move those isolated lines to the next page.

For most documents, you should set both Widows and Orphans to 2, which will prevent single lines from being stranded by themselves. Still, widow and orphan control has its disadvantages. When text is shifted to another page, it can leave gaps at the bottom of a column.

Some users prefer to end all their columns at the same point. In such cases, they don't want Ventura moving text around to control widows and orphans. These users leave the widow and orphan controls off. To turn the controls off, set Widows to 1 and Orphans to 1.

Balancing columns

The Chapter Typography dialog box also lets you set whether or not you want Ventura to balance columns automatically. With Column Balance on, Ventura tries to put an equal amount of text in each column (Figure 5-43).

With Column Balance off, Ventura fills up the first column completely before it puts any text in the second column. It fills up the second column completely before it moves on to the third column, and so on (Figure 5-44).

Tip: Column balance doesn't affect single column documents (there's nothing to balance). Because it requires Ventura to make extra calculations, it slows down formatting and screen redraw. You should only turn it on when you really need it.

Moving down to the first baseline

The Chapter Typography dialog box contains one function that confuses most beginners but has importance to advanced users. The Move Down To 1st Baseline By list box has two settings, Inter-Line and Cap Height.

Figure 5-43. Column balance is on in this example.

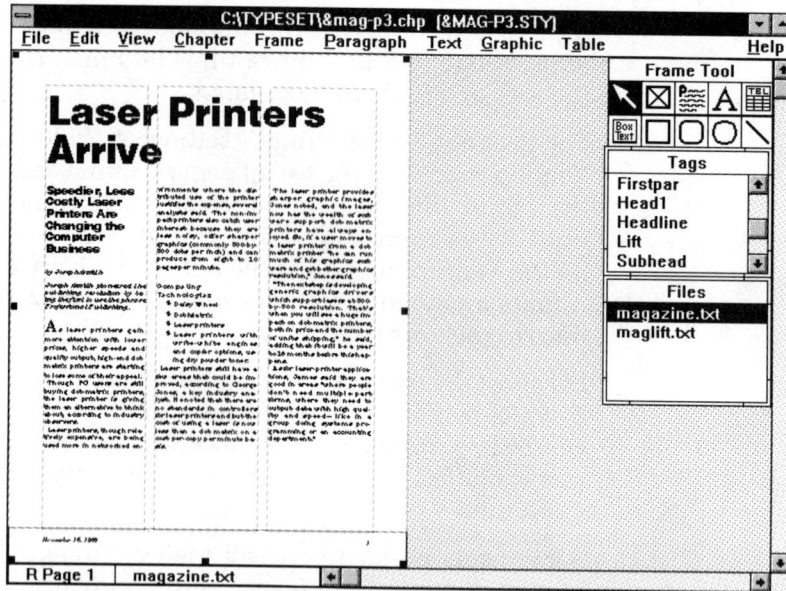

Figure 5-44. Column balance is off in this example.

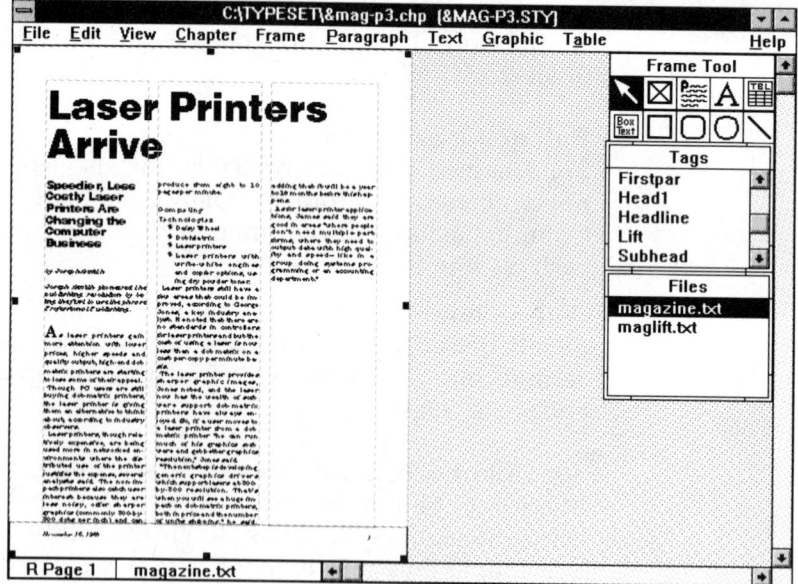

This function controls where Ventura starts the first line of a new page or column. Let's say you are working with 14-point text with an inter-line spacing of 18 points. If you choose Inter-Line, Ventura will count down 18 points before it creates the first line of text. If you choose Cap Height, Ventura will count down 14 points.

Rotating text

Ventura allows you to rotate text in 90 degree increments. You'll find a variety of uses for this feature:

- Run credits vertically alongside photos, drawings, or sample documents, as we do in Chapter 20, "Portfolio."
- Turn the address sideways or upside down for self-mailing brochures and flyers (Figure 5-45).

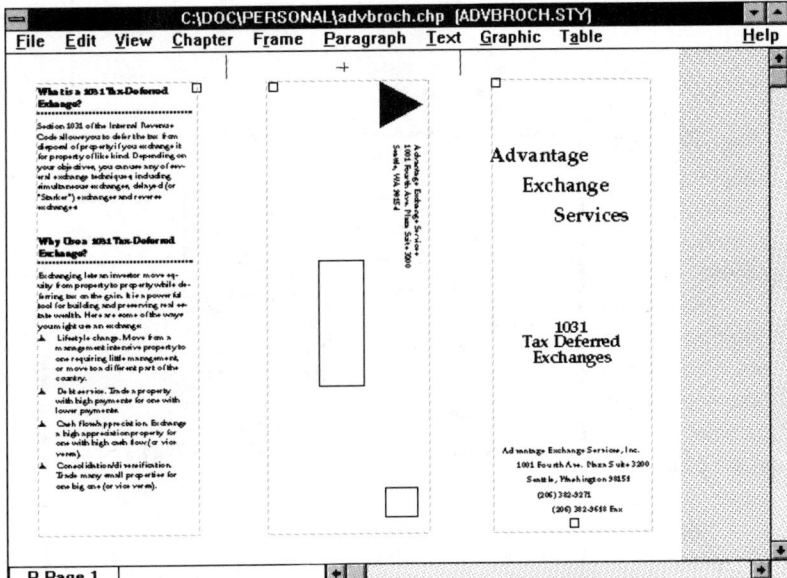

Figure 5-45. With rotated text, you can position correctly on self-mailing brochures and flyers.

- Create unusual and appealing headlines for newsletters or marketing materials.
- Make tables with thin columns more compact and easier to read (Figure 5-46).

You can only rotate entire paragraphs. You cannot rotate a single word or phrase within a larger paragraph. To rotate a text paragraph:

1. Using the Paragraph Tool, select the paragraph.

2. Choose Alignment from the Paragraph menu (Figure 5-47).

3. Select the degree of rotation from the Text Rotation list box.

If you choose 90, the text will run at a right angle to and 90 degrees counter-clockwise from the normal baseline, with the first character at the bottom (see the table example in Figure 5-46) If you

Figure 5-46. Rotated text can sometimes save space in table column heads.

Decimal	Character
35	#
42	*
43	+
155	¢
156	£

Decimal	Character
35	#
42	*
43	+
155	¢
156	£

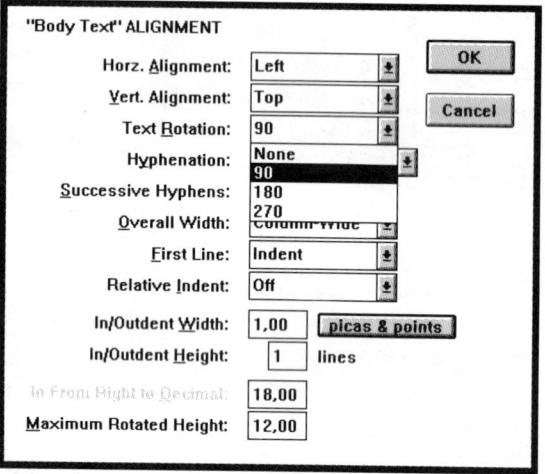

Figure 5-47. You can rotate paragraphs in 90-degree increments with the Alignment dialog box. If you want Ventura to make line-ending decisions, be sure to set the Maximum Rotated Height.

choose 180, the text will turn upside down. And if you choose 270, the text will again run at a right angle to the normal baseline, this time with the first character at the top (see the brochure example in Figure 5-45).

4. Type the line length of the rotated text in the Maximum Rotated Height text box.

To understand the maximum height, think of the right margin in normal text. When you are typing and you reach the right margin, the text wraps down to the next line. When rotated text reaches the maximum height, it wraps to the next line.

When Ventura rotates text, it ignores the normal spacing between lines. It pushes the text below it out of the way to make room for the rotation. The amount of room that Ventura creates is determined by the Maximum Rotated Height you specify.

Tip: If you rotate text and it disappears, your Maximum Rotated Height is not big enough. Reopen the Alignment dialog box and add more space.

Adjusting underlines, superscripts, and other attributes

Every Ventura tag has text attributes associated with it, attributes that can be applied with the Text menu. In addition to such things as bold and italic, these attributes include underlines (single or double), overscores, strike-throughs, superscripts, subscripts, and small caps.

You use the Text Tool and the Text menu to turn on these effects. You use the Paragraph Tool and the Attribute Overrides dialog box to control how they look. In most cases, the default settings are adequate. In some cases, especially underlines and superscripts, you may want to make adjustments. To adjust text attributes:

1. Using the Paragraph Tool, select the paragraph.
2. Select Attribute Overrides from the Paragraph menu (Figure 5-48).

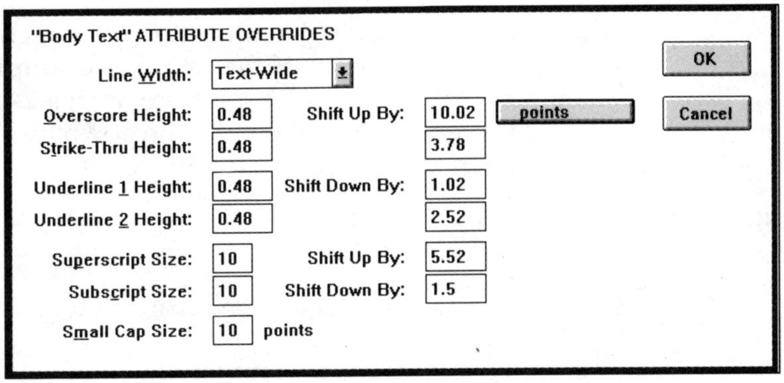

Figure 5-48.
The Attribute Overides dialog box.

"Body Text" ATTRIBUTE OVERRIDES			
Line Width:	Text-Wide		OK
Overscore Height:	0.48	Shift Up By: 10.02 points	Cancel
Strike-Thru Height:	0.48	3.78	
Underline 1 Height:	0.48	Shift Down By: 1.02	
Underline 2 Height:	0.48	2.52	
Superscript Size:	10	Shift Up By: 5.52	
Subscript Size:	10	Shift Down By: 1.5	
Small Cap Size:	10	points	

3. Make the attribute changes you want and click on OK.

Let's quickly discuss each of the attributes so you have some guidance on when and how to make changes:

Line Width controls the length of certain ruling lines, namely underlines, overscores, and strike-throughs. If you choose Text-Wide, the lines will be exactly the length of the letters you select with the Text Tool. If you choose Margin-Wide instead, the lines will stretch from margin to margin, even if you've only selected a single character.

Overscore Height determines the thickness of the ruling line used for the overscore. The *Shift Up By* text box just to the right of the Overscore Height button controls the distance between the baseline of the text and the overscore.

Strike-Thru Height affects the thickness of the ruling line. The *Shift Up By* text box to the right of this button controls the distance between the baseline of the text and the strike-through. Normally, you want to adjust it to appear in the center of the text.

Underline 1 Height and *Underline 2 Height* control the thickness of the lines used for underlines. The *Shift Down By* boxes to the immediate right control the distance between the baseline of the text and the top underline.

Superscript Size and *Subscript Size* control the size of smaller characters above or below the normal baseline. The *Shift Up By* and *Shift Down By* boxes to the immediate right control how far above or below the normal baseline these characters appear.

Small Cap Size affects the point size of text designated as small caps with the Text menu. Usually, the point size should be about 80% of the normal font size.

Example: Ventura's default settings often create underlines that cut off the descenders of the text. For example, let's assume that you want to underline 18-point text with a 2-point underline, and that you want to shift the underline down by four points so it does not overlap the descenders (Figure 5-49).

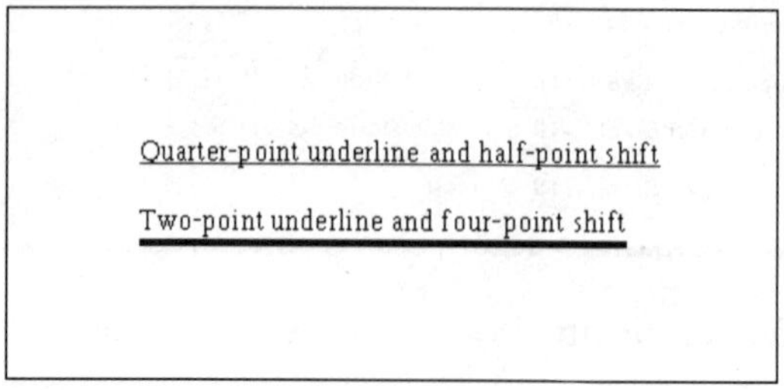

Figure 5-49.
Use the Attribute Overrides dialog box to change the appearance and position of attributes such as underlines.

Quarter-point underline and half-point shift

Two-point underline and four-point shift

To make this change:

1. Using the Paragraph Tool, select the paragraph.
2. Choose Attribute Overrides from the Paragraph menu.
3. Enter an Underline 1 Height of 2.00 points and a Shift Down By of 4.00 points. Click on OK.

Adjusting the space between letters

Ventura provides four methods of controlling the space between letters. Each one has a specific purpose. This section explains all four:

- Automatic pair kerning
- Manual kerning
- Tracking
- Letter spacing

Using automatic pair kerning

Automatic pair kerning is a special capability of certain printers and certain fonts, including most PostScript fonts. These fonts come with *kerning tables* that contain descriptions of letter pairs that need special spacing to look their best. If you enable automatic pair kerning, Ventura can take advantage of this kerning information to improve the look of your pages.

Pair kerning is necessary because different letter combinations need different spacing to look their best. Think of two capital *T*s sitting next to each other. If they are pushed too close together, the crossbars will touch. But now image a capital *T* sitting next to a lowercase *a*. If you used the same spacing as before, the *a* would look too far away from the *T*. This letter pair would look better if the *a* was nudged slightly to the left under the crossbar of the *T*.

Kerning tables list dozens (sometimes hundreds) of such letter combinations, together with spacing instructions for each one. To allow Ventura to make use of this kerning information, you must take two steps. First, you must enable pair kerning for the entire chapter. Second, you must turn it on for each and every tag.

Tip: It makes sense to enable automatic pair kerning for every tag in every document. If kerning information is available for the font you've specified, Ventura will use it. If not, you haven't done any harm.

To turn on pair kerning for the chapter:

1. Choose Chapter Typography from the Chapter menu.
2. Select Pair Kerning: On and click on OK (Figure 5-50).

This step is not enough by itself to make the benefits of kerning appear in your documents. You must also enable kerning for each tag:

Figure 5-50.
The Chapter Typography dialog box controls global settings for the entire document. You can override these settings.

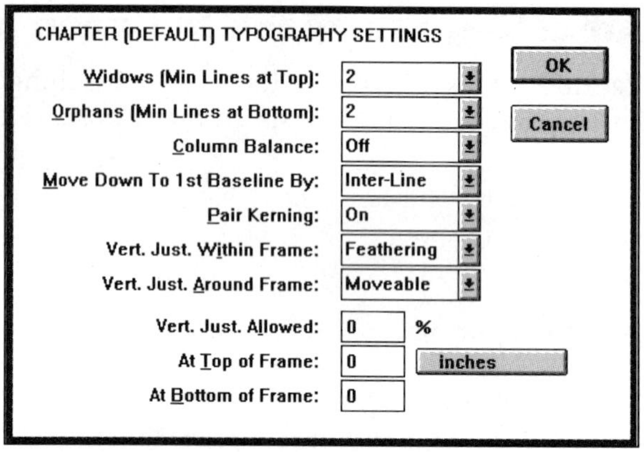

```
CHAPTER (DEFAULT) TYPOGRAPHY SETTINGS
    Widows (Min Lines at Top):     2          OK
 Orphans (Min Lines at Bottom):    2          Cancel
             Column Balance:       Off
   Move Down To 1st Baseline By:   Inter-Line
                Pair Kerning:      On
     Vert. Just. Within Frame:     Feathering
     Vert. Just. Around Frame:     Moveable

         Vert. Just. Allowed:      0    %
            At Top of Frame:       0    inches
         At Bottom of Frame:       0
```

3. Using the Paragraph Tool, select each tag paragraph.
4. Choose Paragraph Typography from the Paragraph menu.
5. Select Automatic Pair Kerning: On and click on OK (Figure 5-51).

Figure 5-51.
The Paragraph Typography dialog box.

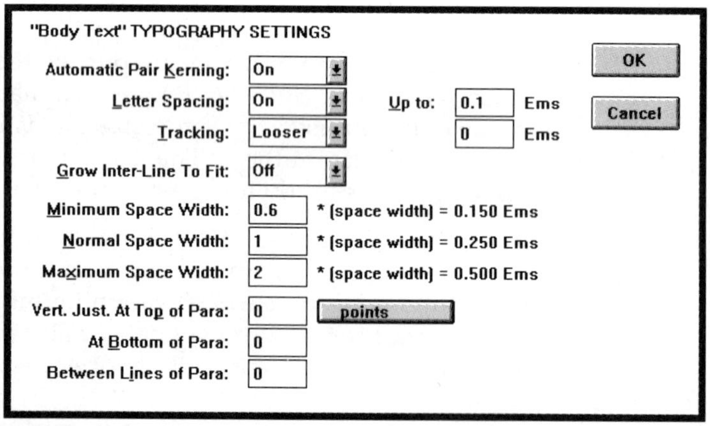

```
"Body Text" TYPOGRAPHY SETTINGS
   Automatic Pair Kerning:  On                              OK
          Letter Spacing:   On     Up to:  0.1  Ems         Cancel
                Tracking:   Looser          0    Ems
     Grow Inter-Line To Fit: Off
     Minimum Space Width:   0.6    * (space width) = 0.150 Ems
      Normal Space Width:   1      * (space width) = 0.250 Ems
     Maximum Space Width:   2      * (space width) = 0.500 Ems
  Vert. Just. At Top of Para: 0    points
         At Bottom of Para: 0
      Between Lines of Para: 0
```

Tip: Even though we recommend automatic pair kerning for the printer, we don't recommend it for small sizes on screen. Showing pair kerning on screen slows down the display. Yet you don't get much in return. The coarse resolution of computer screens makes it extremely difficult to see the differences at sizes below 24 points. We recommend that you use Set Preferences from the Edit menu to set On-Screen Kerning to 24. Ventura will display pair kerning for fonts 24 points or larger, but won't bother for smaller sizes.

Manual kerning

You can think of manual kerning as a synonym for *shifting letters horizontally from their normal positions*. You can shift letters either left or right. If you move letters so they are closer to their neighbors, you are kerning them *tighter*. If you move them further away from each other, you are kerning them *looser*.

Manual kerning comes into play most often for display type. Perhaps you want to improve the look of a headline. Or perhaps you are creating a logo that relies on special spacing effects (Figure 5-52).

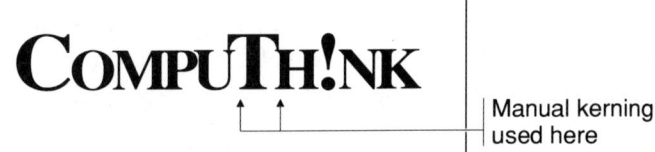

Figure 5-52. Manual kerning moved the letter T closer to the adjacent letters.

Manual kerning can also be valuable when you need to squeeze some text into a space. Perhaps you have a title in a table that won't quite fit into the column. Or maybe you have a three-letter widow that is ruining the look of a paragraph. By selecting the text and kerning it tighter, you can often fit the text into the desired space.

You can kern in two ways: *interactively* with the arrow keys or *numerically* with the Font dialog box. Either way, you must start by using the Text Tool to select the letters you want to kern.

Kerning affects the space to the *right* of the letters you select. For instance, if you wanted to kern the space between the U and T in the CompuTh!nk logo, you would select only the letter U. Then you could kern the space to its right (tighter to reduce the space, looser to increase it). If you wanted to kern that space plus the space between the T and the H, you would select the U and the T.

To kern with the keyboard:

1. Using the Text Tool, select the letter(s) to the left of the space(s) you want to kern.

2. Hold down the Shift key and press the left arrow to kern letters tighter. Hold down the Shift key and press the right arrow to move them further apart (looser).

Each press of the arrow key moves the letters 0.01 to 0.02 ems. An *em*, or *em space*, is equal to the point size of the font. If you are working with 30-point type, the em space is equal to 30 points.

Tip: Interactive manual kerning is best done in Enlarged view. It is only reasonably accurate if you have Adobe Type Manager or another utility that creates accurate screen fonts. Even so, you'll probably have to make some test printouts to get it right. For more information on using screen fonts and Adobe Type Manager, see Chapter 13, "Printing Ventura Documents."

If you prefer, you can type kerning values directly into the Font dialog box:

1. Using the Text Tool, select the letter(s) to the left of the space(s) you want to kern.
2. Choose Set Font Attributes from the Text menu. Click on the Kern: Tight button if you want to move letters closer. Click on the Kern: Loose button if you want to move letters apart.
3. Type in the amount you wish to kern, measured in em spaces.

The values you type in apply to the spaces to the right of the letters you selected. For instance, suppose you select three letters and kern them 0.01 ems tighter. Ventura will subtract 0.01 ems from the spaces to the right of each of the three letters.

Remember that ems are a relative measure. They do not remain the same for every font. As the font gets bigger, the em space gets bigger along with it. It's usually best to work in increments of 0.01 or 0.02 ems. It's rare to kern more than 0.10 to 0.15 ems. Any more than that and the letters are likely to touch.

Warning: It is best not to apply manual kerning (or other text attributes) to frame text or Box Text. Ventura saves the text and its attributes in its caption file, where, for some unknown reason, these attributes sometimes get lost or changed. Rather, use a separate text file, even if you have to create several small files.

Using tracking

To this point, you have learned how to use automatic pair kerning. You have also seen how to use manual kerning to control spacing between a few letters within a word.

Manual kerning adds or subtracts space between the letters you select, and only those letters. By contrast, *tracking* adds or subtracts space between every letter in the paragraph (Figure 5-53).

To apply tracking:

1. Using the Paragraph Tool, select the paragraph.

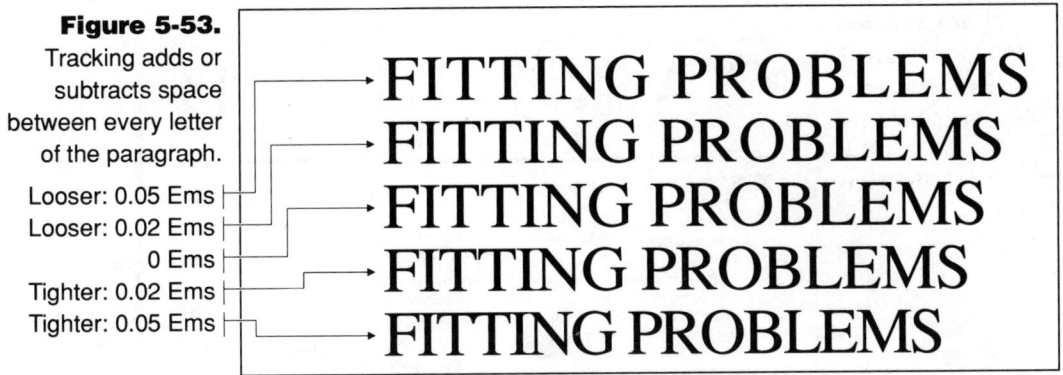

Figure 5-53. Tracking adds or subtracts space between every letter of the paragraph.

2. Choose Paragraph Typography from the Paragraph menu.
3. Select Tracking: Looser to add space between letters. Select Tracking: Tighter to subtract space.
4. Type the amount of space to track, measured in ems.

You can think of tracking as manual kerning applied to the entire paragraph. As with kerning, it is best to work in increments of 0.01 to 0.02 ems or so.

Tracking has several important uses, including better-looking display type and special type effects. For instance, it can help to make display type more attractive and more professional by reducing unsightly gaps at large sizes. The human eye perceives large type differently than small type. The same percentage spacing that looks perfect for 10-point type will look much too open if you enlarge that type to 36 points.

High-end traditional typesetters have an automatic tracking feature. The bigger the type, the more space they subtract. Even though Ventura doesn't have automatic tracking, you can duplicate its effects with manual tracking. Simply apply tracking to any display type over 18 points. Because different fonts need different amounts, we can't give you any hard and fast rules. You will have to experiment until you get it right. As a starting point, try subtracting 0.01 or 0.02 ems from display type between 18 and 30 points, and 0.02 to 0.05 ems from display type above 30 points.

Tracking is also useful for special type effects. Figure 5-54 shows tracking used to add space between letters for a logo design.

Using letter spacing
We've reached the final option in our section on controlling the space between letters. This last feature, called *letter spacing*, gives

Figure 5-54.
Ventura's tracking feature was used to add space between the letters in this logo.

Ventura extra leeway when justifying text. It does not have any effect on paragraphs that are flush left or flush right.

Justification, as you know, makes both the left and right margins even. To do this, Ventura sometimes hyphenates words. It also "stretches" or "squeezes" the text. To be more precise, Ventura adds or subtracts space between words to make the text fit between the margins.

Letter spacing gives Ventura the option of adding space between letters as well. Letter spacing does not require Ventura to add space. It merely gives Ventura the option *as a last resort*. Letter spacing comes into play only if Ventura can't make the text fit by adding space between the words.

To activate letter spacing:

1. Using the Paragraph Tool, select the paragraph.
2. Choose Paragraph Typography from the Paragraph menu.
3. Select Letter Spacing: On. Type the maximum allowable letter spacing into the box labeled Up To. Click on OK.

A typical setting is 0.10. As with kerning and tracking, letter spacing is measured in ems. We recommend that you use letter spacing with all your tags, provided you follow these two guidelines:

- Don't set the maximum letter spacing much past 0.10 ems. Otherwise, the space between letters may begin to look almost as wide as the space between words. The text could become hard to read.

- Check the space widths in the same dialog box. Be sure the minimum width is 0.70 or less. Be sure the normal width is 1. And be sure the maximum width is at least 2.

As explained in the next section, the width settings control how Ventura stretches and squeezes the spaces between words. You want Ventura to have plenty of leeway for word spacing before it has to resort to letter spacing.

Adjusting the space between words

Most users will do fine with Ventura's default word spacing. Advanced users, particularly those with typesetting backgrounds, may want to fine tune word spacing to their preferences. Ventura lets you control the minimum, normal, and maximum settings from the Paragraph Typography dialog box.

Ventura refers to the gap between words as the *space width*. Ventura uses the *normal* space width for unjustified text. For instance, if you look closely you'll see that flush left text has the same amount of space between words on each line.

The *minimum* and *maximum* settings come into play when Ventura justifies text. The program starts by trying to use the normal space width. If it can't get the text to fit the margins, it squeezes or stretches the text to fit. It does so by subtracting or adding space between the words. It uses the minimum and maximum settings as its lower and upper boundaries.

Thus, if you lower the minimum setting, you allow Ventura to squeeze words more tightly (if needed to justify a line). If you increase the maximum setting, you allow Ventura to stretch them more widely apart.

Figure 5-55 shows four examples. The left two columns are justified; the right two are aligned left. Notice that the text in the left column of each pair is spaced more closely together. The right column of each pair has had the settings increased. Notice how the same amount of text takes up more space because of the larger gaps between words.

To adjust the word spacing:

1. Using the Paragraph Tool, select the paragraph.
2. Choose Paragraph Typography from the Paragraph menu (Figure 5-56).
3. Type the settings into the space width text box(es) and click on OK.

Ventura doesn't ask you to specify this space in ems. Instead, it uses what amounts to a percentage of the normal width. It then

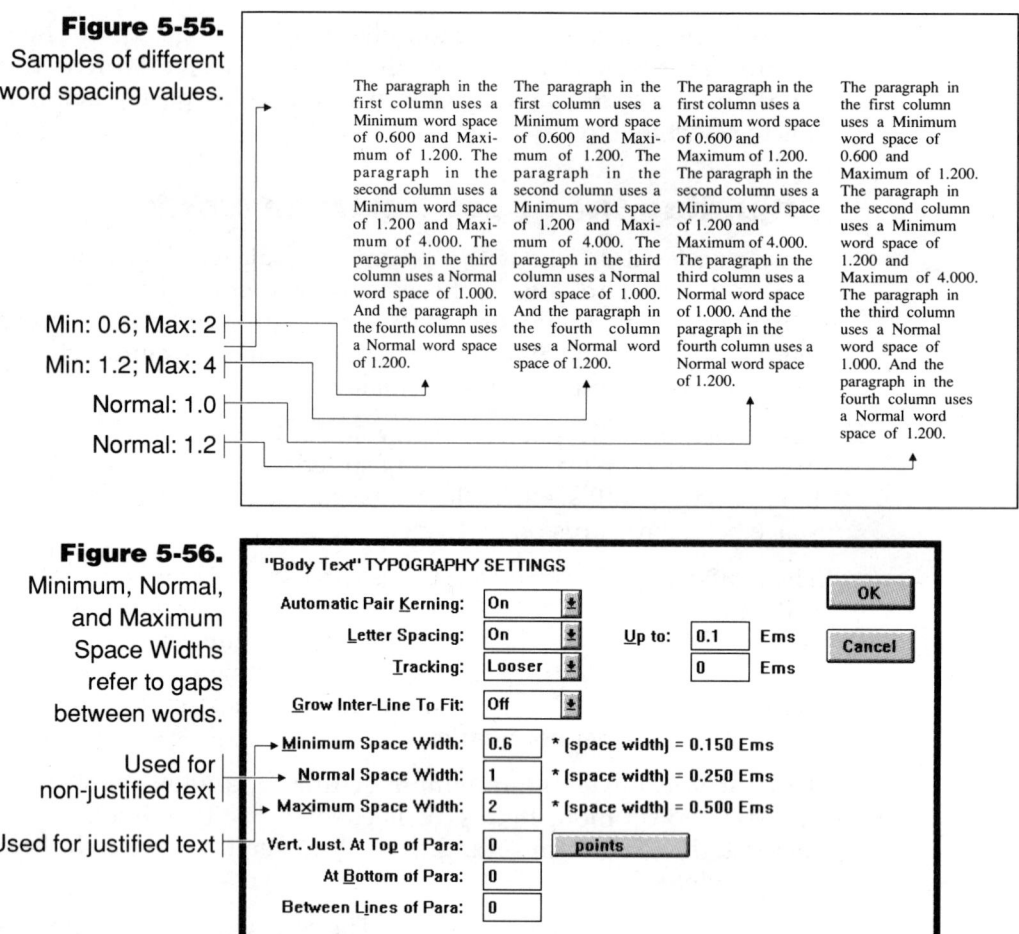

Figure 5-55. Samples of different word spacing values.

Figure 5-56. Minimum, Normal, and Maximum Space Widths refer to gaps between words.

calculates this setting and shows you what it equals in ems. It displays this amount to the right of the text box.

Example: Let's assume that you like a lot of space between words. You decide to double the default settings shown in Figure 5-56, To do so, you would type 1.2 into the Minimum box, 2 into the Normal box, and 4 into the Maximum box.

Tip: If you change the settings, you normally can't see the results in ems until you close and then reopen the dialog box. To see them immediately, click on the measurements button. The act of changing measurement units causes Ventura to recalculate all the values in the dialog box.

Finding and fixing loose lines

In our previous discussion about word spacing, we said that Ventura tries to justify lines with the normal space width. If the text doesn't fit perfectly between the margins, it then tries to add or subtract space between the words. If you've turned letter spacing on, it also adds space between letters if necessary. Ventura will also attempt to hyphenate words to make the margins even.

But what if Ventura does all those things and the text still won't fit? In those cases, Ventura breaks the rules. It stretches the text past the maximum space width.

Most users don't need to worry about these occasional *loose lines*. However, if you create high-end documents such as expensive annual reports or glossy marketing brochures, you'll want to find and fix as many loose lines as possible. This is especially true if you also use narrow columns. Because justification is more difficult in narrow columns, Ventura has to make more compromises.

To find the lines where the space between words exceeds the maximum, simply choose Show Loose Lines from the View menu (Figure 5-57).

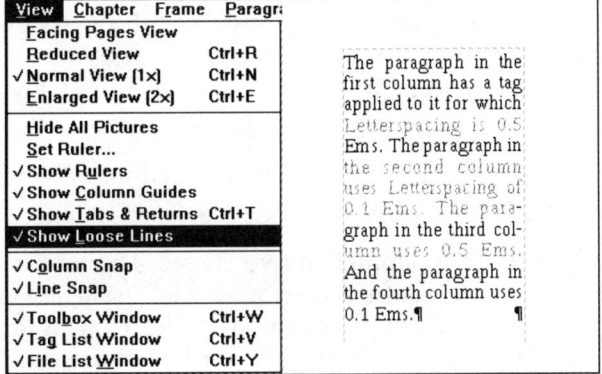

Figure 5-57. Too see where Ventura has been forced to exceed the maximum word space, select Show Loose Lines from the View menu.

If you have a monochrome screen, loose lines show as white text on a black bar. If have a color screen, loose lines show as red. How do you fix loose lines? You have several options:

- You can edit the text to see whether a new combination of words results in better spacing.
- You can try adding hyphenation points manually. Ventura rarely adds incorrect hyphens, but it sometimes misses opportunities.
- You can manually kern the line to take out space between letters and squeeze more text on the line.

Automatically adjusting the space between lines

In this section about text refinements, we've showed you how to control the spacing between letters and words. Ventura's Paragraph Typography dialog box also has an option that automatically adjusts the spacing between lines. Called Grow Inter-Line To Fit, it automatically increases the space between the lines of a paragraph if you insert oversized characters

Normally, you expect all the characters in a paragraph to be the same size. But if you are, for instance, producing a scientific monograph, you may have large symbols and stacked equations within the paragraphs. If you turn on Grow Inter-Line To Fit, Ventura will automatically add extra space to accommodate the big characters.

It doesn't hurt to leave on Grow Inter-Line To Fit. Under normal circumstances it has no effect.

Controlling hyphenation

In this section, we'll show you how to get full control over hyphenation. You will learn to:

- Turn hyphenation on or off for selected paragraphs
- Control ladders (successive hyphens)
- Customize the hyphenation dictionary
- Add or remove hyphenation from specific words

Ventura hyphenates in two stages. The first occurs when you load a text file. Ventura uses a special *hyphenation algorithm* to insert discretionary hyphens into the file. This algorithm is a set of rules for determining the proper hyphenation points in English. Because English isn't always logical, Ventura supplements the algorithm with an exception dictionary. In addition, it also consults a user dictionary, where you can enter words and hyphenation preferences unique to your needs.

Ventura uses the algorithm and the dictionaries to insert *discretionary* hyphens. These hyphens don't require Ventura to break the word and insert a hyphen. They simply indicate where Ventura can hyphenate that word if it needs to reformat a line.

The discretionary hyphens come into play during the second stage, when Ventura justifies text. The program tries to make text fit perfectly between the left and right margins. If it doesn't have enough words to fill up the space, it hyphenates the first word of the next line. It then brings up this partial word to fill out the line.

Note: You often hear Ventura users talking about hyphenation *dictionaries*. In fact, Ventura uses rule-based algorithms for most of its hyphenation. Only the small exception dictionary and user dictionary are truly alphabetic collections of words.

Turning hyphenation on or off

The default setting for hyphenation is on. But certain paragraphs—notably titles, headings, and callouts—should *not* be hyphenated. You can turn hyphenation off (and on again) with the Alignment dialog box (Figure 5-58). As you'll see in a few moments, you can also use this dialog box to control the number of consecutively hyphenated lines.

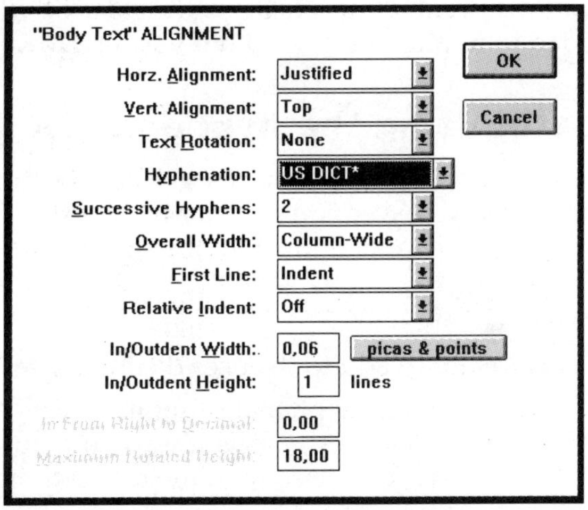

Figure 5-58. In the Alignment dialog box, you can specify which hyphenation dictionary to use, and how many consecutive lines to hyphenate.

To change the hyphenation settings of a paragraph:

1. Using the Paragraph Tool, select the paragraph.

2. Choose Alignment from the Paragraph menu.

3. Select the setting you want from the Hyphenation list box and click on OK.

Select Off if you do not want the paragraph hyphenated. Select the first algorithm, called US DICT*, if you want the default hyphenation for American English. Choose the second algorithm if you want to use a different version.

Note: You won't see a second hyphenation choice in the Alignment dialog box unless you have installed a second algorithm, as instructed below.

Controlling ladders

A *ladder* is a series of successive lines that end with hyphens. Ladders are ugly. In addition, the eye becomes confused when it encounters more than two or three hyphens in a row. You are most likely to encounter ladders in narrow columns, where justification is most difficult and hyphenation is frequent.

Ventura lets you control ladders by setting the maximum number of successive hyphens. Select the paragraph with the Paragraph Tool, open the Alignment dialog box, and select the maximum number from the Successive Hyphens list box. We recommend a maximum setting of two or three. If you allow more than that, the document could become hard to read. If you allow only one, you may force Ventura to create wide gaps of white space where it needed to hyphenate a word but wasn't allowed to.

Customizing the hyphenation dictionary

Ventura includes a small user hyphenation dictionary. Like Ventura's own exception dictionary, words in the user dictionary overrule the default algorithm. If you don't like the way a word is hyphenated, you can change it by entering the preferred method into the user dictionary.

You may want to add to the user dictionary for several reasons:

- To add different hyphenation points than the ones the default algorithm generates (especially for unusual or foreign words that are frequently used in your publications)
- To add additional hyphenation points if it seems the default algorithm is missing opportunities
- To instruct Ventura *not* to hyphenate certain words, such as proper names

The user dictionary is an ASCII file called HYPHUSER.DIC in the \VENTURA directory. It contains several dozen sample words. Here are the first five as they appear in the file:

```
al-go-rithm
auto-mat-ic
bi-no-mial
```

```
bib-li-og-raphy
cen-ter
```

If you plan to add to the user dictionary, it is important to follow the correct format. As you can see, the file is in (1) lowercase letters only and (2) alphabetic order with (3) each word on a separate line and (4) the preferred hyphenation points indicated with hyphens between the letters.

What if you do *not* want a word to hyphenate? For instance, it is good editorial practice not to hyphenate proper names, especially the names of companies and trademarked products. In that case, you type the word without any hyphens. If Ventura's algorithm finds hyphenation points for that word, the user dictionary will override those points and keep the word together. For instance, to keep the name Ventura from hyphenating, you would type:

```
ventura
```

To add to the user dictionary:

1. Make a backup copy of HYPHUSER.DIC in case of mistakes.

2. Open HYPHUSER.DIC with Notepad or any ASCII editor.

3. Type in new words in alphabetic order in lowercase with each word on a separate line. Indicate your preferred hyphenation points with hyphens between the letters. To keep a word from hyphenating, type it onto a line without any hyphens.

4. Save the file in ASCII format.

Adjusting hyphenation for individual words

Even if you customize the user dictionary, you are likely to find words that you want to hyphenate differently. And you will often want to force a breaking word *not* to hyphenate. You can insert additional discretionary hyphens from the keyboard after a text file is imported into Ventura. You can also overrule a hyphenation decision and force a word to stay together.

To hyphenate a word normally, you use the Text Tool to insert a hyphen from the keyboard. This so-called *hard* hyphen will show up on the printed page even if the word appears in the middle of a line. To insert an additional *discretionary* or *soft* hyphen, hold down the Ctrl key while you type the hyphen. A soft hyphen will not show up on your printed page unless the word falls at the end of the line and Ventura needs to break the word to format the line. To see soft hyphens on screen, choosing Show Tabs & Returns from the Edit menu will display soft hyphens as small dots.

To force a word to stay together, insert a soft hyphen *in front* of the word. With the Text Tool, move the cursor immediately to the left of the first letter. Press the hyphen key while holding down the Ctrl key.

Tip: Ventura will sometimes hyphenate the last word in a paragraph. This may leave only three or four letters on the last line. To avoid this unpleasant formatting, you can use your word processor's search and replace function. Create a macro that searches for the last word of a paragraph and then backs up to the front of that word. The macro should then insert a discretionary hyphen in front of the word, which will prevent that word from breaking. The bracket code for a discretionary hyphen is <-> (the hyphen inside angle brackets). For more information on using bracket codes in text files, see Chapter 7, "Creating Text with Other Programs."

Continuing on

In this chapter, we explained quite a few advanced functions. We showed you how to create all sorts of bullets. We taught you how to ornament your chapters with Big First Characters.

We also explained how to work with tabs and leaders. We laid out the procedures for using Auto-Numbering, both for generation of numbers and letters, and for automatically repeated text. We talked about vertical justification: how it works, when to use it, and how to do it. And finally, we showed you how to fine-tune your text by rotating text, adjusting space between letters and words, and controlling hyphenation.

Easy Access

For more info on...	See chapter...
Adding a new tag	3 — Building Basic Styles
Using bracket codes for characters and creating text with a database	7 — Creating Text with Other Programs
Drawing frames, importing pictures, and anchoring frames	11 — Loading and Placing Pictures
Working with screen fonts	13 — Printing Ventura Documents
A table of bullet symbols	21 — Rapid Reference

Part Three:
■ Text

6

Handling Text in Ventura

How to load, create,
and edit text in Ventura

- **Getting text in and out of Ventura** 188
- **Creating text in Ventura** 193
- **Editing text in Ventura** 198
- **Continuing on** 206

In Part Two, you learned how to control the overall look of your documents, using style sheets, tags, and the underlying page. But now it's time to get to the heart of a document—the text.

As you learned in Chapter 3, "Building Basic Styles," Ventura combines multiple files into a single document. There are two ways to create and edit text in Ventura: You can handle text in Ventura itself, or you can use another program such as a word processor to create the text and load it into Ventura.

You'll find that other programs can do certain tasks that Ventura can't do. For example, a database can store and organize large amounts of information; Ventura can't. Other programs such as word processors can automate time-consuming and tedious tasks with powerful features—outlining and search-and-replace, for example. We'll show you how to take advantage of the speed and power of text-handling programs in Chapter 7, "Creating Text with Other Programs."

Clearly, handling large amounts of text is faster and easier using other programs such as a word processor. However, it's much more convenient to make minor text changes and formatting adjustments in Ventura—rather than switching back and forth between Ventura and your word processor. Whereas text-handling is the forte of word processors, Ventura's strength is formatting—fine-tuning the look of text and enhancing it. Ventura's powerful formatting features such as interactive tracking and kerning let you give text just the right look. In this chapter, we'll give you the skills to handle text in Ventura:

- Get text in and out of Ventura
- Create text directly in Ventura
- Edit text in Ventura

Getting text in and out of Ventura

In Chapter 2, "Starting Out Smart," you learned the basics of loading a text file into a Ventura chapter. Now, we'll expand on that knowledge. In this section, we'll teach you how to handle text files in Ventura:

- Loading a text file
- Removing a text file
- Renaming a text file
- Moving a text file
- Converting a text file to a different format

Ventura makes managing your text files easy—you can do all these file functions with commands from the File and Frame menus.

Loading the text file

To load a text file into Ventura, you use the Load Text/Picture command. It's simple. Choose Load Text/Picture from the File menu, select File Type: Text, and select the format of text file (Figure 6-1). Then click on OK and navigate to the directory that contains the text file. Select the filename and click on Open (or double-click the filename).

Figure 6-1. To load text files into Ventura, use the Load Text/Picture dialog box.

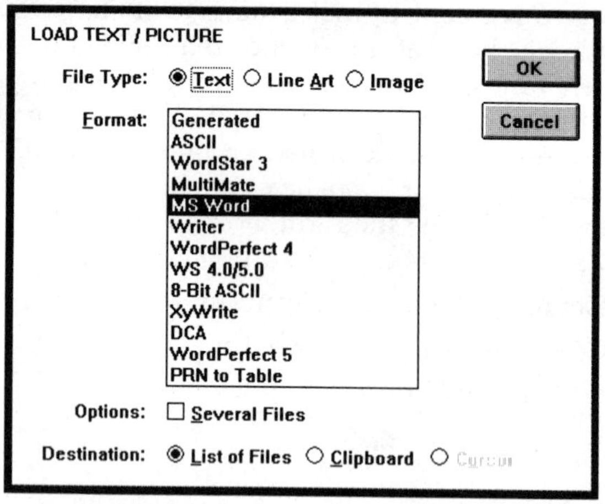

That's the routine. But where Ventura places your text file depends on two conditions: (1) the elements you selected before choosing the Load Text/Picture command and (2) the options you chose in the Load Text/Picture dialog box.

We'll show you how to put your text file right where you want it. There are six possibilities:

- *Loading to the File List only.* Be sure neither the underlying page nor any frames are selected. Then choose Load Text/Picture and select Destination: List Of Files. Continue as usual. To place the file on the underlying page or in a frame, select the page or frame and click on the filename in the File List Window. If you can't see the File List Window on your screen, choose File List Window from the View menu (or press Ctrl-Y).

- *Loading to the underlying page.* Select the underlying page with the Frame Tool. The sizing handles appear on the edges of the page. Choose Load Text/Picture and select Destination: List Of Files. Continue as usual. Ventura adds as many pages as necessary to hold the entire text.

- *Loading to a frame.* Select the frame with the Frame Tool. The sizing handles appear on the frame. Choose Load Text/Picture and select Destination: List Of Files. Continue as usual. If the file contains more text than the frame can hold, Ventura fills the frame and stops. You can use the Frame Tool to expand the frame so that the all the text appears.

- *Threading a text file through multiple frames.* You can thread the text file so that it continues from one frame to another. To thread a text file through multiple frames, load the text file into the frame in which you want the text file to begin. Then select the next frame in which you want the file to continue, and click on the filename in the File List Window. Repeat for all the frames through which you want the file to continue. Ventura threads the text through the frames in the order you load the file in them. You can also make the text jump to frames on subsequent pages (but not previous pages).

- *Loading to the clipboard.* Use the Load Text/Picture dialog box and select Destination: Clipboard. Continue as usual. The file will not appear in the File List Window. To bring it onto the page, select the Text Tool, place the text cursor at the point where you want to place the text, and choose Paste from the Edit menu (or press Insert). The text becomes part of the file in which you inserted it.

- *Inserting a text file into existing text.* Select the Text Tool and place the text cursor where you want to place the text file within the text. Choose Load Text/Picture, and select Destination: Cursor. Continue as usual. The text becomes part of the file in which you inserted it and does not appear in the File List Window.

Note: If you select Options: Several Files, the Open File dialog box will continue to appear, so that you can load more files to the destination you specified. After loading the last file, click on Cancel. If you selected Clipboard or Cursor as the destination, Ventura adds files to the end of the previously loaded files.

Tip: Load files from the hard drive instead of floppy disks. This will speed up the time it takes to open a chapter—Ventura can load files quicker from the hard drive.

Example: Loading a text file is pretty simple. But if you've never threaded text through multiple frames before, this technique can be baffling. After you've tried it once, you'll understand how it works. Let's begin by creating an example chapter that you can use throughout this chapter. If you have any problems setting up the example chapter, see Chapter 2, "Starting Out Smart." Then we'll thread a text file through three frames:

1. Start Ventura and choose New from the File menu.
2. Use Load Diff. Style from the File menu to load DEFAULT.STY from the \TYPESET directory.
3. Use Save Style As from the File menu to rename the style sheet as MYCHAP3.STY.
4. Use Save As from the File menu to save the chapter as MYCHAP3.CHP.
5. Use Load Text/Picture to load the ASCII text file BOOK.TXT from the \TYPESET directory.
6. Press Ctrl-S to save the chapter.

Now you're ready to thread a text file through multiple frames.

7. Select the Add Frame tool, place the cursor where you want the upper left corner to appear, hold down the left mouse button, drag the cursor to the lower right corner, and release the mouse button. Use this technique to draw three frames on the page: one at the top, one in the middle, one at the bottom. Make them any size you like.
8. Using the Frame Tool, select the top frame and click on the filename BOOK.TXT in the File List Window. Then select the middle frame and click on BOOK.TXT again. Do the same for the bottom frame.

Your chapter should look similar to Figure 6-2. The text continues from one frame to the next. Don't worry if our example chapter doesn't look exactly like yours—your frames and our frames differ in size; therefore, they won't contain the same amount of text.

9. Choose Revert To Saved from the File menu to return your chapter to its previous condition.

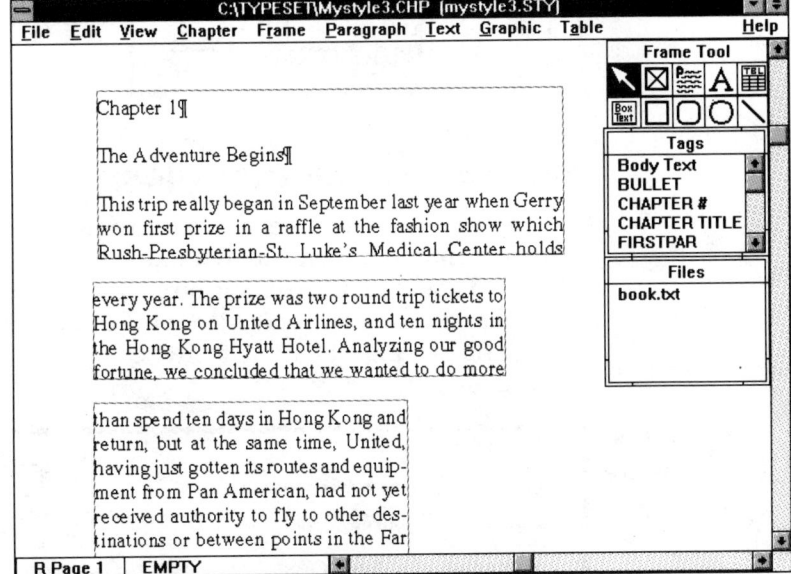

Figure 6-2.
Your example chapter should look similar to (but not exactly like) ours.

Removing text files

Now, you know how to load files and place them on the underlying page and in frames. But how do you get rid of unwanted text files? There are two ways to remove a text file from the underlying page and from frames:

- *Replace the file with another one from the File List.* Using the Frame Tool, select the underlying page or the frame that contains the file you want to remove. In the File List Window, click on the name of the new file. The new text file replaces the original file in the underlying page or frame. However, the original file remains in the File List.

- *Remove a file without replacing it.* Using the Frame Tool, select the underlying page or the frame that contains the file you want to remove. Choose the Remove Text/File command from the Frame menu. The Remove File dialog box appears (Figure 6-3). To remove the file from the frame only (but not the File List), select Remove From: Frame. To remove the file from both the frame and the File List, select Remove From: List Of Files. Then click on OK.

Figure 6-3.
The Remove File dialog box.

Renaming, relocating, and converting text files

You can rename a text file, move it to a new directory, or convert it to a different file format—all without having to leave Ventura. With the File Type/Rename dialog box, you can do most of your file management for your text files (you can't use this command for picture files) without having to switch to MS-DOS or File Manager (Figure 6-4).

Figure 6-4.
The File Type/Rename dialog box.

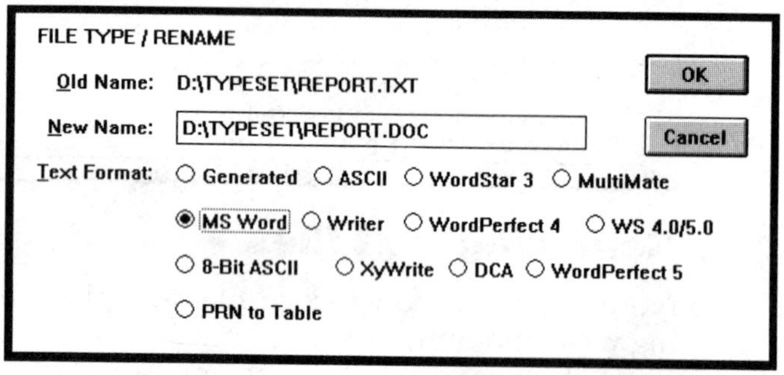

It's simple. You use the Frame Tool to select the underlying page or the frame containing the text file. Next, you choose File Type/Rename from the Frame menu. The File Type/Rename dialog box appears. The full path and filename for the currently selected file appears in the Old Name text box. To give you a head start, Ventura has that same path and filename in the New Name text box. Then you make your changes (rename, move, or convert the file). Finally, you click on OK.

Here's how to make changes to a text file with the File Type/Rename dialog box:

- To rename the file, delete the filename in the New Name entry box and type the new name.
- To move the text file to a new directory, delete the path and type a new path.

- To convert the text file to another file format, click on the desired file format button from the Text Format buttons. By default, the current file format is already chosen for you.

Note: When you convert to another file format, you must change the filename extension to match the new format. Otherwise, Ventura will keep the current filename extension.

Warning: The changes you make to the text file do not take place until you save the chapter. To be sure these changes are made, press Ctrl-S to do a quick save immediately after using File Type/Rename.

Example: If you're following along with our example chapter, try renaming the text file BOOK.TXT as MYBOOK3.TXT. First, select the underlying page with the Frame Tool, click on the filename BOOK.TXT in the File List Window, and choose File Type/Rename from the Frame menu. The Old Name text box should contain the BOOK.TXT text file with its pathname preceding it. Change the name in the New Name from BOOK.TXT to MYBOOK3.TXT. Click on OK. Press Ctrl-S to save your changes. The filename MYBOOK3.TXT should appear in the File List Window.

Creating text in Ventura

Although word processors give you more features for creating and editing text, Ventura's Text Tool can be more convenient for creating short documents and adding text to loaded text files. In addition, you'll see the text in its final WYSIWIG format.

In this section, we'll show you how to create text on the underlying page and in frames. Then we'll teach you how to insert special characters within the text.

Typing on the underlying page

Creating text on the underlying page is easy. You simply select the Text Tool, position the text cursor on the page, and type the text. Using the same method, you can also type text into frames. By typing text on the underlying page, you can easily add text to an existing text file or even create a new text file. Here's how:

- To add text to a text file that has already been loaded on the underlying page, you select the Text Tool and place the text cursor at the point where you want to insert text. Then type the additional text. This text will be added to the existing text file automatically when you save the chapter.

- To create a new text file within Ventura, you choose New from the File menu, select the Text Tool, click on the underlying page, and begin typing. When you save the chapter and name it, Ventura saves the text file with the same filename that you gave the chapter file (except the extension). Ventura also gives it the same format as the most recently loaded text file and uses that format's extension. If no files have been loaded, it will save the text as an ASCII file with the TXT extension.

Warning: If a text file with the same name already exists in the same directory as the chapter file, Ventura will warn you that you are about to overwrite the old file with the new one.

Typing in a frame

If you have a text file loaded into a frame already, you can add text to that file just as you did with a text file on the underlying page—select the Text Tool, position the text cursor, and begin typing the additional text.

However, you can't create an individual text file by typing into an empty frame—as you could by typing on the underlying page. When you type onto the underlying page of a new chapter, Ventura creates a file for the text. When you type into a frame, Ventura puts the text into an internally generated caption file—along with other frame text, Box Text, and, of course, captions—all in the order that they appear in the chapter.

However, there is a way to save text in a frame as a new text file. You use the Frame Tool to select the frame and then use the File Type/Rename dialog box from the Frame menu to save the frame text as a text file. Do this before you save the chapter.

Inserting special characters

Sometimes, you need special characters that aren't on your computer's keyboard: special letters, numbers, and symbols such as the symbol for pi (π), and a ballot box (☐). In this section, we'll give a quick lesson on how to create these special characters.

Note: You can also create special characters directly in the text file with your word processor by using bracket codes. In addition, Ventura also lets you create footnotes and equations, which are treated as special characters within the text. For more information on bracket codes, see Chapter 7, "Creating Text Files with Other Programs." For more information on footnotes and equations, see Chapter 15, "Creating Footnotes and Equations."

Creating non-keyboard characters

You can create more characters than are found on the standard keyboard. What these characters look like depends on the *font* you choose. A font is a specific size and style of type. We'll tell you more about fonts later. The list of characters that a font contains is called the *character set*. Most fonts use the International character set, where each character corresponds to a numerical code. Ventura uses two common coding systems: ASCII (American Standard Code for Information Interchange) and ANSI (American National Standards Institute). Both systems can generate most of the characters in the International character set. For a complete list of the ASCII and ANSI codes for the International character set, see Chapter 21, "Rapid Reference."

So what do these codes mean to you? You use ASCII and ANSI codes to generate special characters such as foreign language characters and symbols. In general, you use the ANSI codes to generate non-keyboard characters in Ventura. However, some dialog boxes may use ASCII codes (or a mixture of the two). But you always use ASCII codes in bracket codes to generate characters in text files.

The most difficult part of creating special characters is figuring out which code to use. However, once you know the code, creating the character is easy. There are two ways to do it in Ventura:

- Hold down the Alt key and type the ANSI number on the numeric keypad (not on the main keyboard). When you release the Alt key, the character will appear on the screen.
- You can also use keyboard shortcuts to produce the commonly used characters, which are summarized in Table 6-1. For a complete list of keyboard shortcuts for special characters, see Chapter 21 "Rapid Reference."

Warning: Some symbols in the ASCII character set do not exist in the ANSI character set—such as the dagger † and the double dagger ‡. Ventura for Windows cannot generate these characters.

Table 6-1. *Keyboard shortcuts for common characters*

Character	Key combination
Copyright mark	Ctrl-Shift-C
Discretionary hyphen	Ctrl- - (hyphen)
Em dash	Ctrl-]
En dash	Ctrl-[
Em space	Ctrl-Shift-M
En space	Ctrl-Shift-N
Figure space	Ctrl-Shift-F
Thin space	Ctrl-Shift-T
Non-breaking space	Ctrl-spacebar
Open quotation mark	Ctrl-Shift-[
Closed quotation mark	Ctrl-Shift-]
Registered trademark	Ctrl-Shift-R
Trademark	Ctrl-Shift-2

Example: If you're following along with our example chapter, try adding a few special symbols to your text. Select the Text Tool and place the text cursor anywhere within the text. Now create the British pound symbol (£) by holding down the Alt key and typing 0163 on the numeric keypad. Create a paragraph symbol (¶). (Hint: the code is 0182.) Choose Revert To Saved from the File menu to return the chapter to its previous condition.

Creating special symbols

Depending on your printer, you may have fonts that contain nothing but symbols and special characters. For example, PostScript printers usually have two resident fonts called Symbols and Zapf Dingbats. For more information on fonts, see Chapter 13, "Printing Ventura Documents." The Symbol font contains Greek, mathematical, and ornamental characters. Zapf Dingbats has special characters that can be used for bullets. For more information on creating bullets, see Chapter 5, "Building Advanced Styles."

You create the characters from these fonts in much the same way you did with International characters—except you must change the font to the one you want. You can change the font for either the whole paragraph or selected text within a paragraph. For more information on changing the font for a paragraph tag, see Chapter 3, "Building Basic Styles."

To create characters from these special fonts within a paragraph, you select the Text Tool and place the text cursor where you want to insert the characters. Then you type each character using its ANSI code. These characters will appear on screen as characters from the International character set. Using the Text Tool, you select these characters and choose Set Font Attributes from the Text menu. The Font Setting For Selected Text dialog box appears. Now, you select the font that you want from the Face list box. You can also adjust other attributes such as size, color, shift, and so on. We'll give you details on how to use the Set Font Attributes command later in this chapter. Finally, you click on OK.

Note: Unless you have special screen fonts that allow you to display these characters on screen, they will still appear on the screen as International characters. However, they will appear in the correct font when you print your document—if that font is installed on your printer.

For a complete list of ASCII and ANSI codes for the Symbol and Zapf Dingbats fonts, see Chapter 21, "Rapid Reference."

Creating ballot boxes and filled boxes

Ballot boxes and filled boxes are special characters that are used often in questionaires, checklists, or bullet lists. You can insert ballot boxes (Ventura calls them hollow boxes) and filled boxes into text quickly by using the Box Char option of the Insert Special Item command from the Text menu (Figure 6-5). Here's how:

1. Select the Text Tool and position it at the exact point in the text where you want to insert a box.

2. Choose Insert Special Item from the Text menu.

3. Select Box Char from the flyout menu. A VP Alert box will appear prompting you to select a Hollow or Filled box, or to cancel the command (Figure 6-6).

4. Click the button of the type of box you want to insert: Hollow or Filled. The box appears in the text and has the same point size as the surrounding text.

Figure 6-5.
Use the the Box Char option from Insert Special Item to create hollow and filled boxes.

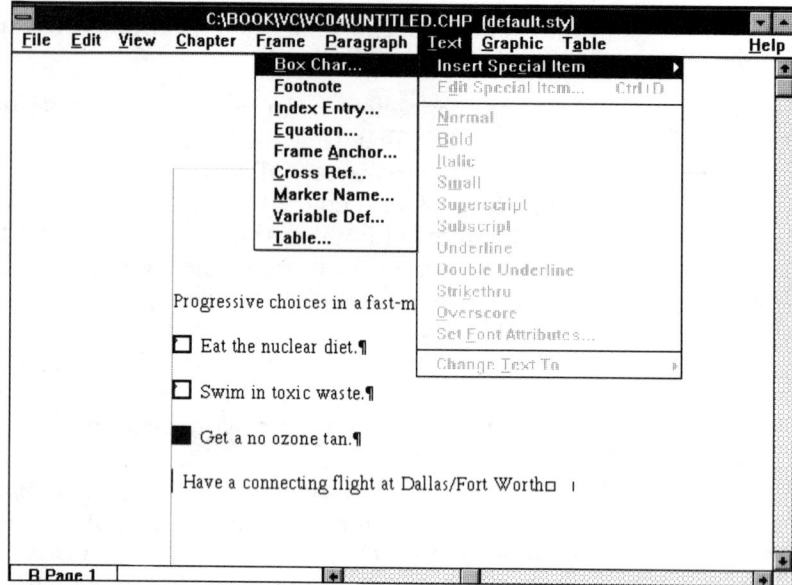

Figure 6-6.
This VP Alert box the Box Char option from Insert Special Item.

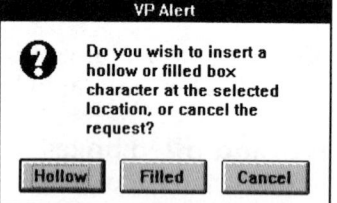

Editing text in Ventura

Although Ventura doesn't have the powerful editing functions of a word processor, such as search-and-replace or a spellchecker, you can use Ventura's Text Tool as a built-in word processor. In this section, you'll learn these text editing skills:

- Selecting, cutting, copying, and pasting text
- Changing text attributes
- Changing font settings
- Using interactive font sizing, kerning, and tracking
- Editing tabs, paragraph markers, and other symbols

Selecting, cutting, copying, and pasting text

Ventura's text mode follows most of the same conventions as most Windows programs—except for shortcut keys. You select text as you do in most Windows programs. It's easy. You simply use the Text Tool. There are two methods: (1) dragging the text cursor across the words you want or (2) clicking the cursor where you want to begin your selection, repositioning the cursor at another position, and shift-clicking to select all the text in between.

Note: You can only select text from one page or frame at a time.

If you're using the Edit menu, you cut, copy, and paste the selected text just as you would with most other Windows program. Here's a quick review of the basics:

- *Deleting text.* Select the text, and choose Cut Text from the Edit menu (or press Del). The selected text is deleted from the page and moved to the clipboard where it remains until you cut or copy more text or turn the computer off.
- *Copying text.* Select some text, and choose Copy Text from the Edit menu (or press Shift-Del). A copy of the text is stored in the clipboard until you cut or copy another item (more text, frames, tags or graphics) or turn the computer off.
- *Pasting text.* Position the cursor where you want to place the cut or copied text and choose Paste Text from the Edit menu (or press Insert).

Tip: With the Text Tool and the Edit menu, you can move text between text files with different file formats. By using the clipboard, you don't have to worry about file conversion because Ventura merges text from the clipboard directly into the text file.

Changing text attributes

Using the Text Tool, you can change the attributes of any block of text. Simply select the text with the Text Tool and choose an attribute (Bold, Italic, and so on) from the Text menu (Figure 6-7). You can add as many of these attributes to the selected text as you want. Table 6-2 lists all the attributes and their effects on text.

To remove these attributes, you return the text to the attributes of the paragraph tag by choosing Normal from the Text menu. This

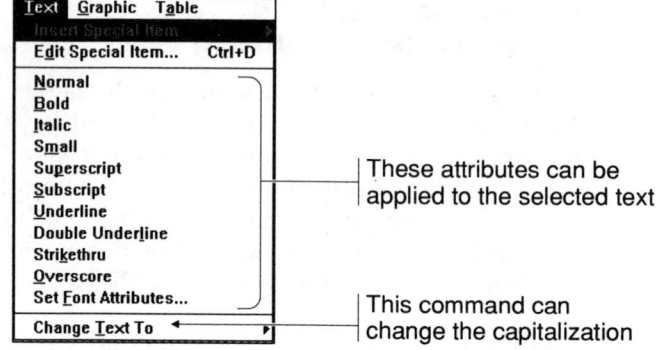

Figure 6-7.
Select the text and choose the attribute you want to apply from the Text menu.

Table 6-2. *Text attributes*

Name in Text menu	Effect	Example
Normal	Removes all attributes and returns the selected text to the attributes associated with the tag that is currently applied	Sample Text
Bold	Applies the Bold attribute to the selected text	**Sample** Text
Italic	Applies the Italic attribute to the selected text	*Sample* Text
Small	Applies a smaller point size font to the selected text	Sample Text
Superscript	Applies a smaller point size font and shifts up the selected text	Sample Text
Subscript	Applies a smaller point size font and shifts down the selected text	Sample Text
Underline	Applies a single line directly underneath the baseline of the selected text	Sample Text
Double Underline	Applies two closely spaced lines directly underneath the baseline of the selected text	Sample Text
Strikethru	Applies a single line through the selected text	~~Sample~~ Text
Overscore	Applies a single line immediately above the selected text	Sample Text

removes all the attributes that you added with the Text menu. Then you re-apply the attributes that you want to keep.

You can also change how the selected text is capitalized. With Change Text To from the Text menu, you can make the text all uppercase or all lowercase, or capitalize the first letter of each word (initial caps). Just select the text, choose Change Text To from the Text menu, and select Upper Case, Lower Case, or Capitalize (for initial caps) from the flyout menu. Table 6-3 shows the effects of each Change Text To option.

Table 6-3. *Capitalization of text*

Upper Case	Changes selected text to all uppercase characters	SAMPLE TEXT
Capitalize	Changes the first character of every word of the selected text to uppercase characters	Sample Text
Lower Case	Changes the selected text to all lowercase characters	sample text

Changing font settings

So far, you've learned how to apply basic attributes to selected text. Now, you'll see how to change the font settings for selected text. There are many situations where local font changes make more sense than changing the whole tag. For example, you could change to the Symbol font to create a few Greek characters and leave the text for rest of the paragraph alone. Using Set Font Attributes from the Text menu, you can adjust seven font settings (Figure 6-8).

Figure 6-8. Changing font and other attributes with Set Font Attributes from the Text menu.

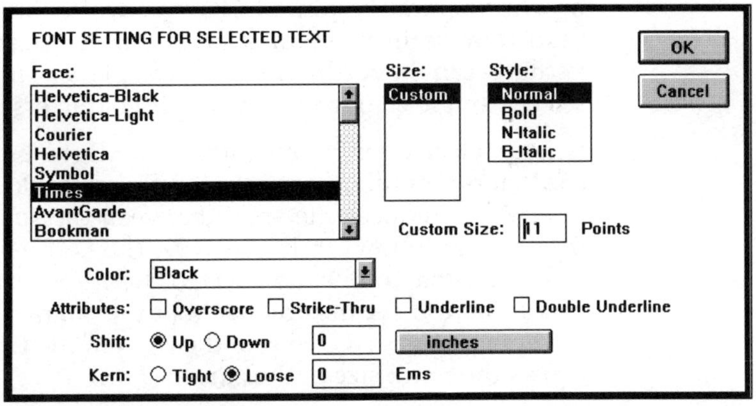

It's simple. To adjust the font settings, simply select the text with the Text Tool and choose the Set Font Attributes from the Text menu. The Font Setting For Selected Text dialog box appears. Make the settings that you want. Then click on OK.

Here's what each option in the Font Setting For Selected Text dialog box controls:

- *Face* is the type family, such as Helvetica or Dutch.
- *Size* is the point size of the text. Depending on your printer, you can select the size from the Size list box. Or you might see the word Custom in the Size list box. In that case, type the size in the Custom Size text box.
- *Style* is the type style (weight and slant of the text), such as Bold or N-Italic (normal italic).
- *Color* is the color of the text, such as Black.
- *Attributes* are special type effects added to the text, such as Overscore and Underline.
- *Shift* is the distance the text is moved above or below the baseline, such as Shift: Up 5 points. To shift the selected text, select the direction you want to shift from the Shift buttons (Up or Down). Then click on the measurements button until it displays the units you want. We suggest Points. Type the amount of shift in the text box to the left of the measurements button.
- *Kern* is the spacing between the characters of the text, such as Kern: Tight 0.1 em spaces. An em space is a unit of measure equal to the point size of the current font. For example, 0.1 ems is 1 point if the current font is 10 point.

Kerning is more complex. But don't worry. We'll unravel the mystery behind kerning. In its broadest definition, kerning is the reduction or increase of space between characters. In Ventura, kerning can have different effects, depending on whether you select a single character or multiple characters.

If you select a single character, the Tight button moves all the characters that follow the selected character closer to that character. In effect, it reduces the space between the selected character and the one that follows it (Figure 6-9). The Loose button moves all the characters that follow the selected character further away from that character. You set the amount that the characters are moved with the Ems text box (which is to the right of the Loose button). An em equals the point size of the current font.

If you select multiple characters, the Tight button reduces the space between the characters in the selected text *and* moves the characters that follow closer to that text. The Loose button increases the space between the text characters *and* moves the following charac-

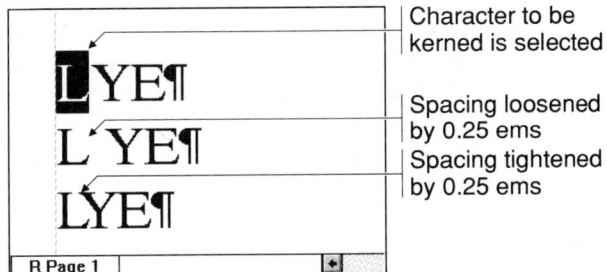

Figure 6-9.
You can reduce (tighten) or increase (loosen) the space between a character and the ones that follow it (kerning).

ters further away. When you kern multiple characters, the process is called *tracking*. Again, the amount is entered in the Ems text box.

Using interactive font sizing, kerning, and tracking

Now that you've learned how to change the font size, adjust the kerning for a character, and adjust the tracking for a group of characters, you're ready to learn some shortcuts. Ventura allows you to change the font size of, kern, and track selected text one unit at a time—without using the Set Font Attributes command. In addition, you'll be able to see the changes immediately on the screen (interactive change). It's fast and easy. You simply select the text, hold down the Shift key, and use the arrow keys to make your changes. Here's how:

- To change font size of selected text, use the Text Tool to select the text. To increase the point size, hold down the Shift key and press the up arrow key. To decrease the point size, hold down the Shift key and press the down arrow key. Each time you press the arrow key, you change the point size of the selected text by one point.

- To kern a selected character, use the Text Tool to select the character. To move all the characters that follow the character closer, hold down the Shift key and press the left arrow key. To move the following text away from the character, hold down the Shift key and press the right arrow key. In general, each time you press the arrow key, you move the text one unit in that direction. For the most part, Ventura moves the text 0.02 ems the first time you press the arrow key; after the first time, it moves the text in 0.01 em increments. When you're done with your kerning, check your settings in the Set Font Attributes dialog box.

- To adjust the tracking of selected text, use the Text Tool to select the text. You must select more than one character; otherwise, you'll simply adjust the kerning for one character. To reduce the spacing between the characters and move all the characters that follow closer to the selected text, hold down the Shift key and press the left arrow key. To enlarge the spacing between the characters and move the following characters farther away, hold down the Shift key and press the right arrow key. The amount of change in the spacing works the same as kerning.

Example: If you're following with our example chapter, experiment with interactive font sizing, kerning, and tracking. Using the Text Tool, select the word "Chapter" in the first line. Increase the font size by holding down the Shift key and press the up arrow key. You'll see the characters grow on screen. Now, select the first character and kern it so that the text that follows is closer (hold down the Shift key and press the left arrow key). Finally, select the whole word "Chapter" again and decrease the size and adjust the tracking so that the character spacing is greater.

Editing tabs, paragraph markers, and other symbols

Ventura uses special symbols to represent spacing and breaks, such as tabs, spaces, and paragraph markers. Ventura also uses a degree symbol to mark most items that have been inserted with the Insert Special Item command from the Text menu (Figure 6-10). When you insert or delete these symbols, you insert or delete their format, that is, the effect they have on surrounding text. Unfortunately, these symbols are often small or invisible. But we'll show you some tricks, so that you can handle them. Table 6-4 shows some of the special symbols that Ventura uses.

Figure 6-10.
Ventura marks items that you inserted with Insert Special Item with a degree symbol.

Here are some tips that will help you handle Ventura's special on-screen symbols:

- To see tabs, returns, and special item symbols, be sure that Show Tabs & Returns has a check mark next to it in the View menu (or press Ctrl-T).

Table 6-4. *Ventura's on-screen symbols*

Item	Screen symbol	Current Selection Box
Paragraph	⁀s.¶	Paragraph End
Standard tab	y→t	Horiz. Tab
Equation	$\frac{3}{10}$	Equation
Non-breaking space	]e.(	NoBreak Space

- If you have difficulty seeing these symbols, try choosing Enlarged View from the View menu (or press Ctrl-E).
- To find the special item symbols and identify them, move the text cursor and watch the Current Selection Box. When the cursor is placed just before a special item, or a character (or a group of characters) with attributes applied to it, the Current Selection Box displays either the name for the special item or Text Attr. for attributes applied to characters (Figure 6-11). This is the exact location of the formatting code for the special item. Once you find its location, you can cut and paste it (and its effect) as you would any other character.

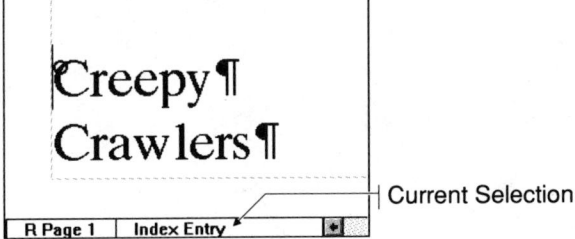

Figure 6-11. To find and identify special items, use the text cursor and Current Selection Box.

Current Selection

Continuing on

In this chapter, you've learned three key skills for handling text in Ventura: working with text files, creating text, and editing text. With these techniques in hand, you can easily and efficiently handle most text tasks in Ventura. However, you'll find it's much faster and easier to use a word processor or other text-handling program to create text files. In the next chapter, we'll teach you how to create text files and preformat them with other programs.

Easy Access

For more info on...	See chapter...
Pretagging and preformatting text files and entering special characters directly into text files	**7** Creating Text with Other Programs
Creating tables	**8** Creating Tables
Drawing Box Text	**12** Enhancing and Editing Pictures

7 Creating Text with Other Programs

How to create and preformat text files for Ventura

- **Choosing a file format** 209
- **Creating the text** 214
- **Using databases and spreadsheets** 216
- **Pretagging text** 220
- **Preformatting text with bracket codes** 223
- **Continuing on** 238

entura can import text files from a long list of word processing programs, databases, and spreadsheets. But unlike some desktop publishing programs, that process is a two-way street: All the words you type in the text file appear in Ventura; and when you save your Ventura file, some of Ventura's formatting information is saved in your text file.

Because of this two-way connection, you can reduce the amount of time you spend formatting in Ventura by inserting formatting codes directly into text files—before you load them into Ventura. In this chapter, we'll show you how to prepare your text files so that Ventura can read text and formatting information from them without a snag.

To create Ventura-compatible text files with outside programs, you follow these steps:

- Use a Ventura-supported file format
- Create the text in the outside program, following the simple guidelines we'll show you
- Add tag codes to preformat paragraphs
- Add bracket codes to preformat individual characters within paragraphs and to create special effects

The last two steps above are optional. But you'll save a lot of time and trouble if you learn these techniques. Don't worry. It's easier than it sounds.

Choosing a file format

Every word processor, database, or spreadsheet supports one or more file formats. You can load any text file into Ventura as long as it is in one of the thirteen file formats that Ventura supports (Table 7-1). In this section, we'll show you three skills that will help you deal with the formats of text files:

- Using Ventura-supported file formats
- Dealing with unsupported file formats
- Following special rules for the ASCII file format

Table 7-1. *Supported word processor format*

Word processor format	Name in dialog box	Default filename extension
Text generated by Ventura	Generated	GEN
ASCII	ASCII, 8-Bit ASCII	TXT
Wordstar	WordStar 3, 4, 5	WS
MultiMate	MultiMate	DOC
Microsoft Word	MS Word	DOC
Xerox Writer	Writer	XWP
WordPerfect	WordPerfect 4, 5	WP
XyWrite	XyWrite	XY
DCA	DCA	RFT
Lotus 1-2-3, ASCII for Ventura tables	PRN to Table	PRN

Using Ventura-supported file formats

So how do you know if Ventura supports your word processor's file formats? Choose the Load Text/Picture command from the File menu and select File Type: Text. If your outside program is supported, its name appears in the Format list box (Figure 7-1).

If your program (or its format) is in the Format list box, you can save the text file in the program's native format and use the default file extension. And when you load the text file into Ventura, you simply select its format from the Format list box.

After you select a name in the Format list box and click on OK, the Open File dialog box appears. The File Name text box shows the Ventura's default file extension for the format you selected.

If your text file is the correct format but has a different extension, you can change the extension so that the default has the new extension. For example, if your company uses both Word for Windows (which Ventura does not support) and Word for DOS (which Ventura supports), the files for each will have the same DOC extension. To make it easy to distinguish the two formats, you can give the Word for DOS files a different extension such as MSW. If so, you'll have to type *.MSW in the File Name text box, so that you can see your Word for DOS files in the the list of files in the Open File dialog box (Figure 7-2).

Figure 7-1.
Open the Load Text/Picture dialog box to verify that your word processor's file format is supported.

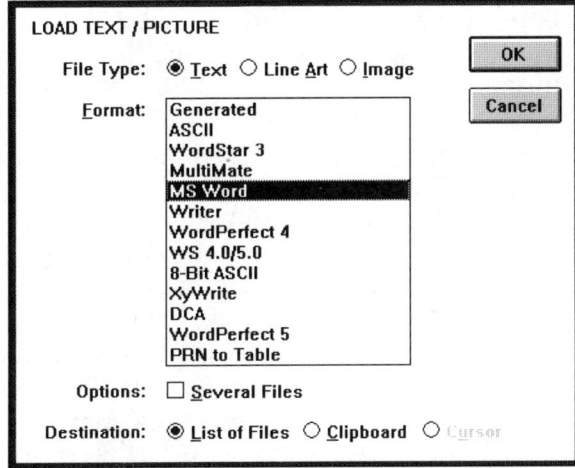

Figure 7-2.
If you use an extension different from the default, replace the default in the File Name text box with your own extension to view your files.

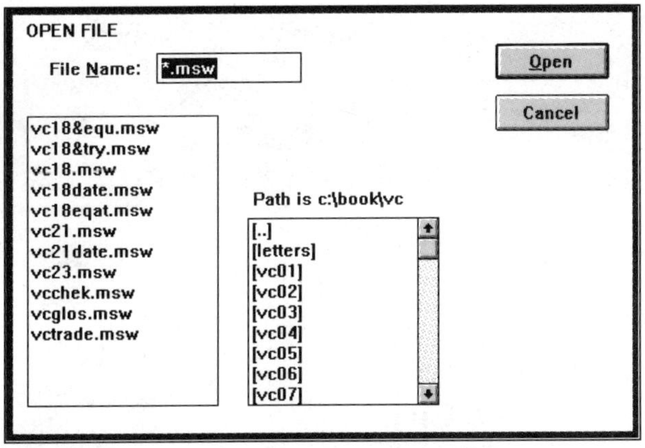

Dealing with unsupported file formats

What if your program isn't listed in the Format list box? Don't worry—you won't have to buy a new program. Even if Ventura can't support the program's own format, there are several ways to get unsupported text files into a format that Ventura will accept. Here are four strategies for converting unsupported text files into a Ventura-supported format:

■ Save to another supported format. Most programs offer optional file formats to save your work. One or more of these formats may be directly supported by Ventura. For example, Word for Windows is not supported by Ventura; however, you can save to either Word for DOS or ASCII formats, which are both supported (Word for Windows calls ASCII "Text Only").

- Use a file conversion utility. Consider using a third-party file utility that specializes in converting between word processor formats. You can buy these utilities at software stores or through magazine ads.

- For smaller amounts of text in Windows programs, use the clipboard. For example, in Word for Windows, select the text you want to transfer, and choose the Copy or Cut command from the Edit menu. Then switch to Ventura. Using the Text Tool, place the text cursor where you want to place the text and choose Paste ASCII Text from the Edit menu.

- Save as an ASCII unformatted text file (or use print-to-file). Virtually all word processors will allow you to save a file to ASCII format. However, the format may have another name. For example, Word for Windows calls the ASCII format "Text Only" (Figure 7-3).

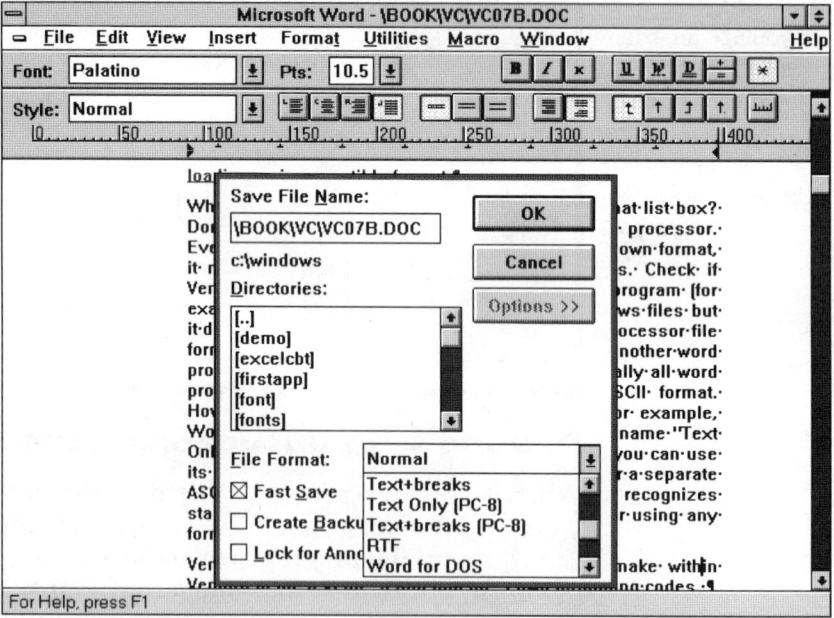

Figure 7-3. If you have an unsupported word processor such as Word for Windows, save the text file in a supported format such as Word for DOS or ASCII ("Text Only").

Following special rules for ASCII files

What if the only compatible file format your outside program can use is ASCII? ASCII is often the only way to transfer text from spreadsheets and databases to other programs such as Ventura. You'll need to follow some special rules for ASCII files. In this section, we'll explain how to deal with ASCII files.

ASCII (American Standard Code for Information Interchange) is a standard code for text files that can be recognized by any computer. For transferring *raw* text between mainframes, minis, and PCs, ASCII has no peer. The trade-off is that ASCII can't support text attributes and other formatting codes the way other file formats can.

In short, ASCII text files are best for tranferring raw text (characters, spaces, and carriage returns), not formatting. There are two important guidelines for creating text for ASCII files:

- *Apply text attributes and other formatting with bracket codes and tag codes.* If you plan to save text in ASCII, don't assign text attributes or any other formatting, especially margins. Any text attribute codes that you have assigned will be lost when you save to ASCII. To apply text attributes in an ASCII text file, use Ventura's bracket codes as part of the text. Bracket codes are discussed later in this chapter.

- *Use two carriage returns at the ends of paragraphs.* The lines in an ASCII file end with a carriage return. This "freezes" the text in the line widths that existed at the time it was saved. Because each line ends with a single carriage return, Ventura expects paragraphs to end with two consecutive carriage returns. Therefore, you must enter an extra carriage return between paragraphs if you intend to keep the paragraphs distinct from each other when you load the file into Ventura.

Although ASCII is about as standard as things get in the world of computers, many programs make subtle variations. Ventura recognizes two types of ASCII file formats:

- *ASCII.* This is the "standard" ASCII that we have just covered. It's sometimes called 7-bit ASCII because it takes 7 bits in binary code to obtain 128 possible number values.

- *8-bit ASCII.* This is a special version of ASCII that uses the 8th bit in a data word to describe an additional 128 "extended" or "special" characters. The extra 128 character codes can support characters and symbols that don't usually appear on the keyboard (foreign language characters, mathematical and scientific symbols, and so on).

Tip: If you have an ASCII file from a database or spreadsheet program where each line (a row or record) that ends with a single carriage return should be treated as a separate paragraph, load the file using the WordStar 3 file filter instead of ASCII.

Creating the text

So far, you've learned how to get your text into a supported file format. Now, we'll give you guidelines for creating text files. First, we'll give you important rules to follow when you prepare text with word processors so that the text will flow smoothly into Ventura. Then we'll give you some tips for creating text files with databases and spreadsheets.

No single program can do everything well. Ventura's strength is formatting, but one of its glaring weaknesses is working with text and numbers. By using a word processor or other program (rather than Ventura), you can take advantage of the speed, editing functions, and special utilities of other programs. For example, you can use the spellchecker, thesaurus, and search-and-replace functions of a word processor; the sorting and selecting facilities of a database; or the number-crunching power of a spreadsheet. Combine Ventura with these specialized programs and get the best of everything.

Creating the text with word processors

Your word processor gives you the best tools (spellchecking, outlining, search-and-replace, macros) to enter and organize text quickly. But Ventura won't recognize all of your word processor's formatting commands. In fact, some formatting commands may cause undesirable effects (such as unnecessary hyphens) when you load the text file into Ventura.

Don't worry. In this section, we'll give you seven guidelines that will help you get the most out of your word processor's capabilities and prevent you from getting unexpected results in Ventura. Later in this chapter, we'll show you how to preformat text using Ventura's bracket codes and tag codes. These codes tell Ventura exactly how to format text.

But before you learn to preformat your text files, you need to know how to prepare the text for Ventura in your word processor. To create text files that flow smoothly into Ventura, follow these simple guidelines:

1. *Align text "flush left."* Don't use the justification setting in your word processor. Don't center text. Text that has been justified and also contains tabbed material will not align properly. The "center" command in most word processors may result in

unwanted spaces when imported into Ventura. To justify or center text, use Alignment from Paragraph Menu *after* you've loaded the file into Ventura.

2. *Don't indent whole paragraphs.* Paragraph indents created by using spaces will not have consistent widths when used with Ventura's proportional spaced fonts. Indents created with tabs are unnecessary and force you to delete the tab after you bring the text into Ventura. For precise indents, use Alignment and Spacing from the Paragraph menu *after* you load the text file(s) into Ventura.

3. *Use only a single tab between columns* instead of using consecutive tabs to position widely spaced columns in your word processor. The actual position of the tabs must be set in Ventura with Tab Settings from the Paragraph menu. Therefore, extra tabs are unnecessary and cause extra work in Ventura.

4. *Don't use extra spaces.* Don't put extra spaces between words and characters. For instance, don't put two spaces after the period in each space. One space is all you need. In addition, extra spaces that slip in after the last sentence of a paragraph may cause an extra blank line.

5. *Don't use your word processor's hyphenation function.* Ventura automatically hyphenates text files whenever you load a text file or open a chapter. In some cases, hyphens created with your word processor may be carried over into Ventura, adding unnecessary and inappropriate hyphenation.

6. *Don't use extra carriage returns to create spaces between paragraphs.* Ventura doesn't require extra carriage returns to achieve inter-paragraph spacing. If you load a text file that uses extra carriage returns between paragraphs, Ventura will turn the extra returns into blank paragraphs.

7. *Edit and spellcheck your text file before typing Ventura's formatting codes (tag codes and bracket codes).* This speeds up your spellchecker by cutting down the number of unrecognized words that the spellchecker sees as misspelled words.

Tip: Enter Ventura's formatting codes into the spellchecker's dictionary if you plan to do subsequent spellchecks. You gain two advantages: Your spellchecker works efficiently throughout the production cycle (it accepts the formatting codes as defined words) and it detects misspellings of these codes.

Tip: Set the margins in the word processor to the margins setting that you'll use in Ventura. This approximates the page count of your final Ventura document. Note that these margin settings have no effect in Ventura.

Using a word processor to format text

As you've seen, you can use a word processor to produce text for your Ventura documents. In addition, you can use the word processor's built-in commands for attributes such as bold and italic. If you use a supported file format, you can apply some attributes to the text file that Ventura will recognize.

Ventura recognizes the following six attributes for most of the word processors it supports: bold, italic, bold-italic, superscript, subscript, strikethrough, and underline. However, Ventura does not recognize such attributes as small caps and double underlines. These attributes must be applied with bracket codes, as explained later in this chapter.

Using databases and spreadsheets

Database and spreadsheet programs are designed to store information and crunch numbers. You can combine the strengths of a database or spreadsheet with the formatting power of Ventura and get the best of both worlds—each program doing what it does best (Figure 7-4).

Because so many different spreadsheet and database programs are available, we'll explain these procedures in general terms so that you can implement them with your specific program (Figure 7-5). Basically, there are only two steps. First, you extract the correct data from the database or spreadsheet. Then you save that data in a file format Ventura can understand.

Databases and spreadsheets specialize in storing, organizing, and linking information. Each piece of information is stored in a field (or cell). Most databases will allow you to select and sort the fields that you want to export to Ventura and then save them to a text file. Most spreadsheets will allow you to save all or part of a spreadsheet to a text file. The key is to export only the information that you need.

For example, suppose you want to create a telephone directory with Ventura. You have a database file that includes the names and

Figure 7-4.
The data for this directory was maintained in Reflex (A Borland database program). The text file was created with the Reflex report function and imported into Ventura. This directory was created by Art Saffran.

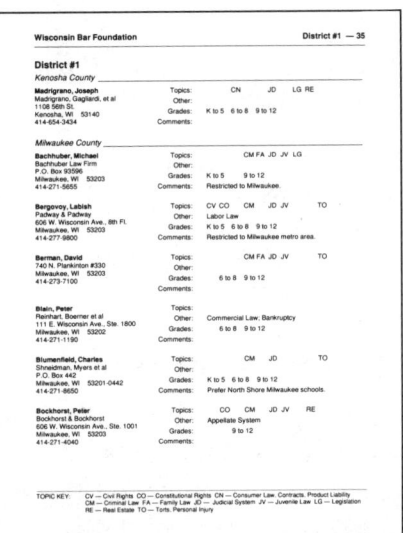

Figure 7-5.
Before and After: database reporting using dBase and Ventura.

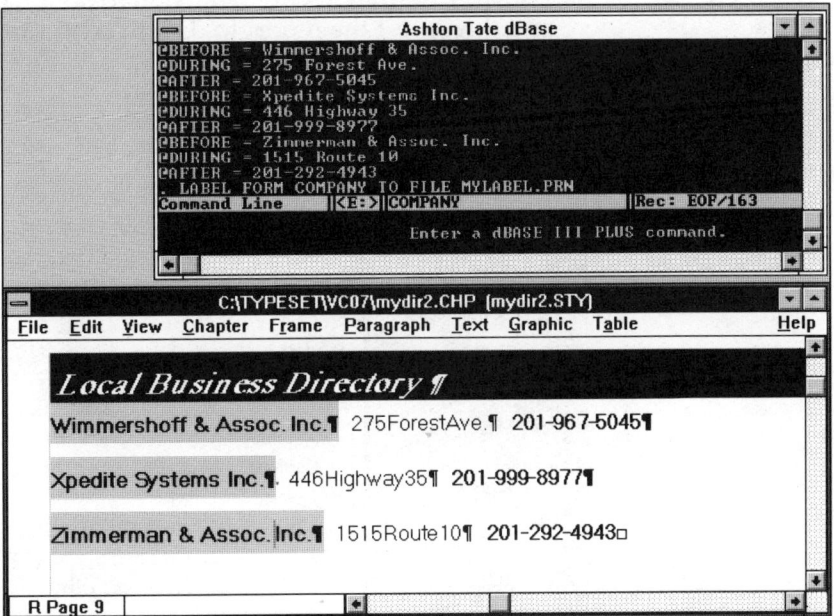

addresses of the people that you want. You would simply extract the information (the names and addresses) that you need, sort it (in alphabetic order of the last names, for instance), and save it as a text file.

How you sort, extract, and re-order fields of data depends on your specific program (and your proficiency with it). In fact, organizing the information with the program is often the easiest part—because that's what it does best. The hard part is saving the information in a format that's right for Ventura.

Note: Using the PRN To Table file filter in the Load Text/Picture dialog box, you can convert a spreadsheet file directly into a Ventura table. However, you must use the Lotus PRN file format or use a specially prepared ASCII file. For more information on creating tables, see Chapter 8, "Creating Tables."

Saving data to a text file

There are two ways to save text from databases and spreadsheets to a file that you can use with Ventura:

- Use the program's Save command to save as an ASCII file (Figure 7-6).

- Use the program's report function to organize your information, and then print the report to disk to create an ASCII file.

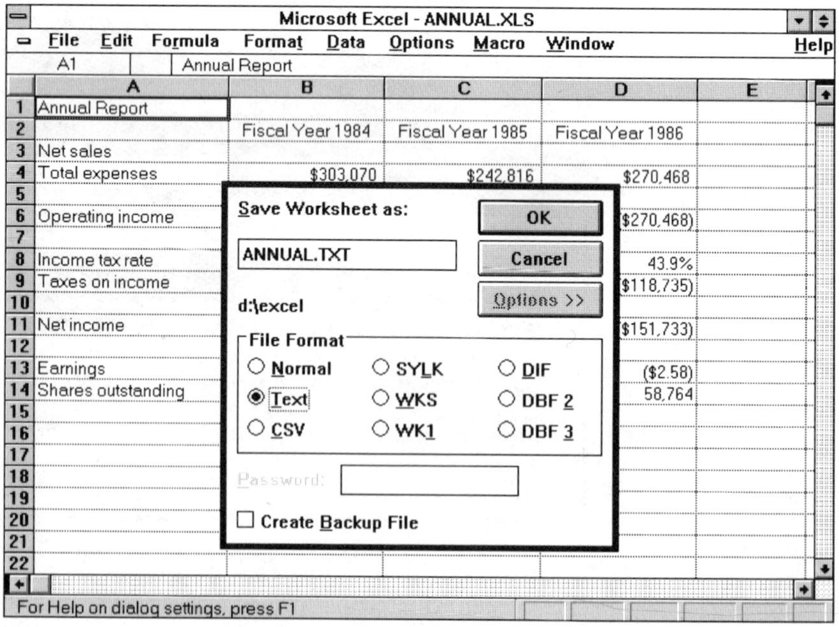

Figure 7-6.
Using Excel to save data in a Ventura-compatible format.

When you save database or spreadsheet text as an ASCII text file, you create a file that you can load into Ventura. However, different programs often have different ways of organizing the text in the file. Most programs place each *record* (a row of data) on a separate line, which ends with a carriage return. Each field in that record is separated by a *delimiter*.

Some database programs let you choose the *delimiter*—the character that separates one field from another. In most cases, you should choose a carriage return (as opposed to a tab character or a comma). By using a carriage return, you place each field in a separate paragraph. This allows you to tag each field with a separate paragraph tag.

Warning: Ventura has a limit for the total number of paragraphs it can have in a chapter. Depending on your computer, 64,000 paragraphs is the maximum. Sound like an inconceivable limit? It's possible to exceed the maximum with a large text file that has carriage returns separating each field of data. If you run into this problem, try breaking the text file into several smaller files. Or use the line break code <R> as the delimiter—this code will place each field on a separate line but keep individual records as paragraphs.

Tip: Use a word processor to clean up ASCII text files created with a spreadsheet or database. You can set up macros to take out unwanted spaces, add or delete extra carriage returns, spellcheck the text, and so on.

Loading the text file into Ventura

Your final step is to load the text into Ventura where it can be placed onto the page. Which file format you use depends on how you've set things up:

- If you've placed a carriage return at the end of each line with one extra return between each paragraph, you can load the file with the ASCII format. When you use the ASCII format, Ventura expects two carriage returns between every paragraph.

- If you've placed only one carriage return between paragraphs, load the file with the WordStar 3 filter instead. When you use the WordStar 3 filter, Ventura expects only one return between paragraphs. For more information on loading text files into Ventura, see Chapter 6, "Handling Text in Ventura."

Pretagging text

In Chapter 3, "Building Basic Styles," you learned how to create tags and apply them to paragraphs in Ventura. But that's not the only way to tag paragraphs. With your word processor (or other program), you can pretag paragraphs in text files. To pretag a paragraph, you type a tag code at the beginning of the paragraph. When you load the file into Ventura, Ventura translates the codes and applies tag formats to the paragraphs. Pretagging has the same effect as selecting a paragraph and then clicking on a tag name in the Tag List Window.

For instance, suppose you type the tag code @HEADLINE = at the beginning of the first line of a paragraph. When you bring that text file into Ventura, you'll discover that the first paragraph is already tagged and formatted as HEADLINE.

Tagging paragraphs with your word processor is simple, but you need to follow a few guidelines to avoid unexpected results.

Note: Using special table tag codes, you can preformat tables directly in the text file. Then when you load the file into Ventura, the table will appear on the page—already formatted. For more information on creating tables, see Chapter 8, "Creating Tables."

Pretagging guidelines

A tag code is composed of the @ symbol and the name of a tag followed by an equal sign. The equal sign must have a space before and a space after it (Figure 7-7). For example, a headline might be represented by an existing tag called @HEADLINE = .

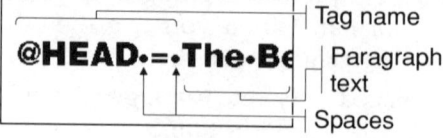

Figure 7-7. A tag code sample.

To pretag a paragraph, you place the tag code at the beginning of a paragraph. That's essentially all there is to pretagging. However, tag codes must follow these rules to be recognized by Ventura:

- The @ symbol must be the first character on the first line of the paragraph (i.e., no spaces should precede it).
- The name of the tag can have up to 13 characters including the spaces and the equal (=) sign.

- One space must precede the equal sign and one space must follow it.
- Do not pretag Body Text. Ventura assumes that anything without a tag code is Body Text.
- The tag codes must match the tag name that you will be using in your Ventura style sheet exactly—letter for letter. That means the two tags below are *not* the same:

    ```
    @NOTETEXT =
    @NOTE TEXT =
    ```

    Ventura tries to match the tag code with the exact tag name—the space between Note and Text in the second tag makes it different from the first. If Ventura can't find the tag name in the style sheet, it will create a new tag, and give that new tag the attributes of the Body Text tag. To avoid misspelled tags, make a list of tags so that you can check the tag names (see the nearby sidebar "Printing out your style sheet").

Tip: In your word processor, turn on the "show spaces as dots" function or equivalent option, so that you can easily see where spaces have been missed or deleted in tags. Space characters are the hardest character to detect, especially with proportional fonts.

Tip: We recommend that you *don't use all caps* when naming tags. When you load text into Ventura, all tag names not found in the current style sheet appear in all caps in the Tag List Window. By leaving at least some characters lowercase, you can quickly spot the tags that weren't in the chapter's style sheet before you loaded the text file.

Tip: Instead of typing the entire tag name for each paragraph, use your word processor's macro or glossary function to insert tag codes. These functions will speed up the entry of tag names and ensure correct spelling.

Example: Suppose you are working on a company newsletter and you want to pretag the text file. Here's how the first three paragraphs might look. Notice that the third paragraph does not have a tag code because it is Body Text:

```
@HEADLINE = ACME President Receives Community Award.¶
@BYLINE = by Tim Toyoshima¶
ACME President John Doe was awarded the annual "Smallville
```

```
Citizen of the Year" prize in a ceremony held last Saturday
at the Smallville Elks Lodge.¶
```

Printing out your style sheet

When you're pretagging paragraphs in your word processor, it's easy to forget the exact tag names that you used in your Ventura style sheet. A list of all the tags will help you avoid misspelling the tag names.

Don't worry you won't have to write all the tag names by hand on a scrap of paper. Ventura has a special Print Stylesheet function that allows you to save the contents of the stylesheet to a text file. Then you can either view this file or print it out on your printer. Here's how:

1. Choose New from the File menu.
2. Use Load Diff. Style from the File Menu to load the stylesheet that you want.
3. Select the Paragraph Tool.
4. Choose Update Tag List from the Paragraph Menu. A VP Alert box asks you to Save or Abandon the chapter. Click on Abandon. The Update Tag List dialog box appears.
5. Click on the Print Stylesheet button. The Save File As dialog box appears.
6. In the File Name text box, type the name for the text file that will contain the list of tag for the current style sheet. Don't include a file extension. Let Ventura automatically add the GEN extension. This extension shows that the text file was generated by Ventura.
7. Click on Save to create the text file. Then click on OK to close the Update Tag List dialog box.

You can load this text file into a Ventura chapter, place it on the underlying page, and format it like any other text file. Then you can print the list. Or you can open the file in your word processor and print it. Like other GEN files, this text file is in the ASCII file format.

Preformatting text with bracket codes

Tag codes let you assign a tag to an entire paragraph. To assign a format to a word or phrase within a paragraph, you use bracket codes. You can also use bracket codes to insert special items such as frame anchors and index references.

Bracket codes are the best way to preformat text in an outside program such as a word processor. If you use an outside program's native formatting functions to format text, the formatting may not be recognized by Ventura or may cause undesirable effects. However, bracket codes tell Ventura exactly what format to apply.

By using bracket codes in your text file, you can create formatting effects that Ventura will understand without a hitch. In this section, you'll learn how to:

- Apply text attributes (such as italic, bold, small caps)
- Change the point size and font
- Control the kerning of text
- Shift text up and down from the baseline
- Create special non-keyboard characters (such as ©, ™, □)
- Create fractions and equations
- Create spaces, breaks, and discretionary hyphens
- Anchor frames
- Insert index and footnote references

Note: You can also add automatic cross-references with bracket codes. These are discussed in detail in Chapter 17, "Power and Speedup Techniques."

That's a long list. But don't worry. The basic process is the same for all the effects. Put simply, Ventura has letter and number codes for every formatting effect. You place those codes within angle brackets (<>). For instance, <B> is the bracket code that turns on the bold text effect.

Before we show you the specifics, we will explain why you should use bracket codes (instead of formatting in Ventura), tell you how they work, and give you some general guidelines that will help you use bracket codes efficiently and avoid unexpected results.

Why use bracket codes?

You don't actually need to use bracket codes, because you can achieve most of the same effects with Ventura's Text menu.

So why use bracket codes at all? First, the best time to apply an attribute to text for emphasis or to add index and footnote references is when you are writing the text in the word processor—before you forget them.

Second, it's faster to type and edit bracket codes in the text file than to use Ventura's Text menu.

And third, bracket codes are the only way to create certain effects (such as text attributes, font changes, or automatic chapter and page numbers) within some of Ventura's dialog boxes (Figure 7-8).

Figure 7-8. You can also use bracket codes in dialog boxes that accept text, such as the Headers & Footers dialog box.

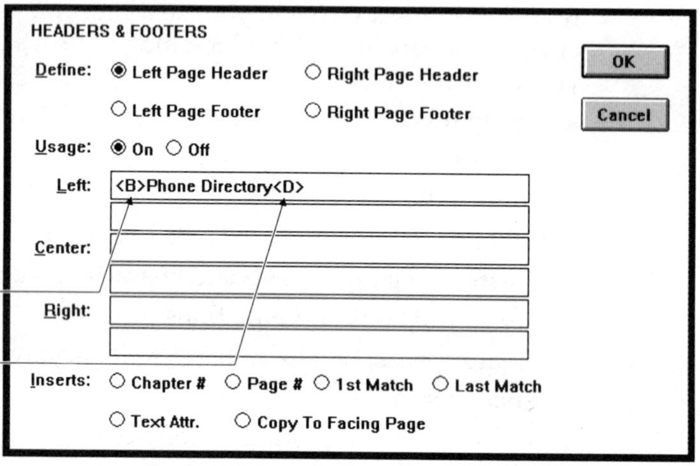

Bracket code turns bold on

Bracket code turns bold off

How bracket codes work

Using bracket codes is as simple as inserting the bracket code in front of the text you want to format and then inserting a return-to-normal code where you want it to stop. Most bracket codes stay in effect until they encounter one of the following conditions:

- A return-to-normal code
- The end of the current paragraph
- Another bracket code of the same type—the old bracket code turns off and the new bracket code takes effect

All these conditions turn off the previously active code. (Bracket codes for index entries, spaces, line breaks, and other special characters do not need to be turned off.)

Later in this chapter, we'll show you how to apply the different types of bracket codes to your text file. But first, you need to learn a few rules that will help you work with bracket codes.

Guidelines for using bracket codes

Follow these rules so that Ventura can read your bracket codes and apply the correct format without a hitch:

- Insert bracket codes immediately before the affected text.

- Enclose formatting codes within angle brackets. On standard keyboards, the open angle bracket is located above the comma, and the close angle above the period.

- Do not add extra spaces before or after the text code enclosed in angle brackets.
    Right: <I>
    Wrong: < I >

- To use more than one bracket code (for text attributes), you must group them together within a single set of angle brackets. For example, text that should have both bold and italic attributes should be preceded by <BI>. The order of codes grouped within brackets is not important.

- If you use more than one consecutive set of angle bracket codes, Ventura will disregard all but the last one (<B>). For example, suppose you have embedded two sets of attribute changes:
    <BI><B>big and beautiful<D><D>
 Only the "inner" set will affect the text (big and beautiful will appear in bold, not bold italic).

- If you want to use angle brackets within the text, you must type double sets of brackets. For example, if you want to set off the word "Return" from the rest of the text by using angle brackets, type <<Return>> (double brackets). Ventura will display and print this as <Return> (single brackets).

Using bracket codes for text attributes

The bracket codes for text attributes are the easiest to use, and the ones you'll use most often. You just turn them on with a bracket code (Table 7-2) and then turn them off with the return-to-normal code <D>.

Table 7-2. *Bracket codes for text attributes*

Text attribute	Bracket code
Light weight	<L>
Medium weight	<M>
Bold weight	<B>
Italic	<I>
Small caps	<S>
Superscript	<^>
Subscript	<v>
Underline	<U>
Double Underline	<=>
Strikethru	<X>
Overscore	<O>
Return to normal	<D>

Note: The return-to-normal code <D> is used to return to the default attribute of the current paragraph. This code must be used to turn off any of the text attributes listed above. The only circumstance where you don't need to use this code is when you want the attribute to last until the end of the current paragraph. A different set of return-to-normal codes are used for font, point size, and color attributes. We'll cover those codes for those attributes in the next section.

Example: Try to create a text file in Windows Notepad using bracket codes to apply attributes to the text, and then load it into Ventura. Before you start this example, be sure that you've installed Ventura's example chapters and stylesheets. Then follow these steps:

1. Start the Windows Notepad. Choose New from the File menu.
2. Type this sentence: "Jesse kicked Scott in the calf, and he had a cow."
3. Use bracket codes to make "Jesse" and "Scott" bold. (Hint: use the <B> and <D> codes.)
4. Use bracket codes to make "calf" and "cow" italic (Hint: use the <I> and <D> codes.)

5. Choose Save from the File menu. In the Filename text box, type C:\TYPESET\COW.TXT. Click on OK. Now you've saved your text as an ASCII file with the name COW.TXT in the C:\TYPESET directory. Your text file should look similar to the one in Figure 7-9.

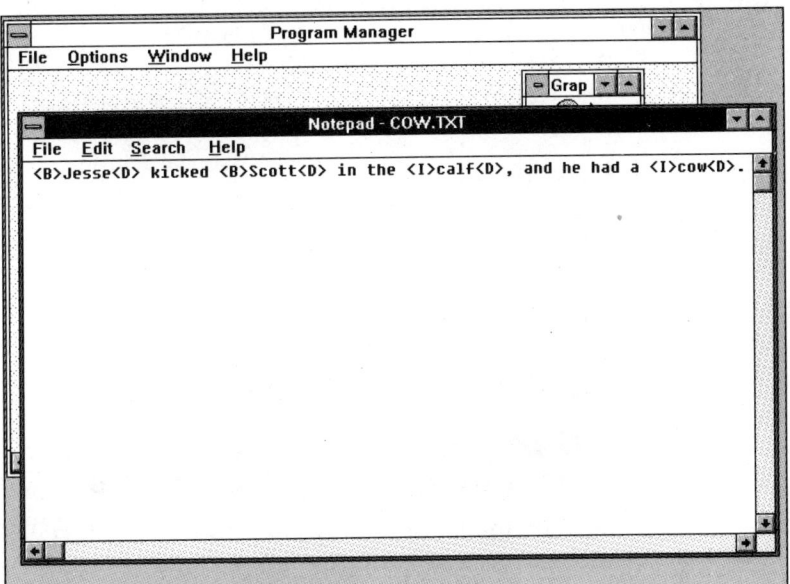

Figure 7-9. Create a text file in Windows Notepad and apply some text attributes with bracket codes. Then see your results when you load the file into Ventura.

6. Choose Exit from the File menu.
7. Start Ventura. Choose New from the File menu. Be sure that Toolbox Window, Tag List Window, and File List Window have a check mark next to them in the View menu.
8. Use Load Diff. Style from the File menu to load SAMPLE1.STY from the C:\TYPESET directory.
9. Use Load Text/Picture from the File menu to load the text file (COW.TXT from the C:\TYPESET directory) that you've just created. Remember that the Format is ASCII.
10. Using the Frame Tool, select the underlying page. Then Click on COW.TXT in the File List Window. The text should appear on the page with the text attributes you applied in the text file (Figure 7-10).

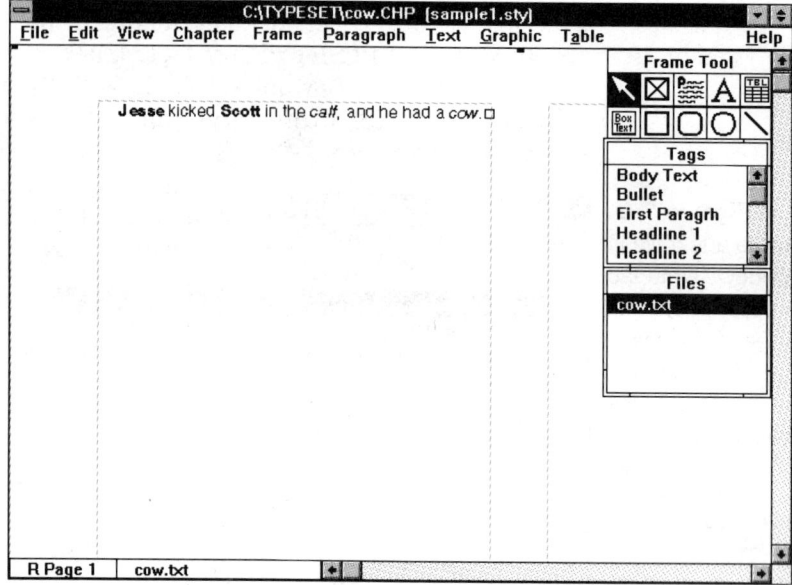

Figure 7-10. After you place your text file on the page, your text should have the attributes that you applied with bracket codes.

Using bracket codes for changing font settings

Remember the Font dialog box? (If not, see Chapter 3, "Building Basic Styles.") Anything you can do in that dialog box, you can do with bracket codes. You can change the typeface, point size, and color of text. Again, you simply turn the command on with a bracket code and turn it off using a return-to-normal code.

However, these three font commands are more complex than text attributes. A font bracket code begins with a letter that tells Ventura what to change: typeface (F), point size (P), and color (C). The letter is followed by a special number to specify the typeface, point size, or color that you want. For example, to change the typeface to Helvetica (whose font number is 2), you use this bracket code: <F2>. To change the point size to 12-point, you use this code: <P12>. To change the typeface to white (whose color number is 0), you use this bracket code: <C0>. To turn a font command off, you use a special return-to-normal code for each one: <F255> for typeface, <P255> for point size, and <C255> for color. Table 7-3 gives you the syntax of each font command.

For more information on font and color numbers, refer to Chapter 21, "Rapid Reference."

Table 7-3. *Bracket codes for font changes*

Format change	Bracket code to begin	Replace *n* with:	Bracket code to end
Change typeface	<F*n*>	Font ID number (1 through 254)	<F255>
Change point size	<P*n*>	Point size	<P255>
Change color	<C*n*>	Color ID number	<C255>

Using bracket codes to kern text

Generally speaking, you should kern (adjust spacing between characters) in Ventura rather than in your word processor. (If you don't know how, see Chapter 6, "Handling Text in Ventura.") By adjusting the kerning in Ventura, you can see the results of your adjustments on screen. However, if you already know how much the text needs to be kerned, it's much faster to insert the bracket code directly into the text file.

Here's how it works. The <%*n*> bracket code controls the spacing between letters. The letter *n* represents increments of 1/100 of an em space. Precede the number with + to add spacing or - to subtract spacing between each pair of characters. The <%0> bracket code turns off the kerning. For example, to give the word *WAVE* a uniformly tighter kerning, you would type <%-4>WAV<%0>E in your word processor. This is just an example. The number you actually use varies, depending on the type size and typeface you are using.

Note: The amount of kerning that you use for one group of characters in a specific typeface and size may not be appropriate for other characters or for other typefaces and sizes.

Tip: Some words occur often in headings. For example, the phrase "bracket codes" appears in every second level heading in this section of this book. Suppose that those words need to be kerned tighter in those headings. To find out the correct number that you need for the bracket code, load the text file into Ventura. Be sure you're using the correct style sheet. Then adjust the kerning for the first instance of the phrase in a second level heading. When the kerning looks right, save the chapter. Then open the text file in your word processor. You'll see that Ventura has entered the bracket codes for you. Simply copy the codes and paste them where you need them.

Using bracket codes for baseline jumps

You can make text *jump* above or below its usual resting place on the baseline. The *baseline* is the imaginary horizontal line on which text is aligned.

To make text jump above or below its baseline, you use the <J*n*> bracket code. Unlike the other bracket codes, this code requires you to do some calculations first—before you plug in a number for the letter *n*. You replace the letter *n* with a number between 1 and 255 that represents the vertical displacement of the baseline measured in 1/300 inch. Positive numbers make text jump above the baseline. Negative numbers make text jump below the baseline.

To find the value for shifting text *above* the baseline, use the following formula:

$n = 256 - (300/72 * P)$

Replace the letter P with the amount to shift up in points.

To find the value for shifting text *below* the baseline, use the following formula:

$n = (300/72 * P)$

Replace the letter P with amount to shift down in points.

To turn off the baseline jump code (resets to zero—the original baseline), use the return-to-normal bracket code <J0>.

Working out these formulas may deter you from using baseline jumps. To get rolling, try either of these quick start methods:

- Specify the baseline jump in Ventura (select the text, choose Set Font Attributes from the Text menu and type a value in points for Shift Up or Shift Down). Close the chapter and open the text file in your word processor to see what codes Ventura has placed in the file. Then copy that same code wherever you need the same jump.

- If you don't want to bother making calculations or using Ventura first, you can simply turn to the table of baseline jumps in Chapter 21, "Rapid Reference." This table has a listing of the bracket codes for the most common jumps.

Using bracket codes for spaces, breaks, and discretionary hyphens

Ventura's bracket codes can also control the spacing between characters and words. Other bracket codes can control how words and lines break (non-breaking space, discretionary hyphen, and line break). None of these codes needs to be followed by a return-to-normal code. Table 7-4 lists the bracket codes for spaces and breaks, and their definitions.

Table 7-4. *Bracket codes for spaces and breaks*

Formatting effect	Bracket code	Definition
Em space	<_>	Equals the point size of the current font
En space	<~>	Equals one half the width of an Em space
Figure space	<+>	Provides a common width for all figures in a table
Thin space	<|>	Equals one half the width of an En space.
Non-breaking space	<N>	Prevents the splitting of words or characters or words that include a space but should not be split by word wrap
Discretionary hyphen	<->	Predetermines the point of hyphenation within a word.
Line break	<R>	Forces the end of a line (word wrap) without taking on the extra above/below spacing of a paragraph break (carriage return)

These codes are simple to use:

- The space codes generate (you guessed it) spaces; therefore, you place the code where you want to add the space.
- The discretionary hyphen code can do two things: (1) If you place it within a word, it tells Ventura where to hyphenate a word. Ventura will hyphenate only when the word must be broken (at the end of a line, for example). (2) If you place it directly in front of a word (no space between the code and the word), it tells Ventura *never* to break (hyphenate) the word.
- The non-breaking space code makes a group of words stay together on the same line. You simply place the code <N> between each word.
- The line break code forces the line to end where the code appears and to continue on the next line—without starting a new paragraph. You simply place the code where you want the current line to end.

Using bracket codes for special characters

Need to create a character that's not on the keyboard? No problem. Simply type its ASCII code number within brackets (<>). For example, the ASCII code for the ¥ character is 157, so you use the bracket code <157> to create it in a text file. Table 7-5 gives the codes for some common characters. For a complete table of ASCII codes and the characters they generate, see Chapter 21, "Rapid Reference."

Table 7-5. *Bracket codes for non-keyboard characters*

Name	Character	Bracket code
Opening Quote	"	<169>
Closing Quote	"	<170>
Copyright Symbol	©	<189>
Registered Trademark	®	<190>
Unregistered Trademark	™	<191>
En Dash	–	<196>
Em Dash	—	<197>
Hollow box	☐	<$B0>
Filled box	■	<$B1>

You can also use these ASCII bracket codes with the font change bracket code (<F*n*> where *n* is the font number) to create non-keyboard characters from other fonts such as Symbol and Zapf-Dingbats. You simply type the font change bracket code to change to the desired font, type the ASCII bracket code for the desired character from that font, and type the return-to-normal bracket code <F255>.

For example, suppose you wanted to use a character from the Symbol font. You would follow these steps:

1. Change to the Symbol font, by typing the font bracket code <F128>. The number 128 is the font number for the Symbol font.

2. Type the ASCII code number for the character within a separate set of brackets. For example, the bracket code for ≠ is <153>.

3. Turn off the Symbol font by typing the bracket code <F255>.

Here's how it would look:

```
<F128><153><F255>
```

Creating hidden text

You can also use a bracket code to hide text in Ventura while leaving it visible in the word processor. Hidden text will not appear on the Ventura screen (only a degree symbol appears) or on the printed page, but it will appear when the text file is loaded into a word processor. To create hidden text, use this bracket code:

```
<$!hidden text>
```

Replace the words *hidden text* with the actual text.

Using bracket codes for fractions and equations

Preformatting with bracket codes lets you insert typographically correct fractions and equations in advance.

Fractions

Although you can wait until you load the text file into Ventura and create typographically correct fractions with the Equation Editor (see Chapter 15, "Creating Footnotes and Equations"), it's faster and easier to use a bracket code in your word processor.

There are two types of fractions: (1) fractions with a diagonal fraction bar and (2) fractions with a horizontal fraction bar.

To make a fraction with small numerals and a *diagonal* fraction bar, use this bracket code:

```
<$Enumerator/denominator>
```

Replace the words *numerator* and *denominator* with the actual numbers. For example, typing <$E7/11> in your word processor produces $7/13$ in Ventura.

To make a fraction with large numerals and a *horizontal* fraction bar, use this bracket code:

```
<$Enumerator over denominator>
```

Replace the words *numerator* and *denominator* with the your numbers. For example, the bracket code <$E7 over 11> will produce $\frac{7}{11}$ in Ventura.

Equations

For complex equations, we recommend you use Ventura's Equation Editor, whose preview area lets you see the equation as you type the equation commands. But if you already know the equation commands, you can create equations faster by creating them with bracket codes in the word processor.

To preformat an equation, use the following bracket code:

    <$Eequation>

Replace the word *equation* with the actual equation commands.

The characters $E tell Ventura that the bracket code contains the commands for an equation. Essentially, you use the same commands that you type above the double line in the Equation Editor—with a few exceptions: (1) Use the special Equation Editor codes to apply text attributes and change fonts. (2) Don't use bracket codes within the equation bracket code. (3) Represent the less than (<) or greater than (>) symbols with double angle brackets: << or >>.

For more information on using the Equation Editor and its commands, see Chapter 15, "Creating Footnotes and Equations."

Using bracket codes for frame anchors

A frame anchor links a frame with a specific position within the text. If the text containing the anchor moves to a new page, the frame can be moved to the new page too. Frame anchors are a sure-fire way to keep a frame on the same page as its text reference.

Chapter 11, "Loading and Placing Pictures" explains frame anchoring in detail. In this section, we'll give you a brief summary and show you how to enter the codes directly into the word processing file.

To anchor a frame, you follow these two steps:

1. Give the frame an anchor name.

2. Mark the place in the text with an anchor mark.

To give a frame an anchor name, you must use the Anchors & Captions dialog box (Frame menu) in Ventura. However, you can insert the anchor mark directly into the text file. No return-to-normal code is necessary. You use this bracket code:

    <$&anchorname>

Replace *anchorname* with the actual name of the anchor, which can be up to 12 characters (including spaces).

For example, to create an anchor reference for a frame with the anchor name *dogpix*, you would use the following bracket code:

```
<$&dogpix>
```

You can also add codes after the anchor name. These codes allow you to choose the position of the frame relative to the reference. These four anchor types are the same as the four options for Frame's New Location in the Insert/Edit Anchor dialog box. See Table 7-6 for the syntax of each type of anchor. Figure 7-11 shows an example of each type.

Table 7-6. *Bracket codes for frame anchors*

Type of anchor	Equivalent command in Text menu	Bracket code
Places frame on same page with original position	Fixed, On Same Page As Anchor	<$&*anchorname*>
Places top of frame on the next line below reference	Relative, Below Anchor Line	<$&*anchorname*[v]>
Places bottom of frame on line above reference	Relative, Above Anchor Line	<$&*anchorname*[^]>
Moves frame with reference automatically	Relative, Automatically at Anchor	<$&*anchorname*[-]>

Tip: When using the Relative, Automatically At Anchor option, the frame will reside on the same line as the text reference. This is ideal for small frames that contain icons such as keycaps and other special symbols. To ensure that the frame has enough vertical space to fit between lines, you can choose Paragraph Typography from the Paragraph menu and select Grow Inter-Line To Fit: On.

Using bracket codes for indexing

By using your word processor to pretag index entries, you'll be able to speed up the indexing process. Using a word processor's search function, you can find key words that signal important parts of the text and should be referenced in your index. When you find

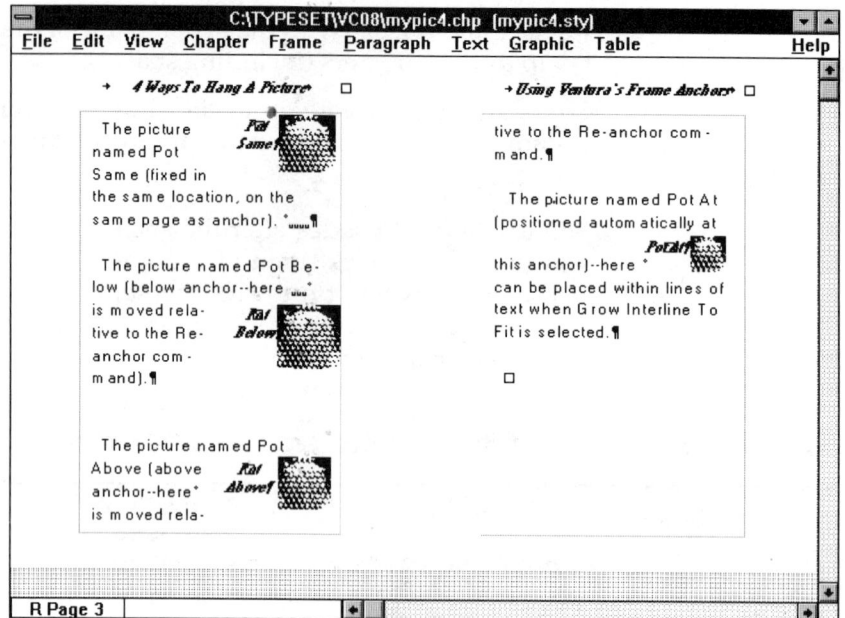

Figure 7-11.
Picture this:
Four ways to
hang a picture.

a word or section you want to index, use a bracket code to insert an index entry at that spot.

With bracket codes, you can create the same effects as the Insert/Edit Index Entry dialog box (Insert Special Item from the Text menu). You can enter both a primary entry (the highest level entry) and a secondary entry (a sub-catagory of a primary entry). In addition, you can enter primary and secondary sorts that tell Ventura to sort the entry using a word or phrase that is different from the primary entry or secondary entry. And that's not all. You can also create *See* and *See Also* references that refer to other entries in the index.

Here's how to create the different types of index entries (replace the italicized words with the actual entries or sorts):

For an index entry with only a primary entry, use this bracket code:

    <$I*primary*>

For an index entry with both primary and secondary entries, separate the two with a semicolon. Use this bracket code:

    <$I*primary;secondary*>

To use the sorting option, use square brackets to enclose the sort and place it after the entry it modifies. Use this bracket code:

```
<$Iprimary entry[primary sort];secondary
entry[secondary sort]>
```

For an index entry intended as a See reference, use this bracket code:

```
<$Sprimary;secondary>
```

For an index entry intended as a See Also reference, use this bracket code:

```
<$Aprimary;secondary>
```

Inserting these codes is simple. But there are a few rules you must follow:

- Use a semicolon to separate primary and secondary entries.
- Do not put any spaces within the brackets, except within the entries themselves. For example, Ventura will accept **<$IBig Flop>**, but it won't accept **<$I Big Flop [Flop] >**.
- Don't place the index entry bracket code before the paragraph tag code.

Using bracket codes for footnotes

In contrast to the many options for an index entry, a footnote reference is a snap. At the point in the text where you want to create a footnote reference, use this bracket code:

```
<$Ffootnote text>
```

Replace the words *footnote text* with the actual text that you want Ventura to place in the footnote frame.

If you turn on the footnote function in Ventura (Footnote Settings from the Chapter menu), a footnote number (or symbol) will appear where you placed the footnote code. For more information on footnotes, see Chapter 15, "Creating Footnotes and Equations."

Continuing on

The Boy Scout motto is "Be Prepared." That's not a bad slogan for desktop publishers as well. Your text files will be much easier to work with in Ventura if you prepare them properly. In this chapter, you've learned the four essential skills for creating text with outside programs:

- Choosing a file format for the text
- Creating the text
- Pretagging text
- Preformatting text with bracket codes

In the next chapter, you'll complete your Ventura text arsenal: you'll learn how to use Ventura's Table Tool for making tables.

Easy Access

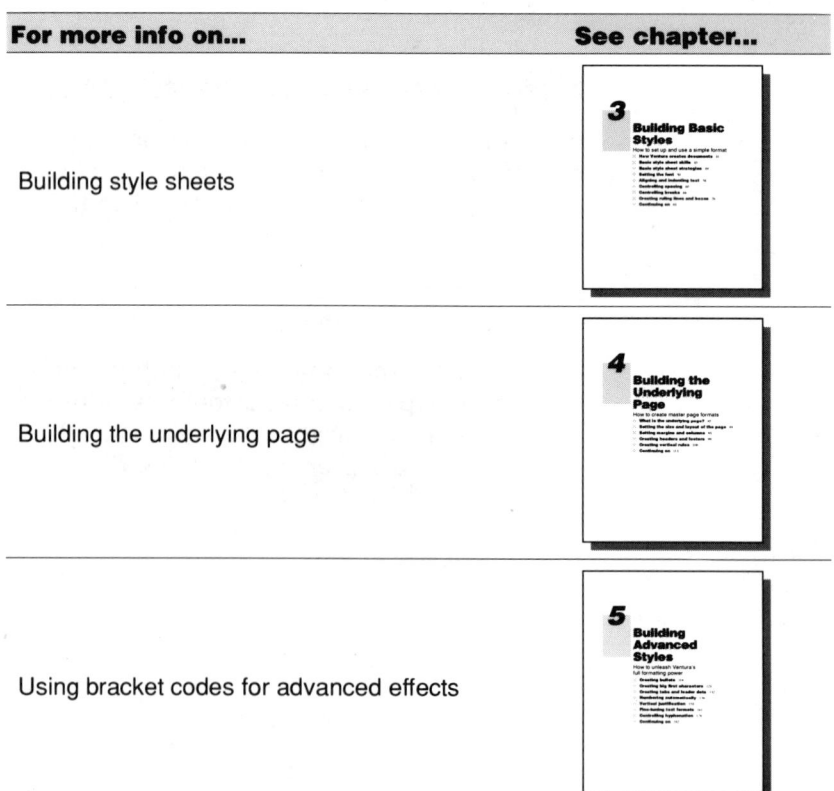

For more info on...	See chapter...
Building style sheets	3 Building Basic Styles
Building the underlying page	4 Building the Underlying Page
Using bracket codes for advanced effects	5 Building Advanced Styles

For more info on...	See chapter...
Inserting special items in Ventura	9 Creating Pictures in Ventura
Creating indexes	14 Creating Indexes and Tables of Contents
Creating footnotes and equations	15 Creating Footnotes and Equations
Inserting automatic cross references	17 Power and Speedup Techniques

8 Creating Tables

How to enhance your documents with attractive tables

- **Inserting a table** 242
- **Adding table text** 250
- **Formatting a table** 250
- **Creating tables in a word processor** 261
- **Creating tables with a spreadsheet** 264
- **Continuing on** 266

The first several chapters of this book taught you how to format your pages and the text that appears on them. But if you really want to communicate information quickly, you'll want pictures and tables as well. This chapter will focus on creating tables. So pull up a chair and get ready to learn your table manners.

You can use Ventura's tab settings to create simple tables if the text for each column is a short entry that does not extend into the next tab setting (or wrap onto the next line). Otherwise, you'll run into formatting problems. For example, if the text in the last column is too long, it will extend past the margin or wrap to the beginning of the next line—that is, it won't stay in the same column.

Here's where Ventura's Table Tool comes to the rescue. With this handy tool, you can create tables composed of *cells* that adjust their vertical size to the amount of text. Each cell in a Ventura Table corresponds to an entry in a column in a simple tab-set table.

The cells in a Ventura table are like spreadsheet cells that hold data at certain locations in a matrix of rows and columns. Like the cells in a spreadsheet, a Ventura table cell can have ruling lines around it, background tint, differently sized cells, and a unique text format (Figure 8-1).

As with text, you can format tables by using tag and bracket codes in your word processor or spreadsheet program. In fact, you can use special table tag codes that Ventura transforms into professional-looking tables when you load the text file.

In Ventura, you create tables with the Insert/Edit Table dialog box. It may look forbidding—but to create a basic table, you just follow these three steps:

1. Insert the table and specify its basic settings
2. Add the text
3. Format the table

After you learn this process, we'll teach you how to prepare Ventura tables in your word processor or spreadsheet program.

Stick with it—after you've mastered the Table Tool, you'll agree that it's one of Ventura's most versatile and valuable features.

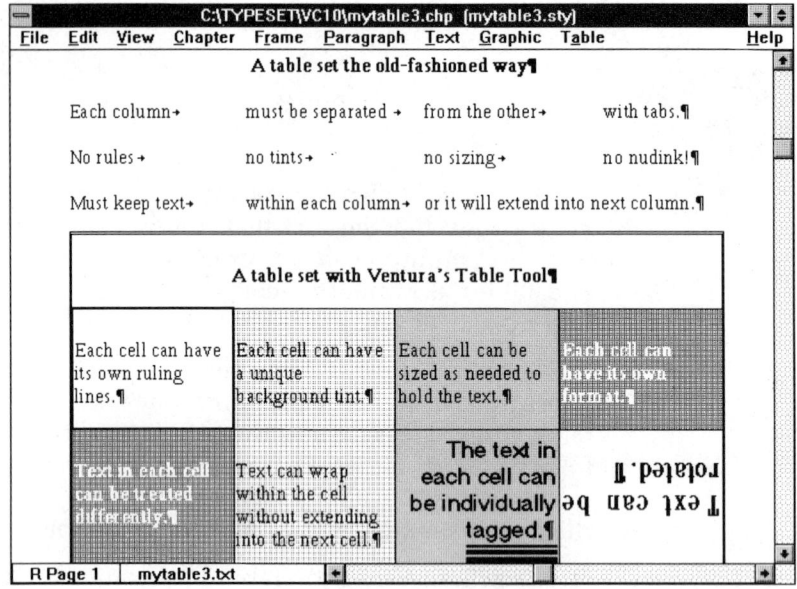

Figure 8-1.
Laying it on the table: regular tabs vs. table with variable size cells, ruling line, and background tint.

Inserting a table

Before you can insert a table, you need text. If you're working with an empty page or frame, you'll have to insert at least one paragraph (or load a text file) before you can add a table. Otherwise, an error message (a VP Alert box) will appear.

When you have some text on the page, Ventura gives you two methods for inserting tables:

- The Table Tool
- The Text menu

Choose the method that suits your task: When you're doing layout (positioning and organizing page elements), use the Table Tool to add tables quickly. When you're editing text in Ventura, use Insert Special Item (Text menu) to add tables while you're still in Text mode.

In this section, we'll teach you each method—both of which use the Insert/Edit Table dialog box (Figure 8-2). For good measure, we'll follow up by walking you through each of the dialog box options. Finally, we'll tell what to do if you change your mind after you close the dialog box.

Ready? Let's get started.

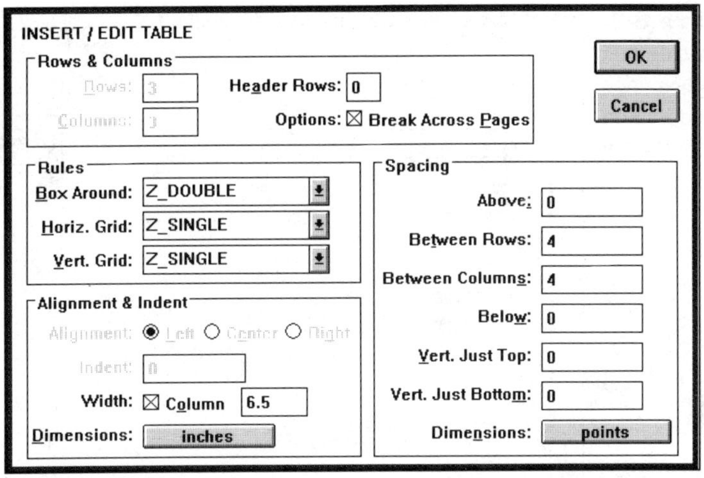

Figure 8-2.
When you insert or edit a table, you select the settings in the Insert/Edit Table dialog box.

Inserting a table with the Table Tool

With the Table Tool, you can insert a table at the top of a blank page, between any two paragraphs, or just before the end-of-file marker at the end of a text file. Just follow these steps:

1. Select the Table Tool from the Toolbox.

2. Click on the location you want for your table: either before the end-of-file marker or just before a paragraph symbol. A horizontal gray bar indicates where the table will be placed.

3. Choose Insert New Table from the Table menu. The Insert/Edit Table dialog box appears.

Note: Then, you set up the table format, using the options in the dialog box. Later, we'll show you how to make and edit the settings in this dialog box.

4. Click on OK.

If you make no changes in the dialog box, a table with the default settings appears on the screen (Figure 8-3).

Note: The default table will fill the width of whatever margins or columns you have established on your page. Therefore, your table may not exactly match the one in Figure 8-3.

Inserting a table with the Text Tool

When you're writing and editing with the Text Tool, it's a nuisance to select the Table Tool and then return to the Text Tool. Luckily,

Figure 8-3.
Ventura's default table settings generate a ruled table with 3 rows and 3 columns.

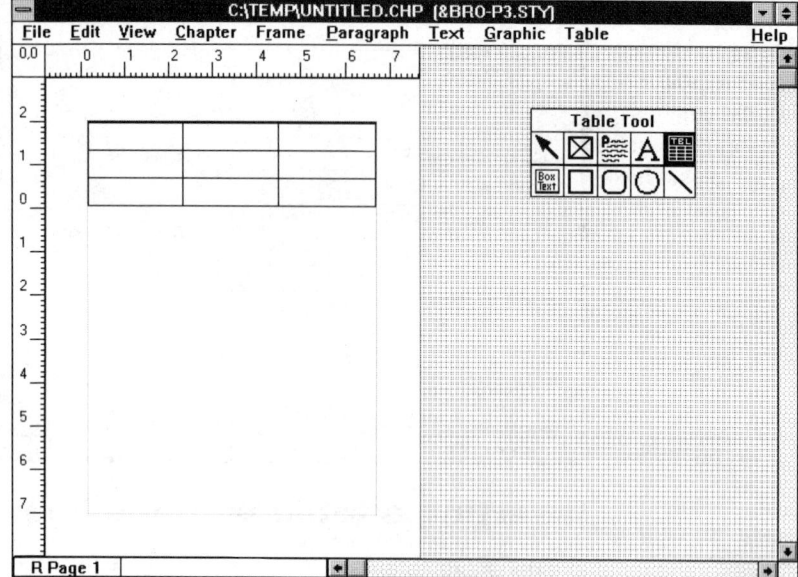

Ventura allows you to insert a table while you're still using the Text Tool. Just follow these steps:

1. Place the Text cursor immediately in front (to the left) of a paragraph symbol or an end-of-file marker.
2. Choose Insert Special Item from the Text menu. A flyout menu appears with a list of special items (Figure 8-4).
3. Choose Table from the flyout menu. The Insert/Edit Table dialog box appears—the same one that appeared when you used the Table Tool.
4. Then set up the table's format, using the options in the dialog box. Later, we'll show you how to make and edit the settings in this dialog box.
5. Click on OK.

Unless you have changed the settings in the Insert/Edit Table dialog box, a table with the default settings appears on the screen (Figure 8-3). (As noted earlier, the precise appearance of this table depends on your page's margins and columns.)

Setting up the table format

So far, you've learned how to create tables with the default format (just click on OK in the Insert/Edit Table dialog box without changing the settings). But you're not stuck with Ventura's default

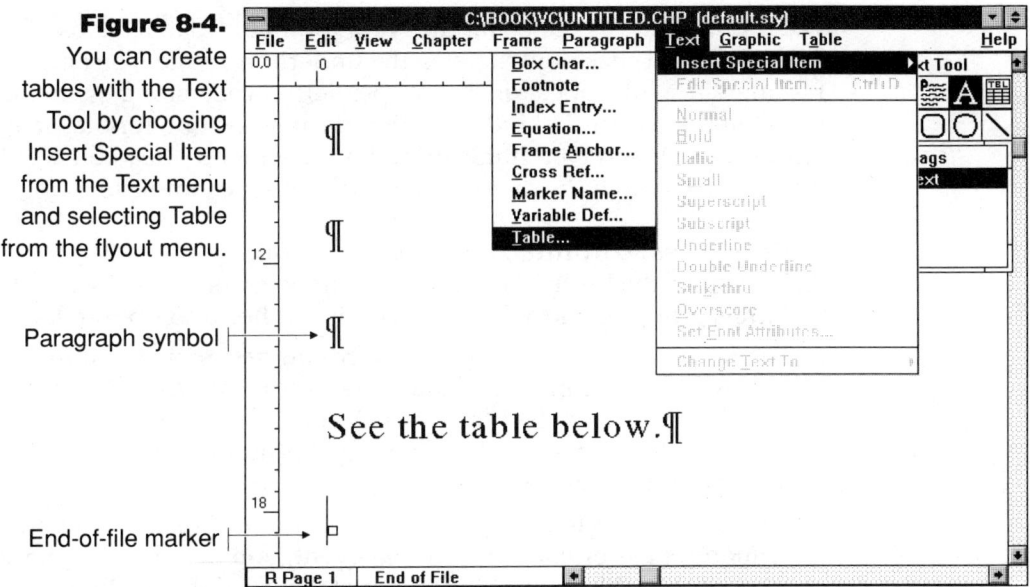

Figure 8-4.
You can create tables with the Text Tool by choosing Insert Special Item from the Text menu and selecting Table from the flyout menu.

Paragraph symbol

End-of-file marker

format—you can customize it when you insert your table or change it later (see the section, "Editing the table format").

We'll guide you through each step of creating a custom table:

- Working with surrounding text
- Setting rows, columns, and break options
- Creating ruling lines
- Determining the overall width and alignment
- Adjusting the spacing

Example: Throughout this section, we'll guide you through an example table. Here's your assignment: place a table at the top of an empty page with two columns and five rows, one header row, and ruling lines. Then give it two headings: Societal ills and Capitalist cures. We'll explain the steps; then you'll have an opportunity to practice them in the Examples.

Working with surrounding text

Where you place your table determines how the text around it reacts: If you put it on the underlying page, your table moves with the surrounding text during edits and repagination. If you put it in a frame, the surrounding text flows around it.

Example: Start by choosing the New command. Then choose the Table Tool and click anywhere on the underlying page. The end-of-file marker will appear in the upper left corner along with the horizontal gray bar that indicates the starting position for the table. Now choose Insert New Table from the Table menu. (Read on; we'll guide you through the dialog box in upcoming examples.)

Setting rows, columns, and break options

At the top of the Insert/Edit Table dialog box, you see the Rows & Columns group. Let's look at what each text box and option does:

- The *Rows* and *Columns* text boxes let you designate the number of rows and columns that the table will have. You can type a number from 1 to 9999 for rows or columns. Typing a 0 (zero) produces the same result as typing the number 1—you get a one-column or one-row table.

- The *Header Rows* text box is useful if your table breaks across two or more pages or columns. In that event, you decide how many rows of the table (from the top down) will automatically repeat on the top of each subsequent column or page that the table occupies. Repeated column headings makes each page of the table easier to read. Note, however, that option will only take effect if you have checked the Break Across Pages option.

- The *Break Across Pages* option lets you choose whether the table should break across pages or columns. By default, this option selected. You should allow breaks across pages when the table is at least one page (or one column) long; otherwise, you should consider keeping the table together—even if it means creating some empty space at the bottom of the previous page (where the full table could not fit).

Note: If you don't know how long your table will be, choose the Break Across Pages option. Otherwise, if your table becomes larger than a page or column, Ventura won't know what to do with it.

Example: If you're following along with our example chapter, the Insert/Edit Table dialog box should still be open on your screen. Make the settings for a two column table with five rows and one header row. Delete the 3 in the Rows text box and type 5. In the Columns text box, replace the 3 with a 2. In the Header Rows text box, delete the default value 0 and type the number 1 in its place.

Creating ruling lines

With the Rules option group, you can select the type of rules that surround a table:

- *Box Around* selects rules for the outer borders of the table.
- *Horiz. Grid* selects rules between each row.
- *Vert. Grid* selects rules between each column.

For each of these options, you can select one of three defaults:

- [NONE] produces no rules around each cell.
- Z_SINGLE produces a single line rule.
- Z_DOUBLE produces a double line rule.

Later in this chapter, you'll learn how to create custom ruling lines of your own and add them to the list boxes in this dialog box. For the moment, just stick with the options discussed here.

Example: If you're following our example chapter, let's stick with the preset values, which are Z_DOUBLE for Box Around; Z_SINGLE for Horiz. Grid; and Z_SINGLE for Vert. Grid.

Determining the overall width and alignment

With the Alignment & Indent group, you determine the horizontal position of the table within the text column. A table can span the width of a column, or it can have a custom width by setting its alignment and indention.

If you want the table to span across the current column's width, select the Width: Column option (the default setting).

To create a custom table width that is independent of the current column, follow these four steps:

1. Disable the Width: Column option (click on the checkbox until the X disappears).
2. Type the custom width of the table in the text box. The Dimensions button below lets you choose the measurement system for all values in the Alignment & Indent group.
3. Align the entire table relative to the current column, using the Alignment buttons to select Left, Center, and Right alignment within the column. The default is Left.
4. Indent the entire table from the left side of the current column, by typing the amount of indention in the Indent text box. The default is 0 (no indention).

Tip: Because the Indent text box only indents from the left, don't use it with the right or center alignment options. You're likely to find the results unpredictable, and it may confuse others who have to work on your chapter file.

Example: If you're following along with our example, keep the default setting of Width: column, which will create a table that spans the entire column width.

Adjusting the spacing

To adjust the padding (spacing) between the table and the paragraphs around it, you use the Spacing group in the Insert/Edit Table dialog box. You can determine the spacing by typing the desired amounts in these text boxes:

- *Above* determines vertical spacing between the top of the table and the bottom of the paragraph above.
- *Below* determines spacing between the bottom of the table and the top of the paragraph below.
- *Between Rows* determines vertical spacing between the rows of the table. This value is affected by the Move Down To 1st Baseline By option in the Chapter Typography dialog box (Chapter menu). If Inter-Line is selected in that dialog box, then the space between rows equals the Inter-Line spacing of the table's first tag plus the Between Rows spacing added here. On the other hand, if Cap Height is selected in the Chapter Typography dialog box, then the total space between rows is the type size plus the spacing designated here. In addition, the spacing options for individual tags in the table can also affect the spacing between rows.
- *Between Columns* determines the spacing added to the left of each column of the table.

The settings that you make here should be similar to those made for paragraph spacing options. The default values are all 0 (zero), except Between Rows and Between Columns, which are set to approximately 4 points.

The last two text boxes relate to vertical justification—the automatic adding of space between paragraphs, tables, and frames, so that text fills the page from top to bottom. If you have enabled vertical justification in the Chapter Typography dialog box (Chapter menu), you can control the maximum amount of space that

Ventura can add to the top and bottom of a table. You type the maximum amounts in these text boxes:

- *Vertical Just. Top* determines the amount of spacing Ventura can insert at the top of the table when vertically justifying a page.
- *Vertical Just. Bottom* determines the amount of space Ventura can insert below the table when vertically justifying a page.

For details on the Move Down To 1st Baseline By option and vertical justification, see Chapter 5, "Building Advanced Styles."

Example: For our example chapter, you can stick with the default settings but consider adding some extra space above and below the table (use some multiple of the inter-line spacing for Body Text). This will add some breathing room between the table and the surrounding text. Click on OK. You are returned to the workspace where you see your new table.

Adjusting the table settings

What if you inserted a table but you don't like some of the settings you chose? Ventura lets you return to the Insert/Edit Table dialog box whenever you want. With one exception, you can change any of the settings to modify your table.

What's the exception? The Insert/Edit Table dialog box won't let you change the number of rows and columns. To add rows and columns to an existing table, you must use Insert Row and Insert Column commands from the Table menu.

Tip: If you have to add lots of rows and columns and you haven't added in the table text yet, it may be faster to start over again and create a new table than to add them from the Table menu.

Here's how to change the table settings:

1. Select the Table Tool.
2. Click once anywhere in the table. It doesn't matter which cell or ruling line you select. Ventura simply needs to know which table you want to change before it can open the Edit Table Settings dialog box.
3. Choose Change Settings from the Table menu.
4. Make the desired changes in the Edit Table Settings dialog box.
5. Click on OK to return to the workspace.

Adding table text

After you've inserted a table into your document, you add text inside the cells. Each cell is a separate paragraph. You can type as much text in a cell as you want because Ventura automatically enlarges the cell and makes sure that the text in every cell remains in its column. It's easy, almost like typing regular text. Just select the Text Tool, move the cursor to a cell, and type.

Note: It's easier to type and edit text if tabs and returns are visible. Choose Show Tabs and Returns from the View menu (Ctrl-T).

However, typing in tables does differ from regular text:

- To start a new line within a cell, don't press Enter; press Ctrl-Enter (a line break).
- Use the arrow keys or the mouse to jump from cell to cell.
- You can select table text with the same techniques you use in ordinary paragraphs—but you can only select the text in one cell at a time. (For more on selecting and editing text, see Chapter 6, "Handling Text in Ventura.")

Example: If you're following our example chapter, type the text for the top two cells. Type "Societal ills" in the left cell and type "Capitalist cures" in the cell on the right. Then add the appropriate comments as table text below each header. Try "Waking up late" for the first Societal ill and "Setting alarm early" for the first Capitalist cure. If you would like to test how the cells grow to fit the text, add an additional line of related complaints in the first cell after "Waking up late." For example, add: "Feeling drowsy and cranky and sorry for myself." Figure 8-5 shows an example of our table with some text added. Your screen may look different.

Formatting a table

When you insert a table, you determine the formatting for the overall table, such as spacing and alignment. But you can also control the formatting of a table's individual elements. In this section, you'll learn the following techniques:

- Formatting table text
- Editing table elements
- Formatting table graphics

Figure 8-5.
Type text into the table cells. The cells automatically grow vertically if the text is too long to fit.

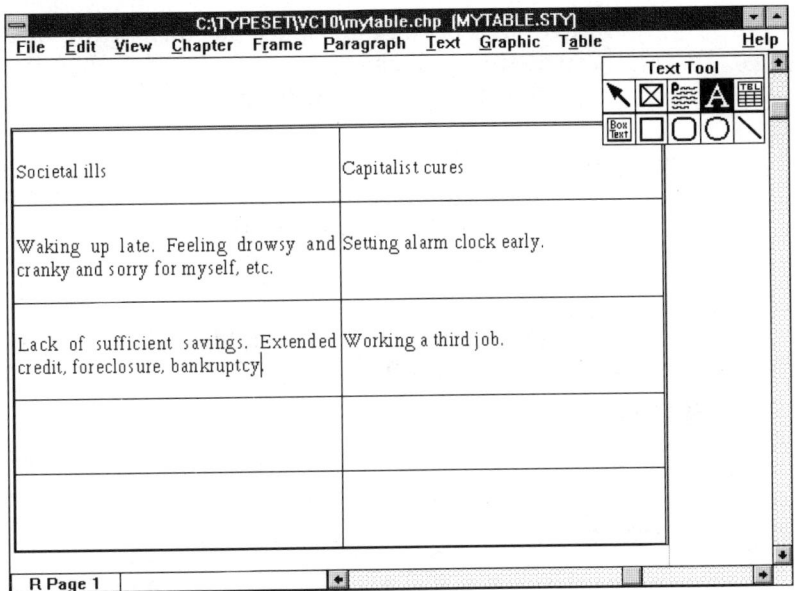

Formatting table text

Although you start out with a default tag for each cell called Table Text (with the attributes of Body Text), you can change the text attributes of any or all cells. As with regular text, you can use the Paragraph Tool to apply tags to paragraphs and the Text Tool to apply character formatting. We'll give you a few helpful tips, but for the whole story on formatting text in Ventura, see Chapter 3, "Building Basic Styles"; Chapter 5, "Building Advanced Styles"; and Chapter 6, "Handling Text in Ventura."

Tip: If you increase the size of some characters in a multi-line cell, the lines may touch or overlap. The solution is to turn on the Grow Inter-Line To Fit option in the Paragraph Typography dialog box.

Tip: If you want leader dots or dashes to mark distances across the table's width, select a cell with the Paragraph Tool and create a new tag. With the new tag still selected, choose Tab Settings from the Paragraph menu. Select a leader character and click on Auto-Leader. Then click on OK. For each empty cell with this tag, you'll have a continuous leader across the cell. For cells whose text have this tag, you'll have a leader extending from the end of the text to the cell's right margin.

Tip: Save horizontal space by formatting your column heads as rotated text. This is especially handy when your heads sport large point sizes or require a lot of text.

Example: For our example, create a tag for your table's column heads. Make the font large and bold. Then add text rotation by choosing Alignment from the Paragraph menu. Select Text Rotation and set it to 90 (for a ninety degree turn to the right) (Figure 8-6).

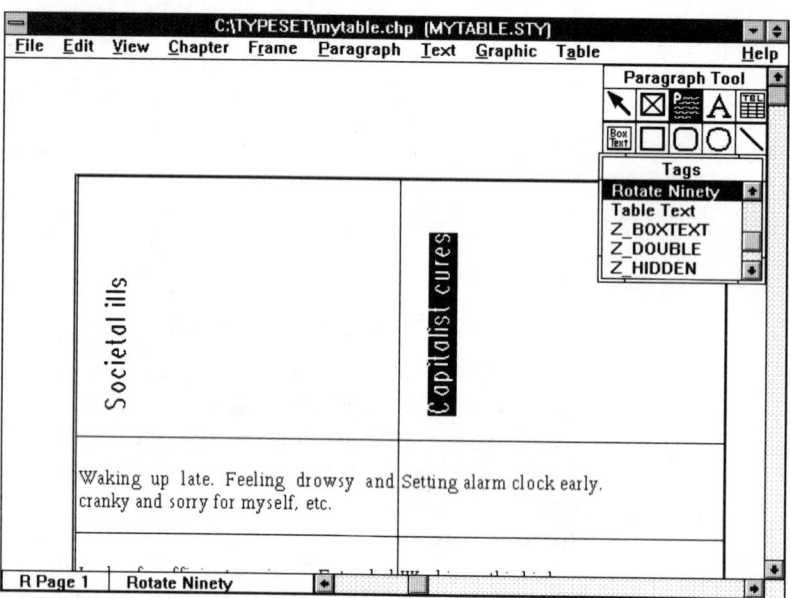

Figure 8-6. By rotating text 90 degrees for table headings, you can have long headings without increasing the column width.

Editing table elements

To edit a table, you need to acquire these skills:

- Selecting cells and ruling lines
- Cutting and copying rows and columns
- Pasting rows and columns

Don't worry. They're easy. We'll teach you each one.

Selecting cells and ruling lines
Selecting cells is simple:

1. Select the Table Tool and click on one corner of a cell you want to select.

2. Drag the mouse to the far corner of the farthest cell of the group of cells you want to select.

3. Release the mouse button. A gray line will highlight the outer border of the area you have selected.

Note: You can also use the Shift-click method to select cells or extend an existing selection. However, you can only select a single block of contiguous cells at one time.

In addition to selecting whole cells, you can also just select one side of a cell or group of cells. (You'll learn why later.) To do this, just drag the Table Tool across the edge of the cells you want to select. The restrictions are:

- You can only select one dimension (horizontal or vertical) at a time.
- You can only select in segments of entire cell sides. That is, you cannot, for example, select half of one side of a cell.

Example: If you're following our example chapter, practice this technique by selecting each of these groups of cells:

- A single cell
- A group of cells
- A horizontal or vertical ruling line between cells
- The whole table

Cutting and copying rows and columns

With the Edit menu (or the keyboard shortcuts) and the Table Tool, you can cut, copy, and paste rows or columns of cells. However, you can't cut, copy, or paste individual cells.

To cut, copy, or paste a row or column of cells, follow these steps:

1. Using the Table Tool, select a single cell.
2. From the Edit menu, choose the command you want—Cut Row/Column or Copy Row/Column. Ventura displays a VP Alert box that lets you choose whether to cut or copy column(s) or row(s) or Cancel the command.
3. Click on the Row(s) button or Column(s) button or Cancel button. Ventura executes the command and returns to the workspace.

When you cut or copy a row or column, all the text in those cells is cut as well. Both the cells and their text will return when you paste. That's next.

Pasting rows and columns

Pasting rows and columns is just as easy as cutting and copying them. Here's how:

1. Using the Table Tool, select a line where you want the column or row to be pasted. (Selecting the length of one cell will do; you don't need to select an entire column or row.)
2. Choose Paste Row/Column from the Edit menu. Ventura displays a VP Alert box that lets you paste in the current location or Cancel the command.
3. Click on the Paste button to complete the operation.

Note: The VP Alert box for pasting columns and rows is weird. It insists on pasting cells "in front" of other cells—which means *to the left* for columns and *above* for rows. If you try to paste cells at the bottom or far right side of a table, it asks if you want to paste these cells in front of a nonexistent row or column. For example, to paste a column at the end (far right) of a two-column table, Ventura asks whether you want to paste a column "in front of COLUMN #3 in your table." This doesn't make sense, but click on Paste anyway. It will work fine.

Formatting table graphics

You've already seen how to customize tables by formatting the text. Ventura also gives you a number of tools for additional effects:

- Adding colors and tints to cells
- Joining cells
- Changing column widths
- Modifying ruling lines
- Creating custom ruling lines

Sound interesting? Then let's dive in.

Adding colors and tints to cells

One of the most striking effects possible with Ventura tables is the ability to change the color and pattern of selected cells. Here's the process:

1. Create a table.
2. Select one or more cells by dragging the Table Tool over the appropriate portion.
3. Choose Set Tint from the Table menu.

4. In the Table Cell Tint dialog box, select a color from the list on the left.
5. Select a pattern from the list on the left.
6. Click on OK.

Tip: If you don't like the Ventura's predefined patterns, you can redefine the default colors as the shade you want. Using any tool, choose Define Colors from the Paragraph menu. Under Color Name, select a color you wish to redefine (one you think you won't ever use). Choose a Color Mode (CMYK is the easiest for gray shades). Then adjust the color scroll bars until the color you want appears in the preview box, or until the desired percentages appear to the right of the scroll bars. Then click on the Rename button and type the name of your new shade. When you click on OK, this shade will appear in dialog boxes in place of the color you redefined. For example, to create a 10% gray pattern, select a Color Name such as Magenta and select the CMYK Color Mode. Set the Cyan, Magenta, and Yellow scroll bars to zero and the Black scroll bar to 10%. Click on Rename and call your new color Gray 10%. Then click on OK and close the dialog box.

Example: For practice, create a table with the default settings. Select the cell in the upper left corner. Choose Set Tint from the Table menu. Then select Black as the color and select the lightest tint, which happens to be white (0% black). Continue across the top row from left to right, and then each of the two rows below—giving each successive cell a darker pattern of black (Figure 8-7). If you decide to add text, create tags whose font color (set in the Font dialog box) complements the background of each cell: black text on white, white text on black, and so on.

Joining cells

Sometimes, the data on a given row (or column) of your table belongs under more than one column (or row). You could type the same data in two cells, but that would be redundant and slow down your readers. Fortunately, Ventura lets you solve this by joining two or more adjacent cells. It's easy:

1. Using the Table Tool, select one or more cells.
2. Choose Join Cells from the Table menu.

That's all it takes. Change your mind or reworking a table to fit new data? Let what has been joined together be split asunder with the Split Cells option:

Figure 8-7.
You can add different shades and colors to each cell with the Table Cell Tint dialog box.

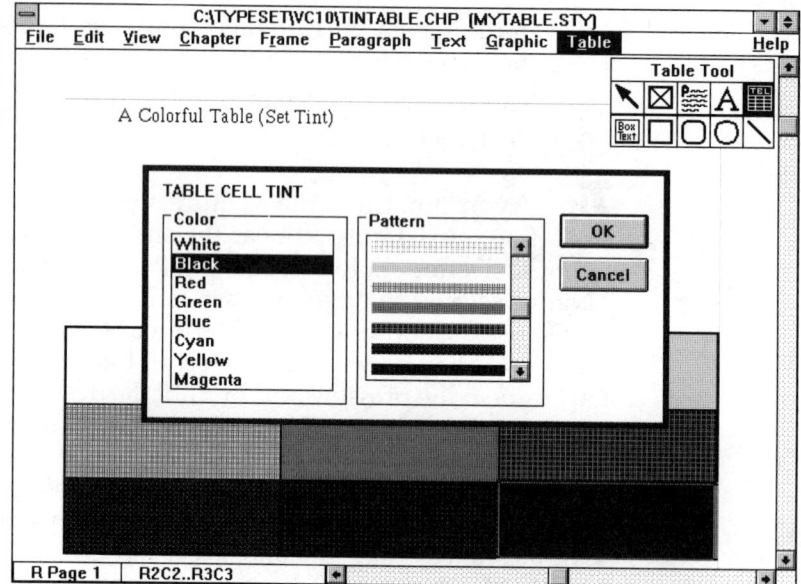

1. Using the Table Tool, select one or more cells that were previously joined with the Join Cells command.
2. Choose Split Cells from the Table menu.

Example: Create a table with three rows and three columns (the default settings will do nicely). Select the center column cells and choose Join Cells from the Table menu to create one large "centerpiece" cell. The result should resemble Figure 8-8. Then practice splitting the joined cells by selecting the same area and choosing Split Cells.

Changing column widths

When you first create your table, you may not know exactly how your text will fit in individual cells. The height of cells changes automatically as you add text. But you may need to adjust columns widths to make text-heavy cells wider than those with little content. You have two methods to choose from. Here's an easy one:

1. With the Table Tool, click once in a cell whose column you want to change.
2. Press and hold the Alt key while you drag the mouse to the right (for wider columns) or left (for smaller columns). Vertical lines guide your movement.
3. When the guides show the width you want, release the mouse button and Alt key.

Figure 8-8.
Use the Join Cells command to join adjacent cells.

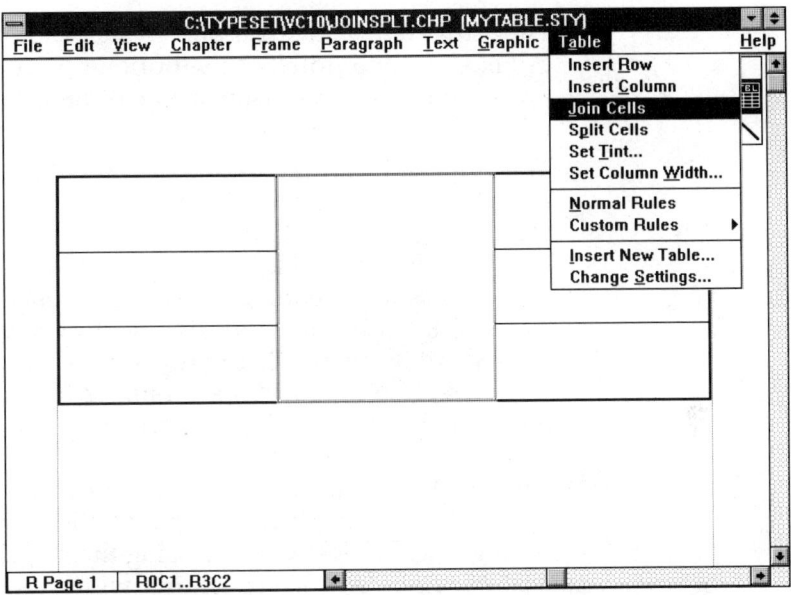

For more precision, you'll need the Set Column Widths command. Just select the Table Tool and click once in a cell whose column you want to change. Then choose Set Column Width from the Table menu. The Table Column Widths dialog box appears (Figure 8-9).

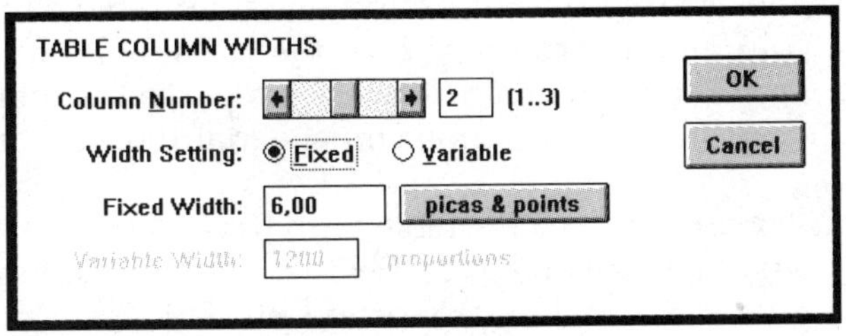

Figure 8-9.
The Table Column Widths dialog box gives you fine control over column widths.

Let's look at the goodies in this box:

- *Column Number* displays the number of the column you selected when you choose the Set Column Width command. To change the widths of other columns, just move the scroll bar until the desired column number appears to its right.

- *Width Setting* options control the way Ventura determines column widths. Each column can be designated as either fixed or variable. You can combine variable- and fixed-width columns in one table, but the proportions you set in the Variable Width text box will only apply to those marked as variable.

- The *Fixed Width* text box is only available on columns designated as Fixed in the Width Setting options. Here you can specify the exact column width in whatever dimensions you choose with the measurements button.

- The *Variable Width* text box is only available on columns designated as Variable in the Width Setting options. Here you can set the column width in proportion to any other variable-width columns in your table. If all variable-width columns have a proportion of 1, Ventura takes the available space (minus any fixed-width columns) and divides it evenly among these variable-width columns. Therefore, to make a column twice as big as all others, you type a proportion of 2 for the big column and a proportion of 1 for each of the others.

Warning: By assigning column widths with the Fixed Width option, you can actually cause a table to stick outside the margin or column guides. Unless you are doing this to achieve some unusual special effect, be sure your column-width totals don't exceed the width of the column where the table is located.

Tip: For Variable width columns, you can tell Ventura to divide the space according to percentages. Just type the proportion (percentage) you want allotted to each variable-width column in the Variable Width box. For example, if your table has two variable-width columns, you can type 25 as the Variable Width for the one column, and 75 for the other. To work properly, the total of all numbers for variable-width columns must equal 100.

Example: Create a table with five columns. Give the first column a fixed width of 6 picas. Set the other four columns as Variable, and give them each a proportion of 25. When you're done, the right four columns of your table should have equal widths.

Modifying ruling lines

You can select and modify a line as small as one side of a single cell or as large as the entire table. Earlier in this chapter, you learned one way to change some of your rules by using the Insert/Edit Table dialog box. Now, you'll learn some techniques that are not only faster but give you more control.

The formatting for table ruling lines are stored in tags similar to the paragraph tags you learned about in Chapter 3, "Building Basic Styles." The main difference: Instead of using the Paragraph Tool and the Tag List Window, you use the Table Tool and the Table menu. Here's how to apply these tags:

1. Using the Table Tool, select the line along one or more cells.
2. Choose Custom Rules from the Table menu.
3. From the flyout menu, select one of the four pre-defined ruling line tags: Z_HIDDEN, Z_SINGLE, Z_DOUBLE, and Z_THICK.

Two of these tags (Z_SINGLE and Z_DOUBLE) are familiar from the Insert/Edit Table dialog box. Let's take a look at the other two:

- Z_THICK is a single thick line that can be applied to any side of a cell, the entire cell, or a selected group of cells.
- Z_HIDDEN renders selected lines invisible. If you apply this tag to the line separating two cells, the cells appear to be joined.

Example: Try it. Re-tag a default three-column, three-row table with Z_THICK. Then re-tag the center cell with Z_HIDDEN. It forms a unique table with a cross interior and 4 outer cells, as shown in Figure 8-10.

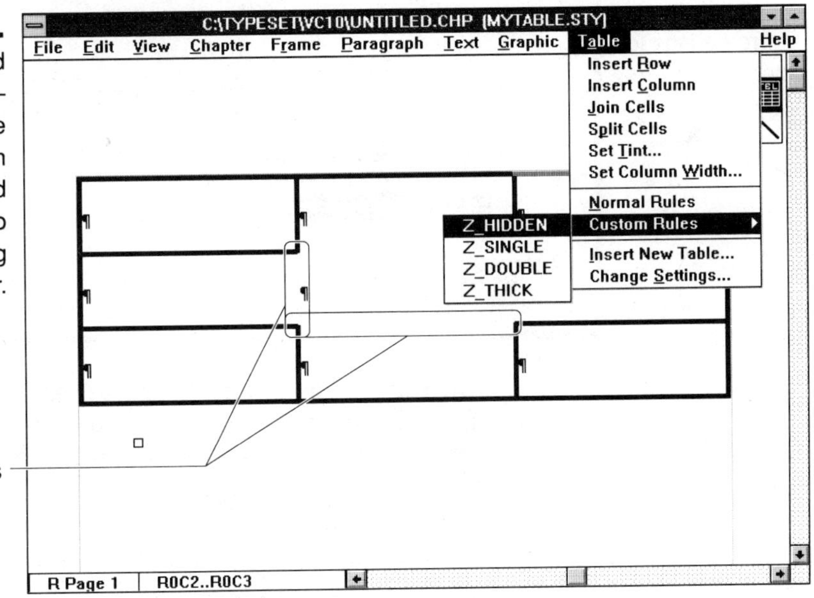

Figure 8-10. A table retagged with Z_THICK—except for the center cell, which has been retagged with Z_HIDDEN to make its ruling lines disappear.

"Invisible" lines

Creating custom ruling lines

As with paragraph tags, you can create new tags for ruling lines that will appear in the Insert/Edit Table dialog box and the Custom Rules flyout menu in the Table menu. Here's the process:

1. Select the Generated Tags: Shown option in the Set Preferences dialog box (Edit menu). This will make ruling line tags initially generated by Ventura visible in the Tag List Window.
2. As an optional assist, choose Show Tabs & Returns from the View menu (unless it already has a check mark).
3. Using the Paragraph Tool, select a paragraph symbol in the table.
4. Click on an existing tag in the Tag List Window (or choose Add New Tag from the Paragraph menu and define a new tag).
5. Choose Ruling Line Above, Ruling Line Below, or Ruling Box Around from the Paragraph menu. Make choices for size, width, color, pattern, and so on.
6. While still in the dialog box, check the Show With Table Rules option (Figure 8-11). Then click on OK.

Figure 8-11. Use one of the ruling line dialog boxes to create tags for custom table rules.

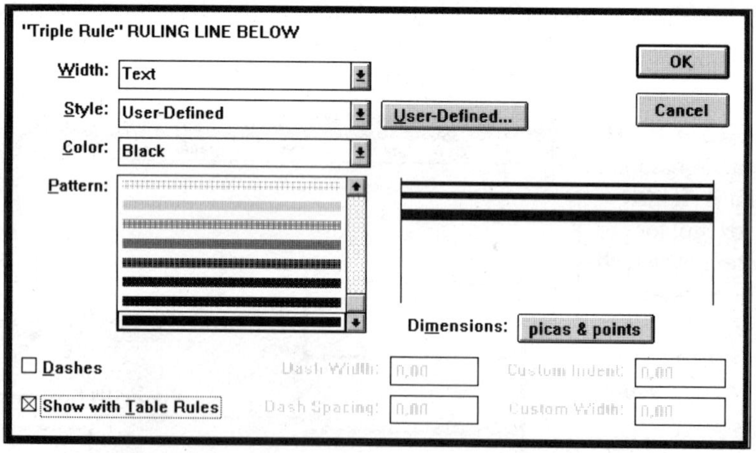

This tag will now be available in the Rules list boxes in the Insert/Edit Table dialog box and on the Custom Rules flyout menu. Any changes you want to make to the tag can be made from the Paragraph menu.

Creating tables in a word processor

Although it is much easier (and more fun) to create tables within Ventura, you can create table text and apply formatting codes with your favorite word processor. However, you must type the tags and text exactly the way Ventura expects it; otherwise, it won't recognize the text as a table.

This section will show you the basic codes to make your word-processing file turn out tables in Ventura. Then we'll show you how to use your word processor to add tags to those tables.

Inserting table tags and data in the word processor

Follow along as we create a table in the word processor using the required tags (table begin, number of columns, and table end) along with the text in the exact format. Then view the results in Ventura.

In the examples below, we'll use Ventura tag codes. You must observe these requirements:

- Start a tag at the beginning of a line.
- Type the tag with the exact spelling as shown.
- Include one space before and after the equal sign.
- End the tag (and the text—if any—that follows it) with a carriage return (by pressing Enter).

For more information on tagging in your word processor, see Chapter 7, "Creating Text with Other Programs."

Now let's cut to the chase, by creating the same table that Ventura makes by default when using the preset values in the Insert/Edit Table dialog box.

1. In the word processor, locate the cursor in the text at the beginning of the line where you want the table to begin.
2. To let Ventura know that this is the beginning of the table and how many columns it will have, type the following, carefully noting the use of spaces (indicated by dots):

    ```
    @Z_TBL_BEG·=·COLUMNS(3) ¶
    ```

3. On each of the following paragraphs, type the actual data (words, numbers, and so on) that you want for each row. Type a comma and a space between the data for each column (cell).

End each line with a carriage return (press Enter). Each line of data you type will create a corresponding row in the table. The form for each row should be:

```
1st column data, 2nd column data, 3rd column data
```

Warning: If you want to use a comma for punctuation within each cell, type two successive commas,, like this,, to let Ventura know this is not a cell break. Otherwise, some of your data could end up in the wrong cells and other parts of it may disappear entirely. If you load text with this problem into Ventura and save it, the data could be lost for good. Commas with no spaces after them (as in 10,000) pose no problems.

Note: If you want a blank row (cells with no data), type only the comma and space for each cell.

4. After you have typed all the rows of data, create a final line to let Ventura know it's the end of the table, type:
```
@Z_TBL_END = ¶
```

5. Now load the text file into Ventura. You'll like the results.

Note: The table you just created will not have any visible ruling lines. You can always add those with the Table Tool as you learned earlier in this chapter. But to learn how to include this formatting in your word processor, see the tip in the next section.

Pretagging options

If you want to specify the table in more detail, you can replace the default tags with your own. Ventura provides two commands that define the tag substitution. These commands are actually tags themselves that are added to the table. The commands are:

- @Z_TBL_HEAD = to change the tag for any column of the header. For example to use tags named TableLeft (for the first column) and TableCenter (for the other columns) in a three-column table, you would type the following line after the Table Begin tag:
```
@Z_TBL_HEAD = TableLeft, TableCenter, TableCenter¶
```

- @Z_TBL_BODY = to change table body tags. For example, you would use this command to tag the body text for the columns with the tags TableBody1 for first column, and so on:
```
@Z_TBL_BODY = TableBody1, TableBody2, TableBody3¶
```

Warning: These two commands are the only two tag codes that can appear in a table. You can specify any other tag name on the same line as the @Z_TBL_HEAD = or @Z_TBL_BODY = commands (as shown above), but you cannot include any other tag codes with the usual @*TAGNAME* = form. If Ventura finds any such tag codes between your @Z_TBL_BEG = and @Z_TBL_END = commands, your table (and possibly Ventura) will crash.

For example, to change the tag for just one cell, you would add a @Z_TBL_BODY = (or @Z_TBL_HEAD =) line to your table just above the line (row) with the cell in question. Specify the unique tag name for the appropriate column. Then, after the line of text that requires the tag, add another a @Z_TBL_BODY = (or @Z_TBL_HEAD =) line to change the tags back to normal. In the example below, only one cell in the third column has the tag WEIRDTAG:

```
1st col. text, 2nd col. text, 3rd. col. text, 4th col. text¶

1st col. text, 2nd col. text, 3rd. col. text, 4th col. text¶

1st col. text, 2nd col. text, 3rd. col. text, 4th col. text¶

@Z_TBL_BODY = Body Text, Body Text, WEIRDTAG, Body Text¶

1st col. text, 2nd col. text, 3rd. col. text, 4th col. text¶

@Z_TBL_BODY = Body Text, Body Text, Body Text, Body Text¶

1st col. text, 2nd col. text, 3rd. col. text, 4th col. text¶

1st col. text, 2nd col. text, 3rd. col. text, 4th col. text¶

1st col. text, 2nd col. text, 3rd. col. text, 4th col. text¶
```

Tip: To learn more of Ventura's table codes and how to include them in your word-processing files, try this: Create a table in Ventura with all the attributes you usually need in your documents. Then save the file. Next, in your word processor, open up the text file for that Ventura chapter. (If you inserted the table in an existing text file, it will be there. If you inserted it in a Ventura chapter with no text files, look in the File List Window for the name of the file containing your table.) You will see all the tags and other information Ventura needs to build that particular table. You can save this file for future reference, or create a macro that inserts all these codes into your text files. Then you just type in your data in the appropriate place. Voila: instant table!

Example: Type the following table in your word processor, carefully duplicating the punctuation, spaces (indicated by dots) and carriage returns (indicated by paragraph marks). Then load it into a Ventura chapter file to see the results. The precise appearance will vary depending on the style sheet of the chapter file you use.

```
@Z_TBL_BEG = COLUMNS(3), DIMENSION(IN), HGUTTER(.0555), VGUTTER(.0
555), BOX(Z_DOUBLE), HGRID(Z_SINGLE), VGRID(Z_SINGLE), KEEP(OFF) ¶
@Z_TBL_BODY = BODY TEXT, BODY TEXT, BODY TEXT¶
Creating Tables:, Pros, Cons¶
Create in Ventura, What you see is what you get, May take longer; req
uires mousing around¶
Create in Word Processor, Can be faster, , especially if done with ma
cros, Can't see what finished table looks like; typos in codes can ca
use problems¶
@Z_TBL_END = ¶
```

Creating tables with a spreadsheet

So far, we've shown you how to create tables in Ventura and in a word processor. You can also build tables in your favorite spreadsheet. It's a fabulous time-saver, but it requires you to follow a few rules. This section covers the two step process: (1) creating the table in your spreadsheet application and (2) importing your spreadsheet table into Ventura.

Creating the table

In order for Ventura to convert your spreadsheets to tables, your spreadsheet software must support the Lotus PRN file format. If it does not, you'll have to save your spreadsheet as an ASCII file and edit it in your word processor. If your software does support the Lotus PRN format, just follow these guidelines:

1. Use little or no formatting: no indents or centering, and so on. It's easier to apply formatting in Ventura. Besides, some formats applied in outside programs can cause unexpected and undesireable results.

2. Be sure that there are at least two spaces between each column. Ventura's PRN To Table file filter (discussed in the next section) requires at least two spaces in this format to recognize where columns begin and end. Format your columns at least two spaces wider than the widest string of text in any cell (Figure 8-12).

3. Create the PRN file. With Lotus, this merely means printing to a file instead of sending the spreadsheet to your printer; Lotus adds the PRN extension automatically. The resulting PRN file is actually an ASCII text file that Ventura and other programs can read.

Now all you have to do is load the text file into a Ventura table. Not sure how? Keep reading.

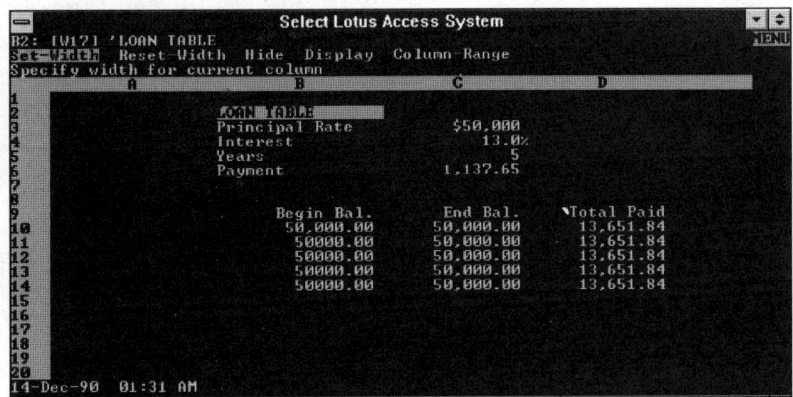

Figure 8-12. Ventura can import Lotus 1-2-3 spreadsheets as tables provided you give the columns enough space.

Bringing a spreadsheet table into Ventura

Here's how to load a spreadsheet file into a Ventura table:

1. Open the chapter in Ventura where you want to use the spreadsheet data.
2. Select the Text Tool and position it at the point where you want the table to begin.
3. Choose the Load Text/Picture command from the File menu.
4. For File Type, click on the Text button.
5. For Format, select PRN To Table.
6. For Destination, click on the Cursor button. Then click on OK.
7. In the Open File dialog box, navigate to the directory where your PRN file is located. Select the filename in the Item Selector Box and click on Open.

The spreadsheet text file will load into Ventura and appear on the screen and be ready to print. Now, you can add further formatting enhancements in Ventura as explained earlier in this chapter (Figure 8-13). Try custom rules, tints, and text formatting for the finishing touches.

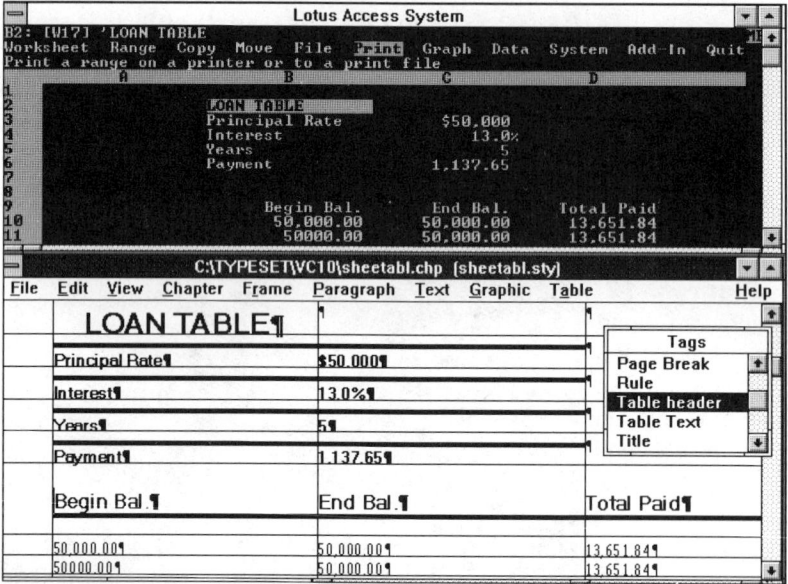

Figure 8-13.
After loading your Lotus spreadsheet into Ventura, you can adjust ruling lines and tags with the Table Tool and Paragraph Tool.

Continuing on

Your table settings are complete and you're now ready to feast on Ventura's more advanced features. No matter how complex the table is, you always use the three basic steps covered in this chapter: inserting the table, adding (or loading) text, and formatting the table. You also learned how to streamline things by preparing tables in your word processor or spreadsheet application before you open Ventura. In the chapters that follow, you'll chow down on another important communication tool: pictures. Bon appétit.

Easy Access

For more info on...	See chapter...
Creating basic style tags	3 — Building Basic Styles
Creating advanced style tags	5 — Building Advanced Styles
Preparing and exporting spreadsheet data for Ventura	7 — Creating Text with Other Programs

Part Four:
Pictures

9 Creating Pictures in Ventura

How to create pictures
with Ventura's Graphic tools

- **Creating simple shapes** 273
- **Advanced tips and tricks** 285
- **Continuing on** 289

You have three choices if you need an illustration for a Ventura document: you can import a file created with an outside program; you can leave a space on the page and paste in an illustration later; or you can draw the picture with Ventura's Graphic tools

In this chapter, you'll learn how to create the five basic shapes: Box Text, rectangles, rounded rectangles, ellipses, and lines. Then we'll show you some advanced tips and tricks you can do with the Graphic tools. First, let's look at the pros and cons of using Ventura's Graphic tools.

Ventura's built-in Graphic tools do have limitations, but despite the shortcomings, they are a handy resource for creating simple pictures (Figure 9-1). They are useful for adding the finishing touches to pictures you import as files. All the callouts in this book were created with Ventura's Add Box Text and Add Line tools.

Figure 9-1.
These two drawings were created entirely with Ventura's Graphic tools, using the techniques you'll learn in this chapter.

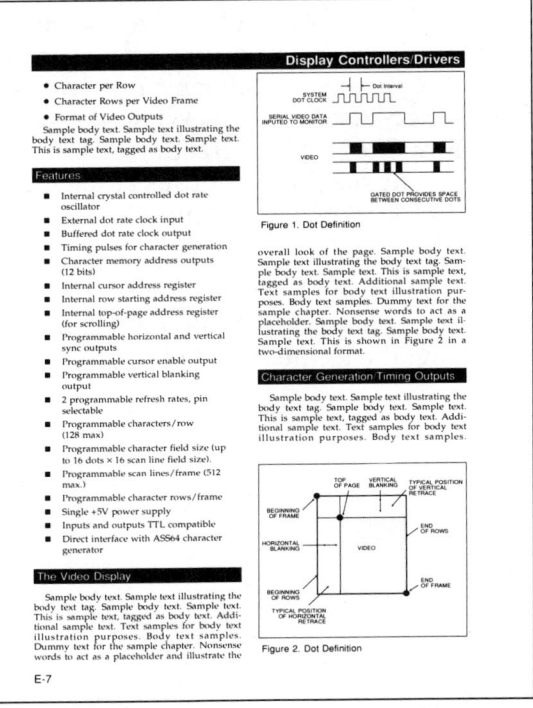

The pros and cons of creating pictures within Ventura

Before you decide to create an illustration with Ventura's Graphic tools, you should have a clear idea of their limitations. In general, anything more complex than simple lines, arrows, and boxes should be built with an outside illustration program, then imported into Ventura.

Ventura has only rudimentary tools. It doesn't offer grouping, polygons, curves, graduated fills, layers, or many of the other functions that make full-scale drawing packages easier and faster to work with. In short, a Ventura drawing will take longer to create and it won't look as good when you're done.

What's more, Ventura drawings aren't very portable. Ventura stores them internally in a special format. You don't end up with a separate file for each picture, as you do when you use an outside program. Nor do you have the option of saving a drawing to a different format. In fact, the only easy way of moving a Ventura drawing is to put it onto the clipboard. Then you can open a different chapter (or a different program) and paste in the drawing.

Still, Ventura's Graphic tools do have some advantages. First of all, they're free. Today's drawing programs go for as much as $800 and eat up as much as 15 MB on your hard disk. Second, Ventura creates vector-based line art. Without repeating the definitions of line art from Chapter 10, "Creating Pictures with Other Programs," suffice it to say that line art prints at the highest resolution of your printer or typesetter, giving smooth, professional-looking results.

So even if you own a full-featured drawing program, you'll find yourself turning to Ventura's built-in Graphic tools for callouts, crop marks, and quick jobs. When you do, you'll get better results by following the techniques and tips in this chapter.

Creating simple shapes

Ventura can draw five basic *shapes*: Box Text, rectangles, rounded rectangles, ovals, and lines. These shapes are available from the second line of the Toolbox. You can combine them to make more complex drawings, as you'll see in our hands-on example.

Ventura's shapes are generally obvious, except for Box Text, which is a hybrid of text and graphics. When you use the Box Text tool, you get a rectangle with the end-of-file symbol inside. By switching to the Text Tool, you can type text inside the box (Figure 9-2).

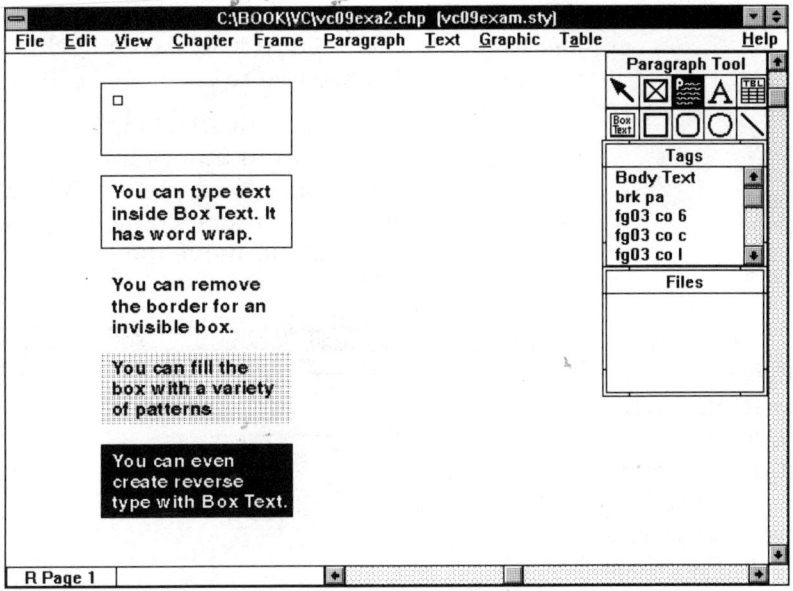

Figure 9-2.
Ventura's Box Text Tool creates graphic shapes that can be filled with text.

Despite its unique ability to contain text, Box Text behaves in every other way like the other graphic shapes.

It's not hard to slap a graphic shape onto a page—just click on the tool and drag with the mouse. But if you want to do things the right way, you'll follow these four steps:

1. Choose the correct parent frame
2. Set up a grid
3. Choose a tool and draw the shape
4. Edit the shape until it looks the way you want

We'll guide you through each step.

Choosing the parent frame

Beginners often fail to realize that *every Ventura graphic shape is attached to a parent frame or page.* Once you grasp this principle, you can use it to your advantage.

What do we mean by *attached*? Simply this: if you move the frame, the shapes move with it. If you copy the frame, the shapes are copied as well. If you delete the frame, the shapes disappear too. The shape doesn't have to be inside the frame or even touching it. The only requirement is that the frame and the shape be on the same page.

When you draw a shape, Ventura automatically attaches it to the last frame you selected. If you haven't selected a frame, Ventura attaches it to the page you're on.

There's nothing wrong with attaching shapes to a page. But often it's better to attach them to frames instead. For instance, suppose you are creating callouts for a picture. You'd want to attach the arrows and labels to the frame containing the picture, not to the page. That way you could move the picture to another page, and the callouts would move along with it (Figure 9-3).

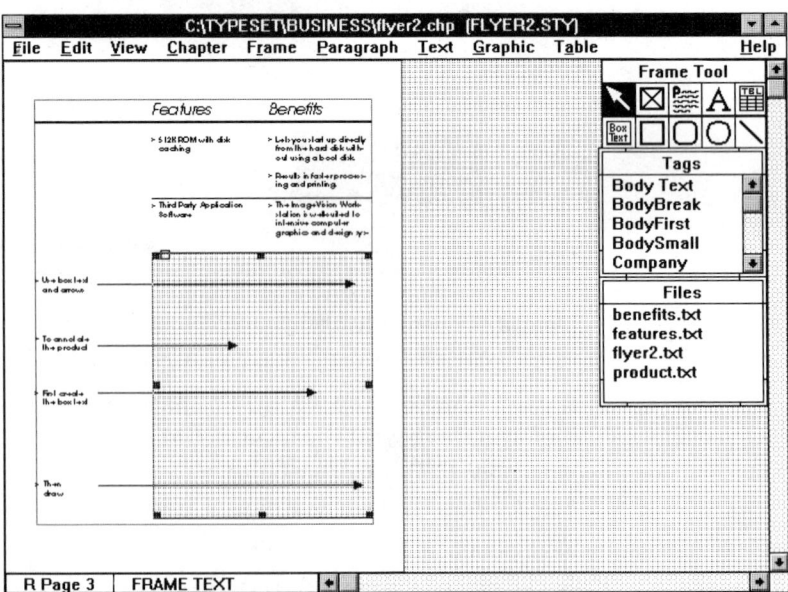

Figure 9-3. The gray rectangle represents a picture inside a frame. The labels and lines are callouts created with Ventura's Graphic tools. The callouts are attached to the picture's frame so they will move along with it.

Here's another example. Let's say you want to group several shapes together to create a drawing. You'd want to attach all of the shapes to the same frame, so you could move, copy, or delete them as a group.

Tip: It's often a good idea to attach Ventura drawings to a separate frame even if you have to build an "invisible" frame to do so. Put a tiny frame with no border and no background somewhere in the margin. Then you can copy or move an entire group of graphic shapes just by copying or moving the frame.

How can you tell for sure which frame is the parent? Whenever you choose one of the five Graphic tools, Ventura puts gray handles around the active frame (blue if you're using a color screen). This is the frame that will become the parent.

Get in the habit of looking for those gray handles before you start drawing. As you draw, move, and stretch shapes, it's very easy to click on the underlying page by mistake. Clicking on the underlying page selects it and makes it the parent frame for the next shape you draw. If you're not careful, you can end up with a group of shapes, half of which are attached to a frame and the other half to the underlying page.

Tip: To attach shapes to the correct parent, use Shift-Click to select all of them and delete them as a group. Then select the correct parent frame. Now paste the shapes you just deleted, thereby attaching them to the correct parent frame.

Set up a grid

Ventura has an optional snap-to grid for its graphics shapes. Think of the light blue lines on a piece of graph paper. Now imagine that those lines were magnetic so they attracted anything that came near. That's how Ventura's grid works. It creates a cross-hatch of invisible lines. Any time you put a shape near a grid line, the shape snaps into position.

You should always set up a grid before you start drawing. A grid makes it easy to size and align shapes. For instance, it can be almost impossible to make two lines meet at a corner on your own. With a grid in place, it's a snap (pun intended). To set up a grid:

1. Select the parent frame with the Frame Tool(see above).
2. Choose Grid Settings from the Graphic menu (Figure 9-4).
3. Select Grid Snap: On.

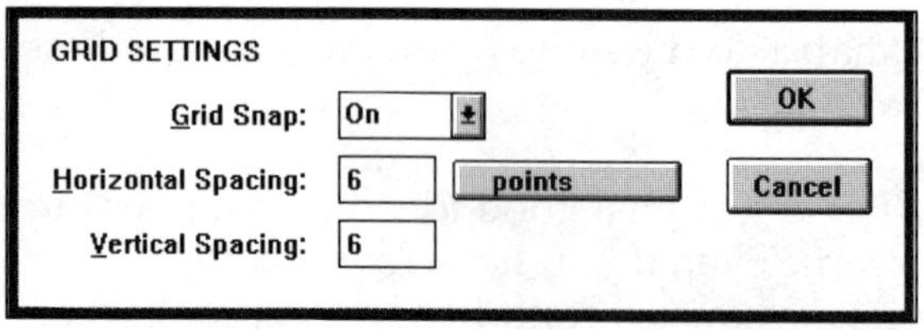

Figure 9-4.
Before you start drawing, use the Grid Settings dialog box to set up an invisible snap-to grid.

```
GRID SETTINGS
    Grid Snap:          On
    Horizontal Spacing: 6      points      OK
    Vertical Spacing:   6                  Cancel
```

4. Click on the measurements button until the measure that you want appears.
5. In the Horizontal Spacing and Vertical Spacing text boxes, type the size of the units in the grid.
6. Click on OK.

What size grid units should you specify? That depends on what you are drawing. If you are creating a series of one inch squares, you'd want both the Horizontal Spacing and the Vertical Spacing to be one inch. For useful positioning, however, you'll usually need smaller units. Since the grid forces you to snap to one of its invisible lines, you want those lines to be close enough together to allow you some latitude.

Tip: Choose the lowest common denominator if you have to draw several shapes in different sizes. For instance, to draw squares of one inch, one-and-a-quarter inches, and one-and-one-half inches, set up a grid with quarter-inch spacing.

We typically use six points (one-half pica) as the starting point for our grids, unless we know we're going to need some special size. The small increments give us lots of leeway to draw and position shapes, but we still have the snap-to alignment benefits of a grid.

You only have to set up the grid once. The settings stay in force for that frame until you change it, and they apply to any shapes you attach to that frame. Be careful if you change the grid. If you move or resize shapes, they will snap to the new grid. As long as you don't touch previously drawn shapes, they will stay at their former positions and sizes.

Using the Graphic tools

So far we've shown you how to select the parent frame and set up the grid. Now all you have to do is draw the shape and enhance it. To draw a shape:

1. Select the parent frame (or page) with the Frame Tool. Remember—if you don't select a parent, Ventura will use the last active frame. If you haven't selected a frame, Ventura will attach the shape to the current page.
2. Select a Graphic tool (Add Box Text, Add Rectangle, Add Round Rect, Add Circle, or Add Line) from the Toolbox.
3. Move the mouse to the beginning point of the shape. Press and hold the left mouse button. Drag the mouse to the desired position and release the button.

Tip: Hold down the Alt key as you drag to constrain the tools. For instance, holding down the Alt key with the Add Line tool draws a perfectly straight line. Holding down the Alt key while using the Add Circle tool creates a perfect circle. And holding down the Alt key with either of the rectangle tools creates a perfect square.

Table 9-1 shows the tools and some of the shapes you can create with them.

Editing the shapes

After you've got a graphic on the page, you can cut, copy, paste, move, or resize it. You can also change its line attributes or its fill attributes. Line attributes control the border of shapes. Fill attributes control the pattern or color of the space inside the borders of a shape.

To cut, copy, and then paste a shape, select it with the Frame Tool, then choose the command from the Edit menu (or use the keyboard shortcuts).

To move a shape, select it with the Frame Tool. Then drag the shape to its new position. If you accidentally resize the shape, move the cursor so it is *not* on top of a handle, then try again.

To resize a shape, select it with the Frame Tool. Then move the cursor until it is over one of the black sizing handles around the edges. Drag the handle to a new location, which will stretch the graphic to a new size. If you move the shape by mistake, reposition the cursor until it is exactly on top of a handle and try again.

Table 9-1. *Ventura's drawing tools*

Name	Toolbox icon	Sample of typical results		
Box Text	[Box Text]	Label ITEM 1	Label inside box ITEM 2	Reversed label ITEM 3
Rectangle	□	Square	Rectangle	Filled rectangle
Rounded rectangle	◻	Rounded square	Rounded rectangle	Filled rounded rectangle
Ellipse	○	Circle	Ellipse	Filled ellipse
Line	◹	Square end line	Arrows	Round end lines

Controlling line attributes

To change line attributes, select the shape, then choose Line Attributes from the Graphic menu. When the Line Attributes dialog box appears (Figure 9-5), make your selection and click on OK.

Obviously, the Line Attributes dialog box controls anything you draw with the Add Line tool. It also controls the border around the other shapes. If you don't see the size you want in the Thickness scroll list, move to the very end, choose Custom and type in the size you want. (Or just type it in. Ventura will automatically change the selection to Custom as soon as you start typing.)

Lines can have three different End Styles: square, arrow, and rounded. You can have any of these three ends at one or both ends. Ventura remembers where you started when you drew the line. The leftmost buttons for End Style always control the starting end of the line. The rightmost buttons control the ending point, regardless of which way the line is actually pointing.

Chapter 9: Creating Pictures in Ventura — Creating simple shapes

Figure 9-5.
The Line Attributes dialog box affects all of Ventura's graphic shapes.

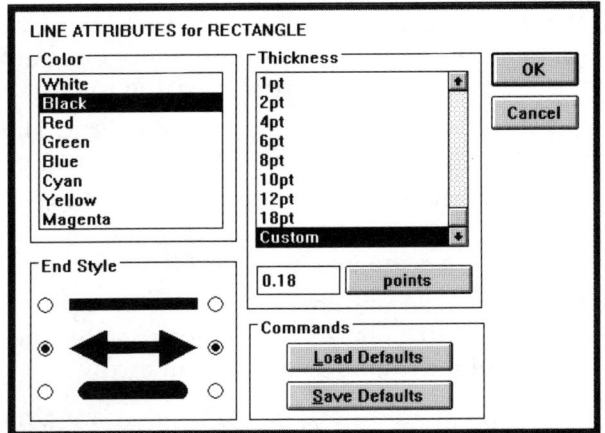

Example: To get a feeling for Ventura's Graphic tools, try building a simple flowchart. Go to a blank page in any chapter. Start by creating the two lines shown in (Figure 9-6).

Figure 9-6.
Want to try a hands-on example? Start by drawing two six-point lines.

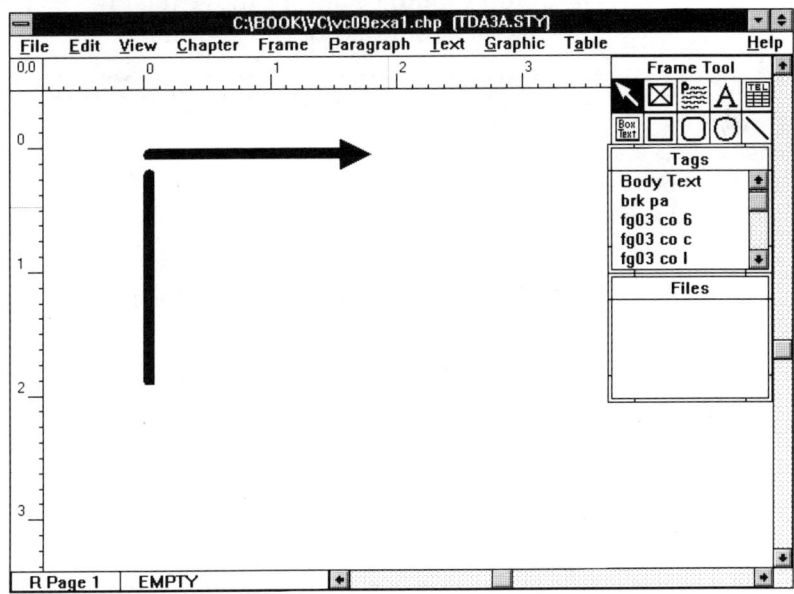

Don't be concerned with exact dimensions. Just try to approximate what you see here by following these steps:

1. Click on the Add Frame tool (second from left in the Toolbox) and draw a small frame anywhere out of the way. This will be your parent frame.

2. With the frame still selected, choose Grid Settings from the Graphic menu. Select Grid Snap: On. Set both the Horizontal Spacing and the Vertical Spacing to six points

3. Use the Add Line tool to draw a vertical line. (Hint: hold down the Alt key as you draw to force it to be perfectly straight)

4. With the new line still selected, choose Line Attributes from the Graphic menu. Make the line six points thick. Give the bottom a square end style. Give the top a rounded end style.

5. Draw a second, horizontal line at right angles to the first. Use Line Attributes to give it the same thickness. Make the left end rounded and the right end an arrow.

Now you should have two lines that are almost touching. If you want to see how graphics attach to the parent frame, try moving the parent frame you drew earlier. You'll see the lines move with it.

6. To see how useful the snap-to grid is, click on either of the lines and move it until it touches the other. With the help of the grid, you should be able to move the lines so the two rounded ends form a rounded corner (Figure 9-7).

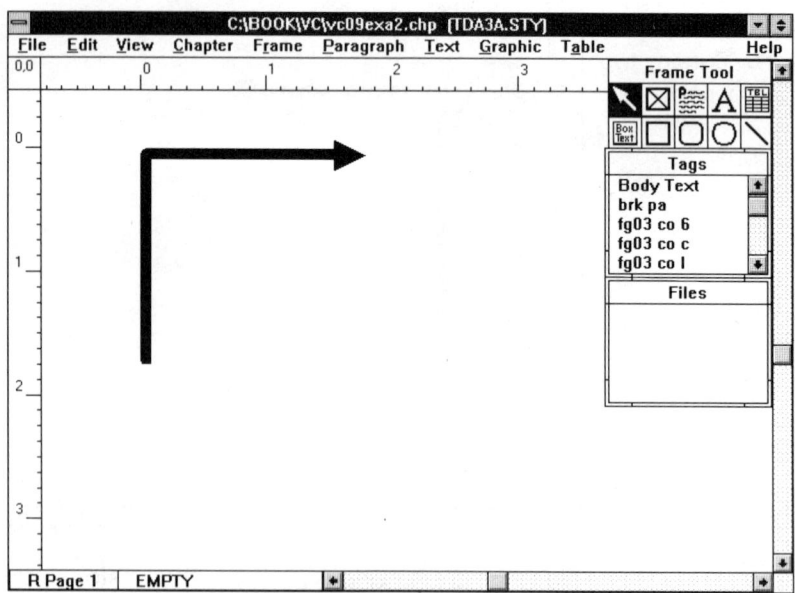

Figure 9-7. Move the lines together until they appear to be one line that turns a corner.

Controlling fill attributes

A line does not have any fill. All the other shapes—including Box Text—can have a pattern and a color inside. To control the fill inside a shape:

1. Select the shape with the Frame Tool.
2. Choose Fill Attributes from the Graphic menu.
3. Select the options you want (Figure 9-8).
4. Click on OK.

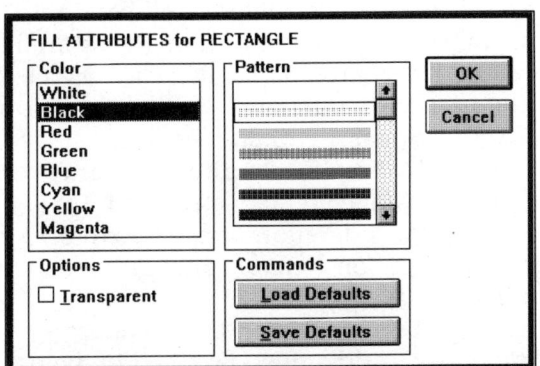

Figure 9-8. Use the Fill Attributes dialog box to control the pattern, the color, and the transparency inside a graphic shape.

You can select any of Ventura's eight colors. The colors you select show up on the screen, but they print out as shades of gray unless you have a color printer.

The color White is useful for creating "electronic white-out" shapes. You can use these white shapes to block out unwanted portions of a drawing, or to cover up unwanted labels on spreadsheet charts imported from other programs.

The color Black is useful in combination with the nine patterns to create gray screens. Select the pattern you want by clicking on a bar in the Pattern scroll box. The top pattern is clear. The bottom color is solid.

Notice the Transparent checkbox in the lower left. Sometimes you want one shape to show through another. Or you want text on the page to show through a graphic shape. The only way to achieve true transparency is to select both the Transparency checkbox *and* the empty pattern (the topmost choice in the Pattern scroll box, which looks like a blank line).

If you do not select Transparent and the empty pattern, your lines and shapes will be opaque—that is they will block out whatever is behind them. This is true even if the color is white. Note, however, that PostScript printers cannot reproduce most transparent effects.

Tip: If you don't like the Ventura's predefined patterns, you can redefine the default colors as the shade you want. Using any tool, choose Define Colors from the Paragraph menu. Under Color Name, select a color you wish to redefine (one you think you won't ever use). Choose a Color Mode (CMYK is the easiest for gray shades). Then adjust the color scroll bars until the color you want appears in the preview box, or until the desired percentages appear to the right of the scroll bars. Then click on the Rename button and type the name of your new shade. When you click on OK, this shade will appear in dialog boxes in place of the color you redefined. For example, to create a 10% gray pattern, select a Color Name such as Magenta and select the CMYK Color Mode. Set the Cyan, Magenta, and Yellow scroll bars to zero and the Black scroll bar to 10%. Click on Rename and call your new color Gray 10%. Then click on OK.

Example: Let's add a filled Box Text to the flowchart example we began earlier:

1. Select the Add Box Text tool.
2. Starting at the point of the arrow, drag diagonally down and to the right to form a box approximately three-fourths of an inch wide and one inch long. The exact size is not important.
3. With the Box Text you just drew still selected, choose Fill Attributes from the Graphic menu. Select the color Black and the second pattern. Then click on OK.

When you've finished, your screen should resemble Figure 9-9.

Formatting Box Text

Ventura assigns a tag called Z_BOXTEXT to any text you type inside a Box Text. You can format this tag as you would any other—by clicking on it with the Paragraph Tool and using the commands from the Paragraph menu. If you need more than one formatting style for Box Text, you can retag the text.

For callouts, put text inside a Box Text with no pattern and no line. To improve the appearance of your callouts, be sure to set up a grid, so they will all start from the same point. If your callouts appear to the left of pictures, consider aligning them flush right.

Box Text is useful for more than just callouts. It is also a quick, convenient way to produce labeled flowcharts.

Chapter 9: Creating Pictures in Ventura   *Creating simple shapes* **283**

Figure 9-9.
Draw a Box Text shape and fill it with a black pattern.

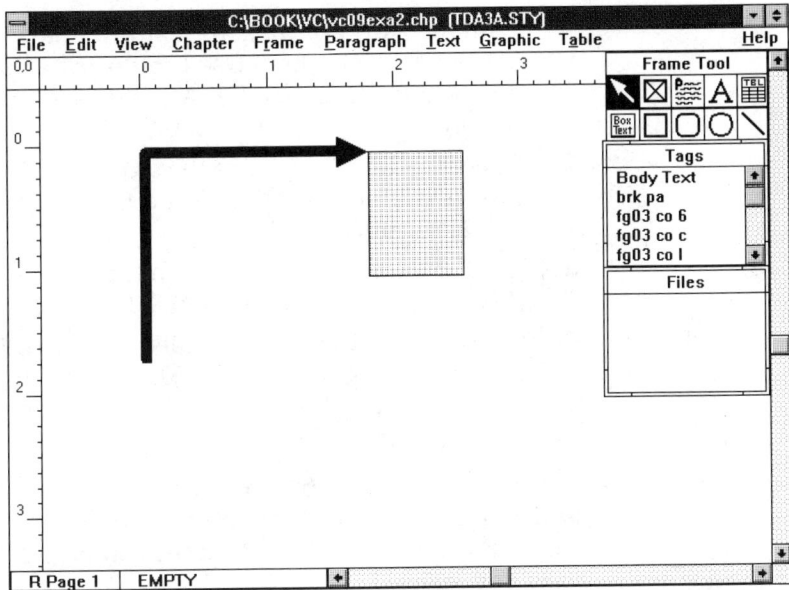

***E*xample:** Let's continue with the flowchart example we started earlier. Try adding a label to the horizontal line and to the filled rectangle to make the picture resemble Figure 9-10.

Figure 9-10.
Use Box Text to add labels. Format the labels with the Paragraph Tool.

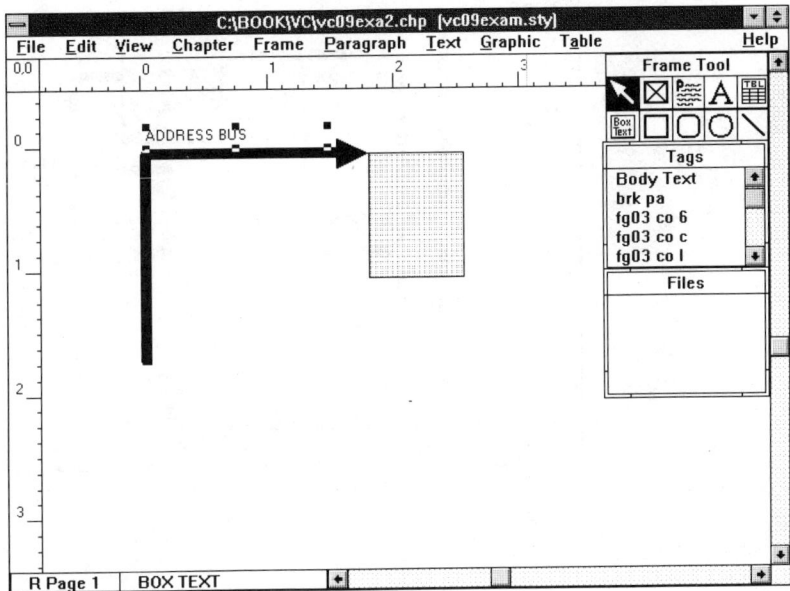

1. With the Add Box Text Tool, draw a narrow box along the top of the horizontal line. Use Line Attributes to make sure it has no line around it. Use Fill Attributes to make sure it has no fill pattern.
2. Select the Text Tool. Type the words "ADDRESS BUS" into the Box Text along the line. Type the words "MEMORY CARD 701-2120" into the filled box.
3. Use the Paragraph Tool and the Paragraph menu to format the Box Text along the line as flush left 12-point Helvetica (Swiss).
4. Select the text inside the filled box with the Paragraph Tool. Add a new tag. Call it Z_BoxCenter or something similar. Use the Paragraph Tool to format it as centered 12-point Helvetica (Swiss) Bold.

Ambitious? Want more practice with Ventura's Graphic tools. Figure 9-11 shows how you might extend the flowchart example we've started. Everything you see can be created with the techniques you learned above.

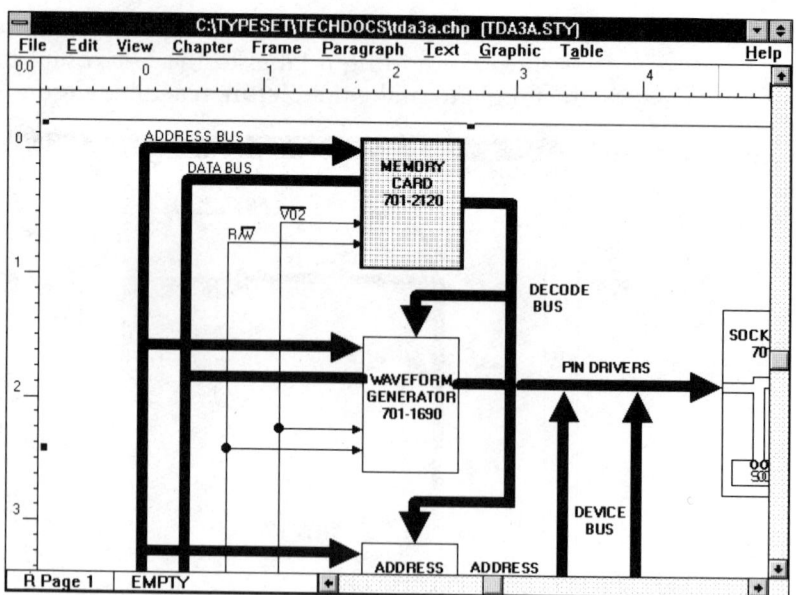

Figure 9-11.
A continuation of our flowchart example.

Advanced tips and tricks

The first part of this chapter set out the basic procedures for creating graphics with Ventura's built-in tools. Those steps will suffice if you use the Graphic tools once in a while. But if you find yourself using them frequently in your daily desktop publishing, you'll want to avail yourself of the speed and efficiency of the techniques explained below.

Using the defaults to save time

You've already seen the basic process for getting a graphic shape to look the way you want it. First, you draw the shape. Then you modify it with the Line Attributes and Fill Attributes dialog boxes.

But what if you, for instance, want all your rectangles to have a one-point line and a gray fill pattern? Why should you have to draw and change them one by one? You don't.

One way to save yourself some work is to draw one rectangle, copy it to the clipboard, then paste it in as many times as necessary. Another way to save time is to change the default settings so every rectangle has the attributes you want right from the start.

Setting default fill and line attributes

Each tool is independent of the others and has its own defaults. And each tool has two defaults, one for Line Attributes and one for Fill Attributes (except for the Add Line tool, which cannot have a fill). Setting defaults works identically in both the Line Attributes and the Fill Attributes dialog boxes. To change the defaults:

1. Select a shape with the Frame Tool.
2. Choose Line or Fill Attributes from the Graphic menu.
3. Change the settings to the way you want the defaults to appear from now on.
4. Click on Save Defaults (Figure 9-12).
5. If you want to apply these defaults to the currently selected shape, click on OK. Otherwise, click on Cancel.

Even if you click on Cancel, Ventura remembers the defaults you set. Every shape you draw from now on will have the new settings.

Figure 9-12.
To create and apply default settings for attributes, use the Commands buttons.

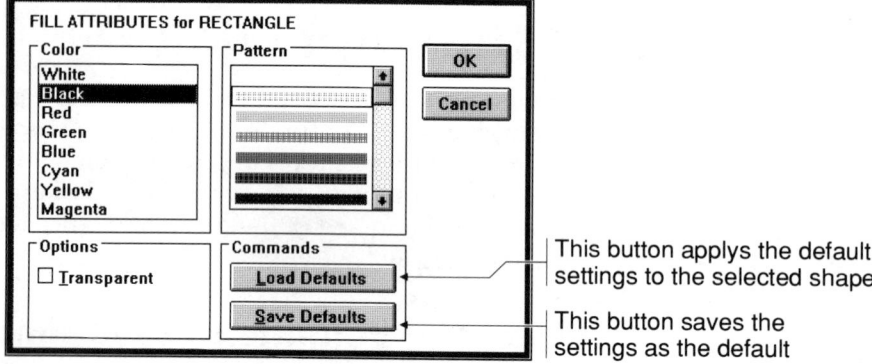

Example: Try resetting the default fill attributes so rectangles are solid black. Click on a rectangle (or draw one if you don't have one on the page). Now choose Fill Attributes from the Graphic menu. Set the color to black and the pattern to solid (the last bar in the Pattern scroll box). Click Save Defaults, then click on Cancel.

The rectangle should still look the way it did before. But if you now draw a new rectangle, it will have a solid black fill.

Copying from the defaults

Suppose you've already drawn 17 black rectangles and you change your mind. Now you want them all to have a two-point line and a white fill pattern. To speed the process of changing them, you can copy from the defaults you set up:

1. Set the defaults to the new settings (see above).
2. Select the shape (or shapes) you want to change.
3. Choose Line Attributes from the Graphic menu. Click on the Load Defaults button. Then click on OK.

You can do the same for the Fill Attributes dialog box. The default settings will be applied to the shape(s).

Tip: Don't forget that you can change shapes as a group. Use Shift-Click to highlight them all. Then use Line Attributes and Fill Attributes as you would for a single shape.

Repeating graphics on every page

With a simple command, you can cause any shape to appear on every page in the document:

1. Draw the shape.

2. With the shape still selected, choose Show On All Pages from the Graphic menu.

Repeating graphics are especially useful for custom crop marks and registration marks. Because they appear in the same place on every page, offset printers can use them for accurate positioning.

To stop a shape from repeating on every page, select the shape, then choose Show On This Page from the Graphic menu. Now the shape will show only on the current page.

Stacking and combining graphics

For more advanced effects, you can stack and combine graphic shapes. One common technique is to offset a white rectangle on top of a black one, to create a shadow. Another popular technique is to mask out unwanted portions with white shapes (Figure 9-13).

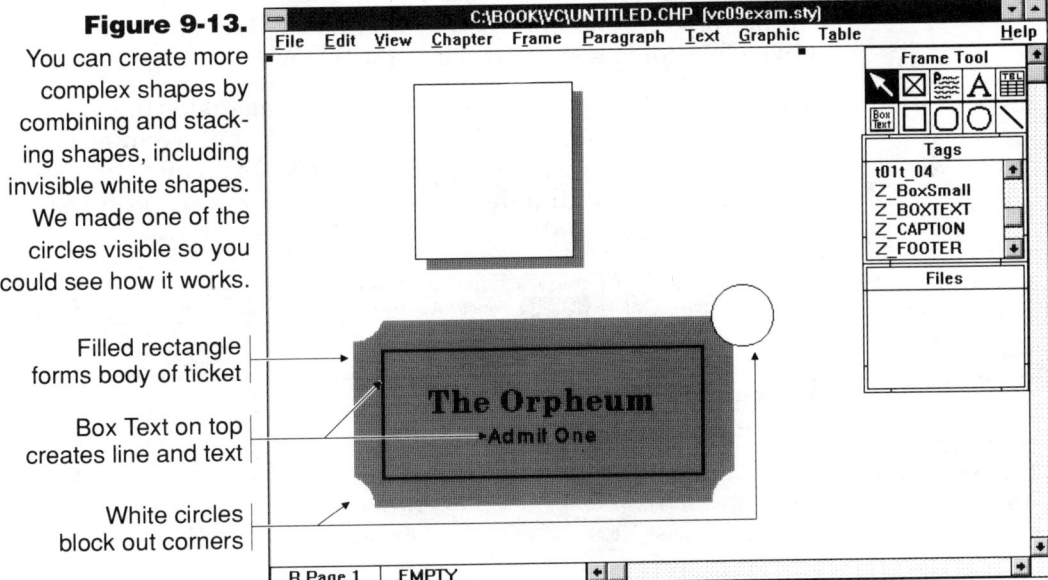

Figure 9-13. You can create more complex shapes by combining and stacking shapes, including invisible white shapes. We made one of the circles visible so you could see how it works.

Filled rectangle forms body of ticket

Box Text on top creates line and text

White circles block out corners

Remember these things when combining and stacking objects:

- You can change the stacking order with the Send To Back and Bring To Front commands in the Graphic menu.
- If a shape gets buried under several others, you don't have to move all the ones on top to get to it. Put the cursor over the spot where you know the shape to be. Now hold down the Ctrl key as you click on the left button of the mouse. Ventura will cycle

through the layers of shapes, one each time you click. Stop when you get to the one you want.

- Although you cannot group objects, you can attach them all to the same parent frame, so they will move as a group.
- You can duplicate many of these stacking effects with frames, which can also have fills (using the Frame Background command from the Frame menu).

Positioning graphics with frames

Often you don't need more than the ruler and the snap-to grid to position your graphics. In other cases, however, it may be essential to be precise. For instance, if you are drawing crop marks or registration marks, they must be in exactly the right place.

If you need this kind of precision, attach the graphic shapes to an invisible frame, then use the frame to position the graphics. Frames can be moved with the mouse, of course. But they can also be moved by typing coordinates into the Sizing & Scaling dialog box.

The X and Y coordinates in the Sizing & Scaling dialog box apply to the upper left corner of the frame. For this reason, we suggest that you attach the shapes to the upper left corner of an invisible frame. Then you can move the shapes by specifying new coordinates for the frame (Figure 9-14).

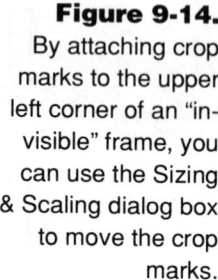

Figure 9-14. By attaching crop marks to the upper left corner of an "invisible" frame, you can use the Sizing & Scaling dialog box to move the crop marks.

Continuing on

This chapter has explained the essentials of Ventura's built-in Graphic tools. You learned how to choose the parent frame, set up a grid, draw a shape, and edit it. You also saw how to save time by using the default attributes, and how to create advanced effects with repeating graphics, stacked graphics, and precise positioning. In the next chapter, you'll learn how to work with pictures created with outside programs.

Easy Access

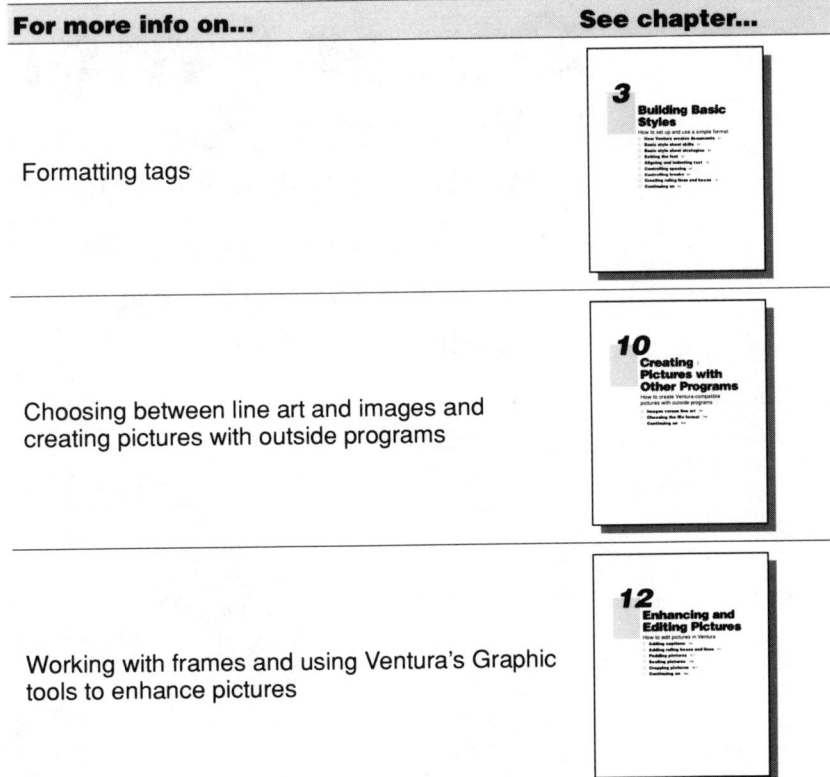

For more info on...	See chapter...
Formatting tags	3 — Building Basic Styles
Choosing between line art and images and creating pictures with outside programs	10 — Creating Pictures with Other Programs
Working with frames and using Ventura's Graphic tools to enhance pictures	12 — Enhancing and Editing Pictures

10 Creating Pictures with Other Programs

How to create Ventura-compatible pictures with outside programs

- **Images versus line art** 291
- **Choosing the file format** 298
- **Continuing on** 308

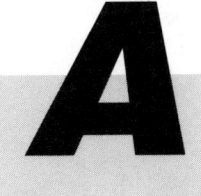As you saw in the previous chapter, you can produce rudimentary pictures with Ventura's built-in Graphic tools. But most Ventura users need pictures from outside programs for their documents—technical illustrations for their manuals, clip art for their flyers, scanned photographs for their company newsletters, and so on. Fortunately, Ventura is compatible with many different picture file formats from many different programs.

But Ventura's versatility has a price—the burden of making the right choices. First, you have to decide which type of graphics to use (Ventura accepts two kinds). Then you must choose the best file format, because most outside programs have several options.

In this chapter, you'll learn how to make those decisions. You need these skills *even if you aren't the one who does the actual drawing*. As the Ventura operator, it will be up to you to tell illustrators which file formats to use, choose the right type of clip art, or figure out the best way to capture computer screens for your document.

This is not a step-by-step chapter, because we hardly have room to go through the dozens of graphics programs on the market. Rather, it's a collection of strategies and shortcuts that make it easier to coexist with the outside world. In this chapter, we'll begin with an explanation of how Ventura distinguishes between *line art* and *images*. Then we'll look at these two kinds of pictures in more detail, with ideas on which file formats work best for which situations.

Images versus line art

You can import two types of pictures into Ventura: *line art* and *images*. The rest of the graphics world uses these words to mean other things, so it's important to understand Ventura's definitions. Indeed, you have to know the differences just to bring in a picture. The Load Text/Picture dialog box requires you to choose the type of picture before you can select a file format and load the picture (Figures 10-1 and 10-2).

We'll give you a brief definition of each type of picture and its pros and cons so you know how to choose the one that suits your needs.

Figure 10-1.
You have to choose between line art and images to load a picture

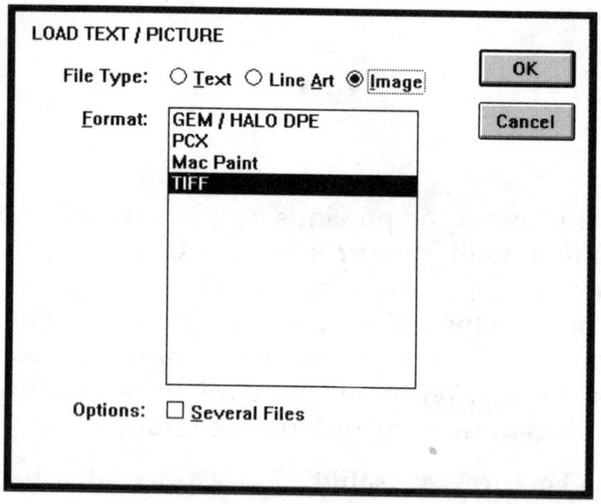

LOAD TEXT / PICTURE

File Type: ○ Text ○ Line Art ● Image

Format: GEM / HALO DPE
PCX
Mac Paint
TIFF

Options: ☐ Several Files

[OK] [Cancel]

Figure 10-2.

LOAD TEXT / PICTURE

File Type: ○ Text ● Line Art ○ Image

Format: GEM
Windows Metafile
AutoCad .SLD
Lotus .PIC
VideoShow
Mac PICT
CGM
PostScript
HPGL

Options: ☐ Several Files

[OK] [Cancel]

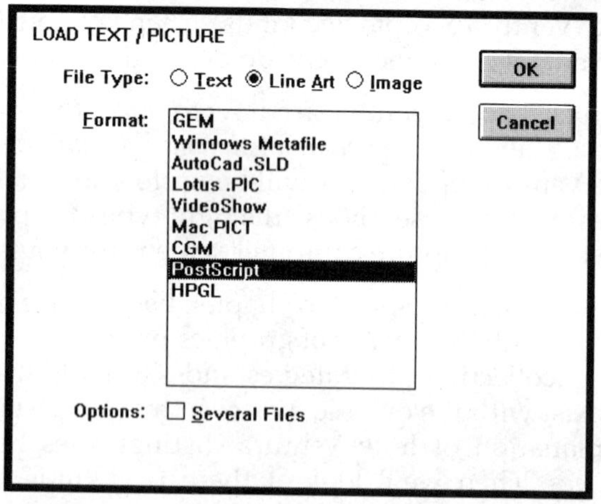

Line art defined

Line art is a mathematical description of a picture. You may see it referred to as *vector-based* art. Programs that produce line art are usually called *draw* programs. Corel Draw is one popular example. Programs that produce bit-mapped images (which we'll discuss in the next section), are called *paint* programs. The Paintbrush accessory that comes free with Windows is an example.

If you tell a draw program to produce a line, it sends a mathematical description to the printer. The printer then does the best job it can of interpreting that description. A low-resolution 300 dots per inch (dpi) laser printer will interpret it at 300 dpi. A high-resolution typesetter might interpret that same description at 2540 dpi.

By contrast, the resolution (the dots per inch) of an image never varies. If you send a 72 dpi line to a laser printer, it will come out at 72 dpi. Send that same line to a high-resolution typesetter and it will still print at 72 dpi (see Figure 10-3).

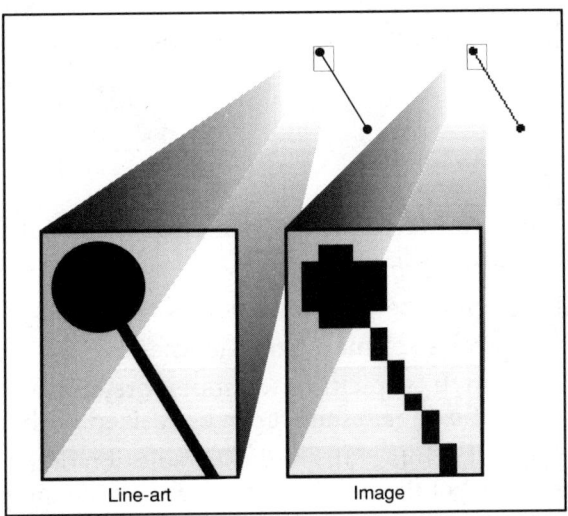

Figure 10-3. Line art (left) is a mathematical description, so it is reproduced at the highest resolution of the printer. Images (right) are instructions to turn dots on or off, so they look jagged when enlarged.

Line art has several advantages. It looks smoother, because it always prints at the highest resolution of the printer. And tints (gray areas) stay as fine, even if you enlarge or reduce the picture (Figure 10-4).

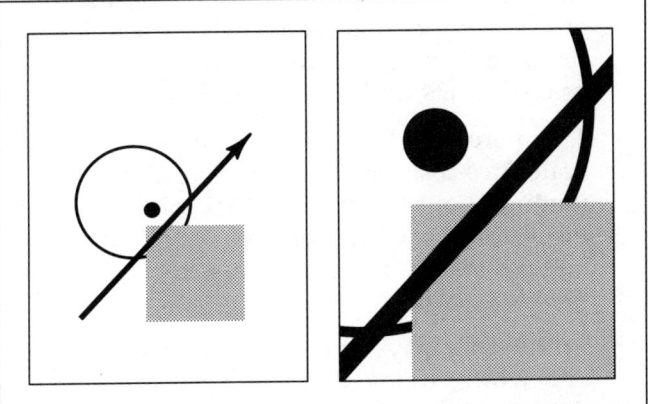

Figure 10-4. Shapes produced by a line-art program. Note the smoothness of lines, even when enlarged, and that the tint resolution remains the same.

By contrast, the tints in an image change, because they are made up of dot patterns. If you enlarge the picture, the dots that make up the picture become larger, as does the space between the dots (Figure 10-5).

Figure 10-5.
Shapes produced by an image program. Note the jagged edges of the lines (especially when enlarged) and the change in tint resolution.

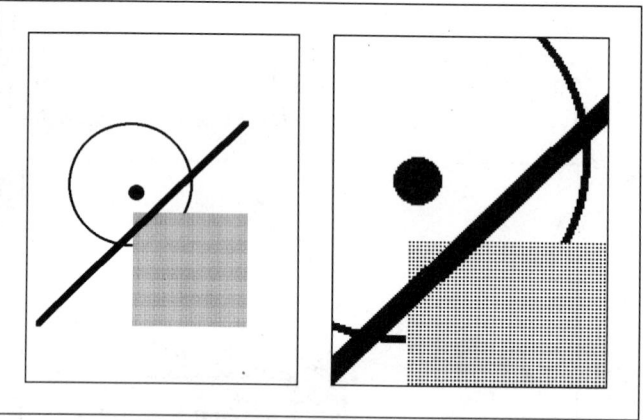

Let's summarize the strong points of line art:

- Line art looks smoother than images.
- You can draw pictures without worrying about the size they will be on the page. Line art can be resized without a loss in quality.
- Line art prints at the highest resolution of the output device. You always get the best picture your printer can produce.
- Drawing complex shapes is faster because line-art objects are moveable and can be sized without loss of quality.

Bit-mapped images defined

In Ventura, an image is a *bitmap*. A bit-mapped image is like a piece of graph paper that has some squares filled and some empty (Figure 10-6). These squares are called *pixels*. A computer screen is a grid of pixels, and a bit-mapped image is a recording of that grid.

There are two types of bit-mapped images: two-color and gray-scale. *Two-color* or *black-and-white* images record only on/off information about each pixel. Each pixel, then, must be either either black (on) or white (off). *Gray-scale* images contain information about shading. Each pixel can be black, white, or some shade of gray in between.

In the early days of desktop publishing, most images were black and white. Today, however, gray-scale images are important for such things as scanned photographs and screen captures. For instance, the computer screens in this book were captured with gray-scale information. That is why the buttons have the same shaded appearance they do on screen. If we had used a black-and-white image instead, the buttons would have been black. Ventura accepts

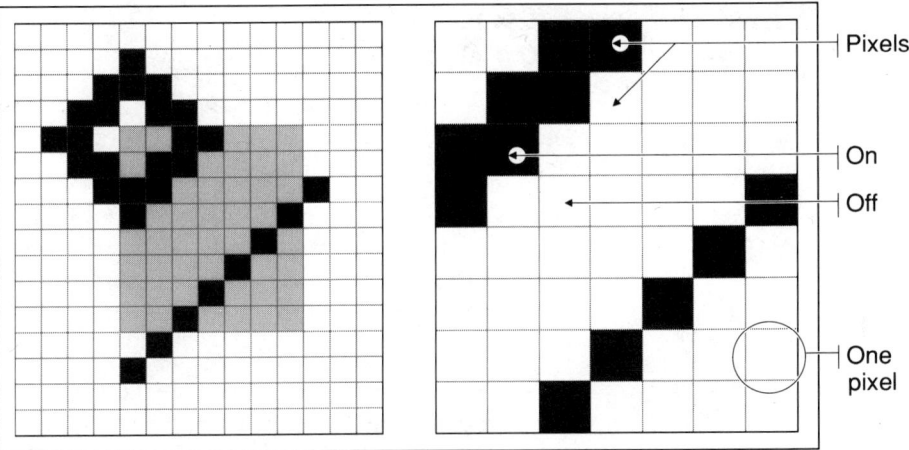

Figure 10-6.
Think of bit-mapped images as graph paper with some of the squares filled in. When a bit-mapped image is enlarged, each pixel is enlarged, which, on diagonals and curves, leads to an effect known as the "jaggies."

one image format (TIFF) that can contain gray-scale information. (More on that later in the chapter.)

As you have seen, line art has many advantages. If you have the choice, it's often the best way to go. But there are some times when you don't have that choice. If you need to bring in a sample computer screen, for instance, it will have to be an image. There are several other situations that call for images:

- When you need to scan a photograph or drawing from paper. A scanner is a device that converts a paper image into electronic form. It does this by turning it into a bitmap (see the nearby sidebar "Understanding scanners" to learn how this happens).
- When you want texture effects like those from the side of a crayon, the strokes of a paintbrush, or the pen and ink technique known as stipple (Figure 10-7).

Figure 10-7.
Example of how a bit-mapped image can faithfully reproduce a *stipple* effect.

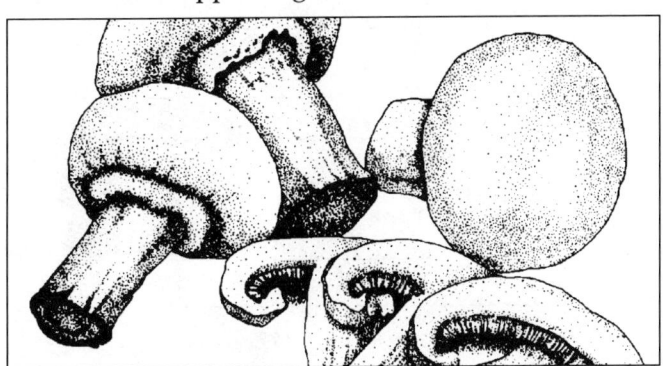

Understanding scanners

One of the best ways to get existing artwork into Ventura is to use a scanner. A scanner has an optical sensing device that looks at a picture and converts it to electronic form.

However, many otherwise experienced desktop publishers don't understand how scanners work. In particular, they are confused by the differences between *black-and-white* scanning, *gray-scale scanning*, and *dithering*. Don't worry. In this sidebar, we'll clarify the differences.

Let's assume that we want to digitize a printed picture that has a continuous range of tones, from light gray at the left to black at the right. A scanner would divide this picture into tiny cells. Then it would look at each cell to determine how to render it (Figure 10-8).

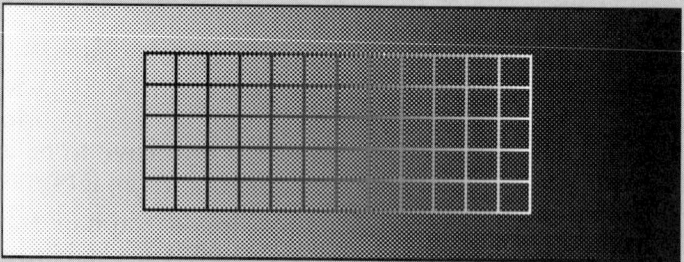

Figure 10-8. Digitizing involves a mechanical (scanner) perception of small units of an image, as though in a grid.

In a black-and-white (or "two-color") scan, the only decision is whether to make the cell black or white. Figure 10-9 shows what would happen if we scanned the picture from our first example in black-and-white mode. As you can see, anything below a certain amount of gray is rendered as white. Anything above that threshold comes out as black.

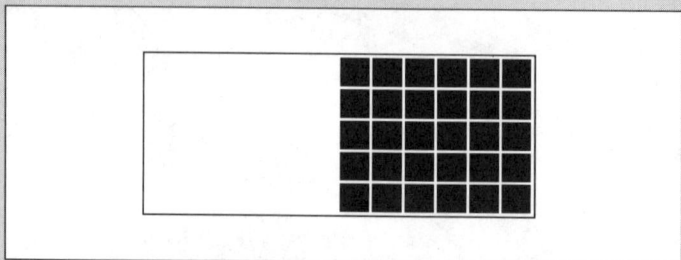

Figure 10-9. A black and white (or "two-color") scan requires grays to be converted to one or the other— no in-betweens.

If we now perform a gray-scale scan instead, the scanner will look at each cell and record its gray-scale value (Figure 10-10). The more shades of gray the scanner can perceive, the better the quality of the resulting picture. A scanner capable of 16 shades of gray can perform basic functions, but you need one capable of distinguishing 256 shades to get decent results from photographs.

Figure 10-10. A gray-scale scan compares the perceived gray of each unit to one of the available shades of gray (16 here) and picks the closest.

Some scanners can simulate gray through a process called dithering. Dithering doesn't use actual gray values. Rather, it groups pixels into larger clumps or cells. Then it turns some of the pixels white and some black to simulate gray when viewed from a distance (Figure 10-11). To show a light gray, the clump of cells would have many white pixels and a few black ones. To show a dark gray, it would have many black pixels and a few white ones.

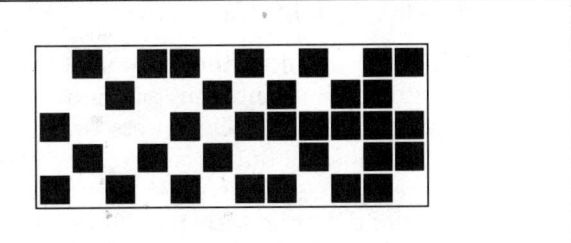

Figure 10-11. A dithered scan mimicks the perceived gray by alternating black and white dots.

- When you need to create a quick sketch in a hurry. So-called *paint* programs—which produce images—are usually easier to learn and use than *draw* programs, which produce line art.
- When money is an issue. Paint programs are less expensive than draw programs. Windows even comes with a free paint program called Paintbrush.

However, bit-mapped images have disadvantages, too:
- They tend to appear of lower quality because of the jaggies—the stair-step appearance of diagonal lines and circles.
- The aspect ratio (the proportion of width to height in a picture) is hard to control. A circle that looks round on screen may be flattened or elongated when it prints.
- Large images, particularly those with gray-scale information, take a long time to load and print.

In summary, then, you should use line art when quality and accuracy are required: for technical drawings, product illustrations, glossy advertising materials, and so on. You should use an image when ultimate quality isn't essential—a church flyer, for instance—and for scanned photographs and computer screen captures.

Choosing the file format

You've just learned the differences between line art and images. Even after you've chosen which type you want, you still need to decide which file format to use.

You need to know the format of picture files so that Ventura can recognize them and convert them. The file extensions are usually a clue to the format. Designers often refer to picture file formats by their extension. But be careful, because two programs can generate files with the same extension but a different format, such as VideoShow and Lotus with the PIC extension. For a table to help you remember which extensions belong with which formats, see Chapter 21, "Rapid Reference.")

In addition to recognizing the formats of files given to you by others, you may need to choose a format for your own drawings. Many programs can generate more than one format. For instance, PC Paintbrush can generate and edit both PCX and TIF images. Corel Draw can generate PCX, EPS (Encapsulated PostScript), TIF, GEM, and more.

If you're stuck with a program that can't create a format Ventura recognizes, check the nearby sidebar "Working with unsupported formats" for suggestions.

To help you handle file formats correctly, let's look at them in more detail, first for line art and then for images.

Choosing a line art format

When you click on the Line Art button in the Load Text/Picture dialog box, Ventura presents you with nine options:

1. GEM
2. Windows Metafile
3. AutoCad .SLD
4. Lotus .PIC
5. VideoShow

Working with unsupported formats

You should always check to see if a graphics program can save to a format supported directly by Ventura. But if it cannot, you can still find a way to use your creations. Obviously, you should first check to see if the program can save files to a supported format. If not, here are a four things to try:

- Use the "print to disk" function. If the program supports PostScript, choose PostScript as the printer and print to a disk file.

- Use a screen capture program. If you have a screen capture program such as Tiffany, you can create a bit-mapped image of a picture directly from the program's screen.

- Use the clipboard. Press the PrintScreen key and an image of the screen will be placed on the clipboard. Open the Paintbrush accessory (or another Windows paint program) and choose Paste from the Edit menu to bring the picture in from the clipboard. Now save the file in PCX format and load it into Ventura.

- Use a third-party file conversion program such as HiJaak from Inset Systems. Such programs can transfer files back and forth between many different formats.

6. Mac PICT
7. CGM
8. PostScript
9. HPGL

Most of these formats are associated with a specific file extension—GEM with the (you guessed it) GEM extension, Windows Metafile with the WMF extension, and so on.

Most draw programs can produce files in several different formats. Which one should you use? You don't always have a choice, especially if you're an editor who gets files from outside illustrators. Because you may run into any or all of these formats during your desktop publishing career, we're going to discuss all nine to show you their strengths and weaknesses.

However, when you *do* have a choice, the three best options are PostScript, HPGL, and Windows Metafile.

Warning: In theory, each file format is standardized. In practice, they come in different "flavors." Sometimes Ventura can't handle a file even though it's in one of the supported file formats. If you can't bring a file in, or if the picture looks wrong (black and white are reversed, for instance), you may need to go back to the graphics program and try a different format.

The GEM format

Although Ventura now runs under Windows, it was originally written for GEM, an alternative operating system. Ventura still uses the native GEM format internally for many line art functions.

Because GEM is Ventura's "preferred" format, a GEM picture loads and prints more quickly. However, the GEM format is limited. It does not offer the rich shading, texturing, filling, and font options of other formats such as PostScript. In addition, it is not supported by a wide range of programs.

Still, you should consider using the GEM format if (1) the outside program supports it and (2) the picture does not contain complex shading or textures.

The Windows Metafile format

Windows own Metafile format (WMF extension) has some unique advantages. The Metafile format is used by Windows' Clipboard. This lets you trade pictures between programs without saving them to a separate file. Suppose you've created an illustration in a draw program. You can then copy it to the Clipboard, switch to Ventura, and paste it into a frame directly. You name the file at the time you paste it.

In addition to the Clipboard method, you can also use the WMF format the way you would any other format—save to a WMF file, then bring it into Ventura with the Load Text/Picture dialog box. For more information on loading picture files, see Chapter 11, "Loading and Placing Pictures." Popular draw programs such as Corel Draw, Micrografx Designer, and Arts & Letters export to the Windows Metafile format (WMF).

Unfortunately, WMF has some problems. Its files can get unwieldy. Text characters often suffer undesirable side effects with WMF. Colors are not always interpreted correctly. In addition, Ventura doesn't support embedded images or all the Metafile special effects. But if your line art contains no characters and no unusual special effects, you can have pictures with this format that are equivalent in quality to EPS (PostScript) format files, which are usually used as the benchmark for quality.

The AutoCad .SLD format

There are several ways to get drawings from AutoCAD to Ventura Publisher. An AutoCAD slide file (SLD extension) is generally the worst option. This format can distort dimensions. It can also lose some of the text and fill information. We recommend the PostScript or HPGL formats instead.

The Lotus .PIC format

You probably know that you can use the Lotus 1-2-3 spreadsheet to generate text files for Ventura. You can also turn a Lotus spreadsheet into graphs and charts that can then be loaded into Ventura as line art.

To create a Lotus graph or chart, load the spreadsheet file that contains the data. Type /G to access the graph menu. Select the type of graph and the range of data. To see the graph, choose View from the Graph menu. To save the graph to a file, choose the Save command. Lotus will save the graph in PIC file format, which loads directly into Ventura.

Lotus charts have some limitations. The shading and cross-hatching is crude compared to some other spreadsheets. More importantly, the chart's labels come in with the rest of the chart, whether you want them or not. Their appearance usually does not fit with the rest of your document.

Tip: If you don't like the position or appearance of the Lotus labels (and you probably won't), cover them up with an opaque white rectangle. Then use Box Text to add your own labels. For help in drawing rectangles and Box Text, see Chapter 9, "Creating Pictures in Ventura."

The Mac PICT format

Ventura's support of the PICT format is designed to let you accept files created on a Macintosh. In practice, however, most people use the PostScript (EPS) format instead. It's more accurate and has fewer limitations. Any Macintosh drawing program can create a PostScript file.

If you decide to try the PICT format, be aware that Ventura will automatically convert any text to Times or Helvetica. (By contrast, a PostScript file can specify any type size or style.) In addition, Ventura cannot accept bit-mapped images embedded within a PICT file.

The VideoShow format

The VideoShow format was originally developed for slide presentations. It was in wide use by MS-DOS presentation programs such as Lotus Freelance Plus. Today, most MS-DOS programs can produce files in formats better suited to Ventura. Although Ventura can bring in simple VideoShow files, it cannot convert some of the things people take for granted in presentations these days, such as 3D bars.

The CGM format

The CGM file format was an early attempt at a graphics file standard (the initials stand for Computer Graphics Metafile). But different companies implemented the standard in different ways. As a result, Ventura may be able to read and convert one CGM file but not another. Even if the file reads in successfully, you may not be able to print the page.

The CGM format is fine when it works, but frustrating when it doesn't. Don't be afraid to experiment with it, but if you experience problems, switch to another format.

The PostScript format

Almost all programs can produce PostScript files, which usually have the EPS extension (for Encapsulated PostScript). For instance, any Windows program can produce PostScript files by using Windows' built-in EPS capability. You simply install a PostScript printer driver (even if you don't actually own a PostScript printer). Then you use the Printer Setup command to go to the printer options to send the output to an Encapsulated PostScript file instead of to a printer.

If you have a PostScript-compatible printer, EPS is the best format for Ventura for three reasons:

- EPS files will generate the most accurate reproduction of your artwork.
- EPS files have superior text handling capabilities.
- EPS files can be sized and scaled without regard for the original size of the artwork.

But PostScript does have two big disadvantages. First, it cannot be printed on non-PostScript machines, such as the popular Hewlett-Packard LaserJet series. Second, a PostScript file does not show up on screen. It displays as a large X, making it difficult to preview your pages.

There is a partial solution to both problems. Some drawing packages can generate a TIFF file to go along with the EPS file. (TIFF is one of the bit-mapped image formats discussed later in the chapter.) This TIFF file—called an *image header*—is a "copy" of the EPS drawing. Ventura can use the TIFF version to display on screen, and to print out to non-PostScript printers.

We called this a partial solution because the on-screen version does not always correspond accurately to the line art (EPS). As a result, any positioning you attempt in Ventura may be off. For instance, if you use callouts and arrows to point to parts of the picture, they may not be accurate.

In addition, the printed TIFF file will not have the same high-resolution as a PostScript file. However, the TIFF image header option is a good way to proof PostScript files on a non-PostScript printer. For instance, you could use your LaserJet to proof a brochure before you sent it to a service bureau for high-resolution PostScript typesetting. When you send the same file to a PostScript device, it automatically prints the PostScript file.

Tip: Users of CAD packages can create a PostScript file by installing a PostScript printer driver and printing to a disk file. They can also buy a supplemental DeskConvert utility from Generic Software that converts drawings into PostScript files. DeskConvert can also generate a bit-mapped PCX file.

The HPGL format

HPGL stands for Hewlett-Packard Graphics Language. It was developed to control the plotters used by computer-aided drafting and design (CADD) programs. (A plotter is a device that uses pens to produce marks on paper. It can print on the oversize paper needed for blueprints and engineering diagrams).

The HPGL format doesn't do a good job with text, shades, and patterns. For instance, it translates each letter into a tiny drawing, not into a standard font. So it's not the right choice if you are doing graphics arts illustrations with programs such as Corel Draw.

But HPGL may be the best option for users of CADD software who produce technical drawings. Ventura lets you control how the file is converted. For instance, most plotters use more than one pen. Ventura lets you assign each pen a different line width and color. You can make these settings in a dialog box that appears after you've loaded the file with the Load Text Picture dialog box. With some experimentation, you can get a picture into Ventura with the precision and detail necessary for engineering applications.

You don't have to own a plotter to use HPGL format. Simply configure the software for an HP plotter, then print to a file.

Choosing an image format

Ventura can import four image formats:
1. GEM/HALO DPE
2. PCX
3. Mac Paint
4. TIFF

Below we've explained the pros and cons of each one so you can make the right selection.

Tip: To save disk space and speed up Ventura, keep image files as small as possible by using a small page size. Even if most of the page is blank, those white pixels still take up space in the picture file. If you have a small image, paste it onto a small page.

The GEM/HALO DPE format

This menu selection refers to the historical origins of the format rather than to its common name. It refers to the IMG format, which has advantages when working in Ventura, but some disadvantages when working with other programs.

As mentioned earlier, Ventura was originally written for the GEM operating environment, which works with the IMG format. Although Ventura has been redesigned to run under Windows, it still uses the IMG format internally. Because IMG is Ventura's native format, it's the easiest one to use. It loads, redraws on screen, and prints faster than any other. And it takes up less disk space than the other three formats. In fact, when you use the PCX and TIFF format (see below), Ventura creates a duplicate file in IMG format, so you end up using almost twice the disk space as you would if you had started with IMG in the first place.

As far as Ventura is concerned, the IMG format is the cleanest solution. Unfortunately, it has drawbacks when working with outside programs. Very few paint packages can import and export IMG files. And the IMG format cannot contain gray-scale information, only black-and-white. For these two reasons, you may not be able to use the IMG format.

The PCX format

The PCX format offers the advantage of compatibility. It was established as a standard many years ago by ZSoft's PC Paintbrush program. It is now supported by many other programs. All paint programs support it, including Windows' built-in Paintbrush program. In addition, virtually all desktop publishing programs and even some word processing programs can import PCX files. Almost all scanners can create PCX images. And even draw packages, which produce line art, can import PCX files for tracing or for embedding within a line art file.

However, there are some negative points to the PCX format. First, it often takes up more disk space than the corresponding IMG file. To compound this, Ventura can't display PCX on screen, so it makes a copy in IMG format. You end up with two files instead of one (Ventura uses the same name, but gives the second one the IMG extension).

In addition, Ventura accepts only black-and-white PCX files. There is a color PCX format, but Ventura will not accept it. Even if you only draw in black-and-white, you cannot save the image as a color PCX file if you want Ventura to use it. This limitation also means that you cannot get any gray-scale information in a PCX file. For gray scale pictures, you must use the TIFF format.

MacPaint

This format comes from Macintosh paint programs such as MacPaint and SuperPaint. It often has the MAC extension. Unfortunately, files in this format transfer as letter size pages, even if you only want a small section. Usually, you have to transfer the image to the PC from the Mac, open it in a PC paint program, and cut out the piece you want. Otherwise, you end up with a small picture swimming in a sea of white.

These days, most Macintosh paint programs can also save files to the TIFF format, which is generally more useful (see below).

The TIFF format

TIFF stands for Tagged Image File Format, a specification developed by Microsoft and Aldus. Files in this format, that originate on MSDOS systems, usually have the TIF extension. It has gained widespread acceptance and is now supported by most graphics and desktop publishing programs on both the IBM PC-compatible and the Macintosh platforms.

The TIFF format is your only option for electronic halftones (scanned photos) and gray-scale screen captures. For instance, the sample screens in this book were captured with a program called Tiffany. Tiffany converted the colors on the screen to shades of gray.

TIFF is the only format that can retain gray-scale information from scanned photos or screen captures. Ventura even lets you change the angle and resolution of the dots that make up a TIFF gray scale image. No other format gives you this control. To use this capability, you select the frame containing the TIFF image and choose Image Settings from the Frame menu (Figures 10-12 through 10-14).

Controlling image settings is an advanced function that rarely comes into play. First of all, it applies only to gray scale images printed on PostScript printers. Second, Ventura's default options are the best choice for most situations. These defaults are stored in the printer and optimized for that particular device.

Still, there may be a few instances in which you wish to modify the defaults with the Image Settings dialog box. For instance, you can use it to create special effects (Figures 10-13 and 10-14). Consult with an experienced printer or graphic artist for more details on

Figure 10-12. Ventura allows you to change the screen type, the angle of the screen, and the number of lines per inch (see Figures 10-13 and 10-14).

Figure 10-13. This image uses the default settings for screen type, angle (00) and lines per inch (0000). This is how it would appear on a 300 dpi printer.

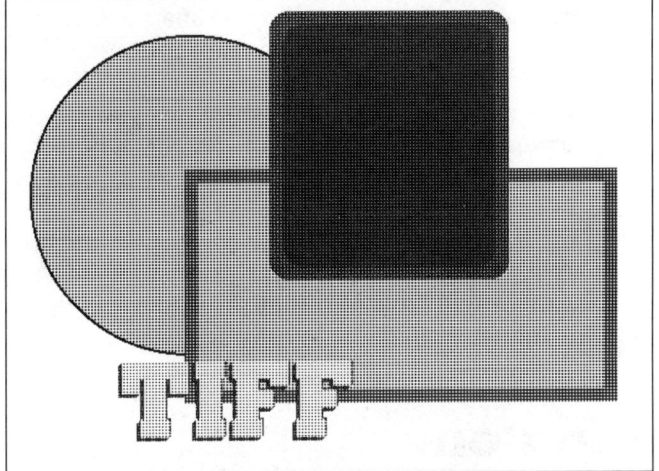

Figure 10-14. This image uses the Line type of screen, at a 45 degree angle and at 25 lines per inch.

how to change the appearance of a gray-scale picture by altering its screen type and angle with the Image Settings dialog box.

On the down side, a gray-scale TIFF file takes up a lot of space on the disk and takes a long time to print. In addition, Ventura creates an IMG file to display on the screen—just like a PCX file. If you don't need gray shades, be sure to save in a black-and-white TIFF format, not in a gray or color TIFF format.

Tip: Need to put a picture of a computer screen in your manual? You don't need a Polaroid. You can use the Windows Clipboard or a screen capture utility. Screen capture programs run in the background, ready and waiting to snap a digital picture of the screen. They save the picture as a file. Commercial utilities like Tiffany—the one we used in this book—let you choose which file format to save in. Most of them also allow you to choose the area of the screen to capture. You can get the whole thing, just the smaller active windows, or some smaller area you select by drawing a box.

Tip: If you are scanning photographs, use the TIFF format if possible. If you use the black-and-white PCX or IMG formats, the scanner will have to dither them to simulate grays. The quality will be higher with the true gray scales available in the TIFF format.

Continuing on

Now you have the complete picture about working with outside graphics programs. You learned that Ventura categorizes all pictures as line art or images. And you know how to decide which type is best for your needs. In addition, you found out how to determine which file format to use.

After you've created a picture with an outside program, you'll want to load it into Ventura and place it on the page. You may also want to edit and enhance the picture. You'll learn those skills in the next two chapters.

Chapter 10: Creating Pictures with Other Programs

Easy Access

For more info on...	See chapter...
Drawing pictures with Ventura's built-in Graphic tools	9 — Creating Pictures in Ventura
Loading and placing pictures on the page	11 — Loading and Placing Pictures
Enhancing and editing pictures	12 — Enhancing and Editing Pictures
Learning by example—real-life samples of documents with outside pictures	20 — Portfolio
Using the correct file extensions	21 — Rapid Reference

11

Loading and Placing Pictures

How to import picture files
into a Ventura document

- **Creating frames** 311
- **Loading pictures into frames** 324
- **Adding margins inside frames** 328
- **Anchoring frames** 331
- **Continuing on** 338

In the previous chapter, you found out that you can use outside programs to create pictures for Ventura documents. In this chapter, you'll learn how to load those pictures into a chapter and place them onto the page. Adding a picture involves four steps:

- Creating a frame to contain the picture
- Loading the picture into the chapter and putting it into the frame
- Putting margins inside the frame (optional)
- Anchoring the frame (optional)

We're going to step you through this process. We've also included a hands-on example you can follow through the whole chapter.

Example: To get a feel for working with frames, create a practice chapter that you can use throughout the chapter for our frame experiments. Open the example chapter &PRPT-P2.CHP from the \TYPESET directory. Use Save As from the File menu to save it as FRAME.CHP. (If you did not install Ventura's examples, do so now.) Next, select the existing frame in the right column and press the Delete key to remove it from the page. Finally, go to the View menu and be sure that Column Snap and Line Snap are *not* selected (do not have a checkmark next to them). Now you have a chapter ready and waiting, so that you can try each skill that you learn in this chapter.

Creating frames

Before you can put a picture onto a page, you have to create a container for it. This container forms a boundary for the picture and separates it from other text and graphics.

You create that container by drawing a frame. But there's more to it than simply slapping a frame down onto the page. In many cases, you also need to change its size or position. You can also make frames repeat on every page of the chapter.

Drawing frames

If you've been through Chapter 9, "Creating Pictures in Ventura," then you already know how to draw a frame because it is almost identical to using Ventura's Add Rectangle tool to create a rectangle. But even though the process is the same—choose a tool and drag with the mouse—the resulting frame is different from a graphic rectangle.

Like graphic rectangles, frames can appear anywhere on the page. They can have ruling lines around them. They can have backgrounds (colors and patterns) inside.

So far, frames sound like the rectangles you draw with Ventura's Add Rectangle tool. But frames have additional capabilities that set them apart. They can contain other files (either text or pictures). And they also have margins and columns inside, as well as padding outside (Figure 11-1).

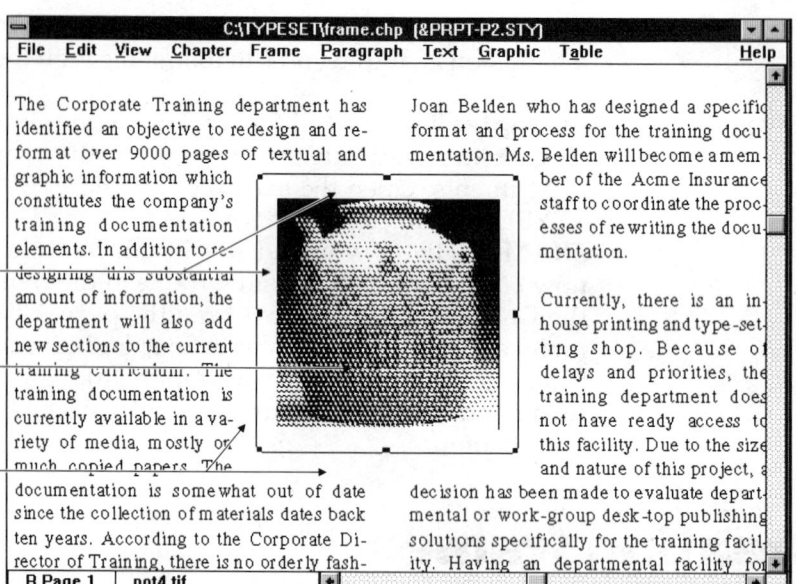

Figure 11-1. Frames can contain files. They can have margins inside and padding around the outside.

Margin inside the frame

Picture file inside the frame

Padding outside the frame keeps text from touching

To draw a frame:

1. Select the Add Frame tool from the Toolbox.
2. Place the cursor where you want the upper left corner of the frame to appear.
3. Drag the mouse down diagonally to the right.

4. When you've stretched the frame to its full size, release the mouse button.

Tip: Work in Reduced View to draw frames in their approximate size and position. Then switch to Normal View for fine tuning.

Tip: To draw several frames in a row, hold down the Shift key as you draw the frames with Add Frame Tool. When you release the mouse button, the cursor will remain in its Add Frame shape, so you can draw another frame without reselecting the Add Frame tool again.

Example: If you're following along with our practice chapter, try drawing a frame before we move on to sizing and positioning frames. Here's how:

1. If the column guides are not already visible, choose Show Column Guides from the View menu, so that you can see the columns of the underlying page and use them as guides. Then choose Reduced View from the View menu.
2. Select the Add Frame tool from the Toolbox.
3. Move the mouse cursor just below the first long text paragraph in the first column, against the left edge of the column.
4. Hold down the left mouse button as you drag the cursor across both columns and down to the lower right corner of the right column. Release the mouse button (Figure 11-2). Don't bother to match the sample screen exactly. In a few moments, we're going to show you how to adjust the size and position with complete precision.

Changing the size of frames

When you create a frame, you want its size to relate to the picture that will go inside. If you plan to insert a picture of the Empire State Building, you don't want a frame that is short and squat. If you plan to insert a 3 x 5-inch photo, you want the frame to be exactly 3 x 5 inches. In our practice chapter, we wanted to put in a picture that's wider than it is tall, so we drew a frame to match.

But you don't have to worry about exact sizing when you first draw the frame. Ventura makes it easy to change the size: You can type the exact dimensions in a dialog box. So as you draw frames, just try to approximate the final size and position. Then you can fine tune them with the procedures we're going to teach you next.

Figure 11-2.
After deleting the frame in the original chapter, use the Add Frame tool to draw a new one.

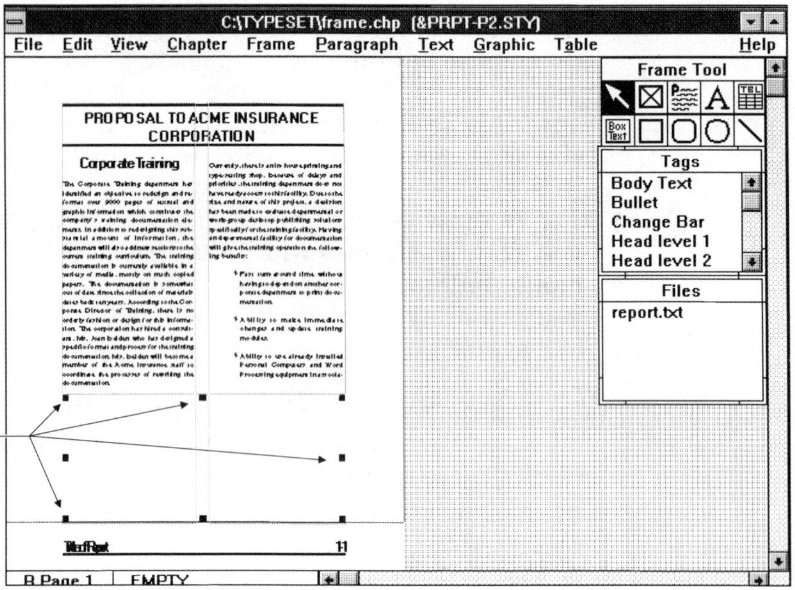

Sizing handles

Sizing frames with the mouse

The easiest way to change the size of a frame is to use the mouse to grab one of the sizing handles around the edges. Then you can stretch the frame to its new size.

It's a breeze. Simply select the Frame Tool, place the cursor over one of the sizing handles, hold down the left mouse button, drag the handle until its the size you want, and release the button. The sizing handles on the sides control only one dimension. For instance, you use the top middle handle to size a frame vertically. The sizing handles at the corners can control two dimensions—both the vertical and horizontal size of a frame..

*E*xample: If you're following with our practice chapter, try changing the size of the frame you just drew. Put the cursor over one of the corner sizing handles and hold down the left mouse button. Drag it diagonally to change both the horizontal and the vertical dimensions at the same time. (If it doesn't work, position the cursor more carefully and try again.) Now put the cursor over the middle handle on the lower side. Drag up and down to change the vertical size.

Warning: Although we haven't put anything into our frame yet, we want to make you aware that resizing affects the picture inside, not just the frame that contains it. In the case of bit-mapped images, the resizing must be planned very carefully to avoid unpleasant side effects. For more information on sizing images, see Chapter 12, "Enhancing and Editing Pictures."

Using column and line snap

Ventura gives you two tools that make it easier to draw and resize frames with the mouse: column snap and line snap. Both of them are turned on or off from the View menu.

Column snap makes the edges of the columns and margins "magnetic." If you come near an edge while drawing or moving a frame with the mouse, it snaps to the edge for perfect alignment. You should almost always have column snap on, except in those rare cases when you deliberately want a frame to violate the boundaries created by your margins and columns.

Line snap, on the other hand, is not something you should always use. Line snap restricts the vertical size of the frame to increments that match the inter-line spacing of Body Text. You can't change the size of this snap unit except by changing the inter-line spacing of the Body Text tag. This spacing applies throughout the document.

For instance, suppose that Body Text had an inter-line spacing of 12 points. With line snap on, you could draw a frame that was 12 points high, or 24 points high, or 36 points high, or any other increment of 12 points. Or, to think of it another way, your frames can only be drawn in increments of one line. You can have a frame that is one line high, or 30 lines high, but there is no way to accidentally draw a frame that is 10 ⅔ lines high.

When and why would you use line snap? Primarily to make columns align at the bottom. Perhaps you have crafted a spacing scheme so that all the columns in your newsletter end at the same point. You don't want to throw that spacing off with a frame that deviates a few points. By turning line snap on, you guarantee that the frames you draw will always be in perfect step with Body Text.

You can use both snap functions to help you move and resize existing frames as well as draw new frames.

Note: If you draw frames and then turn on the snap functions, the existing frames do not move automatically. Likewise, if you change the inter-line spacing of Body Text, existing frames do not automatically snap to the new spacing. They remain in their current positions until you move or resize them.

Example: If you're following our practice chapter, get a feel for the snap functions by playing with the frame you drew in the previous example. First, go to the View menu and activate Column Snap and Line Snap so they both have check marks next to them. Now grab the middle button on the right side and drag it to the left. Notice how the frame snaps over each time it gets close to a column guide. Next, grab the center handle on the top and stretch the frame upward. Notice how it "jerks" as you drag the mouse. The frame is snapping to the inter-line spacing of the Body Text (14 points in this particular style sheet).

Sizing frames with a dialog box

Resizing with the mouse is fine for some applications. But when you want a frame to be an exact size, the Sizing & Scaling dialog box is the way to go. Here's how it works:

1. Using the Frame Tool, select the frame.
2. Choose Sizing & Scaling from the Frame menu.
3. Click on the measurements button until it displays the units you want.
4. In the Frame Width text box, type the width that you want for the frame.
5. In the Frame Height text box, type the height that you want for the frame.
6. Click on OK.

When you change the size of a frame with the Sizing & Scaling dialog box, the upper left corner of the frame remains in its original place. The other corners move as necessary to make the frame the specified size.

***E*xample:** If you're following our example chapter, try using the Sizing & Scaling dialog box to resize the frame you've created. Select the frame. With the mouse, drag the lower right handle up and to the left to create a very small frame in the first column. (Exact size isn't important.) Now choose Sizing & Scaling from the Frame menu. Be sure that the measurements button reads Picas & Points. Make the frame 36,00 picas & points wide and 16,04 picas & points high (Figure 11-3). This makes the frame same width as the columns (36 picas & points).

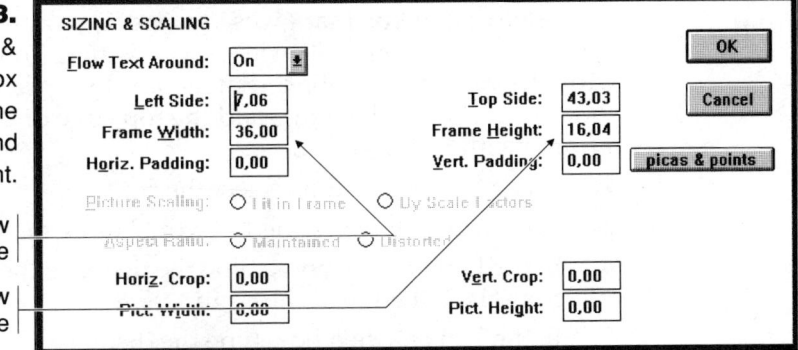

Figure 11-3.
Use the Sizing & Scaling dialog box to change the frame's width and height.

Enter the new width here

Enter the new height here

Positioning frames

You just learned how easy it is to draw and size frames. It's equally easy to move them around—to another spot on the same page, to another page, or even to another chapter.

Moving frames with the mouse

To move a frame with the mouse:

1. Using the Frame Tool, place the mouse cursor anywhere inside the frame boundaries. Do not put it over a handle or you will resize the frame instead of moving it.

2. Hold down the left mouse button. A four-way cursor appears.

3. Drag the frame to its new location and release the button.

If you have turned on line and column snap, the movement will be jerky as the frame attempts to snap to the nearest edge or line.

When you move a frame, you automatically move everything associated with it. If you went through Chapter 9, "Creating Pictures in Ventura," then you know that you can attach lines, arrows, Box Text, and other shapes to a frame. You can also put things inside, such as a background, a text file, or a graphics file. All of these things move when the frame moves.

Tip: Use Ventura's rulers for more accurate positioning when working with the mouse. Choose Show Rulers from the View menu. If you now move, for instance, the left edge of the mouse cursor to the left edge of the frame, the guideline on the upper ruler will indicate how far the frame is from the left edge of the paper.

Moving frames with a dialog box

The same dialog box that gives you precise control over the size of a frame also lets you control its exact position. You position a frame with the Sizing & Scaling dialog box by specifying how far it should be from the left edge and the top edge of the page. To move a frame with Sizing & Scaling:

1. Using the Frame Tool, select the frame.
2. Choose Sizing & Scaling from the Frame menu.
3. In the Left Side text box, type the distance the frame should be from the left edge of the page.
4. In the Top Side text box, type the distance from the top edge of the page.
5. Click on OK.

Example: If you're following our practice chapter, try using this method to move the frame you've been working. Select the frame and choose Sizing & Scaling from the Frame menu. Be sure Left Side has 7,06 picas & points. This will place the frame exactly between the column guides. Change Top Side to 6,00 picas & points. This will move the frame just above the middle of the document. Click on OK. The frame appears on the screen with left corner position that you specified. With the frame still selected, choose Sizing & Scaling again, change Top Side to 43,03 picas & points. This places the frame at the bottom of the page and aligns it with the bottom margin. Click on OK. Your results should look similar to (Figure 11-4).

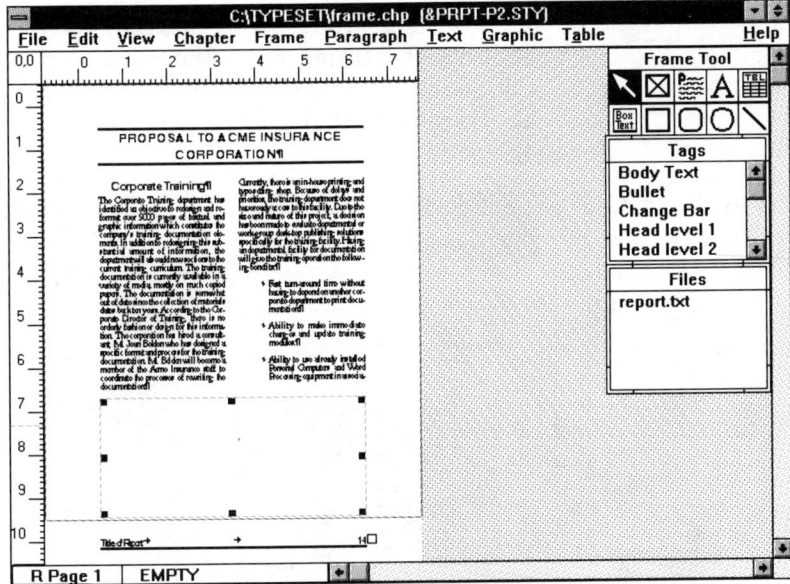

Figure 11-4.
After you change the Top Side of the frame to 43,03 picas & points, your practice chapter should look similar to this.

Cutting, copying, and pasting frames

You can move frames anywhere on the same page with the mouse or with the Sizing & Scaling dialog box. However, if you want to move a frame to another page, you must use the Cut Frame, Copy Frame, and Paste Frame commands from the Edit menu. Moving a frame is simple. First, you select the frame with the Frame Tool, and then cut or copy it to the clipboard. Then you can move to the new page and paste the frame.

Cutting and copying affect the frame, its contents (picture or text file), and its attached graphics. When you cut or copy a frame, all these items move to the clipboard. Here's how these two commands work:

Cutting a frame deletes it from the page and places it on the clipboard. If there is a picture inside the frame, the picture disappears from the page, too. The picture's file, however, is not deleted from the chapter. It is still on the File List, and can be placed into another frame if you want.

Copying a frame leaves it on the page and places a copy of it on the clipboard.

To cut or copy a frame:

1. Using the Frame Tool, select the frame.

2. Choose Cut Frame from the Edit menu (or press Delete) to remove the frame from the page and put a copy onto the clipboard. Choose Copy Frame (or press Shift-Delete) to leave the frame on the page while putting a copy onto the clipboard (Figure 11-5).

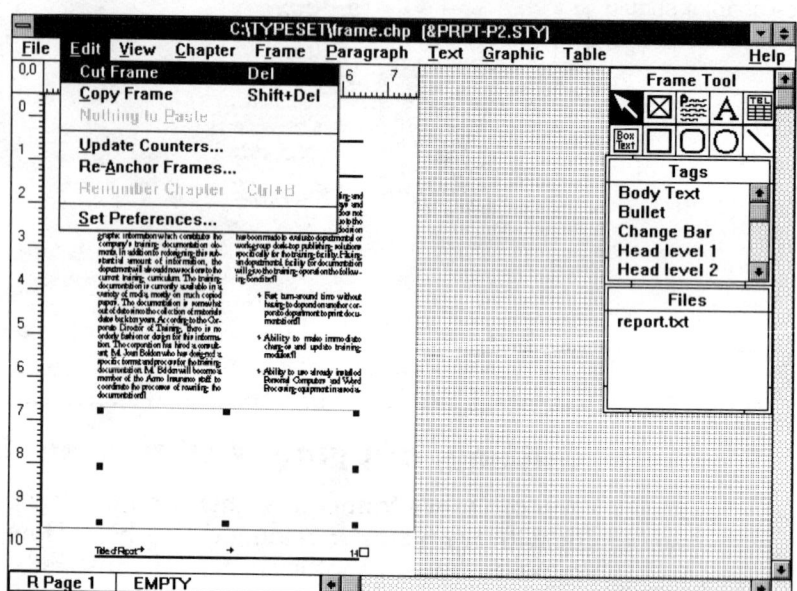

Figure 11-5. You cut, copy, and paste frames with the Edit menu.

Note: Ventura's Cut, Copy, and Paste commands have keyboard shortcuts that differ from those of most other Windows programs. Be sure you learn these differences.

Pasting a frame places the frame that you cut or copied to the clipboard onto the current page. When you paste a frame, it appears at the same relative position from which it was cut or copied. If it was at the bottom on the old page, it will appear at the bottom when you paste it onto the new page. After you paste it on the desired page, you can move it where you want it.

It's possible to copy a frame and then paste additional copies on the same page. Each of those copies will appear in the same position as the original, so you have to be careful. You won't be able to see the copies until you move them to one side, so that you can see the frame (or frames) underneath.

To paste a frame:

1. Cut or copy a frame to the clipboard.

2. Move to the page where you want to place the frame that you cut or copied.
3. Choose Paste Frame from the Edit menu (or press Insert).

You can cut, copy, and paste more than one frame at a time. The frame (or frames) you put onto the clipboard stay there until you cut or copy something else.

Warning: If you are switching from the GEM version of Ventura, then you are used to three separate clipboards, one for frames, one for text, and one for graphic shapes. The Windows version of Ventura does not have this luxury. There is only one clipboard. If you cut or copy anything else, you replace what was there before. If, for instance, you put a frame on the clipboard and then cut some text, the text will replace the frame.

Although the Windows Clipboard has some limitations compared to the GEM version, it also has some advantages. In particular, it can trade data with other Windows applications. You can, for instance, open a word processor and put text on the clipboard. Then you can open Ventura and paste that text directly into a Ventura document.

You can move certain pictures to Ventura with the clipboard. For instance, you can trade line art with Windows programs such as Arts & Letters, Corel Draw, and Micrografx Designer. You put the drawing onto the clipboard, switch to Ventura, and paste the drawing into a frame. A dialog box appears so you can save the file in the Windows Metafile (WMF) format.

However, you cannot use the clipboard to transfer bit-mapped images from other programs.

Tip: Can't remember what you put on the clipboard? Check the Edit menu. The third option down reads Paste Frame, Paste Text, or Paste Graphic depending on what's currently on the clipboard.

Tip: Use the clipboard when you need to move frames from one chapter to another. Open the first chapter and put all the frames onto the same page. Select them all. Now copy them to the clipboard. Close the first chapter and open the new one. Paste the frames into the new chapter. Now that they are in the right chapter, you can move them one by one to the pages where you want to place them.

Creating repeating frames

Suppose you had a picture (a logo or another graphic that illustrates the theme of the document) that you wanted to repeat on every page. How would you do it? It would be time-consuming and tedious to draw a frame on every page and load the picture into each frame.

Never fear. Ventura allows you to create a frame once and then automatically repeat it on every page. It's simple. You draw the frame as usual. Next you can load the picture file into frame (or you can load the file later). Then you follow these steps to make the frame repeat:

1. Using the Frame Tool, select the frame.
2. Choose Repeating Frame from the Frame menu. The Repeating Frame dialog box appears (Figure 11-6).
3. Select the pages where you want the frame to appear from the For All Pages buttons:

   - *Off* turns off the repeating frame function.
   - *Left* makes the frame repeat on left pages only.
   - *Right* makes the frame repeat on right pages only.
   - *Left & Right* makes the frame repeat on all pages—left and right.

4. Click on OK.

Figure 11-6.
The Repeating Frame dialog box.

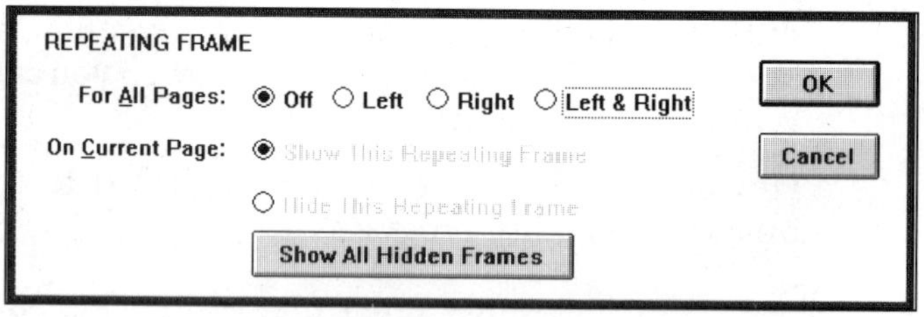

When you have single-sided documents, or select the Left or Right options, the frame will appear at the same position on every page.

However, if you specify Left & Right, you may not get what you expect. With this option, Ventura places repeated frames in mirrored positions on opposite pages (Figure 11-7). For example, if you place a repeating frame on the outside of a left page, it will also appear on the outside of the right page—not on the left side.

To place the repeating frame at the exact same position on both left and right pages, you must specify a different repeating frame for the left page and the right page. Sound like a pain? It's really pretty

Figure 11-7.
Facing pages with repeating frame (containing the spray can picture) at mirrored positions (on the outside in this case).

A repeating frame that uses Left & Right option

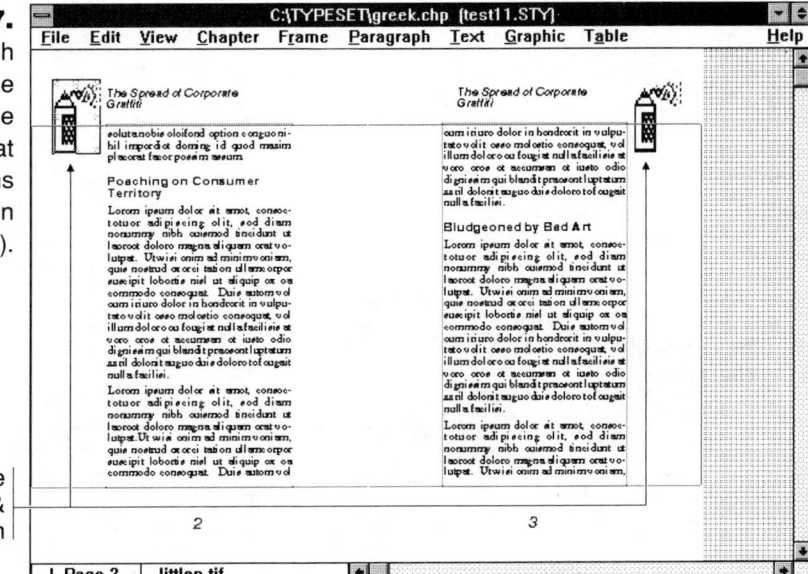

simple. First, place the frame where you want it to appear on the left page. Then copy the frame to a right page. Select the frame on the left page, choose Repeating Frame and select For All Pages: Left. Then select the frame on the right page, choose Repeating Frame and select For All Pages: Right. This will make the frames appear at the same postion on each page—no matter if it's left or right (Figure 11-8).

You can also turn off the repeating frame for specific pages. To turn off a repeating frame for a specific page, go to the page where you don't want the repeating frame to appear. Select the frame, choose Repeating Frame from the Frame menu, select On Current Page: Hide This Repeating Frame, and click on OK.

To make the repeating frame reappear on the page, go to the page with the hidden frame, choose Repeating Frame, and select On Current Page: Show This Repeating Frame. If you want all the hidden repeating frames to reappear, click on the Show All Hidden Frames button. Then click on OK.

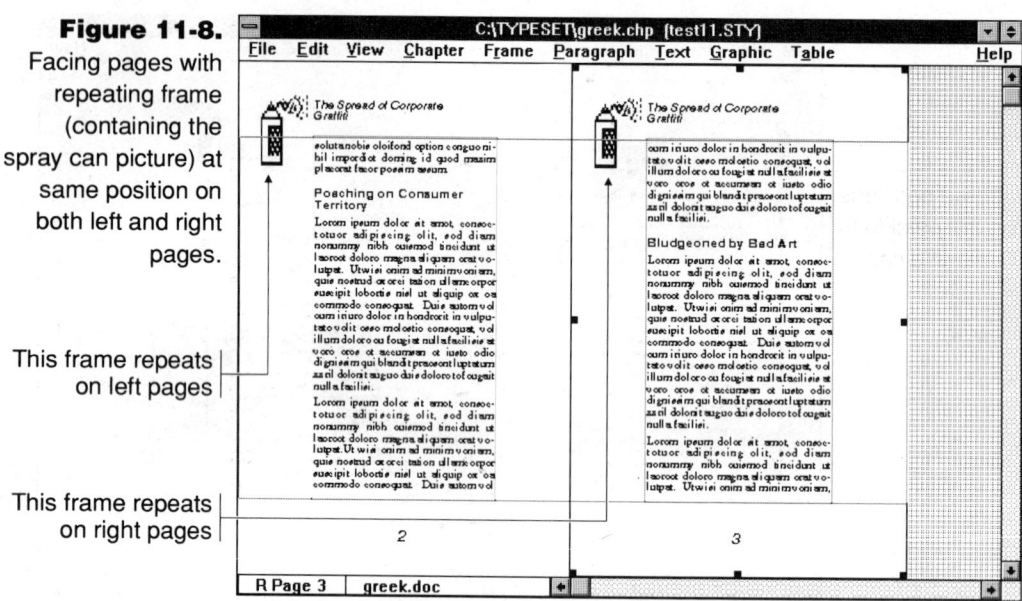

Figure 11-8. Facing pages with repeating frame (containing the spray can picture) at same position on both left and right pages.

Loading pictures into frames

After you've drawn a frame, you can put a picture inside. To do that you (1) load the picture into the chapter and (2) place it inside the frame. You can load more than one picture at a time. And once a picture appears on the File List, you can reuse it in as many frames as you like.

Loading pictures into the chapter

Ventura uses the same dialog box to load pictures as it does to load text. As you learned in the previous chapter, Ventura has filters to convert files from most of the leading graphics formats. To load a picture file, all you have to do is decide what type of picture to use (Line Art or Image), specify the file format, and tell Ventura if you want to load more than one picture at a time:

1. Choose Load Text/Picture from the File menu (Figure 11-9).

2. Select the type of file from the File Type buttons.

3. Select the file format from the Format list box. If you need help understanding the different file types and formats, see Chapter 10, "Creating Pictures with Outside Programs."

Figure 11-9.
The Load Text/Picture dialog box.

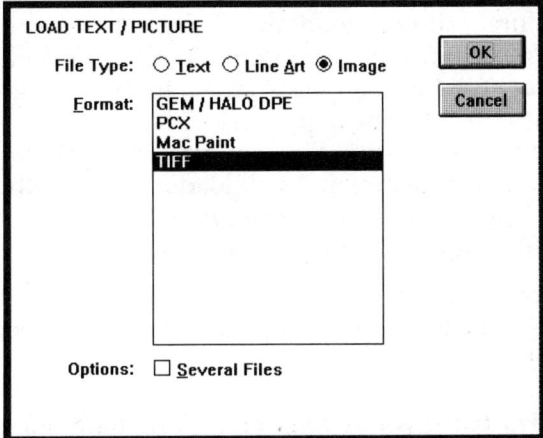

4. Click on the checkbox next to Options: Several Files if you want to load more than one picture at a time. If you only want to load one file, leave the checkbox blank.

5. Click on OK.

Ventura now brings up the Open File dialog box so you can choose the file. Ventura will automatically filter the File List with an extension, depending on the file format you've chosen. For instance, if you choose the GEM line art format, it will filter the list with the GEM extension (Figure 11-10). For a list of recommended extensions for text and graphics files, see Chapter 21, "Rapid Reference."

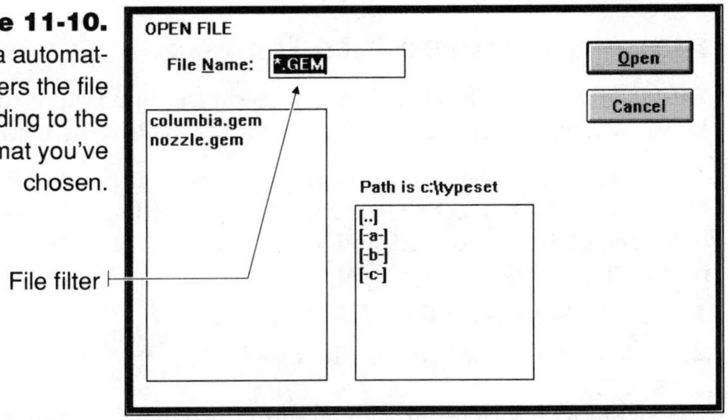

Figure 11-10.
Ventura automatically filters the file list according to the file format you've chosen.

File filter

6. If necessary, navigate to the drive or directory where the file you want is located. Select the file and click on OK (or double-click on the filename).

Ventura will now load and (if necessary) convert the picture file. For more information on how (and why) Ventura converts certain picture file formats, see Chapter 10, "Creating Pictures with Other Programs." If you happened to have a frame selected when you loaded the picture file, Ventura will assume that's where you wanted the picture and will load it inside. Otherwise, the filename will appear immediately on the File List, but the picture won't be visible until you load it into a frame.

If you chose to load several files, Ventura will return you to the Open File dialog box to load another. It will keep bringing you back until you've loaded all the files you need and you click on Cancel.

Example: If you're following along with our example chapter, try loading a picture into the chapter. We'll use the picture of a nozzle, one of the Ventura example files.

1. Be sure that the frame you drew earlier is *not* selected. If it is, click elsewhere on the workspace to deselect it.
2. Choose Load Text/Picture from the File menu.
3. Select File Type: Line Art and Format: GEM. Leave the Options: Several Files checkbox blank. Click on OK. The Open File dialog box appears.
4. Move to the \TYPESET directory. Double-click on the file NOZZLE.GEM. This filename then appears in the File List Window, indicating that the file is loaded in the chapter.

Placing pictures into frames

After you've loaded a file, it appears on the File List. Now you tell Ventura where you want it by placing the picture in a frame.

As we mentioned earlier, you can place the picture at the same time you load it. Just select the frame first, then choose Load Text/Picture. The picture you load will automatically appear in the selected frame. It only takes two steps:

1. Using the Frame Tool, select the frame.
2. Click on the filename in the File List.

Tip: Don't forget that you can change the size of the File List. If you have a long series of files to place, grab the bottom of the File List with the mouse cursor and drag it down to enlarge the list so you can see more of the files at one time.

Example: If you're following along with our practice chapter, try placing the NOZZLE.GEM picture file into the frame you've created. Select the frame at the bottom of the page with the Frame Tool. Now click on the filename NOZZLE.GEM in the File List. The picture appears in the frame (Figure 11-11).

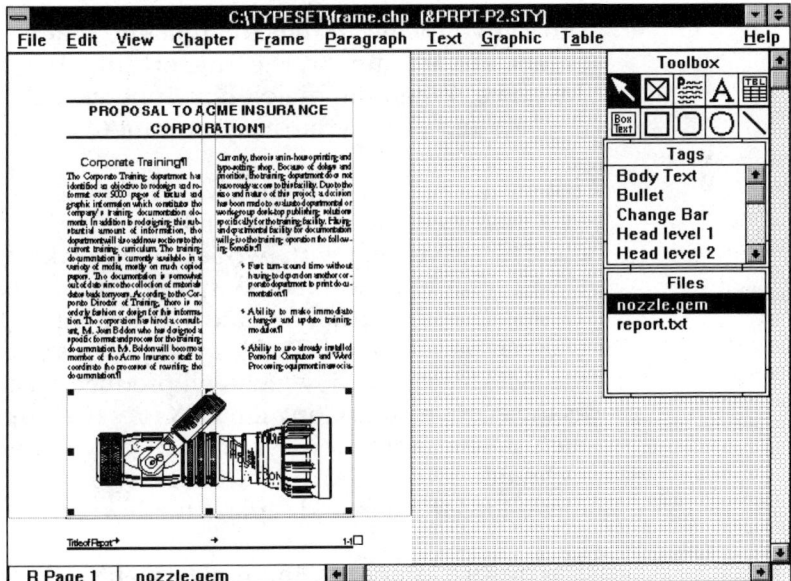

Figure 11-11. Our example chapter after loading and placing a picture.

Removing pictures

Change your mind? Did you load the wrong picture file? Or put the picture into the wrong frame? You can remove a picture either from the document or just from the frame:

1. Using the Frame Tool, select the frame containing the picture.

2. Choose Remove Text/File from the Frame menu. When the Remove File dialog box appears (Figure 11-12), the name of the picture file automatically appears in the File Name text box.

Now you must tell Ventura whether to remove the picture from the entire chapter, or just from this frame.

3. Go to the Remove From list box. Select List Of Files if you want to remove the picture from the document. Select Frame if you want to remove it from the current frame but leave it on the File List for use later.

4. Click on OK.

Figure 11-12.
Remove Text/File to removes a file from a frame or chapter.

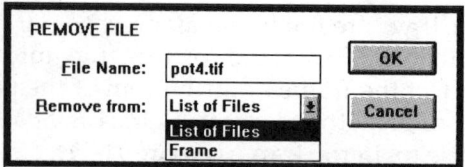

What if you want to remove a picture that is not inside a frame? Select any frame or the underlying page. Choose Remove Text/File. When the dialog box appears, delete the filename that appears and type in the one you want to remove.

Tip: In the previous chapter, we explained that Ventura converts PCX files to its own native IMG format by producing a duplicate file. This leaves you with two sets of files taking up twice the space. If you want to conserve disk space, you can load in the PCX files. That will automatically create a matching set of IMG files. Now you can remove the PCX files with Remove Text/File and load in the IMG files instead, which will produce exactly the same picture as the PCX version. Copy the PCX files to a floppy disk for backup, then delete them from your hard drive. You can also use this technique with CGM line art files, which are re-created as GEM files—load them in and replace them with the GEM files.

Warning: Do not use the replacement technique with TIFF files. Although Ventura creates an IMG file to display TIFF files on the screen, TIFF files contain gray-scale information that is used when you print the picture—this information won't be in the IMG file.

Adding margins inside frames

Margins keep pictures away from the inside edge of a frame. They have several important uses. They prevent a picture from overlapping and obscuring a ruling box around the frame (we'll get into ruling boxes in the next chapter). And they let you control how a picture appears inside the frame. For instance, you can use them to reserve a blank area inside the frame for labels and callouts. Or you can increase one or more margins to cover up a portion of the picture (Figure 11-13).

You can set the margins before or after loading a picture into a frame. It's usually easier to see what's going on if you do it after you've got a picture inside. To set the margins:

1. Using the Frame Tool, select the frame.

Figure 11-13.
Margins inside a frame add to your control over the appearance of the picture inside.

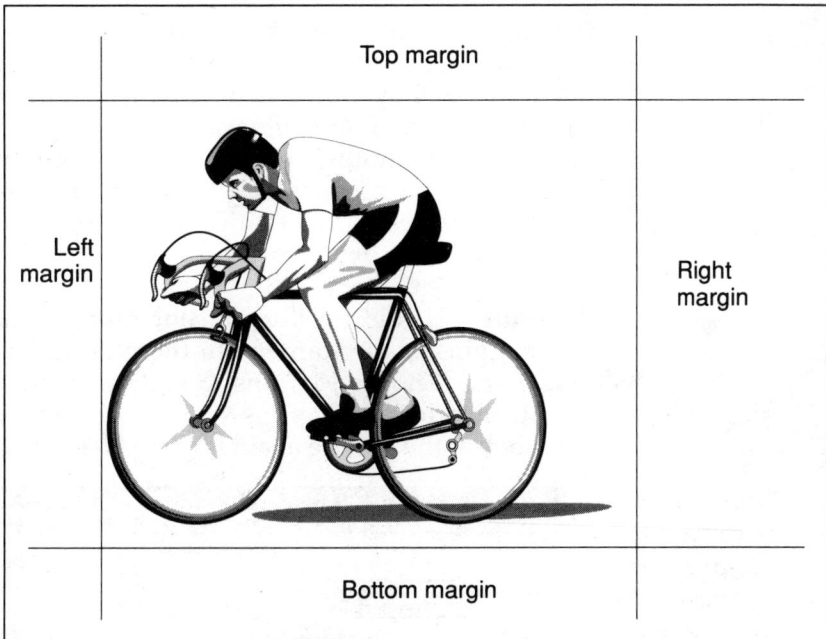

2. Choose Margins & Columns from the Frame menu. The Margins & Columns dialog box appears (Figure 11-14).
3. Type the sizes of the margins in the Margins text boxes: Top, Bottom, Left, and Right.
4. Click on OK.

Figure 11-14.
You've seen the Margins & Columns dialog box used for the underlying page. But it is also used to control the inner margins of the frames you draw to contain pictures.

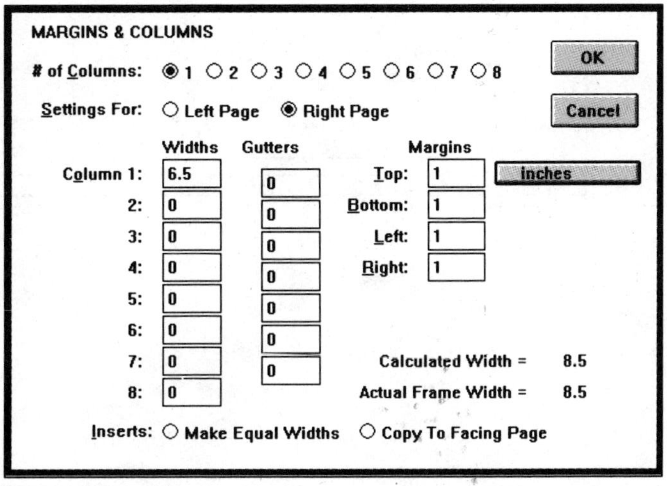

Tip: If you have a ruling box around the frame, add inner margins equal to the height of the ruling box. Otherwise, the picture inside the frame will overlap and obscure the ruling box. For instance, if you have a one-point ruling box, add a one-point margin on all four sides. Naturally, you can use an even larger margin if you want white space to appear between the picture and the ruling box. For more information on ruling boxes, see Chapter 12, "Enhancing and Editing Pictures."

Example: If you're following along the practice chapter, try adding margins to the frame with the NOZZLE.GEM picture. Select the frame. Choose Margins & Columns from the Frame menu. Create margins of 3,00 picas & points on all four sides. Click on OK and look at the picture again (Figure 11-15). See the difference?

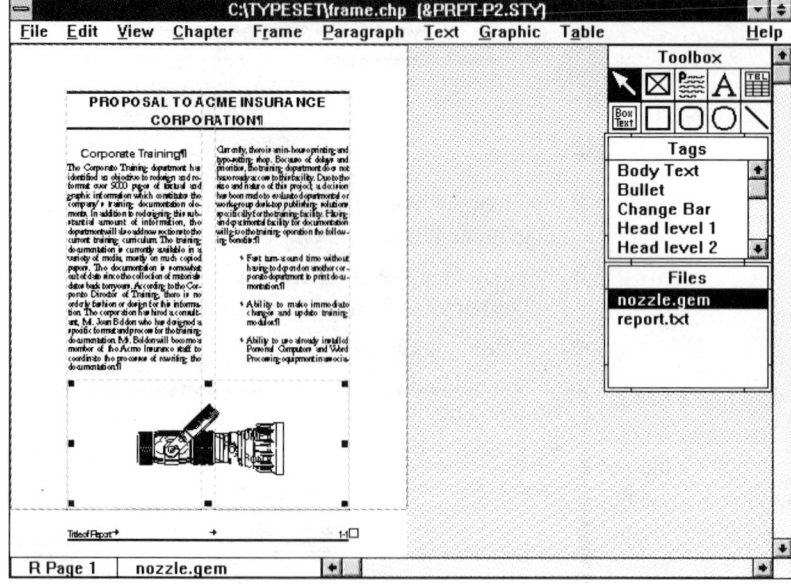

Figure 11-15. After you've added 3,00-pica & point margins to the nozzle frame, your chapter should look similar to this.

Anchoring frames

After you've gone to the trouble of loading and placing pictures, you may want to make sure they stay in the right place. Ventura provides a handy anchoring feature that helps keep a picture close to the text that describes it. It's not completely automatic—you still have to make some adjustments—but it's a big help, especially if you create long documents with many pictures.

Ideally, a picture should be as close as possible to the text that talks about it. When we discuss the Margins & Columns dialog box in this book, for instance, we want its picture to show up nearby, not five pages later.

But if you make changes to the text after putting in the frames, the text may flow to another page, while the picture stays behind. And that's where anchoring comes in. Once a picture is anchored, you can issue a command to move it to the same page as the text.

In a way, the name is misleading, because *anchoring* implies that the picture always stays in the same place. A better name might have been *linking*. What actually occurs is that the picture and the text are "connected" so the the picture can automatically be pulled to the same page as the text.

Creating an anchor takes two steps:

1. Give the frame an *anchor name*. Until you name the frames, Ventura has no way to tell them apart.

2. Put an *anchor marker* into the text. This marks the spot to which the frame will be linked.

After you've done these two things for all the frames, you can issue the Re-Anchor Frames command from the Edit menu. Ventura will look at the frames and match them up with their markers in the text, moving them to the correct pages. Ventura even gives you four different anchor types to choose from. One of them moves the picture automatically every time you move the text. The others wait for you to issue the Re-Anchor Frames command before they move the frames.

Assigning the anchor name

It's best to start by assigning the anchor name to the frame first. Then you can place the anchor marker into the text. As you'll see, following this order (assign anchor, then place the marker) will save you some typing. To assign the anchor name:

1. Using the Frame Tool, select the frame.
2. Choose Anchors & Captions from the Frame menu. The Anchors & Captions dialog box appears (Figure 11-16).
3. In the Anchor text box, type the anchor name you want to give the frame.
4. Click on OK

Figure 11-16. Use the Anchors & Captions dialog box to assign an anchor name to the frame.

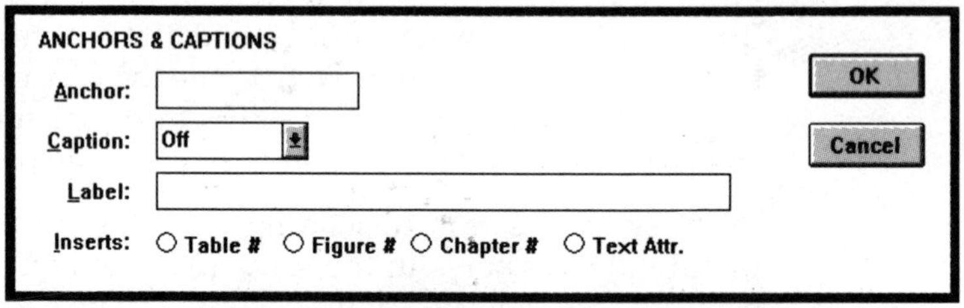

You can use any name up to 16 characters, as long as you don't use the same name twice. You may want to write the name down, because you must use the exact name when you create the anchor marker. Ventura matches the spelling, but it ignores capitalization.

Tip: What should you use as anchor names? We think the smartest idea is to use the name of the picture file contained within the frame. Because filenames must be unique, you don't run any risk of duplicating names.

Example: If you're following our practice chapter, try giving an anchor name to the nozzle picture you loaded earlier. Select the frame, choose Anchors & Captions from the Frame menu, and type the name "nozzle" in the Anchor text box. Click on OK. Later, we'll re-anchor this frame, using the anchor marker you'll create in the next section.

Don't be intimidated by these vague names. The four choices are quite straightforward:

Fixed, On Same Page As Anchor puts the frame on the same page as the text marker. The frame appears in the same position as it had on the original page. You can then move it to adjust it to its new surroundings.

Relative, Below Anchor Line puts the frame below the anchor marker and on the same page if possible. Where Ventura actually places the frame depends on where the marker occurs on the page. For example, if the marker is on the last line of a page, Ventura usually puts the frame on the next page.

Relative, Above Anchor Line puts the frame above the text marker and on the same page if possible. Again, where Ventura actually places the frame depends on where the marker occurs on the page.

These first three options don't take effect until you issue the Re-Anchor Frames command.

Relative, Automatically At Anchor moves the frame along with the text. This option takes effect automatically every time the text moves.

After you close the dialog box, you will see a small degree symbol where you placed the anchor marker. (If you can't see it, choose Show Tabs & Returns from the View menu.) To delete an anchor marker, you delete this symbol. To edit an anchor, place the text cursor next to the symbol. Use the arrow keys to move backwards or forwards until you see the words "Frame Anchor" in the Current Selection Box at the bottom of the screen. Then select Edit Special Item from the Text menu to open the Insert/Edit Anchor dialog box and make your changes.

Example: If you're following along with our example chapter, try inserting an anchor marker for the nozzle frame. We've already given the frame the anchor name "nozzle." Now let's anchor it to the text. Move to the second page. Place the text cursor at the end of the second to last paragraph, right after the words "productivity in the workgroup." Use Insert Special Item from the Text menu to bring up the Insert/Edit Anchor dialog box. Type the name "nozzle" in the Frame's Anchor Name text box. Select Anchor's New Location: Fixed, On Same Page As Anchor and click on OK. Now you have a frame on one page and its anchor marker on another. In a moment, we'll let Ventura move the frame to the same page as the anchor marker.

Inserting the anchor marker

After you name the frame, you must mark a spot in the text. From then on, the frame will be linked to that spot. You can put the marker anywhere, but it should be as close as possible to the text describing the picture. If you use text references, such as "See Figure A," then the best place to put the anchor marker is directly after the reference. A standard location also makes it easier to find the markers later, if you need to edit or delete them.

To insert an anchor marker:

1. Using the Text Tool, place the text cursor where you want the anchor marker to appear.
2. Choose Insert Special Item from the Text menu. Then select Frame Anchor from the flyout menu to bring up the Insert/Edit Anchor dialog box (Figure 11-17).
3. In the Frame's Anchor Name text box, type the anchor name for the frame. If there is a frame on the same page with an anchor name, Ventura will insert it for you, saving you the trouble of typing. If you want a different frame instead, or if the name doesn't appear, just type it in.
4. Choose the kind of anchor you want from the Frame's New Location buttons.
5. Click on OK.

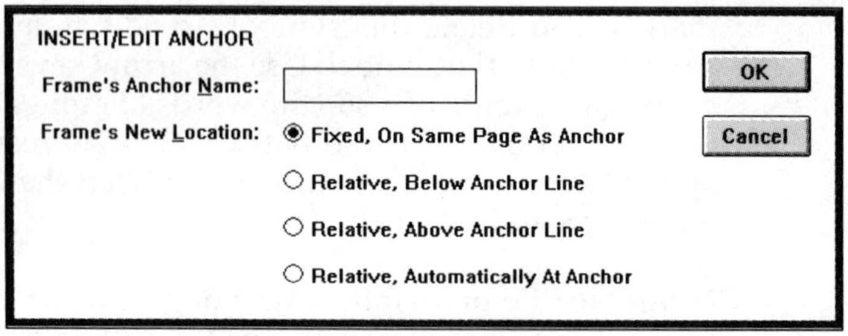

Figure 11-17. Use the Insert/Edit Anchor dialog box to put an anchor marker into the text.

The Insert/Edit Anchor dialog box let's you choose from four different types of anchors:

- Fixed, On Same Page As Anchor
- Relative, Below Anchor Line
- Relative, Above Anchor Line
- Relative, Automatically At Anchor

Re-anchoring frames

The Re-Anchor Frames command moves frames to the same page as their text marker. There's no need to do this if the chapter remains unchanged and all the pictures are where you want them. But if the text grows or shrinks, you may want to re-anchor to get the pictures rearranged on the right pages again.

To do so, choose Re-Anchor Frames from the Edit menu. Ventura presents you with a VP Alert dialog box that has three options (Figure 11-18).

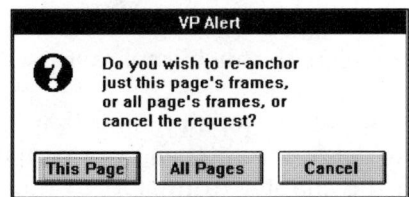

Figure 11-18.
The VP Alert box for re-anchoring frames.

Cancel exits you out of the dialog box without doing anything. If you select either of the other two, Ventura examines the text for anchor markers. It then moves frames so they are on the same page as the markers.

This Page re-anchors the frames for markers on the current page only. If there are no anchor markers on this page, no frames will appear. This option lets you fix a page without moving the anchored frames on other pages.

All Pages re-anchors the frames for every page in the document.

If you re-anchor frames often, you're likely to get a VP Alert box like the one in Figure 11-19. It's easy to spell the anchor name one way in the Anchors & Captions dialog box and another way in the Insert/Edit Anchor dialog box. If you get even one letter wrong, Ventura won't be able to match the frame with the text marker.

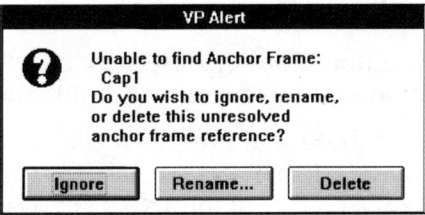

Figure 11-19.
This VP Alert box appears if Ventura can't find an anchor frame.

Ventura brings up this VP Alert box if it finds an anchor marker without a matching frame. Sometimes, it's possible to guess what went wrong. Here's some common solutions:

- If Ventura says it can't find an anchor and you see an obvious misspelling, then select Rename. Ventura will let you type in a correction, and then it will try again to find a frame for the corrected anchor marker.

- If you can't figure out why the names don't match, then select Ignore. Ventura will pass over that marker and attempt to match up the rest of them. You can go back later and manually resolve the discrepancy that kept the re-anchoring from working.

- If you want to delete the anchor marker itself, select Delete.

Tip: Often, the best way to repair a long chapter is to re-anchor all the pages once to get frames in their approximate places. Then you can go through the chapter from start to finish to put frames in their final positions. As necessary, you can re-anchor for an individual page to bring in a frame without moving any of the other frames you've already positioned.

Example: If you're following along with our practice chapter, try re-anchoring the chapter. Choose Re-Anchor Frames from the Edit menu. You will see an error message for an unresolved marker called Cap1. This is left over from the frame we deleted from the example document at the very beginning of this chapter. Click on Ignore. Ventura will now move the nozzle picture to the second page to join its anchor marker (Figure 11-20).

Working with automatic anchors

The first three anchor types don't take effect until you issue the Re-Anchor Frames commands. The last anchor type (Relative, Automatically At Anchor) doesn't require a command. The picture floats along with the text, moving when it does.

But pictures are almost always larger than text, so you may need to take special precautions when using automatic anchors.

For example, suppose you are producing a computer manual. In the place of words like Enter or Tab, you have anchored small frames that have a picture of the actual key. Use the Paragraph Tool to select the tag (or tags) that contain these small pictures. Choose Paragraph Typography from the Paragraph menu. In the dialog box, select Grow Inter-Line To Fit. Ventura will automatically in-

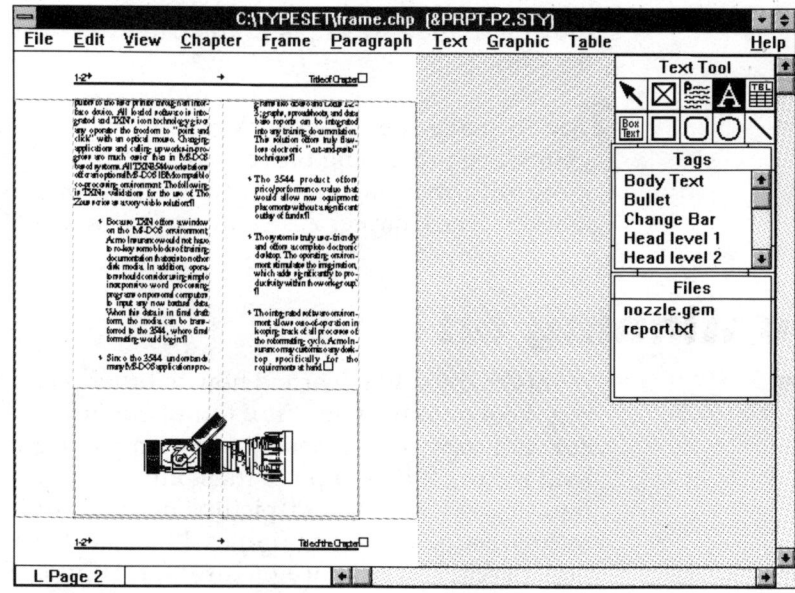

Figure 11-20.
After you choose Re-Anchor Frames, the nozzle frame is re-anchored (moved) on the second page, where its anchor marker is located.

crease the space between lines if the pictures are too big for the normal line spacing.

One other case requires special precautions. If you are using automatic anchors with large pictures that fit between paragraphs, you need to put a line break just before the anchor marker. You also need to make sure the frame is on a line by itself. This gives Ventura somewhere to split the text and the frame if it finds it impossible to fit them both on the same page or column.

Tip: You can use automatic anchors for marginal icons. For instance, suppose you want a picture of a burning match in the margin every time you have a "hot tip" in your computer manual. Draw the picture of the match, put it in a small frame, and anchor the frame to the text that describes the tip. Put the anchor at the front of the first line. In essence, you're treating the picture as if it were the first character in the paragraph. Now outdent the first line to push the picture into the margin. For information on using pictures as bullets, see Chapter 5, "Advanced Styles."

You can reuse an automatically anchored frame over and over again, without making copies. For instance, consider the marginal icons explained in the previous paragraph. You only need one picture of a burning match in your chapter. Every time you use that same anchor name, Ventura will make a copy of the frame and move it to the correct page. You can even have multiple copies on the same page.

Tip: To make life easier in Ventura, put the anchor markers into your word processing files before you bring them into Ventura. For more information on using a word processor to insert anchor markers, see Chapter 7, "Creating Text with Other Programs."

Continuing on

In this chapter, you learned how to bring pictures into Ventura and put them onto the page. You found out how to draw, size, position, cut, and copy the frames that contain pictures. You learned how to load picture files and place them into frames. You learned why and how to add margins to picture frames. And you picked up the techniques of anchoring frames. In the next chapter, you'll discover how to edit and enhance pictures for truly professional results.

Easy Access

For more info on...	See chapter...
Using bracket codes to insert frame anchors directly into word processing files	**7** Creating Text with Other Programs
Using Ventura's built-in drawing tools	**9** Creating Pictures in Ventura
Creating Ventura-compatible pictures with standalone graphics programs and saving graphics files in different formats	**10** Creating Pictures with Other Programs
Changing the size of a picture inside a frame	**12** Enhancing and Editing Pictures
Recommended extensions for graphics file formats	**21** Rapid Reference

12
Enhancing and Editing Pictures

How to edit pictures in Ventura

- **Adding captions** 341
- **Adding ruling boxes and lines** 351
- **Padding pictures** 357
- **Scaling pictures** 358
- **Cropping pictures** 363
- **Continuing on** 366

In the previous chapter, you learned how to load pictures into Ventura and place them into frames on the page. These basic skills may be all you need for simple documents.

But for more sophisticated results, you'll want to use some of Ventura's more advanced capabilities. For instance, you may want to add a caption to the photographs in your newsletter; put a ruling box around the product illustrations in your instruction manual; put padding around the outside of frames, so that the text doesn't bump into the pictures. You'll learn these skills in this chapter.

In addition, you'll learn how to control the size and appearance of the picture inside the frame. You'll find out how to scale pictures (how to change their size) and how to crop pictures (how to change which portion of the picture can be seen). We've also included a hands-on example for those who like to learn by doing.

Many of Ventura's dialog boxes combine several functions. For instance, you can use the Anchors & Captions dialog box to give frames anchor names, to tell Ventura where to put the caption frame, to create a caption label, and to set up automatic figure numbering. We think it's confusing to get bombarded with all these options at one time, so we've chosen to teach each task separately. After you've mastered the skills, you can combine operations for more efficiency.

Note: Here's the beauty of the Ventura approach to pictures—you can use all the techniques we'll show you here without affecting the original picture files. The only thing that changes is the way the picture displays inside the Ventura document.

Adding captions

In this section, we'll show you the mechanics of adding and formatting captions. At the end of the section, we'll show you several real-life examples of different caption styles.

A *caption* is a text description that accompanies a picture frame. Ventura provides a convenient way to link captions to pictures, so that they always remain together. First, you attach a *caption frame* to the picture frame. Then you type *caption text* inside the caption frame. If you want automatic numbering, you can also add an optional *caption label* inside the caption frame (Figure 12-1).

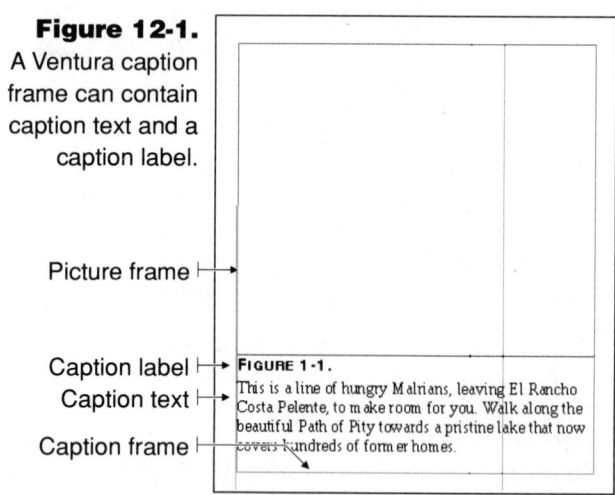

Figure 12-1. A Ventura caption frame can contain caption text and a caption label.

In this book, which was formatted with Ventura, the caption frame normally appears along the left side. The caption label (for instance, "Figure 12-1") appears at the top of the caption frame. The caption text (for instance, "A Ventura caption frame can contain...") appears directly beneath the caption label.

After you attach a caption frame, it travels along with the picture. If you move the picture frame, the caption frame moves with it. If you delete the picture frame, you automatically delete the caption frame and everything inside it.

To create a caption:

1. Attach the caption frame, using the Anchors & Captions dialog box.

2. Add a caption label, using the same dialog box (optional).

3. Type text into the caption frame, using the Text Tool (optional).

Attaching the caption frame

Your first step is to attach a caption frame. Your only decision is which side of the picture frame to put it on. The most common position is below the picture frame, but you can also put it above or on either side. To attach a caption frame to a picture frame:

1. Using the Frame Tool, select the picture frame.
2. Choose Anchors & Captions from the Frame menu.
3. Use the Caption list box to select where to put the caption frame (Figure 12-2), and then click on OK.

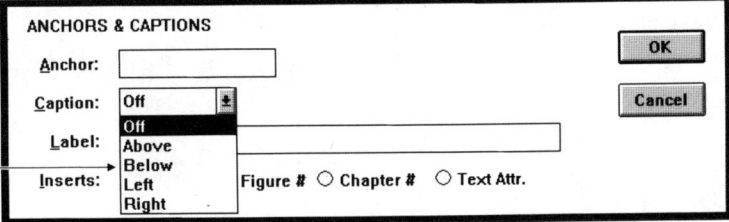

Figure 12-2. The Anchors & Captions dialog box.

Click here to tell Ventura where the caption frame goes

The size of the caption frame depends partly on the size of the picture. If you attach the caption frame to the bottom of the picture frame, the caption frame will be the same width as the picture frame. Ventura will assign an arbitrary height to the caption frame, which you can change as needed. If you later change the width of the picture, the caption frame changes automatically along with it. The two frames are linked.

Except for being linked on one side, a caption frame behaves like any other frame. For instance, you can put a ruling box around it. You can give it margins inside, or padding outside. The settings you make for the caption frame do not affect the picture frame.

Example: If you'd like to try these techniques as we go along, open the example chapter &MAG-P3.CHP from the \TYPESET directory. Rename the style sheet and the chapter file to avoid altering the originals. Use Save Style As from the File menu to save the style sheet as TESTING.STY. Use Save from the File menu to save the chapter as TESTING.CHP. (If you didn't install Ventura's example chapters, you can do so now.) Delete both frames on the page. Now draw a frame at the upper right of the two rightmost columns. Load the GEM line-art file NOZZLE.GEM from the \TYPESET directory and place it in the frame. Save the chapter. You have just prepared an example document you can use throughout this chapter to test your skills.

With the picture frame still selected, choose Anchors & Captions from the Frame menu. Select Caption: Below and click on OK. Your page should resemble Figure 12-3.

Figure 12-3.
Draw a frame, load and place the NOZZLE.GEM picture file, then use Anchors & Captions to attach a caption frame below the picture.

Picture frame

Caption frame

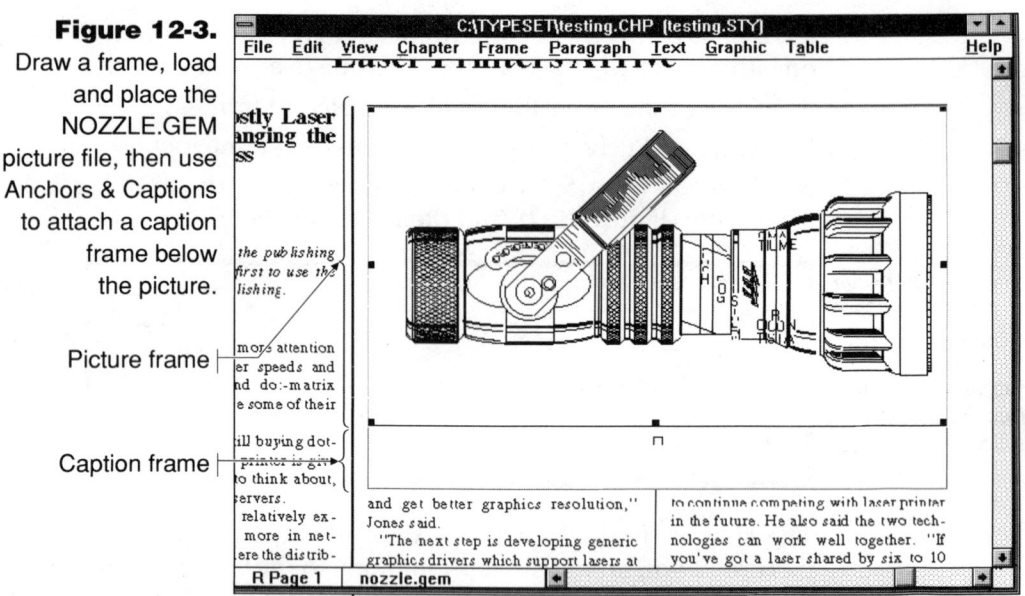

For more information on loading pictures, see Chapter 11, "Loading and Placing Pictures."

Adding a caption label

A caption label is a short description you type into Ventura's Anchors & Captions dialog box. After you close the dialog box, Ventura puts a label into the caption frame. It puts this label into a separate paragraph, which precedes the ordinary caption text. Thus, if you want both a caption label *and* caption text, the label always precedes the text.

Because the caption label is a separate paragraph, you can easily format it differently from the caption text. Look again at the captions in this book. The caption labels are formatted in bold with vertical alignment at the top. The caption text, on the other hand, appears directly below the caption label. Because the label and the text are separate tags, we can quickly and easily change their formatting. For instance, it would only take one command to change the style of every caption label in the entire book from bold to normal text.

In theory, you can type any label into the Anchors & Captions dialog box, up to the 60-character limit. In practice, *you should only use caption labels for automatic figure numbering*. If you want to add other text, use ordinary caption text as explained below.

Why do we suggest restricting the use of caption labels to figure numbering? For one thing, the caption label is limited in length. But more importantly, you can only edit the label by reopening the dialog box—you can't edit it with the Text Tool. However, with caption text, you can easily edit the text with the Text Tool.

To add a caption label:

1. Using the Frame Tool, select the picture frame or the caption frame (it doesn't matter which one).
2. Choose Anchors & Captions from the Frame menu.
3. In the Label text box, type in the label you want. Add numbering and text attributes to the label (we'll show you how in the next section).
4. Click on OK.

Automatic figure numbering

When you add the label, you can also enable automatic figure numbering. With automatic figure numbering, Ventura keeps track of the frames and numbers them in order. If you add, delete, or rearrange frames, Ventura renumbers them for you automatically.

To see what we're talking about, glance at the pictures in this book. Notice how they have captions such as "Figure 12-1." Ventura created those numbers automatically for us. We typed the following phrase into the dialog box:

```
Figure [C#]-[F#]
```

Where we placed the code [C#], Ventura inserted the number of the current chapter. Where we had put the code [F#], it inserted the sequential number of the current frame. Thus, the third frame in the first chapter became "Figure 1-3." If we later moved that frame to seventh position, Ventura automatically would renumber it to become "Figure 1-7."

Ventura lets you have two separate numbering sequences active at the same time. You can, for instance, number all the tables in order (assuming you've put the tables into separate frames). Then you can separately number all the illustrations, without disturbing the order and sequence of the tables. Ventura refers to the first numbering sequence as "Table #" and the second as "Figure #."

Note: You don't have to use figure numbering for figures and table numbering for tables. These numbering techniques simply count the occurrences of [F#] (or [T#]) in separate frames and print the respective number. You could, for instance, use figure numbering to sequentially number all the flowcharts and table numbering to sequentially number all the programming examples (assuming those examples were inside separate frames). The only requirement is to use them consistently throughout the document for the same type of illustration.

To add automatic numbering, you put codes into the Label text box. Ventura provides buttons on the Inserts line of the Anchors & Captions dialog box to insert the codes for you. To add the number of the chapter, place the cursor at the desired spot in the Label text box and click on the Chapter # button. To add the number of the frame, click on either the Table # or Figure # buttons.

If you just want numbers, put the codes on the line by themselves. If you want a phrase to accompany the numbers, type it in as you want it to appear. Be sure to include spaces and punctuation.

In addition to automatic numbering, the Label text box can also include special text attributes. In Chapter 7, "Creating Text Files with Other Programs," you learned that you can control a wide variety of text effects with bracket codes. You can, for instance, change the font or point size, or make the text bold or italic.

Those same bracket codes work in the Anchors & Captions dialog box. To turn on a text effect, you type its bracket code. To turn it off, you type a return-to-normal code. For instance, here's how to make the chapter and figure number bold, but not the rest of the label:

```
Figure <B>[C#]-[F#]<D>
```

The <B> code turns bold on and the <D> code turns it off. To save the trouble of typing the brackets, you can click on the Text Attr. button at the bottom right. Ventura will insert the letter D between the brackets. Erase the D and type in the bracket code you want.

For more information on using bracket codes, see Chapter 7, "Creating Text Files with Other Programs." For a handy chart of bracket codes, see Chapter 21, "Rapid Reference."

Example: Return to the example chapter we created earlier. Select the frame containing the picture of a nozzle. Choose Anchors & Caption from the Frame menu. Now add a caption label that includes both chapter and figure numbers with a hyphen in between. While you're at it, give the word "Figure" an initial capital letter, and use bracket codes to make the rest of the word small caps. Figure 12-4 shows you what the dialog box should look like. If you are not familiar with bracket codes (the <S> and the <D>), you can leave them out.

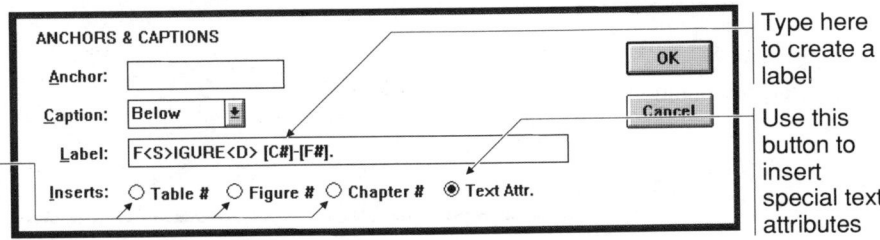

Figure 12-4. Adding a label to the caption.

Use these buttons to insert automatic numbering

Type here to create a label

Use this button to insert special text attributes

Changing the numbering style

Unless you tell it otherwise, Ventura uses Arabic numerals and starts with the number one. You can change these defaults if you want. For instance, you might prefer Roman numerals or letters. Or you might want to number the figures sequentially throughout a long document. If the first chapter had seven pictures, then the second chapter's pictures would need to start with eight to keep the sequence intact. To change the numbering style:

1. Choose Update Counters from the Edit menu.

2. Select Which Counter: Initial Figure.

3. To manually start at a number other than one, select Update Method: Restart Number. In the Restart Number text box type the number you want to start with instead. It's up to you to know the correct number.

4. To ask Ventura to number sequentially across chapter boundaries, select Update Method: Previous Number +1. Ventura will look at the last number in the previous chapter and add one to it to preserve the correct sequence. It's up to you to put the chapters in the correct order in your publication when you print them with Manage Publication from the File menu.

5. To use something other than Arabic numerals, select the format from the Number Format list box. You can select letters, Roman numerals, or spelled out words in a variety of capitalization styles. For instance, to use capital letters instead of Arabic numerals, select *A,B* from the Number Format list box (Figure 12-5).

6. Click on OK.

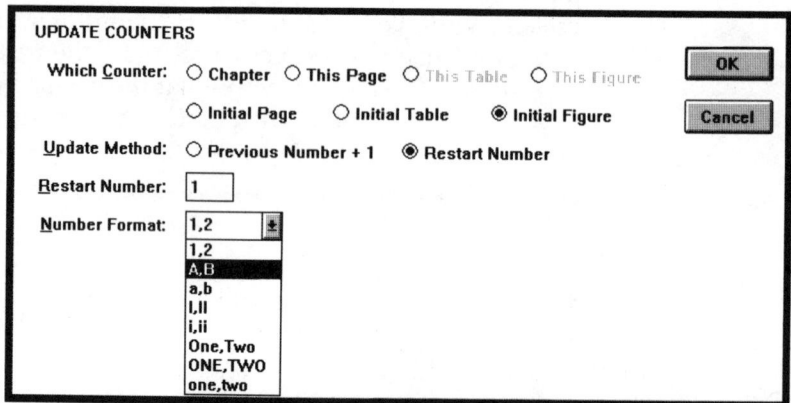

Figure 12-5.
The Update Counters dialog box allows you to change the way figures and tables (and chapters and pages, for that matter) are numbered.

Adding caption text

When you attach a caption frame, Ventura automatically puts a paragraph inside that frame. Ventura marks the paragraph with an end-of-file symbol—a hollow box.

To add caption text for a picture, you simply type inside the frame. Using the Text Tool, place the text cursor just to the left of the end-of-file symbol inside the caption frame. Then type the text (Figure 12-6).

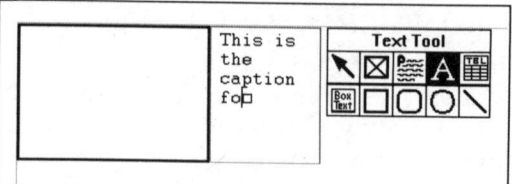

Figure 12-6.
Use the Text tool to type caption text directly into the caption frame.

If you can't see the end-of-file symbol, choose Show Tabs & Returns from the View menu. If you still can't see it, use the mouse to enlarge the caption frame until the marker is visible.

You can have caption text by itself, or you can combine it with a caption label (as we've done for the pictures in this book). As mentioned earlier, the caption text appears *after* the caption label. If you haven't created a caption label, then the caption text is the only thing inside the caption frame.

Example: If you are following our hands-on example, try putting caption text alongside the caption label you created in the previous section. Position the Text Tool inside the caption frame just to the left of the end-of-file symbol. Type "A sample of caption text." Don't worry about formatting—we'll cover that in the next section. At this point, the example should look similar to Figure 12-7.

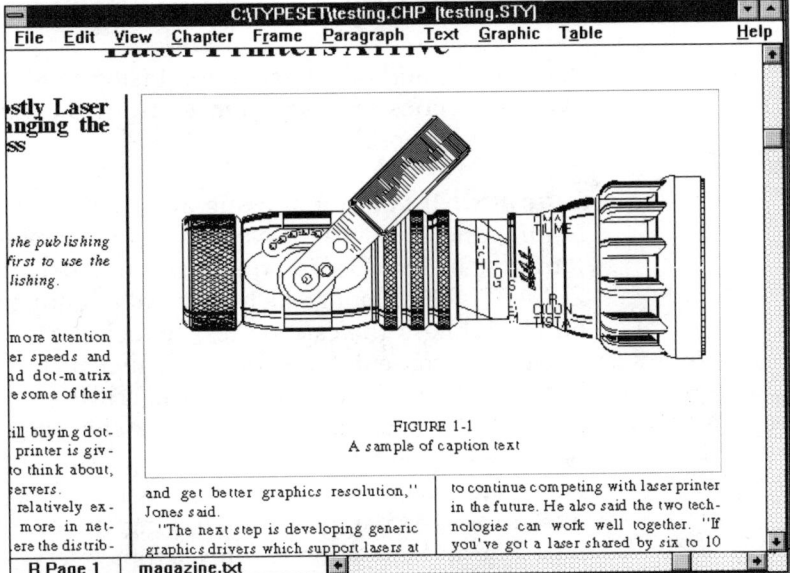

Figure 12-7. Continue with the hands-on example by typing text into the caption frame.

Tip: Ventura stores the captions you type in a separate text file, which has the CAP extension. For instance, if your chapter is called REPORT.CHP, the captions will be in a file called REPORT.CAP. You can edit and spellcheck this ASCII-format file, *but use caution*. Ventura keeps track of captions by their order in the file. If you add or delete so much as a single carriage return, you'll throw off the order and the captions will appear with the wrong pictures.

Formatting caption labels and text

As Ventura creates caption labels and text, it automatically assigns them one of four different tag names:

- Z_LABEL CAP for labels without numbers
- Z_LABEL FIG for labels that include figure numbering
- Z_LABEL TBL for labels that include table numbering
- Z_CAPTION for caption text

You can retag the paragraphs with different names if you prefer, but usually there's no reason to do so.

You can use these tags to change the style and appearance of caption labels and caption text. With the Paragraph Tool, click on the paragraph. Then use the Paragraph menu to change the formatting. For detailed instructions on changing tags, see Chapter 3, "Building Basic Styles."

Tip: If these and other generated tags don't appear in the Tag List Window, choose Set Preferences from the Edit menu and select Generated Tags: Shown.

Example: If you're following along with our example, try reformatting the label and the caption text you created earlier. Using the Paragraph Tool, select the caption label, which is tagged as Z_LABEL FIG. Change its horizontal alignment from center to left. Now, highlight the caption text, which is tagged as Z_CAPTION. Use the Alignment dialog box to change its horizontal alignment to left, turn the relative indent on, and create a first line indent of 1,00 picas and points. Now open the Breaks dialog box. Select Line Break: After and click on OK. By putting a line break after the paragraph (instead of before), you have removed the break between the two paragraphs, allowing them to reside on the same line. The indents keep the text from overlapping. When you're finished, your page should look similar to Figure 12-8.

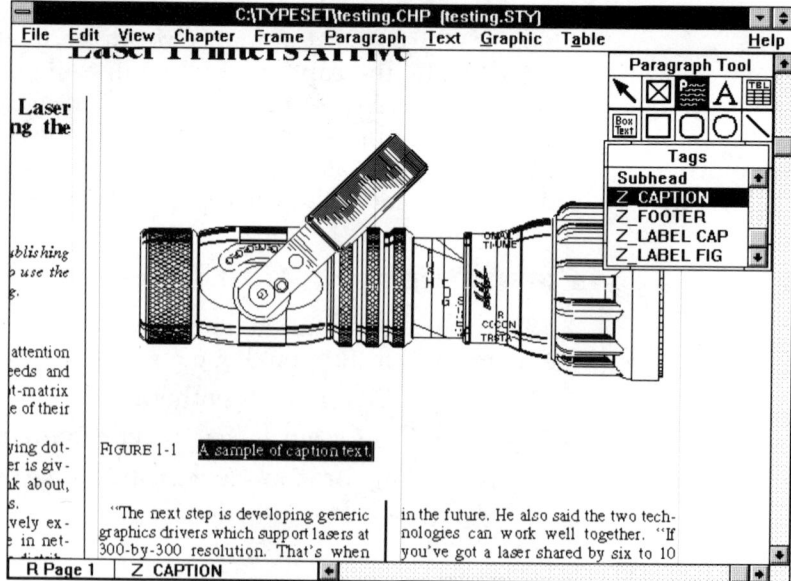

Figure 12-8. The example chapter after reformatting the caption label and caption text.

Figure 12-9.
You can apply a shade to the picture frame, the caption frame, or (as in this case) to both.

Caption samples

Now that you have the mechanics of captions under your belt, we thought you might like to see a few examples of caption styles. The three samples in Figures 12-9 through 12-12 were created entirely in Ventura. They imitate some well-known magazines. The captions were built using the techniques explained above.

Adding ruling boxes and lines

You'll often want borders to set your pictures off from the rest of the document. Ventura lets you put up to three ruling boxes around a frame. If you prefer, you can put ruling lines along the top, along the bottom, or both (Figure 12-11).

Figure 12-10. You can change the size of caption frames and you can put them on any side of the picture frame.

ARTIFICIAL INTELLIGENCE

MIND GAMES:
For this Soviet Scientist, there's more to computer games than graphics

Lorum ipsum dolor sit amet, con; minimum venami quis nostrud laboris nisi ut aliquip ex ea com color in reprehenderit in voluptate nonumy. Lorum ipsum dolor sit amet, con; minimum venami quis nostrud laboris nisi ut aliquip ex ea com color in reprehenderit in voluptate nonumy. Minimum veniami ex ea con dolor in reprehenderit in voluptate nonumy.

This is a line of Milano cookies, bearing all their belongings, having been evicted from Pepperidge Farms.

Lorum ipsum dolor sit amet, con; minimum venami quis nostrud laboris nisi ut aliquip ex ea com color in reprehenderit in voluptate nonumy. Minimum veniami ex ea con dolor in reprehenderit in voluptate nonumy. Minimum veniami ex ea con dolor in reprehenderit in voluptate nonumy.

Tetris for Windows provides all the action of the original release of the program, but allows the use to modify the background of each level of play to display any .BMP file.

The windless city

Lorum ipsum dolor sit amet, con; minimum venami quis nostrud laboris nisi ut aliquip ex ea com color in reprehenderit in voluptate nonumy. Lorum ipsum dolor sit amet, con; minimum venami quis nostrud laboris nisi ut aliquip ex ea com color in reprehenderit in voluptate nonumy. Minimum veniami ex ea con dolor in reprehenderit in voluptate nonumy.

Lorum ipsum dolor sit amet, con; minimum venami quis nostrud laboris nisi ut aliquip ex ea com color in reprehenderit in voluptate nonumy. Lorum ipsum dolor sit amet, con; minimum venami quis nostrud laboris nisi ut aliquip ex ea com color in reprehenderit in voluptate nonumy.

Lorum ipsum dolor sit amet, con; minimum venami quis nostrud laboris nisi ut aliquip ex ea com color in reprehenderit in voluptate nonumy. Lorum ipsum dolor sit amet, con; minimum venami quis nostrud laboris nisi ut aliquip ex ea com color in reprehenderit in voluptate nonumy.

An order of hashbrowns on the sidewalk

Lorum ipsum dolor sit amet, con; minimum venami quis nostrud laboris nisi ut aliquip ex ea com color in reprehenderit in voluptate nonumy. Lorum ipsum dolor sit amet, con; minimum venami quis nostrud laboris nisi ut aliquip ex ea com color in reprehenderit in voluptate nonumy. Minimum veniami ex ea con dolor in reprehenderit in voluptate nonumy.

Lorum ipsum dolor sit amet, con; minimum venami quis nostrud laboris nisi ut aliquip ex ea com color in reprehenderit in voluptate nonumy. Lorum ipsum dolor sit amet, con; minimum venami quis nostrud laboris nisi ut aliquip ex ea com color in reprehenderit in voluptate nonumy. Minimum veniami ex ea con dolor in reprehenderit in voluptate nonumy. Lorum ipsum dolor sit amet, con; minimum venami quis nostrud laboris nisi ut aliquip ex ea com color in reprehenderit in voluptate nonumy.

Sizzling sassafrass

Lorum ipsum dolor sit amet, con; minimum venami quis nostrud laboris nisi ut aliquip ex ea com color in reprehenderit in voluptate nonumy. Lorum ipsum dolor sit amet, con; minimum venami quis nostrud laboris nisi ut aliquip ex ea com color in reprehenderit in voluptate nonumy. Minimum veniami ex ea con dolor in reprehenderit in voluptate nonumy.

Lorum ipsum dolor sit amet, con; minimum quis nostrud laboris nisi ut aliquip ex ea com color in voluptate. Lorum ipsum amet, con; nostrud laboris ex ea com color in in nonumy. Minimum veniami ex.

16 OMNI

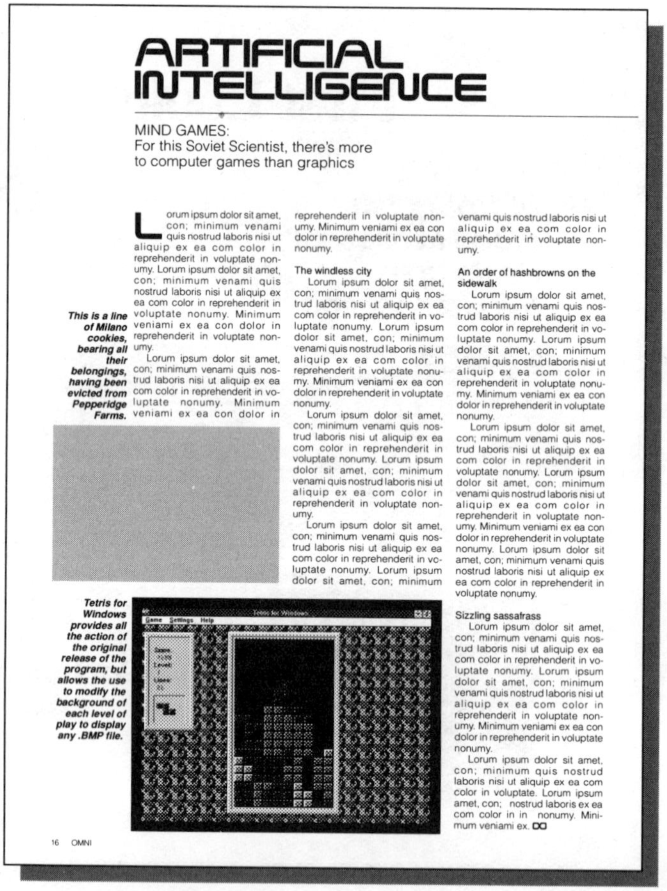

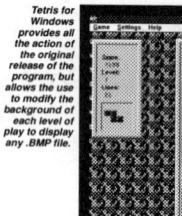

Figure 12-11. A few of Ventura's options for adding borders and lines to pictures.

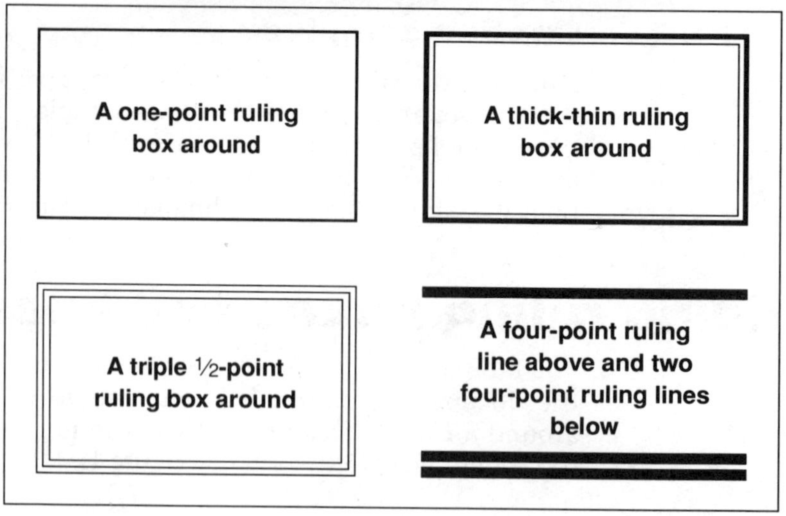

Figure 12-12. These captions use a short ruling line to separate them from the main text. It is created with a second paragraph in the caption frame, either above or below the caption text, that has a ruling line applied with the paragraph menu.

The picture frame and the caption frame are treated separately. You can put a ruling box around them both. Or you can put a ruling box around the frame but not around the caption, as we've done for the pictures in this book.

In this section, we'll explain how to attach a ruling box to a picture frame. Ruling lines work in the same fashion, except that they appear above or below the frame instead of all the way around. To create a ruling box:

1. Using the Frame Tool, select the frame.
2. Choose Ruling Box Around from the Frame menu (Figure 12-13).
3. Select Width: Frame. Until you make this selection, you can't work with the rest of the dialog box.

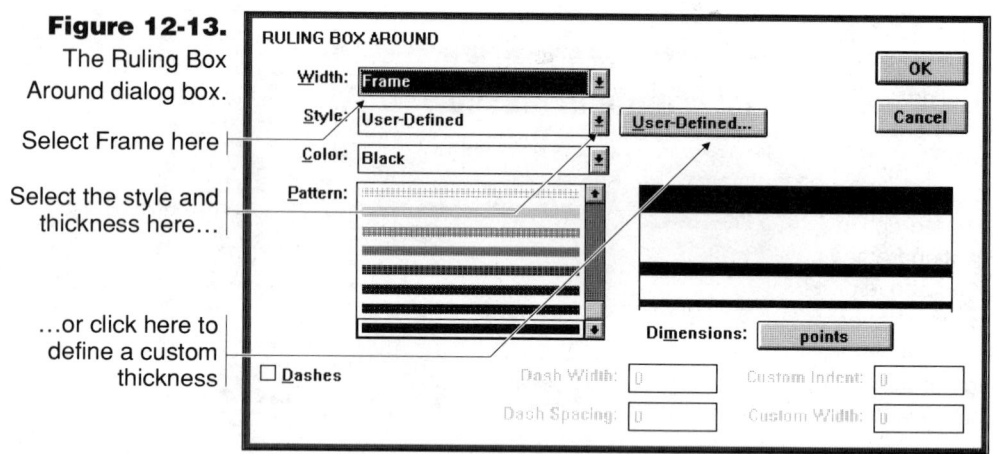

Figure 12-13.
The Ruling Box Around dialog box.

Select Frame here

Select the style and thickness here...

...or click here to define a custom thickness

4. To use a predefined style, select the one you want from the Style list box. (The word *Style* refers to the number of lines and their thicknesses).

5. To create a style of your own, select User-Defined from the Style list box. Then click on the User-Defined button to bring up the secondary dialog box (explained in detail below).

6. Select the color you want from the Color list box. Most ruling lines and boxes are black.

7. Select the pattern you want from the Pattern list box. If you want a solid rule, select the line on the very bottom.

8. If you want a dashed line, click on the Dashes check box. If you don't like the default version, you can control both the width of the dashes and the space between them with the Dash Width and Dash Spacing text boxes.

9. Click on OK.

As you make your selections, you will see a portrayal of the ruling box in the Preview Box. This preview is not completely accurate, but it does give you a rough idea of what you are seeing. After you click on OK, the ruling box will appear around your frame.

Note: The screen version of the ruling line is only approximate. It is particularly inaccurate for thin rules, because of the coarse resolution of the screen pixels. In addition, the thicknesses will vary according to the type of printer you use. Only a high-resolution typesetter can produce true hairlines. In general, a 300-dpi laser printer can only produce lines of a quarter point or larger.

Example: Try a one-point ruling box around the nozzle picture we've been working with in our example chapter. Select the frame, and then choose Ruling Box Around from the Frame menu. Select Width: Frame, Style: 1 point, Color: Black, and Pattern: Solid. Click on OK. Your results should look similar to Figure 12-14.

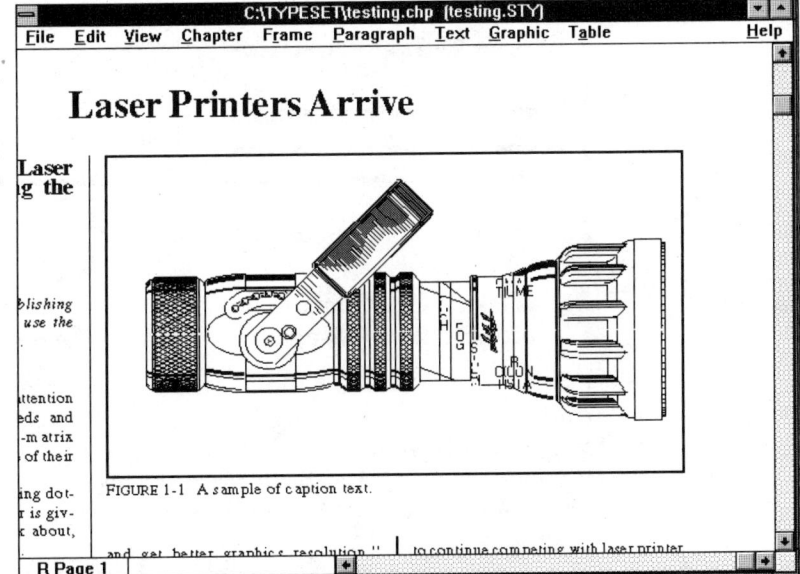

Figure 12-14. Our hands-on example chapter after putting a one-point ruling box around the picture of a nozzle.

Creating a user-defined line style

If you don't like the predefined line styles, you can create one of your own. You can control the number of lines, their thickness, and the space between them.

To create a user-defined style, follow the instructions above. Make all your choices except for the Style. Then choose User-Defined from the Style list box and click on the User-Defined button. The User-Defined Ruling Style dialog box appears (Figure 12-15).

This dialog box refers to the outermost line as Rule 1, the next one as Rule 2, and the innermost line as Rule 3. In most cases, however, you will only want to use a single ruling box around a picture. But even if you are only using a single ruling line, you must still access this dialog box to create a custom thickness.

To create custom ruling boxes with this dialog box:

1. Type the thickness of each line in its Height text box.

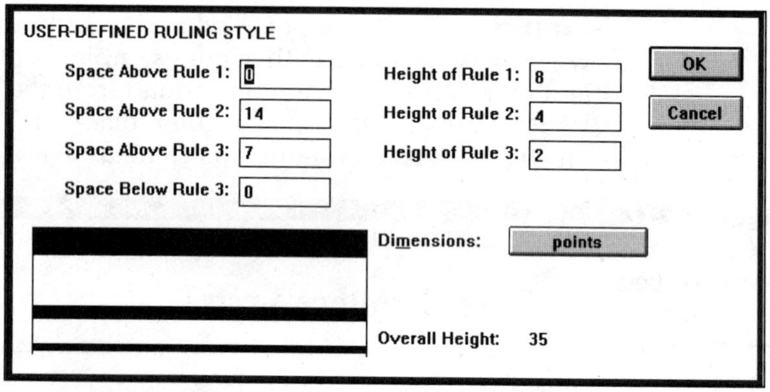

Figure 12-15. With this dialog box, you can create a unique style for ruling boxes and lines around picture frames.

2. Type the space above or below each line (if any) in the Space text box.

3. Click on OK. Clicking on OK returns you to the original dialog box. Click on OK again to return to the workspace.

Putting space above Rule 1 puts a gap between the edge of the frame and the first ruling line. In most cases, you should not use any space above Rule 1 when creating a ruling box around a frame. If you want to create a buffer zone so text does not touch the ruling box, you should use the padding feature, as explained later in this chapter.

Putting space above Rule 2 creates a gap between the outermost ruling line (Rule 1) and the second line (Rule 2). Putting space *below* Rule 3 creates a gap between the innermost ruling box and the picture within the frame.

As you make your choices, you can see an approximation of the results in the Preview Box in the lower left.

Warning: When you add ruling boxes to frames that have pictures inside, you should add a margin to the inside of the frame. Otherwise, the picture may overlap and obscure the ruling line (Figure 12-16).

Tip: If you want the picture to be flush against the ruling box, make the margin equal to the thickness of the ruling box. For instance, if you have a one-point ruling box, make the margin one point on all sides. If you want white space between the ruling box and the picture, then you should make the margins larger.

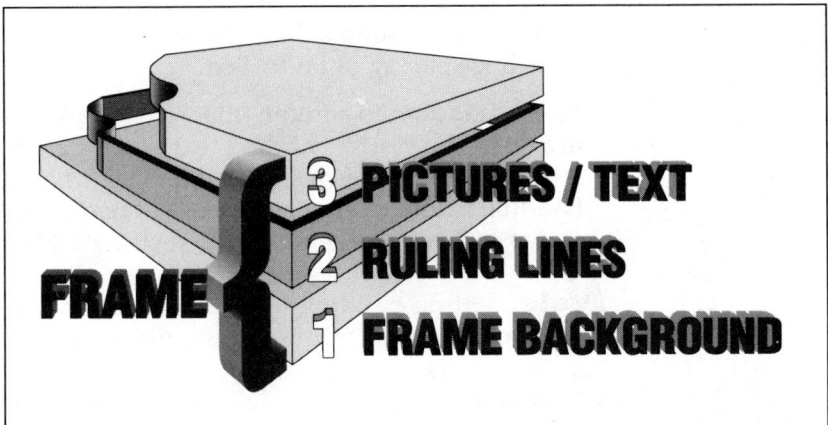

Figure 12-16.
This is an edge-view representation of a frame. Pictures and text, being on the top layer of a frame, can obscure both ruling lines and the frame background unless margins are applied.

Padding pictures

Padding keeps text from colliding with the edges of frames. It is the spacing between the outside of the frame and the text around it (Figure 12-17).

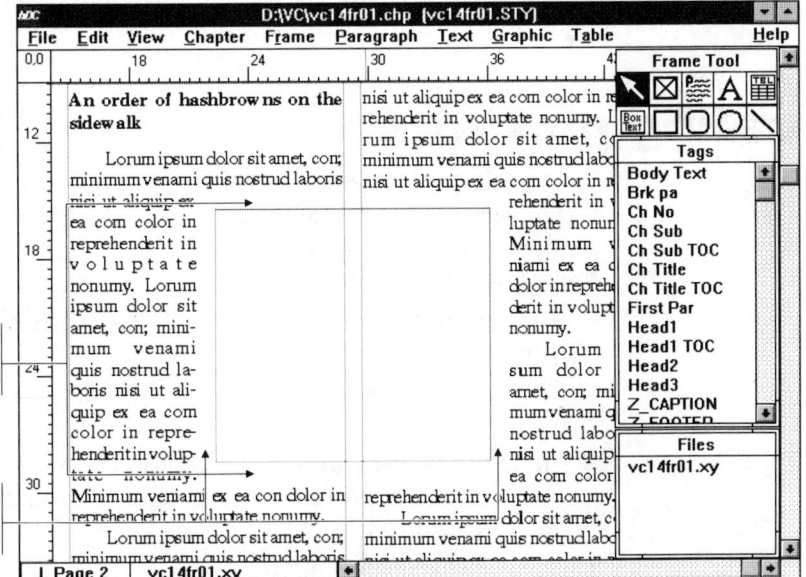

Figure 12-17.
Padding forms an invisible boundary outside the frame into which text may not penetrate.

Vertical padding area

Horizontal padding area

You should use padding whenever your frames intrude into the text area. It is not necessary if text is confined within frames or columns and cannot touch the picture. But if the picture frame is inside a text frame area, set the padding to at least one half the inter-line spacing of Body Text.

To add padding to a frame, choose Sizing & Scaling from the Frame menu. In the Horiz. Padding text box type the amount of padding that you want on each side (left and right) of the frame. In the Vert. Padding text box type the amount of padding that you want to add above and below the frame. Then click on OK.

Note: Setting padding for a picture frame does not automatically set it for a caption frame—you must set it separately.

Example: In our example chapter, the column boundaries keep the text from touching the sides of the picture. The caption frame, however, could use some padding to ensure the text is not too close to the caption. As it stands, the caption frame is about three lines deep, even though the caption is only one line deep. Use the mouse to resize the caption frame so that it is only one line deep. With the caption frame still selected, choose Sizing & Scaling from the Frame menu. Add vertical padding of 7 points and click on OK. Can you see the extra space that has opened up below. Now try it with 28 points of vertical padding. See the difference?

Scaling pictures

In Chapter 11, "Loading and Placing Pictures," you learned how to resize picture frames with a mouse or with a dialog box. In this section, you'll find out how to change the size of the picture inside the frame. For instance, you can:

- Ask Ventura to stretch or shrink the picture, so that it fills the frame completely
- Enlarge or reduce the picture manually, without affecting the frame
- Make the picture larger than the frame and show only a portion of it through a process called *cropping* which we'll cover in the next section.

These options apply whether you are using images or line-art. For more information about the difference between images and line art, see Chapter 10, "Creating Pictures with Other Programs."

When you change the size of a frame, Ventura calls it *sizing*. When you change the size of the picture inside, Ventura calls it *scaling*.

Look at the Sizing & Scaling dialog box (Figure 12-18). The top half has to do with the size and position of the frame. The bottom half controls the appearance of the picture inside.

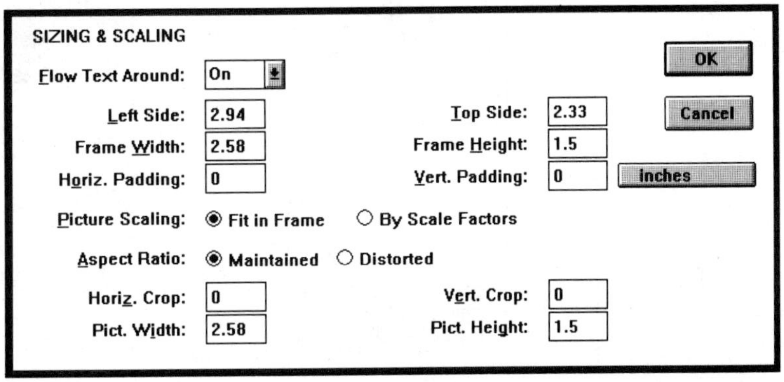

Figure 12-18.
Use this dialog box to size frames and scale pictures.

SIZING & SCALING				
Flow Text Around:	On			OK
Left Side:	2.94	Top Side:	2.33	Cancel
Frame Width:	2.58	Frame Height:	1.5	
Horiz. Padding:	0	Vert. Padding:	0	Inches
Picture Scaling:	● Fit in Frame	○ By Scale Factors		
Aspect Ratio:	● Maintained	○ Distorted		
Horiz. Crop:	0	Vert. Crop:	0	
Pict. Width:	2.58	Pict. Height:	1.5	

Before we step you through the process of scaling a picture, let's examine the four key options in this dialog box.

Picture Scaling: Fit In Frame tells Ventura to resize the picture automatically. If you change the size of the frame, Ventura will change the size of the picture to match.

Picture Scaling: By Scale Factors tells Ventura you want to resize the picture manually. You type in the measurements you want. From then on, the picture stays the same size even if you resize the frame.

Aspect Ratio: Maintained tells Ventura that, if Scaling is set to Fit In Frame, it can change the size of the picture as long as it doesn't distort the original proportions (the ratio of height to width). You'll use this option for product illustrations, CAD drawings, technical drawings, and other applications where accuracy is essential. Be aware that you may end up with extra white space. Ventura will enlarge or shrink the picture as much as possible, but it will leave white space in the frame if necessary to avoid distorting the aspect ratio.

Aspect Ratio: Distorted tells Ventura it can change the size of the picture any way it wants, even if it stretches the picture out of its original proportions. This option always fills the frame completely so that there is no unwanted white space. You'll use it when you don't care if the picture is slightly disfigured.

You can combine these options to create the four effects shown in Figure 12-19.

Figure 12-19.
Ventura's four different picture scaling effects.

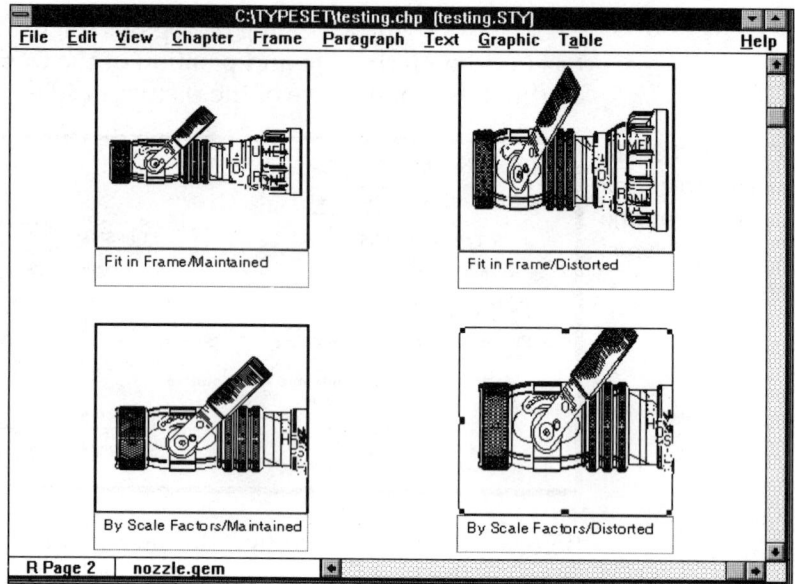

The upper left example combines Fit In Frame with Aspect Ratio: Maintained. As you can see, Ventura tries to fill the frame, but it has to leave some space at the top and bottom because it is not allowed to distort the original proportions.

The upper right example combines Fit In Frame with Aspect Ratio: Distorted. Notice how the picture fills the whole frame. Notice as well that the picture has been deformed, because we told Ventura it could distort the original proportions if necessary.

The lower left example combines By Scale Factors with Aspect Ratio: Maintained. We instructed Ventura to increase the width by about 50%. It enlarged the picture while keeping the proportions as they were in the original.

The lower right example combines By Scale Factors with Aspect Ratio: Distorted. Once again we instructed Ventura to increase the width by about 50%. As you can see, this time it distorted the height as well.

Scaling a picture to fit in the frame

Scaling a picture to fit in the frame is easy because Ventura does the calculations. You click on the correct buttons, and Ventura figures out how to stretch the picture to fit the boundaries of the frame. To scale a picture to fit in the frame:

1. Using the Frame Tool, select the frame containing the picture.
2. Choose Sizing & Scaling from the Frame menu.
3. Select Picture Scaling: Fit in Frame.
4. If you want to preserve the original proportions, select Aspect Ratio: Maintained. If you don't care if the picture is stretched out of its original shape, choose Aspect Ratio: Distorted.
5. Click on OK.

Tip: You should always maintain the aspect ratio of gray-scale images to avoid unpleasant moire patterns.

Example: Try scaling the nozzle picture in our example chapter. Select the frame, and then choose Sizing & Scaling. You'll see that the current combination is Fit In Frame/Maintained. Select Fit In Frame/Distorted instead and click on OK. Notice the difference in the picture? The nozzle picture has been elongated or compressed to fit within the frame.

Scaling a picture manually

Scaling a picture manually requires you to do a small amount of math, but it gives you complete control over the dimensions.

Scaling a picture manually starts by selecting Picture Scaling: By Scale Factors in the Sizing & Scaling dialog box. As soon as you make this selection, Ventura displays two numbers in the Pict. Width and Pict. Height text boxes. These numbers represent the original dimensions of the picture. To change size, you type in the new numbers you want.

For instance, suppose you have a picture that is two inches wide. To double its width, you would make its width four inches. To cut its size in half, you would make the width one inch.

You can scale a picture with the aspect ratio maintained, or with the aspect ratio distorted. If you maintain the aspect ratio, Ventura will only let you change the width. After you tell it what the new width should be, it calculates the new height necessary to keep the proportions exactly as they were before. If you scale a picture with the aspect ratio distorted, Ventura lets you change both the width and the height. Here's how:

1. Using the Frame Tool, select the frame containing the picture.
2. Choose Sizing & Scaling from the Frame menu.

3. Select Picture Scaling: By Scale Factors.

4. To preserve the original proportions, select Aspect Ratio: Maintained. Then type a new width into the Pict. Width text box. Ventura will calculate a new height for you. If you don't need to preserve the original proportions, select Aspect Ratio: Distorted. Now type the new width and height you want in the Pict. Width and Pict. Height text boxes.

5. Click on OK.

Ventura enlarges or reduces the picture regardless of the size of the frame that contains it. After you choose By Scale Factors, Ventura maintains the picture's size until you change it. Resizing the frame will not change the size of the picture.

Because the picture is now independent of the frame, you may need to adjust the size of the frame. For instance, if you reduce the picture, you could end up with a tiny picture inside a large frame. If you enlarge it, you could end up with a picture that is much larger than the frame.

If the picture is larger than the frame, Ventura shows as much of it as possible, starting with the upper left corner. You can choose to display a different portion of the picture by cropping it, as explained in the next section.

***E*xample:** Try enlarging the line-art illustration of a nozzle in our example chapter. Select the frame, and then choose Sizing & Scaling from the Frame menu. Select Picture Scaling: By Scale Factors and Aspect Ratio: Distorted. Now experiment with different values in the Pict. Width and Pict. Height dialog boxes. For instance, try making the picture smaller by typing a width and height of 15,00 picas & points. Make it larger by typing a width and height of 35,00 picas & points.

***W*arning:** When scaling a bit-mapped image, always try to enlarge or reduce it by whole numbers. For instance, enlarge a picture by 2, or by 3, or by 4, but not by 1⅞. Otherwise, you may see unwanted patterns appear in the picture. These considerations do not apply to line art, which can be enlarged or reduced without any of these problems.

As you learned in Chapter 10, "Creating Pictures with Other Programs," a bit-mapped image is like a piece of graph paper with some squares black and others white. If you produce that image at its original size, the image's pixels will translate directly to the output device (1 pixel = 1 pixel). Likewise, if you enlarge or reduce by whole numbers, the output device can easily make the translation (1 pixel = 2 pixels, for instance).

But if you enlarge or reduce a bit-mapped image by a fractional number, you'll cause problems. An output device can only print whole pixels. It can't print half pixels or any other fraction. For instance, if you print an image 1⅔ times its original size, the output device tries to represent each original pixel with 1⅔ pixels. Because it can't do that, it has to round it up or down to the nearest whole pixel value.

Rounding off the numbers introduces errors. Sometimes, the printer rounds up and sometimes it rounds down, distorting the original pattern. Figure 12-20 shows what can happen if you take a regularly spaced checkerboard pattern and enlarge it 1⅔ times its original size.

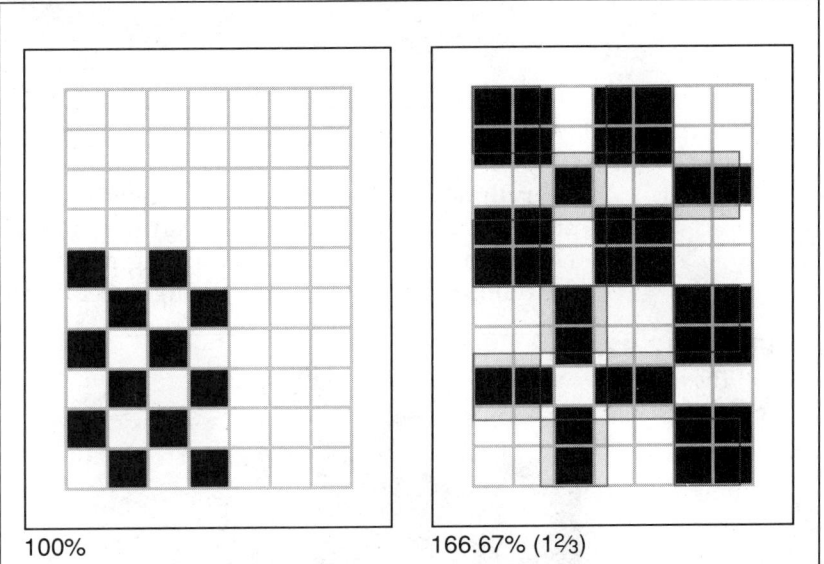

Figure 12-20. This shows enlargment of an image to 1⅔ times its actual size. The light gray areas, surrounded by a dark gray line, show an actual 1⅔ enlargement. Note that areas with less than half a pixel covered with gray have not turned black, whereas those more than half gray have "rounded up," and are black.

Cropping pictures

Often you want to use a picture — but only a portion. You can show the part you want and eliminate the rest with *cropping*. You can crop pictures with the mouse, or you can crop them by typing numbers into the Sizing & Scaling dialog box.

Imagine a picture the size of a piece of notebook paper. Now suppose you have a piece of cardboard the same size, with a two-inch square cut in the center. If you put the cardboard over the picture, you'll only be able to see what shows through the two-inch square. The square provides a "window" onto the larger picture.

When you crop a picture in Ventura, you usually make the picture bigger than the frame. Then you decide what part of the picture to show. Initially, Ventura puts the "window" at the upper left corner of the picture. You can move it around if you want to show a different portion instead (Figure 12-21).

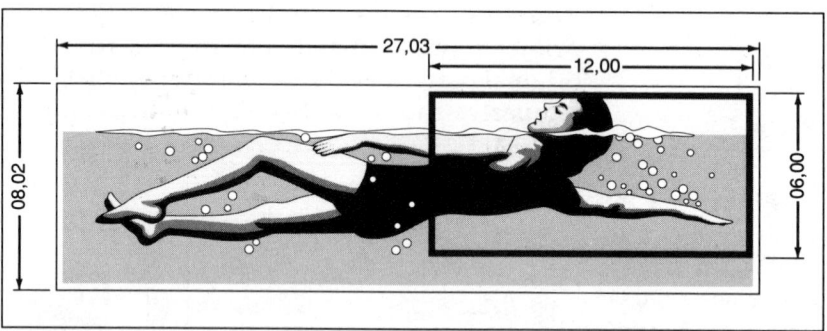

Figure 12-21.
The gray box shows the portion of this larger picture we want to show in the frame.

Everything in the "window" shows on the screen and on the printed page. The rest of the picture is not visible (Figure 12-22). There are two methods for cropping pictures in Ventura: (1) using the mouse and (2) using the Sizing & Scaling dialog box.

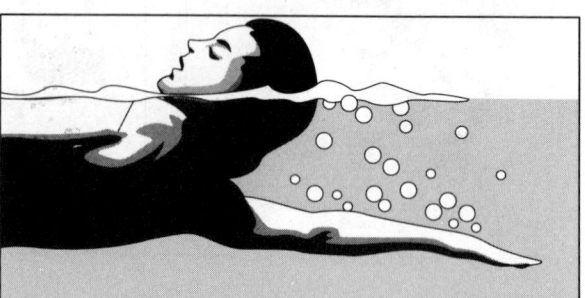

Figure 12-22.
The resulting cropped picture.

Note: Cropping a picture doesn't delete the unused portions. The rest of the picture is still there, it simply doesn't display or print. The original picture file is not changed in any way.

Cropping with the mouse

We just explained that you crop a picture by making it larger than the frame, and then deciding which part to show. That's what usually happens. You can also crop a picture that is smaller than the frame. If you want to move a small picture, so that it appears in a different part of the frame, you can do so by cropping.

But most people use cropping to eliminate unwanted portions of a picture by pushing them into the area that doesn't show. They also use it to spotlight key sections of a picture, by enlarging that section and eliminating the rest of the picture.

To crop with the mouse:

1. Using the Frame Tool, place the frame cursor anywhere inside the frame containing the picture.
2. While holding down the Alt key, hold down the left mouse button. The cursor changes to a small hand, which shows you that you can "push" the picture within the frame to crop it.
3. While still holding down the Alt key and the left mouse button, move the mouse to move the picture inside the frame.
4. Release the button when you've got the picture positioned the way you want it.

*E*xample: If you're following along with our example chapter, try cropping the nozzle picture with the mouse. First, select the picture frame. Then scale the picture so that it has a width and height of 35,00 picas & points. To do this, choose Sizing & Scaling from the Frame menu and type 35,00 in the Pict. Width and the Pict. Height text boxes. Then click on OK. Now use the mouse to push the picture left and up until the front part of the nozzle shows inside the frame.

Cropping with the
Sizing & Scaling dialog box

If you need more precision, you can crop pictures with the Sizing & Scaling dialog box. You type numbers to tell Ventura how far to push the picture and in which direction. To crop a picture with the dialog box:

1. Using the Frame Tool, select the frame containing the picture.
2. Choose Sizing & Scaling from the Frame menu.

3. Type the amount of cropping in the X Crop Offset and Y Crop Offset text boxes.
4. Click on OK.

The X Crop Offset and Y Crop Offset entries are not very intuitive, but they are relatively easy to use once you understand how they are set up:

- *X Crop Offset* moves the picture horizontally. It measures the distance from the left of the frame. A positive value moves the picture to the *left*. A negative value moves the picture to the *right*. A value of zero restores the picture to its original position with the left edge of the picture next to the left edge of the frame.

- *Y Crop Offset* moves the picture vertically. It measures the distance from the top of the frame. A positive value moves the picture *up*. A negative value moves the picture *down*. A value of zero restores the picture to its original position with the top of the picture next to the top of the frame.

Note: If the frame has margins applied to it, the X Crop Offset and Y Crop Offset measure from the left and top margins, respectively, instead of the edge of the frame.

Continuing on

In this chapter, you learned how to add the finishing touches to pictures and how to add caption frames, caption text, caption labels, and automatic numbering. You saw how to add borders, and padding to frames. And you learned how to change the size of a picture and choose which portion will display and print. In the next part, you'll learn how to print your documents and use Ventura's advanced features.

Easy Access

For more info on...	See chapter...
Using the Breaks dialog box to put two paragraphs on the same line	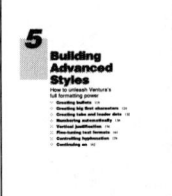
Using bracket codes for text attributes	
Bringing pictures into a chapter	
Remembering the correct bracket codes and choosing the line style you want	

Part Five:
Printing and Advanced Features

13
Printing Ventura Documents

How to print documents
and work with fonts

- **Understanding printing** 371
- **Preparing to print** 378
- **Printing a single chapter** 391
- **Printing multiple chapters** 397
- **Printing special jobs** 400
- **Continuing on** 415

Printing seems deceptively simple in Ventura, but there's a lot going on. In this chapter, we'll show you how to exploit all of Ventura's printing power. First, we'll explain how Ventura and Windows cooperate to put characters onto the page. Then, we'll show you how to set things up in advance, so that you don't get any unexpected surprises. We'll even explain those mysterious *width tables* that perplex people so much. Next, we'll step you through the process of printing one or more chapters. Finally, we'll cover a handful of circumstances that require special techniques.

Ventura works slightly differently than most Windows applications, so you need to start by learning how Ventura prints pages. Once you understand the process, you can achieve superb control over the appearance of your printed pages.

Understanding printing

Even the most basic printing tasks are easier if you know what's happening behind the scenes. And if you need to do advanced printing—use downloadable soft fonts, print to disk files, and so on—this knowledge is mandatory.

The key is realizing that printing is a cooperative effort between Ventura and Windows. Every time it starts up, Ventura queries Windows' initialization file, called WIN.INI, to find out what printing resources are available.

How Ventura works with WIN.INI

Ventura doesn't print on its own. Instead, it uses Windows' printing resources. To find out what's hooked up to your system, Ventura looks in a special file called WIN.INI.

When Ventura starts up, it examines WIN.INI to see which printers and fonts it can use. WIN.INI is a text file located in the \WINDOWS directory. It lists Windows devices, settings, and preferences. When you use Windows Control Panel, the changes you make are saved in the WIN.INI file. You can also make changes manually by editing WIN.INI just as you would edit any other ASCII file. As you'll see later, certain advanced printing functions *require* you to manually edit WIN.INI.

You can look at the WIN.INI file for your computer by opening it with the Notepad accessory or any word processor (Figure 13-1).

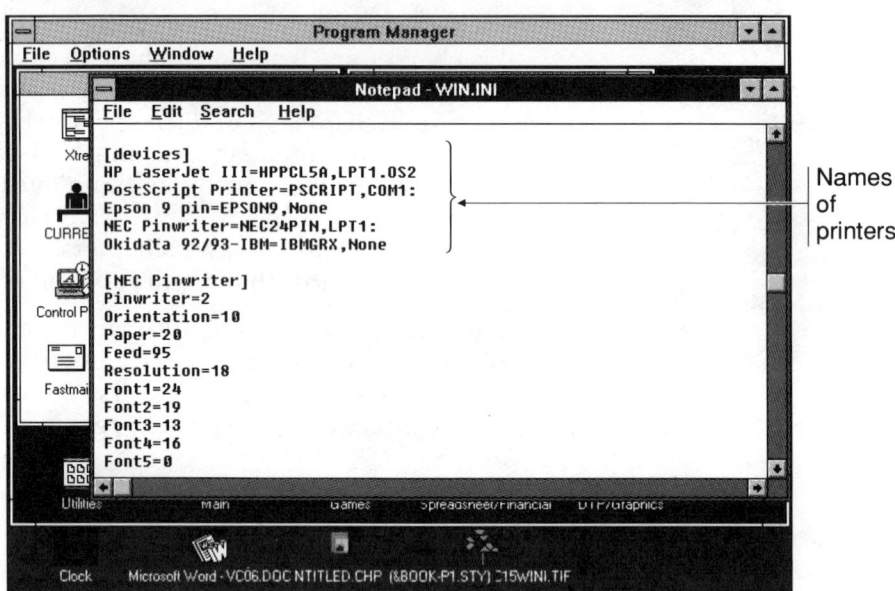

Figure 13-1.
The WIN.INI file lists (among other things), the printers and fonts Ventura can use. This particular computer has five devices (printers) available.

WIN.INI is divided into sections. Each section controls one aspect of the environment. This is not the place to explain all of WIN.INI's options. But we do want to acquaint you with the five sections that have to do with printing. Many printing problems can be traced back to these sections.

Table 13-1 summarizes the five printing-related sections and what they contain. Study this table for a moment. We will refer to it later in the chapter.

How Ventura works with fonts

Ventura needs three kinds of information to work with fonts:

1. Which fonts are available (for a particular printer)

2. How much space to give each character

3. Which screen font to use to imitate the printed characters on the screen

Table 13-1. *WIN.INI sections that affect printing*

Name	What it does	How it affects Ventura
[devices]	Defines the printers available to Ventura.	Unless a printer is listed here, Ventura can't use it.
[ports]	Defines which ports are available. Think of a port as a "pipe" or "channel" through which Ventura can pour information.	Ventura can change the port you are using, but only if the new port is listed in this section. For instance, you can't send information to a file unless File is listed as one of the ports.
[PrinterPorts]	Windows restricts you to one active printer per port. This section defines which printer is active for each port.	Ventura doesn't even show printers unless they are active. If you've installed a printer but you can't access it in Ventura, its name is probably missing from this section.
[fonts]	The fonts in this section are used mostly for screen display (and for a few dot-matrix printers). Most *printer* fonts, by contrast, are defined separately in the [Printer Name] section.	Affects which fonts Ventura uses on screen.
[Printer Name,Port]	A special section for each printer you install. For instance, a PostScript printer would have a section called [PostScript,COM1] or something similar. An HP LaserJet III would have a section called something like [HPPCL5A,LPT1]. This section lists the settings and the soft fonts available for that printer.	Tells Ventura which printer driver to use. Ventura gets much of its font information from this section.

Oddly enough, Ventura doesn't need to know how each character is shaped. That work is done for Ventura by the printer and the screen fonts. Suppose you tell Ventura to put a 24-point letter *A* in Times Roman on the page. When it comes time to print, Ventura simply tells the printer "Build me a 24-point Times Roman *A*" and the printer does the heavy lifting. Likewise, to show the letter on screen, Ventura gets a screen font.

But Ventura *does* need to know which fonts it can use, how much space to give each character, and which screen font to use. This information is stored in separate places. If Ventura can't find everything it needs, it won't be able to print correctly. Let's look at each of these three factors to see how they affect printing in Ventura.

How Ventura knows which fonts are available
In Table 13-1, we described the sections of the WIN.INI file that Ventura uses to get printing information. As you saw, each printer has its own [Printer Name,Port] section. This section has a lot to do with which fonts you can use.

First, each [Printer Name,Port] section tells Ventura which *printer driver* to use. This printer driver not only controls the printer, but also tells Ventura which fonts are built-in (resident). If the printer also had additional fonts on a plug-in cartridge, that information is also shown in the [Printer Name,Port] section. After Ventura knows which fonts are resident, it makes them available for your documents. That's why the names change in the Font dialog box when you switch printers. Ventura is showing you which fonts are available for that particular printer.

In addition, the [Printer Name,Port] section lists *soft fonts*. Soft fonts are the typefaces available to that printer beyond the ones built into the printer. Soft fonts are stored on disk, then sent to the printer before printing in a process called *downloading*. If Ventura sees soft fonts listed in the [Printer Name,Port] section, it will show them in the Font dialog box, so you can use them.

Figure 13-2 shows a sample [Printer Name,Port] section for a PostScript printer. It includes soft fonts, which are listed at the end of the section.

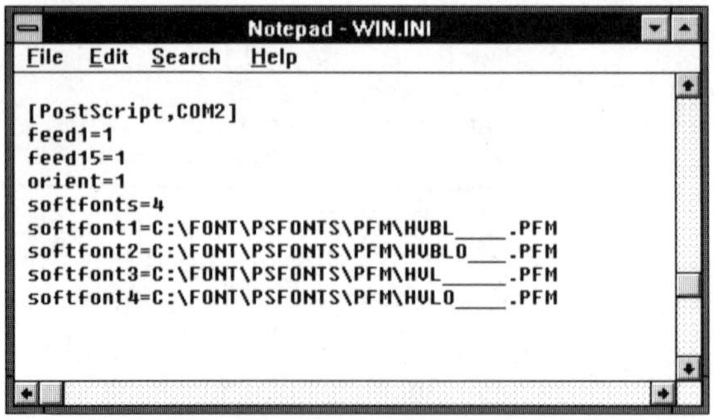

Figure 13-2.
A typical [Printer Name,Port] section.

```
[PostScript,COM2]
feed1=1
feed15=1
orient=1
softfonts=4
softfont1=C:\FONT\PSFONTS\PFM\HUBL____.PFM
softfont2=C:\FONT\PSFONTS\PFM\HUBLO___.PFM
softfont3=C:\FONT\PSFONTS\PFM\HUL____.PFM
softfont4=C:\FONT\PSFONTS\PFM\HULO___.PFM
```

How Ventura figures out character spacing

After Ventura knows which fonts are available, it still needs to know exactly how much space to allow for each character. As you have undoubtedly realized, different letters take up different amounts of space. A capital W, for instance, is much wider than a lowercase i (Figure 13-3). And the same letter in a wide font like Bookman takes up more room than the same letter in a narrow font like Times.

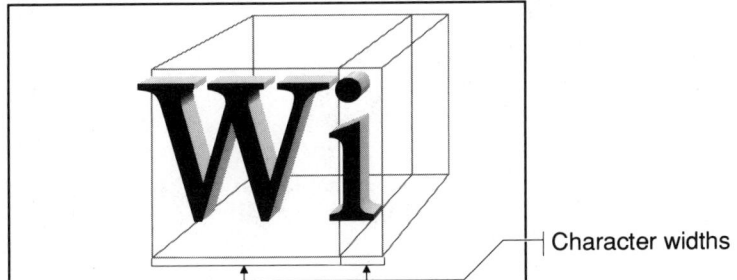

Figure 13-3. Different letters take up different amounts of space, so Ventura builds a *width table* that contains the spacing information.

How does Ventura know how much space to assign to each letter in each size in each typeface? Simple—it reads the information from a *width table*. Every time you load Ventura, it creates a new width table called ENVIRON.WID. Ventura reads the printing sections of WIN.INI, finds out what the default printer is, and builds a width table containing information about every single font available to that printer. You'll see later in the chapter when, why, and how to use ENVIRON.WID to build your own width tables.

Ventura uses the same spacing information for the printed page and for the screen (that's why they match). Where does Ventura get this information? The printer driver contains width information for built-in fonts. The width info for soft fonts, however, is in separate files. The widths for PostScript soft fonts, for instance, are in PFM (Printer Font Metrics) files. That's why the [Printer Name,Port] section of WIN.INI not only lists names of soft fonts, but also tells Ventura where to find the width information files.

How Ventura gets screen fonts

So far, you've learned how Ventura finds out which fonts it can use and how much space to allot for each character. Ventura also needs to know how to represent each font on screen.

When Ventura receives instructions to put a letter on screen, it looks at the [fonts] section of WIN.INI. If Ventura finds a screen font for that particular font in that particular size, it uses that font for the screen display. If Ventura can't find an exact match, it uses one of the generic screen fonts that come with Windows to create an on-screen approximation. (In reality, Ventura does most of this lookup in advance and stores the information in a font cache. But this is the general concept.)

The generic Windows fonts are adequate (barely) at medium sizes, but they don't make the grade for smaller and larger sizes. Indeed, you'll probably be disappointed with Ventura until you substitute better screen fonts.

How do you improve the screen font situation? You have two options. First, you can build substitutes for the sizes you use most often. Second, you can use a *font rasterizer*, which is a utility that builds screen fonts for you when you need them. We believe the best way to solve the screen font problem is with a font rasterizer. But if that option is not available to you, you can build a collection of screen fonts to use in place of the generic Windows fonts. Let's examine both options.

Building screen fonts

You probably know that a laser printer forms characters by putting dots into patterns. Likewise, an on-screen character is also a collection of dots. In the case of a computer display, these dots are called *pixels* (short for *picture elements*).

For example, you may have received a Bitstream Fontware starter set with your version of Ventura. The Bitstream Fontware package is a MS-DOS utility that build fonts for both printers and screens. You can use it just to build screen fonts and thereby obtain a dramatic improvement in your display.

The Bitstream company is known for the fonts it sells for printers. But you can use Bitstream screen fonts even if you're not using the company's printer fonts. To use Fontware, you must install it onto your hard disk, load it, and then tell it which fonts to make in which sizes. Once you've done that, you can remove it from your hard disk to regain the space.

In theory, you could make a separate set of screen fonts for each printer font. In practice, several things make that unrealistic. First, the Fontware starter kit that comes with Ventura doesn't include many fonts, so you would have to buy extras from Bitstream. Second, when you build screen fonts with Fontware, you must build separate representations for each font in each size. In other words, you must build a bit map for 10-point Dutch normal, one for 10-point Dutch bold, one for 10-point italic, and one for 10-point bold-italic. And then you must build one for 11-point normal, and one for 11-point bold, and so on, and so on.

Consequently, bit-mapped screen fonts take up a lot of room on the hard disk. If you built, for instance, a full set of screen fonts for every font on an Apple LaserWriter Plus, you would take up many megabytes of disk space.

So the best solution is to build screen fonts just for the three starter fonts that come with the Bitstream kit. Ventura will then use those fonts in place of the standard Windows fonts. It will use the serif font (Dutch) to represent any serif font you ask for. It will use the sans serif font (Swiss) for any sans serif font. And it will use Courier for every monospaced font.

The key is to build those fonts in many different sizes. That way, whenever Ventura needs to put a font on screen it can find a close match. When Ventura can't find a good match, it scales fonts on its own, creating crude approximations that are hard to read. We recommend the following sizes: 6, 7, 8, 9, 10, 11, 12, 13, 14, 18, 20, 24, 30, 36, 72.

Tip: Be sure you also build a screen font for any unusual type sizes you frequently use. If, for instance, the newsletter you work on all the time has a 64-point nameplate logo, you should create a 64-point screen font.

Warning: Use restraint if you are short on disk space. In particular, minimize the large sizes you build. Small sizes don't take up much room. But screen fonts in large sizes can take up hundreds of kilobytes each.

Using a font rasterizer

Building screen fonts in advance is one way to get a better display. But, as discussed above, it has disadvantages. A better solution is to use a font rasterizer, a utility that creates screen fonts on the fly when and as you need them.

You can buy font rasterizers from many different companies. One of the most popular is the Adobe Type Manager (ATM) from Adobe Systems, Inc. We've used ATM to illustrate the process in this section, but the same general principles apply to other font rasterizers as well. (These principles also apply to TrueType, the built-in font rasterizer that Microsoft expects to include with the ersion of Windows.)

When you buy ATM, you also buy and install font outlines. These outlines describe the shape of each character. When you need a screen font, ATM uses the outline to construct a temporary screen representation in the size you specified. (The reality is more complex than our simplified explanation, but you get the idea.)

After ATM builds the screen fonts, it stores them in a font cache, a section of temporary memory. ATM can then reuse them later without rebuilding them from scratch. That's why you see a slight delay the first time you ask for a font when using ATM. That delay represents the time it takes ATM to build the screen version. The next time you ask for the same font and size, the results are almost instantaneous, because ATM simply fetches it from memory.

Note: ATM does more than rasterize fonts for the screen. It can also rasterize them for a printer. In practice, this means that you can use PostScript fonts on non-PostScript printers such as the Hewlett-Packard LaserJet series. The nearby sidebar, "How to use ATM with Ventura for Windows" explains how to get the two programs to cooperate.

After you install ATM, it shows up as an icon in the Windows Program Manager. You can access the ATM Control Panel by double-clicking on the icon. After you've started using ATM for screen display, you should always use the ATM Control Panel to install new PostScript soft fonts. That way you not only make the soft fonts available to your printer, but you also tell ATM about the fonts, so that it can use them to create screen versions.

Preparing to print

In the first part of this chapter, you learned what's going on as Ventura prints. That knowledge will help you prepare for printing. Before you start printing, you must:

1. Select the right printer.
2. Set it up for the print job at hand.
3. Be sure you are using the right width table.
4. Be sure the right fonts are in the printer.

Selecting a printer

You can skip this section if you have only one printer. But anyone who has more than one printing device installed must be sure to pick the right one in advance. At first glance, selecting a printer seems extremely simple. You select Printer Setup from the File Menu. Then you click on the Printer you want to use (Figure 13-4).

Figure 13-4.
Use Printer Setup from the File menu to pick the printer you want to use.

But there can be complications that require you to use Windows Control Panel to get things working correctly. Specifically, you may need to use Windows to activate a printer, to make a printer the default device, to add a printer, or to change a printer's port.

Activating a printer

Some Windows users go to Ventura's Printer Setup dialog box only to discover that some of their printers have "disappeared." They are accustomed to the Printers portion of Windows Control Panel, which lists all installed devices, whether or not they are active. Ventura, by contrast, only shows active devices.

The issue of active and inactive printers only comes up if you have more than one device attached to the same port. Windows will only let you have one active printer per port. Any other devices that are installed for the same port must be inactive.

Example: Let's say you use a dot matrix printer on LPT1 for most of your everyday correspondence. But when you work in Ventura, you use a laser printer, also through LPT1. To make the laser printer show up in Ventura, you must activate it. To do that, you must go to Windows Control Panel and click on the Printers icon. (The Control Panel icon is usually placed in the Main group.) When the Printers dialog box appears, select the laser printer, then click on the Active button (Figure 13-5).

Selecting the default printer

If you have more than one printer on your system, one of them will be designated as the default printer. When you select a default printer, you are telling Windows, "Always use this printer unless I tell you otherwise."

If you start using Ventura on a regular basis, you may want to change the default printer, so that you're not always running to the

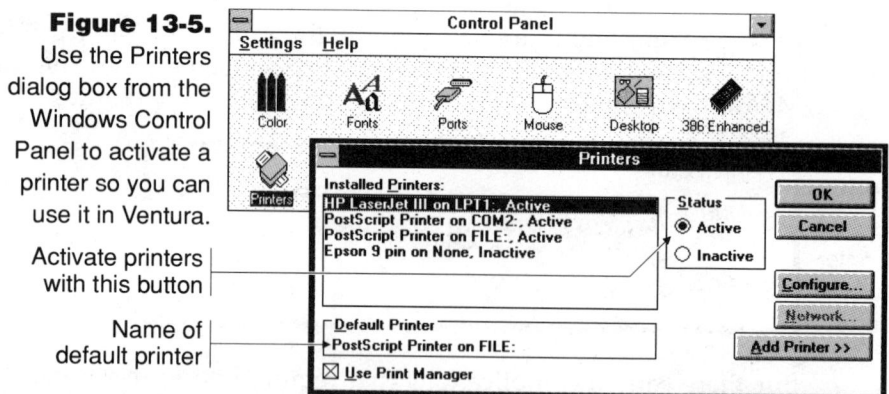

Figure 13-5. Use the Printers dialog box from the Windows Control Panel to activate a printer so you can use it in Ventura.

Activate printers with this button

Name of default printer

How to use ATM with Ventura for Windows

A font rasterizer is a great convenience for any Ventura user. The idea of What You See Is What You Get is central to desktop publishing. But without a rasterizer, Windows' screen displays are abysmal.

There are at least 10 font rasterizers on the market. As of this writing, Adobe Type Manager is our favorite. But Ventura and ATM won't coexist properly unless you take two steps. First, you must be sure there aren't already any extra screen fonts referenced in WIN.INI. Second, you must be sure ATM does not accidentally put in references to PostScript fonts that are already built into your printer. Here's what to do:

1. Remove any screen fonts you built with Fontware or any other utility. ATM also supplies screen fonts to Ventura. If Ventura sees two screen fonts, it doesn't know which one to use. When we say remove, we mean take out the references in the [fonts] section of WIN.INI. These references look something like this:

```
;Bitstream Dutch Roman - 6,7,8,9,10,11,12,13,
14,18,20,24,30,36,72 pts. in
;     ai000waj.fon
```

When you are deleting the screen fonts, be careful not to delete the standard fonts that come with Windows. These fonts look something like this in WIN.INI:

```
Helv 8,10,12,14,18,24 (VGA res)=HELVE.FON
Courier 10,12,15 (VGA res)=COURE.FON
Tms Rmn 8,10,12,14,18,24 (VGA res)=TMSRE.FON
```

Printer Setup dialog box to select a different device. But you can't do that from Ventura. To select the default printer, open the Windows Control Panel and double-click on the Printers icon. Then select the printer you want as the default and *double-click* on its name. There is no button for selecting the default device.

Adding a printer

It's not unusual for desktop publishers to buy and install new printers. But don't forget that Ventura doesn't manage its own printing resources. To add a printer to Ventura, you must install it for Windows and then activate it.

```
Symbol 8,10,12,14,18,24 (VGA res)=SYMBOLE.FON
Roman (All res)=ROMAN.FON
Script (All res)=SCRIPT.FON
Modern (All res)=MODERN.FON
```

You can leave the actual screen font files on your hard disk if you want, but you'll just be wasting disk space. You won't need them any more with ATM.

2. If you have a PostScript printer, open WIN.INI after installing ATM. Go to the [PostScript] section. Remove any references to the fonts built into your PostScript printer. If you only have ATM, this will probably just include Helvetica, Times Roman, and Courier. If you have also installed fonts from Adobe's Plus Pack, you'll also need to delete references to Avant Garde, New Century Schoolbook, Bookman, Zapf Dingbats, and Zapf Chancery (assuming these are built into your printer).

If you leave these duplicates in WIN.INI, you'll get incorrect font sizes when you go to print because of the overlap. Be sure to (1) leave in the references to any soft fonts that are *not* built into the printer and (2) adjust the number on the "softfonts=" line. This line tells Windows and Ventura how many soft fonts to look for. If you delete soft font references, you need to change this number, so that it's accurate again.

To install a printer in Windows, go to the Printers dialog box in the Control Panel. Click on the Add Printer button. A list of printers appears at the bottom of the dialog box. Select the one you want to install and click on the Install button. Windows instructs you to insert the disk containing the printer driver for that printer.

After installing a printer, be sure to activate it if you want it to be available in Ventura (see above).

Note: If you don't see the printer you want to install on the list, scroll all the way to the bottom. There you will see a option called Unlisted Printer. Select this option and click on the Install button. When instructed, place the disk with the printer driver into a floppy drive, so that Windows can copy it to the hard disk.

Setting up a printer

After selecting a printer, you still have to be sure it's set up correctly. If you always print the same way—on the same size paper, from the same tray, in the same orientation—you won't have to worry about this. But if you ever do anything besides letter-size documents in portrait orientation, you'll have to set up the printer before you start.

Here are some of the reasons that may need to set up a printer:

- *To print to a different "flavor" of the same device.* For instance, the PostScript printer driver has several versions for specific brands, which you specify when you set up the printer.
- *To use a different paper source.* Some printers have more than one tray. You can, for instance, have letterhead in the upper tray, plain paper in the lower tray, and envelopes in the envelope feeder.
- *To pick a different paper size.* Although Ventura has a command for the paper size (Page Size & Layout from the Chapter menu), you must also set up the printer for the same size before you print.
- *To use a different orientation.* As with paper sizes, Ventura has its own commands for portrait (tall) versus landscape (wide) orientations in the Page Size & Layout dialog box. Before you print, however, you must set up the printer, so that its orientation matches the one you chose in Ventura.
- *To scale the printout.* PostScript printers can enlarge or reduce pages by a percentage.
- *To print more than one copy.*

How do you accomplish this setup in Ventura? Ventura has a command that takes you directly to Windows' printer dialog boxes, where you can pick what you want. To set up a printer:

1. Choose Printer Setup from the File menu.
2. Select the printer you want to work with from the list and click on Setup.
3. When the setup dialog box appears (Figure 13-6), select the options you want. (You can also get to this same dialog box from the Setup button in the Print dialog box. It doesn't matter which route you take).
4. Click on OK.

Figure 13-6.
The printer setup dialog box for a PostScript printer.

Type number of copies here

Example: Suppose you've been working with an Apple Laser-Writer PostScript printer, and you've been assigned to create a newsletter. It will be sent to a high-resolution Linotronic imagesetter using 11 x 17 tabloid pages in landscape orientation. To set up the printer correctly, select Printer Setup from the File menu. When the dialog box appears, select the PostScript printer and click on the Setup button. When the PostScript Printer dialog box appears (Figure 13-6), make the following selections:

1. Select Linotronic 300 from the Printer list box.
2. Select Tabloid from the Paper Size list box.
3. Click on the Landscape button.
4. Confirm that the Paper Source is Upper Tray, the Scaling is 100 percent, and the Copies are 1.
5. Click on OK to exit the dialog box. Click on OK again to to exit the Printer Setup dialog box.

Note: Just because you've set up the printer correctly doesn't mean you can ignore Ventura's page layout commands. You must also select matching settings from Ventura's Page Size & Layout dialog box. If you don't, you'll get a warning message when you try to print (Figure 13-7).

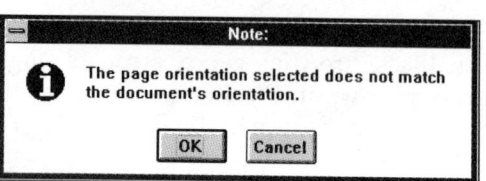

Figure 13-7. Printer and Ventura page sizes and orientations must match before you print.

Note: If you are planning to print your pages to a Linotronic imagesetter and want to use Ventura's automatic crop mark feature, you must choose the "extra" sizes (Letter Extra, Tabloid Extra, and so on). Otherwise, Windows will assume there isn't enough room for the crop marks and not print them.

Working with width tables

Part of preparing to print is being sure you have the right width table. Beginning and intermediate users can get by with Ventura's default width table. Advanced users, on the other hand, may want to build and use their own width tables.

We explained width tables in the first section of this chapter. To review: A width table contains information about the spacing (widths) of characters. Ventura uses it to know where to put each character on the screen and on the page. Ventura's default width table is called ENVIRON.WID. Ventura creates this default table by finding out what fonts are available from Windows, and then building a table that includes the width information for each one of those fonts.

When and why to change width tables

Why create and change width tables? Why not just use one width table that contains all your available fonts? Several reasons:

- *To ensure consistency between computers.* To be sure another computer can reproduce your document, you must create a width table and attach it to the chapter. Otherwise, the other computer will use ENVIRON.WID. Remember: Ventura builds ENVIRON.WID by reading and converting the environment's printing resources. If the other computer doesn't have the same kind of printer, it won't have the same width table.

- *To improve system speed.* Ventura rebuilds ENVIRON.WID scratch each time you start up or change printers. But if you build and specify a different width table, Ventura simply reads it.
- *To create a new, streamlined width table.* You can save memory and time by removing unnecessary fonts from the width table and saving it under a new name.
- *To increase operator speed.* For a particular project, you may use only two fonts that are at opposite ends of the font list. This makes for a lot of mousing around. By removing unnecessary fonts, those that you use will be near the top of the list.
- *To preserve special effects.* If you've modified the kerning tables for a specific project, you will want those kerning values in effect for only that project; therefore, you'll need a different width table.
- *To preserve disk space.* If you have created a special width table, for whatever reason, you will need to be sure it follows the chapter files, wherever they go—onto floppy disks, if that's how you backup your data. A streamlined width file takes up less disk space, thus allowing more room for your other data.

Creating and changing width tables

Ventura doesn't come with any width tables. Under default conditions, it rebuilds ENVIRON.WID from scratch each time you use the program or change printers. To use additional width tables, you must create and name them first. Then you can specify them when and as you want.

To create a new width table, specify the printer as the default printer in Windows. Then use the Manage Width Table dialog box to rebuild ENVIRON.WID, thereby capturing the font information for that printer. Next, make any changes you want (such as removing fonts) and save the width table with a new name.

Example: Assume that you want to create a PostScript width table that includes special soft (downloadable) fonts called Helvetica Black and Helvetica Light, but does not include the resident fonts you never use, such as Avant Garde, Bookman, and Zapf Chancery. Here's how you'd build and name a new width table:

1. Install the downloadable fonts. Use ATM's Control Panel if you have ATM on your system. Otherwise, use the installation method recommended by the font manufacturer.
2. Go to the Printers section of the Windows Control Panel. Select the PostScript printer and double-click on it to make it the default device.

3. Start Ventura and choose Manage Width Table from the File menu.

4. When the Manage Width Table dialog box appears (Figure 13-8), select Use Environment's Width Table. This causes Ventura to read the font information and rebuild ENVIRON.WID.

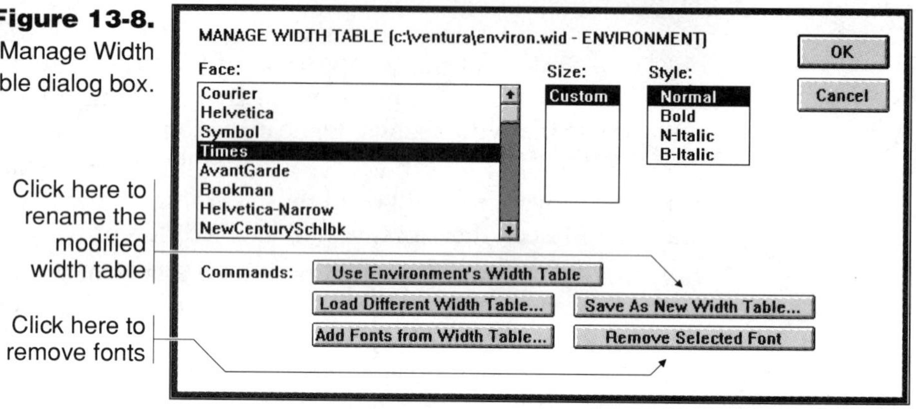

Figure 13-8.
The Manage Width Table dialog box.

Click here to rename the modified width table

Click here to remove fonts

By installing the soft fonts in advance and rebuilding ENVIRON.WID, you have automatically "installed" those fonts into the width table. Now, all you have to do is remove the fonts you don't want and rename the width table.

5. Select the font you want to remove, then click on Remove Selected Font. If the font has different styles (normal, italic, bold, bold-italic), you must do this once for each variation. Repeat until you have deleted all versions of Avant Garde, Bookman, and Zapf Chancery.

6. Click on Save As New Width Table. Give the width table a new name in the \VENTURA directory, such as PS.WID.

Using different width tables

Each time Ventura starts up, it defaults to ENVIRON.WID. To use a different width table, go to the Manage Width Table dialog box and make the switch with the Load Different Width Table button.

The next time you save your chapter, this new width table will be attached to your chapter. From then on, whenever you load that chapter (or any chapter that uses the same style sheet), Ventura will automatically use the new width table you specified. And if you use Ventura's Manage Publications function to copy the chapter, the width table will automatically be copied along with the rest of the chapter.

Warning: Any time you add new fonts to Windows, you must rebuild any width tables that are supposed to use that font. If you do not rebuild them, they won't know about the new font. This is not necessary for Windows ENVIRON.WID, which rebuilds itself. For any other width tables, however, you must (1) make the printer the default printer in Windows, (2) use Manage Width Table to rebuild ENVIRON.WID for that printer by selecting Use Environment's Width Table, and (3) save the rebuilt width table under its old name again.

Preparing the fonts

If you use your printer's resident fonts, you don't have to worry about preparing them. They are ready and waiting inside the printer. But if you use soft fonts, you have to be sure those fonts get sent (downloaded) to the printer. You can download fonts manually or automatically. Your choice affects how you set up your WIN.INI file.

Let's quickly review how WIN.INI handles soft fonts before we discuss the differences between manual and automatic downloading. The [Printer Name,Port] section of WIN.INI lists any soft fonts available for that printer. If the listing includes both the font metrics files *and* the font outline files, Windows will download the outlines to the printer automatically as needed. If the listing includes only the font metrics files, Windows assumes that the fonts have already been sent to the printer.

Example: Here's how WIN.INI might look for a PostScript printer with six Adobe soft fonts set up to automatic download:

```
[PostScript,COM1]
feed1=1
feed15=1
softfonts=6
softfont1=c:\psfonts\pfm\hvbl    .pfm,c:\psfonts\HVBL    .PFB
softfont2=c:\psfonts\pfm\hvblo   .pfm,c:\psfonts\HVBLO   .PFB
softfont3=c:\psfonts\pfm\hvl     .pfm,c:\psfonts\HVL     .PFB
softfont4=c:\psfonts\pfm\hvlo    .pfm,c:\psfonts\HVLO    .PFB
softfont5=c:\psfonts\pfm\bdps    .pfm,c:\psfonts\bdps    .PFB
softfont6=c:\psfonts\pfm\tjrg    .pfm,c:\psfonts\tjrg    .PFB
```

In this example, the PFM files are the Printer Font Metrics files with width information. The PFB files are the Printer Font Binary files with the character outlines. To set up Windows for automatic downloading, the outline files must follow the width files on the same line, separated by a comma with no space.

Fonts from companies other than Adobe may use different file extensions, but they follow the same principles.

Tip: If you own a Hewlett-Packard LaserJet, rejoice! You will probably never have to edit your soft font lists in WIN.INI. Just use the Printer Font Installer dialog box for all your font handling situations. To learn more about this dialog box, keep reading.

Downloading fonts manually

Manually downloading fonts usually saves time. You do it once at the beginning of the day, and then you don't have to worry about it again. By contrast, automatic downloading occurs each time you start a new print job. It can waste a lot of time with repetitious downloading of the same fonts over and over again.

To download fonts manually, you send them to the printer before you start printing. They remain in the printer's memory until you turn it off. For this reason, many desktop publishers start their days by turning on the laser printer and downloading the fonts they will need. They leave the printer on all day to avoid losing the fonts they've sent over.

If your printer belongs to the Hewlett-Packard LaserJet family, you can download fonts from within Ventura by accessing Windows HP printer driver dialog box. Follow these steps:

1. Choose Printer Setup from the File menu.
2. With your HP printer selected in the Printer Setup dialog box, click on Setup.
3. When the dialog box appears, click on the Fonts button.

The Printer Font Installer dialog box appears (Figure 13-9). The fonts you have installed appear in the box on the left.

Note: Unlike PostScript printers, you cannot download scalable font outlines to a Hewlett-Packard LaserJet. You can only download bit-mapped fonts, which means a particular type style in one particular size. This is why you see each size of each typeface listed separately in the Printer Font Installer dialog box.

Figure 13-9.
The Printer Font Installer dialog box for Hewlett-Packard LaserJet printers.

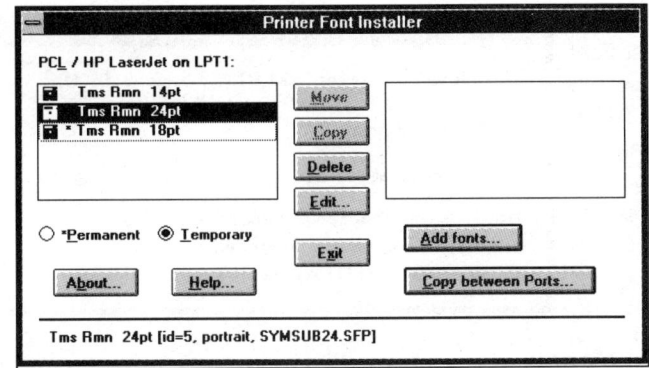

Note: If you haven't installed any fonts, you can do so now by inserting the font disk in your floppy drive and clicking on the Add Fonts button. Follow the subsequent dialog box prompts to install your fonts. Then read the note below.

Note: If you have installed fonts on your hard drive but the box on the left is empty, click on the Add fonts button. When prompted, type the path where your fonts are located on your hard disk and click on OK. The fonts names appear in the box on the right. Select the ones you want and click on the Add button near the top center of the dialog box. Those fonts appear in the left box. The fonts are now set up for your printer at its current port assignment.

4. Select a font you want to manually download and click on the Permanent button under the list.

A message box appears the first time you do this to remind you that the fonts are only "permanently" downloaded until you turn off your printer.

5. Repeat the last step for each font you wish to download. (You are forced to do this one font at a time.)

6. When you are finished, click on the Exit button.

The Download Options dialog box appears (Figure 13-10).

7. To download fonts for the current session only, be sure only the Download Now check box is checked and click on OK.

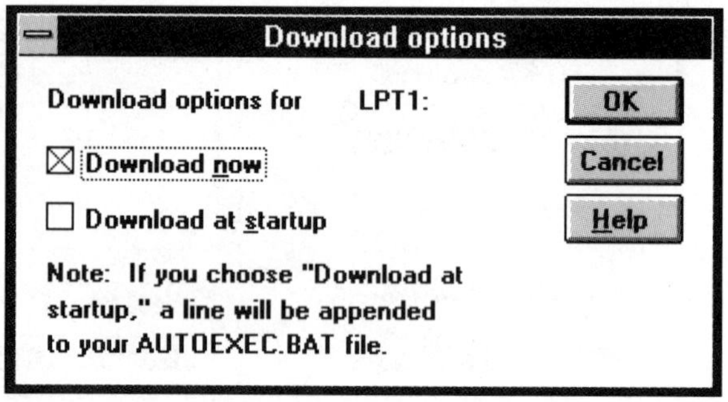

Figure 13-10.
Exiting the Printer Font Installer dialog box with one or more fonts designated for permanent downloading produces the Download Options dialog box.

```
                    Download options
Download options for      LPT1:              [ OK ]
☒ Download now                               [ Cancel ]
☐ Download at startup                        [ Help ]
Note: If you choose "Download at
startup," a line will be appended
to your AUTOEXEC.BAT file.
```

Note: If you check the Download At Startup option, Windows will (1) create a batch file that will send your fonts to your printer and (2) insert a line in your AUTOEXEC.BAT file to run this batch file every time you start your computer. That's great if you always want the same fonts downloaded every day. (And if you do, be sure to turn on your printer before starting your computer or the download will fail.) Otherwise, stick to downloading only when you need it.

That's the LaserJet side of things. If you use a PostScript printer, we have some bad news: The PostScript driver for Windows 3.0 does not have a built-in font downloader. That means you will have to use a utility program like Adobe's PSDOWN (if your printer is hooked up to a serial port) or PCSEND (if your printer is on a network or hooked up to a parallel port). Fortunately, these programs are included with all Adobe fonts you buy. Because neither are Windows programs, you will have to run your chosen utility by creating a PIF file, double-clicking on the MS-DOS icon in Program Manager (if you have created one), or using the utility before you start Windows. For more information on running MS-DOS programs with PIF files, consult your *Windows User's Guide*.

In addition to using a downloading utility, you must also set up WIN.INI for manual downloading. Fortunately, this usually means no setup at all, because most PostScript font installation utilities set things up that way anyhow. But it never hurts to peek inside WIN.INI to be sure things are the way you want them.

To ensure manual downloading for a PostScript printer, the width files (font metrics files) for the soft fonts must be listed in the [Printer Name,Port] section of WIN.INI. However, the files for the character outlines must *not* be listed. Therefore, if you want to download fonts manually, check your WIN.INI file and remove the outline files if you find them listed.

Example: Here's the same WIN.INI file you saw before, this time set up for manual downloading. Notice that the PFB files are no longer listed.

```
[PostScript,COM1]
feed1=1
feed15=1
softfonts=6
softfont1=c:\psfonts\pfm\hvbl____.pfm
softfont2=c:\psfonts\pfm\hvblo___.pfm
softfont3=c:\psfonts\pfm\hvl_____.pfm
softfont4=c:\psfonts\pfm\hvlo____.pfm
softfont5=c:\psfonts\pfm\bdps____.pfm
softfont6=c:\psfonts\pfm\tjrg____.pfm
```

Downloading fonts automatically

Manual downloading is faster and more efficient than automatic downloading. Still, there may be times when you are forced to use automatic downloading. For instance, perhaps you share a networked printer. Because there is no way to know which fonts other people may have downloaded to the machine, you may have to take the precaution of downloading them automatically with every print job.

To cause Windows and Ventura to send the fonts to the printer along with the rest of the print job, modify WIN.INI, so that the [Print Name] section lists not only the width files, but also the files that contain the actual description of the character shapes. See the preceding section for details.

Warning: If you create print files to take to an imagesetting service bureau, be sure to set up for manual downloading. Otherwise, Ventura will send the font information to the print files, resulting in large files and slow print times.

Printing a single chapter

In this section, we'll explain how to print a single chapter in Ventura. We'll also show you how to work with Windows Print Manager in the event you experience printing problems. To learn how to print multiple chapters, turn to the section that follows. And to learn how to handle special printing jobs such as oversize pages, crop marks, and color overlays, turn to the final section in the chapter.

This section assumes that you understand how Ventura prints and that you've prepared everything correctly—selected the correct printer, set it up to match the document, and so on. Those subjects were covered in the first part of this chapter. If you haven't read those sections yet, please do so before you try to print for the first time.

To print a single chapter in Ventura:

1. Open the chapter.
2. Choose Print from the File menu to bring up the Print dialog box (Figure 13-11).
3. Select the options you want.
4. Click on OK.

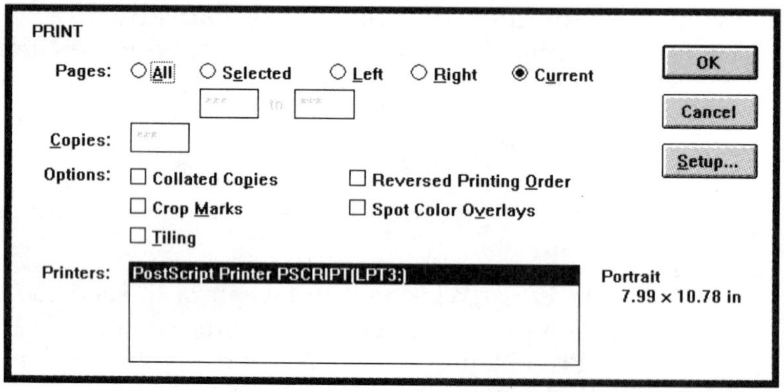

Figure 13-11. You choose your print options from the Print dialog box.

Selecting your print options

This section explains how to use Ventura's Print dialog box for printing one chapter at a time. It summarizes your options briefly and mentions potential problems.

Note: Certain options, such as multiple copies and printing to a file, require you to use other dialog boxes, as explained later in the chapter.

Choosing which pages to print

Click on the All radio button to print every page in the document. Click on the Selected button to print a range of pages, and then type in the beginning and ending numbers of the range in the text boxes immediately below the Selected button. Click on the Current button to print the page you are on right now.

The Left and Right buttons are used to for double-sided printing, as explained in the final section of this chapter.

Tip: If you don't want some of the pages at the beginning, but you do want everything else and you've forgotten the last page number—not to worry. Just type a number that is obviously higher than your last page number, such as 999. When Ventura gets to the last page of the chapter, it will stop automatically.

Printing a single page

There will be many occasions when all you want to print is a single page. Sometimes, that's all you have. Other times, you will be making minor modifications to a page and will want to check it periodically.

The simplest way to print a single page is to move to that page, either with the Page Up, Page Down, Home, or End keys, or by using the Goto Page function, so that the page you want to print is on the screen.

If you have a long chapter, moving to the page you want to print can take a long time. Therefore, you may want to consider another method of printing a single page.

From the same Print dialog box, you can click on the Selected button. This is normally how you would specify a *range* of pages, but there's certainly no law (real or imagined) preventing you from selecting a range of 1 to 1, or 53 to 53.

Controlling the number of copies

If you select Collated from the Options section of the Print dialog box, you can control the number of copies from the Print dialog box. Simply type in the number of copies you want into the Copies text box.

However, if you want multiple copies of uncollated chapters, you must make this setting in the Windows printer dialog box for that printer. To print multiple copies of an uncollated chapter:

1. Choose Print from the File menu.

2. Select the printer you will be using and click on Setup.

3. When the printer setup dialog box appears, type the number of copies you want into the Copies text box at the lower right.

4. Click on OK to return to the Print dialog box and proceed with your print job.

Warning: You cannot see the number of copies you have selected in the Print dialog box. What's more, once you set the printer up for multiple copies, it stays that way until you reset it. If you're not sure how many copies you chose last time, click on the Setup button to check. Otherwise, you can end up printing multiple copies when you didn't want to.

Collating copies

Collating refers to printing multiple copies in order. Let's say you are printing three copies of a chapter. You can print uncollated, in which case the printer will put out three copies of page 1, three copies of page 2, and so on. Or you can print collated, in which case the printer will produce the entire chapter in order, then start from the beginning and print it over again in order, and then print it in order a third time.

Collating greatly increases print time. We recommend that you print with Collated Copies off (no check mark) and shuffle the pages by hand. We think most people can collate by hand considerably faster than the printer can. But, if you *insist*:

1. While in the Print dialog box, click on the Collated Copies check box. An X appears in the check box, and the Copies text box is activated.
2. In the Copies text box, type the number of copies you want.
3. Click on OK (or press Enter).

Reversing the print order

Some printers, like the Hewlett-Packard LaserJet III, eject pages face down. That way they are in the right order when you remove them from the tray. Other printers eject pages face up. When you take them out, they are in reverse order and have to be shuffled.

If you have a face up laser printer, you can click on the Reversed Printing Order check box to cause Ventura to print from the back of the chapter to the front. As a result, your chapter will be in the correct order when you remove it from the tray.

Note: We don't recommend using Reversed Printing Order because it increases printing time. For each page, Ventura goes to the beginning of the chapter and recalculates all the line endings. With a long chapter, this can double or triple the time it takes to print.

Other printing options

The Print dialog box also contains several options that do not pertain to the everyday printing of chapters. These special options, including Crop Marks, Tiling, and Spot Color Overlays options are covered separately in the final section of this chapter.

Working with Print Manager

So far, you've seen how to send a single chapter to the printer using Ventura Print dialog box. But sooner or later you're going to experience printing problems. When you do, you'll need to know how to work with Windows Print Manager. Remember that Ventura doesn't print on its own. Unless you've modified the Windows default setup, Ventura doesn't send documents to the printer. Instead, it sends them to Windows Print Manager.

In essence, then, Ventura prints to a file, not directly to the printer. Print Manager takes over from there. It doles out that file to the printer as needed. Meanwhile, you can go back to work in Ventura. Print Manager will keep working in the background as long as necessary to complete the printing job. You can even send over several print jobs. Print Manager will put them in line and print them in order.

For the most part, all this is transparent to you. Occasionally, however, problems cause the printing to stop—paper jams, forgetting to turn on the printer, running out of paper, and so on. If Print Manager can't send the document to the printer, it will alert you with an error message in the middle of your Ventura screen. In those cases, you need to know how to get to Print Manager to check on the difficulty.

When you print from Ventura, Windows automatically opens Print Manager and puts its icon onto the desktop. You may not be able to see it if Ventura's window is taking up the whole screen, but it's there. To work with Print Manager, you must open the Print Manager window (Figure 13-12).

To control printing with Print Manager, you simply highlight the print job you want to work with. Then you click on one of the buttons at the top. You can:

- Pause a job to stop it temporarily
- Resume a printing job that was interrupted
- Delete a printing job to cancel it permanently

Figure 13-12.
You can monitor and control printing from Windows' Print Manager screen.

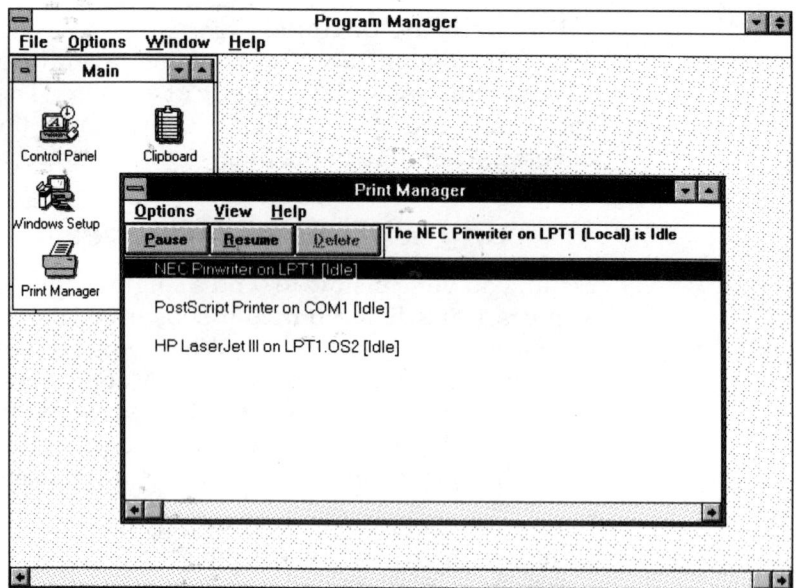

Example: Suppose you've sent a long report to Print Manager and you're back in Ventura. Print Manager alerts you that it is having trouble sending to the printer. You check the printer and realize that it's out of paper. Here's how you correct the problem:

1. Refill the paper tray.
2. Minimize Ventura and open the Print Manager window.
3. Select the print job that was interrupted.
4. Click on Resume.
5. Return to Ventura.

Tip: If you want to monitor the progress of a long printing job, size Ventura's window, so that there is space at the bottom. Then, double-click on the Print Manager icon to open it up *before* you start printing. Size the Print Manager window so it fits in the space below Ventura's window. Now return to Ventura and print. Print Manager constantly updates the percentage of completion, so you'll be able to follow along (Figure 13-13).

Figure 13-13.
If you open Print Manager's screen and position it where you can see it, you can monitor the progress of long printing jobs as you continue to work in Ventura.

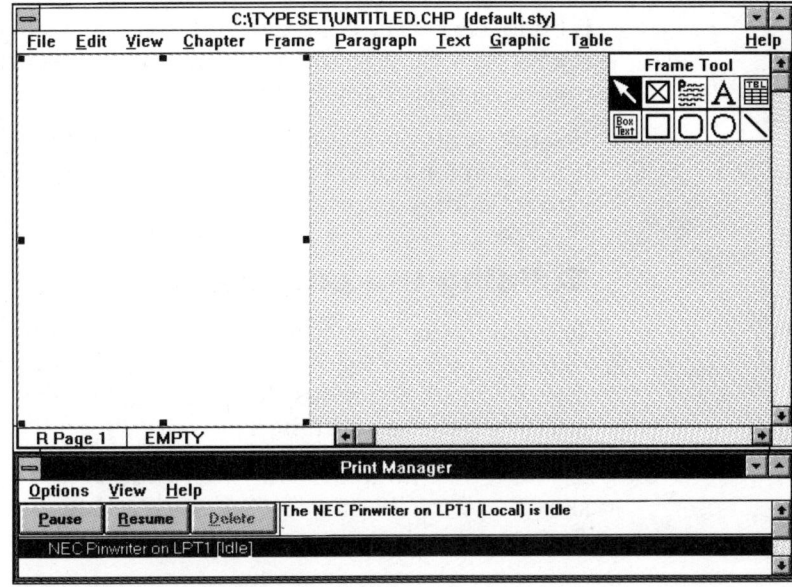

Stopping a print job

The rest of Ventura should be so easy. As soon as a print job begins, Ventura pops up a message box (Figure 13-14). To stop printing, just click on the only button—Cancel—and get back to work.

Figure 13-14.
Click Cancel to stop printing.

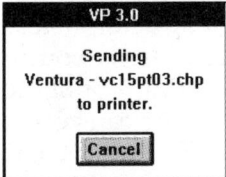

As long as the alert box is on the screen, Ventura has not finished sending the file to Windows Print Manager. If you cancel during this time, Ventura takes care of telling Print Manager to halt the job. After the message disappears, it means that the print file is now in the hands of Print Manager. To stop it now, you must go to Print Manager. Click on the name of the print job and choose Pause to stop it temporarily or Delete to stop it permanently.

Printing multiple chapters

You've already seen how to print all or part of a single chapter in Ventura. Ventura also lets you print a series of chapters. All you do is build a list of the chapters, and issue the print command. Ventura opens each chapter in turn, sends it to the printer, closes it, and opens the next chapter.

Printing multiple chapters involves three steps. First, you build the list of chapters, called a *publication*. Second, you prepare the publication. Third, you print it.

Building the publication

To build the list of chapters, you create a publication using Manage Publication from the File menu. A publication is a list of chapters that can be used, not just for printing, but also for copying and for building indexes and tables of contents.

If you're not familiar with publications and how to build them, skip ahead to Chapter 16, "Managing Ventura Files," where you'll find complete instructions.

Preparing the publication

As you'll see in a moment, printing multiple chapters is very simple—basically, you click on one button. The important part is to get the publication set up correctly before you start.

We don't want to repeat the instructions from other sections, so we're not going to go into great detail here. But we are going to summarize the steps and precautions you must take to prevent unpleasant surprises when printing a publication. (In parentheses, we've listed the chapters where you can get extra help in case some of these tasks are new to you.) These are the things you should do before you commit your computer and your printer to the potentially time-consuming task of printing a whole publication. Be careful—*the order in which you take these steps is important*:

1. *Individually auto-number the chapters.* If you have used Auto-Numbered paragraphs in the chapters of your publication, and have edited the text file(s) with a word processor *since* the last time you had the chapter open in Ventura, reopen the chapter and check your page breaks and anchored frame positions. Auto-Numbering, because it adds a paragraph, can cause these things to change, and, among other things, potentially change the number of pages in your chapter. (refer also to Chapter 5, "Building Advanced Styles.")

2. *Individually update the counters.* If you are manually numbering your chapters using Update Counters, or manually number-

ing the initial page, figure, and/or table of each chapter, be sure you have done this for all chapters. Even if you are allowing Ventura to figure the initial page number (from the last page of the previous chapter), it is a good idea to check each chapter to ensure the settings are correct. If the page numbering is wrong, you'll have to reprint the whole thing. (Chapter 5, "Building Advanced Styles.")

3. *Arrange the chapters in order.* Put the chapters in the order you want them printed (and numbered if you want Ventura to do the numbering across chapter boundaries). Ventura prints and numbers by starting at the top of the list and working down to the bottom. (Chapter 16, "Managing Ventura Files.")

4. *Renumber the publication.* If you are numbering pages across chapters, or if you have any cross references in your chapters, you must renumber from the Manage Publication dialog box. Just be sure to have things set up the way you want them in the Update Counters dialog box (Edit menu) *before* you click on Renumber. (Chapter 16, "Managing Ventura Files.")

5. *Make the TOC.* If you plan to use Ventura's table-of-contents function from the Manage Publication dialog box, now's the time. The reason to wait until now is to be sure all the page numbers have been updated. A TOC with wrong page numbers isn't high on the list of useful research tools. (Chapter 14, "Creating Indexes and Tables of Contents.")

6. *Make the index.* If there is any chance that even one page has been added or removed from your publication, do the index over. (Chapter 14, "Creating Indexes and Tables of Contents.")

7. *Print the publication.*

Printing the publication

This section explains how to print a publication. It assumes that you've already built the publication and prepared it as explained above. Printing a publication is very much like printing a single chapter, except that you get there by a different route.

To print a publication:

1. Choose Manage Publication from the File menu. The Multi-Chapter dialog box appears (Figure 13-15).
2. Click on Open, and pick the publication you want to print.
3. Click on the Print button.

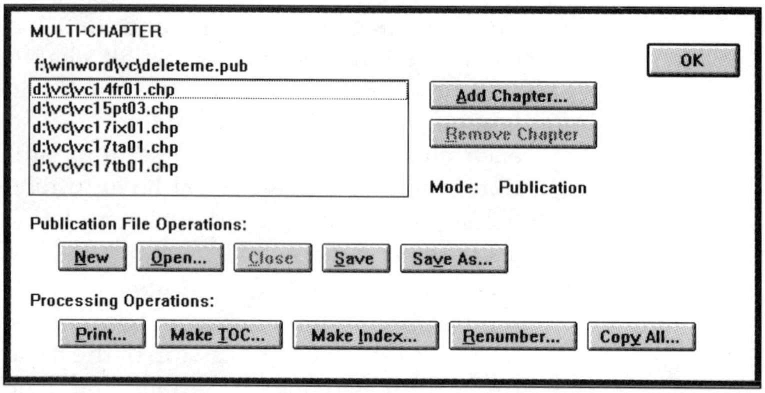

Figure 13-15.
The Manage Publication dialog box.

The Print dialog box appears. From here, the process works just as though you had chosen Print from the File menu.

Printing special jobs

This section explains how to handle five special printing situations:

- Large pages on small printers
- Double-sided pages
- Crop marks
- Color overlays
- Print files

Printing large pages on small printers

If you are lucky enough to own a printer or imagesetter that can print large pages, you don't need to take any special steps. Specify the page size you want in the Page Size & Layout dialog box, then print as normal. But there are situations when you may wish to print a page size that is larger than the paper in your printer.

For instance, perhaps you want to proof a large-page project with your letter-size laser printer. Ventura gives you two choices in that case. You can *tile* the pages, printing the large page onto several overlapping letter-sized pages that you then tape together. Or, if you use a PostScript printer, you can *scale down* (shrink) the big page to fit onto a small one.

Printing tiled (overlapped) pages

You can use Ventura's Page Size & Layout dialog box to specify a page size larger than the paper in the currently installed printer. But if you try to print this oversize page on your letter-size laser printer, an alert box pops up and asks how to handle the situation.

If you have specified an 11 x 17-inch page, and your installed printer uses 8.5 x 11-inch paper, the VP Alert box looks like Figure 13-16. You have only two choices: normal or overlap on four pages. The Normal button will print a page that looks as though it's been cut right out of the middle of the 11 x 17 page. Not much use unless you are printing to a file. If you choose Overlap, Ventura will print on four pages that you can piece together.

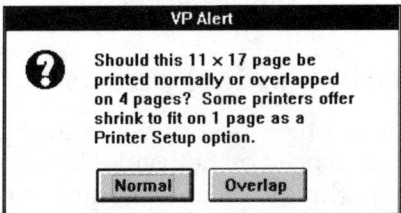

Figure 13-16.
The VP Alert box for 11 x 17-inch pages.

If you have specified an 18 x 24-inch page (broadsheet), and your installed printer uses 8.5x11-inch paper, the VP Alert box looks like Figure 13-17. Note that the Overlap button now bears the trailing ellipses meaning—you guessed it—another dialog box!

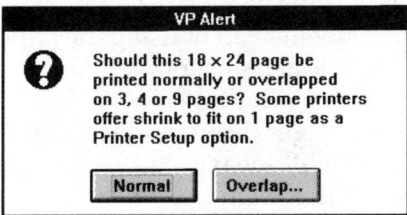

Figure 13-17.
The VP Alert box for broadsheet pages.

When you click on the Overlap button, another VP Alert box pops up (Figure 13-18).

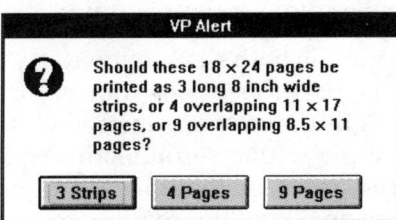

Figure 13-18.
The VP Alert box for tiling options.

This dialog box offers you one of three choices for tiling:

- *3 Strips*—for output on certain typesetters.
- *4 Pages*—for output on any output device that supports 11 x 17-inch paper size.
- *9 Pages*—for output on letter-size 8.5 x 11-inch paper.

If you have a standard 8.5 x 11-inch printer, you can't do much with any but the last button, 9 Pages. And, alas no, Ventura won't tile an 11 x 17 page on three sheets of legal (8.5 x 14-inch) paper.

If you choose to proof large pages in this manner, be sure you are really ready to print before you begin this procedure. Your laser printer must assemble the image once for each sheet it prints—that's nine times for one broadsheet page.

Printing double-sided pages

In order to print double-sided pages with regular laser printers (ones not designed to print on both sides in one pass), print once on one side. Then you flip the pages over and put them back into the printer and print the other side. To do this you use the Right and Left buttons in the Print dialog box. You click on Right to print all the right-hand pages in the first pass. Then you turn the paper over and click on Left to print all the left-hand pages on the next pass.

Some laser printers do not tolerate pages that have already been printed on one side. Your pages may wrinkle or jam, forcing you to feed them in manually instead of using the paper tray. Or they may come out dirty (with toner smears).

Warning: Running pages through twice may void the warranty of your laser printer. By all means, check the fine print in your warranty before you try this technique.

Quite frankly, the easiest way to handle double-sided printing is to print on one side. Then take these single-sided originals to your local copy shop and ask for double-sided copies. Many modern photocopiers can handle this chore automatically.

If you decide to print on both sides anyway, try a small chapter first to see how well the paper feeds—if your printer misfeeds only *one* sheet, if it jams or grabs two sheets instead of one, every page from then on will have the wrong second side. You also need to know how to replace the pages, so that they print on the correct side on the second pass. Some printers require you to put pages in face down. Others require pages face up. In addition, you may have to reshuffle the pages to get them in correct printing order.

Printing crop marks

Crop marks are tiny lines at the outside of a page to indicate its finished size. Usually, crop marks show the corners of the finished size, which is also known as the *live area* or *image area* because it's the part of the paper that actually receives ink, as opposed to the rest of the paper, which is trimmed off (cropped). Sometimes, however, crop marks indicate only the top, bottom, or center.

Ventura has an automatic crop mark function you can activate at print time. If you don't like the way Ventura's automatic crop marks look, you can also draw crop marks of your own. We'll explain both methods in this section.

First, some general information. You can only print crop marks if the size of your page is smaller than the size of the paper in your output device because crop marks fall outside of the final printed area. So if you are printing 8.5 x ll-inch pages on a 8.5 x ll-inch laser printer, you can't print the crop marks. They won't show up.

But what if you are printing an 8 x 10-inch page. That would give you enough extra room to show the crop marks, right? Not necessarily. Laser printers have a *dead zone*, a strip around the outside where the printer cannot produce any marks (Figure 13-19).

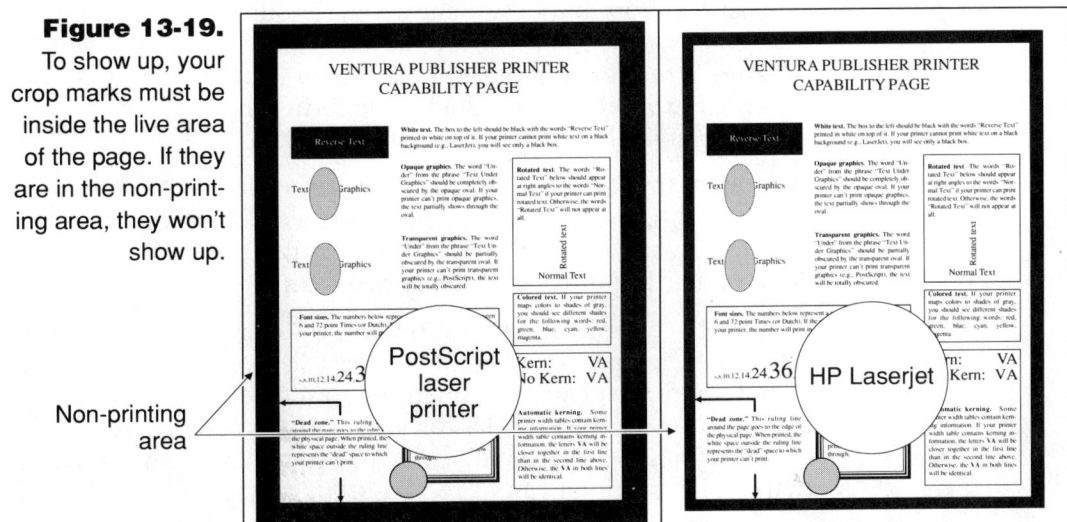

Figure 13-19. To show up, your crop marks must be inside the live area of the page. If they are in the non-printing area, they won't show up.

There's a further complication with Ventura's automatic crop marks. Their closest point to the image area is one-quarter of an inch (Figure 13-20).

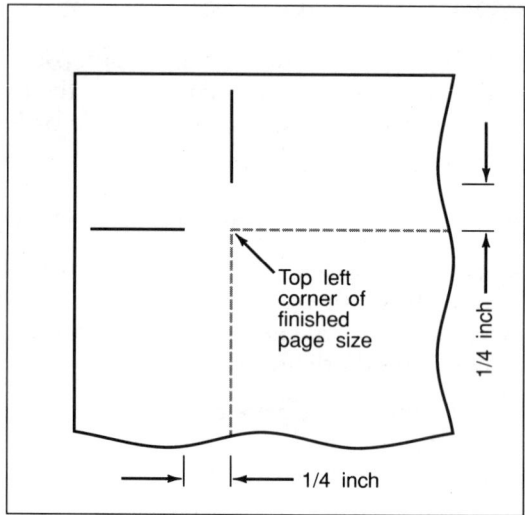

Figure 13-20. Ventura's automatic crop marks are positioned a quarter inch away from the live area, so you must provide for this extra space.

In addition, if you manually create a smaller page size, Ventura starts out by positioning it in the upper left corner of the larger sheet of paper. That means you would have room for crop marks on the bottom and the right, but not at the top and left. In most cases, you should center the smaller page inside the larger paper size, so the crop marks can show on all four sides (Figure 13-21). Incidentally, when you choose the Half (5.5 x 8.5 inches) size from the Page Size & Layout dialog box, Ventura automatically centers it for you. For more information on centering the page on the paper, see Chapter 4, "Building the Underlying Page."

What's all this mean in practice? Quite simply, unless your page size is 7 x 10 inches or smaller, Ventura's automatic crop marks won't show up. You can use a slightly larger page size if you draw the crop marks yourself, as explained later.

Because the most common printing job is letter-size pages on letter-size paper, it may sound as if crop marks aren't very useful. But even though you can't see them on your laser-printed proof, you should turn on crop marks for jobs you are sending to a service bureau. Imagesetters have wider paper that will show the crop marks a laser printer can't produce—but only if you specify one of the "extra" sizes (Letter Extra, Tabloid Extra, and so on) in the

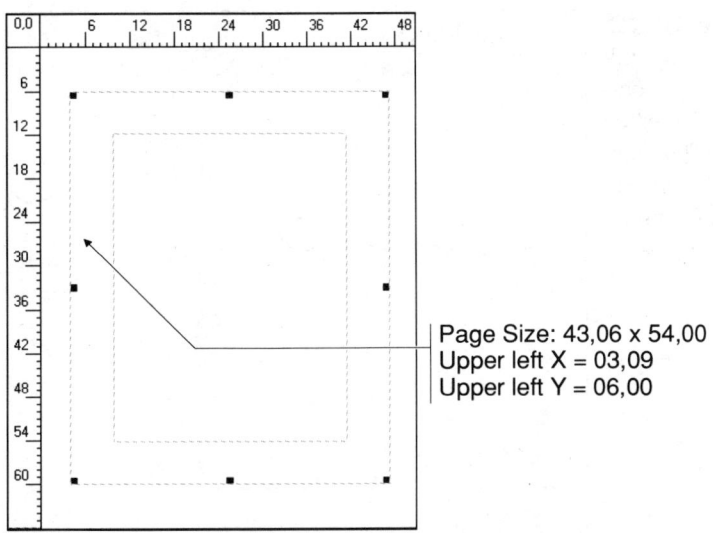

Figure 13-21.
If you want crop marks to show on all four sides, you must center your page horizontally and vertically.

PostScript printer setup dialog box. For more information, see the section on "Setting up a printer," on page 382.

Note: If you're creating camera-ready pages for offset printing, talk to the print shop about crop marks. The operators will tell you whether or not they require crop marks and what kind they prefer.

Using the Automatic Crop Marks option

Despite the detail of the information that lead up to this, the actual procedure for enabling Ventura's Automatic Crop Mark feature is quite simple. While in the Print dialog box, click on the check box next to Automatic Crop Marks, and proceed to print. The crop marks will show up on the finished pages.

How to manually create crop marks

If your offset printer prefers a different style of crop mark, or if you want crop marks that are closer to the page, or if you just plain detest the appearance of Ventura's automatic crop marks (and you wouldn't be alone), there is an alternative. You can draw crop marks with Ventura's Graphic tools. Then you can set the marks to repeat on every page with the Graphics menu. For more information on creating crop marks with Ventura's Graphic tools, see Chapter 9, "Creating Pictures in Ventura."

If you draw the crop marks yourself, you can put them anywhere you want in any style you want. Figure 13-22 shows three styles created solely with Ventura's Graphics mode.

Figure 13-22.
Three crop mark styles you can create yourself by drawing lines and telling Ventura to repeat them on every page.

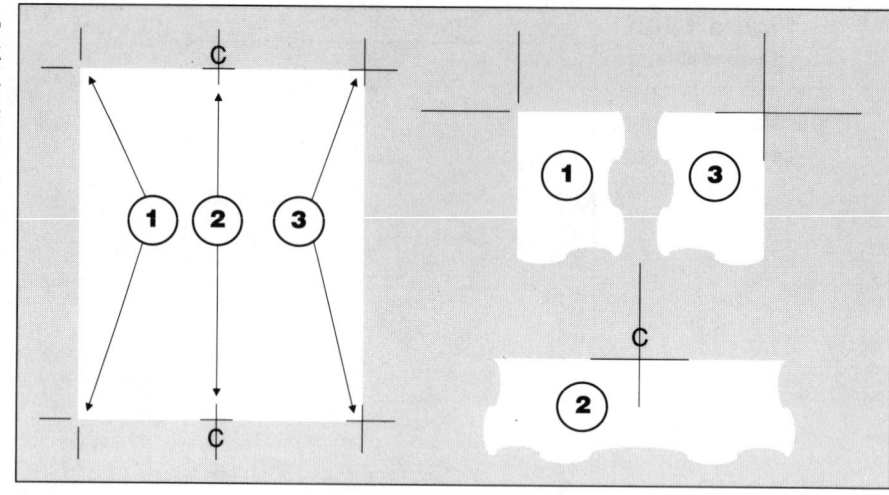

The simplest of these crop marks is similar to Automatic Crop Marks, but differs in one important respect—the marks are nearer the corner of the page. If your project is to be printed on a printing press, the crop marks can be inside the image area. The print shop can remove marks from the printing plate once it has been aligned on the press—but you *must* instruct the pressperson to do so.

Warning: If you are printing spot-color overlays, crop marks drawn in Graphic mode will only show on the page for that color. The pages for the other colors will not have any crop marks. For instance, if the lines are black, they will show up on the black pages, but not on the pages for red and blue. For an advanced solution to this problem, see the nearby sidebar, "Creating crop marks for spot-color overlays," on page 408.

Printing color overlays

One of Ventura's touted features is its ability to print spot-color overlays. For instance, if you have a project that will be printed with a second color of ink, Ventura can create separate printouts for both colors, plus a third combined printout (Figure 13-23). The printouts will all be black, but there will be a separate page for each color. Your print shop can use these overlays to create printing plates for the different colored inks. To use the overlays feature:

1. Define the colors you want to use.
2. Assign those colors to page elements (paragraph tags, frame backgrounds, lines).

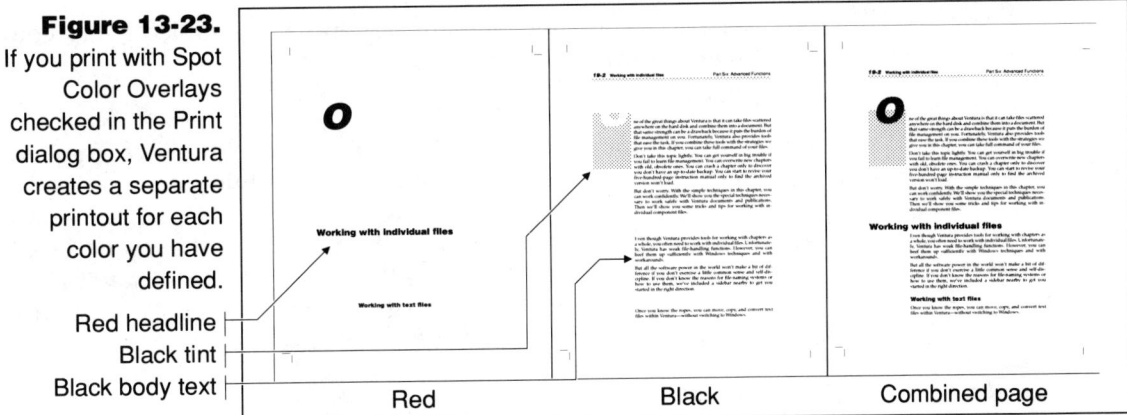

Figure 13-23. If you print with Spot Color Overlays checked in the Print dialog box, Ventura creates a separate printout for each color you have defined.

3. Check the Spot Color Overlays check box in the Print dialog box.

Commercial printers don't need separate color overlays when the different colors are widely separated. In such cases, you can simply mark which elements are to be in color and which should be in black. But overlays are valuable when colors touch or overlap (note the drop-cap letter *O* against the gray tint in Figure 13-23. Because printing inks are translucent, any black printed behind a red will show through. Ventura's overlay feature knocks out the color that is behind, so that there is no overlap and no overprinting.

Define the colors

If you want to print overlays, you must tell Ventura which colors you plan to use. Actually, your most important job is to tell Ventura which colors *not* to use. *Ventura prints a separate sheet for every color that is enabled, whether or not you use that color in the document.* Ventura's default condition is for all eight colors to be enabled. Consequently, if you print overlays without disabling the colors you're not using, you will end up with eight printouts per page.

Ventura won't let you disable black or white. But you can and should disable any of the other six colors that you are not using. Here's how:

1. Select Define Colors from the Paragraph menu. The Define Colors dialog box appears (Figure 13-25).
2. Click on the down arrow in the Color Name list box. Select the color you want to disable.
3. If there is an X in the Enabled check box, click on the check box to clear it. The word Enabled is now gray.

4. Repeat the last two steps until you have disabled every color except the ones you are using.
5. Click on OK (or press Enter).

The Define Colors settings are specific to the style sheet. They will not affect other chapters that use a different style sheet.

Tip: You can use the slide bars at the bottom of the dialog box to change the way colors appear on the screen or to create your own colors. You can, for instance, create an on-screen color that more closely matches the final printed color.

Creating crop marks for spot-color overlays

This is an advanced tip for those who frequently create color overlays that require crop marks or registration marks so that the commercial printer can match up the different overlays for accurate printing. Unfortunately, Ventura's automatic crop marks aren't the kind most print shops need. So you'll draw your own marks, you say? But crop marks applied with Graphic mode will only show on the page for the color applied to the crop marks. For instance, black crop marks (the default color) will only show up on the black page.

Figure 13-24 shows a method of creating crop marks, with Graphic mode lines, that prints crop marks on *all* pages. If you frequently do color work, you can build these crops marks once, store them in a chapter, and copy them to new chapters when needed.

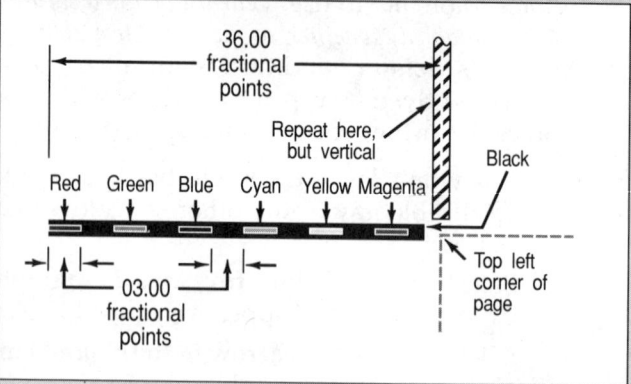

Figure 13-24. Colored lines are 00.50 fractional points; black lines are 01.50 fracitonal points. After drawing all colors, draw a black line and send it to back.

Assign the colors
After you've defined the colors you want to use, you can assign them to different page elements. You can assign colors to text (with the Font dialog box), to ruling lines and boxes, to graphic lines and shapes, to frame backgrounds, and to graphic fills. Simply open the dialog box and select the color you want to use.

Print the overlays
Don't try to print overlays until you've defined the colors and assigned them to the page elements. Then you can print by clicking on the check box next to Spot-Color Overlays in the Print dialog

The illustration uses white lines to show where one color ends and another begins. You only need use as many colors as you have enabled. Rarely will you need more than one or two colors.

Basically, you draw short colored lines and cover them with a longer black line. Then you send the black line to the back. This doesn't have to be a lot of work. Make one set of horizontal and vertical lines for each corner. Attach each line for each corner to a separate frame. Make the frames small enough that they will fit outside the boundaries of the page.

And here's another tip. Attach the crop marks to the upper left corner of each small frame. That way you can position your crop marks by positioning the upper left x and y values of the frame (in the Sizing & Scaling dialog box). If you've ever had to create unusual page sizes, you'll appreciate how much easier it is to type values into the Sizing & Scaling dialog box than to get things exactly right with the mouse on the screen. for more information on creating crop marks with Ventura's Graphic tools, see Chapter 9. "Creating Pictures in Ventura."

Now, save your work as a template chapter. Whenever you need color crop marks, open the template chapter, copy the frames, open the chapter you want to work on, and paste the frames on the page. You can then move them wherever you want. To make the marks appear on every page, you can turn the frames into repeating frames. Or you can the graphics from each, paste them onto the underlying page, and then use the Graphic menu (choose Show On All Pages) to make them to repeat on all pages.

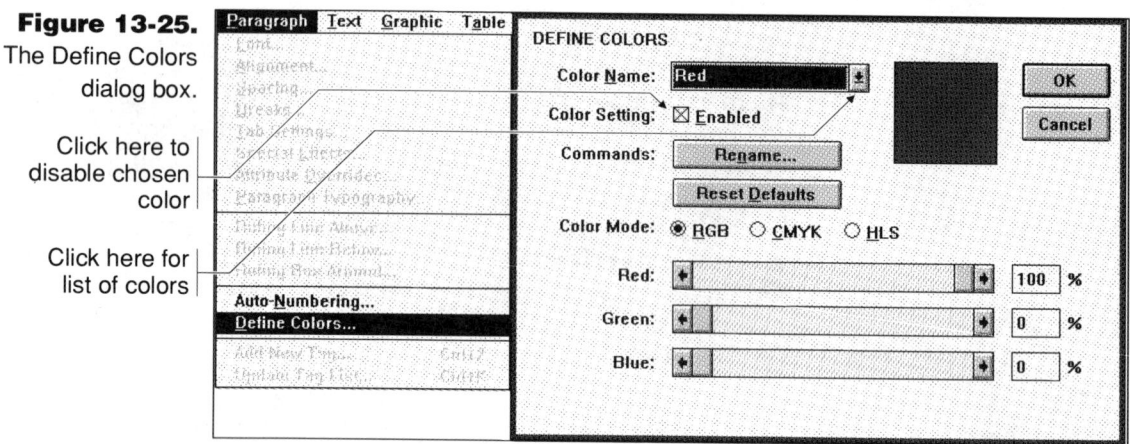

Figure 13-25.
The Define Colors dialog box.

Click here to disable chosen color

Click here for list of colors

box. Click on OK to start printing. Be prepared for an extra delay, because Ventura recomposes the page for each separate color.

Printing to a file

In this section, we'll explain when and why you should print to a file instead of to a printer; how to set up your printer so things work right; and how to handle large pages and multiple chapters.

When and why to print to a file

What do *print to file* and its synonym *print to disk* mean? It means fooling Windows into thinking it is printing when actually you are recording it in a file. Because that file is in a printer language (usually PostScript), it can later be sent to an output device—for instance to the high-resolution imagesetter in a service bureau.

Printing to file, then, is an electronic means to deliver documents to a typesetter. But why not just send the service bureau your Ventura chapters? A few service bureaus offer that service, but they are rare. Most prefer to receive PostScript print files, which are relatively straightforward to handle.

Even if your service bureau *could* print using your chapters, would you want to risk it? What if they had an older, incompatible version of Ventura? What if they were using different hyphenation dictionaries? What if they made changes that threw the entire chapter off? When you print to a file, you eliminate the risk of the service bureau printing the wrong pages, or printing the wrong spot-color overlays, or a myriad of other problems that may arise. The responsibility falls on you to get it right.

Setting up the printer

This section explains how to set up a PostScript printer to print to file. Almost all service bureau printing is done via PostScript files. There are a few typesetters that can speak other printer languages, notably PCL Level 5. The same general procedures apply.

Before you can print a file, you must use Windows Control Panel to (1) direct your printer's output to a file and (2) adjust the printer setup to fit the printer you or your service bureau will use.

The hard way to do this is to constantly change these settings every time you make a print file. Forget that. The easy way is to install two print drivers—one for regular printing and one for printing to file. Here's how:

1. Open Windows Control Panel by double-clicking on the Control Panel icon in Program Manager.
2. In the Control Panel, double-click on the Printers icon.
3. In the Printers dialog box, click on the Add Printer button to expand the dialog box.
4. Select the printer you want to install from the List of Printers and click on Install.

If the printer you choose requires a different driver than one already installed, you will be prompted to insert the appropriate Windows disk in your floppy drive. If, however, you choose a printer that speaks the same language as your current printer (such as a Linotronic when you've already installed an Apple LaserWriter, or an Agfa Compugraphic Genics when you've already installed an HP LaserJet), Windows asks you if want to use the current driver or install a new one (Figure 13-26).

5. Either insert the proper disk in the floppy drive or click on Current, depending on the message you receive. Your newly installed printer appears in the list of Installed Printers at the top of the dialog box.
6. With the printer name still selected in the Installed Printers list box, click on the Configure button.
7. In the Printers - Configure dialog box, scroll through the list of Ports and select File (Figure 13-27).

You're almost done. Just a few more steps:

8. While still in the Printers - Configure dialog box, click on the Setup button.

Figure 13-26.
When you install a typesetter for output to file, Windows points out that same-language printers use the same driver.

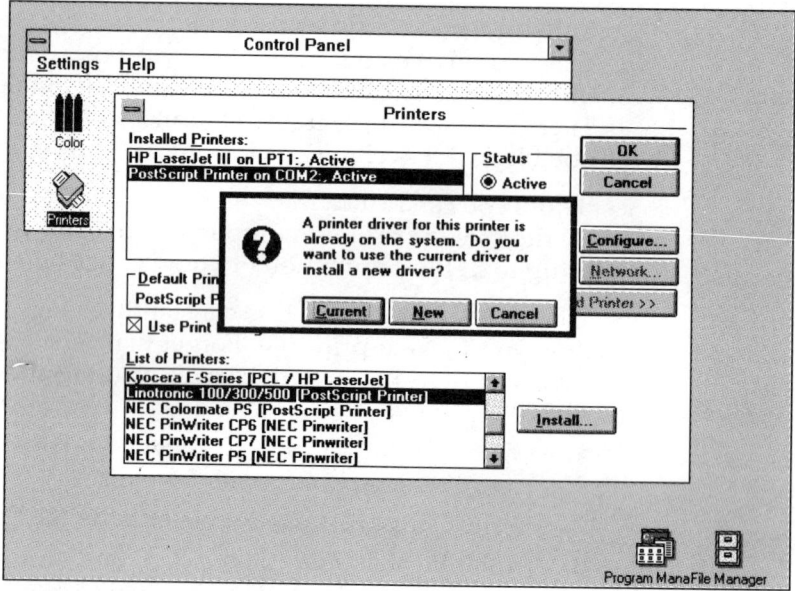

Figure 13-27.
Designating FILE: as your output port is the crucial step in getting Ventura to send printer output to a file.

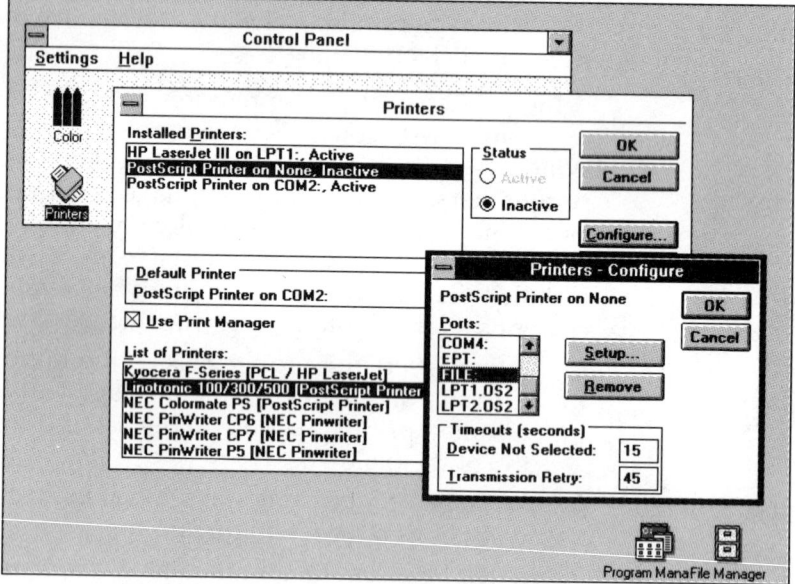

9. When the dialog box appears (Figure 13-28), select the correct output device from the Printer list box. Make any other adjustments (like choosing a larger paper size) you need. Then click on OK, and OK again to return to the Printers dialog box.

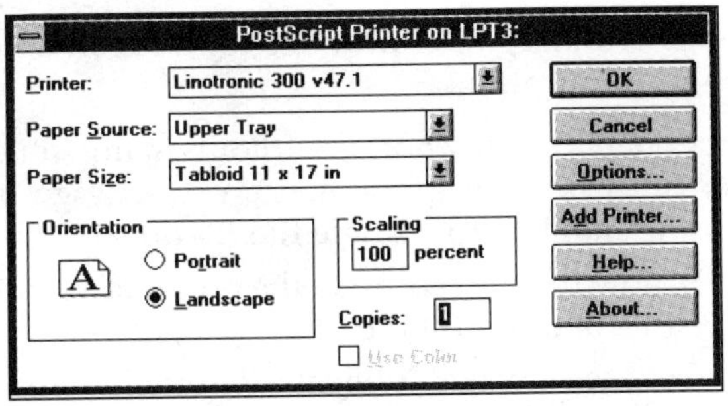

Figure 13-28.
Select the correct version of PostScript from the Printer list box. This example is set up for a Linotronic 300 imagesetter.

10. Finally, with your printer "on FILE:" still selected in the Installed Printers list, click on the Active button in the status section. This is necessary in order to access this new printer from Ventura. Then click on OK and close Control Panel.

You're all set up. Now, when you go to print from Ventura, you'll see another printer listed in the Printers list of your Print dialog box. You'll recognize it by the word "File" that appears in parentheses to the right of the name. Select that printer and print as usual. When you click on OK in the Print dialog box, another dialog box pops up and asks you for the destination file. Type in the full pathname of the file. If you type in a name without a page, the file will be written to the \VENTURA directory.

To switch back to printing to your old printer, just select its name in Ventura's Print dialog box the next time you go to print. From now on, switching from printing to a file or printing to your regular printer is that simple.

Printing multiple chapters to a single file
It's usually not a good idea to print multiple chapters to a single file unless they are very short.

If you are sending your print files to a service bureau, check to see how many pages they want in each file. Some service bureaus have a page limit imposed by the capacity of the light-tight box that receives the exposed photopaper or film.

Print files can be very large, especially if your chapters include bit-mapped images. A 20MB file is not uncommon for a publication with lots of illustrations. If you print your whole publication in one file, and it turns out to be 20MB, how are you going to get it to the service bureau? Modem? That would take nearly one full day to transmit at 2400 baud! Disk? No floppy disk will hold it. Face it, if you can't get it there, you can't get it printed! Therefore, you should print large publications to file as individual chapters—not a single publication.

For smaller publications, without many illustrations (trial and error must be your guide here), you may get away with printing multiple chapters to a single file. To do so:

1. Follow the procedure in the previous section for setting up the name of the print file.
2. Choose Manage Publication from the File menu.
3. Open the publication you want to print.
4. Click on the Print button, make your choices in the Print dialog box.
5. Click on OK.

Printing large pages to a file

In order to print large pages to a file, Ventura and Windows still need to know what output device is going to be on the receiving end. If you choose a page size not supported by the currently installed printer, you know what happens—you saw all the VP Alert boxes in the last section.

Again, you must use Printer Setup to change the printer, if necessary, to the one on which your file will be printed. The printer you install will, as part of the install procedure, automatically tell Ventura and Windows about its available paper sizes (or film sizes, in the case of some high-resolution printers). If you are unfamiliar with the installation procedure, refer to the section, "Selecting a printer," on page 378.

Also, from the Printer Setup dialog box, you should check the orientation to be sure that it is the correct one for your page layout: portrait or landscape. And, as we have said before, be sure to select "extra" sizes for Linotronic imagesetters if you want your print files to include automatic crop marks.

When all that is correct, "OK" your way out of the Printer Setup maze and begin your print procedure.

Printing large chapters to file

Some chapters may create files that are too large to handle. They may be too large to fit on the disks your service bureau accepts; or they may exceed the service bureaus page length limitations.

One solution to a disk space crisis is to use a file compression utility. Print the file to your hard disk. Then use the utility to compress it to a smaller size that will fit on a floppy. Be sure to use a compression utility that is compatible with the one your service bureau uses. As an alternative, most compression utilities let you create self-extracting files that decompress themselves.

But in many cases, your only choice is to print the chapter in pieces. You can do this by specifying page ranges in the Print dialog box.

Continuing on

It doesn't matter how good your documents look on screen if you can't get them onto paper. As you've seen, there's a lot more to printing with Ventura that simply clicking on the OK button in the Print dialog box. In this chapter, you learned how Ventura works together with Windows to print your pages. You found out about the all-important preparation phase that must occur before you start printing. You learned the steps you must take to print one or more chapters. And you picked up pointers on special jobs such as oversize pages, crop marks, color overlays and print files.

Next, you'll add some advanced skills to your DTP arsenal. In the next chapter, you'll learn how to create indexes and tables of contents.

Easy Access

For more info on...	See chapter...
Working with automatic numbers	5 — Building Advanced Styles
Managing files and publications	16 — Managing Ventura Files

14

Creating Indexes and Tables of Contents

How to automate indexing and contents listings

- **Creating an index** 418
- **Creating a table of contents** 440
- **Continuing on** 452

anually compiling an index or a table of contents (TOC) is a time-consuming chore. Luckily, you can use Ventura to automate the most tedious parts of the process. This chapter shows you how to generate indexes and tables of contents in Ventura. You'll also learn formatting tips that will make those listings more useful for your readers.

Indexes and tables of contents are closely related. In both cases, you use Manage Publication from the File menu to create a publication that contains the chapters you want to work on. You can only generate an index or TOC for a publication—even if the publication contains only one chapter. Ventura goes through the chapters in the publication, looking for the things you want to list. Each time it finds an item, it records the page number.

When it's all done, Ventura puts the listings and the page numbers into a separate file. You can then format that file just like you'd format any other Ventura document (Figure 14-1).

Figure 14-1.
Ventura creates indexes and tables of contents by scanning a chapter and creating a separate file. Then you format that file to achieve the appearance you want.

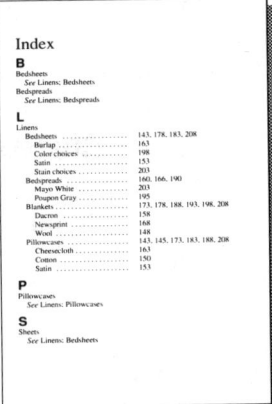

Creating an index

In this section, you'll learn how to plan, produce, and format an index. A good index accomplishes several important jobs. First, it gives readers page numbers so they can turn directly to the information they want. Second, it subdivides big topics, so readers can pinpoint a specific subtopic. And third, it lists topics under alternate names, so readers can find a subject even if they can't remember the "official" terminology. Ventura helps you with all three functions.

In this section, we'll show you how to create an index by following these three steps:

1. Insert the index entries into the chapter.
2. Generate the index file.
3. Format that file to create the final index.

We'll also show you how to edit index entries. And, for those who prefer to work with a word processor, we'll show you how to insert index entries directly into text files.

When you finish this section, you'll have all the skills you need to generate and format a professional-looking index. But no matter how easy it was to produce, an index won't help readers unless it is carefully planned. For some useful guidelines, refer to the sidebar, "Planning an Index," on page 420.

Inserting index entries in Ventura

When you insert an index entry, you are accomplishing two functions. First, you are marking the spot, so Ventura can find the right page number when it generates the separate index file. Second, you are telling Ventura how you want the index to read.

It's easy to insert index entries in Ventura documents. You use the Text Tool and the Insert/Edit Entry dialog box (Figure 14-2) to perform these four steps:

1. Mark the index reference in the text.
2. Define the type of index entry.
3. Create primary and secondary entries.
4. Define how the entries are sorted.

Marking the index reference

First, you need to insert marks that your index will reference. Ventura uses these marks later, to generate the index file. It looks through the chapter, finds all the marks, and records the page number on which they occur. At the time you insert marks, you tell Ventura how to display it in the index. Here's how it works:

1. Select the Text Tool.
2. Place the text cursor immediately in front of the word or phrase you want to index.
3. Choose Insert Special Item from the Text menu. A flyout menu appears.
4. Select Index Entry from the flyout menu.

The Insert/Edit Index Entry dialog box appears (Figure 14-3). With this dialog box, you define the type of entry, specify the primary and secondary entries, and tell Ventura how to sort the entry.

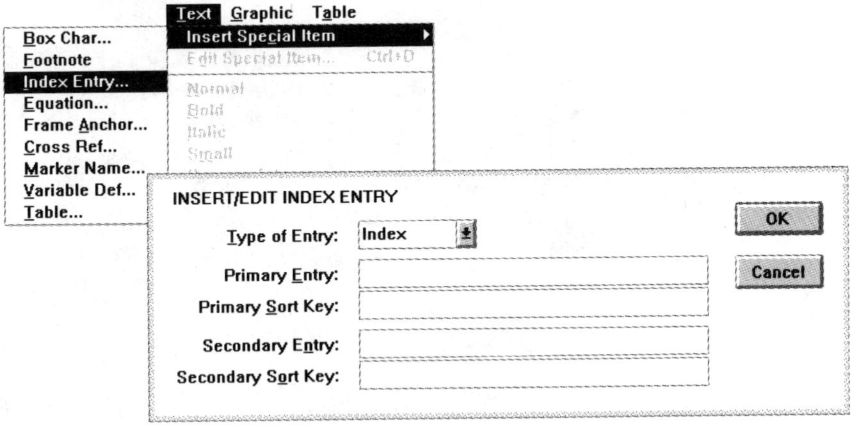

Figure 14-2.
The Insert Special Item menu and the Insert/Edit Index Entry dialog box.

We'll guide you through this dialog box so you understand its options. Then you'll create some index entries on your own.

Figure 14-3.
Select the kind of index entry from the Type Of Entry list box.

Defining the type of entry

The first choice you must make in the Insert/Edit Index Entry dialog box is the type of entry. There are three types of index entries: a basic index entry, a "See" entry, and a "See also" entry.

A basic index entry appears as a primary entry and an optional secondary entry with a page reference. For instance, here's how a primary entry might look in an index:

    Donuts 125-137

And here's a primary entry with two secondary entries:

    Donuts
        Chocolate 126, 133
        Jelly 129-131

Planning an index

When you plan an index, you should imagine you are a naive reader, and then you should anticipate where and how that reader would search for a piece of information.

Choosing topics

When deciding what to index, it is better to err on the side of excess. Having lots of information in the index is no problem for most readers—it's alphabetized and easy to scan. However, an incomplete index is virtually useless. Put yourself in the position of the reader and anticipate key words that relate to topics. If you're writing about donuts, include "donuts" in the index. Put in an entry for "pastries." If that's the only section in the book about food, also include an index entry for "food." Though this is an extreme example, consider including "food with a hole in the middle." When in doubt, include it in the index.

Compiling partial indexes to keep track of your work

When working with long documents, especially ones with multiple chapters, it's hard to remember all the topics you've already indexed. Here's a handy trick: Compile the index before all index entries have been inserted in the text files and print out the partial index for your own reference. If you're inserting index entries with your word processor, display the generated index file in a separate window alongside the window containing your main text file. Then you can easily check for consistency in spelling and capitalization.

A *See* entry tells the reader to look for information under a different topic. In your final index, the primary entry is still listed, but the secondary entry appears with the word "See" preceding it (with no page reference). Here's a See entry for Donuts (primary) and Pastries (secondary):

    Donuts
        See Pastries

Maintaining consistent entries
Be sure that you use plurals, tense, syntax, and capitalization consistently in your index entries. Any deviation causes entries to be listed in the generated index file in a different way than you expect them to be. For example, an index entry for "Donuts" would not be considered the same as either "donuts," "donut" or "Donut." Even extra word spaces can cause an extra listing. Fortunately, after you have compiled the index, you have a guide that tells you which pages contain the inconsistencies.

Using *See* references
See index entries direct the reader to a synonymous key word. They place the page numbers under one entry with all other key words refering to that entry, rather than listing page numbers for each possible key word. If you're writing about donuts and have no other reference to pastries, include "donuts" in the index and use a *See* entry for "pastries." If the reader looks under pastries, the index shows "See donuts."

Because the location of *See* index entries within the text file has no effect on the generated index file (no page numbers are referenced), put them all either at the beginning or the end of the file so that you have them all in one place.

Using *See also* references
See also index entries direct the reader to related topics that they can look up in addition to the current entry. To continue in the caloric vein, if you list "Pastries" in the index, you might refer the reader to "Sweet breads" or "Cakes" (or both).

A *See Also* entry tells the reader where to find more information. In your index, the secondary entry has the words "See Also" preceding it (with no page reference). Here is a typical See Also entry:

Donuts
  Chocolate 126, 133
  Jelly 129-131
  See Also Twin Peaks

Note: You never have to type the words "See" or "See Also." Ventura inserts those words for you automatically. You can also use other phrases instead, as you'll learn later.

Creating the primary and secondary entries

A typical index entry has two parts. The *primary entry* is the general category. Primary entries are the highest level heading in the index. The *secondary entry* is the specific topic. The secondary entry is listed beneath the primary entry and is followed by the page reference. Here's a primary entry (Donuts) with two secondary entries (Chocolate, Jelly):

Donuts
  Chocolate 126, 133
  Jelly 129-131

As you can see, Ventura combines the page references for identical entries. It's important to understand that there must be one index entry for every page number. Thus, in the example above, you would have created one entry for chocolate donuts on page 126 and another on page 133. And you would have typed in three entries for jelly donuts, on pages 129, 130, and 131.

To create primary and secondary entries, you type them into the Primary Entry and Secondary Entry text boxes in the Insert/Edit Index Entry dialog box. For instance, Figure 14-4 shows how the dialog box would look for either of the chocolate donut entries.

Figure 14-4. An Insert/Edit Index Entry dialog box for a basic index entry with a primary entry and a secondary entry.

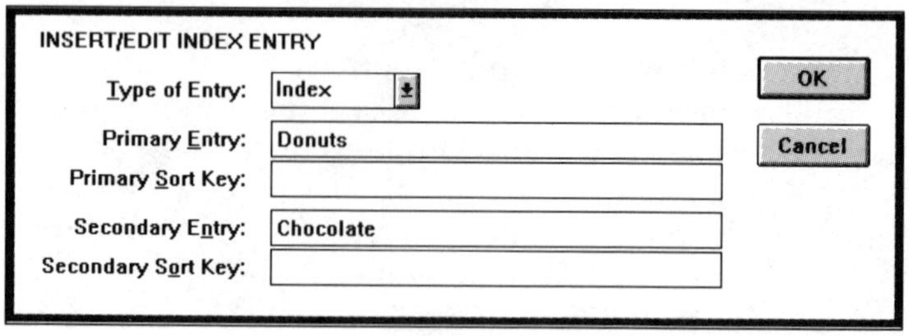

INSERT/EDIT INDEX ENTRY

Type of Entry: Index
Primary Entry: Donuts
Primary Sort Key:
Secondary Entry: Chocolate
Secondary Sort Key:

OK Cancel

Warning: Ventura won't combine the page references unless the entries are identical. You must be extremely careful to spell and capitalize entries the same each time you type them into the dialog box. To Ventura, the words "donut," "donuts," "Donut" and "Donuts" are separate and distinct. They would result in four separate entries, not in a combined listing.

Defining how entries are sorted

In most cases, you don't need to worry about how entries are sorted. If you leave the Sort Key lines blank, Ventura lists the entries in alphabetic order—and that's usually what you want. Ventura places entries that begin with symbols (in their ASCII code sequence) before those that begin with letters. For example:

Donuts
    Chocolate 126, 133
    Jelly 129-131
    Varieties 125
    Whole Wheat 132

Eclairs
    Chocolate 139
    French 141

Still, there are several instances that require an entry to be sorted differently from the way it is spelled. The most common is the case of See Also entries. If you don't specify a different sort key, the See and See Also entries will be listed alphabetically under the letter *S*:

Donuts
    Chocolate 126, 133
    Jelly 129-131
    See Also Desserts
    See Also Twin Peaks
    Varieties 125
    Whole Wheat 132

But most editors prefer that all of these entries be grouped together at the beginning or end of the listing:

> Donuts
>   Chocolate 126, 133
>   Jelly 129-131
>   Varieties 125
>   Whole Wheat 132
>   See Also Desserts
>   See Also Twin Peaks

There are also other cases. Some entries contain words that shouldn't be indexed. For instance, you want "The Whole Earth Catalog" to appear in the *W*s for "Whole," not in the *T*s for "The."

And some entries contain numbers—21st Century, for instance, or 640K RAM. Others reference symbols. For example, a document explaining how to use a calculator might index the symbols for each calculator key, such as an asterisk (*).

To sort an entry as it appears on the Entry lines, leave the Sort Key lines blank. To sort an entry differently from the way it is spelled on the Primary or Secondary Entry lines, type the correct sort instructions onto the Primary or Secondary Sort Key lines. If Ventura sees something on either line, it ignores the Entry spelling and uses the Sort Key spelling instead.

Let's return to some of our previous examples and see how you'd use the Sort Key. To place a See Also reference at the end of the entries, you could type "ZZZ" as the sort key (Figure 14-5).

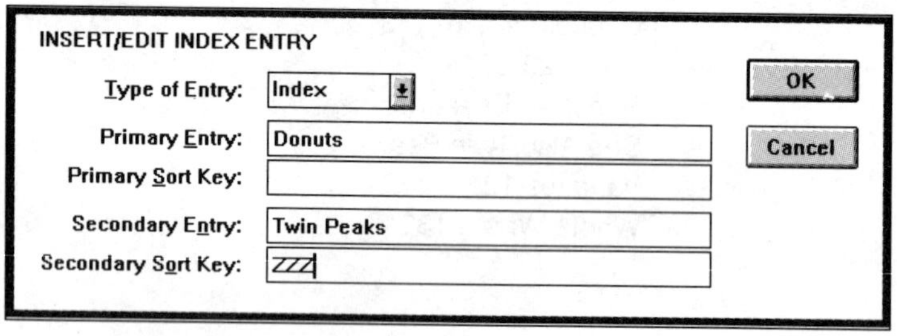

Figure 14-5. Use *ZZZ* as the sort key to make a See Also entry appear at the end of the list. Use *AAA* to make it appear at the top.

INSERT/EDIT INDEX ENTRY

Type of Entry:	Index
Primary Entry:	Donuts
Primary Sort Key:	
Secondary Entry:	Twin Peaks
Secondary Sort Key:	ZZZ

To make "The Whole Earth Catalog" appear with the *W*s, you'd type "Whole Earth Catalog" as the sort key.

To make "21st Century" appear with the *T*s, you'd use "Twenty-First Century" as the sort key.

If you wanted to list the asterisk as a spelled word under the *A*s, you would use the appropriate Sort Key text box to type the word "asterisk."

In the example in Figure 14-6, the Primary Entry contains a number as the first character ("3"), and it is spelled out in the Primary Sort Key text box ("three").

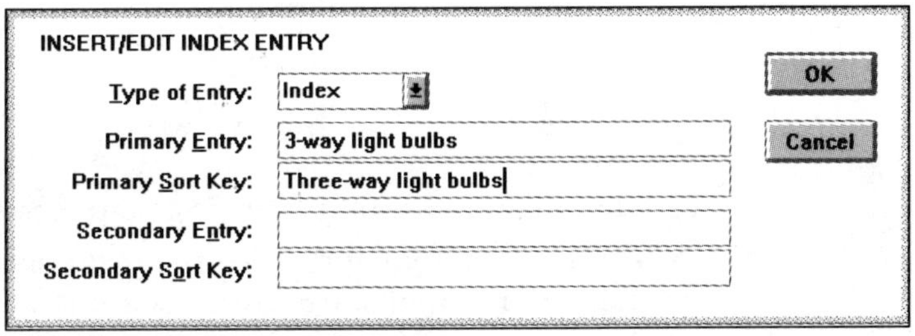

Figure 14-6.
To sort this entry under *T*, instead of the number *3*, spell out "Three" in the Primary Sort Key text box.

INSERT/EDIT INDEX ENTRY		
Type of Entry:	Index	OK
Primary Entry:	3-way light bulbs	Cancel
Primary Sort Key:	Three-way light bulbs	
Secondary Entry:		
Secondary Sort Key:		

Leaving the dialog box

After you've selected the type of entry, created the primary and secondary entries, and created different sort keys (if needed), you can click on OK to return to the workspace. The Current Selection Box at the bottom of the screen now reads "Index Entry." You will also see a small degree symbol in the text file to mark the spot where the index entry resides (Figure 14-7).

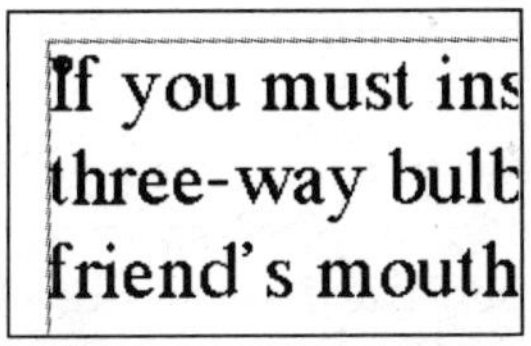

Figure 14-7.
Choose Show Tabs & Returns to display the degree symbol.

If you must ins
three-way bulb
friend's mouth

Note: If you can't see the degree symbol, choose Show Tabs & Returns from the View menu.

Example: To get the hang of things, try inserting a few index entries of your own. Load Ventura. Create a chapter called IN-DEXTST.CHP in the \TYPESET directory, using the SAMPLE1.STY for the style sheet and loading SAMPLE.TXT on the underlying page (both these files come from Ventura's example files).

Because we're using such a short document, all of your entries will have page 1 as their page reference. But even though you wouldn't really need to index such a short document, it's worthwhile to get hands-on practice. Later in the chapter, we'll show you how to use these practice entries to generate an index file and format it. As a preview, here's how the entries might look in the printed index:

Formatting
    See Tagging

Paragraph Tagging tool 1
    See Also Tagging

Tagging
    Bullets 1
    Headlines 1

That's where you're headed. The first step is to insert the entries:

1. Select the Text Tool and place the text cursor at the beginning of the sentence that starts with "Enable the Paragraph Tagging tool...."

2. Choose Insert Special Item from the Text menu. Select Index Entry from the flyout menu. The Insert/Edit Index Entry dialog box appears.

3. For Type Of Entry, select Index. For Primary Entry, type Paragraph Tagging tool. Leave the Secondary Entry blank.

4. Click on OK. Do you see the small degree symbol that marks where you inserted the entry? (If not, choose Show Tabs & Returns from the View menu). Look at the Current Selection Box at the bottom of the screen. It now reads "Index Entry."

5. Next add a See Also entry: Press the right arrow key once so that the words "Index Entry" disappear from the Current Selection Box. Now open the Insert/Edit Index Entry dialog box again. For Type Of Entry, select See Also. For Primary Entry, type Paragraph Tagging tool. For Secondary Entry, type Tagging. For Secondary Sort Key, type ZZZ. Click on OK.

6. Let's add two more entries: Move the text cursor to the beginning of the next sentence, which starts with "Tag the paragraph above...." Open the Insert/Edit Index Entry dialog box. For Type Of Entry, select Index. For Primary Entry, type Tagging. For Secondary Entry, type Headlines. Click on OK.

7. Move the text cursor several paragraphs down to the beginning of the sentence that starts with "For instance, you can take the following list of features...." Open the Insert/Edit Index Entry dialog box. For Type Of Entry, select Index. For Primary Entry, type Tagging. For Secondary Entry, type Bullets. Click on OK.

8. Finally, try adding a See reference. Move the cursor anywhere else in the text file (the location doesn't matter). Open the Insert/Edit Index Entry dialog box. For Type Of Entry, select See. For Primary Entry, type Formatting. For Secondary Entry, type Tagging. Click on OK.

9. Choose Save from the File menu to save your work.

Editing index entries in Ventura

So far you've learned how to create an index entry that Ventura can find later when it generates the index file. But what if you decide you want to change an entry? Or what if you need to correct the spelling of an item? To edit an index entry, follow these steps:

1. Choose Show Tabs & Returns (View menu) so you can see the degree symbol that marks the location of the index reference.

2. Using the Text Tool, place the text cursor to the left of the index entry symbol (degree symbol). If you have trouble with this, place the text cursor to the right of the index entry symbol and press the left arrow key until the Current Selection Box at the bottom of the screen shows "Index Entry" (or "See" or "See Also" (Figure 14-8).

Figure 14-8. Use the Current Selection Box to find index entries.

3. Choose Edit Special Item from the Text menu (or press Ctrl-D).

Example: Try retrieving the final entry you made (Formatting, See Tagging). Place the cursor at the spot marked by the degree symbol. Use the arrow key to move left or right until "Index—See" appears in the Current Selection Box. You can practice changing the index, but press Esc to cancel what you do.

In many cases, you'll have several index entries at the same location and it will be difficult to tell which one you've selected. If this happens, start at the far right entry, press Ctrl-D, and check the Insert/Edit Index Entry dialog box to see if it's the one you want. If it isn't the correct one, press Esc, use the left arrow key to move to the next entry, and check again.

Tip: Because it can be difficult to find the index entry you want, many publishers prefer to insert and edit index entries directly into the word-processing file, where they can see what they're doing. We'll show you how later in this chapter.

Deleting an index entry

To delete an index entry, place the cursor to the left of the entry you wish to remove (Figure 14-8). Press Ctrl-D to bring up the dialog box to check that you have the correct entry. Press Esc (or click on Cancel) to return to the workspace. Upon finding correct the entry, press the Delete key, or choose Cut Text from the Edit menu.

Moving or copying an index entry

Moving an index entry is as simple as editing one. After you've found the right index entry, choose Cut Text from the Edit menu. Place the text cursor at the new spot in the text. Choose Paste Text from the Edit menu to insert the index entry at the new location.

To copy an index entry, follow the same procedure, but use the Copy Text command instead of Cut Text.

Tip: You'll find the keyboard shortcuts for the menu commands on the right side of the menu (Figure 14-9). Memorize the ones for Cut, Copy, and Paste. You'll use them constantly to delete, move, and copy page elements quickly.

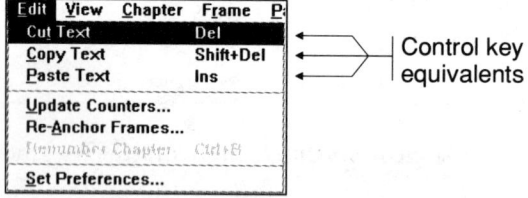

Figure 14-9. You cut and copy index entries just as you do text.

Inserting index entries with a word processor

Instead of laboriously inserting each individual index entry in Ventura, you can insert entries with your word processor. However, you cannot use a word processor's native indexing function. You must use Ventura's bracket codes.

For more information on using bracket codes, see Chapter 7, "Creating Text with Other Programs." In this section, we'll give you a brief summary of the codes and procedures for indexing.

Here are the rules:

- Put the bracket code immediately in front of the word or phrase you want to index.
- Put angle brackets (< >) around the entire entry.
- The first character inside the brackets should be a dollar sign ($). The second character should be one of the three indexing code letters: *I* for a basic index entry, *S* for a See entry, and *A* for a See Also entry.
- After the two code letters, type in the primary entry, followed by a semicolon. Then type in the secondary entry. Do not put a space between the entries.

Here's how some of the entries you saw earlier would look in bracket codes. A basic index entry looks like this:

<$I*Tagging;Headlines*>

A See entry looks like this:

<$S*Formatting;Tagging*>

And a See Also entry looks like this:

<$A*Paragraph Tagging tool;Tagging*>

To use sort keys, put the primary sort and secondary sort keys in square braces ([ ]) immediately following the entries. For instance, to sort the previous See Also entry as if it were spelled ZZZ, you'd put that sort key in braces:

<$A*Paragraph Tagging tool;Tagging[ZZZ]*>

Tip: Create a list of topics as you insert entries in your text files so that you can use the list to search (using your word processor's text search feature) for all other occurrences of those same topics.

Generating the index

So far, you've learned how to insert index entries. But you don't have an index yet—you just have the pieces. You still need to assemble all your entries (and their page numbers), put them in alphabetic order, and make a file for them. It's a lot of work. But don't worry, Ventura will do most of it for you.

To generate an index, you first open the Multi-Chapter dialog box by choosing Manage Publication from the File menu (Figure 14-10). There you create what is known as a *publication*—a Ventura file containing a list of one or more chapter files. For more information on creating and working with publications, see Chapter 16, "Managing Ventura Files."

Figure 14-10.
The Multi-Chapter dialog box lets you assemble a publication and index its chapters.

After saving, click here to begin indexing functions

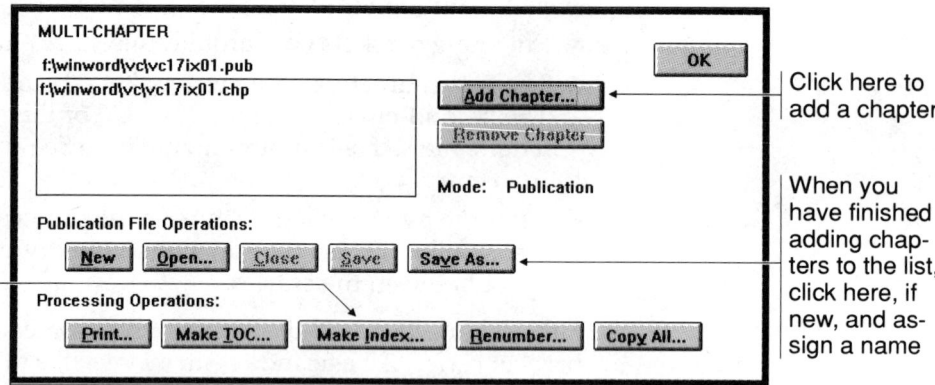

Click here to add a chapter

When you have finished adding chapters to the list, click here, if new, and assign a name

Next, in the same dialog box, click on the Make Index button to open the Generate Index dialog box (Figure 14-11). Here you control several important aspects, including the placement and format of the page numbers that follow each index entry. What you put in the text boxes determines how the index will appear (although you can add finishing touches when you format the index file).

Figure 14-11.
The Generate Index dialog box is where you set up the arrangement of the index.

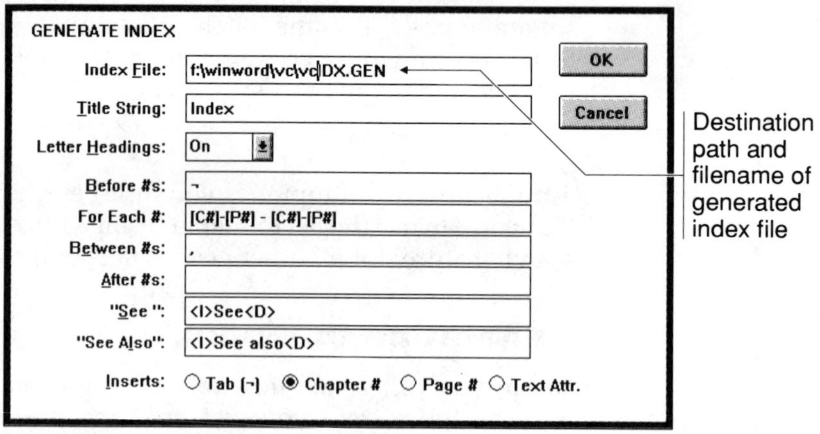

Destination path and filename of generated index file

The Generate Index dialog box intimidates most Ventura users. (It still makes Jesse nervous, and he's been using it to construct indexes for 700-page books for five years.) The best way to overcome this hurdle is to skim the explanations, and then try it out on your own. We'll guide you through the steps:

1. Name the index file.

2. Give the index a title.
3. Define letter group headings.
4. Determine what separates an entry from its page references.
5. Determine what page numbers look like.
6. Determine how page numbers are separated.
7. Determine what appears after the last page number.
8. Define the words that precede See and See Also entries.

Sound tough? It doesn't have to be because *Ventura has default settings for all the steps.* To generate a standard index, simply click on OK. But if you want to know how to make changes, here's how.

Naming the index file
As you know by now, Ventura scans the chapter looking for index entries and records their page numbers. Then it puts these entries in alphabetic order and stores them in a separate file. In this first line of the dialog box, you tell Ventura what to name that file.

Unless you tell it otherwise, Ventura automatically uses the name of the publication, replaces the last three characters with *IDX*, and creates a GEN extension. It also places the index file in the same directory as the publication file. For example, Ventura would generate the index file EXAMPIDX.GEN for EXAMPLE.PUB. You can change the filename in the Index File text box. But we suggest you keep the name that Ventura generates.

Giving the index a title
By default, Ventura gives provides the title "Index." Frankly, we're not quite sure what else you *could* call it, since "A detailed alphabetic listing of names, places, and topics along with the numbers of the pages on which they are mentioned or discussed" seems a little awkward. However, if you can think of a better title, you can include it by typing it in the Title String text box in place of "Index."

Defining letter group headings
You can place the letter of each alphabetic group above that group. For example, you can have a C above the index entries that begin with C, a D above D entries, and so on. You use the Letter Headings list box to turn this option On or Off.

Separating an entry from its page references
By default, Ventura separates the index entry from its page references with a tab. The arrow that appears on the Before #s line

stands for the tab character. Using tabs as separators results in an index that looks something like this:

> Formatting
>   See Tagging
>
> Paragraph Tagging tool   1
>   See Also Tagging
>
> Tagging
>   Bullets   1
>   Headlines   1

Tabs also let you insert leader dots between the entry and the page number—like this:

> Formatting
>   See Tagging
>
> Paragraph Tagging tool 1
>   See Also Tagging
>
> Tagging
>   Bullets 1
>   Headlines 1

Although tabs are nice for small indexes, they can cause problems in larger indexes where you may have many page numbers on the same line. They also make the index harder to use if there is a lot of space between the entries and the numbers. (The reader's eye gets confused and doesn't know which number belongs with which entry.) For these reasons, many people prefer to format indexes with spaces between the entries and the numbers:

> Formatting
>   See Tagging
>
> Paragraph Tagging tool 1
>   See Also Tagging
>
> Tagging
>   Bullets 1
>   Headlines 1

To change the separator, delete the tab character and type in a new separator such as a single space.

Determining what page numbers look like

To control how page numbers appear, you use the For Each # text box. In this text box, you determine what kind of numbering to use and how to separate ranges of numbers.

You can include a chapter number *and* the page number, or just the page number. By default, Ventura assumes *chapter-by-chapter* numbering (each chapter begins at page 1). It uses the code [C#]-[P#] to generate entries like this:

    Formatting
      See Tagging

    Paragraph Tagging tool 3-1
      See Also Tagging

    Tagging
      Bullets 3-1
      Headlines 3-1

If you include the chapter number, you must also define the punctuation that separates the chapter number from the page number. The default is a hyphen. To change the separator, replace the hyphen between [C#]-[P#] with the desired symbol.

The [C#] represents the chapter number; the [P#] represents the page number. If you don't want chapter-by-chapter numbering, you must delete the two [C#]'s and the hyphens so that you are left with [P#]-[P#] in the For Each # text box. This results in the *sequential* numbering that is standard in most books.

Tip: Use the Insert buttons as a shortcut for inserting items such as tabs, chapter number codes ([C#]), page number codes ([P#]), and text attributes.

When index entries occur on more than two consecutive pages, Ventura doesn't show all the pages, only the first and last. You can determine how the range is indicated. By default, it is a hyphen. Thus, if you had listings for jelly donuts on pages 129, 130, 131, and 132, Ventura would create something like this:

    Donuts
      Chocolate 126, 133
      Jelly 129-132

If you don't like the default hyphen, you can substitute something else—for instance, an en dash, an em dash, or the word "to." The word "to" is most appropriate in chapter-by-chapter numbering, where too many hyphens can confuse the reader. For instance:

Donuts
    Chocolate 3-12, 3-13
    Jelly 3-14 to 3-17

If you want spaces before and after the separator, be sure to type them on this line.

Tip: Later in the chapter, we'll show you how to format the index with the Paragraph Tool. At that time, you'll choose a font for the entire listing. But sometimes, you may want the page numbers to be in a different format from the rest of the index. You can get this effect by putting bracket codes before and after the page number symbol. For instance, to make the numbers bold, you'd use the bracket code <B> to turn bold on and <D> to turn it off. To make the page numbers a different size, you'd use the bracket code <P*nnn*> where *nnn* is the desired point size.

Place bracket codes after the tab. If you insert the codes before the tab, any leader dots will also have the new size and formatting. For more information on using bracket codes for text attributes, see Chapter 7, "Creating Text with Other Programs."

Separating page numbers
By default, Ventura uses a comma and a space to separate page numbers from each other, like this:

    Donuts 1, 10, 15

To change the separator, you use the Between #s text box. Delete the default comma and space and type in the separator you wish to use instead. For example, you could use a semicolon and a space. The result would look like this:

    Donuts 1; 10; 15

Determining what follows the last page number
By default, Ventura puts a blank space after the last page reference in an entry. But you can add a special character after an entry's page references to indicate the end of the entry. For example, you

could use a ballot box or a bullet. If you changed the size of the font for the page numbers, you could also use this text box to type the code that changes the font back to the default size: <P255D>.

Defining the words that precede "See" and "See Also"

By default, Ventura precedes See and See Also entries with the words "See" and "See Also" (funny how that worked out, isn't it?). But you can change these words or their formatting.with the "See" and "See Also" text boxes. Whatever text (and text attributes) that you put in the "See" and "See Also" text boxes will be inserted immediately before each cross reference in the index file. For example, you could change See to "Refer to."

Normally, See and See Also references appear in the same typeface as the rest of the index listing. However, it's a good idea to set off the words by making them italic while leaving the rest of the listing in normal type. You do this by putting bracket codes into this text box. For example, you could make the word "See" italic by adding the bracket code <I> to turn on italics and <D> to turn it off. Then the "See" text box would look something like this:

```
<I>See<D>
```

If you did the same thing in the "See Also" text box, you'd get an index that looked something like this:

Formatting
   See Tagging

Paragraph Tagging tool 1
   See Also Tagging

Tagging
   Bullets 1
   Headlines 1

Warning: Be sure to put a space after the word in the text box. Otherwise, the words "See" or "See Also" will run together with the reference itself.

Generating the index file

After you've made the changes to the Generate Index dialog box, hit OK to start the process. Ventura will load the first chapter in the publication, scan it, and create an index file with alphabetized listings and page numbers. Then it will move on to the next chapter and add its listings to the file. Ventura continues until it has done all the chapters.

Example: If you followed along with our previous example, you've already inserted five index entries in a chapter which you can now use to practice generating an index. True, it will be a tiny index, but it will give you a chance to try things. Here's what to do:

1. Choose Save to save any changes you've made to your chapter. Then choose Manage Publication from the File menu. Click on New. Add the test chapter you worked with before (our suggested name was INDEXTST.CHP). Now you have a publication with only one chapter. Click on Save As and name the publication INDEXTST.PUB. Then click on Save.

2. Click on Make Index. (If the INDEXTST.CHP filename is selected, this button will not be active. Deselect the filename by clicking on it once.) The Generate Index dialog box appears. Change the Title String from "Index" to "Index Test." In the Before #s text box, delete the tab character and replace it with a space. Then in the For Each # text box, delete the chapter number codes and hyphens, so the line reads "[P#] - [P#]."

3. Click on OK and wait as Ventura loads the chapter, scans it, and builds the index file.

4. If you're curious to check your results, use Windows' Notepad accessory to view the resulting file. If you used the names and locations we recommended, this file will be called \TYPESET\INDEXIDX.GEN.

What's it all mean? The text consists of the title of the index, the letter headings, and the actual index listings, including the page numbers (in this case, they are all on page 1). The tag names are *generated tags* created automatically by Ventura. In the next section, we'll show you how to use these tags to format the index.

Formatting the index

You've put in your index references in your text and generated your index file. Now you're ready to put on the finishing touches by formatting your index.

After you've generated your index file, you simply treat it like any other text file. You load it into a chapter file and use the Paragraph Tool and the Paragraph menu to format it like you would any other chapter. In other words, select a paragraph with the Paragraph Tool and use Font, Alignment, Spacing and the other Paragraph menu options to alter the appearance of the text. For more information on formatting and style sheets, see Chapter 3, "Building Basic Styles," and Chapter 5, "Building Advanced Styles,"

Tip: Because you usually want the index to resemble the rest of the document, make a new style sheet for the index that's based on the document's style sheet. Then you can add tag settings for the generated index tags without affecting or adding to the tags in the main style sheet.

For the most part, formatting an index is just like formatting any other document. However, you need to remember several things:

- There are only three paragraph tags: Z_INDEX TITLE, Z_INDEX LTR, and Z_INDEX MAIN.
- All the index entries under a given letter are in a single paragraph. (That's right, a single paragraph—even if there are dozens of entries under that letter.)
- Secondary entries are preceded by a tab character.

You can change these things, as explained in the section, "Going beyond the standard format," later in this chapter. For the moment, let's focus on a standard, two-level Ventura index. ("Two-level" means the index has primary and secondary listings.)

The tab settings are the source of most problems when building indexes. Most Ventura indexes have two of them: one before the secondary entry and one after.

The tab in front lets you indent the secondary listings. To create an indent, click on any @Z_INDEX MAIN paragraph with the Paragraph Tool and choose Tab Settings (Paragraph menu). Set the first tab slightly to the right of the left margin. Traditional indexes usually indent the secondary entries one em space. An em, if you recall, equals the point size. An index in 10-point type, therefore, would have a tab setting of 10 points to create a one-em indent.

Unless you have changed the default setting, you will also have a second tab between the entries and the first page number. To format this second tab, use the Tab Settings dialog box to set a value for Tab Number 2. Most people create a right-aligned tab at the right margin. Thus, if your right margin was 15 picas from the left margin, you'd set Tab Number 2 at 15 picas, right-aligned.

Going beyond the standard index

Three-level and four-level indexes can be a problem. Ventura treats all index entries under a specific letter as one paragraph. But what if you need an index with more than two levels (Figure 14-12)?

Figure 14-12.
This index uses more levels than are available with the standard generated index.

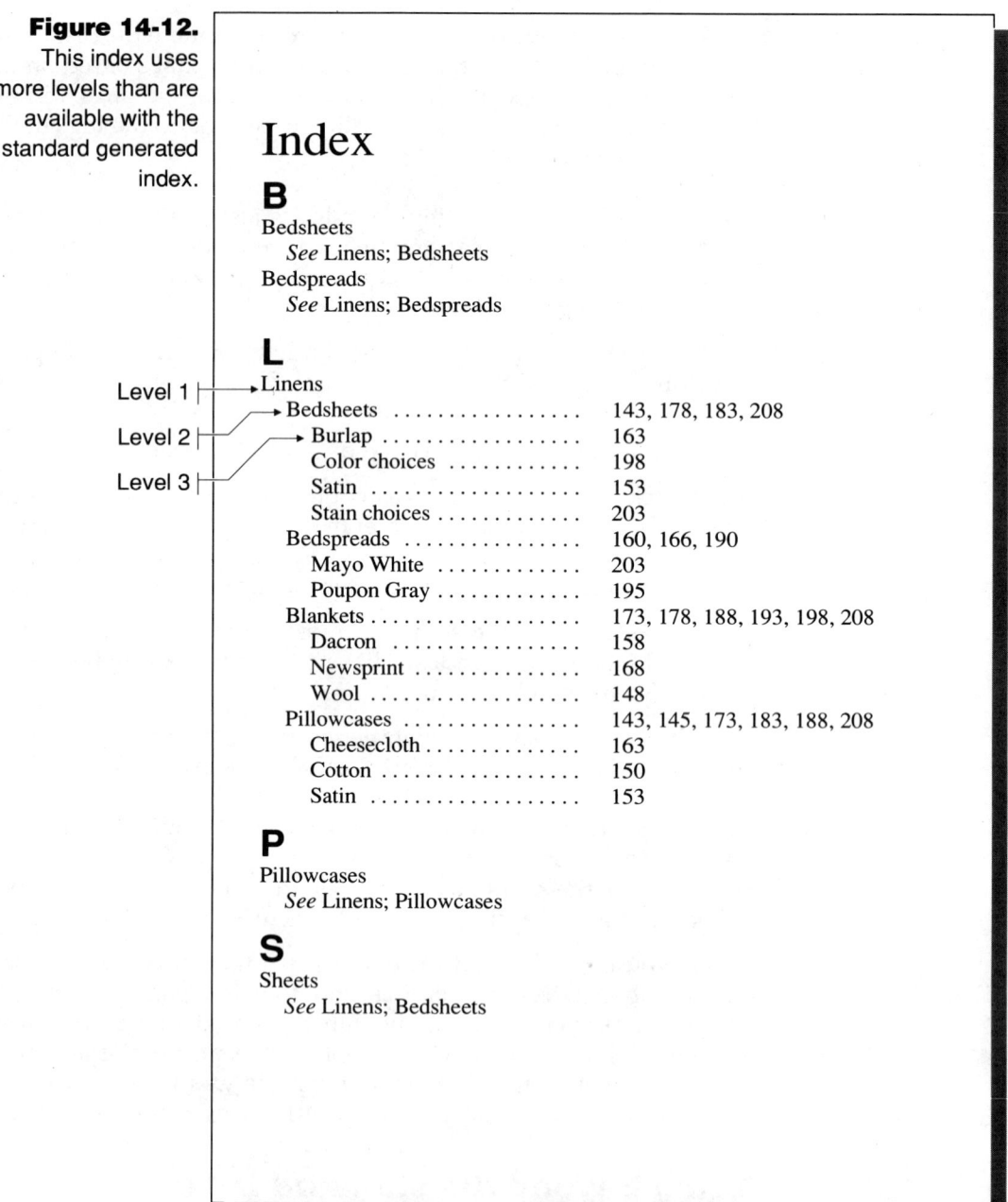

We're going to finish up the indexing section by explaining a technique developed by Byron Canfield that goes beyond Ventura's standard two-level index.

Here's how it works:

1. Because Ventura doesn't have provisions for a third level, put the second and third level entries on the same line.
2. Separate the second and third level entries with an unusual character that you can find with your word processor's search and replace function (we used an asterisk).
3. Generate the index file.
4. Use a word processor to perform a series of search and replace operations to separate first, second, and third levels from one another and to give each level a separate and distinct tag.
5. Format the new file.

For instance, here's a typical two-level entry:

```
Type Of Entry: Index
Primary Entry: Linens
Secondary Entry: Bedsheets
```

And here's a three-level entry, using the asterisk to separate the second and third levels on the same line:

```
Type Of Entry: Index
Primary Entry: Linens
Secondary Entry: Bedsheets*Burlap
```

We've given you more specific instructions in Table 14-1. This is an advanced technique, so you'll have to follow along with care. And you'll probably have to modify our method slightly for your own word processor and your own preferences.

Inevitably, documents change at the last minute, requiring you to rebuild the index file. The temptation, when you've made many individual adjustments to an index file, is to *not* regenerate it because that would mean doing all the adjustments again. You'll also be tempted to insert new numbers manually. But don't let these apparently easy solutions lead you astray—no matter how pretty the format, if the page numbers are wrong, it's useless.

Tip: Use macros to automate adjustments and avoid making them one by one. Then if you must regenerate the index file (thereby destroying any adjustments), you can recreate them easily.

Table 14-1 summarizes the steps you must take. It makes the following assumptions:

- That you typed in second-level and third-level entries on the same line separated by an asterisk

- That you are sure that all second-level entries occur at least once *without* a third-level entry attached to them
- That you generated an index file with Ventura
- That you opened the index file with your word processor
- That you will tag first, second, and third-level entries as Z_INDEXL1, Z_INDEXL2, and Z_INDEXL3, respectively

Please note that arrow symbols represent tabs, the ¶ symbols represent carriage returns, and small dots represent spaces.

Warning: We've used an asterisk as the separator in our examples. If you have any asterisks in your index, you must use a different symbol. Or you can use an unusual combination of symbols—such as }*{ —to avoid any possibility of confusing the separator symbol with a character in the index.

Creating a table of contents

In this section, you'll learn how to generate and format a table of contents (TOC). A successful table of contents accomplishes many of the things an index does: It guides readers to the information they want, and it divides topics into accessible chunks. In this section, we'll show you how to create a successful TOC by following these steps:

1. Place the chapters you want to work on in a publication.
2. Organize and preformat the TOC.
3. Generate the TOC file.
4. Format the TOC file to create the final TOC.

Ventura's Generate Table Of Contents dialog box is the key to creating a table of contents. However, this dialog box can be intimidating (Figure 14-14). But after you learn your way around, it's a powerful tool. This dialog box tells Ventura five important facts:

- The name of the TOC file (and where to put it)
- The TOC title that appears on the first page
- The tags that Ventura applies to the TOC entries
- The order of the TOC entries (TOC heading levels)
- The numbering style for TOC entries

After you've given Ventura instructions via the Generate Table Of Contents dialog box, it scans each chapter in the publication, finds

Table 14-1. *Building a three-level index*

Steps		Search text	Replacement text
1	Start at the top of the index file		
2	Separate second level entries from main index entry and tag them by replacing the line breaks with carriage returns and naming the tag Z_INDEXL2	`<R>¶→`	`¶¶@Z_INDEXL2·=·`
3	Search forward for the separator character	`*`	
4	After the separator has been found, search backward for the tag name and then move the cursor to the end of the tag name	`INDEXL2`	
5	Delete the 2 and insert a 3		`3`
6	Select the text from the character that follows the 3 to the separator character		
7	Delete the selected text		
8	Reinsert the spaces and the equal sign so the tag will be in Ventura format		`·=·`
9	Repeat steps 3-8 until no more separator characters are found		
10	Return to top of file		
11	Apply the new first-level tag to the first-level entries by searching forward for line breaks followed by carriage returns and replacing them with two carriage returns and the new tag	`<R>¶`	`¶¶@Z_INDEXL1·=·`
12	Return to the top of the file		
13	Rename the remaining original main tags to match the new names by searching forward for the old tag and replacing it with the new one	`@Z_INDEX·MAIN`	`@Z_INDEXL1`

the search tags for each level, records their text and page numbers as TOC entries, and applies tags to each entry. Then it records this information in a separate file. To create the actual TOC, you load this pretagged file into a document and format it.

For instance, suppose you had a manual with ten chapters. Let's say that each chapter title was tagged with the name CHAPTITLE. To build a TOC containing only the chapter names, you'd tell Ventura to look for (you guessed it) the CHAPTITLE tag. Each time

Ventura found this tag it would record the title itself (the contents of the tagged paragraph) and the page it was on. It would store what it found as ten separate paragraphs in the TOC file.

In real life, many TOCs have more than one level. The TOC of this book, for instance, includes not just chapter names, but chapter numbers and first-level headings (Figure 14-13) as well. Each one of these three elements—chapter number, chapter title, headings—is a separate level in Ventura's TOC dialog box (Figure 14-14).

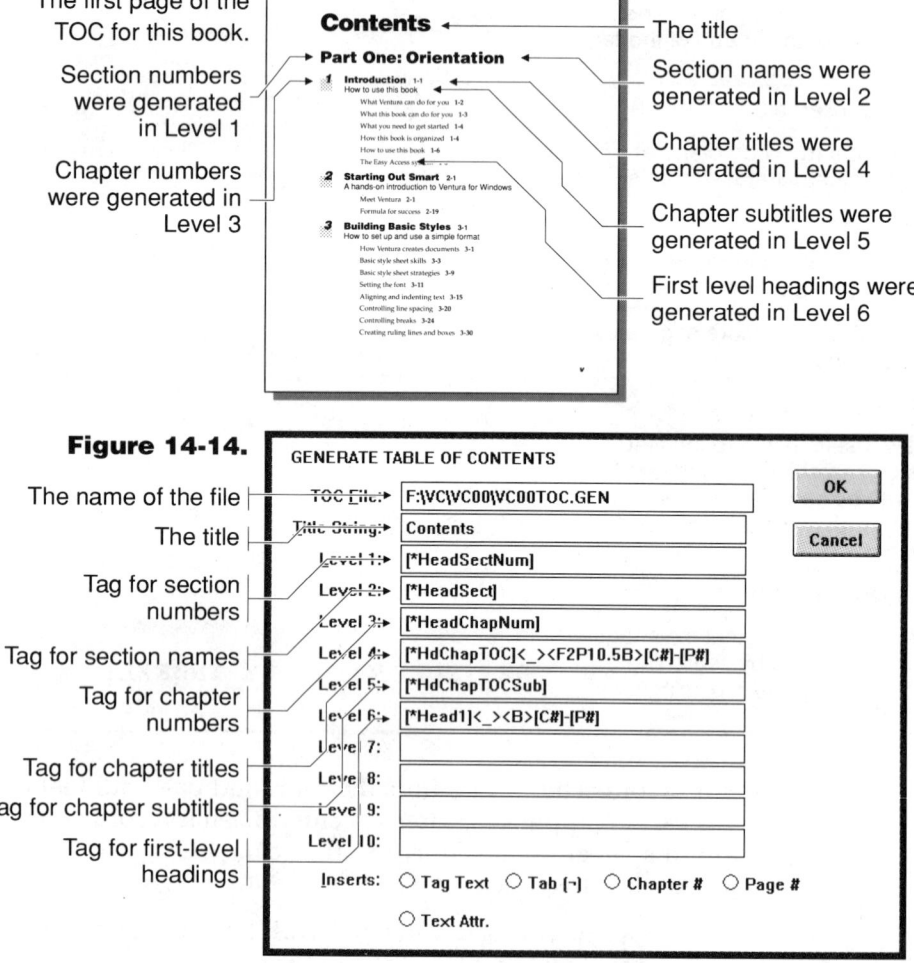

Figure 14-13. The first page of the TOC for this book. Section numbers were generated in Level 1. Chapter numbers were generated in Level 3. The title. Section names were generated in Level 2. Chapter titles were generated in Level 4. Chapter subtitles were generated in Level 5. First level headings were generated in Level 6.

Figure 14-14. The name of the file. The title. Tag for section numbers. Tag for section names. Tag for chapter numbers. Tag for chapter titles. Tag for chapter subtitles. Tag for first-level headings.

The different levels let you choose what order to list things in your TOC. Because we wanted the chapter number to come first, we put it on Level 1 of the dialog box. We wanted the title second, so we put its tag name on Level 2. The third item, the first-level headings, went on Level 3. Ventura puts each level in a separate paragraph and gives each one a separate tag name. Level 1 items are tagged as Z_TOC LVL1, Level 2 items as Z_TOC LVL 2, and so on.

Working with the TOC dialog box

In this section, you see how to use the Generate Table Of Contents dialog box to create a TOC file. To generate a table of contents:

1. Choose Manage Publication from the File menu. The Multi-Chapter dialog box appears.

2. Create a publication that contains all the chapters you want to include in the TOC (Figure 14-15). Save the publication.

For instance, if your book has ten chapters, the publication should include all ten. For more information on building and working with publications, see Chapter 16, "Managing Ventura Files."

Figure 14-15. Be sure the publication includes all the chapters.

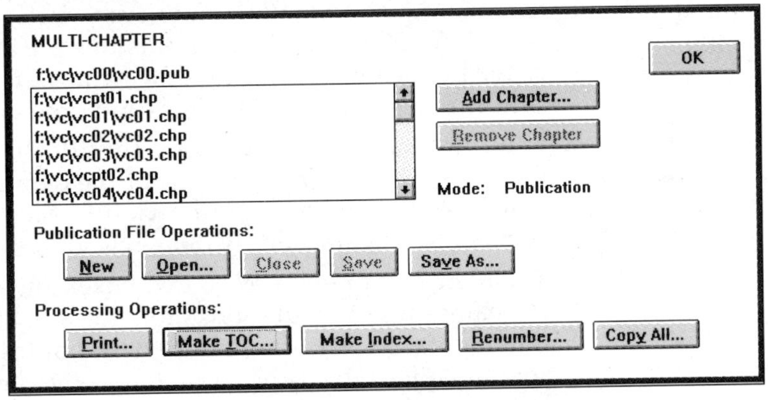

3. Click on the Make TOC button. The Generate Table Of Contents dialog box appears (Figure 14-16).

4. Use the text boxes in the Generate Table Of Contents dialog box to name the TOC file, create the TOC title, and define the TOC entries for each level (we'll guide you through each text box). Then click on OK.

Let's examine the text boxes in the Generate Table Of Contents dialog box in more detail:

- The *TOC File* text box contains the default name of the TOC file. Ventura bases this name on the name of the publication. It simply adds the letters *TOC* to the end of the publication's name and

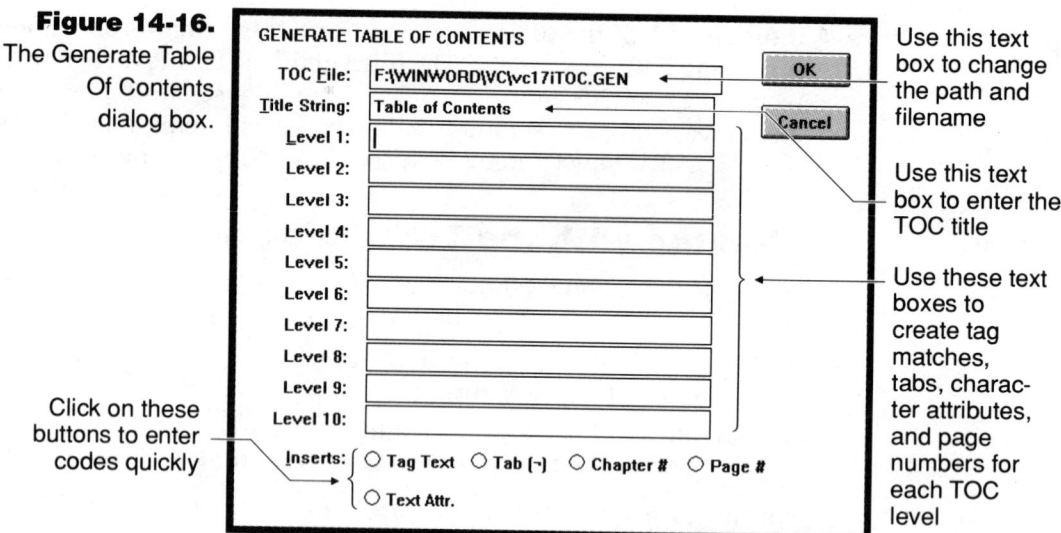

Figure 14-16.
The Generate Table Of Contents dialog box.

Click on these buttons to enter codes quickly

Use this text box to change the path and filename

Use this text box to enter the TOC title

Use these text boxes to create tag matches, tabs, character attributes, and page numbers for each TOC level

replaces the extension with *GEN*. Thus, if your publication is called MANUAL.PUB, Ventura will call the TOC file MANUATOC.GEN. Ventura puts this file in the same directory as the publication. To change the name of the file or its location, simply delete the current names and type new ones.

- The *Title String* text box contains the title that Ventura will put at the top of the file. You can accept the default of "Table of Contents" or you can create your own title. Most people change it to "Contents." Again, simply delete the old and type in the new.

- The *Level 1* through *Level 10* text boxes allow you to specify the tag names that Ventura looks for. You can also specify the page numbering style and apply text attributes. You do this with special codes. You type these codes by clicking on the *Inserts* buttons at the bottom of the dialog box.

For instance, on Level 2 of the TOC dialog box for this book, we gave Ventura instructions that told it to "look for every instance of the tag called HeadChap. Each time you find it, record the text of the tagged paragraph. Then put two tab characters after the text and record the page number you found it on." The actual instructions looked like this in the Level 2 text box:

[*HeadChap]→→[P#]

Here's how you'd type those instructions into the dialog box:

1. Move the cursor to the Level 2 text box. Click on the Tag Text button. The code [*tag name] appears in the text box.

2. Delete the text "tag name" without deleting the rest of the code. Replace it with the actual tag name—in this case, "Head-Chap."
3. Click on the Tab button twice to create two tab characters.
4. Click on the Page # button to insert the code for page numbers.

Whatever you type on these lines will appear in the new file. For instance, if you want a single space between the text and the page numbers, you would type a space on the line right after the tag name code. If you wanted a period after each page number, you would type the period right after the page number code. If you wanted the word "Page" to appear in front of each page number, you would type it in the text box right in front of the page number code.

You can also use the Text Attr. button to add bracket codes to these lines. The button inserts the bracket code <D> each time you type it. You can then erase the *D* and type in the code you really want.

With those bracket codes, you can make one part of a line look different from the rest. If you wanted an entire line to be bold, you would use the Paragraph Tool (see below). But if you wanted only the page numbers bold while the rest of the line was normal, you would surround the page numbers with bracket codes. For instance, to make the page numbers bold, you use the code <B> to turn bold on and the code <D> to turn it off again.

In the same fashion, you can use bracket codes to change the point size, to change to a different font, to shift text from the baseline, and to create any of the effects explained in Chapter 7, "Creating Text with Other Programs."

Generating the new file

After filling in the Generate Table Of Contents dialog box as explained above, click on OK. Ventura then loads each chapter in the publication, one after another. It scans each file, looking for the tag names you listed in the dialog box. Each time it finds one, it records the text and the page number in the file.

If you are working with a large publication or long chapters, the process can take several minutes. When it is complete, Ventura returns you to the Manage Publication dialog box. Click on OK to return to the workspace.

Note: The settings you choose in the Generate Table Of Contents dialog box remain with the publication. This means you can regenerate the TOC over and over again without changing the dialog box each time. You can use this feature to create a quick rough draft TOC. When you're ready for the final TOC, just open the Generate Table Of Contents dialog box and click on OK.

Formatting the table of contents

So far, you've learned how to fill in the Generate Table Of Contents dialog box to tell Ventura how to build the TOC. And you've seen that Ventura uses these instructions to build a separate TOC file.

After you've generated the file, all you need to do is give the TOC the right look. You simply load the new TOC file into a chapter and format it with the Paragraph Tool, as you would with any text file.

We won't repeat the formatting instructions found in Chapter 3, "Building Basic Styles," and Chapter 5, "Advanced Styles." The techniques that work on other text work the same on the TOC file. We do, however, want to alert you to several important issues.

Loading the TOC file

Where should you load the file? You have several choices. First, you can treat it as a separate chapter. Second, you can load it into the same document inside a separate frame (or frames if it is longer than one page). The first and second options are good choices if you expect the TOC to change. Because the TOC file is not renamed or made part of any other file, you can regenerate it as many times as you need. As long as you give it the same name and location, Ventura will load in the updated TOC file. You won't have to take any special steps to be sure the TOC information is up to date.

Your third choice is to make it part of the original text file. You do this by choosing Destination: Clipboard or Destination: Cursor in the Load Text/Picture dialog box when you bring in the TOC file. Either of these two options lets you put the TOC text into the existing text file. The next time you save the file, the TOC text is saved along with the rest of the file.

This third method makes it harder to revise the TOC. If you have to regenerate the TOC file, you'll have to delete the TOC text you originally inserted and then load in the new TOC text.

For more information on loading text files, see Chapter 7, "Creating Text with Other Programs."

Choosing the style sheet

What style sheet should you use? Because the TOC usually has a strong resemblance to the rest of the document, most people use the same style sheet for the TOC as they do for the rest of the document. They simply add the tags for the TOC to the original style sheet.

However, most people prefer to treat the TOC as a separate document. They start with the document's style sheet, but they rename it so their changes won't affect the original. This method insulates the original document from any chapter-wide changes you make, such as the margins or columns. In addition, it helps keep the number of total tags down in the style sheet used for the main chapters—long documents are often very close to Ventura's tag limit of 128. On the other hand, you have to remember to update two different style sheets if you later make changes to the overall look of the document and you want the TOC to match.

The TOC text will contain one tag for the title and one for each level you specified. The title is tagged as Z_TOC TITLE. Level 1 is Z_TOC LVL 1, Level 2 is Z_TOC LVL 2, and so on.

Tip: Create the TOC tags *before* you bring in the TOC text. After you bring in the text, the TOC tags will be part of the style sheet. If you don't define them in advance, Ventura will give them all the same parameters as Body Text. You'll have to change them one by one. But if you build them in advance, you can apply the proper tab settings to the first TOC tag (Z_TOC LVL 1) and then copy the others from it.

Deciding where to put page numbers

Where do you put the page numbers? Should you use leader dots? The most common format calls for tabs between the text and the numbers, with the numbers aligned right. Some TOCs, however, have the page numbers separated from the text only by a space. Remember—you decide the separator in the Generate Table Of Contents dialog box. If you want a space, type it into the text box. If you want a tab character, create it by clicking on the Tab button at the bottom of the dialog box.

Some TOCs use leader dots to guide the eye from the text to the numbers. You create leader dots with the Paragraph Tool and the Tab Settings dialog box. For more information on creating leader dots and setting tabs, see Chapter 5, "Advanced Styles."

Tip: To make the right-hand ends of the dot leaders align in a table of contents, insert *two* tabs between the tag match and the page number. Then format so that the first tab is aligned right at a position just short of the longest page number (Figure 14-17).

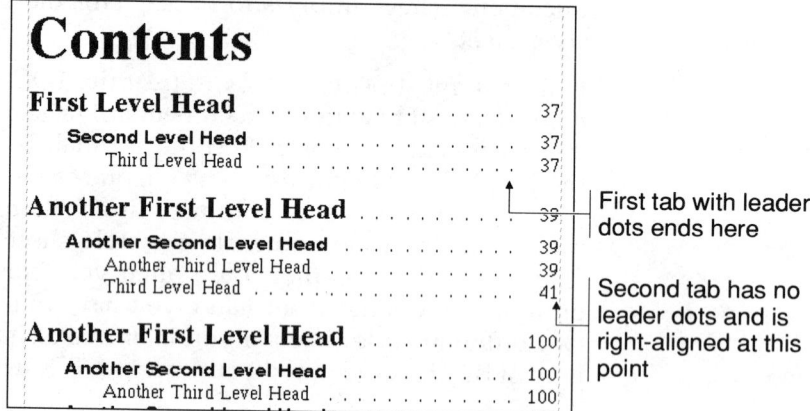

Figure 14-17. Use two tabs to make leaders dots more attractive.

Going beyond the standard table of contents

You can create extraordinary TOCs by using more than one level in the dialog box for each entry in the TOC. Here are some examples.

Different text treatments in the same entry

In Figure 14-18, notice the three distinct treatments of text for each chapter entry. The chapter number, the chapter title, and the chapter subtitle all have different attributes.

This could be done to a single paragraph of normal text with character attributes, tabs, and line endings. But you cannot generate these entries with just one line in the Generate Table Of Contents dialog box. Why? Because you can't fit that many character attributes on a single line. Yes, you could add all the extra coding after the fact. But then you would have to do it to each line one at a time. And you would have to redo it each time the table of contents was updated.

Tip: You can overcome the length limitation of the dialog box by opening the PUB file in an ASCII editor such as Notepad and adding more character attributes there. However, the PUB file contains vital information about the publication, which can be damaged if you make careless (or inadvertent) changes to the codes within it.

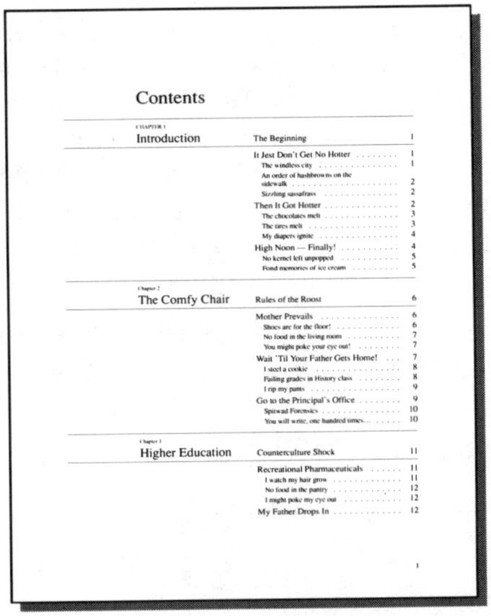

Figure 14-18.
Here is an instance where the normal chapter title and headline paragraphs cannot be used for the tag match in the table of contents because it is in all uppercase in the chapter, but initial caps in the table of contents (see Figure 14-20).

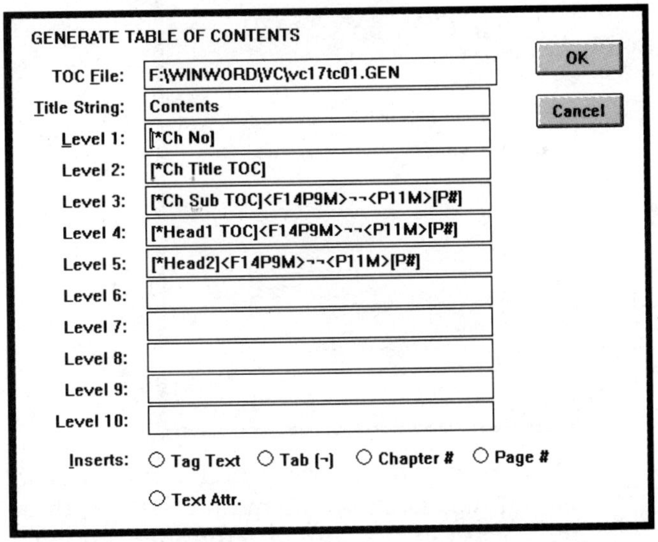

Figure 14-19.
The Generate Table Of Contents dialog box for the example in Figure 14-18.

However, it *can* be done in an automated fashion—as separate paragraphs. There is no requirement that every level generate a page number. Take a look at Figure 14-19. Levels 1 and 2 do not include the page number code. Therefore, they do not create any page numbers, they just echo the text. Level 3 generates a page number, and then, using Spacing and Breaks, the three paragraphs are arranged in the desired places. For more information on placing paragraphs on the same line, see Chapter 3, "Building Basic Styles."

Using invisible paragraphs for tag matches

It's great the way Ventura can pull text from the pages of your chapters and stick it into the TOC. But there are disadvantages. The text in the TOC is going to match the text in the chapter *exactly*. If you want to make changes—for instance, if you want the capitalization different—you have to make the changes manually to the TOC. Unless, that is, you use "invisible" paragraphs to contain the text you want to appear in the TOC.

Compare the TOC in Figure 14-18 with Figure 14-20, one of the chapters listed in that TOC. Look closely—do you see the differences in capitalization in Chapter 2? The TOC shows the title, subtitle, and headings in upper and lowercase. The chapter shows them in uppercase.

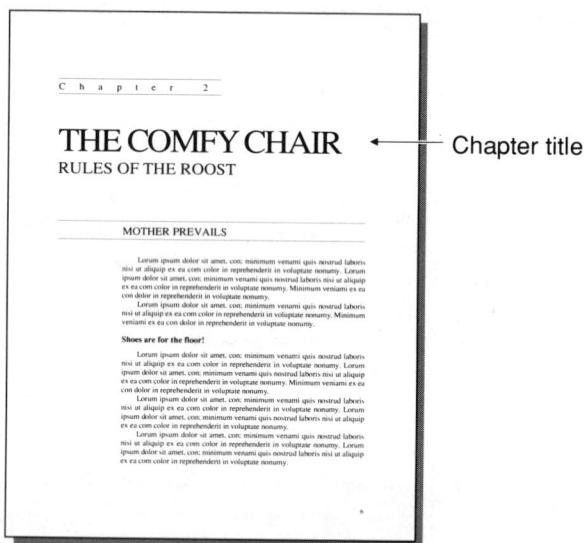

Figure 14-20. Compare the capitalization and entries in this chapter with its TOC (see Figure 14-18).

This trick was accomplished with "invisible" paragraphs. Although you can't see them on the page, these paragraphs contain the correct capitalization. How did we make the paragraphs invisible? By giving them a color of white and a line spacing of zero.

Then, in the Generate Table Of Contents dialog box, we instructed Ventura to look for the invisible paragraphs instead of the actual title, subtitle, and heading.

Using the TOC function for figure and table lists

You can generate figure lists and table lists with the Generate Table Of Contents dialog box. We refer to figure lists in this section, but our comments apply equally to table lists.

Figure lists are handy for readers, particularly in scientific and research documents. They make it easy to reference important illustrations. Besides, some people just want to look at the pictures (come on, admit it—the first thing you did when you picked up this book was check out the pictures). Figure lists usually show the figure number, the page number on which it occurs, and the caption as well (Figure 14-21).

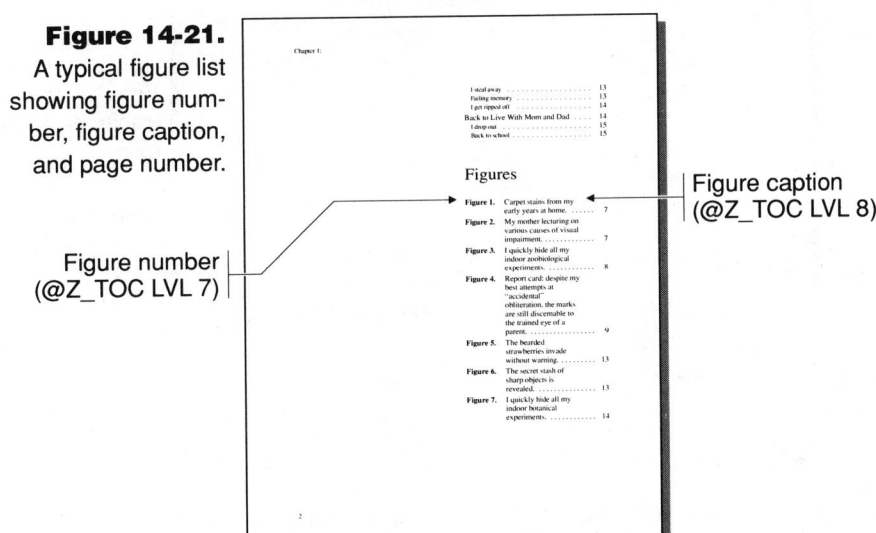

Figure 14-21.
A typical figure list showing figure number, figure caption, and page number.

Figure number (@Z_TOC LVL 7)

Figure caption (@Z_TOC LVL 8)

If you don't mind that the figure list looks identical to the TOC, you can use the same levels. Remember that each level gets a unique tag: Z_TOC LVL 1 for the first level, Z_TOC LVL 2 for the second, and so on. You can generate multiple TOC files using the same levels. Just type different tag names in the text boxes, and give the files different names. In this fashion, you can use the Generate Table Of Contents dialog box once to create a TOC, once for a figure list, and once for a table list.

Usually, however, you want the figure list to be a little more subdued than the TOC. You might think this would require a separate style sheet. But if you practice restraint, and don't use all ten levels for the TOC, you can use the remaining levels to build a figure list.

If your TOC uses only Levels 1 through 5, you have five levels left for building a figure list. You can't do this with the same PUB file, of course; otherwise, the figure listings would be interspersed with the TOC. But all you have to do is have one PUB set up for the TOC (using Levels 1-5) and another PUB set up for the figure list (using

6-10). Figure 14-22 shows the settings for the figure list PUB to create the sample shown in Figure 14-21.

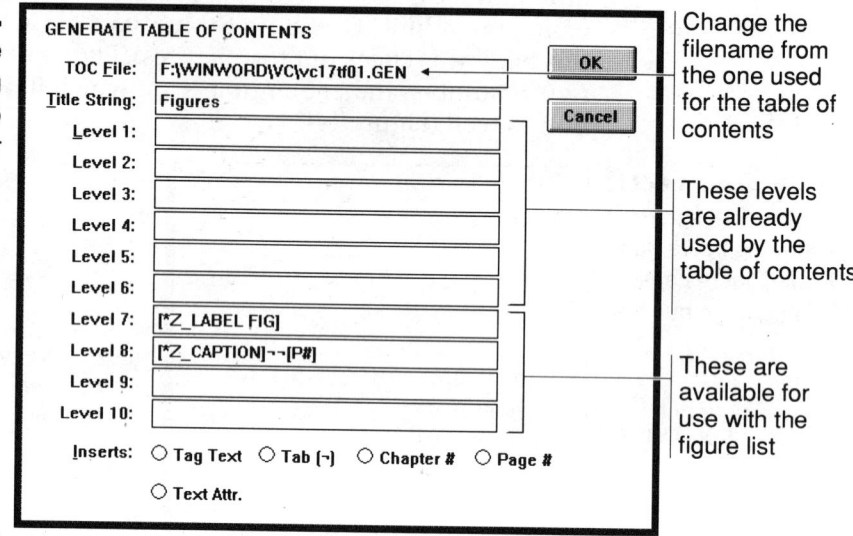

Figure 14-22. The Generate Table Of Contents dialog box is used to search for paragraph tags.

Continuing on

Now you know how to take the drudgery out of making indexes and tables of contents—well, at least *most* of the drudgery. You've learned how to plan them for maximum value, generate them for maximum efficiency, and format them for maximum appeal. Spend a little time to automate the procedure. Remember that the key to effective indexing and tables of contents is planning.

Easy Access

For more info on...	See chapter...
Formatting and using style sheets	4 — Building the Underlying Page
Using bracket codes to apply text attributes	7 — Creating Text with Other Programs
Creating publications	16 — Managing Ventura Files
Bracket codes for indexing	21 — Rapid Reference

15 Creating Footnotes and Equations

How to add footnotes and equations to Ventura documents

- **Creating footnotes** 455
- **Creating and editing equations** 471
- **Continuing on** 478

cholarly, technical, and scientific documents often need footnotes and equations. Thanks to Ventura, these otherwise cumbersome formats are easy to create. In this chapter, we'll show you how to use two of Ventura's most powerful tools: the footnoting function and the Equation Editor.

Ventura automates much of the troublesome formatting involved with creating footnotes. You simply insert footnote references in the main text. Then you use the Footnote Settings dialog box (Chapter menu) to tell Ventura how to handle the footnote reference that appears in the main text and the footnote text that can be placed at the bottom of the page or at the end of the chapter. Ventura will automatically number the footnotes (in the manner you specified) and place the footnote text for you (Figure 15-1).

Ventura also makes it easy to handle equations. Using Ventura's Equation Editor, you can insert equations into the main text without interrupting its flow. Other DTP programs handle equations as complex graphics that are difficult to edit and difficult to integrate with the main text. However, Ventura treats equations as a special kind of text that can easily be edited and placed within the main text (Figure 15-1).

Creating footnotes

Footnotes let you refer to supplemental information (such as bibliographical notes, definitions, and comments) without interrupting the flow of the text.

But before you work with footnotes, you need to understand Ventura's terminology. In Figure 15-2, you get a visual definition of all the footnote terms.

You also need to know the difference between a number and a symbol—the two ways to mark a footnote reference within the main text. When you turn on the footnoting function, Ventura lets you decide whether you want to signal footnotes with numbers[1] or with symbols.*

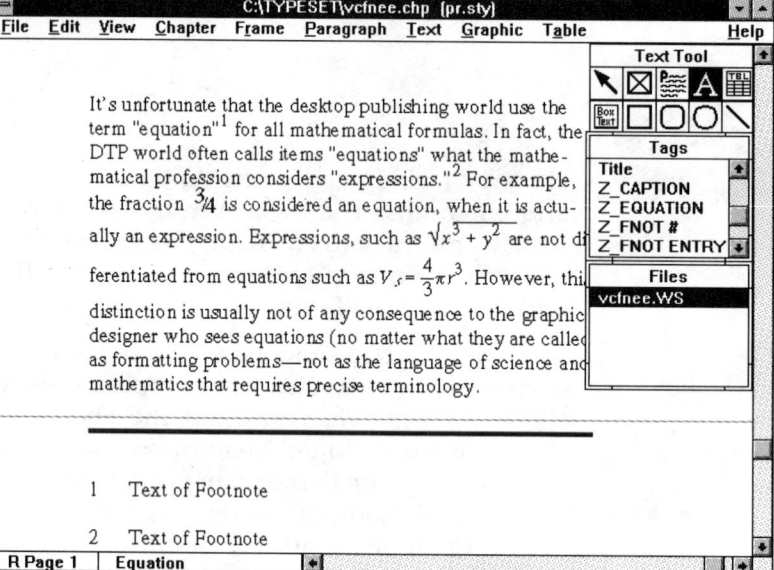

Figure 15-1. Ventura gives you the tools to handle both footnotes and equations.

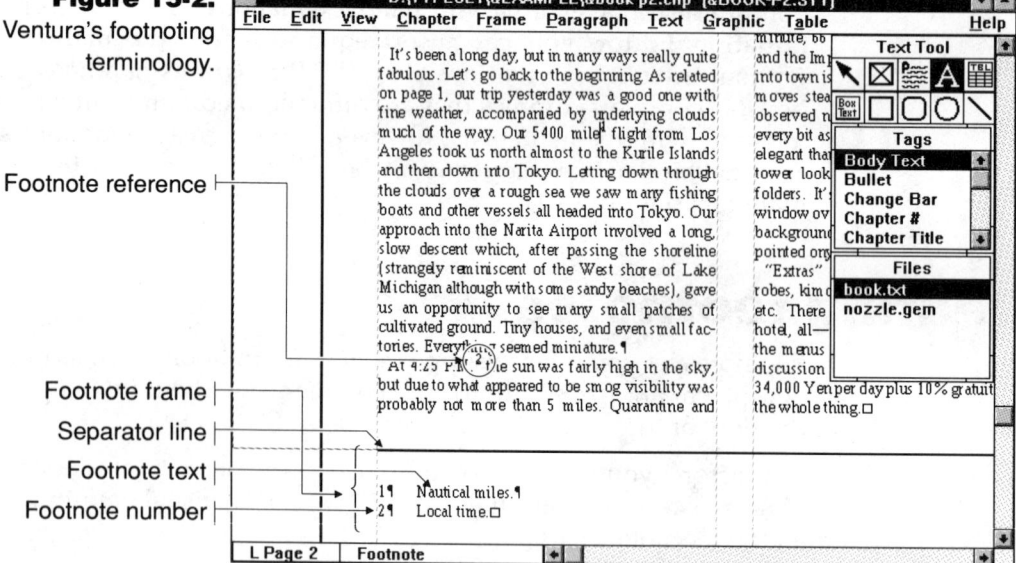

Figure 15-2. Ventura's footnoting terminology.

Now that you know the terms, you're ready to start learning about Ventura's footnoting function. With Ventura's footnoting function, you can place either symbols or numbers next to the item (within the main text) that you want to footnote. After you've chosen your settings for the footnoting function, Ventura automatically creates a footnote frame for any page that contains footnote references and places all the footnote text in that frame. You can tell Ventura to place the footnote frame at the bottom of the page where the footnote is referenced or assemble them all in a single frame at the end of the chapter. If you add more footnotes, Ventura automatically resizes the frame or continues the footnote text in a frame on the next page.

To create a footnote, you follow these four steps:

1. Turn on the footnote function.
2. Insert the first footnote *reference* in the text.
3. Type the footnote *text*.
4. Format the footnotes.

Turning on the footnote function

To turn on the footnoting function, you choose the Footnote Settings from the Chapter menu (Figure 15-3). Then you select one of the footnote reference options from the Usage & Format buttons. As you can see from Figure 15-3, there is no "On" button. To turn on the footnoting function, select one of the three different numbering formats.

In the Footnote Settings dialog box, you also make these three formatting choices:

- Use symbols or numbers for footnote references
- Control how the footnote reference looks in the main text
- Use a separator line to keep the footnote text distinct from the main text

This dialog box looks intimidating. But never fear. We'll take you step by step and show you a clear and orderly path through its mysterious symbols and terms.

Choosing the type of footnote reference

To turn on the footnote function, you must select the numbering format for your footnotes. You have three choices:

- # From Start Of Page (1,2,3)
- # From Start Of Page (User-Defined)
- # From Start Of Chapter (1,2,3)

The # From Start Of Page (1,2,3) and # From Start Of Chapter (1,2,3) options give you two ways to use numbers (digits) for footnote

Figure 15-3.
The Footnote Settings dialog box.

These buttons create footnotes with numbers

This button creates footnotes with symbols

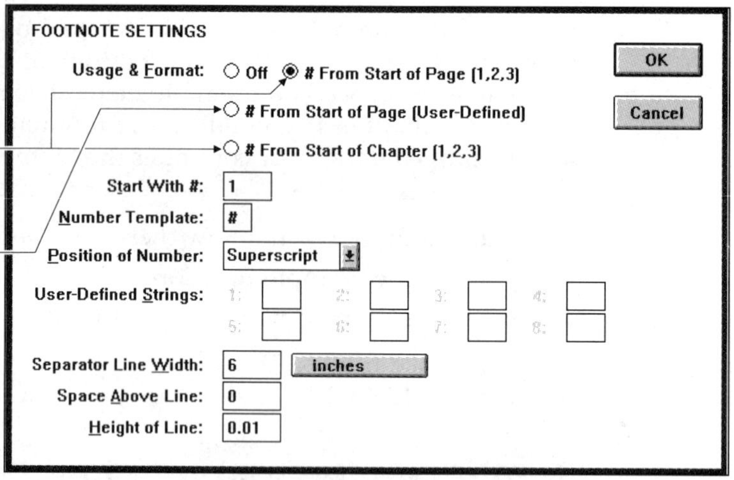

FOOTNOTE SETTINGS

Usage & Format: ○ Off ⦿ # From Start of Page (1,2,3)
○ # From Start of Page (User-Defined)
○ # From Start of Chapter (1,2,3)

Start With #: 1
Number Template: #
Position of Number: Superscript
User-Defined Strings: 1: _ 2: _ 3: _ 4: _
5: _ 6: _ 7: _ 8: _
Separator Line Width: 6 inches
Space Above Line: 0
Height of Line: 0.01

OK   Cancel

references. The # From Start Of Page (User-Defined) allows you to use symbols for references. First, we'll show you how to use numbers and then symbols.

Using numbers for footnote references

To use numbers for footnote references, you follow these steps:

1. Choose Footnote Settings from the Chapter menu.

2. Select one of the two numbering options for Usage & Format: # From Start Of Page (1,2,3) or # From Start Of Chapter (1,2,3). Here's how the two options work:

- The *# From Start Of Page (1,2,3)* button begins numbering all footnotes that occur on a single page with the number one. This option is the most common.

- The *# From Start Of Chapter (1,2,3)* button begins numbering at the beginning of the chapter and continues to the end. Use this option when you want the footnotes to appear as "endnotes" that are assembled at the end of the chapter.

3. In the Start With # text box, type the number you want the references to start with. The default is 1. If you selected # From Start Of Page (1,2,3), Ventura numbers the references on each page beginning with the number in this text box. If you selected # From Start Of Chapter (1,2,3), it begins with this number at the beginning of the chapter.

4. In the Number Template text box, type any symbols or punctuation that you want to appear with the number. The # symbol represents the actual number. For example, you could add parentheses around each reference by typing them in this text box. You can have up to three characters including the # symbol. The default is no punctuation—only the number.

5. In the Position Of Number list box, select the vertical position of the reference: No Shift, Superscript, or Subscript. The default is No Shift, which is aligned with the paragraph text. You can fine tune the size and shift of the reference number later with the Paragraph Tool and the Attribute Overrides command from the Paragraph menu (see the section, "Formatting the footnote references").

6. Click on OK.

Example: Try it. Set up numbered footnote references that begin numbering at the start of each page with the number 1, appear in the main text with square brackets around the number, and have no shift. But before you start, let's create a test chapter that you can use for the examples throughout this footnoting and equations chapter. If you haven't loaded the Example chapters from the Examples Disk that came with Ventura, do so now. Then start Ventura. Choose New from the File menu. Load the style sheet SAMPLE1.STY from the \TYPESET directory, using Load Diff. Style from the File menu. Load the ASCII text file SAMPLE.TXT, using the Load/Text File command. Name the chapter TEST.CHP, using Save As from the File menu. Now you're ready to set up your footnote references. Choose Footnote Settings from the Chapter menu. Select # From Start Of Page (1,2,3) for Usage & Format. Type 1 for Start With #; type [#] for Number Template; and select No Shift for Position Of Number. Your dialog box should look like Figure 15-4. Click on OK. Press Ctrl-S to save your chapter. Now you've turned on the footnoting function and set up the footnote references—however, Ventura won't do anything until you've inserted a reference within the text. You'll learn how in the upcoming section, "Inserting footnote references in the main text."

Note: We'll be using the chapter you just created to give you hands-on experience with footnoting—and later with equations.

Using symbols for footnote references

If you don't want to use numbers for your footnote references, you can use symbols instead. However, you should use symbols only when a maximum of eight footnotes can occur on any page. Ventura lets you define only eight footnote symbols. If you have nine or more, Ventura will begin using the same symbols again starting with the ninth footnote. This makes it difficult for the reader to

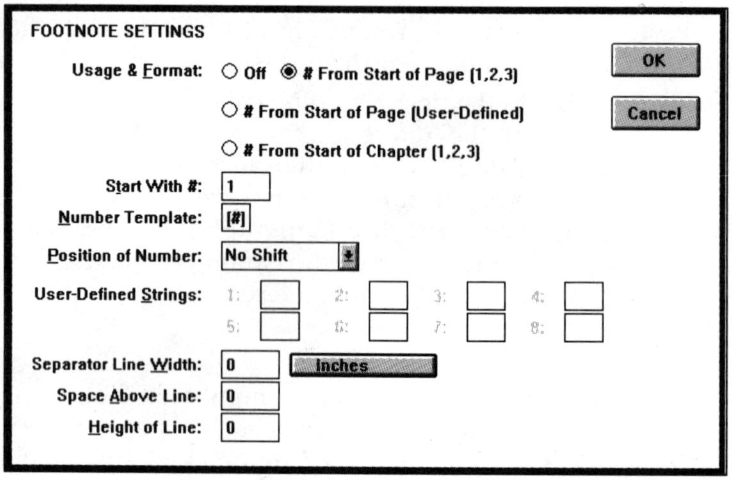

Figure 15-4.
Make these settings in the Footnote Settings dialog box for the example chapter TEST.CHP.

match the footnote reference with the correct footnote text. In short, if you have a lot of footnotes, play it safe and use one of the numbering options.

Warning: Because Ventura uses the same ANSI character set as Windows, you can't specify the "dagger" (†) "double-dagger" (‡) or "section" (§) symbols for footnotes.† But there are plenty of other characters you can use as footnote symbols.

To use symbols for footnote references, follow these steps:

1. Choose Footnote Settings from the Chapter menu.

2. Select # From Start of Page (User Defined) for Usage & Format. Ventura's default symbols should appear in the User-Defined Strings text boxes, which are numbered in the sequence that the symbols will be used (Figure 15-5). Notice that you don't have to use just one symbol—you can use a combination of symbols for a reference.

What if you don't want Ventura's default symbols? Don't panic. If you want to use a keyboard character, just delete the old symbol and type the new character into the text box. If you want to use a non-keyboard character such as £, delete the old symbol and then hold down the Alt key and type the ANSI code for the symbol, using the numeric keypad. For the list of codes for the ANSI character set, see Chapter 21, "Rapid Reference."

---

† The final production on this book was done with the GEM version of Ventura—which is why you can see these characters here.

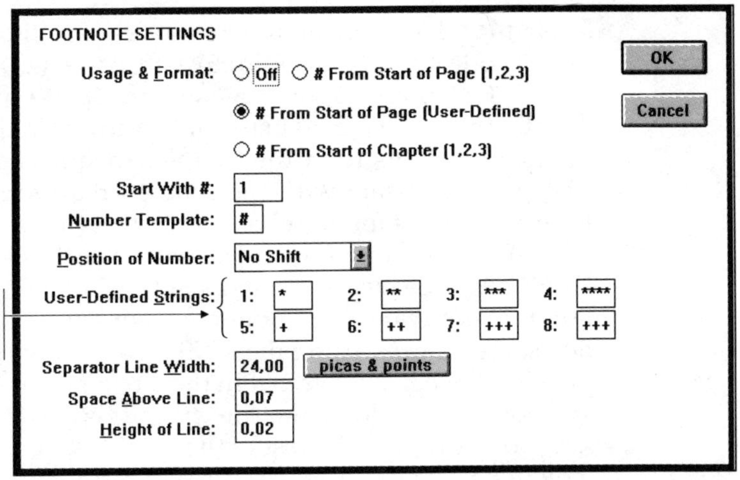

Figure 15-5.
When you select # From Start Of Page (User-Defined), Ventura's default symbols appear in the User-Defined Strings text boxes.

Ventura's default symbols

[Figure 15-5: FOOTNOTE SETTINGS dialog box showing Usage & Format options with "# From Start of Page (User-Defined)" selected; Start With #: 1; Number Template: #; Position of Number: No Shift; User-Defined Strings: 1: *, 2: **, 3: ***, 4: ****, 5: +, 6: ++, 7: +++, 8: +++; Separator Line Width: 24,00 picas & points; Space Above Line: 0,07; Height of Line: 0,02]

3. Type the symbols (or hold down the Alt key and type ANSI codes with the numeric keypad if you want non-keyboard characters) that you want in the User-Defined String text boxes.

4. In the Position Of Number list box, select the vertical position of the reference: No Shift, Superscript, or Subscript. You can fine tune the size and shift of the reference number later with the Paragraph Tool and the Attribute Overrides command from the Paragraph menu (see the section, "Formatting the footnote references").

5. Click on OK.

Table 15-1 lists ANSI codes for some characters that are commonly used as footnote symbols.

Table 15-1. *ANSI character set (excerpt)*

ANSI code	Character	ANSI code	Character
35	#	0165	¥
42	*	0164	¤
43	+	0191	¿
0162	¢	0223	ß
156	£	0182	¶

Example: Try it. Set up footnote references that use the symbols * (ANSI code 42), £ (156), ¥ (0165), ¤ (0164), + (43), Ç (0199), ø (0248), and ß (0223), and appear as superscripts. Open the TEST.CHP chapter that you created in the first example in this chapter. Choose Footnote Settings from the Chapter menu. The Footnote Settings dialog box appears with the settings that you made for the last example. Type # for Number Template. Select # From Start Of Page (User-Defined) for Usage & Format. Select Superscript for Position Of Number. Leave the symbols in the 1 and 5 text boxes (they are the ones we want). Type the new symbols into the User-Defined Strings text boxes, using the ANSI codes we've given you. Start by deleting the current symbol in the 2 text box and then typing the £ symbol, holding down the Alt key and typing 156 with the numeric keypad. Now type the rest of the symbols. Your dialog box should look like Figure 15-6. Click on OK. Press Ctrl-S to save your chapter. You've turned on the footnoting function and set up footnote references that appear as symbols. Next you'll learn how to insert these references into the main text.

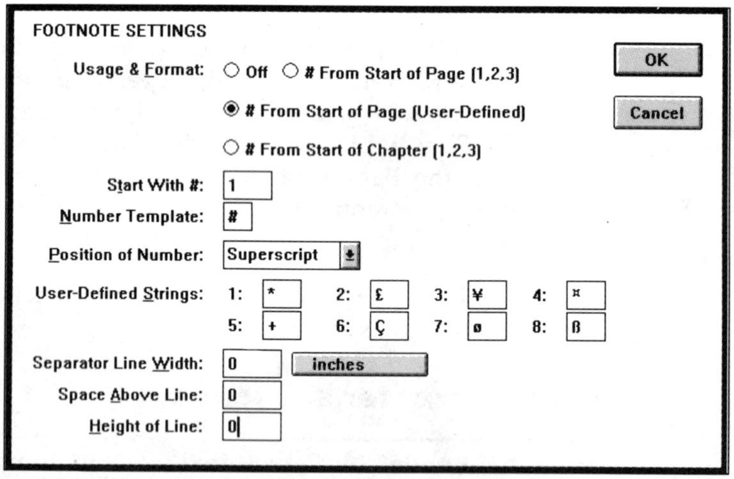

Figure 15-6.
Make these settings in the Footnote Settings dialog box for the example chapter TEST.CHP.

Inserting the footnote reference within the main text

After you've turned on the footnoting function and selected the type of footnote reference, you insert the footnote references in the main text, using the Text Tool and the Edit menu. Here's how:

1. Using the Text Tool, position the text cursor at the place in the text where you want the footnote reference to appear.

2. Choose Insert Special Item from the Text menu (Figure 15-7). A flyout menu appears.

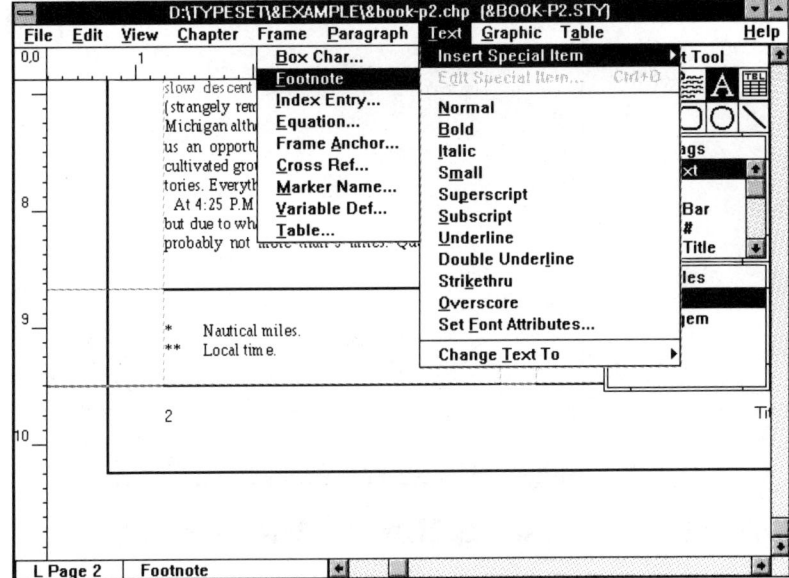

Figure 15-7.
The Insert Special Item menu.

3. Select Footnote from the flyout menu.

At this point, two things happen:

- The footnote reference appears on the page at the text cursor—either a number or symbol, depending on your choices in the Footnote Settings dialog box.
- A footnote frame appears at the bottom of the page. (If the footnote reference is not the first on the page, the frame is already there and enlarges to contain the additional reference.)

Example: Try it. In the TEST.CHP chapter, add footnote references in the sixth, seventh, and eighth paragraphs after the words "picture," "fonts," and "WYSIWYG." Open the TEST.CHP chapter. Using the Text Tool, place the text cursor directly after the word "picture" in the sixth paragraph. Choose Insert Special Item (Text menu). Select Footnote from the flyout menu. A footnote reference appears after the word. The footnote frame also appears at the bottom of the page. Now add footnote references for fonts and WYSIWYG. If you've gone through all the examples in this chapter, your TEST.CHP chapter should have a footnote frame that looks similar to Figure 15-8. Next you'll add the footnote text.

Figure 15-8.
The footnote frame for the example chapter TEST.CHP should now look like this.

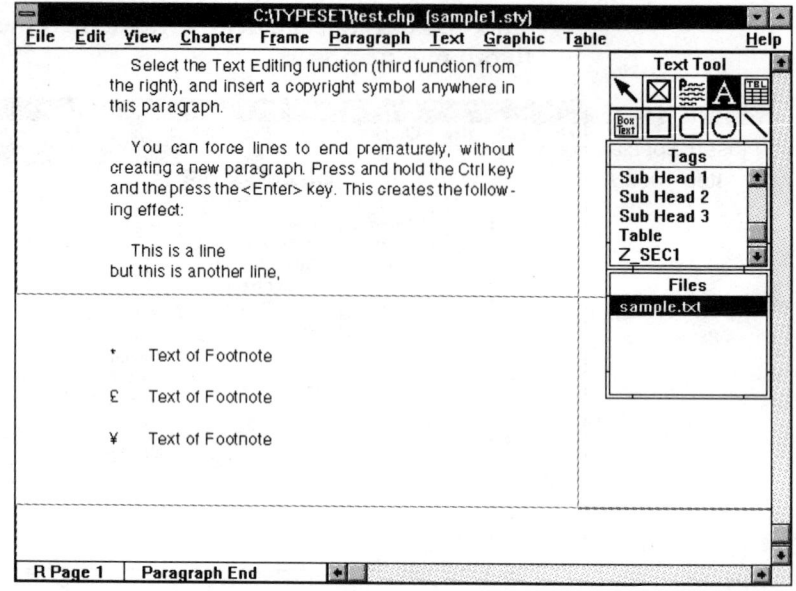

Adding the footnote text

After you insert a footnote reference in the text, Ventura automatically opens a footnote frame at the bottom of the page, which contains a footnote number or symbol that matches the one in the text, and is followed by the words "Text of Footnote" (Figure 15-9). Using the Text Tool, you simply delete these words and type in the text for the footnote.

If you add more footnotes to the page, they will appear inside the same frame. Ventura can enlarge this frame to contain lengthy footnotes. If all the footnote text cannot fit on a page, it will continue in the footnote frame on the next page.

Creating a separator line

When you turn on the footnote function, Ventura automatically creates a frame for the footnote text at the bottom of each page that contains a footnote reference. You can add a separator line that creates a visual border between the footnote text and the main text.

If you want to create a separator line, choose Footnote Settings from the Chapter menu and use these three text boxes to make your changes:

■ *Separator Line Width* sets the length of the line beginning from the left margin of the footnote frame. The separator line will

Figure 15-9.
Initially, the footnote text appears with the words "Text of Footnote." Replace these words with the actual footnote text that you want to use.

Footnote text, tagged as Z_FNOT Entry— select this text, delete it, and type the actual footnote text

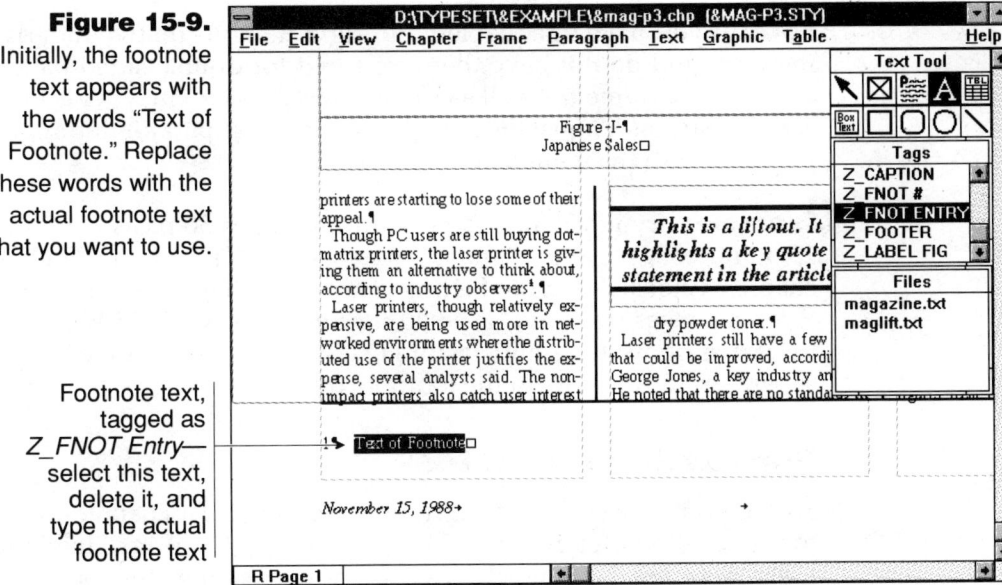

always start at the left margin of the footnote frame, but it *can* go past the right margin of the footnote frame.

- *Space Above Line* sets the distance from the top of the footnote frame to the top of the separator line (Figure 15-10). This does not affect the position of the footnotes—the line moves independently.

- *Height Of Line* sets the thickness of the separator line.

Figure 15-10.
Space Above will push the separator line down from the top of the footnote frame.

Separator line 3 points from top of frame

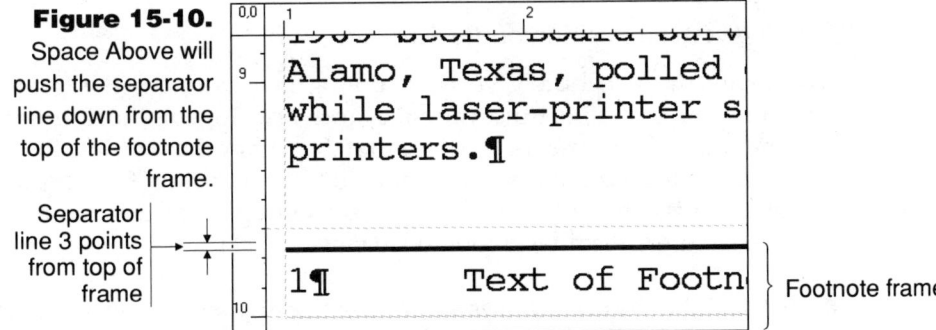

Tip: If you don't want a separator line, make the settings in these three text boxes 0.

Note: If you have unequal left and right margins on the underlying page and do not have them mirrored for double-sided pages, the footnote frame (as well as footers and headers) may reflect the wrong margins. Adjust the margins so that the separator line aligns properly with the main text.

Example: Try it. Create a separator line that is 30 picas long, has 15 points of space above, and is 6 points wide. Open the TEST.CHP chapter. Choose Footnote Settings from the Chapter menu. Select Picas for measurements. Type 30 for Separator Line Width, 01,03 for Space Above Line, and ,06 for Height Of Line. Click on OK. The separator line appears in the footnote frame.

Formatting footnotes

So far, you've seen how to turn on footnotes for a chapter, insert footnote references in the text, and type footnote text into the footnote frame. Now we'll show you how to change the format of all these elements.

Formatting the footnote reference

With the Footnote Settings dialog box, you can also control the formatting of the footnote reference that appears within the main text. In the section, "Choosing the type of reference," we showed you how to determine these three attributes:

- The beginning number
- Additional punctuation
- The vertical position of the number

By using the Attribute Overrides dialog box from the Paragraph menu, you can fine tune the size and position of the footnote references—the numbers (or symbols) that mark the footnote in the main text. The size and vertical position of footnote references are controlled by the Size and Shift Up By settings for Superscript in the Attribute Overrides dialog box (Figure 15-11).

Note: Make the settings for size and vertical position the same for all paragraph tags that are applied to paragraphs containing footnote references; otherwise, your footnotes will look inconsistent.

To adjust the size and position of footnote references within the main text, follow these steps:

1. Using the Paragraph Tool, select the paragraph containing the footnote reference.

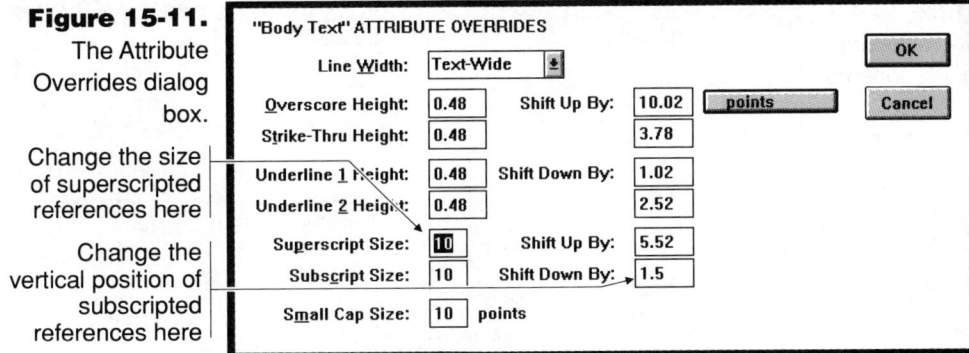

Figure 15-11.
The Attribute Overrides dialog box.

Change the size of superscripted references here

Change the vertical position of subscripted references here

2. Choose Attribute Overrides from the Paragraph menu.

3. In the Superscript Size text box (or Subscript Size if your footnote references appear as subscripts), type the point size of the footnote reference (typically ½ to ⅔ the point size of the paragraph text).

4. In the Shift Up By text box immediately to the right of the Superscript Size text box (or Shift Down By if you're using subscripts), type the amount you want to shift the footnote reference from the baseline of the paragraph text (⅓ to ¼ the point size of the paragraph text) and click on OK.

Check the size and position of the footnote reference in Enlarged view (or print it) and make any necessary adjustments again in the Attribute Overrides dialog box.

***E*xample:** Try it. Adjust the footnote references for TEST.CHP so that they are superscript, have a size of 6 points, and are shifted up 3 points. Open the TEST.CHP. Using the Paragraph Tool, select the paragraph containing the word "picture," to which you added a footnote in a previous example. Choose Attribute Overrides from the Paragraph menu. Select Points for measurement. Type 6 for Superscript Size and 3 for Shift Up By. Click on OK. You've adjusted the size and position of footnote references (and other items that are superscripted) for all paragraphs that use this tag.

Formatting the footnote number and text

Ventura creates two distinct paragraphs for every footnote in a footnote frame: one for the footnote number and one for the footnote text (Figure 15-12). It applies different tags to these two types of paragraphs. The footnote number has the Z_FNOT # tag and the text paragraph has Z_FNOT ENTRY (Figure 15-12).

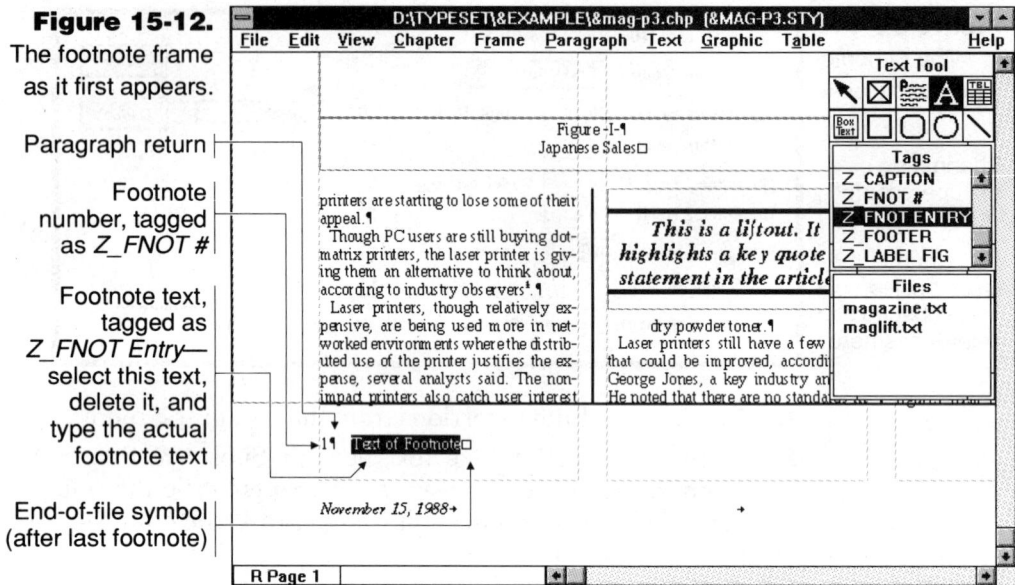

Figure 15-12.
The footnote frame as it first appears.

Paragraph return

Footnote number, tagged as Z_FNOT #

Footnote text, tagged as Z_FNOT Entry— select this text, delete it, and type the actual footnote text

End-of-file symbol (after last footnote)

You can change the formats of the footnote number and footnote text by changing their tags with the Paragraph Tool and the Paragraph menu—just as you would with any other tag. For more information on modifying tags, see Chapter 3, "Building Basic Styles." With the Paragraph menu, you can give the footnote number and footnote text the Font, Spacing, and Alignment that you want. However, Ventura won't let you attach a different tag to these generated footnote paragraphs.

By default, the footnote number and footnote text paragraphs will have breaks and horizontal spacing that place the two paragraphs side by side. To adjust them, you modify the Spacing and Alignment of one or both paragraphs. For more information on placing paragraphs side by side, see Chapter 3, "Building Basic Styles."

Example: Try it. Make the footnote number 5 point and the footnote text 8 point. Open the TEST.CHP chapter. Using the Paragraph Tool, select a paragraph containing a footnote number in the footnote frame. Choose Font (Paragraph menu). Type 5 for Custom Size. Click on OK. Now select a paragraph containing footnote text. Choose Font from the Paragraph menu and give it a size of 8 points. Click on OK. Your footnote frame should look similar to Figure 15-13. You've adjusted the size of the footnote number and text.

Figure 15-13.
The footnote frame for the example chapter TEST.CHP should now look like this.

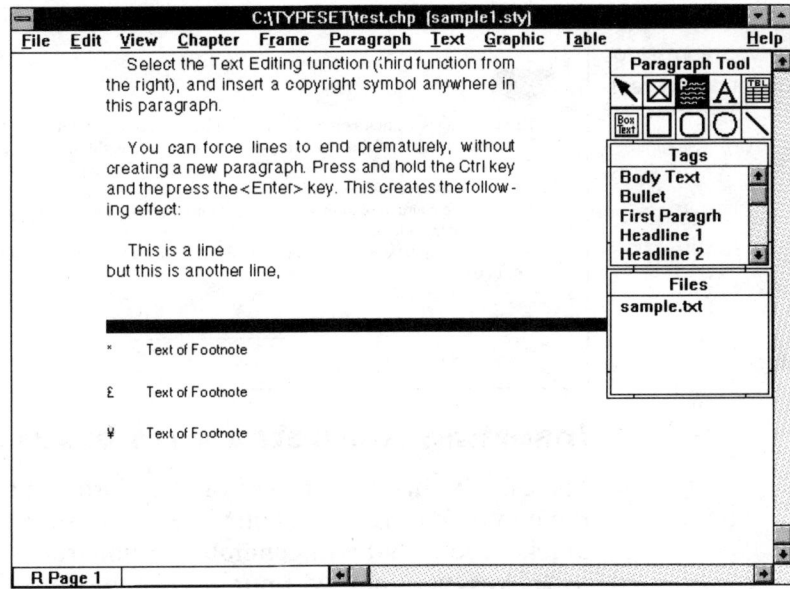

On your own

Now use the skills that you've learned in this section to experiment with footnote formats. Figures 15-14 and 15-15 show a couple of possibilities. The specifications for these examples are explained in the actual footnote text of each picture—so look at them closely and try to create these formats on your own.

Figure 15-14.
Use punctuation and indents for a scholarly look.

> Lorum ipsum dolor sit amet, con; minimum venami quis nostrud laboris nisi ut aliquip ex ea com color in reprehenderit in voluptate nonumy.
>
> ———————————
>
>   1. These footnotes are numbered using the Number Template set to generate the number and the period "#.".
>   2. This footnote uses a separator line 23,00 picas wide. The separator line is 00.50 points high and has a Space Above Line setting of 03.00 points.
>   3. Other Footnote settings are the same as the first sample.
>   4. Here, the footnote numbers use a In From Left space of 00,06 picas, and the footnote text has a relative indent for the first line only, after which, it returns to the left margin.
>
> ——— 2 ———

Figure 15-15.
Vary your format for a contemporary feel.

a These footnotes are numbered with user-defined characters (eight letters) using the default Number Template. Because of this, there must be no more than eight footnotes per page.
b This footnote uses a separator line 02,00 picas wide. The separator line is 12.00 points high and has a Space Above Line setting of 03.00 points.
c The footnote characters in this frame (footnote frame) are simply made italic to distinguish them from the footnote text.
d Here, the footnote letters are flush against the left margin, and the footnote text has an In From Left of 07.00 points.

———— 2 ————

Inserting footnotes with bracket codes

You can also insert footnotes directly into text files before you load them into Ventura. With your word processor, you type the special bracket codes that will generate footnote references, numbers, and text. However, they will not appear until the footnote function is turned on—although the footnoting information will be there ready and waiting. For more information on using bracket codes to insert footnotes into text files, see Chapter 7, "Creating Text with Other Programs."

To insert a footnote in your text file, you type this bracket code at the point where you want the reference to appear:

    <$F>

After the letter F, you can type the footnote text for that footnote. Be sure to type the footnote text directly after the letter F (no space). For example, if you wanted to add two footnotes—such as High Radiation and Drippy Catsup—to a text file, you would type these codes directly after the words that you want to footnote:

    <$FHigh Radiation>
    <$FDrippy catsup>

We inserted the above codes into an ASCII file and then loaded the file into Ventura. Then we turned on the footnoting function. For the result, see Figure 15-16. For a table of bracket codes, see Chapter 21, "Rapid Reference."

Figure 15-16.
These footnotes were created with bracket codes in a text file and then loaded into Ventura with the footnoting function turned on.

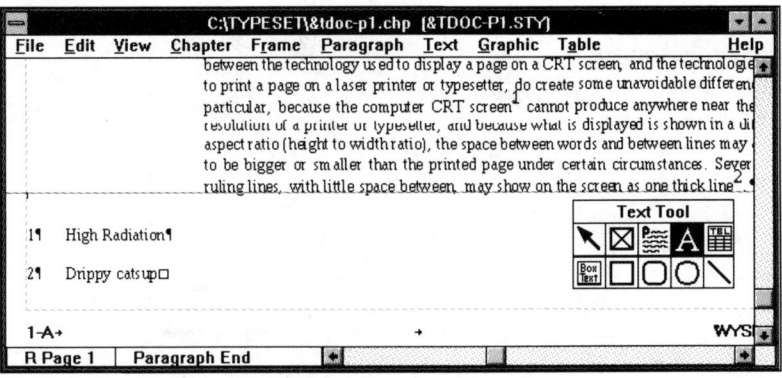

Creating and editing equations

With Ventura's equation editor, you can create complex scientific and mathematical equations that are part of the normal text stream. They move along with the rest of the text, and you can change them at any time. Unlike other programs, you are not forced to treat them as complex graphics that must be changed with a special graphics program. With Ventura's equation editor, you can treat equations as a special kind of text that can easily be changed.

There are two ways to create equations:

- Build equations with Ventura's Equation Editor
- Use bracket codes to type equations directly into a text file

In this section, we'll show you both methods. You'll learn how to create and format equations, using true fractions, Greek characters, and mathematical symbols.

Creating equations with Ventura's equation editor

To build an equation in Ventura, you follow these steps:

1. Using the Text Tool, place the text cursor where you want to create the equation.
2. Choose Insert Special Item from the Text menu. A flyout menu appears.
3. Choose Equation from the flyout menu (Figure 15-17). The Equation Editing screen appears.
4. At the Equation Editing screen (Figure 15-18), type the codes that describe the equation above the double line. You can

Figure 15-17.
Using the Text menu to open the Equation Editor.

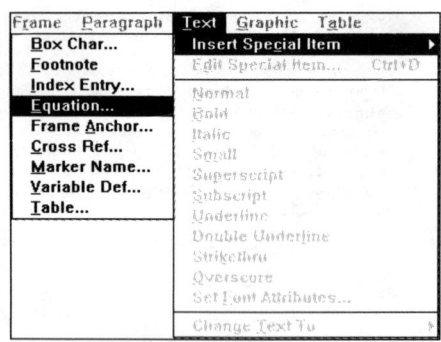

choose the Insert Special Item command again to access a menu of common equation commands. A preview of the actual equation appears below the double line (Figure 15-18).

Figure 15-18.
The Equation Editing screen.

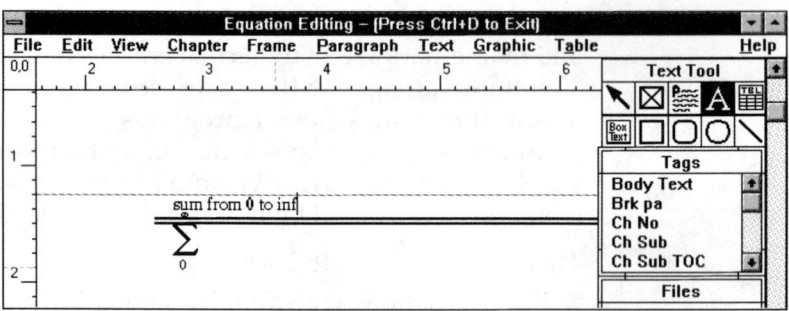

5. Close the equation editor by choosing Exit Equation Editing from the Text menu (or by pressing Ctrl-D). The equation appears where you had placed the text cursor.

Creating a simple equation

The most common equations, though almost too simple to be considered equations, are regular fractions. The Equation Editor makes it possible to have true fractions: "½" instead of "1/2".

We'll start you off by showing you how to create the simplest equations—fractions. Here's how:

1. Using the Text Tool, place the text cursor where you want to create the fraction. Then open the Equation Editor by choosing the Insert Special Item command (Text menu). The Equation Editor appears on the screen.

2. Choose Insert Special Item again from the Text menu. The flyout menu that appears contains nine of the most common equation codes (Figure 15-19).

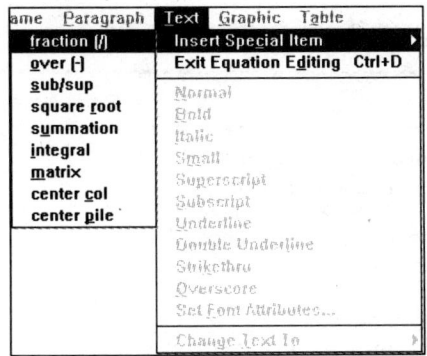

Figure 15-19.
While using the Equation Editor, some common equation commands are available through the Text menu's Insert Special Item command.

3. Select Fraction from the flyout menu. Ventura will generate the fraction ½ both above the double line and below it. Delete the 1 and 2, and create your own fraction. Create the fraction 5/22. A preview of the fraction appears below the double line.

4. Exit the Equation Editor by pressing Ctrl-D. The fraction appears where you had placed the text cursor.

Creating complex equations

To create equations, you use special *codes* that describe the mathematical symbols and *commands* that manipulate words, numbers, and codes. Most of the codes are really just abbreviations of what they represent (for example, code SQRT for square root). Most commands modify the attributes of the elements that follow it (for example, the command FAT makes all words, numbers, and symbols that follow it boldface) or create special symbols (for example, the command SYMBOL P generates the pi symbol π).

You type combinations of these codes and commands above the double line to make a complete equation. Then Ventura generates the actual equation below the double line. For example, the command SQRT X generates $\sqrt{x}$. For examples and definitions of the common equation codes and commands from the flyout menu, see Table 15-2. For a complete listing of all equation codes, see Chapter 21, "Rapid Reference."

How do codes and commands work? An equation code or command operates on the *expression* that directly follows it. In Ventura, an expression is a character, a group of characters that are not separated by spaces, a word, or anything placed inside braces ({}). You use spaces to keep expressions distinct from one another—but the spaces do not appear in the actual equation.

Table 15-2. *Common equation commands*

Command	Function	Example	Result
fraction bar [/]	This command, the forward slash, is placed between two expressions and makes a superscript out of the first, making it the numerator, and a subscript out of the second, making it the denominator	`1/2`	½
over [-]	This command is placed between two expressions; it centerstacks the first expression over the second expression and separates them with a horizontal bar	`1 over 2`	$\frac{1}{2}$
sub/sup	These two commands make *sub*scripts and *super*scripts of any character or expression	`x sub {i^+^1} sup {n^+^1}`	x_{i+1}^{n+1}
square root	This command places a square root symbol over the expression that follows it	`sqrt x`	$\sqrt{x}$
summation	This command creates the summation symbol and is generally used with the *from* command, followed by a range expression	`sum from 0 to inf i`	$\sum_{0}^{\infty} i$
integral	This command creates the integral symbol and is generally followed by an expression	`int sub 0 sup 1 {x^dx}`	$\int_{0}^{1} x\,dx$
matrix	This command creates a matrix out of the expression that follows it, with even vertical spacing between rows, regardless of the height of each expression; in contrast, the *pile* command bases the vertical spacing on the height of the expressions	`matrix{ccol{a above b}~ccol{c above d}}`	a c b d
center col	This command aligns an expression in a centered column; also available are *lcol* and *rcol*, which align left and right, respectively	`ccol{a above b}`	a b
center pile	This command is the same as the pile command and vertically stacks a set of expressions so that they are center-aligned above one another; also available are *lpile* and *rpile*, which align left and right, respectively	`cpile{a above b above c}`	a b c

You have two special codes that help you handle expressions:

- Braces ({}) to group elements of the equation as a single expression. A code or command usually modifies only the expression that directly follows it. If you want a code or command to operate on a group of expressions, you must enclose the group within braces. For example, to generate $\sqrt{x^2 + y^2}$, you must group x^2 together with y^2; otherwise, you'll get $\sqrt{x^2} + y^2$ because the SQRT command simply places the next expression (x^2) underneath the square root sign. Here's the correct code:

```
sqrt {x sup 2 ~+~ y sup 2}
```

- Tilde (~) to create a normal space in the actual equation. While using the Equation Editor, you create spaces with the tilde (~), *not* the space bar. Use the circumflex (^) to add a thin space. Use the space bar to create spaces that keep elements distinct from each other—these spaces will not appear in the equation.

Tip: Place the tilde before and after the plus sign (+) to create space between the elements, making them more readable.

Rules for creating equations

- You must place a space both before and after all codes, words, and commands. If in doubt, add more spaces—they won't affect the final appearance.

- To add a space between characters and words, use these special characters for the space desired: the tilde (~) for a normal space; and a circumflex (^) for a thin space. Normal spaces typed with the space bar in the Equation Editor do not print.

- Most codes and commands affect the elements that follow—not the preceding elements. However, diacritical marks are an exception: they affect the expression that directly precedes them. For example, the command abc bar generates $\overline{abc}$.

- Do not use tabs to add spaces to equations or to align equations within a paragraph.

- In the actual equation, all characters are italicized—except for mathematical operators such as "cos," "tan," "log," and so on. These operators appear in Roman type (normal).

- Equations can use up a lot of vertical and horizontal space. Select Grow Inter-Line To Fit: On in the Paragraph Typography dialog box (Paragraph menu) so that the line spacing will automatically expand to accommodate big equations.

Example: Try building an equation on your own, using the sample codes and commands we supply below. Simply open any chapter (such as the TEST.CHP chapter). Using the Text Tool, place the text cursor where you want to place the equation. Choose Insert Special Item from the Text menu. Select Equation from the flyout menu. Type the commands and codes for the equation. A preview of the equation will appear. Press Ctrl-D to exit the Equation Editor. The equation appears where you placed the text cursor. Repeat these steps for the other two sample equations. See Figure 15-20 to check your results.

1. `1/2`
2. `sum from i=0 to inf`
3. `cos ( theta sub 1 ) ~+~sin ( theta sub 2 )`

Figure 15-20. The finished equations.

1. $\frac{1}{2}$
2. $\sum_{i=0}^{\infty}$
3. $\cos(\theta_1) + \sin(\theta_2)$

Formatting the equation

When it comes to formatting, Ventura treats an equation as though it were one text character. You use the Text Tool and Text menu to change the text attributes of the entire equation (Figure 15-21).

You can also make formatting changes within the equation, using the Attribute Overrides dialog box (Paragraph menu) and special commands in the Equation Editor.

Equations use the paragraph tags that are assigned to the paragraph in which they are inserted. You can use the Paragraph Tool and Attribute Overrides dialog box (Paragraph menu) to modify the format of equations. For example, you can adjust the size and position of superscripts in the equation with the Superscript Size and Shift Up By text boxes. But remember you're altering the attributes of the paragraph tag—the changes will also affect other superscript characters (such as footnotes) within that paragraph.

Figure 15-21.
Use the Text Tool to select the equation and the Text menu to change the attributes for the entire equation.

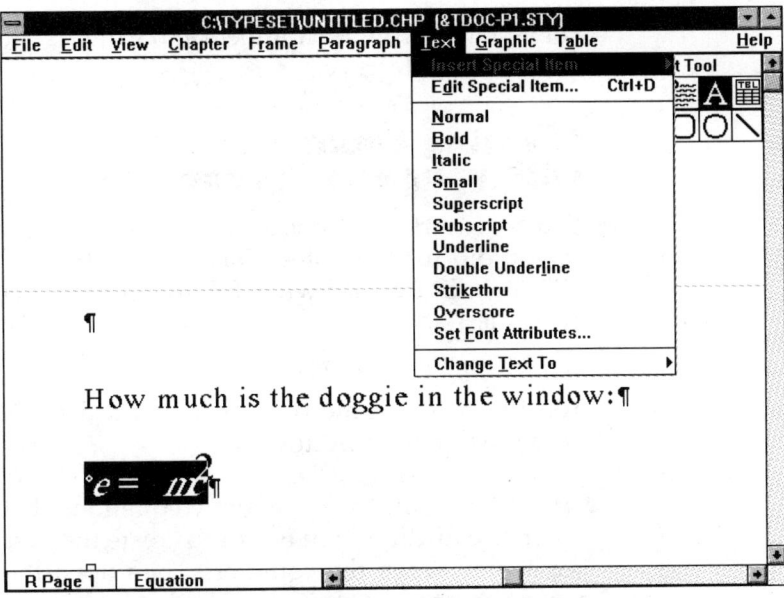

To apply formatting to an individual character, word, or expression within the equation, you place a text attribute code in front of it. For example, the code ROMAN makes the expression normal instead of italic. See Table 15-3 for the syntax of these attributes.

Table 15-3. *Equation Editor text attributes*

Effect	Command	Example	Result
Color change	color *n*	These~words~ color 0 { are invisible } .	These words
Different font	font *n*	Font~is~ font 55 { Helvetica~Black }	Font is **Helvetica Black**
Bold text (italic)	fat	This~word~is~ fat BOLD .	This word is **BOLD**.
Roman (normal)	roman	This~is~ roman NORMAL ~text.	This is NORMAL text.
Bold text (normal)	fat roman	This~is~ fat { roman { BOLD~NORMAL } } .	This is **BOLD NORMAL**.
Font size change	size *n*	These~are~ size 18 BIG ~and~ size 6 small .	These are BIG and small.
Symbol font	symbol *x*	symbol p ^r^ sup 2	$\pi\, r^2$

n = a number from 0 to 8 for color, and 1 through 255 for font ID number
x = a character in the standard character set that corresponds to one in the Symbol font.

For a table of Font ID numbers and Color ID numbers, see Chapter 21, "Rapid Reference."

Creating equations with your word processor

You can insert equations directly into your word processor files just as you did for footnotes. This time, instead of an "F," you use an "E" to indicate that what follows is an equation. The complete syntax is:

```
<$EText of equation>
```

You follow the same rules that you did for equations you made with the Equation Editor.

Tip: If you want to create many equations that are similar to each other, use the Equation Editor to create the first one so that you can see a preview of the equation. Then open the text file with your word processor and use the bracket code generated for this equation as a template for your other equations—just copy it and make the necessary changes to the bracket code. You'll find this technique is much faster than using the Equation Editor (where it takes a lot of time to generate equations) and much more accurate than using just bracket codes (where you can't see your results until you load the text file into Ventura).

Continuing on

Initially, footnotes and equations can seem daunting. But don't let them get you down. After you know the basic features of the footnote function and Equation Editor, you can create even the most complex footnotes and equations without a hitch. In this chapter, we've given you the essentials of creating and formatting footnotes and equations. We also showed you how to insert them directly into your text files. Now you have the skills to handle almost any footnote or equation—no matter how complex.

Easy Access

For more info on...	See chapter...
Modifying tags	2 — Building Basic Styles
Preformatting text files using bracket codes	7 — Creating Text with Other Programs
A table of bracket codes	21 — Rapid Reference

16
Managing Ventura Files

How to take control of your document files

- **Working with chapter files** 481
- **Working with publication files** 486
- **Continuing on** 492

ne of the great things about Ventura is that it can take files scattered anywhere on the hard disk and combine them into a document. Furthermore, Ventura provides tools to manage all those files. If you combine these tools with the strategies we give you in this chapter, you can take full command of your files.

Don't take this topic lightly. You can get yourself into big trouble if you don't manage your files wisely. For instance, you can overwrite new chapters with old ones. But with the simple techniques in this chapter, you can safely handle your Ventura files. First, we'll show you how to copy and move a chapter and its component files. Then, we'll show you how to assemble chapters into a single group, called a *publication*, so that you can handle many chapters all at once.

Working with chapter files

In Part One of this book, you learned how Ventura works with files and how it assembles all the files each time you open a chapter. The individual files that make up a chapter can be anywhere on your hard drive and Ventura will simply find and load them.

But how do you find all the individual files to copy them to a floppy disk or delete them from your hard disk?

You can't use standard utilities or MS-DOS commands to move Ventura documents around—at least, not without special precautions. Because Ventura documents are made of many individual files, you can easily forget to move one of the essential component files. Ventura chapter files contain *links* to all the other component files (Figure 16-1). If you move or rename a file (or change the file type) without changing the links in the chapter file, Ventura won't be able to find the file when it needs it. When you open the chapter, Ventura will display a VP Alert box that tells you it can't find the file.

But what if you want to change the links, so that Ventura, for example, will look in a different directory for your files? In this section, you'll learn to use Ventura's Manage Publication command to copy chapters and all their component files safely.

Figure 16-1.
The chapter file (CHP) contains links to all the other component files wherever they are on the disk.

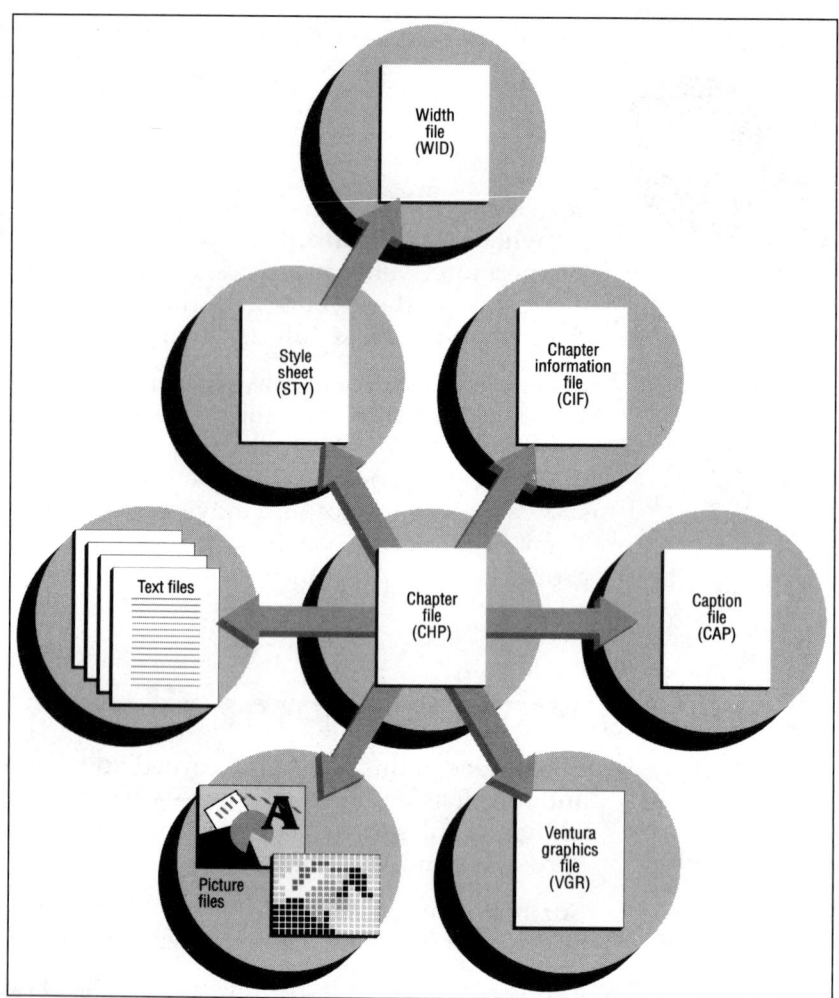

Note: To understand how Ventura puts chapters together, you may want to review the beginning of Chapter 3, "Building Basic Styles." For a quick summary, see Table 16-1.

Copying a chapter with Ventura

To copy chapters safely, you must use the Manage Publication command in the File menu. After you choose the Manage Publication command, you'll see the Multi-Chapter dialog box, which allows you to copy and move your chapters. Don't let the Multi part fool you. You use the Multi-Chapter dialog box for individual chapters as well as publications made up of multiple chapters.

Table 16-1. *How Ventura assembles documents*

Category	Type	Contents	Extension(s)	Typical name
Chapter files	Chapter file	Pointers to the other files plus formatting information	CHP	SAMPLE.CHP
	Style sheet	Formatting information	STY	SAMPLE.STY
	Chapter information file	Date of last save, last print, and other programming info	CIF	SAMPLE.CIF
	Ventura graphics file	Graphics created with Ventura's built-in drawing tools	VGR	SAMPLE.VGR
	Caption file	Captions, Box Text, and frame text	CAP	SAMPLE.CAP
Document files	Text file(s)	Text created with other programs	TXT, DOC, WP, etc.	SAMPLE.TXT
	Graphics file(s)	Pictures created with other programs	PCX, GEM, EPS, etc.	PICTURE.PCX
Multi-chapter files	Publication file	Pointers and information about the chapters that make up the publication	PUB	SAMPLE.PUB
	Generated files	Index and table of contents text and information generated by Ventura	GEN	SAMPLIDX.GEN (index) SAMPLTOC.GEN (table of contents)

Why work with Ventura instead of your usual file utility or MS-DOS command? When you copy a chapter file with a Windows or MS-DOS utility or command, you copy just the chapter file—without copying its component files with it. However, Ventura's Copy All option in the Multi-Chapter dialog box copies all the component files with the chapter file. More importantly, Copy All changes the links in the chapter file, so that Ventura knows the new locations of the component files and can reassemble the whole document. If you moved a component file with Windows or MS-DOS, Ventura won't know where to find it because the links haven't been changed.

To copy a chapter to a new location, just follow these steps:

1. Choose Manage Publication from the File menu.

2. If you haven't saved the current chapter, a VP Alert box appears. You can save the current chapter by clicking Save. Or you can abandon any changes you've made since the last time you saved by clicking on Abandon. After you've saved or abandoned, the Multi-Chapter dialog box appears.

3. If the chapter you want to copy is not present in the list box, click on Add Chapter. The Open File dialog box appears.

4. Navigate to the directory where the desired chapter file is located. Select the file and click on Open.

5. With the filename selected in the Multi-Chapter dialog box, click on Copy All (Figure 16-2).

Figure 16-2.

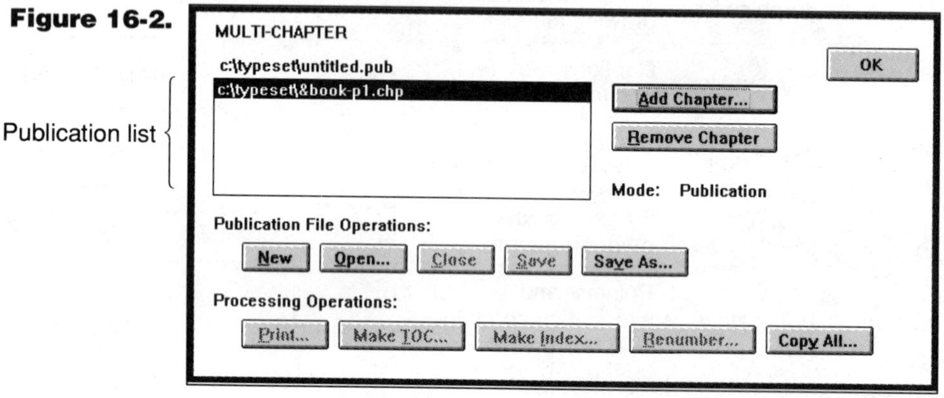

Publication list

```
MULTI-CHAPTER
c:\typeset\untitled.pub                                           OK
c:\typeset\&book-p1.chp                    Add Chapter...
                                           Remove Chapter

                                           Mode:  Publication

Publication File Operations:
  New    Open...    Close    Save    Save As...

Processing Operations:
  Print...   Make TOC...   Make Index...   Renumber...   Copy All...
```

6. In the Pub & Chps text box, delete the current drive and path. Then, type the drive and path where you want to copy the chapter (Figure 16-3).

Note: Be sure that the path ends with a backslash (\); otherwise, Ventura displays a VP Alert box that tells you that destination directories should be prefaced with a drive and path. This simply means that you typed the drive or path incorrectly—usually because the last backslash is missing.

7. Click on Make All Directories The Same As The First. This optional step tells Ventura to copy all graphic, text, and other component files to the same directory as the one specified in the Pub & Chps. Click on OK.

As Ventura copies all the files for the chapter, it will display message boxes (for each file) that tell you that the file is being "archived." The word "archive" is simply Ventura's terminology for "copy."

Figure 16-3.
Use the Copy All dialog box to tell Ventura where to put the component files.

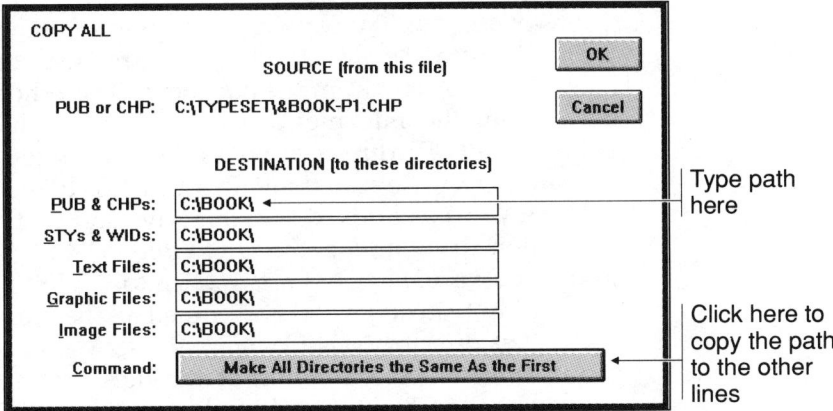

Using the Copy All is simple. However, to get the results that you want, you should know these three things about Copy All:

- If you specify a destination directory that does not exist, Ventura will automatically create it—even if it you didn't want it to. So be sure that the pathname is correct.
- Any text file, picture file, or style sheet can be used by more than one chapter. Before you delete files, be sure those same files are not *also* being used by other chapters—especially style sheet (STY) files.
- Ventura does not *move* files. It merely copies them. You will still have the original files in the directory from which you copied them. If you want to move a chapter to a new location, you must first use the Manage Publication command to copy it, then delete all files from their original location. However, be sure that the files you delete are not being used by other chapters.

Tip: When you perform a Copy All of a chapter (or publication), the associated width (WID) file is copied to the destination as well. The new WID file isn't necessary; therefore, you can delete it (unless you are sending the copied files to someone who needs the information in your width file, such as special fonts). If you're keeping the copy yourself or if you have moved a chapter on your hard disk, you should delete the width file in the new location. Otherwise, you'll have duplicate width files on your floppy disks or scattered all over your hard disk.

For more tips on managing files, see the nearby sidebar, "Tips for managing files and chapters," on page 486.

Example: Try copying a chapter to a new directory. Be sure that Ventura's example chapters are installed on your computer. Choose New from the File menu. Then choose Manage Publication from the File menu. Click on Add Chapter. Navigate to the \TYPESET directory. Select the chapter file &BOOK-P1.CHP. Click on Open. Be sure that &BOOK-P1.CHP is still selected. In the Pubs & Chps text box, delete the drive and path. Then type the destination drive and path: C:\TYPESET\&EXAMPLE\. Click on OK. You've just created a new directory \TYPESET\&EXAMPLE (if it didn't already exist) and copied all the files for &BOOK-P1.CHP to that directory. Use Windows File Manager (or your favorite file utility) to see a listing of the files that have been moved to the \TYPESET\&EXAMPLE directory.

Tips for managing files and chapters

- Keep all files for a specific project—style sheets, chapter files, pictures, and text files—in the same directory.

- When possible, use the same style sheet for all chapters of the same project. Using multiple style sheets makes it difficult to update tags. You would need to make the changes in *all* style sheets, instead of just one.

- Set up and *use* a strategy for naming files. For more information on creating a file naming system, see Chapter 17, "Power and Speedup Techniques."

- Don't create a lot of small text files if it's not necessary. The more files you have, the more chances you'll forget one and lose it.

- Make backups regularly and often. You can buy insurance for all your computer hardware, but this is the *only* way to insure your data.

Working with publication files

The Manage Publication command makes it easy to manage the individual files of multiple chapters as one group. It lets you collect chapters into a single publication and then make a table of contents for, index, print, renumber (page, table, and figure numbers), and cross-reference those chapters as a single entity. In this section, we'll show you how to assemble publications, save them, load them, and copy them to new locations. Then we'll show you how to reorder and renumber the chapters in a publication.

Creating a publication

The Manage Publication command allows you to work with one large group of chapters at one time. But before you can effectively use this function, you need to know how to group the chapters together into a publication. Here's how:

1. Choose Manage Publication from the File menu.
2. If the New button is available (indicating that a publication is already open), click on that button. The New button then turns gray (indicating that you are starting a new publication). The dialog box should look similar to Figure 16-4.

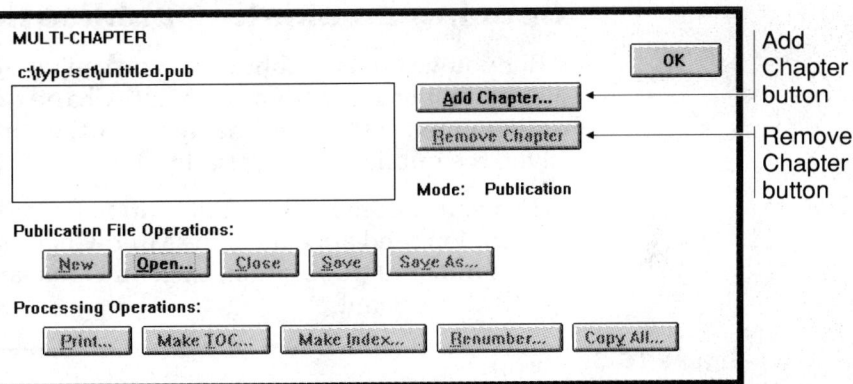

Figure 16-4. You add and rearrange chapters in a publication with the Multi-Chapter dialog box.

3. Click on Add Chapter. Navigate to the directory that contains the chapter that you want to add to the publication. Double-click on the filename for that chapter.
4. Click on Add Chapter again and use the same process to add the rest of the chapters you want to include in the publication.
5. Click on Save As. Be sure you are in the same directory that contains the example files.

To remove a chapter from your publication, simply select that filename in the list and then click on the Remove Chapter button. If you try to close the Multi-Chapter dialog box after adding or removing a chapter, Ventura will ask if you want to save or abandon the changes you made. Be sure to save if you want to keep your changes.

Example: Try creating a publication using Ventura's example chapters. Be sure that Ventura's example chapters have been installed on your computer. Choose New from the File menu. Then choose Manage Publication from the File menu. Click on Add Chapter. Navigate to the \TYPESET directory. Double-click on the chapter file &BOOK-P1.CHP. Now add three other chapters: &BOOK-P2.CHP, &BRO-L2.CHP, and &BRO-P3.CHP. Click on Save As. Be sure that the you are in the \TYPESET directory. In the File Name text box, type the filename PUBTEST. (You don't need to type the extension—Ventura will take care of that for you.)

The publication you've just created is a group of unrelated chapters; therefore, you wouldn't want to generate a table of contents or index for it. For more information on what you can do with publications, see the Easy Access table at the end of this chapter.

Opening an existing publication

After you've built a publication, you can use it over and over again just by reopening it from the Multi-Chapter dialog box. Just click on the Open button and navigate to the directory in which you saved the publication (Figure 16-5).

When you choose Manage Publication from the File menu, the last publication used appears in the Multi-Chapter dialog box. To work with a different publication, click on Open, and select the publication that you want.

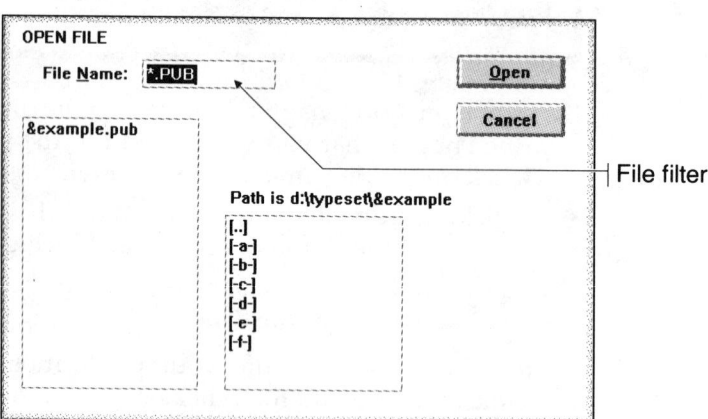

Figure 16-5. When you click on Open in the Multi-Chapter dialog box, the files are filtered so that only publication files are displayed.

Copying a publication

By clicking on the Copy All button in the Multi-Chapter dialog box, you can copy all the files from all the chapters in your publication. Copying a publication works just like copying a single chapter, except that you're copying a group of chapters and their component files as well as changing their links. However, you must be sure that none of the chapters is selected; otherwise, only that chapter will be copied. To deselect chapters (selected chapters are highlighted), double-click on the chapters, so that they are no longer highlighted.

Note: If you try to copy a publication to a floppy disk that doesn't have enough storage space available, Ventura displays a VP Alert box that tells you to insert another disk. Simply put in another formatted disk into that disk drive. That's why it's a good idea to have extra blank formatted floppy disks on hand *before* you start copying your publication. If you try to copy to another directory on your hard disk (or another hard disk) that doesn't have enough space, you'll have to cancel the command and remove some files from that destination and then do the Copy All procedure again.

Changing the links for a publication

As you recall, the Copy All option changes all the links for all the chapter files in the specified publication. However, a special exception exists for the *publication file* itself. A publication file is nothing more than a text file that contains the links to all the chapters in a publication. The Copy All option updates these links, but unfortunately it doesn't update the link pointing Ventura to the location of your generated index files or table of contents files.

To change these links after a Copy All option, use Windows Notepad (or any text editor) to open the publication file in the new location. You will recognize it by the PUB extension. The links to your table of contents and/or index files appear as pathnames at the top of the file. Figure 16-6 shows an example of a publication with the links for the generated table-of-contents file (recognized by the GEN extension) pointing to the C:\TEMP directory.

After you've spotted the proper filenames, just use your text editor to change the pathnames to the new location and then save the publication file. That's all there is to it. For more information on these GEN files, see Chapter 14, "Creating Indexes and Tables of Contents."

Figure 16-6.
Using Notepad, you can edit the links in your publication file.

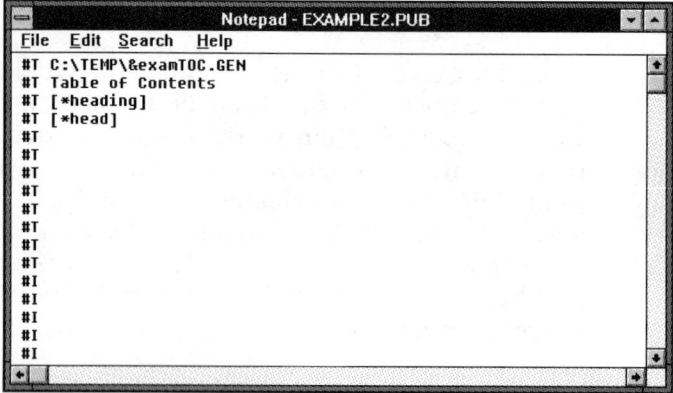

Reordering your publication

Certain commands in the Multi-Chapter dialog box are affected by the order in which the chapters appear in the chapter file list box. For example, you may want to use the Renumber option to update Ventura's automatic page numbers and cross references across an entire publication. If so, you need to arrange those chapter files in the right order in the publication. Ventura will renumber the chapters in the order they appear in the chapter file list box.

Similarly, if you click on the Print button, Ventura will print your publication in the order it appears in the chapter file list box. If you want the publication printed in a different order, you'll have to rearrange the chapters in the list box. The Make TOC button also requires the proper order.

How do you rearrange the chapters in a publication? In the chapter file list box in the Multi-Chapter dialog box, simply select the file you want to move. Then move the cursor through the list and stop at the point where you want to move the chapter. Notice that as you move the cursor between filenames, it changes to a horizontal bar. With this new cursor showing, click once on the new location. The selected chapter file will move to that position.

Renumbering your publication

So far, you've learned how to create and reorder your publication and use the Copy All option. (You learned how to use the Print, Make TOC, and Make Index buttons in previous chapters.) That leaves the Renumber button.

Renumber updates all of Ventura's automatic numbers for chapters, pages, tables, and figures across an entire publication. Most of the time, you'll probably enter the chapter number manually. And most books restart the numbering of figures and tables at the beginning of the chapter. But even so, the Renumber function is valuable if you want to have consecutive page numbers across an entire publication. And, if you've used Ventura's automatic cross references, the Renumber button will update those as well.

For example, suppose you're working on a manual with three chapters. Chapter 1 ends on page 8. You would want Chapter 2 to start on page 9. Ventura's Renumber function will handle this automatically, provided you set things up correctly in advance.

To use the Renumber function for consecutive page numbers, you must first set up each chapter following these steps:

1. Open one of the chapters from the publication and choose Update Counters from the Edit menu (Figure 16-7).

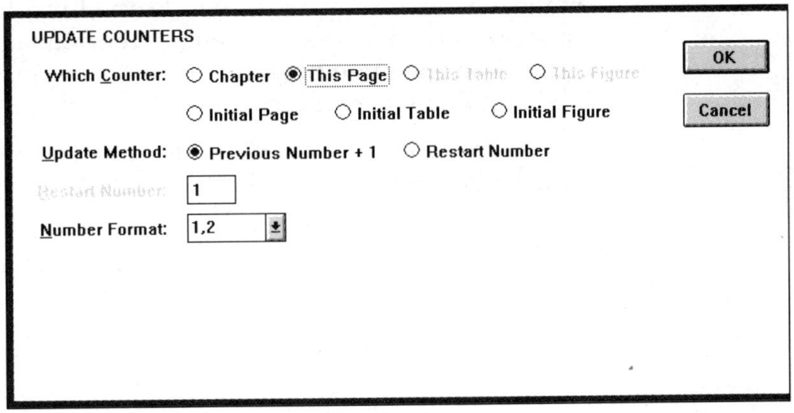

Figure 16-7.
To specify consecutive page numbering across a publication, start with the Update Counters dialog box.

2. Select Which Counter: This Page.
3. Select Update Method: Previous Number + 1.
4. Click on OK.
5. Repeat steps 1-4 for each chapter.

Now you can use the Renumber function to renumber all the chapters, so that the page numbers are consecutive:

6. Choose Manage Publication from the File menu.
7. Open or create your publication. Be sure the chapters in the publication are in the correct order.
8. Click on Renumber. Click on OK.

For more information on using page numbers in headers and footers, see Chapter 4, "Building the Underlying Page." For more information on Ventura's automatic numbering features, see Chapter 5, "Building Advanced Styles." For more information on creating automatic cross references, see Chapter 17, "Power and Speedup Techniques."

Continuing on

The more documents you build, the more you need to understand and use proper file management. Many desktop publishing problems are related to file management. People can't find the files they need, they don't back up their work, or they move files without changing the links in the chapter file.

As you now know, the key is to use Ventura's Multi-Chapter dialog box to move or copy chapters. It's the most trouble-free way to manage your files. And, as you learned in Chapter 14, "Creating Indexes and Tables of Contents," the Manage Publication command also gives you powerful cross-chapter functions for indexing and building tables of contents.

If you think that was neat, wait until you see the next chapter, which offers time-saving shortcuts from seasoned Ventura pros.

Easy Access

For more info on...	See chapter...
Learning how Ventura builds documents	3 — Building Basic Styles
Automatic numbering	5 — Building Advanced Styles
Printing	13 — Printing Ventura Documents
Creating Indexes and Tables of Contents	14 — Creating Indexes and Tables of Contents
Manually changing chapter links	17 — Power and Speedup Techniques

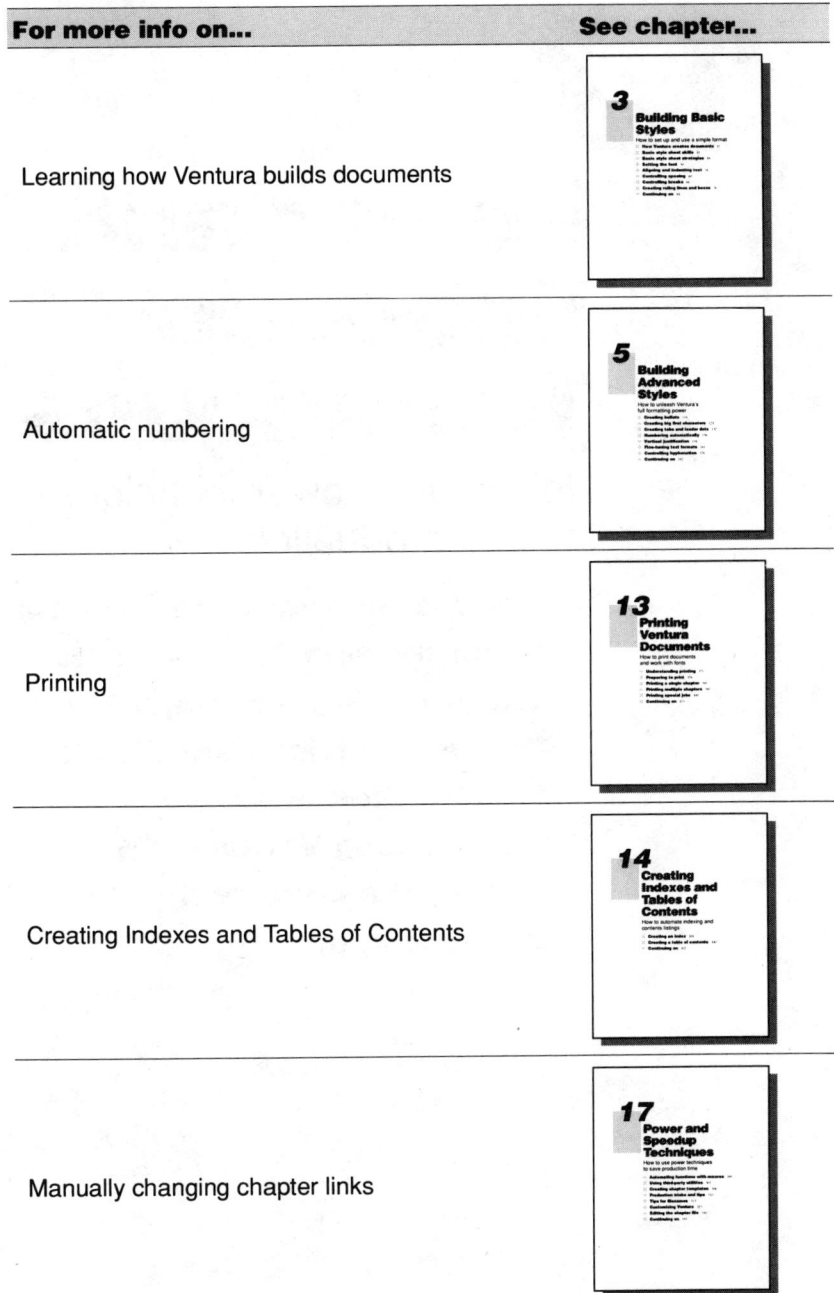

17

Power and Speedup Techniques

How to use power techniques
to save production time

- **Automating functions with macros** 495
- **Using third-party utilities** 501
- **Creating chapter templates** 506
- **Production tricks and tips** 510
- **Tips for filenames** 513
- **Customizing Ventura** 525
- **Editing the chapter file** 530
- **Continuing on** 535

asten your seat belts. We're going to take Ventura to full speed. This chapter contains tips and workarounds that can vastly improve your work style. It contains favorite techniques developed by power users all over the country. Think of it as a menu of possibilities. Browse it for ideas that relate to your situation, then try out your favorites. Here are some of the possibilities:

- Using macros to perform repetitive tasks
- Using third-party utilities to supplement Ventura's functions
- Using chapter templates to speed up production
- Using handy production shortcuts to save time
- Using power tips, tricks, and workarounds to wring extra power from Ventura

All set? Then let's rev her up.

Automating functions with macros

One big advantage of using Ventura for Windows is that you can easily use Windows accessories such as Recorder. Windows' Recorder takes the tedium out of time-consuming and repetitive chores by capturing all your steps and playing them back at the touch of a key. This section will give you an overview of making Recorder macros for Ventura and some suggestions on using macros to make your life with Ventura easier.

Tip: We suggest you read over this section and give Recorder a run for its money. But if you find that Recorder's features aren't powerful enough for you, check out the powerful Windows scripting and programming capabilities of Publishing Technologies' BatchWorks, Softbridge's Bridge, or Hewlett-Packard's NewWave.

Creating Windows macros

For a full discussion of Windows' Recorder, you should turn to your *Microsoft Windows User's Guide*. But here's a quick review of the steps you need to follow to record a macro for Ventura:

1. Start Recorder by double-clicking on its icon in the Program Manager.
2. Start Ventura and set it up just the way you expect it to appear when you execute the macro. For example, if you want a macro that makes format changes on selected text, open a chapter containing some text and then select some part of it.
3. Switch to Recorder by pressing Ctrl-Esc. The Task List box appears. Select Recorder. Then click on Switch To.
4. In the Recorder window, choose Record from the Macro menu. The Record Macro dialog box appears (Figure 17-1). Type a name for the macro in the Record Macro Name text box, specify a shortcut key in the Shortcut Key text box, and set the Record Mouse and Playback options you want. Also give a brief description in the Description text box to help others who use your macro understand what it does and how it works.

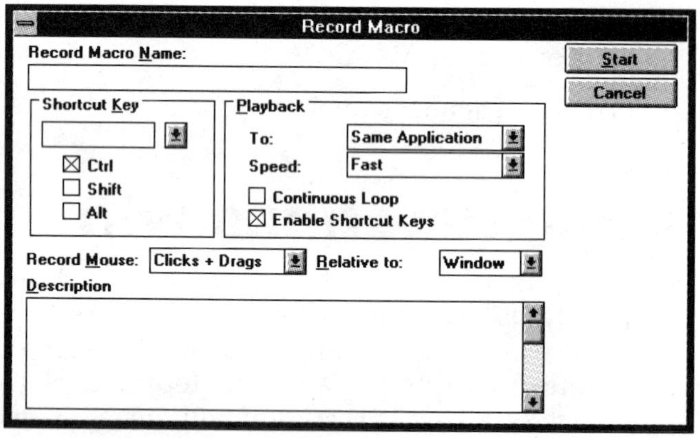

Figure 17-1.
Use the Record Macro dialog box to give your macro a name, keyboard shortcut, and a description. You can also control how it records mouse movements and how the macro plays back.

Tip: To save time, enter only the macro name and Record Mouse options at this time. You can come back and change all the other settings later. If you add everything to the dialog box now and then have to cancel the macro recording, all that work will be wasted.

5. Click on Start. You return to the Ventura Window.
6. Carefully perform the steps you want to record. If you chose Recorder's "Ignore Mouse" option, use Ventura's keyboard shortcuts; otherwise, the steps won't be recorded correctly.
7. When you're finished, press Ctrl-Break. A message box appears and announces that recording has been suspended.
8. Choose the Save Macro option and click on OK.

9. If you didn't finish filling out the macro's dialog box before, switch to Recorder again, select your macro, and choose Properties from the Macro menu. Then modify or add the shortcut key, description, and other options you want.

10. Choose Save from Recorder's File menu to name and preserve the file containing your macros.

Tip: We find the Ignore Mouse option in the Record Mouse section gives us the most trouble-free macros. This ensures that your macro will work no matter how you've sized your windows or what screen you play it back on. (This is useful if more than one person wants to use your macros.) If you really need to use the mouse, try the Clicks + Drags option. That way, it only records the mouse actions when the mouse buttons are pressed.

Tip: Whenever you assign a keyboard shortcut to a Recorder macro, that shortcut no longer performs any of the functions it once had in Ventura or any other application. To restore a shortcut's former function, you must either close Recorder or turn off its shortcut keys in the Recorder Options menu. To avoid this bothersome task, choose shortcut keys you don't otherwise use. Alt-Shift-Ctrl combinations are the safest, because few applications use them. Many Ctrl-Shift combinations are available as well. You may also find certain keys on your keyboard never get used—such as Scroll Lock. If so, they are prime targets for a macro.

Using Windows macros

Okay, you've recorded your macros just the way you want them. What's left? There are just three requirements for your macros to work properly:

1. You must have Recorder running as an icon on your desktop (Figure 17-2).

2. You must have the file with your macros loaded into Recorder. (Use the Open command from the Recorder's File menu.)

3. You must set up Ventura in conditions similar to those that you had when you recorded your macro. For example, if you recorded your macro in a maximized Ventura window, don't expect it to work with Ventura minimized. If you recorded a macro that acted on selected text, don't expect it to work if you have no text selected. And so on.

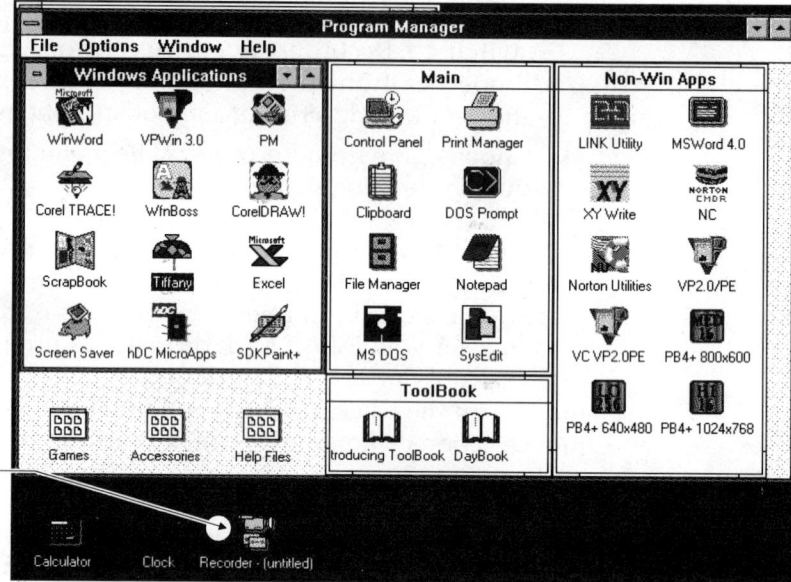

Figure 17-2.
To use Windows macros, activate the Recorder and minimize it to an icon.

Recorder icon

Tip: If you only have one macro file, the easiest way to keep your macros active is to have Windows load them automatically at startup. To do this, start Notepad, and open the WIN.INI file in your \WINDOWS directory. Near the top you'll see a line that says load=. Add the name of your macro file to that line. For example, if your macro file was named MACROS.REC, your load= line would look like this:

```
load=macros.rec
```

The next time you start Windows, Recorder will be sitting on your desktop with your macros loaded and ready to go.

Tip: To open and use multiple macro files easily, use Program Manager's Copy command from the File menu to make multiple copies of the Recorder icon. Then, for each one, select the icon and choose Properties from the File menu. In the Command Line text box, type RECORDER.EXE MACROS.REC where MACROS.REC is the name of the macro file you want to open with that icon. (Change the Description box as well, so that you can tell one icon from another.) The next time you double-click on that icon, you'll open that macro file in Recorder. To change macro files, simply double-click on a different Recorder icon (Figure 17-3). This saves you the trouble of mucking around with menus and dialog boxes—and you don't even have to close the previous macro file.

Figure 17-3. Create different icons for each macro in Program Manager. Then all you need to do is double-click on the specific macro's icon to use the macro. You can even create a program group that keeps all your macro icons in one place.

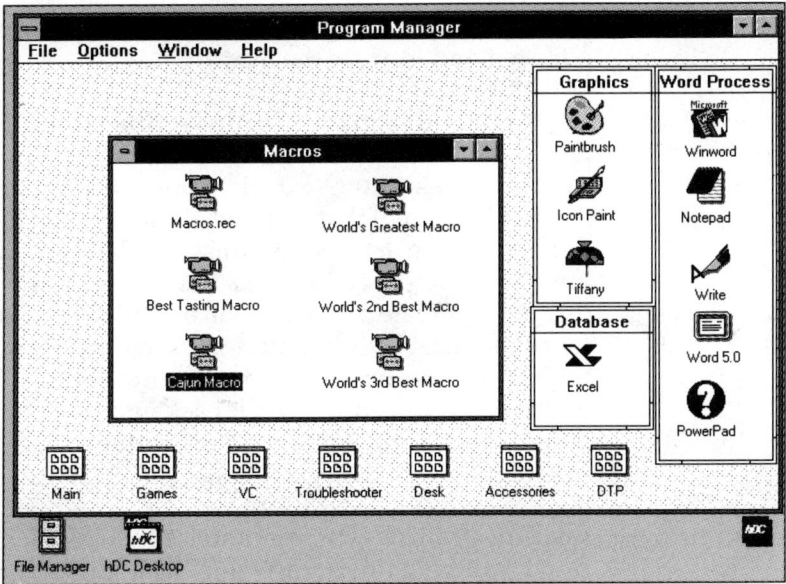

Tip: Using the New command from the File menu in Program Manager, you can also create a separate program group for all your macro files (Figure 17-3).

Macro brainstorms

Now you've mastered macro making. But what kinds of procedures should you record? Record anything that you do over and over again—let the macro do the busy work. Here are some ideas to get you started.

Setting font attributes

If you have to use the Set Font Attributes command to format only specific words inside a paragraph (something tagging won't do), automate the procedure with a macro. You can make a macro apply any formats accessed through the Set Font Attributes command (including typeface, style, size, color, kerning, and even baseline shift) to selected text.

Fixing frames

Maybe you have many frames in a document that need some attribute changed in a consistent manner, such as changing the Style of ruling boxes or changing the Image Settings of TIFF files. If so, you can automate the changes with a Recorder macro. After this macro is recorded, you just select each frame that needs to be adjusted and execute the macro.

Secret decoder macro for invisible notes

One way editors can communicate with production artists is through notes in the text file. You could have a tag (with a name such as EditNote) that displays these notes in big bold type, so that the production artist won't miss it in Ventura and the editor won't miss it on the proof. To make the paragraphs containing the notes disappear, create a macro that modifies the EditNote tag, so that those paragraphs are placed in an empty margin (small font size, no leading, no breaks) and made invisible (set the font color to white). If you need to switch back and forth between seeing these notes and hiding them, create another macro that restores the "visibility" attributes for that tag.

Scaling pictures by percentages

Don't you wish Ventura would scale pictures by percentages, instead of making you figure out the picture dimensions? Now it can. For a fun challenge, try this macro. You'll have to figure out the details, but here's an outline:

First, the preparation stage. Before recording, start up both Windows' Calculator and Ventura. Be sure that your Sizing & Scaling dialog box has By Scale Factors for Picture Scaling and Maintained for Aspect Ratio. Then select a frame containing a picture.

Now switch to Recorder and start your recording. Open the Sizing & Scaling dialog box and select the Picture Width (Alt-I). Then press Ctrl-Insert to copy the number to the clipboard. Use Windows' Task Manager to switch to Windows' Calculator, and press Shift-Insert to paste the number. Perform your calculation—double the size, reduce it by one-half, or whatever you want. Press Ctrl-Insert to copy the new value to the clipboard, and then Alt-Esc to return to Ventura. (The old Picture Width value should still be selected.) Shift-Insert pastes the new value into the text box. But because the new value gets pasted in with a leading space, you'll have to press Home to move to the beginning of the number and press Delete to get rid of the space. Press Enter and stop recording (press Ctrl-Break).

That's it! Now just assign some logical shortcut like Ctrl-Shift-2 for 200% scaling, Ctrl-Shift-3 for 300% and so on. You can make a series of macros for the percentages you use most often.

Using third-party utilities

By its very nature, Ventura expects you to use other software: A word processor for your text, a drawing program for line-art pictures, or a gray-scale editor for bit-mapped images. How you get along with Ventura depends a lot on these other programs. If you use the right combination of programs, you'll all be pals for life. Get the wrong mix, and you'll never quite be satisfied.

We can't take the space here to review all the countless graphics and text programs available. It's up to you to read the trade magazines, talk to professionals, check out demonstration copies, and then decide for yourself. However, we will tell you about some Windows accessories that will make your life with Ventura easier. Some of these handy programs are right under your nose (they come with Windows); others you'll have to buy—but you'll find that the convenience they provide you is well worth the price. We'll also tell you about shareware utilities that you may otherwise never hear of. These shareware programs are designed for Ventura and do only a few specific tasks—but they do them well.

Windows utilities

You can make your work simpler and more efficient with a number of programs developed specifically for Windows. Let's look at some of the Windows utilities that work well with Ventura.

Windows accessories

The first and best place to look for Windows utilities is Windows itself. Its built-in accessories give you many handy features at no extra cost. Does that sound like a commercial? Maybe. But it's true.

First, there's Recorder. If you read the first part of this chapter, you already know how useful it can be in automating Windows and Ventura functions. You also know that Calculator can help you scale pictures automatically. Later in this chapter, we'll look at Notepad, a handy tool for editing CHP files. Finally, there's Paintbrush. Though modest in its features, Paintbrush does let you import, export, create, and edit both BMP and PCX bit-mapped images. If you're clever, you can find good uses for other Windows accessories as well.

Tip: To avoid moire patterns in printing bit-mapped images, you need to size your pictures to correspond to the resolution of your printer. For more information on sizing pictures, see Chapter 12, "Enhancing and Editing Pictures." In making these calculations, Paintbrush can come to your aid by providing the actual pixel dimensions of BMP and PCX image files. To find out a picture's size in pixels, select its filename in the File Open dialog box and click on the Info button.

Tip: If you're using Paintbrush to edit or convert the format of full-sized screen shots, you may run into a problem: When you paste images from the clipboard, Paintbrush can't import images any larger than its screen display. Consequently, if you paste in a full-screen image, Paintbrush will lop off the edges. To avoid this problem, do the following:

1. Choose Zoom Out from the View menu.
2. Paste your image into Paintbrush (Paste from the Edit menu).
3. Click on any tool to complete the paste.
4. Choose Zoom In from the View menu.

You can now edit and save your complete image without losing any of the edges.

Adobe Type Manager

We strongly recommend you invest in one of the font rasterizers available for Windows, such as Adobe Type Manager (ATM). Not only does ATM let you print Adobe fonts on non-PostScript printers, it also improves your screen display immensely. That's not just an aesthetic issue either: A good screen display can help you make kerning and other adjustments in less time and with fewer wasted proofing prints. For more information on using ATM with Ventura, see Chapter 13, "Printing Ventura Documents."

hDC FirstApps

FirstApps from hDC is a collection of "MicroApps" designed to enhance your Windows computing (Figure 17-4). Some of these are just revved up versions of Windows accessories—for example, Alarm Clock (a Clock clone) or System Enhancer (a Task Manager clone). Others are fun, but not terribly functional—for example Art Gallery (a graphics file manager) or Desktop (a screen saver and wallpaper enhancement). But others can be useful.

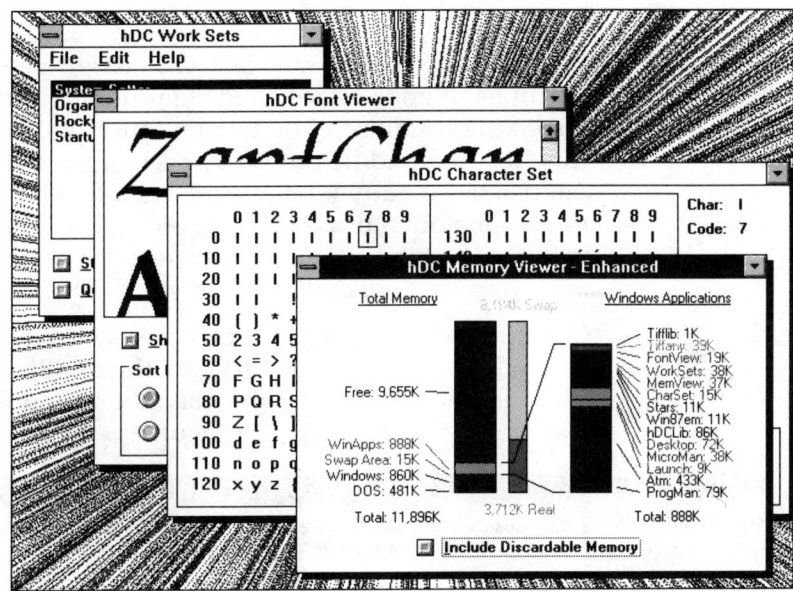

Figure 17-4.
FirstApps offers a number of mini-applications to enhance your Windows computing.

Here are our favorites:

- *Auto Save.* Do you forget to save your Ventura chapter from time to time? Auto Save will do it for you at specified intervals. Concerned that this will keep you from reverting to a previous version? Not to worry; you can also set Auto Save to prompt you and get your permission before it saves your chapter.

- *Character Set.* If your documents use foreign words or unusual characters, Character Set lets you consult the ANSI and traditional OEM character sets without running to your Windows manual each time. It also lets you copy any of these characters and paste them into Ventura or other Windows applications.

- *Font Viewer.* Unlike Control Panel, whose Font section only shows you installed screen fonts, the hDC Font Viewer will also show what fonts are available on your printer.

- *Memory Viewer.* This utility gives you a bar graph of your RAM and maps which program is using what. This is a handy tool for diagnosing which of your applications is hogging all your RAM.

- *Work Sets.* Perhaps the best of all, this MicroApp memorizes your desktop so you can later reopen all your windows just the way you like them. You can set up multiple work sets for different projects or users. This is handy for anyone who does a lot of multitasking or is finicky about window arrangement.

Whiskers

Whiskers is a utility that lets you assign a number of different functions to your middle and right mouse buttons (if you have a three-button mouse). For two-button users, Whiskers provides a way to add a middle button by clicking both buttons at once. You can use these buttons to execute such functions as cut, copy, and paste. Or you can assign "Shift-left click" to your right mouse button to extend a selection in text mode. The possibilities are numerous (but not endless) (Figure 17-5).

Our favorite use: Assign Reduced View to Ctrl plus the right button and Normal View to Ctrl plus the middle button. This lets us zoom in and out easily with the mouse and Ctrl key, instead of reaching for the keyboard shortcut.

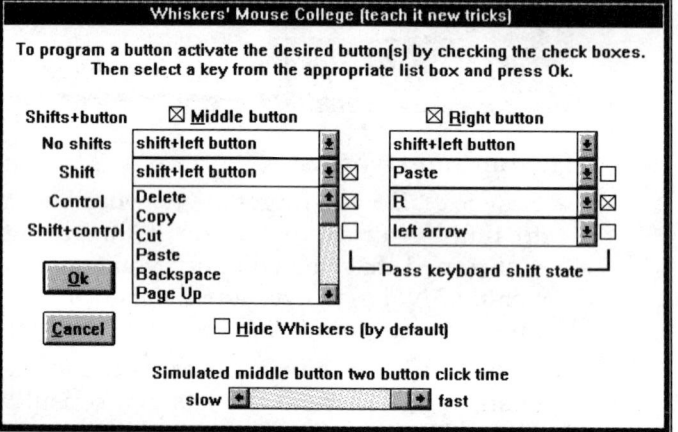

Figure 17-5.
Whiskers dialog box lets you program a number of keystrokes into seldom-used mouse buttons.

Shareware utilities

Sometimes good things come in small packages. Some of our most useful adjuncts to Ventura have been inexpensive shareware or commercial products that do just a few things—but do them very well. Most popular shareware products are available on a number of electronic bulletin boards. If you don't have a modem, contact your local Ventura users' group. Here are our favorites.

Change it with CHANGE.COM

CHANGE.COM is a shareware utility that performs multiple search-and-replace operations on ASCII files 64K or smaller. You can search for any character by typing in the character or its ASCII number. You can even search for hex codes and use wildcards.

Why would you want such a utility? Why not use a word processor? Because CHANGE.COM can search for characters that you can't necessarily change in your word processor—for example, line feeds (ASCII value 10). And CHANGE.COM works on binary files as well. That means you can use it to search-and-replace the disk drive letter of a width file in a Ventura style sheet file.

Fix it with FIXCHP.EXE

Another shareware utility, FIXCHP.EXE, circumvents the need to use Ventura's Multi-Chapter Copy All function. If your only purpose is to change the pathname pointers in the CHP files to a single directory, FIXCHP.EXE can save you the trouble of loading up Ventura. Just use the DOS COPY command to copy the chapter to the directory where you want Ventura to look for its constituent files. Then, at the DOS prompt, type FIXCHP and the chapter name. FIXCHP changes all the pointers to the current directory. That means that if you want the pointers changed to more than one directory, you'll have to edit the CHP file with a text editor or resort to Ventura's Multi-Chapter Copy All function. But for copying chapters to a floppy disk and then changing the pointers, FIXCHP.EXE makes it a snap.

Greek it with GREEKER.COM

Still another shareware utility we use is GREEKER.COM. This friendly little program does nothing but generate a file containing dummy text (often called "Greek" text even though it's pseudo-Latin). Just type GREEKER at the DOS prompt. It will ask you to specify:

- The size of the file you want (in kilobytes)
- Whether to include double carriage returns between paragraphs
- Whether to include a headline
- The name of the file

This program is handy if you're developing a rough layout for a client and need some dummy text for your design.

Tip: If you give your Greek file a name that's used for the final text file, you can save the trouble of removing the Greek text and loading the genuine text later on. When you get the final text file, just rename it, so that it copies over the Greek file. Then when you open your Ventura chapter, the genuine text will already be loaded on the page.

Creating chapter templates

If you only learn one time-saving technique, learn this one. Using chapter templates is a widely used, time-tested way to save thousands of hours in duplicated effort and frustration. In this section, you'll find out what a chapter template is, what it should contain, and how to create and use one.

Understanding chapter templates

What is a chapter template? Think of it as a collection of molds into which you pour the parts of your document. It's much more than a regularly used style sheet. It's essentially a blank chapter containing only text and empty frames that you use each time you create a new document. It may even have specific picture files, captions, or other text that you use repeatedly. Give this template chapter a new name. Then all you need to do is "fill in the blanks."

Let's take newsletter production as an example (Figure 17-6). A publisher or production department can save time by creating a blank chapter that contains elements that are always the same:

- Issue information (Volume number and date of issue)
- Masthead
- Banner or nameplate
- Contents
- Departments
- Self-mailer information (return address and permit number)
- Graphics used in every issue: logos or regular advertisements

When do you use chapter templates? Any time you produce multiple documents that require a consistent appearance, you can benefit from a chapter template. That means multiple chapters in a book, multiple issues in a periodical, multiple reports for a single company, and so on.

Creating a template

Here's how to create a chapter template.

First, decide how you want it to look. Make some thumbnails, roughly sketching the position of various elements. Work small, maybe 25% actual size—if you make your thumbnails too large, you'll be tempted to spend too much time on detail.

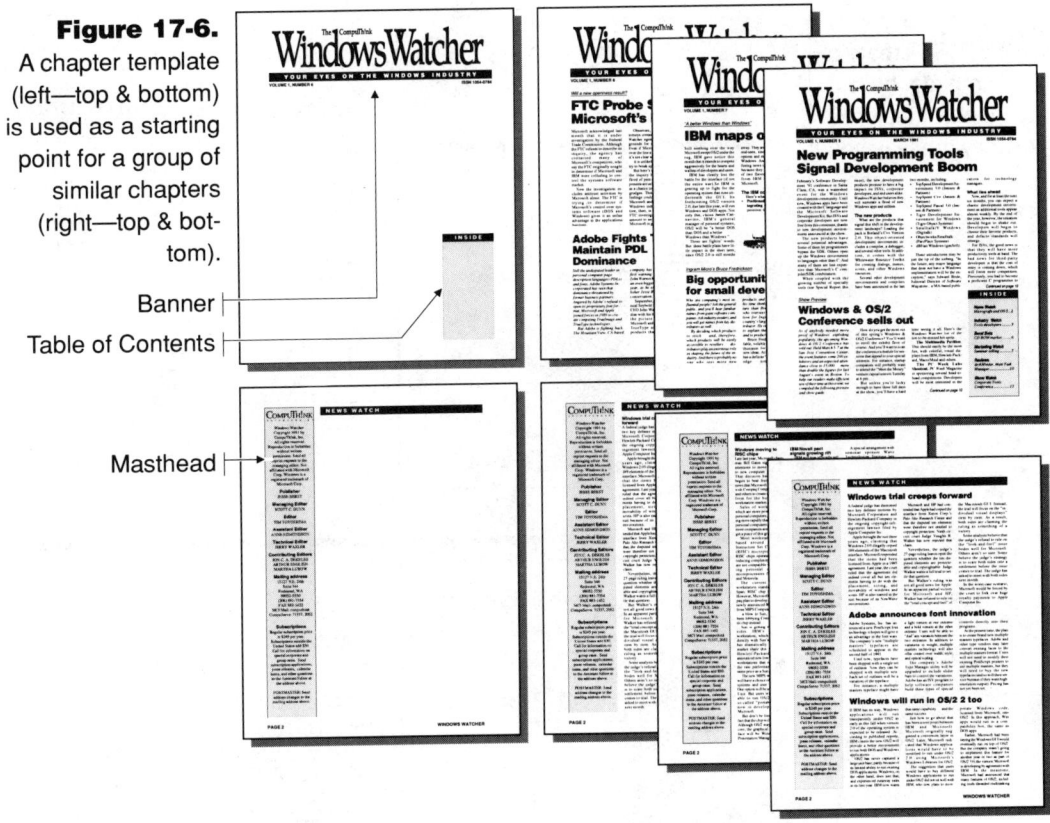

Figure 17-6.
A chapter template (left—top & bottom) is used as a starting point for a group of similar chapters (right—top & bottom).

Banner
Table of Contents
Masthead

Second, build a chapter that looks exactly the way you want (Figure 17-7). For a list of things to consider when building a chapter template, see the *Template checklist* sidebar, on page 510.

Finally, when the chapter has the look that you want, remove any text or picture files (files that won't be used in every document) from the chapter and save it. Voila! Now you have a chapter that you can use as a template: Just open the template, save it as a new chapter, and then load text and picture files into it (Figure 17-8).

Using the template

Now comes the easy part. To make a new chapter using the template, follow these steps:

1. Open the template chapter.
2. Save the chapter with the Save As command, giving it the name of the actual document you want to create.

Figure 17-7.
To create a template, build a chapter that looks exactly the way you want it.

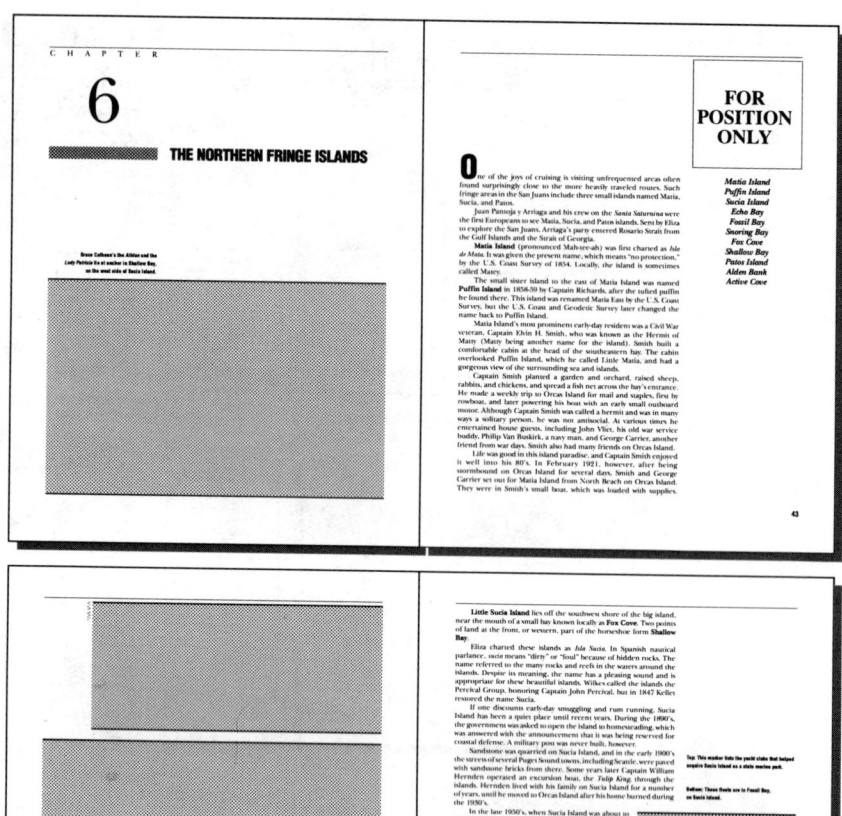

3. Load the text file for the underlying page.
4. Copy frames as needed for other text and picture files.
5. Save the chapter.

Now, you only need to fine-tune the elements in your new chapter, by repositioning frames, copyfitting, and proofing. Most of your design and formatting will have already been done. Every time you use this template, you're saving hours of design, layout, and formatting work.

Figure 17-8.
Empty out frames to create frame templates within the chapter template.

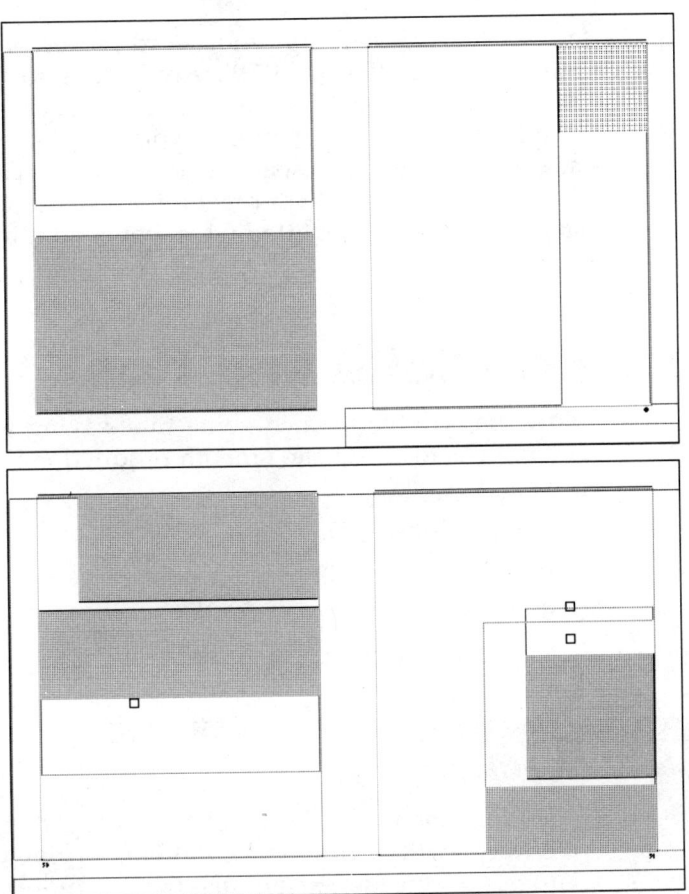

Tip: To change the elements of a template chapter, so that it affects all other chapters, you can use one of these two methods: (1) Make the same changes to all the other chapters as well as the template. (2) Make the changes to the template chapter and recreate all previously completed chapters. Neither of these options is very inviting. Fortunately, you can make certain changes to the chapter and template files without even opening them in Ventura. In the section, "Editing chapter files," later in this chapter, we'll show you how to make changes (such as editing your headers and footers) directly in the CHP file.

Tip: Create templates for your word processor, such as a standard business letter (Figure 17-9). Apply tags to the text in Ventura, delete text that won't appear in every letter leaving empty paragraphs, and save the chapter. In your word processor, type the text next to the tags. Then load the text file into the template chapter. The key is to enter all your text into the text file with the tag codes so it's already be formatted when you load it into Ventura.

Production tricks and tips

Now that you've learned some time-saving techniques, here are some tricks to speed and smooth production in specific situations:

- Newsletters
- Long documents
- Pictures
- Style sheets
- Keyboard shortcuts

Template checklist

Every document is different, so we can't give you hard and fast rules for what belongs inside. But we can give you a list of page elements to consider. Remember that the more elements you can put into the template, the less work you'll have to do later.

Special issues to consider when setting up a template:

- Chapter numbering
- Page headers and footers
- Page numbering, by chapter or consecutive through the whole publication
- Figure and table numbering, by chapter, or consecutive through the whole publication
- Representative frames of each type used, including all their attributes, so that you can simply copy the kind you need
- Repeating frames
- Crop marks

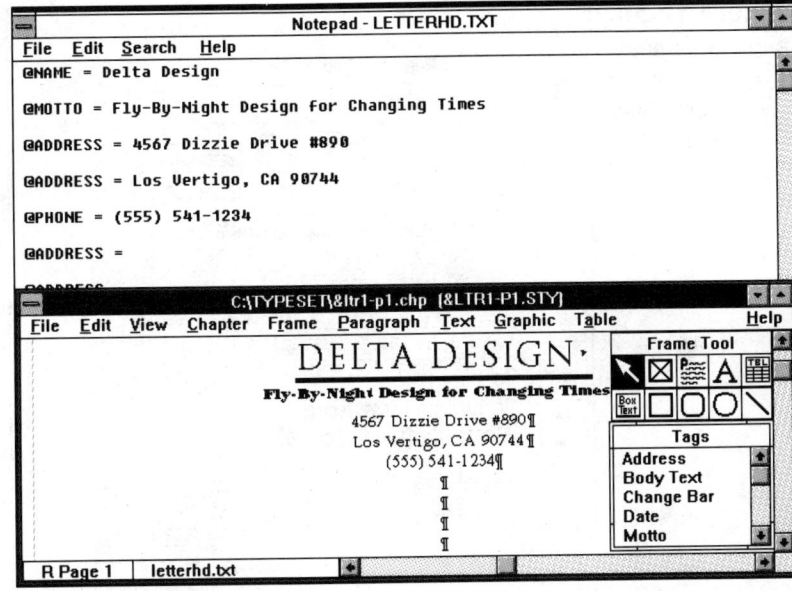

Figure 17-9.
One way to create word processing templates: save the chapter and then return to the word processor to see which codes Ventura has left behind.

Newsletter tips

You've already learned how to save time on your newsletter by using a chapter template. Here are some more of our favorite tricks: saving stock frames and re-using the same filenames for chapters and text files.

Saving stock frames

Keep frames in your template chapter that have ruling lines, margins, and the number of columns preset for all possible column widths. When you need to load a text file into a frame, select the type of frame you need, copy it, and then load the text file into it.

Here's one approach:

1. Make one frame for each type of frame that you use—one frame for a one-column story, another for a two-column story, and so on. Be sure each frame has the attributes (margins, columns, rules, and so on) you'll need.

2. Using the Frame Tool, size each frame, so that it's small and unobtrusive, and place it in the margin of your template.

3. Use Ventura's Add Box Text tool to label each frame, so that you can tell which frame is which.

When it's time to load text, simply make a copy of the frame, enlarge it, and then move it to the proper position (Figure 17-10).

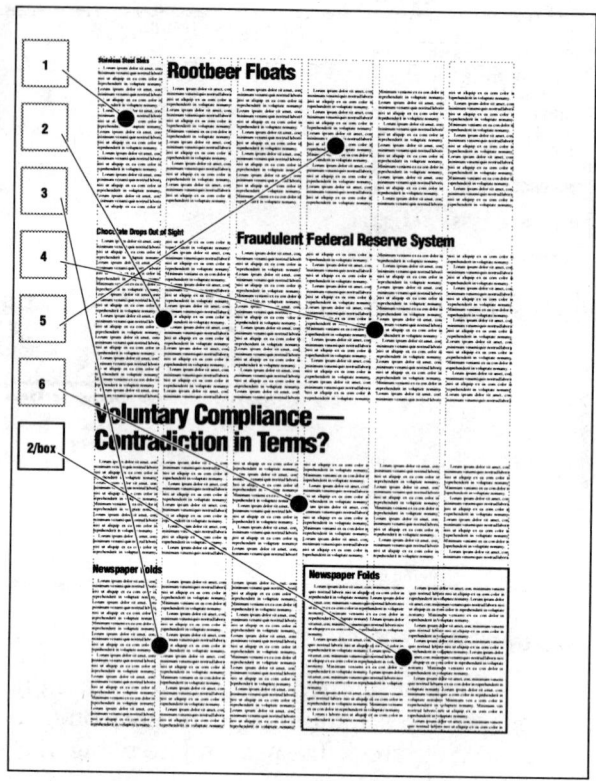

Figure 17-10. Keep stock frames handy to speed newsletter production.

Re-using the same filenames

If you keep all your past issues intact on your hard disk, you can make it easier to identify and track your files by incorporating the date of your newsletter into the chapter name. This system can also display the chapter files in your disk directory in chronological order. Here are three possibilities:

- Use a six-digit "reverse notation" date such as NL910118.CHP, which is a newsletter chapter (NL) from January 18, 1991 (910118).

- If the newsletter is a weekly, use the number of the week: NL9125.CHP, which is the newsletter chapter for the 25th week of 1991.

- If the newsletter is a daily, use the number of the day: NL91067.CHP, which is the newsletter chapter for the 67th day of 1991.

However, if you handle a large number of Ventura documents, you'll want to archive back issues to floppy disks and reserve your hard drive for current projects only. In that case, you can profit by keeping the same filenames from issue to issue. Here's how:

1. Use generic names for chapter, text and graphic files: LEAD1.TXT, INTERVW.TXT, ARTICLE1.TXT, and so on.
2. When an issue is finished, copy these files to a backup floppy disk. You may want to rename the files on the backup floppy so that they reflect the name or number of the specific issue. Leave the original on your hard drive.
3. Have your writers and artists use the same filenames for the next issue. When you copy them to the hard drive, they will overwrite your old articles. (For example, the new ARTICLE.TXT will take the place of the old ARTICLE.TXT.)
4. When you're ready, open your newsletter chapter file. All of the new articles will already be loaded.

Naturally, you'll have to move and resize frames, and do some copyfitting. But you'll have saved the trouble of loading different text and pictures for each issue.

Tips for filenames

Use the way that DOS and Ventura's File List Box list your files to your advantage. Both DOS and the File List Box automatically list files alphabetically. Actually, the filenames are listed in the order of their ASCII codes; therefore, some symbols whose ASCII codes have lower values than the letters (such as &) appear at the head of the list. Those with higher values appear at the end. By choosing the characters that you use in your filenames wisely, you can control how the files are listed and grouped when you do a DOS DIR command to list the files in a directory, and when you view your files in the File List Box.

When we produced this book, we used one main text file per chapter. But we included many sidebars that were separate text files. These files were named so that they would be grouped together in the File List Window. All files had VC as the first two characters. All files for a given chapter used the number of the chapter for the next two digits: 17 for this chapter. For the text files of sidebars, we made the fifth character an ampersand (&), which appears higher in the list.

You can place files that do *not* change (or change very little) toward the end of the list by using characters in the filenames that occur later in the list, such as the curly brace (}). For example, if you are producing a catalog called the *Victoria Directory*, you might give all the files in your project the two-letter code *VD*. Divisions of the catalog would be named VD01, VD02, and so on. Then name the template VD!!.CHP if you want it at the top of the File List, or VD{{.CHP if you want it at the bottom.

Cross-referencing

What is cross-referencing? Cross-referencing is the way Ventura gets information about another element (such as a figure, table, or text) that's in another location in the same document. The information you could get from a cross reference could be the number of the chapter in which it is contained, the page number where it occurs, or the number of a figure or table. When you edit a document, you move text, tables, pictures, and other elements to different places in the document. Keeping track of the exact locations and content of all these elements would be a gruesome job. Fortunately, the cross-referencing feature is ready to do the dirty work.

The easiest way to use cross-referencing is to add special bracket codes into the text file with your word processor. To make a reference to a page number where an element occurs, follow these steps:

1. In your word processor, open the text file.

2. Place a marker at the location you want to reference, using the bracket code:

`<$M[label]>`

Replace the word "label" with the name that you want to give the marker.

3. Insert a reference to the page where the marker occurs, using the bracket code:

`<$R[P#,label]>`

Replace the word "label" with the marker name of the item you want to refer to.

4. Create a publication that contains all your chapters, using the Multi-Chapter dialog box. Then select Renumber to make Ventura replace the reference codes with the actual page numbers.

To reference the page number of a frame, you follow the same steps—except you don't add a marker. Instead, you use the frame's anchor name as the "label" in the reference code:

`<$R[P#,anchorname]>`

The word "anchorname" is the anchor name that you've given the frame with the Anchors & Captions dialog box. For more information on anchoring frames, see Chapter 11, "Loading and Placing Pictures."

Sound a little confusing? Let's go through an example. Imagine you're producing a scientific book, *The Migratory Patterns of Pigeons*, and in chapter 15, you mention the Spotted Laundry Pigeon, which you covered in great detail in chapter 7. To refer to that chapter and page, you need to perform three steps:

1. Insert a marker at the location in chapter 7 where you discuss the Spotted Laundry Pigeon:

   `<$M[spotlaundry]>`

2. Insert a reference to the marker in chapter 15, one for each, if you need both the chapter number and the page number:

   `as discussed in chapter <$R[C#,spotlaundry]>, on page <$R[P#,spotlaundry]>.`

3. Finally, when all your chapters are finished (before you create a table of contents or index), you create a publication that contains all the chapters with Manage Publication from the File menu, and then select Renumber.

But what if you add another chapter before the current chapter 7? What if you add pictures or text, changing the page on which you discuss the Spotted Laundry Pigeon? Not to worry. Ventura's Renumber function will update the reference, so that it displays the correct numbers. Just open the publication again with Manage Publication from the File menu, and click Renumber.

You can also use cross referencing to connect the first part of an article to a continued section in the same chapter, as in Figure 17-11. For a complete listing of cross-referencing bracket codes, see Chapter 21, "Rapid Reference."

Picture tips

As you've seen in previous chapters, handling and enhancing pictures and other graphics can be complex. Here are a few of the tricks we've picked to make life with graphics a little easier.

Frame scrapbooks

The key to efficient desktop publishing is to avoid repeating complex and time-consuming tasks unnecessarily. Macros and chapter

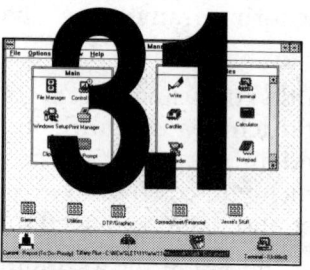

Figure 17-11.
Why put page numbers in manually? Ventura can do the work automatically—no matter how many times you change the chapter.

Numbers inserted by Ventura

templates let you take advantage of your previous work. You can do the same for frames and graphics.

Wouldn't it be nice to have a place to keep blank frames that were already sized and formatted (with preset ruling lines, captions, figure numbers, and so on) and graphics that you use over and over? Then all you would have to do is copy them to your chapter when you needed them. Well, you can. Just create a chapter that serves as a scrapbook for frames and graphics. You can even have one scrapbook chapter for frames and another for graphics.

Here's how:

- Create a scrapbook chapter by choosing New from the File menu and then saving it as FRAMELIB.CHP.
- Open a chapter that contains frames that you want to put into your scrapbook chapter, copy the frames (select multiple frames or do one at a time), open the scrapbook chapter, and paste them in. Repeat this copy/paste process for each chapter that has frames that you want in your scrapbook chapter. Using the Text Tool, type directly into the frame to label each frame, so that you can tell which frame is which. Now you can simply copy frames you need from this scrapbook chapter.

Building a frame scrapbook is pretty simple. When you copy a frame to the clipboard, you preserve most of its settings and attributes. For example, the Sizing and Aspect Ratio information is preserved—even if you remove the picture file from the frame. In fact, if you place another picture in the frame, it will still have the settings (for Sizing and Aspect Ratio) of the picture that was previously in the frame. This can be handy when you're loading numerous screen captures of the same size (such as full-screen captures).

However, you can't copy all settings and attributes of a frame. Here are the exceptions:

- Anchor names can't be copied. A given anchor name can exist only once in a chapter.
- Grid Settings for graphics won't be preserved unless a graphic element is linked to a frame.
- Image Settings for gray-scale pictures won't be preserved if the frame no longer contains the TIFF file.

The picturemark paragraph

As you should know by now, you can anchor frames to special codes inserted anywhere in your text (use Insert Special Item from the Text menu). Unfortunately, after you've inserted those anchors, they are either invisible (if you've turned off Show Tabs & Returns) or difficult to see (if you've turned on Show Tabs & Returns, it appears as a tiny degree symbol). Using the Text Tool, you can move the text cursor until you find one—you'll see the words "Frame Anchor" in the Current Selection Box. But moving the text cursor through the entire document is a tedious and inefficient way to find frame anchors.

The best way to keep track of frame anchors is to create a separate paragraph that only holds this anchor and the text of the anchor's name. We give this paragraph a special tag called "PictureMark." For example, if we had a picture file named SHUTTLE.GEM, we would name the anchor Shuttle.GEM, create a paragraph with the anchor name, and tag it as PictureMark. In a word processor, the tag, paragraph, and anchor codes would look like this:

```
@PICTUREMARK = Shuttle.GEM<$&Shuttle.GEM[v]>
```

In your Ventura document, the PictureMark paragraph might look similar to Figure 17-12.

Tip: You can save a lot of headaches if you follow our example above and use the picture filename as the anchor name. Then, there's no confusion about which picture belongs to which anchor.

Figure 17-12.
A PictureMark paragraph to hold a frame anchor provides a visible placeholder for the picture's name. Later, you can make the paragraph invisible.

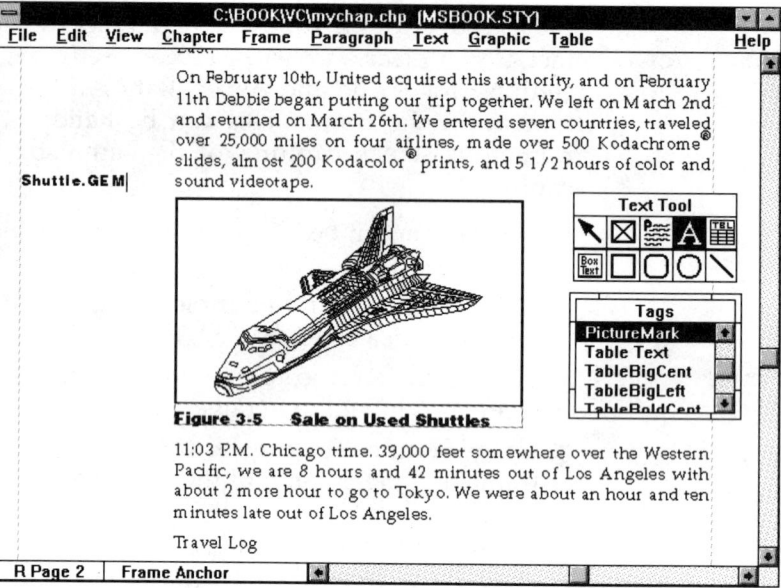

To work efficiently, the PictureMark paragraph must have the proper formatting. Set the spacing, so that the paragraph's text sticks out into a margin or empty companion column. That way, you can change the tag's text color to white, rendering it invisible when you print. To keep the PictureMark paragraph from taking up any vertical space, select the paragraph, choose Breaks from the Paragraph menu, and make these settings:

- Select Line Break: No.
- If pictures go below anchors, Select Next Y Position: Beside Last Line Of Prev. Para.
- If pictures go above anchors, type Inter-Line space: 00,00.

Now you have a PictureMark paragraph that you can use as a visible place-marker for your frames.

Assembly line importing

If you're dealing with a large chapter with lots of pictures, you can speed up picture and frame placement chores by grouping and performing similar tasks all at once. Here's the process we follow:

1. Import all picture files at once. (Check the Several Files option in the Load Text/Pictures dialog box.)

2. Copy the frames you'll need from your frame scrapbook chapter and paste them all on the first page of your current chapter.

Don't worry if they're all stacked on top of each other—it's actually faster that way.

3. Place pictures into frames by selecting the top frame, then clicking the filename on the bottom of the File List. Ctrl-click to select the next frame in the stack. Then load the next picture, moving up the File List. Continue until all pictures are loaded in their frames. Don't be intimidated by all these pictures and frames. When you select a frame, you can see the filename of the picture it contains in the Current Selection Box.

4. After all the pictures are placed in their frames, open the Anchors & Captions dialog box from the Frame menu and type the picture name in the Anchor text box. Click on OK (or press Enter). Then select the next frame with a Ctrl-click and repeat the process until you've assigned an anchor name to each frame.

5. If your text is already on the page with all the anchor codes, all you have to do is choose Re-Anchor Frames from the Edit menu. If not, you can load in the text, add anchors (if you haven't already added them in your word processor), and re-anchor later.

Now all that's left is some minor repositioning and sizing of individual frames, and scaling of individual pictures.

Snapping pictures to half-line positions

Because the Line Snap function always uses the value of the Inter-Line spacing for the Body Text tag, you may face some frame positioning problems. There is a solution:

1. Open your chapter template.
2. Using the Paragraph Tool, select a paragraph of Body Text. Then add a new tag (press Ctrl-2) called BODY. Because you copied it from the Body Text tag, it has identical attributes.
3. Retag the paragraph as Body Text. Then with the paragraph still selected, choose Font from the Paragraph menu and change the size of the type to 6 points (or half their current size, if you prefer). Click OK.
4. Choose Spacing from the Paragraph menu. Change the Inter-Line space to 06.00 points (or half the current leading, if you prefer).

Your frames will now snap vertically in ½-pica (6-point) increments. "But," you say, "the type is all wrong now!" Read on.

5. Open your word processor. If it runs under Windows, you won't even have to quit Ventura.

6. Load the text file into your word processor and perform a search-and-replace, so that every paragraph begins with the text @BODY = . Be sure to include the "space-equals-space". (In most word processors, you replace every paragraph symbol with a paragraph symbol *plus* the text @BODY =).

Now you have a new problem: The BODY tag appears in some places where it shouldn't. For example, it shows up in front of all the other paragraph tags, i.e. @BODY = @HEADLINE = . Easy enough to fix. Note that in all cases where the BODY tag should *not* appear, it is immediately followed by another @ sign, regardless of the tag name that follows. Therefore, you can:

7. Perform a search and replace, replacing every occurrence of @BODY = @ with @. Save the file and you're done.

The next time you open the chapter, all paragraphs formerly Body Text will now be tagged "Body," and you will have far more control over the placement of frames.

Tip: If you have a color monitor and are using the above technique for changing the Line Snap value, change the Body Text tag to green or blue, so that you will be sure to see and change any paragraphs accidently left as Body Text. Don't use red. Using red can cause some confusion because red is also used by the Show Loose Lines function.

Saving time with dummy pictures

Are you tired of wasting time waiting for Ventura:

- Waiting for all those pictures to load and waiting for Ventura to convert file formats every time you open a chapter?

- Waiting for pages to print, when the only changes in your chapter are to the text? Sure, you could Hide All Pictures, but all the data in every picture file still gets sent to the printer; it's just covered up afterwards by a black block—saving absolutely no time to print.

- Having your clients mark the same impossible changes on the pictures for the third time in a row?

Why not just blank them out? (The pictures, that is—not your clients.) We'll show you how.

Warning: Don't try to solve this problem by moving files or copying them to floppies and deleting them. There are two reasons why this doesn't help matters:

- If you open the chapter after such a deletion, the chapter will stop for *every* missing picture, telling you that it can't find it.
- If, after opening the chapter, you purposely or accidentally save the chapter, all links between frames and the pictures they're supposed to contain will be removed. You'll have to flow the pictures in all over again.

The safe and easy way to reduce loading and printing time is to replace the pictures with tiny picture files having the same names. Just follow these steps.

1. Make backup copies of all your pictures on floppy disks.

Warning: Don't skip this step. If you don't keep your original files in a safe place, you could end up confusing them with the dummies and lose your work. If you're not sure which files are which, check the file size in your DOS directory listing. That's the quickest way to discover the "forgeries."

2. Create tiny graphics files and give them the same names as the picture files used in your document.

3. Copy the dummies over the originals on your hard drive.

You can now load your document in a much shorter time than before. And printing proofs will speed up dramatically as well.

4. When it comes time to print the final copy, get out your backup disks and copy the real pictures back over the dummies.

Here's an example. Suppose you have a TIFF picture called ELEPHANT.TIF, that you have already placed and sized. It takes up 327,680 bytes on your hard disk and takes 30 seconds to load into Ventura. Just copy that file to a floppy disk or to a different directory, and replace it with another file, also called ELEPHANT.TIF. The difference: The new ELEPHANT.TIF is actually a copy of another very small file called MOUSE.TIF, containing only 512 bytes. This replacement file will load so fast, you'll just barely see the name flash by on the screen. It will also print fast.

This gimmick works because Ventura doesn't really care what's in the file—mouse or elephant, it's all the same. All it cares about is finding a file by a specific name in a specific directory on a specific disk drive and inserting that file into a specific frame.

So where do you get the tiny file? You'll probably need to create it, and that may require some extra software. Here are your best bets:

- For TIFF files, you will need one of these items: a scanner and scanning software that allows you to create small files; a TIFF file editor, such as PC Paintbrush IV+; or a screen-capture utility that can capture tiny regions and save them in TIFF format.
- For PCX files, you can use Windows' Paintbrush.
- For EPS and C00 files, you can substitute an ASCII file containing only two lines of text:

```
%!PS-Adobe-2.0 EPSF-2.0
%%BoundingBox: 0 0 12 12
```

This trick can save you a lot of time loading documents and printing proofs on your printer, particularly when you're working on long documents with lots of pictures. It can also free up some space on your hard drive (temporarily at least).

Style sheet tips

With a few tricks, you can make your style sheets more efficient and easier to use. Some of these ideas may not work for you because of the particular type of documents you produce or your personal working style. But in general, they speed up and smooth out your work with style sheets.

Tag scrapbook

You've learned how to set up a scrapbook chapter that contains often-used graphics and frames. Why not create a tag scrapbook, too? With the Paragraph Tool, Ventura lets you copy and paste tags from one style sheet to another. Using this technique, you can keep all your favorite tags in one scrapbook style sheet, and then copy the ones you need.

Here's what you do. First, create a Ventura chapter file containing dummy text to which you can apply the tags in your scrapbook style sheet. Either create the tags in this file, or copy them from other files. (We'll cover the details of tag copying in a minute.) When you're satisfied, save that file and its style sheet.

Now let's pretend you're working on another document and you decide you need one of the tags from your tag scrapbook. How do you bring the tag into your current document? Here's one way:

1. Save your current chapter.

2. Open the Ventura chapter file containing your tags and the dummy text.
3. Using the Paragraph Tool, select the paragraph that has the tag you want to copy. You can also select multiple tags by using the Shift-Click technique to select different tags.
4. From the Edit menu, choose Copy Tag (or press Shift-Delete).
5. Open the chapter file where you want to paste the tag.
6. Choose Paste Tag from the Edit menu (or press Insert).

A new tag suddenly appears in your Tag List.

Tip: Because tags reside in the style sheet rather than the CHP file, you can also move tags without the slowdown of opening and closing multiple chapters. Here's the speedy way:

1. Save your current chapter.
2. From the File menu, choose Load Diff. Style to load the style sheet from your tag library.
3. Using the Paragraph Tool, select a paragraph whose tag you want to change. Then apply the tag you want to copy.
4. Choose Copy Tag from the Edit menu (or press Shift-Delete).
5. Choose Load Diff. Style from the File menu to load the original style sheet again.
6. Choose Paste Tag from the Edit menu (or press Insert).

The new tag appears on your style sheet and is already applied to the paragraph you selected.

Note: If the new tag you paste in has the same name as a tag already in the current style sheet, the new tag from the tag library will overwrite the old. So check tag names and make necessary changes before borrowing from your tag library.

Tip: You can also use the Windows' Clipboard to save multiple tags. Just select all the tags that you want to save (select the tags using Shift-Click). Open the Clipboard and save the tags (which are in the Clipboard buffer) as a CLP file. When you need this group of tags, you open this CLP file in Clipboard and simply paste the tags into the style sheet of your current chapter.

Special tags

You can use tags to do a variety of things—not just paragraph formatting. Try these ideas for tags and tag management:

- Create a tag to track the date when the style sheet was last modified. You never apply this tag to text, you just leave it showing in the tag window, where its name displays the date. For example, the tag !V910618 indicates that the style sheet was last modified on June 18, 1991. The exclamation point keeps the tag at the top of the list. You have to remember to rename this tag as you make changes; it will not update automatically.

- If you have tags that perform similar functions, be sure that their names use the same first two or three characters. That way, they will always be grouped together in the Tag List Window.

- When you name tags that you seldom use, follow the example of Ventura's own generated tags—they all begin with a "Z" and an underscore character. You could name your seldom-used tags starting with an "X" and an underscore. This will make them occur immediately above the generated tags, but at the bottom of the Tag List Window.

- When you load a text file that contains tag names Ventura doesn't recognize (that is, tag names not in the current Tag List), Ventura adds the new tag names to the Tag List, using all capital letters. For example, if you have a Headline tag, but accidently typed it "Haedline" in your text file, it will show up in your Tag List as an extra tag: HAEDLINE. To be able to spot these tags quickly, use at least one lowercase letter in all your tag names. That way the new tags will stand out like a sore thumb.

Keyboard tips

Menus are an easy way to navigate through Ventura's functions. But keyboard shortcuts save time—and once you're familiar with them, they're actually even easier. Here are some fundamental shortcuts that every Ventura power user should know by heart:

- To open the dialog box that you last used, press Ctrl-X. This makes it easy to switch from adjusting settings in a dialog box (for paragraph tags and frames, for example) to seeing their results in the workspace, and back to the dialog box again.

- To select all the text in a text box, use the tab key to move to that text box. To select all the text in the first text box, press the Tab key once, then hold down the Shift key and press Tab again.

- To cancel a dialog box, press the Esc key.

- To access menus with the keyboard, press the Alt key and then press the underlined letter in the menu that you want from the menu bar. To choose commands from the menu, press the underlined letter from the command that you want. If the command opens a dialog box, you have to use the Alt key again to select the dialog box options whose shortcuts are indicated by underlined letters.

For lists of more shortcuts, see Chapter 21, "Rapid Reference."

Customizing Ventura

Take control of Ventura. You can customize Ventura to fit your preferences or to set up different versions of Ventura for different projects or different people. In this section, we'll show you how to tailor Ventura to your needs and preferences.

Setup strategies

Ventura lets you customize a number of settings to suit your needs. How you set up these options depends on your personal taste. But to give you some ideas, we'll show you three different setups, which we call *speed*, *accuracy*, and *WYSIWYG* (What You See Is What You Get).

Look at Table 17-1, you'll notice several options that are the same for every setup. If you have any questions on how these options work, use the index to find where we covered the details. Which setup is right for you? You can pick the one that fits your work style best, or you can mix and match to create a custom setup. You'll probably find yourself changing back and forth.

Now on to our three set-ups:

- The *speed* settings are ideal if you have a slower computer and slower display. They reduce the number of things that Ventura has to draw on screen. The fewer things Ventura has to draw, the faster it responds. The more often you have to page back and forth in a long document, the more you'll appreciate the speed settings.

- The *accuracy* settings put as many guidelines onto the screen as possible. These guidelines help you align and position page elements more accurately. You'll use these settings most often during the early stages of document creation.

Table 17-1. *Customizing Ventura*

Menu	Command	Function	Options	Speed	Accuracy	Wysiwyg	Effect
Edit	Set Preferences	Generated Tags	Shown	■	■	■	Tag List Window shows Ventura's generated tags
			Hidden				
		Text to Greek	None			■	Size at which Ventura uses tinted blocks to represent text instead of actually drawing it
			2				
			4				
			6		■		
			8				
			10				
			All	■			
		On-Screen Kerning	None	■			The kerning of letters on screen (doesn't affect kerning on printed page)
			36		■		
			24			■	
			18				
			14				
			10				
			All				
		Auto-Adjustments	None				Automatic adjustment of spacing if you change font and convertion of quotes and double dashes to true typographic characters
			Styles				
			" and - -	■	■	■	
			Both				

■ The *WYSIWYG* settings make the screen resemble the printed page as closely as possible, so that What You See Is What You Get. If you know about these settings, you can minimize the number of test printouts.

Customizing for different users

So you've got Ventura set up just right. Then along comes Susan, who shares the Ventura workstation with you. She changes inches

Table 17-1. *Customizing Ventura* (continued)

Menu	Command	Function	Options	Speed	Accuracy	Wysiwyg	Effect
View		Show/Hide All Pictures	Hide (no check)	■			Display of pictures on screen
			Show (check)		■	■	
		Show Rulers	Off (no check)	■		■	Display of on-screen rulers at top and left
			On (check)			■	
		Show Column Guides	Off (no check)	■		■	Display of non-printing guidelines around columns
			On (check)			■	
		Show Tabs & Returns	Off (no check)	■		■	Display of paragraph marks that indicate returns, tabs, line breaks, and end of file
			On (check)			■	
		Show Loose Lines	Off (no check)	■		■	Display of lines that needed extra spacing for justification
			On (check)			■	
		Toolbox Window	Off (no check)	■		■	Display of Toolbox
			On (check)			■	
		Tag List Window	Off (no check)	■		■	Display of list of tag names
			On (check)			■	
		File List Window	Off (no check)	■		■	Display of list of files
			On (check)			■	
Chapter	Chapter Typography	Move Down to 1st Baseline By	Inter-Line	■	■	■	Calculation of spacing
			Cap Height				
		Pair Kerning	On	■	■	■	Pair kerning for the chapter as a whole
			Off				

to picas & points, moves the Toolbox, turns off the rulers, and hides all the pictures. When you get back, you've got to spend the first few minutes restoring Ventura to the way you like to do things.

Fortunately, there's a simple way to retain your settings. You simply make new icons or "Program Items" in Windows Program Manager for each person using the same Ventura workstation. Here's how:

Ventura remembers how you set things up. It stores these settings in a file called VPWIN.INF. These settings include the choices you've made in the View menu, the Toolbox, and the measurement systems for each dialog box. It also provides a way to store VPWIN.INF in a different directory. By giving each user a different directory, you can keep multiple settings separate but easily accessible. For instance, Jesse, Byron, and Paul could store their individual versions of VPWIN.INF in directories called \JESSE, \BYRON, and \PAUL.

Now all we have to do is tell Ventura which version of VPWIN.INF to use each time it starts up. When you click on the Ventura icon, it activates a command line that loads Ventura. You can view this command line by clicking once on the icon in Program Manager, then choosing Properties from the File menu. Right now, it probably looks something similar to this:

```
C:\VENTURA\VPWIN.EXE /I=C:\VENTURA
```

The last part of the line (starting with "/I=") tells Ventura to look in the C:\VENTURA directory for the initialization file. To create an icon telling Ventura to use Jesse's version of VPWIN.INF, select the Ventura icon in Program Manager and choose Copy from the File menu. Designate the program group for the new icon and click on OK. You now have a second Ventura icon, which you can modify to suit your needs. After creating the directory C:\JESSE, select the icon and choose Properties from the File menu. Then change the Command Line to read:

```
C:\VENTURA\VPWIN.EXE /I=C:\JESSE
```

While you're at it, you can change the Description line. Get yourself an icon-drawing program (like the shareware product Icondraw) and you can even create a custom icon. For example, if Byron and Paul also created their own icons, you'd have three versions of Ventura peacefully coexisting on the same machine (Figure 17-13).

Customizing for different projects

Just as you can create different versions of Ventura for different users, you can also create different versions for different projects. You can even auto-load a document at the same time.

Let's say you divide your time between a short company newsletter and a long service manual. You might want very different

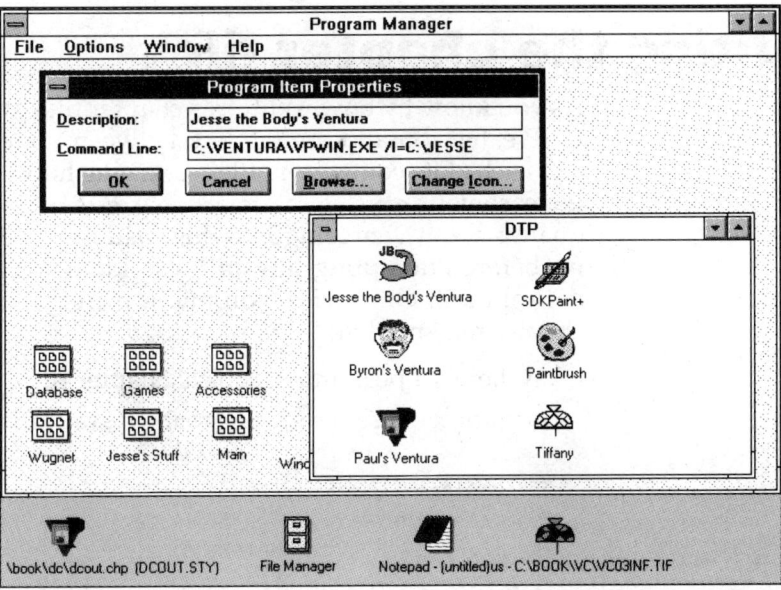

Figure 17-13.
To create custom versions of Ventura, use Properties from the File menu to change the Command line so Ventura looks in a different subdirectory for the VPWIN.INF file.

settings for the two projects. You might also want Ventura to load the right document when it starts.

To set this up, create two icons in Program Manager, one for the newsletter and one for the manual. Using Properties from the File menu, you'd name the first one "Newsletter Ventura" or something similar on the Description line. Then you'd type a Command line that looked similar to this:

```
C:\VENTURA\VPWIN.EXE \NEWSLET\NEWSLET.CHP
/I=C:\NEWSLET
```

Notice that this Command line uses the *I* switch to tell Ventura to look in the \NEWSLET directory for VPWIN.INF. It also instructs Ventura to automatically load a chapter called \NEWSLET\NEWSLET.CHP.

Likewise, you could create an icon called "Manual Ventura" with a Command line similar to this:

```
C:\VENTURA\VPWIN.EXE \MANUAL\MANUAL.CHP
/I=C:\MANUAL
```

Naturally, you'd substitute your own directory and chapter names when setting up a system like this on your own.

Editing the chapter file

As you know by now, Ventura's chapter files are recognized by the CHP extension and are the link between your Ventura document and each of its component files. Learning how to edit these files can increase your efficiency remarkably. But beware: if you have any qualms about venturing into this shadowy realm, perform a backup before attempting any of these ideas (or at least backup the critical files). Otherwise, you might increase your deficiency—the chapter may not load!

Okay, here's a peek into a typical chapter file:

```
#D·1001·032E·0013·000D·02·02·00·0000·000A·F:\WINWORD\VC\VC19.STY·¶
___·..*..*..*..*.*.*.*.¶
#G·07·F:\WINWORD\VC\VC19PUB1.C00·*·*·*·¶
#G·07·F:\WINWORD\VC\VC19CHAP.EPS·0040·0150·018B·¶
#T·01·F:\WINWORD\VC\NEWPAGES.TXT·*·*·*·¶
#I·03·F:\WINWORD\VC\VC19SUBB.TIF·0010·00C6·0096·¶
#I·03·F:\WINWORD\VC\VC19SUBA.TIF·0010·00C6·0096·¶
#I·03·F:\WINWORD\VC\VC19RENB.TIF·0012·00AB·0114·¶
#I·03·F:\WINWORD\VC\VC19RENA.TIF·0012·021C·00FA·¶
#I·03·F:\WINWORD\VC\VC19MUL4.TIF·0010·01E4·0150·¶
#I·03·F:\WINWORD\VC\VC19MUL2.TIF·0010·0220·0152·¶
#I·03·F:\WINWORD\VC\VC19MU1D.TIF·0010·026A·013A·¶
#I·03·F:\WINWORD\VC\VC19MU1C.TIF·0010·01E4·0150·¶
#I·03·F:\WINWORD\VC\VC19MU1B.TIF·0010·026A·013A·¶
#I·03·F:\WINWORD\VC\VC19MU1A.TIF·0010·00E1·0122·¶
#I·03·F:\WINWORD\VC\VC19LODP.TIF·0010·01E4·0150·¶
#I·03·F:\WINWORD\VC\VC19FMNB.TIF·0010·01AE·009F·¶
#I·03·F:\WINWORD\VC\VC19FMNA.TIF·0010·0280·01E0·¶
#I·03·F:\WINWORD\VC\VC19FMFB.TIF·0012·01E4·0150·¶
#I·03·F:\WINWORD\VC\VC19FMFA.TIF·0012·01B8·016E·¶
#I·03·F:\WINWORD\VC\VC19FMAN.TIF·0010·01AE·009F·¶
.
.
.
```

Does this just look too scary for words? Don't have a heart attack—the CHP file is just a plain ASCII file. You can edit it the way you edit any ASCII file—in your word processor. If your CHP file is under 64K (most of them are), you can edit it in Windows' Notepad. We'll show you how and why.

Warning: The placement of spaces in the CHP file is critical. That's why we've shown them here as small dots (·). We've also shown the paragraph returns as the standard paragraph symbol (¶), although your word processor may not show them. Our notation also lets you see the space that immediately precedes each paragraph return.

Changing the file type and extension

Among the things in the CHP file that can be edited are the names, paths (locations), and file types of any files used in a chapter. If you want to substitute a text file from a different directory but of the same name, you can simply change the path on the line that contains that filename. If you want to substitute a file with a different name, change that too.

What if you want to substitute a file of a different type? That's a little trickier, but not much. That's because when you load a file into Ventura, it asks you what type of file you plan to load, and gives you three general categories:

- Image files
- Line-art files
- Text files

Each of these file types corresponds to a special code in the CHP file—#T for text, #I for image art, and #G for line art. You'll find it at the beginning of each line that contains a file's name. In addition, you'll find a two-digit number corresponding to the type of file within each category.

Changing image files

Now, let's put this knowledge to some practical use. If you use a lot of PCX files in a chapter, you know that Ventura performs a conversion that creates a file with the same filename, but with the IMG extension. Every time a chapter imports a PCX file, there's that pesky IMG file hanging around.

The IMG file, however, once created by Ventura, can be used in place of the PCX file. But who wants to go through the whole chapter, possibly multiple chapters, removing the PCX files and replacing them with the IMG files? By editing the CHP file, you can change all of these, and Ventura will never know the difference. Here's how:

1. Load the CHP file into your word processor.

2. Perform a search-and-replace, replacing every occurrence of .PCX with .IMG. Don't add or remove any spaces.

3. Then perform another search-and-replace, replacing all occurrences of #I 01 with #I 00. Again, be sure there is a space between the #I and the two-digit number.

The next time you open your chapter, Ventura will dutifully load all the IMG files and place them in the appropriate frames, properly sized, as though that's what it's been doing all along.

For a list of the image file codes used in the CHP file, see Table 17-2.

Table 17-2. *Image file codes for CHP files*

CHP Code	File Type	Default Extension
00	GEM / HALO DPE	IMG
01	PCX (PC Paintbrush)	PCX
02	Mac Paint	PNT
03	TIFF	TIF

Changing line-art files

There probably won't be many times that you'll want to substitute one format of line-art file for another, but the steps are the same. The only thing different is the code at the beginning of each line. It starts with "#G" and also includes a two-digit code that represents the file type. For a complete list of these codes, see Table 17-3.

Table 17-3. *Line-art file codes for CHP files*

CHP Code	File Type	Default Extension
00	GEM	GEM
01	Windows Metafile	WMF
02	AutoCad .SLD	SLD
03	Lotus .PIC	PIC
04	VideoShow	PIC
05	Mac PICT	PCT
06	CGM	CGM
07	PostScript	EPS
08	HPGL	HPG

Changing text files

Just like the image and graphics files, text files can be changed in the CHP file, as well. Table 17-4 has a list of codes used for file types. We recommend changing some of Ventura's default text file extensions. For example, we like to be able to distinguish between WordPerfect 4 and WordPerfect 5 files (because Ventura does). And because a number of word processors use the DOC extension (including MultiMate, Word for DOS, and Word for Windows), we've come up with custom extensions of our own.

Table 17-4. *Text file codes for CHP files*

CHP code	File type	Default extension	Recommended extension
00	Generated	GEN	—
01	ASCII	TXT	TXT or ASC
02	WordStar 3	WS	WS3
03	MultiMate	DOC	MM
04	MS Word	DOC	MSW
05	Writer	XWP	XWP
06	WordPerfect 4	WP	WP4
07	WS 4.0/5.0	WS	WS4 or WS5
08	8-Bit ASCII	TXT	TXT or ASC
09	XyWrite	TXT	XY
0A	DCA	RFT	RFT
20	WordPerfect 5	WP	WP5

Changing header and footer information

Why mess around with headers and footers in the CHP file when Ventura's dialog boxes are relatively direct and easy? Two reasons:

- Typing text directly in the CHP file allows you type more text than the dialog box.
- If you have to change the text in the page headers or footers of lots of chapters, it can be done faster with a word processor.

The following example shows how the header and footer section of the CHP file looks for this book:

```
#LH·"<P12F55I>[C#]-[P#]<P10D><+><+>[<Head1]<F255P255D>"·¶
#LH·""·¶
#LH·""·¶
#LH·""·¶
#LH·"<P10>[<P#h1]·[<Pth1]<D>"·¶
#LH·""·¶
#LF·""·¶
#LF·""·¶
#LF·""·¶
#LF·""·¶
#LF·""·¶
#LF·""·¶
#RH·"Chapter·[C#]:·[<HeadChap]"·¶
#RH·""·¶
#RH·""·¶
#RH·""·¶
#RH·"<I>[<Head1]<D><+><+><P12F55I>[C#]-[P#]"·¶
#RH·""·¶
#RF·""·¶
#RF·""·¶
#RF·""·¶
#RF·""·¶
#RF·""·¶
#RF·""·¶
```

There are four main sections, distinguished by the first three characters on the line: #LH and #LF for the left page header and footer, and #RH and #RF for the right page header and footer. There are six of each to represent the six lines available with each selection in the Headers and Footers dialog box. Their position in the CHP file duplicates their order in the dialog box: For each six-line set, the first two lines are for text that goes to the left; the next two for centered text; and the last two for text that goes on the right.

Now that you know where the header text goes in the chapter file, you can add and delete information from this file just as you would in Ventura—only this time you have the power of your word processor and its search function to help you. There are only two things to keep in mind:

- When typing or editing these lines, be sure to keep all text you add within the quotation marks.

- Be careful not to delete any of the characters outside the quote marks.

Happy editing!

Continuing on

Having completed this chapter, you now have a wide array of power techniques at your disposal. You know how to build chapter templates, how to use macros, when to consider third-party utilities, and how to add power techniques to your arsenal. Though some of these techniques may seem a bit obscure, they can make your production jobs a lot easier, especially if you are a professional desktop publisher.

There are two common apprehensions about performing some of these techniques:

First, you may not remember exactly what you're supposed to do. Solution: hold onto this book and then you won't *have* to remember everything the first time around.

Second, you may be afraid of destroying valuable data. Solution: make backup copies of the files on which you experiment. The only serious mistake you can make is to fail to make backups. After you have copies of your files, you can experiment to your heart's content—and then if you make a fatal mistake, you can always bring the original back to life.

Easy Access

For more info on...	See chapter...
Creating and modifying tags	3 Building Basic Styles
Using advanced style sheet tricks	5 Building Advanced Styles
Creating, sizing, and loading pictures into frames	11 Loading and Placing Pictures
Scaling pictures	12 Enhancing and Editing Pictures
Working with Ventura files	16 Managing Ventura Files

For more info on...	See chapter...
Creating a newsletter	**19** Building a Newsletter
For tables listing cross-referencing bracket codes and keyboard shortcuts	**21** Rapid Reference

Part Six:
Hands-On

18
Building a Business Proposal

How to build a single-column report or proposal

- **Planning the proposal** 542
- **Loading the files** 544
- **Setting up the underlying page** 547
- **Applying and refining the style sheet** 549
- **Adding pictures** 557
- **Printing the proposal** 559
- **Continuing on** 560

Reports and proposals are the lifeblood of business communications: They circulate within the organization itself, to customers, to stockholders, and to the general public. As a result, the document you work on today could be directly responsible for your next raise or your company's next big job.

Thanks to Ventura Publisher, you can give these important documents the competitive edge by providing a polished look while still meeting short deadlines. In this chapter, you'll create a format that makes your reports and proposals stand out from the crowd (Figure 18-1). You'll build this document all on your own, following our step-by-step, illustrated instructions.

Figure 18-1.
This chapter will guide you through the steps to build this proposal.

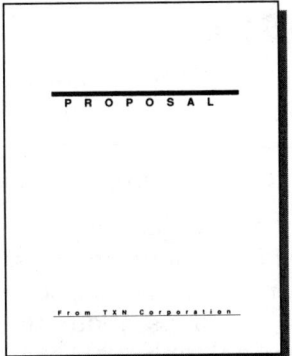 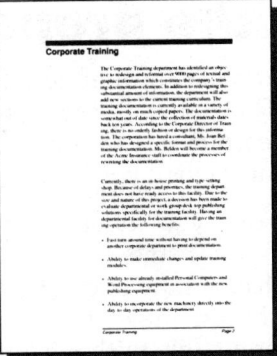

If you've read Chapter 2, "Starting Out Smart," you already know the procedure for creating a Ventura document. We'll follow a similar game plan for this proposal:

1. Plan the document.
2. Load and place text files.
3. Set up the underlying page.
4. Apply and refine the style sheet.
5. Place the pictures.
6. Print the proposal.

Note: Because the text for this project consists of a single file, we'll take the shortcut of loading and placing the text file simultaneously. In a complex document with several text files, we recommend the extra step outlined in Chapter 2, namely, placing text files *after* setting up the underlying page.

Warning: This proposal example has over 70 steps. Although there's no law that keeps you from dipping into the example at any point, we recommend that you follow the example all the way through—and in order. Otherwise, your results may not match those depicted in this book.

This chapter assumes that you understand basic Ventura techniques. Some of you may have turned here before completing the previous chapters. For more information on fundamental Ventura skills and techniques, see Chapter 2, "Starting Out Smart."

Planning the proposal

You may be tempted to skip the planning phase if you're in a hurry. That's fine. But you should return here—the planning skills you'll learn in this section will save you time and keep you out of trouble later when you're laying out your proposal in Ventura.

First, you must identify the target audience and determine the content (the source of the text and graphics). Then you should decide how to create, name, and store the source files. Finally, you should make the basic decisions about the underlying page, preferably with the help of a thumbnail sketch.

For this hands-on tutorial, we'll assume that you work for TXN, a manufacturer of graphic workstations, and that your readers are the business executives of the Acme Insurance Corporation. You want to show them why your 3544 DTP system is the solution to their problems. And you want to create an appealing document that makes it easy to find key information while creating a professional image for your company.

For the source documents, you'll use the REPORT.TXT text file and the NOZZLE.GEM graphics file stored in the \TYPESET directory created when you installed Ventura. Although we constructed this tutorial using sample text and pictures that come with Ventura, you can easily use your own files. Simply substitute another path and filename for those of the sample files.

Now you are ready to decide the format for the underlying page:

- Page size
- Single or double-sided pages
- One or more columns
- Headers and footers

Reports and proposals are typically created with office laser printers and reproduced with copiers on one side of the paper. Your readers expect and prefer to see these documents on standard letter-size sheets. For these reasons, we have chosen a single-sided, one-column format. But, as you will see, we've improved on the basic letter-size document. We've made this proposal more readable by shortening the line length. We've made it more accessible by providing headings and page numbers. And we've made it more attractive by using graphic devices and typestyles that work together.

If you were planning this proposal on your own, you'd be smart to create a thumbnail sketch. As explained in Chapter 2, "Starting Out Smart," a sketch lets you experiment on paper quickly. That way you don't waste time in Ventura. In this case, the reduced view picture of the document in Figure 18-2 can act as our thumbnail.

Figure 18-2. We'll use this picture of the screen as our thumbnail.

Loading the files

Now that you have your plans laid out, it's just a matter of beginning construction from the ground up. Start Ventura, load the files you want to use, and begin building the chapter. The order that you load your files doesn't really matter. In this section, we'll use the following procedure:

- Load and rename the style sheet
- Load, place, and rename the text files
- Rename the picture file
- Load the picture files
- Save the chapter

If you were working from your own files, you would already have named them the way you wanted them, preferably according to a company-wide system. In this case, we'll use files that came with Ventura, so we'll rename them as we go along. It's good practice anyway. Out in the real world, authors and contributors often submit files with all sorts of crazy names, forcing you to rename them to make sense of things.

Let's create a simple file-naming system now. Let's assume that all proposals get the two-letter prefix PR, and that we do one proposal each month. Table 18-1 shows what we might end up with.

Table 18-1. *Names for the proposal files*

Type of file	Name of file
Chapter file for December's proposal	PR12.CHP
ASCII text file for December's proposal	PR12.TXT
GEM graphics file of a nozzle for December's proposal	PR12NOZZ.GEM
Style sheet (reused for all proposals)	PR.STY

For more information on naming and managing files, see Chapter 16, "Managing Ventura Files."

Load and rename the style sheet

We've determined that the Ventura example chapter &PRPT-P1.CHP is the best match. It has the basic single-column look we're after. Let's get going.

1. Start Ventura (or clear the current chapter by choosing New from the File menu).

2. Choose Load Diff. Style from the File menu and use the Item Selector to load the &PRPT-P1.STY from the \TYPESET directory (Figure 18-3).

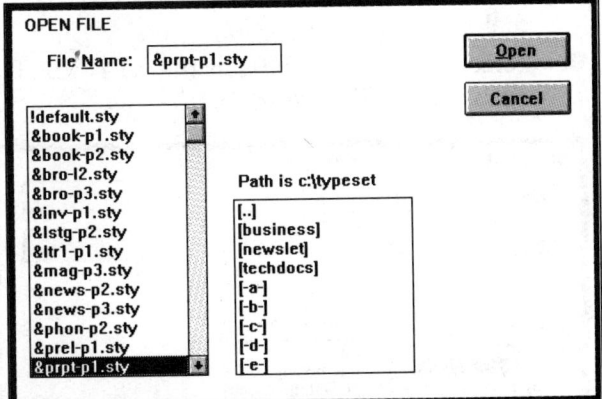

Figure 18-3. Load the style sheet as the starting point for your proposal.

Note: This style sheet should be found in the \TYPESET directory that was created during installation. If you can't find it there, copy the &PRPT-P1.STY and REPORT.TXT from the \EXAMPLES directory of Disk 2 that comes with Ventura to the \TYPESET directory.

To prevent overwriting the original, you must save the style sheet that you have just loaded before making any changes.

3. Choose Save Style As from the File menu. The Save File As dialog box appears with *.STY highlighted in the File Name text box.

4. To create the new name, simply type the new filename (up to eight characters). We chose PR.STY.

5. Click on the Save button to execute the command.

For more information on loading style sheets, see Chapter 3, "Building Basic Styles." For more information on copying chapters, see Chapter 16, "Managing Ventura Files."

Load, place, and rename the text file

Now you can load the text file you plan to use. If you follow the steps we explain below, you can place it on the page at the same time you load it.

6. Using the Frame Tool, click once on the workspace to select the underlying page.

7. Choose Load Text/Picture from the File menu. The Load Text/Picture dialog box appears.

8. Select Text for the File Type, ASCII for the Format, and List Of Files for the Destination. Then click on OK. The Open File dialog box appears.

9. Select REPORT.TXT from the \TYPESET directory, and then click on OK (Figure 18-4).

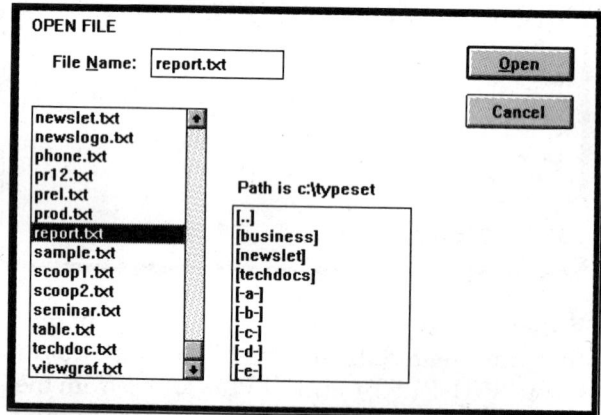

Figure 18-4. Next you load the text file.

The text appears on the page and the filename appears in the File List Window. (If the text doesn't appear on the page, click once on the page with the Frame Tool, then click once on the filename in the File List Window.) Now you should rename the text file to match our naming system.

10. With the page and the sample file still selected, choose File Type/Rename from the Frame menu. The File Type/Rename dialog box appears.

11. Place the cursor in the New Name text box. Delete the current name and type in the new name: PR12.TXT. Then click on OK.

For more information on loading and renaming text files in Ventura, see Chapter 6, "Handling Text in Ventura."

Rename the picture file

Before loading the last file you'll need, the example picture file called NOZZLE.GEM, we'll give you some practice in using a consistent naming system, and in using Windows to supplement Ventura. You'll make a copy of the file and rename it *before* loading it into Ventura.

12. Switch to Windows' File Manager. Use it to make a copy of the graphics file NOZZLE.GEM in the \TYPESET directory, but name the copy PR12NOZZ.GEM.

Load the picture file

You're now ready to load the picture file in Ventura.

13. Return to Ventura. Use Load Text/Picture from the File menu to load PR12NOZZ.GEM. (Hint: Choose File Type: Line Art and Format: GEM.)

The filename PR12NOZZ.GEM appears in the File List Window.

Save the chapter

Save the chapter before going on.

14. Choose Save As from the File menu to save the chapter in the \TYPESET directory with the name PR12.CHP.

Tip: Periodically during the rest of this tutorial, you should use the keyboard shortcut Ctrl-S to save what you've done up to that time.

Setting up the underlying page

With the files loaded, you have the raw material to build your foundation—the underlying page. To do this, you follow three basic steps:

- Make the page settings
- Set the margins and columns
- Create the footers

In other words, you will build the basic framework for the entire document. All the tools you need are in the Chapter and Frame menus.

Make the page settings

First, be sure the underlying page has the correct basic structure.

15. Choose Page Size & Layout from the Chapter menu. The Page Layout dialog box appears. Select Portrait for the Orientation, Letter for the Paper Type & Dimension, Single for the Sides, and Right Side for Start On (Figure 18-5). Then click on OK.

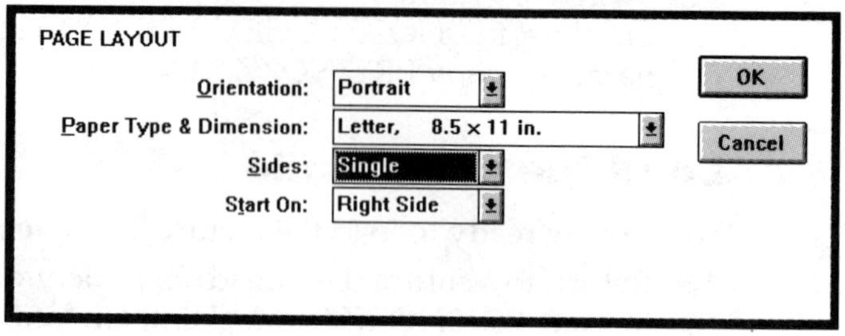

Figure 18-5.
Setting the layout and orientation of the underlying page.

Set the margins and columns

The example style sheet you loaded as your starting point already had the margins and columns set. You'll change those settings to make your proposal more readable by increasing white space and decreasing the line length. You'll also enlarge the left margin so you can bind the report along the left side.

16. Using the Frame Tool, select the underlying page, and choose Margins & Columns from the Frame menu. Click on the measurement button until it displays Inches. Select 1 for the # Of Columns, Right Page for the Settings For, and the following margin settings (in inches) for the Margins: Top, Bottom, and Right: 1.25, Left: 1.50 (Figure 18-6). Then click on OK.

Create the footers

Later, you'll change the format of the footer text, but for now just be sure that the footer frame is in place and shows what you want.

17. Select Headers & Footers from the Chapter menu. Select the Right Page Footer button from the Define buttons. Select the On button from the Usage buttons.

So far you've turned on the footer feature. Now make the document easier to reference by putting the main headings into the footer. That way readers can scan the bottom of the page to see what section they are in.

Figure 18-6.
Setting the margins and columns for the report.

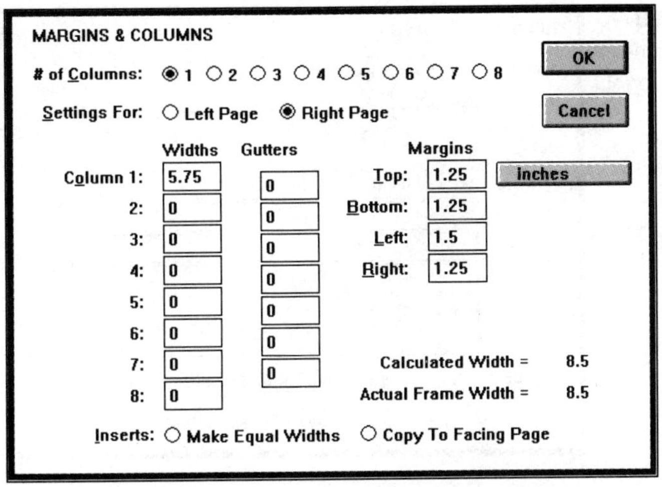

[Dialog box: MARGINS & COLUMNS
# of Columns: ● 1 ○ 2 ○ 3 ○ 4 ○ 5 ○ 6 ○ 7 ○ 8
Settings For: ○ Left Page ● Right Page
Widths | Gutters | Margins
Column 1: 5.75 | 0 | Top: 1.25 — Inches
2: 0 | 0 | Bottom: 1.25
3: 0 | 0 | Left: 1.5
4: 0 | 0 | Right: 1.25
5: 0 | 0
6: 0 | 0
7: 0 | 0 | Calculated Width = 8.5
8: 0 | | Actual Frame Width = 8.5
Inserts: ○ Make Equal Widths ○ Copy To Facing Page
OK / Cancel]

18. Place the cursor in the Left text box and click on the 1st Match button. The code [<Tag Name] appears in the text box.

Ventura places a code onto the line. You will replace this code with the actual name of the tag for the main headings. That way Ventura will look at each page, find that tag, and insert the current main heading into the footer.

19. Delete the words "Tag Name" from inside the square brackets and type in the words "Head level 1."

Now add a page number:

20. In the Right text box, type "Page" and a space.

21. Select the Page # button from the Inserts buttons.

The Page # button inserts the Ventura code [P#], which displays and prints the correct page number. Your dialog box should resemble Figure 18-7.

22. Click on OK.

For more information on headers and footers, see Chapter 4, "Building the Underlying Page."

Applying and refining the style sheet

With the basic foundation in place, you can now flesh out the details with the Paragraph Tool. Because you loaded a pretagged text file and a predesigned style sheet, the text is already formatted.

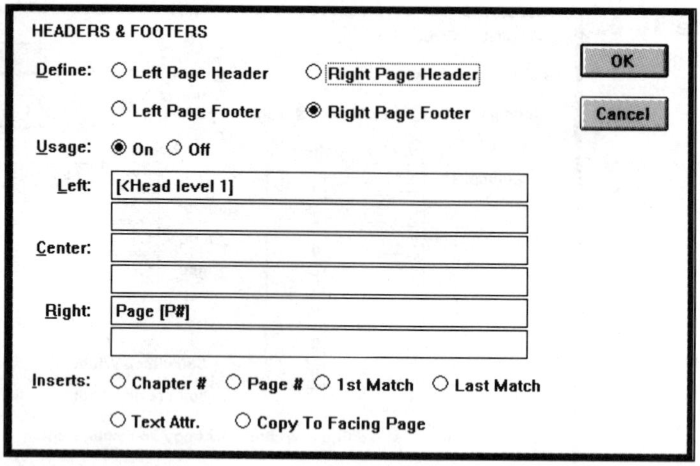

Figure 18-7.
Creating the footers for the proposal.

```
HEADERS & FOOTERS
Define:  ○ Left Page Header    ● Right Page Header     [ OK ]
         ○ Left Page Footer    ● Right Page Footer     [ Cancel ]
Usage:   ● On  ○ Off
Left:    [<Head level 1]
         
Center:  
         
Right:   Page [P#]
         
Inserts: ○ Chapter #  ○ Page #  ○ 1st Match  ○ Last Match
         ○ Text Attr.  ○ Copy To Facing Page
```

You don't have to apply the style sheet, you just have to refine it so it looks the way you want it.

You'll change the appearance by fine-tuning the body text and the bullet lists. Then you'll spruce up the title, and the headers and footers. And finally, you'll make some minor adjustments so that all the elements fit together elegantly.

Define the body text

Currently, the Body Text tag has full-column spacing with 12 point Times Roman type (called Dutch if you are working with a Hewlett-Packard LaserJet or compatible printer). You'll make your proposal more readable with these adjustments:

- Shorten the line length. You apply this design principle by indenting all body text with a "temporary" margin. This gives you more white space. It also makes the headings easier to find, because they project out into this white space.

- Change the text alignment from justified to left aligned (ragged right margins) to create uniform spacing between words.

Tip: The easiest way to work with Ventura is to march in order down the Paragraph menu. That way you don't have to worry that you've overlooked any key attributes.

Note: For the rest of this chapter, we will be referring to the Times Roman and Helvetica typefaces. If you are working with an HP or compatible printer, substitute Dutch for Times Roman and Swiss for Helvetica.

Now let's get to work:

23. Using the Paragraph Tool, select any paragraph of Body Text.

24. Choose Font from the Paragraph menu. Confirm that Body Text is set for 12-point Times Roman Normal. If it is not, change it now and click on OK.

25. With Body Text still selected, choose Alignment from the Paragraph menu. Then select Left from the Horz. Alignment list box. Click on OK.

26. Choose Spacing from the Paragraph menu. Set Above to 14 points, Inter-Line to 14 points, Inter-Paragraph to 0, and In From Left to 10 picas & points. Your dialog box should resemble Figure 18-8. When you're done, click on OK.

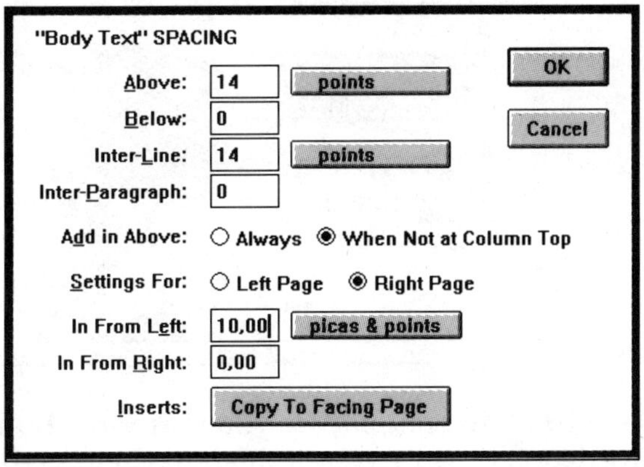

Figure 18-8.
Change the spacing commands for Body Text.

These settings (12-point type with 14 points of leading and 14 points of space between paragraphs) give your document an open spacious look.

For more information on applying and changing tags, see Chapter 3, "Building Basic Styles."

Change the bullet tag

Now follow the same basic procedures to improve the Bullet tag.

27. With the Paragraph Tool, select any bullet paragraph. Then check the Font, Alignment, and Spacing dialog boxes in turn from the Paragraph menu to make the following settings:

- Font dialog box—12-point Times Roman normal
- Alignment dialog box—Horz. Alignment: Left

■ Spacing dialog box—Above: 7 points, Below: 7 points, Inter-Line: 14 points, Inter-Paragraph: 0 points, In From Left: 10 picas.

When you've finished changing the Body Text and Bullet tags, your page should look something like Figure 18-9.

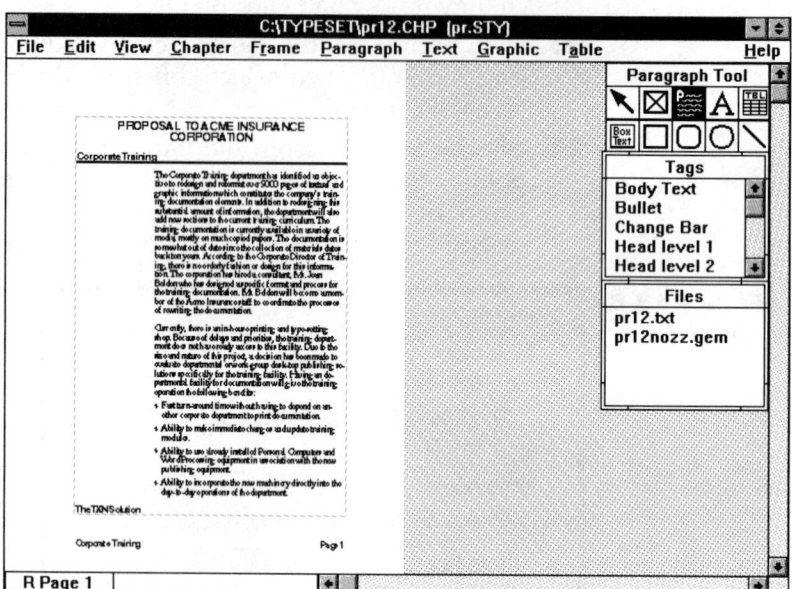

Figure 18-9.
Your page should look like this after setting the underlying page and changing the Body Text and Bullet tags.

Tip: Notice how the spacing you set for the Bullet tag makes it sit a a little closer to the paragraph above than to the paragraph below. This is a good technique for any kind of bullet or numbered list. It makes the list look as if it belongs to the preceding paragraph.

For more information on creating bulleted lists, see Chapter 5, "Building Advanced Styles."

Redesign the title and subtitle

Now you're ready to improve the title. Here's how:

28. If you can't see the paragraph symbols that end each paragraph, choose Show Tabs & Returns from the View menu.

29. Using the Text Tool, place the text cursor just before the paragraph symbol that ends the title. Backspace to delete the words and spaces "TO ACME INSURANCE CORPORATION" so the title contains only the word "PROPOSAL." Press Enter.

30. On the line you just created, type "From TXN Corporation."

Now you can make some eye-catching changes to the title and subtitle. More than that, you can establish a graphic signature, a device you can repeat elsewhere to give the proposal a unified look. In this case, we will use ruling lines.

31. With the Paragraph Tool, select the title ("PROPOSAL"). Confirm that it is tagged as Title.

32. Choose Font from the Paragraph menu. Make the title 24-point Helvetica Bold and click on OK.

33. Choose Alignment from the Paragraph menu. Set Horz. Alignment to Center and click on OK.

34. Choose Spacing from the Paragraph menu. Use these settings: Above: 9,00 picas & points (1.5 inches), Below: 0, Inter-Line: 24 points, Inter-Paragraph: 0, Add in Above: Always, In From Left and Right: 0. Then click on OK.

35. Choose Paragraph Typography from the Paragraph menu. Set the Tracking to Looser: 1.2 Ems. This step puts space between the letters for a custom look. Then click on OK.

36. Choose Ruling Line Above from the Paragraph menu. Give the tag a 10-point, frame-wide, black ruling line above. Then click on OK.

This step gives the title a signature graphic look that we'll echo later for the proposal's headings.

Now format the subtitle you just typed in.

37. With the Paragraph Tool, select the paragraph "From TXN Corporation."

38. Use the Add New Tag command from the Paragraph menu to create a tag called "Subtitle."

39. Choose Font from the Paragraph menu. Set the Font to 14-point Helvetica Bold and click on OK.

40. Choose Alignment from the Paragraph menu. Set the Horz. Alignment to Center and the Vert. Alignment to Bottom. Setting the vertical alignment to the bottom of the page forces the rest of the text to the next page, creating a standalone title page. When you're done, click on OK.

41. Choose Spacing from the Paragraph menu. Set the Spacing to Above: 0, Below: 0, Inter-Line: 14 points, Inter-Paragraph: 0, Add in Above: When Not At Column Top, In From Left and Right: 0. Then click on OK.

42. Choose Paragraph Typography from the Paragraph menu. Set the Tracking to Looser: 0.9 Ems and click on OK.

43. Because you copied the Subtitle tag from the Title tag, you need to remove the line. Choose Ruling Line Above from the Paragraph menu and set Width to None. Click on OK.

44. Choose Ruling Line Below from the Paragraph menu. Apply a 1-point, frame-wide, black ruling line below. Click on OK.

Once again, you've put space between the letters for an attractive look and added a ruling line. At this point, your page should look similar to Figure 18-10.

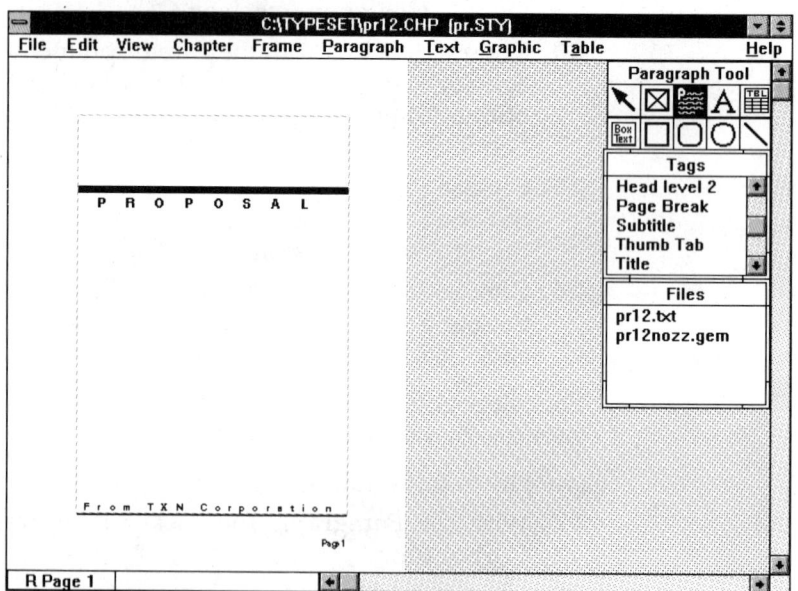

Figure 18-10. Your document after creating the title page.

For more information on creating new tags, see Chapter 3, "Building Basic Styles."

Modify the footer

As noted earlier, specifying footers is not enough. You have to refine the footer's tag. Here's how:

45. While you are still on the Title page, turn off the unneeded footer there by choosing Show Page Footer from the Chapter menu (so that the check mark is no longer visible).

46. Press Page Down to move to page 2.

47. Use the Paragraph Tool to select the footer.

48. Choose Font from the Paragraph menu. Make the footer 9-point Helvetica N-Italic. Then click on OK.

49. Choose Spacing from the Paragraph menu. Set Above: 0, Below: 0, Inter-Line: 11 points, Inter-Paragraph: 0, and In From Left: 10,00 Picas & Points. Then click on OK.

50. Choose Ruling Line Above from the Paragraph menu. Give the footer a 1-point, text-wide, black ruling line. Click on OK.

The footer should now resemble the one shown in Figure 18-11.

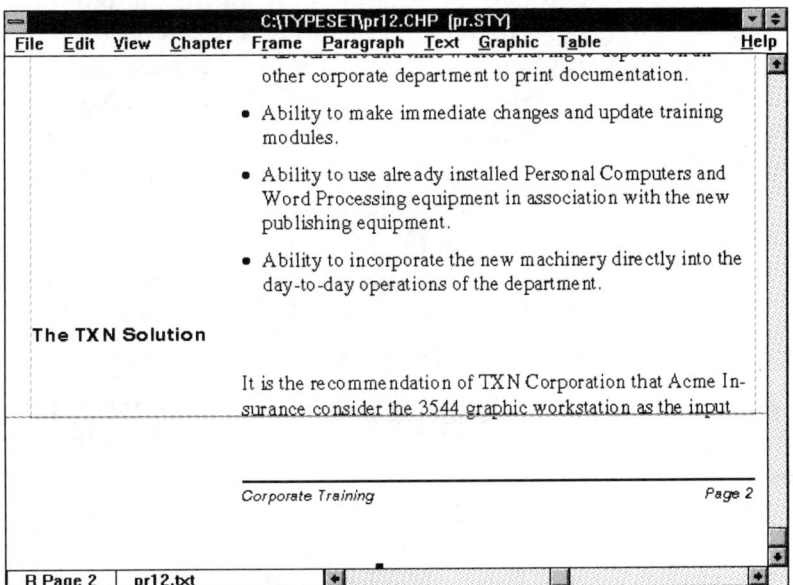

Figure 18-11. The correctly formatted footer. Because the ruling line is text-wide instead of frame-wide, it doesn't extend all the way to the left margin.

Format the headings

Now let's change the two headings so they match the graphic style we established on the title page.

51. Using the Paragraph Tool, select the Head level 1 paragraph ("Corporate Training").

52. Choose Font from the Paragraph menu. Make the tag 18-point Helvetica Bold. Click on OK.

53. Choose Alignment from the Paragraph menu. Be sure Horz. Alignment is set to Left. Click on OK.

54. Choose Spacing from the Paragraph menu. Set Above: 42 points, Inter-Line: 21 points, and Add in Above: When Not At Column Top. Click on OK.

55. Choose Ruling Line Above from the Paragraph menu. Create a frame-wide, 10-point ruling line and click on OK.
56. Choose Ruling Line Below from the Paragraph menu. Set Width to None and click on OK.
57. With the Paragraph Tool still active, select the Head level 2 paragraph ("The TXN Solution").
58. Choose Font from the Paragraph menu. Make this tag 14-point Helvetica Bold. Click on OK.
59. Choose Alignment from the Paragraph menu. Be sure Horz. Alignment is set to Left. Click on OK.
60. Choose Spacing from the Paragraph menu. Set Above: 28 points, Inter-Line: 14 points, and Add in Above: When Not At Column Top. Click on OK.
61. Choose Ruling Line Above from the Paragraph menu. Create a frame-wide, 1-point ruling line and click on OK.
62. Choose Breaks from the Paragraph menu. Select Keep With Next: Yes. This will prevent the Head Level 2 paragraph from being stranded at the bottom of a page.

Your second page should now resemble Figure 18-12.

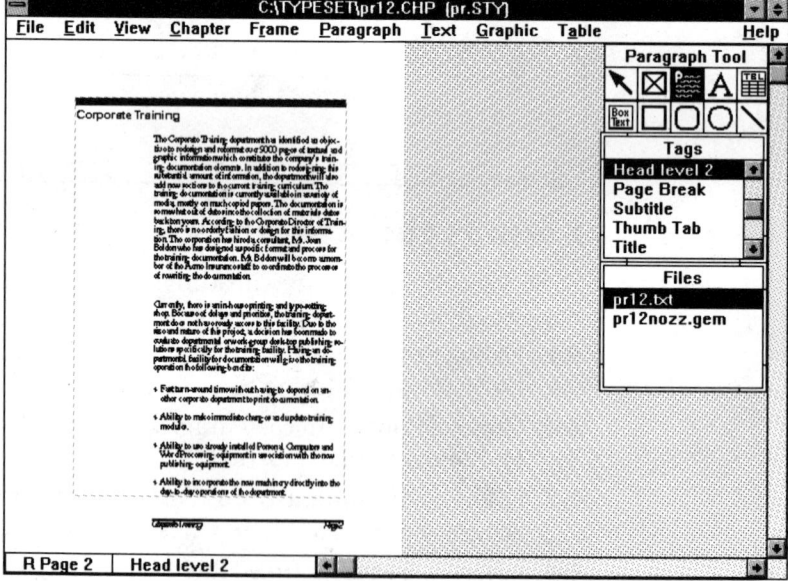

Figure 18-12. The second page should look similar to this after refining the style sheet.

Adding pictures

Now it's time to add a picture. First, you'll draw, size, pad, and position a frame on the second page. Next, you'll place the picture and add a caption.

Draw the frame

Filling in dialog boxes and clicking on menu options—though simple and intuitive—do not provide the tactile pleasure of drawing and sizing objects by hand. Drawing a frame is done much quicker by hand. After you've got an approximation on the page, you can fine-tune the frame with the Sizing & Scaling dialog box.

63. Press Page Down to move to page 3.

64. If you have not already done so, choose Reduced View from the View menu. While you're in the View menu, be sure that Show Column Guides and Column Snap are active (indicated by check marks).

65. Select the Add Frame tool and position the cursor about three-fourths of the way down the page. Now drag the cursor diagonally down to the right. Release the button when you reach the bottom right corner of the column.

66. With the new frame still selected, choose Sizing & Scaling from the Frame menu. Make the frame 25,00 picas & points wide and 14,00 picas & points high. Give the frame 1,02 picas & points of vertical padding. Then click on OK.

67. Choose Ruling Box Around from the Frame menu. Add a black hairline ruling box around the frame and click on OK.

68. If necessary, drag the frame until it sits in the lower right corner of the column as shown in Figure 18-13.

Place the picture

Now you are ready to put the picture inside the frame.

69. Using the Frame Tool, select the frame. Then click on the filename PR12NOZZ.GEM in the File List Window.

For more information on loading and placing pictures, see Chapter 11, "Loading and Placing Pictures."

Figure 18-13.
Drawing a frame on the third page.

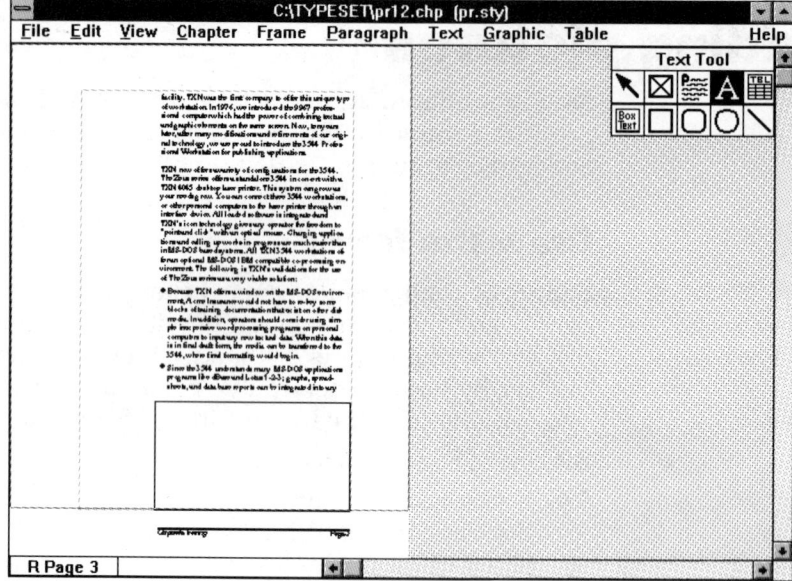

Add a caption

It's time to create a caption frame for this picture. Here's how:

70. With the frame still selected, choose Anchors & Captions from the Frame menu. Select Left from the Caption list box and click on OK.

When you return to the workspace, you'll find a newly created caption frame on the left side of the picture frame.

Tip: If you get tired of waiting for the nozzle picture to redraw each time you make a change, select the frame and choose Hide This Picture from the View menu.

71. Grab the left center handle of the caption frame and resize it until the caption frame is flush with the left column guide.

Inside the caption frame is an end-of-file symbol (hollow box). This area is reserved for the caption text that you type in. If you click the Text Tool on this spot, you'll notice the Z_CAPTION tag is highlighted in the Tag List. The attributes of this default tag will be immediately apparent when you type a caption.

72. Using the Text Tool, place the text cursor immediately to the left of the end-of-file symbol.

73. Type in the following caption text:

```
A technical drawing of the ACME nozzle created
with the 3544 graphic workstation.
```

74. Using the Paragraph Tool, select the caption paragraph. Use the commands on the Paragraph menu to make the font 9-point Helvetica N-Italic, flush left, with 11-point Inter-Line spacing. Set the first line indent to 0 in the Alignment dialog box. The result should resemble Figure 18-14.

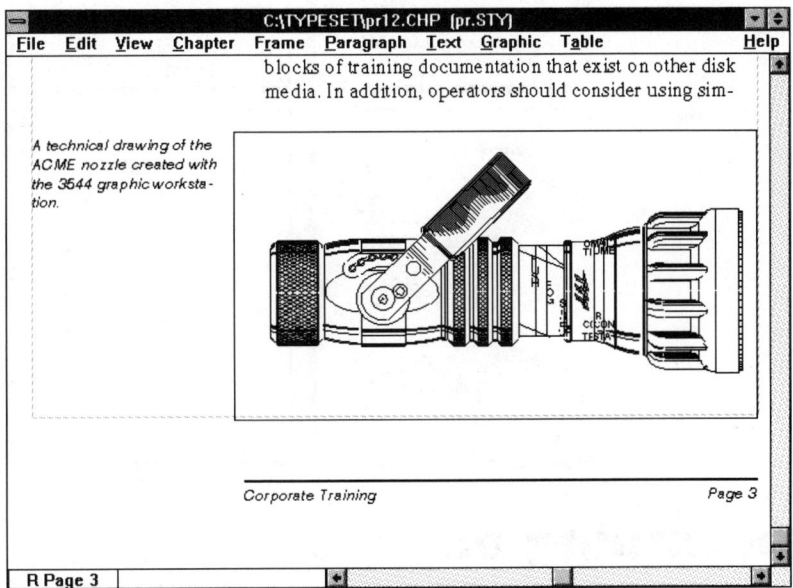

Figure 18-14.
The completed caption.

For more information on enhancing pictures, see Chapter 12, "Enhancing and Editing Pictures."

Printing the proposal

Save your work and try printing the proposal out now to see how you did.

75. Choose Print from the File menu. Print all the pages.

Your final result should resemble Figure 18-15.

For more information on printing, see Chapter 13, "Printing Ventura Documents."

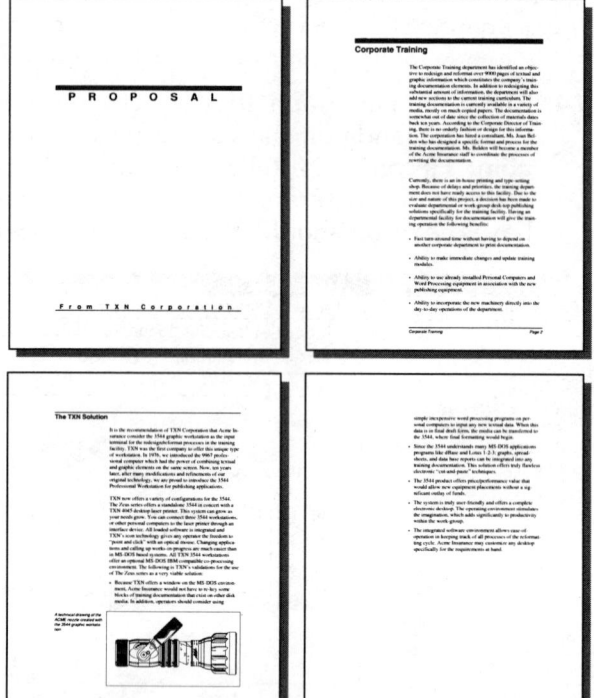

Figure 18-15.
The finished proposal.

Continuing on

This chapter has walked you through the essential steps to creating a handsome business proposal. If you've got extra time, you can advance your Ventura skills even further by using this proposal as the jumping off point for further experimentation. Collect good-looking documents and borrow the effects you like. To see samples from professional designers, see Chapter 20, "Portfolio."

Naturally, business documents are only one of the many kinds of publications you can produce with Ventura. In the next chapter, you'll get some hands-on experience in creating another useful project—a newsletter.

Easy Access

For more info on...	See chapter...
Sampling Ventura's fundamental techniques and procedures	2 — Starting Out Smart
Mastering the fundamentals of style sheets and tags	3 — Building Basic Styles
Loading and renaming text files in Ventura	6 — Handling Text in Ventura
Loading and placing picture files into Ventura	11 — Loading and Placing Pictures
Printing your business report	13 — Printing Ventura Documents

19 Building a Newsletter

How to build a three-column newsletter

- **Planning the newsletter** 564
- **Loading the base document** 565
- **Setting up the underlying page and text frames** 567
- **Loading text** 577
- **Refining the style sheet** 578
- **Loading and adjusting pictures** 587
- **Copyfitting and final touch-ups** 593
- **Continuing on** 598

The newsletter is second only to reports as the most common desktop published document. In this chapter, you'll create the most popular and versatile format, the three-column newsletter. We'll spend much of our time on issues specific to newsletters, such as jumping text files from frame to frame, creating a table of contents, and arranging pictures on the page.

We'll also show you how to combine the underlying page with frames to create a versatile template that you can use again and again for each issue of a newsletter. Instead of filling each column on the underlying page, we'll use a popular variation: a two-column frame for the text and a companion column for supplementary items. In addition to providing space for pictures and short items, the companion column adds white space and lends a clean, airy look to the design.

Ordinarily, you'd set up your underlying page first and create frames for pictures last. But because this newsletter will use text frames as well as picture frames, it makes sense to treat the frames as part of the underlying structure. Our general procedure will be similar to the one we used for the business proposal in the last chapter. Here are the steps:

1. Plan the document.
2. Load a template or base document.
3. Format the underlying page and frames.
4. Load text.
5. Refine the style sheet.
6. Load and adjust pictures.
7. Make final copyfitting adjustments.

Now roll up your shirt-sleeves. We're going to lead you through all the steps that professional designers go through when creating a real-life newsletter.

Planning the newsletter

If you prefer, you can jump straight to the hands-on practice that follows. But to know how and why we made our design decisions, read this section.

First, you must identify who the target audience is and how the newsletter will be distributed. This information affects all your other decisions. For example, a newsletter intended for children will probably use more white space and graphics than an internal newsletter at an accounting agency. Similarly, if you distribute your newsletter by mail, size and weight will affect your distribution costs.

For this tutorial, assume that you are producing a corporate newsletter for a manufacturer of "widgets." It will be produced on a laser printer and then photocopied or printed for in-house distribution.

Knowing this, you can make some initial decisions about the underlying page. For this tutorial, you'll use a double-sided 8.5 x 11-inch format. This size is easy to print on a laser printer and easy to reproduce by photocopying or printing four pages onto a 11 x 17-inch signature sheet and then folding each signature. We've also chosen a dignified but attractive corporate design:

- An eye-catching nameplate that features the company logo and establishes the corporate identity
- Two text columns and one companion column (divided by vertical rules) to provide striking asymmetry and page-to-page variation
- Margins that create needed white space around dense text
- Serif body type and sans serif headings that follow a proven formula for readable body type with attention-grabbing headings
- Newsletter design elements such as a logo, a banner, a table of contents, a masthead, pictures, captions, pull quotes, and jump line text that aid readers while adding to page-to-page variety

Your first task is to construct a thumbnail sketch of your newsletter to guide you in developing the final format. Such a sketch will give you a goal to shoot for. In this case, we want the finished product to resemble the one in Figure 19-1. (In real life, of course, you'd start with a hasty sketch.)

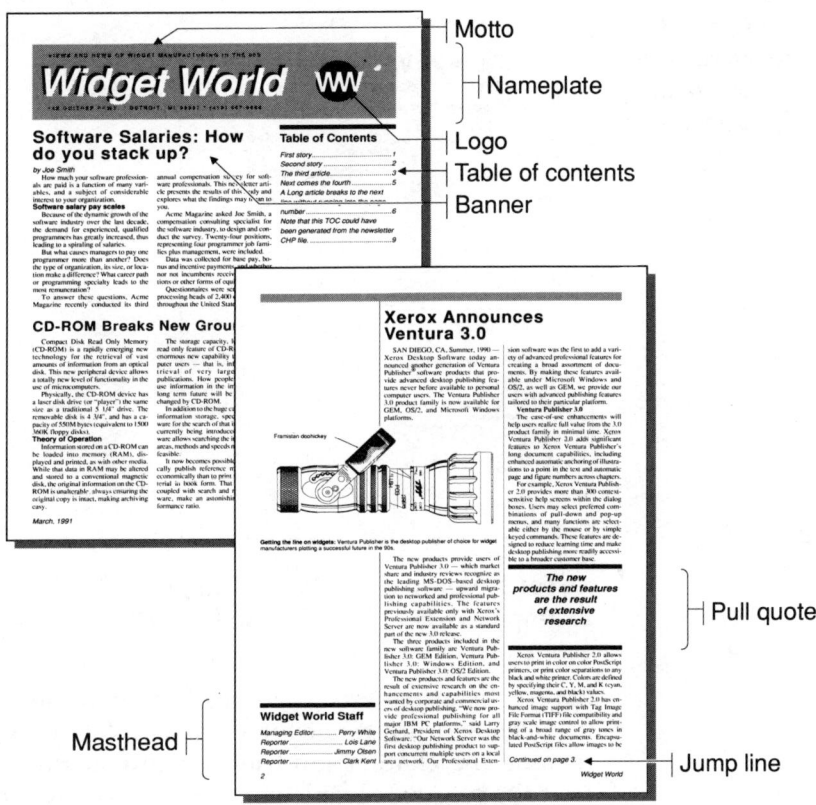

Figure 19-1.
The newsletter you construct in this chapter will contain all the major newsletter elements.

Flabbergasted by newsletter terminology? You're not alone. Designers and editors use some of terms in Figure 19-1 interchangeably. To get a grasp on what these terms mean, see the nearby sidebar, "Newsletter terminology."

Loading the base document

The most efficient way to build a chapter is to use an existing chapter as a template and make modifications to it. For our newsletter, we have Ventura's three sample newsletter chapters available to us. Of the three, the &NEWS-P2.CHP offers the "best match" for our design criteria. It contains most of the page elements that we want; moreover, it loads text into frames rather than directly onto the underlying page (Figure 19-2).

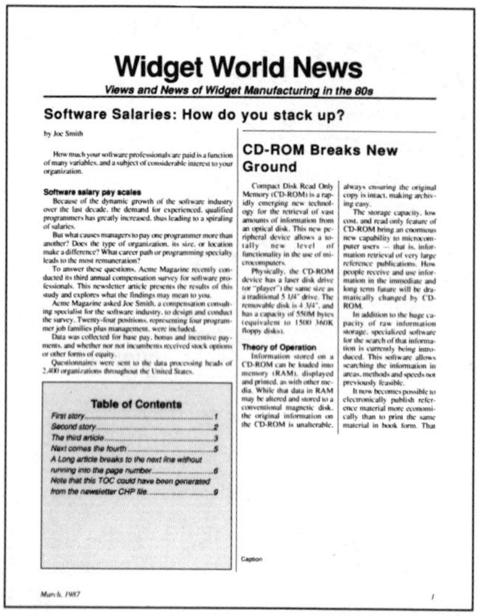

Widget World News

Views and News of Widget Manufacturing in the 80s

Software Salaries: How do you stack up?

by Joe Smith

How much your software professionals are paid is a function of many variables, and a subject of considerable interest to your organization.

Software salary pay scales

Because of the dynamic growth of the software industry over the last decade, the demand for experienced, qualified programmers has greatly increased, thus leading to a spiraling of salaries.

But what causes managers to pay one programmer more than another? Does the type of organization, its size, or location make a difference? What career path or programming specialty leads to the most remuneration?

To answer these questions, Acme Magazine recently conducted its third annual compensation survey for software professionals. This newsletter article presents the results of this study and explores what the findings may mean to you.

Acme Magazine asked Joe Smith, a compensation consulting specialist for the software industry, to design and conduct the survey. Twenty-four positions, representing four programmer job families plus management, were included.

Data was collected for base pay, bonus and incentive payments, and whether nor not incumbents received stock options or other forms of equity.

Questionnaires were sent to the data processing heads of 2,400 organizations throughout the United States.

Table of Contents

First story.....1
Second story.....2
The third article.....3
Next comes the fourth.....5
A Long article breaks to the next line without running into the page number.....6
Note that this TOC could have been generated from the newsletter CHP file.....9

CD-ROM Breaks New Ground

Compact Disk Read Only Memory (CD-ROM) is a rapidly emerging new technology for the retrieval of vast amounts of information from an optical disk. This new peripheral device allows a totally new level of functionality in the use of microcomputers.

Physically, the CD-ROM device has a laser disk drive (or "player") the same size as a traditional 5 1/4" drive. The removable disk is 4 3/4", and has a capacity of 550M bytes (equivalent to 1500 360K floppy disks).

Theory of Operation

Information stored on a CD-ROM can be loaded into memory (RAM), displayed and printed, as with other media. While that data in RAM may be altered and stored to a conventional magnetic disk, the original information on the CD-ROM is unalterable, always ensuring the original copy is intact, making archiving easy.

The storage capacity, low cost, and read only feature of CD-ROM bring an enormous new capability to microcomputer users — that is, information retrieval of very large reference publications. How people receive and use information in the immediate and long term future will be dramatically changed by CD-ROM.

In addition to the huge capacity of raw information storage, specialized software for the search of that information is currently being introduced. This software allows searching the information in areas, methods and speeds not previously feasible.

It now becomes possible to electronically publish reference material more economically than to print the same material in book form. That

Caption

March, 1987 1

Figure 19-2. This sample Ventura chapter will be our starting point.

Note: If you haven't copied the sample chapters from Ventura's Examples disk to the \TYPESET directory, you must do so now to create our newsletter.

Let's get started. First, you need to open the chapter you want to use as a starting point for your template (&NEWS-P2.CHP) and rename the chapter (and its constituent files) so that you won't alter the original sample chapter. Just follow these steps:

1. Choose Open Chapter from the File menu and load &NEWS-P2.CHP from the \TYPESET directory.
2. Choose Save Style As from the File menu. Save the style sheet (&NEWS-P2.STY) under the name MYNEWS.STY in the \TYPESET directory.
3. Using the Frame Tool, select the top frame, which contains the NEWSLOGO.TXT file. Choose File Type/Rename from the Frame menu. Rename and save the file as MYNLOGO.TXT in the \TYPESET directory. Keep the file format as ASCII.
4. Repeat the renaming procedure for the NEWSLET.TXT file (rename it as MYNEWS1.TXT) and the NEWSLTOC.GEN file (rename it as MYNTOC.GEN).
5. Choose Save As from the File menu to save the chapter with a unique, yet descriptive name such as MYNEWS.CHP in the \TYPESET directory.

Note: All of the sample files described above should be in the \TYPESET directory that was created when you installed Ventura. If you didn't install the examples or if you have erased them, you can copy the &NEWS-P2.CHP and SCOOP.CHP files (using the MS-DOS COPY command) to the \TYPESET directory.

For more information on managing files, see Chapter 16, "Managing Ventura Files." For more information on loading and saving style sheets and chapters, see Chapter 3, "Building Basic Styles" and Chapter 4, "Building the Underlying Page." For more information on loading and placing text files, see Chapter 6, "Handling Text in Ventura."

Setting up the underlying page and text frames

You need a foundation before you begin building a house. Likewise, you need a foundation for your newsletter before you add text, pictures, and other elements. In the previous section, you used one of Ventura's sample chapters as a starting point for our newsletter. Now you'll learn how to create a template chapter for our newsletter that contains elements that appear in every issue such as margin and column settings, ruling lines, headers, and text frames. You can use this template chapter as a starting point—instead of recreating all these elements for each issue of the newsletter. Here's what you'll be doing:

- Getting your bearings
- Laying a foundation
- Adding pages
- Setting up frames

Let's get started.

Getting your bearings

Before you start, take a look around. Using the Frame Tool, click on some of the frames that contain text on the first page. Notice the filename that appears in the Current Selection Box. The newsletter's top headline, first story, and second story are all one file threaded through several frames. By "threading," we mean that a file is loaded into multiple frames and the text continues from one frame to the next. This is a common way to load text into a newsletter. Sometimes it's the only way to place multiple stories and pictures on a single page. But you should avoid having more frames on the page than necessary—they'll just get in the way.

So what's the first thing we do? Get rid of the extra frames:

6. Choose Reduced View from the View menu so that you can see the whole page.

Newsletter terminology

There's a lot of confusion about newsletter terminology. For instance, the words "nameplate," "logo," "banner," and "masthead" are often used interchangeably. We use these terms to describe separate elements, each serving a unique purpose. In alphabetic order, here are some key terms for newsletters you should know:

banner —a headline that stretches across more than one column.

dateline —a line on the front page identifying the date and volume number of the issue.

jump line —a short, descriptive phrase that directs readers within an article that jumps from column to column and page to page. Jump lines usually consist of phrases such as "continued on page #" and "continued from page #."

logo —a special design identifying a company. It optionally appears in a newsletter's nameplate.

masthead —a small box containing identifying information about the publisher, such as the address, the names of the editors, subscription information, legal disclaimers, and so on.

motto —the verbal equivalent of the logo. It is usually a short, catchy phrase that projects the company's identity.

nameplate —the large, identifying name of the newsletter. Often it appears at the top with the name of publication, the company logo, and a motto.

pull quote —an enlarged quotation from the body of an article, often set off by ruling lines or boxes. Also called a *teaser* or a *lift out*.

table of contents —(TOC) is a list of the newsletter's contents and the page numbers.

Tip: Throughout this chapter, we may occasionally prompt you to change views to help with your work. But you should also feel free to change views as often as necessary to help you build your newsletter. The same goes for the Show Tabs & Returns command on the View menu; it lets you see spaces, paragraph symbols (carriage returns), tab symbols, and end-of-file symbols. But sometimes these get in the way, so turn this option on and off as you please.

7. Using the Frame Tool, select and delete the banner headline frame (which says "Software Salaries: How do you stack up?") and the frame for the first story (which begins with "by Joe Smith").

The text from these frames flows into the remaining frame on the right. When you finish, the page should look similar to the one in Figure 19-3.

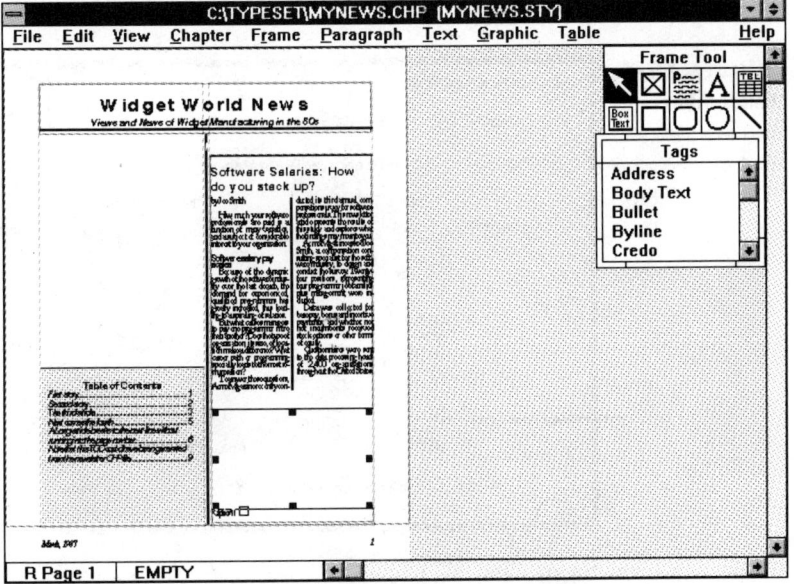

Figure 19-3. After deleting the banner and first story frames, your page should have frames for the nameplate, one story, the TOC, and an empty picture frame (bottom right).

Laying a foundation

Before you do any frame juggling, you need to set up your underlying page to match our design criteria. To create an underlying page, you have to establish the margins and columns, set ruling lines, and create headers. Because you're using a chapter with most of these elements already created for you, you'll only have to make a few modifications to them. Here's how.

Get a grid on things

The underlying page is an essential part of your *grid*—a framework that helps you arrange and align page elements. The margin and column settings for the underlying page can help you align elements on the page. You just turn on the Show Column Guides and Column Snap commands from the View menu to use the margin and column settings as a visual, snap-to guide for aligning frames and graphic elements. Start with the page's margins and columns.

8. Using the Frame Tool, select the underlying page and choose Margins & Columns from the Frame menu. Change # Of Columns to 3. Click on the measurement button until it changes to Picas & Points—the measuring system most designers use. The Margin settings should be 4,06 on the Top, Bottom, Left, and Right; and the Column Width should be 13,04 with Gutters of 1,00 pica. Your settings should match those in Figure 19-4. After you have everything set, select Copy To Facing Page at the bottom of the dialog box. Then click on OK.

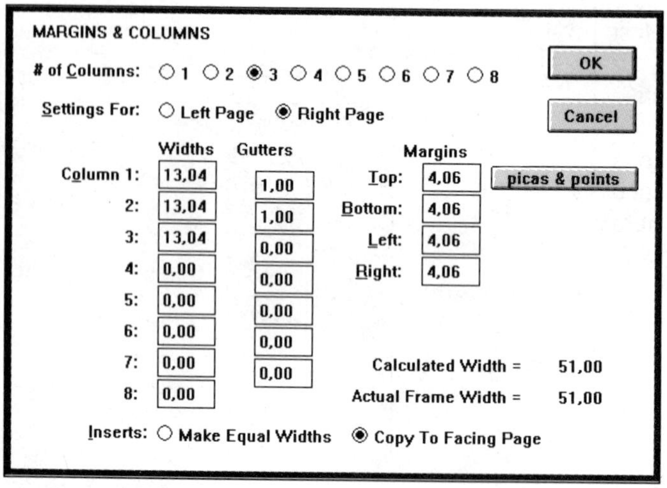

Figure 19-4.
Match these settings in the Margins & Columns dialog box.

Make the rules

Now let's fix the ruling lines that separate the columns. The Inter-Col. Rules option should already be On, but the width is a little coarse for our tastes.

9. Select the underlying page and choose Vertical Rules from the Frame menu. Click on the measurements button next to the Rule 1 Width text box until it changes to Points. (The top button controls measurements for position.) Change the width to 0.24 in the Width text box just above the top measurements button. Click on Copy To Facing Pages (so that both left and right pages have the same vertical rule settings) and then click on OK.

Header late than never

Fortunately, your chapter already has a footer to announce the date and page number, so you can just leave them alone for now. Remember that the thumbnail calls for a nameplate in a gray box—so you should make the headers for each page consistent with the nameplate to give your readers a sense of continuity. To do that, use a gray ruling line at the top of each page.

Tip: To make a ruling line at the top of each page, use Ventura's header feature, but create the line as part of the Z_HEADER tag. If you create a ruling line on the underlying page or even as part of the header frame, you'll have no control over its width—it'll be frame wide or nothing. On the other hand, the ruling line functions in the Paragraph menu let you determine the length of your ruling line.

10. Select the underlying page and choose Headers & Footers from the Chapter menu. Select Define: Left Page Header and Usage: On. Click on the Left text box and type a space (spacebar). That's all you need to create an invisible header for your ruling line tag. Select Copy To Facing Page and click on OK.

You now have a header frame at the top of your page, and in it you have a header paragraph consisting of a single space. Now create the ruling line:

11. Using the Paragraph Tool, select the header paragraph and choose Ruling Line Below from the Paragraph menu. The "Z_HEADER" Ruling Line Below dialog box appears. Select Width: Margin, Dimensions: Picas & Points, and Color: Black. For Pattern, scroll to the top of the box, and click on the fourth pattern from the top (count the empty pattern at the very top as the first).

12. Click on the User-Defined button. The User-Defined Ruling Style dialog box appears. In the Space Above Rule 1 text box, type 01,00. In the Height Of Rule 1 text box, type 01,00. Click on OK to close the dialog box. Then Click on OK again to return to the document.

One final step. Because the first page will boast a stunning nameplate, you don't need that header to compete with it.

13. Choose Show Page Header (which should now have a check mark to the left of it) from the Chapter menu to turn the header function off for the first page. Be sure that the Show Page Header command doesn't have a check mark next to it. This hides the header for the current page.

Note: Now you're cookin'—but play it safe! Choose Save from the File menu (or press Ctrl-S) to be sure you don't get burned. Do this after completing each major step, just in case you, the computer, or the electric company makes an unrecoverable error.

Adding pages

The basic page is complete. Now add more pages so the newsletter can grow:

14. Choose Insert/Remove Page from the Chapter menu. Select Insert New Page After Current Page, then click on OK.

Voila! You have a second page complete with your header, footer, columns, and rules similar to Figure 19-5.

15. Now repeat the process to add a third page.

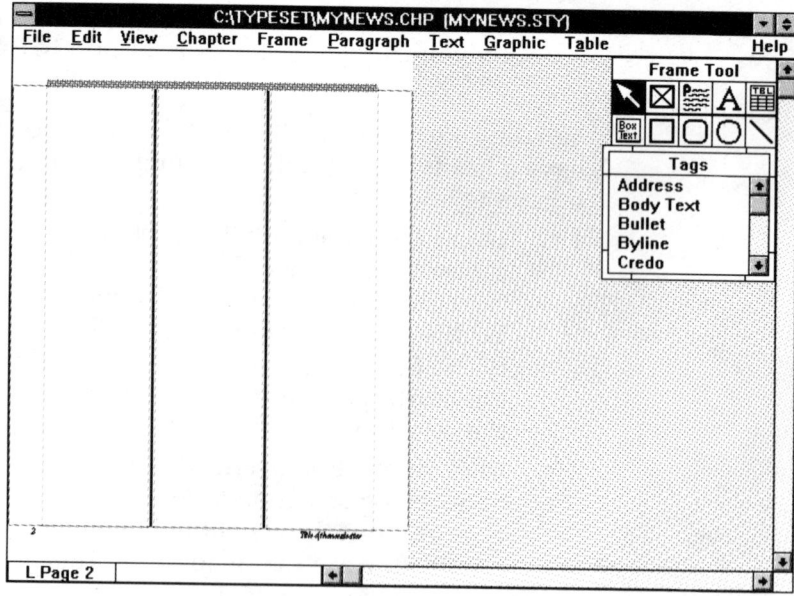

Figure 19-5. The new page you add will have the same characteristics as the underlying page.

Your underlying page is set up. Now all you have to do is turn it on so you can use it as a grid.

16. Pull down the View menu and be sure Column Snap, Line Snap, and Show Column Guides are checked. If you want to see horizontal and vertical measurements, choose Show Rulers from the View menu.

Setting up frames

Because your text and pictures will be placed into frames, frames are an important part of your grid. Fortunately, we already have several frames on the page, so let's adjust them so that they have the formats that we need.

Formatting frames

Let's start with the story frame:

17. If you have not already done so, press the Home key to return to the first page of the newsletter.

18. With the Frame Tool, select the frame with the "Software Salaries" story, and choose Margins & Columns from the Frame menu. Set all Margins to 0 and Gutters to 1,00 to match your underlying page. Don't worry about the column widths: those will change as you resize the frame. If the columns are currently different widths, click on the Make Equal Widths button. Be sure # Of Columns is 2. Then click on OK.

Tip: Generally speaking, you should keep the formatting of your text frames to a minimum. Instead, control the positioning of text within frames using tag formatting (not frame margins). Otherwise, if you later need to make a change, you'll have to adjust each frame in your document one by one.

Next come the rules. Make the inter-column rule match the ones on the underlying page:

19. With the "Software Salaries" frame still selected, choose Vertical Rules (Frame menu) and select Inter-Col. Rules: On. Click on the two measurements buttons until they both read Points, and set Width: 0.24. Click on Copy To Facing Page in the Vertical Rules dialog box. Otherwise, if you try to copy this frame to another page later, the inter-column rules might not show up. Then click on OK.

20. Finally, get rid of that top ruling line by choosing Ruling Line Above from the Frame menu and selecting Width: None. Click on OK.

That should do it for the story frame. Press Ctrl-S to save the changes you've just made. Now let's get a head start on your new nameplate. You'll do the text formatting when you work on the style sheet, but for now let's give the frame a tasteful, businesslike gray background:

21. Using the Frame Tool, select the nameplate frame and choose Frame Background from the Frame menu. Select Color: Black. For Pattern, select the fourth one from the top of the box. Click on OK.

Now, retouch the table of contents (TOC) frame. Because you have a gray background for the nameplate, you don't want a similar page element on the same page to compete with it. Here's how:

22. Using the Frame Tool, select the TOC frame and choose Frame Background from the Frame menu. For Pattern, select the top (empty) pattern and click on OK. The TOC frame should now have a white background.

One last change: Get rid of the box around the TOC:

23. Because its frame is still selected, all you have to do is choose Ruling Box Around from the Frame menu and select Width: None.

Sizing and positioning frames

Now for some practice in resizing and moving frames. You can change the size of a frame by dragging one of its sizing handles or by specifying values in the Sizing & Scaling dialog box. Try both methods.

For starters, resize the top frame containing the hideous nameplate, "Widget World News." You'll fix it later, but for now give yourself some breathing room:

24. Using the Frame Tool, select the nameplate frame and choose Sizing & Scaling from the Frame menu. Remember to set measurements to Picas & Points. Type 9,03 in the Frame Height text box. The Frame Width should already be okay—42,01 picas so that the nameplate frame will span all three columns.

Now resize the rest of the frames with some down-and-dirty dragging around:

25. Using the Frame Tool, select the frame with the "Software Salaries" story and drag it so its left side clings to the left page margin and its top edge touches the bottom of the nameplate frame.

Note: Did you activate Show Column Guides and Column Snap from the View menu? If not, do so now—so you can use the grid from the underlying page to align your frames quickly.

Next move the table of contents (TOC) frame out of the way:

26. Using the Frame Tool, select the TOC frame and drag it to the upper right corner of the page, flush with the right margin on the right, and just under the nameplate frame.

Now let's try the other method for resizing:

27. With the TOC frame still selected, shrink the frame so it fills only the right column by dragging one of the sizing handles on its left side.

28. Select the empty picture frame at the bottom of the page and resize it so that it also fits into the right column. Finally, select the story frame and drag it to fit the left two columns. Size it vertically as well, so its bottom edge touches the bottom margin of the underlying page.

29. Press Ctrl-S to save your work. When you're finished, your first page should resemble Figure 19-6.

Copying frames to other pages

You'll also need frames on the other pages of our newsletter. The easiest way to do that is just to "clone" the frames from the first page (with the exception of the nameplate frame). It's simple:

30. With the Frame Tool, select one of the three frames below the nameplate. Hold down the Shift key and select each of the other two frames so that all three frames have their sizing handles showing. Choose Copy Frame from the Edit menu (or use the shortcut, Shift-Delete). Move to page two by pressing the Page Down key. Choose Paste Frame from the Edit menu (or press the Insert key).

As you probably expected, the same three frames appear on page two. However, there's one thing that needs fixing. De-select the three frames (click on the underlying page) and select either the story frame or the TOC frame. You'll see the name of their text files

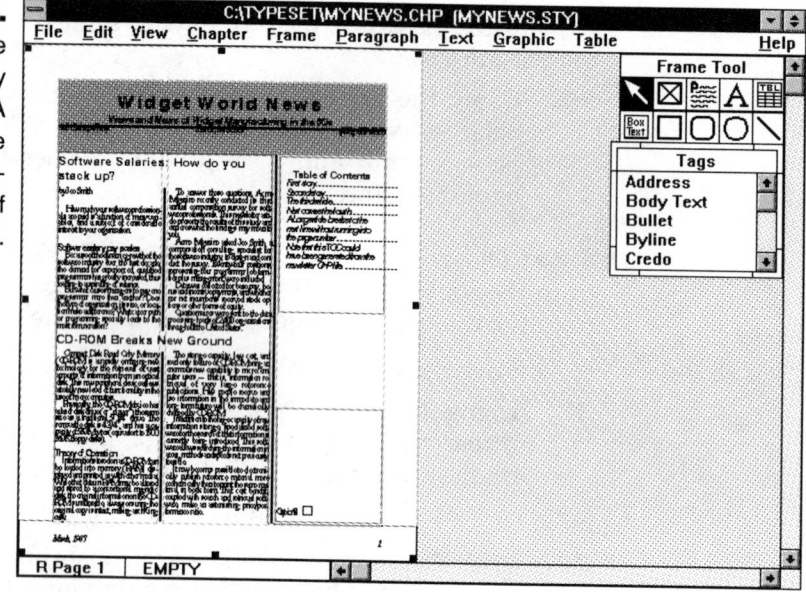

Figure 19-6.
Move and resize your frames so they look like this. A screen shot of the newsletter at the current stage of development.

in the Current Selection Box. That's to be expected. Ventura will thread a text file through as many "child" frames as you create by copying the "parent" frame—even if there's not enough text to fill them. You'll want to load new articles into each of these frames, so let's clean them out:

31. Select the two-column story frame and choose Remove Text/File from the Frame menu. Select Remove From: Frame. Then click on OK. The Current Selection Box should now read Empty.

32. Repeat the above procedure for the TOC frame. This little frame will be used for the masthead later on.

You still have some more moving and resizing to do. The current arrangement was fine for your first page. But because the finished newsletter will be two-sided, you'll want to place your companion column on the outside margin to create a symmetrical arrangement.

Tip: After you've moved your frames around, a smaller frame may get covered by a larger one and become hard to select. Just hold down the Ctrl key while you click on the frame. Ventura will then skip down to the next layer to select the frame.

33. Using the Frame Tool, move the masthead (formerly TOC) frame to the bottom of the left column. Move the empty story frame to the right two columns. Move the picture frame to the middle of the left column (we'll worry about it's exact position later). As a final touch, stretch the story frame vertically so it fills both right columns from top to bottom.

Now try page three on your own:

34. Copy the story frame from page two, paste it on page three, and move it to the left two columns to keep your companion column on the outside margin. Now press Ctrl-S to save your work.

Hey, this baby is really starting to take shape! You've completely formatted your underlying page and all the frames you'll need for stories, masthead, TOC, and even pictures. Now let's add some more words.

Loading text

Things are looking good. So far, you've created a format that can serve as a template for a future newsletter. Now let's do something about those empty frames:

35. Press Page Up to go to page two. Using the Frame Tool, select the big story frame.

36. Choose Load Text/File from the File menu. Select File Type: Text, Format: ASCII, and Destination: List Of Files. Click on OK. Navigate to the \TYPESET directory and click on the SCOOP1.TXT text file. Then click on Open.

37. With this frame still selected, choose File Type/Rename from the Frame menu and rename it MYNEWS2.TXT. Click on OK.

You're all done loading text files (easy, wasn't it?). For a larger publication, you would load your text files into the File List all at once and then place them into individual frames later.

Loading files isn't the only way to add text: you can also type in text during layout. For example, the text for the masthead is short enough to type directly into the frame:

38. Using the Text Tool, place the text cursor in the small frame on the lower left of page two. Type in the title: Widget World Staff and press Enter. On the next four lines, type in the job title and name for each member of your small staff. Separate the job title and name with a single tab. In the example below, the arrow and paragraph symbols represent tabs and carriage returns, respectively.

Note: If you want to be able to see carriage returns and tabs in Ventura, be sure Show Tabs & Returns is checked in the View menu. While you're using the View menu, you may also wish to change to Normal or Enlarged view to check your typing.

```
Widget World Staff¶
Managing Editor→Perry White¶
Reporter→Clark Kent¶
Reporter→Lois Lane¶
Photographer→Jimmy Olsen¶
```

After you type in your masthead, all that remains is some tag touch-ups. That's next.

Refining the style sheet

It's much easier to change a style sheet that's already close to what you have in mind than to start from scratch. From here on, you just look at all the possibilities and choose the formats that fit your needs. In this section, you'll refine the style sheet, which will complete most of your formatting work.

The good news is that for our purposes some of the tags from the original style sheet can stay the same. For instance, the Body Text tag can remain the same because it has the conservative format that we want for this newsletter.

The bad news is that you'll have to modify most of the tags to get just the right look. But it's not hard. You simply use the Paragraph Tool to select the paragraph that contains the tag you want to change and then use the Paragraph menu to make your changes. It's easy. Let's start out with the tags that need only a little tinkering.

Subhead tag

Helvetica Bold subheads provide an attractive contrast to the body text: they grab your attention but still fit the conservative tone of your newsletter. Fortunately, our style sheet already uses this font, so you won't have to change this setting.

Note: Throughout this chapter, we will be referring to the Helvetica typeface. If you are working with a Hewlett-Packard LaserJet or compatible printer, substitute Swiss wherever this book says Helvetica.

But to make the publication a little more compact, eliminate that huge space above the paragraph:

39. If you have not already done so, press Home to return to page one.
40. Using the Paragraph Tool, select a Subhead paragraph, such as the heading "Software salary pay scales" in the first story.
41. Choose Spacing from the Paragraph menu. Delete the value in the Above text box and type in a big fat 0. Click on OK.

Headline tag

Your headlines should stand out more, so bump them up to 20-point Helvetica Bold:

42. Using the Paragraph Tool, select the Headline paragraph, "CD-ROM Breaks New Ground."
43. Choose Font from the Paragraph menu, select Font: Helvetica, Style: Bold, and Custom Size: 20. Then click on OK.

Note: Depending on the printer or font products you have installed, you may not be able to set custom sizes for your newsletter. If so, use the closest size available in the Size list box.

44. Now Choose Spacing from the Paragraph menu and set Above to 14 points and Inter-Line spacing to 22 points. To ensure a visible connection between a headline and its story, give it less space Below—just 8 points. Select Add In Above: Always. Then click on OK.

Because the first (or lead) story needs to stand out, make it a little different:

45. Using the Paragraph Tool, select the headline that reads, "Software Salaries: How do you stack up?" Use the Add New Tag command from the Paragraph menu to create a tag called "HeadlineBig."

For more information on creating new tags, see Chapter 3, "Building Basic Styles."

46. Now choose Font from the Paragraph menu. We'll leave the font Helvetica and the style Bold. Give it a size of 24 points and click on OK.

47. Choose Spacing from the Paragraph menu, and set space Above to 9, space Below to 8, and Inter-Line spacing to 24. Select Add in Above: Always. Click on OK and you're done.

Byline tag

With the current format, the Byline paragraph prevents the story's column tops from aligning. Let's fix that:

48. Using the Paragraph Tool, select the Byline paragraph, "by Joe Smith."

49. Choose Alignment from the Paragraph menu. Change Overall Width to Frame-Wide. Click on OK.

50. Then, to match your other display type, choose Font from the Paragraph menu. Make the font Helvetica, the Style Italic, and the size 10. Click on OK.

51. Choose Spacing from the Paragraph menu. Make the Inter-Line spacing 11, and remove all spacing Above and Below. Click on OK.

At this point, both the "Salary" and "CD-ROM" stories should fit on your first page. If they don't, try adjusting the spacing Above in your Headline and HeadlineBig or stretching the frame a bit. Now doesn't that look nice?

TOC title tag

Because all your headings are flush left, make the TOC title left aligned as well:

52. Select the TOC title with the Paragraph Tool and choose Alignment from the Paragraph menu. Select Horz. Alignment: Left and click on OK.

53. Choose Font from the Paragraph menu. Use Helvetica Bold to complement your headlines, but keep its size modest (16 points) so that it doesn't compete with them. When you're done, click on OK.

54. Choose Spacing from the Paragraph menu and try your hand at deciding the appropriate spacing. When you're done, click on OK.

55. Finally, for added flair, choose Ruling Line Above from the Paragraph menu. Select Width: Frame, Style: 6 point, and a solid black pattern. Click on OK.

TOC entry tag

The entries for the TOC look pretty good. But when you resized the frame to fit into a single column, the tab settings were thrown off. But it's easy to fix:

56. Using the Paragraph Tool, select a TOC entry paragraph and choose Tab Settings from the Paragraph menu. Set the first Tab Location to 13,04 picas & points (the width of your column). For Tab Alignment, select the Right button so numbers won't move outside the column. Leave the other settings the way you found them and click on OK.

57. Choose Spacing from the Paragraph menu. Set both In From Left and In From Right to 0,00 picas & points. That should improve things considerably.

After you've made the adjustments, the TOC entry tag should resemble those in Figure 19-7.

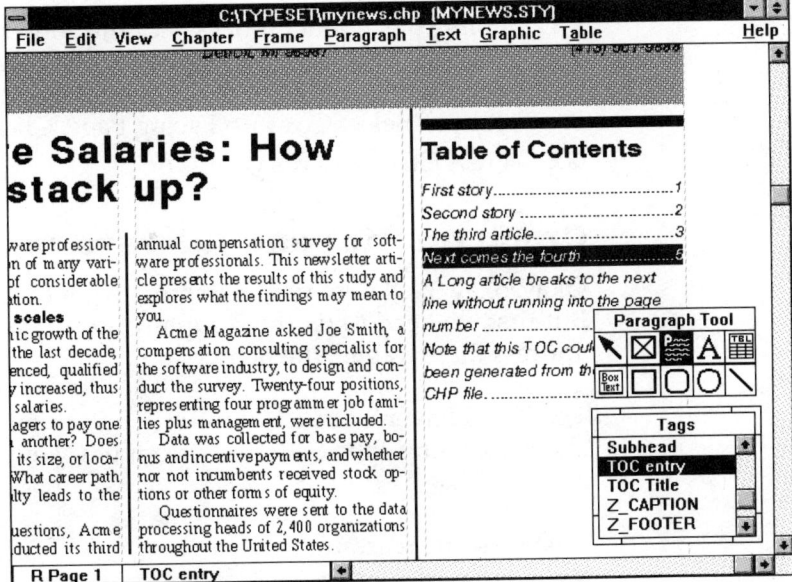

Figure 19-7.
The finished Table of Contents.

Z_FOOTER tag

Ah yes, zee footer. Parlez vous? Ah, no. Then in plain English, let's tinker with the stinker.

58. Using the Paragraph Tool, select the footer paragraph at the bottom of the first page.

59. Choose Font from the Paragraph menu. Make this tag match your other display type by using Helvetica (plain or italic, you decide). And make it a little more modest by reducing the size to 9 points.

60. Next, choose Headers & Footers from the Chapter menu and select Define: Right Page Footer. Delete the contents of the Left text box and replace it with the current month and year. Now select Define: Left Page Footer. Delete the contents of the Right text box and replace it with "Widget World." This automatically puts nameplate and dateline information on every set of facing pages. When you're done, click on OK.

Now adjust the height of the footer on the page. This is important to ensure the text falls more securely in the printable area of most laser printers. Our approach here will be to increase the bottom margin to "push" the footer higher:

61. Using the Frame Tool, select the footer frame and choose Margins & Columns from the Frame menu. Make the Bottom margin bigger (1,00 picas & points) than the top (0,06 picas & points). Select Copy To Facing Page. Click on OK.

62. Press Ctrl-S to save your work.

Credo (motto) and Address tag

Okay, okay. We know you're itching to get to that nifty nameplate. But first we need to fix the company motto (tagged as Credo) and address that "frame" the nameplate.

Tip: If you haven't already done so, you can make editing easier by choosing Show Tabs & Returns from the View menu (or by pressing Ctrl-T).

First do some rearranging:

63. Using the Text Tool, select the credo line ("Views and News of Widget Manufacturing in the 80s"). Be sure you select the entire line, including the paragraph symbol (carriage return) at the end. Cut the credo text by choosing Cut Text from the

Edit menu (or pressing the Delete key). Then position the cursor just in front of the nameplate text ("Widget World News") and paste the credo text by choosing Paste Text from the Edit menu (or pressing the Insert key). The credo line should be just above the nameplate.

64. With the credo text still selected, choose Change Text To from the Text menu. On the flyout menu, choose Upper Case.

Now a little editing:

65. First, use the Text Tool to update the credo to say "90s," not "80s," for crying out loud. Next, insert a space between each pair of letters and three spaces between each pair of words. This nifty designer effect, combined with the upper case, allows you to use small type and still maintain readability. Don't worry if the extra space causes the credo to break into two lines; we'll fix that next.

Tip: For editing individual characters—especially with small type or against a patterned background—position the cursor at that text area and choose Enlarged View from the View menu (Ctrl-E).

Now let's finish up the formats:

66. Using the Paragraph Tool, select the paragraph with the Credo tag.

67. Choose Font from the Paragraph menu and make the tag Helvetica Normal with a size of 7. Click on OK.

68. Choose Spacing from the Paragraph menu. Set the space Above to 10 points, space Below to 0 points, and Inter-Line spacing to 10. For Add In Above, select Always. To center the credo over our two text columns, set In From Right to 14,00 picas & points. Leave In From Left at 0. Click on OK.

69. Finally, choose Ruling Line Below from the Paragraph menu and set Width to None. Click on OK.

70. Now apply this same Credo tag to the address below the nameplate. Just select the address with the Paragraph Tool and click on the word Credo in the Tag List Window.

71. Create the same designer effect in the address: Use the Text Tool to make the address all uppercase, with the letters separated by spaces, and three spaces between words. In addition, delete the tabs and instead separate the groups of words with asterisks flanked by spaces.

When finished, your newsletter should resemble Figure 19-8.

72. If you want, you can also clean up your Tag List by deleting

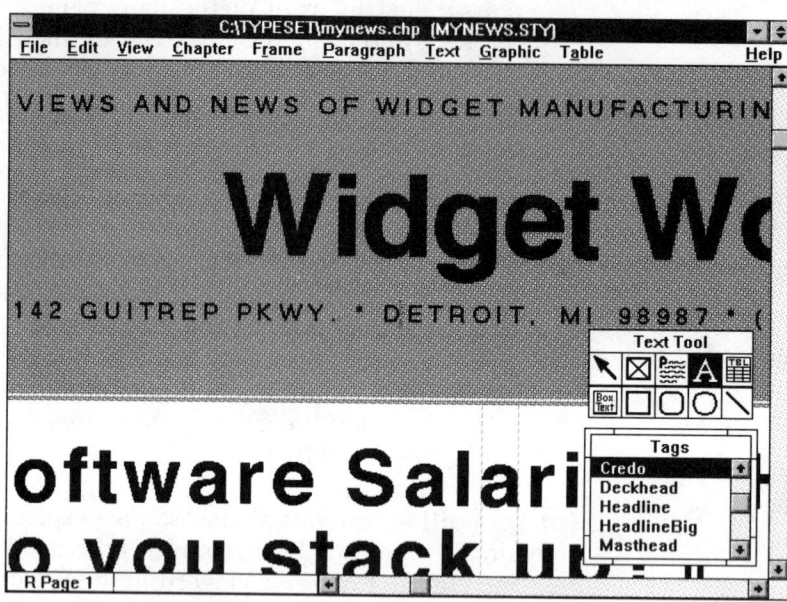

Figure 19-8.
After making changes to the Credo tag, your newsletter should look similar to this.

the Address tag, which is no longer needed. Use the Update Tag List command from the Paragraph menu and save your changes when prompted.

73. Press Ctrl-S to save your work.

Nameplate tag

The nameplate is really starting to shape up. But let's make the name of the publication stand out more from its gray background by making the name white with a black drop shadow. We'll walk you through the steps.

74. First, let's make our newsletter name more concise. Using the Text Tool, select the word "News" and the space before it. Choose Cut Text from the Edit menu or press Delete. When you're finished, the nameplate should read simply, "Widget World."

75. Now let's rename the tag to fit the terminology you learned in the "Newsletter terminology" sidebar. Using the Paragraph Tool, select the words "Widget World." The word "Masthead" should appear in the selection bar at the bottom of the window. Choose Update Tag List (Paragraph menu) and rename the tag to "Nameplate1." When you're done,

click on OK. If you need help with this command, see Chapter 3, "Building Basic Styles."

In real life, a physical body creates a shadow. For our nameplate, we'll defy all the laws of physics by making the shadow text first, and then the "real" text.

76. With the nameplate text still selected, choose Font from the Paragraph menu. Make the nameplate 56-point Helvetica Bold Italic. Then click on OK.

77. Choose Spacing from the Paragraph menu. Set space Above 24 points, Below 0, and Inter-Line 30 points. Select Add In Above: Always. Click on OK.

78. Choose Alignment from the Paragraph menu. Select Horz. Alignment: Left and click on OK.

Now you've got the shadow text. Next, you'll create the primary text that "casts" the shadow text.

Note: If you are planning to print this newsletter on a Hewlett-Packard LaserJet, we have good news and bad news. The bad news is that most LaserJets won't print reverse (white on black) type. That means you can't do the shadow effect described here. The good news is you're now done with the nameplate and can move to the section titled "Other tags."

To create the white text that "casts" the shadow, we have to add some more text:

79. Using the Text Tool, place the cursor at the end of the "Widget World" line, press Enter, and type "Widget World" again (or copy the line and paste it just below the first one).

Tip: The new text will probably be invisible because the frame is too small to hold it all. To see the new line you added, use the Frame Tool to move the story frame for "Software Salaries" down until it is out of the way (you can always move it back later).

The rest of your nameplate should look similar to the one in Figure 19-9.

80. Using the Paragraph Tool, select the lower line that you just created. Choose Add New Tag (Paragraph menu) and create a tag called "Nameplate2." The Copy From list box should show that it is being copied from Nameplate1. When you're done, click on OK.

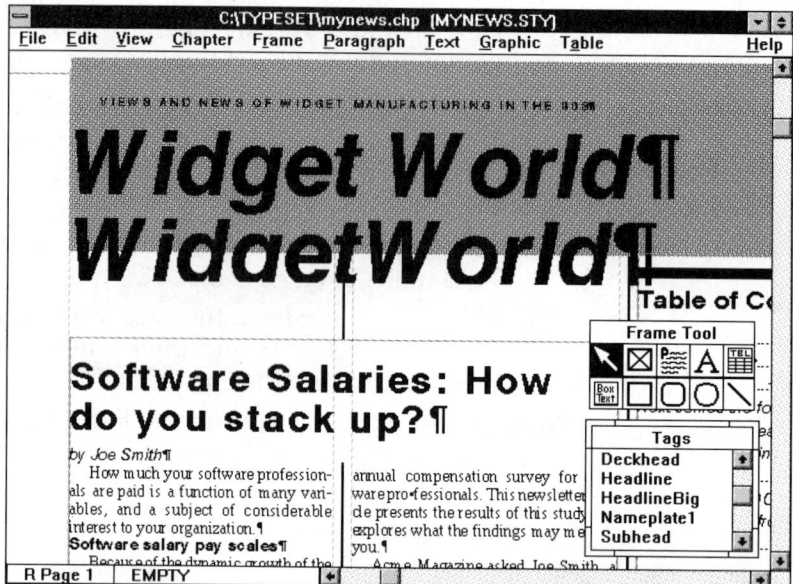

Figure 19-9.
To create a drop shadow, format the shadow text, then duplicate it.

81. With the lower Nameplate2 paragraph still selected, choose Font from the paragraph menu. Change the color to White. Then click on OK.

82. Choose Spacing from the Paragraph menu. To move the text up on top of its shadow, set Inter-Line spacing to 0. In addition, set the space Below to 0. To offset the words a little so the shadow shows, set space Above to 3 points and In From Left to 0,04 picas & points. Click on OK.

Your nameplate should resemble the one in Figure 19-10.

If your shadow effect doesn't look quite right or if you want to change the degree of offset, select the Nameplate2 paragraph, choose Spacing from the Paragraph menu, and adjust the space Above or space In From Left.

Tip: Because no spacing separates the two nameplate paragraphs, it may be difficult to select Nameplate2. To adjust this tag's attributes, apply the Nameplate2 tag to some other text—such as the "Software Salaries" headline below. While it is still selected, change the settings you want. Then retag the text to its former tag. The new attributes will appear on the lower nameplate text.

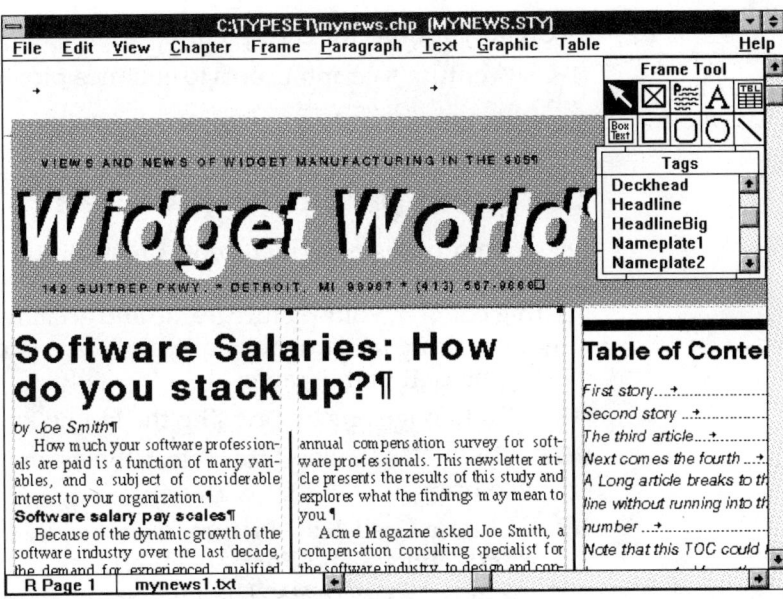

Figure 19-10.
Stacking white on black type produces a shadow effect.

83. If you moved the story frame out of the way before, move it back so it butts up against the bottom of the nameplate frame. Then choose Save from the File menu or press Ctrl-S.

Other tags

Now that you've constructed the basics of the style sheet, you just need to apply those tags to the rest of the newsletter:

84. Press the Page Down key once to move to page two.
85. Apply the HeadlineBig tag to the headline, "Xerox Announces Ventura 3.0."
86. Be sure that the masthead complements your TOC by tagging the paragraph that contains the words "Widget World Staff" with the TOC title tag and the names underneath with the TOC entry tag.

Loading and adjusting pictures

Things are really taking shape. You might be tempted to stop here—but we've got graphical touch-up techniques that will make your newsletter irresistible. Here's what you'll do in this section:

- Illustrate key issues in your articles, using Ventura's sample pictures

- Create captions for each picture
- Use Ventura's Graphic tools to enhance pictures and build a logo

Now it's time to add some visual panache.

Load and place the pictures

Let's begin by using a picture to illustrate the article in the right column on the first page. Because you cleverly began with an existing chapter, your picture frame and attached caption frame are already waiting for you. Now all you have to do is load the picture file and place it in the frame:

87. Go to page one by pressing the Home key.

88. Using the Frame Tool, select the frame in the lower right column.

89. Choose Load Text/Picture from the File menu and select File Type: Image and Format: TIFF. Click on OK. The Open File dialog box appears. The File Name text box should already contain the correct filename extension (TIF). If necessary, navigate to the \TYPESET directory where Ventura's sample files are stored. Then select the POT4.TIF picture file by double-clicking on its name in the Item Selector Box.

Presto—the picture's loaded in the frame that you selected.

90. With the frame still selected, choose Sizing & Scaling from the Frame menu. Be sure the settings Picture Scaling: Fit In Frame, and Aspect Ratio: Maintained are selected. If they aren't, make it so (Aye, Captain). Click on OK.

91. Then drag the top sizing handle and size the frame so that the width of the picture just fills the frame.

Now for page two. The procedure is the same, except you'll be loading a vector graphic:

92. Go to page two by pressing the Page Down key.

93. Select the empty frame in the left column.

94. Follow the same procedure you used for the first picture, but with this difference: Use File Type: Line Art and Format: GEM. The picture you want to load is called NOZZLE.GEM from the \TYPESET directory.

95. After the picture is in the frame, resize the frame so that it extends from the companion column on the left to the first column of text in the "Xerox Announces Ventura 3.0" story.

Position the picture just below the story's first paragraph as shown in Figure 19-11.

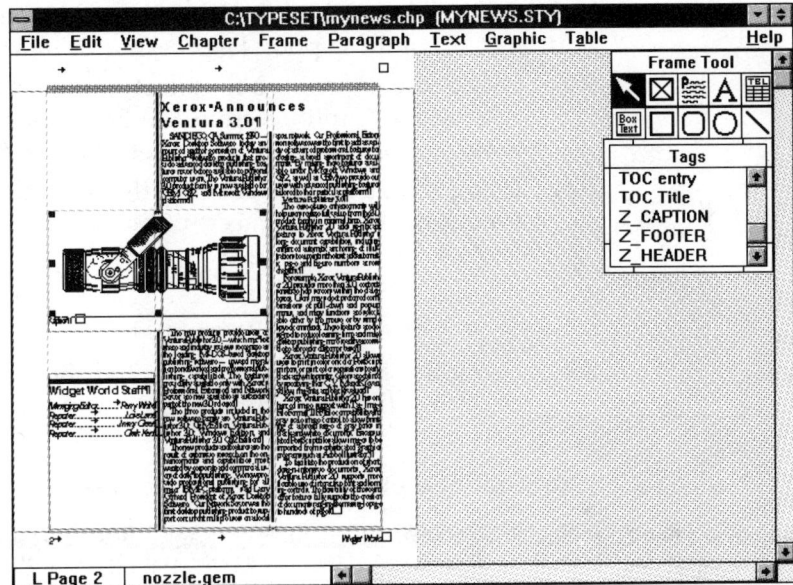

Figure 19-11. A two-column picture integrates text and illustration while making attractive use of the companion column.

Tip: The text of the story should flow around the picture frame. If it doesn't, select the picture frame, choose Sizing & Scaling from the Frame menu, and be sure Flow Text Around is set to On. If the text still does not flow around, the picture frame may be *underneath* the text frame. To bring it forward, select the picture frame, cut it (press Delete) and paste it back in (press Insert). Finally, be sure the caption frame is also set to Flow Text Around: On.

Tip: If some of the story is "leaking" down the side of the picture, select the picture frame, choose Sizing & Scaling from the Frame menu, add 1 or 2 points to the number in the Horz. Padding text box. This will bump the text to the bottom of the box. Repeat the procedure for the caption frame.

Add some captions

As you recall, short "Label" captions can be typed in the Anchors & Captions dialog box; however, they are limited to 60 characters. But you can type in longer captions by positioning your text cursor in the caption frame. Because your base chapter already included caption frames, you're saved the trouble of creating them. You just need to add your caption text. Because you're already on the second page, start by creating a caption for the NOZZLE picture.

Your existing frame already has a caption label that reads "Caption." Get rid of the caption label text:

96. Using the Frame Tool, select the caption frame, choose Anchors & Captions from the Frame menu, and delete the word "Caption" from the Label text box. Click on OK.

97. Using the Text Tool, position the text cursor inside the caption frame and type this caption:

```
Getting the line on widgets: Ventura Publisher is the
desktop publisher of choice for widget manufacturers
plotting a successful future in the 90s.
```

98. Using the Text Tool, select the first five words in the caption ("Getting the line on widgets") and choose Bold from the Text menu.

Your caption should resemble Figure 19-12.

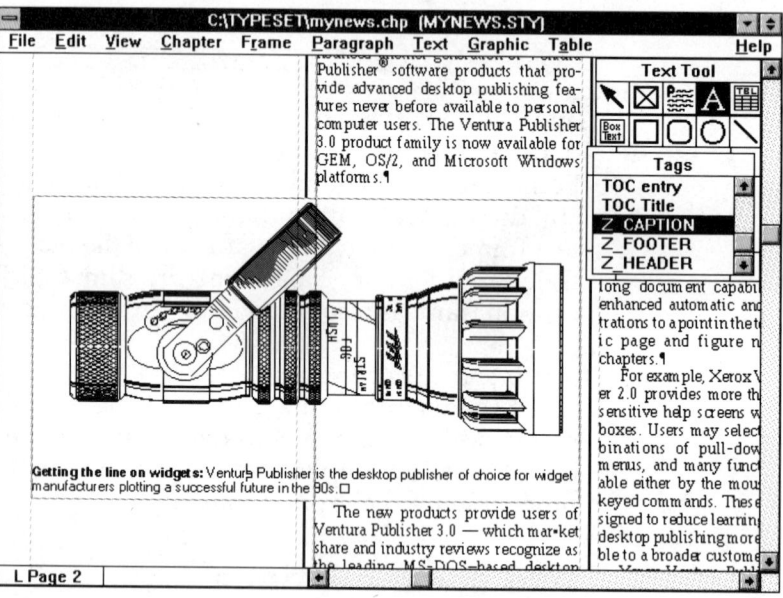

Figure 19-12. After adding the new caption text, the second page of your newsletter should look similar to this.

The caption you created is automatically tagged by Ventura as Z_CAPTION. You can keep the format for this tag. Or you can change it by selecting the caption with Paragraph Tool and making your changes with Paragraph menu. We prefer the following format changes:

99. Using the Paragraph Tool, select the caption and choose Alignment from the Paragraph menu. Set the In/Outdent Width to 0.

100. Now go to the first page and add a caption for the picture there. You can type your own caption in the frame or copy some of the text from the story using the Text Tool.

Create graphics with built-in Graphic tools

Ventura's Graphic tools let you add graphic enhancements without importing art from other applications. With a little ingenuity, you can use these tools to give your document a professional look.

Calling all callouts

A common use for the Graphic tools is the creation of callouts to narrate portions of a picture. For some quick practice, let's add a callout to the picture on page two:

101. Go to page two.

102. Using the Frame Tool, select the picture frame so that any graphics you draw will be attached to that frame.

103. Using the Add Box Text tool, draw a small rectangle above the nozzle and to the left of the lever.

104. Using the Text Tool, place the text cursor in the Box Text that you just created and type in some callout text such as "widget meltdown control" or "framistan prehensile doohickey" (sorry if this is too technical).

105. Using the Add Line tool, draw a line from the callout text to the lever or some other part of the picture. With the line still selected, choose Line Attributes from the Graphic menu and set the Thickness to ½pt. Then, under End Style, select an arrow head for one end of the line. Click on OK.

Note: If you have a ruling box around your Box Text, remove it: Using the Frame Tool, select the Box Text, choose Line Attributes from the Graphic menu, and set the Thickness to None. Then click on OK.

Your newsletter should now look similar to Figure 19-13.

If you like, you can also reformat the Z_BOXTEXT tag or even apply another tag, such as Z_CAPTION.

Figure 19-13.
After adding your callout, page two of your newsletter should resemble the one shown here.

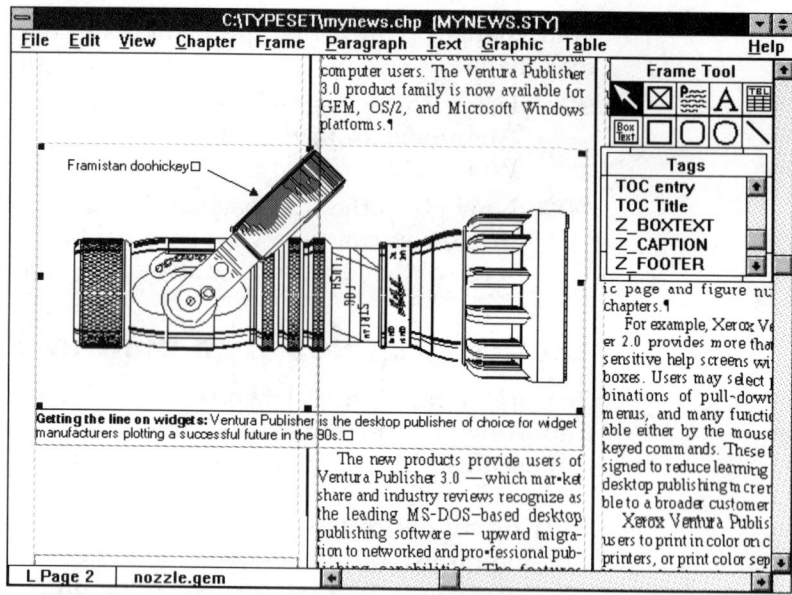

Logo a go go

Logo-typing—it's not just a name, it's a way of life. Some smart folks spend their entire time thinking up unique designs for companies who pay them gobs of money. What do these companies get for their money? Consumers often recognize products by associating a simple design with a company and its products. Image may not be everything—but a memorable logo can get you a long way.

What's in it for you? A distinctive logo can help readers spot your newsletter on a newsstand or in the mailbox. It also adds some visual punch to the first (and all important) page. Here's one way to create a logo, using only Ventura's built-in Graphic tools:

106. Go to page one.

107. Using the Frame Tool, select the nameplate frame so that graphics will be attached to it. To the right of the nameplate, use the Add Circle tool and hold down the Alt key to draw a perfect circle.

108. With the circle still selected, choose Fill Attributes from the Graphic menu, select Color: Black and Pattern: Solid (the last pattern).

Note: As noted earlier, HP LaserJet printers cannot print white-on-dark text. If you are planning to print your newsletter on an HP LaserJet, you will have to redesign the logo with this in mind.

109. Be sure the nameplate frame is selected. Using the Add Box Text tool, draw a box on top of the circle to hold text that will be superimposed on the circle.

110. Using the Text Tool, type the initial letters of the publication title (WW) inside the Box Text.

111. Using the Paragraph Tool, select the logo paragraph. Choose Add New Tag (Paragraph menu) and create a new tag called Logo. As always, click on OK when you're finished.

112. Choose Font from the Paragraph menu. Make your logo 40-point Helvetica Bold. Color it white. Click on OK.

113. Choose Spacing from the Paragraph menu. Select Inter-Line: 40 points.

114. Choose Paragraph Typography from the Paragraph menu. Select Tracking: Tighter and type 0.2 ems in the text box immediately to the right.

Tip: If your logo text doesn't show up inside the frame, it may not be attached to the frame. To attach it, use the Frame Tool to select the Box Text containing the "WW," cut it (press Delete) and paste it in again (press Insert). If it appears but is hidden behind the circle, select the Box Text and choose Bring To Front from the Graphic menu (or press Ctrl-A).

115. Using the Frame Tool, carefully position the Box Text so that the "WW" text is centered within the circle.

Your newsletter now looks stunning. It should resemble the one in Figure 19-14.

Copyfitting and final touch-ups

At this point, your newsletter looks pretty slick. The formatting for pages, frames, and tags is complete and it looks cool. Not only that, you've taken care of all your pictures, captions, and graphics. What more could you want?

The answer, for many kinds of documents, is nothing: that's all there is!

But with newsletters, you have the challenge of fitting copy into snaking columns so that all your copy fits, and your columns all line up. We wish we could tell you that copyfitting only requires

Figure 19-14. You can create your own logo using only Ventura's Graphic tools.

you to press the "Make It Fit" button in some mythical dialog box—but it just ain't so.

However, Ventura's Frame Typography command from the Frame menu does give you some powerful features to help you fit copy: Vertical justification allows you to squeeze in an extra word (preventing widows), and Balance Columns allows you to line up your columns. However, Ventura won't make a long story shorter or a short story longer. And vertical justification, if not used carefully, can make your pages look uneven and unattractive.

In this section, we'll walk you through three common situations and solutions in copyfitting and newsletter layout. They are:

- Squeezing text into smaller spaces
- Expanding text for larger spaces
- Jumping text from page to page

We'll guide you through each situation.

Making the squeeze

In the real world, fitting a story that's a wee bit long is usually solved by the editor, who must choose some words to cut. But Ventura can give you some help, too.

For practice, let's look at the story on page two. If your tags and column widths are like ours, you'll see a divided word ("val-ues") at the end of the third paragraph from the bottom. To editors worth their salt, this looks pretty disgraceful. Moreover, it may be adding a line you don't need. So let's find a way to squeeze this word back on the previous line without changing the whole tag:

116. If you have not already done so, go to page two.

117. Using the Text Tool, select the last few lines of the paragraph.

118. Choose Set Font Attributes from the Text menu.

119. Select Kern: Tighter, and set the kern value to 0.02 ems. Click on OK.

Your paragraph should magically be a line shorter and not have that ugly final word hanging at the bottom.

Warning: Don't abuse this power: We recommend tightening text no more than 0.02 ems for copy fitting purposes. If you have much more than that, the fitted copy will clash with the rest of your type because of the large difference in spacing.

Filling the gap

Sometimes, stories are too short. The most popular trick here is the *pull quote*, a quotation from the text that is highlighted in large type. Pull quotes are valuable design elements by themselves, helping to break up chunks of text. They serve a practical function, too: They draw the audience into the content of the article, enticing them to read. Let's try one.

120. If you have not already done so, go to page two.

121. Using the Add Frame tool, draw a square frame to fill the right column, near the picture we added earlier.

122. With the Frame still selected, choose Ruling Line Above from the Frame menu. Select Width: Frame and Style: 6 points. Give it a solid black pattern. Click on OK.

123. Choose Ruling Line Below from the Frame menu. Create a 6-point frame-wide rule as before and click on OK.

124. Using the Text Tool, select some phrase you wish to use as your pull quote. We've chosen the opening words of paragraph four: "The new products and features are the result of extensive research." Copy the text (press Shift-Delete), select the Text Tool inside the pull quote frame, and paste (press Insert).

125. Using the Paragraph Tool, select the text and choose Add New Tag from the Paragraph menu. Follow the usual procedure, this time to create a tag called "Pullquote."

126. Using the Paragraph Tool, choose Font from the Paragraph menu. Make this tag 14-point Helvetica Bold Italic and click on OK.

127. Now choose Spacing from the Paragraph menu. Give the tag 8 points of space Above and an Inter-Line spacing of 16 points. Choose Add in Above: Always. Then click on OK.

128. Finally, choose Alignment from the Paragraph menu. Set Horz. Alignment to Center and click on OK.

You should now have an attractive pull quote decorating your article (Figure 19-15). Notice how the ruling lines provide continuity with the line above the masthead.

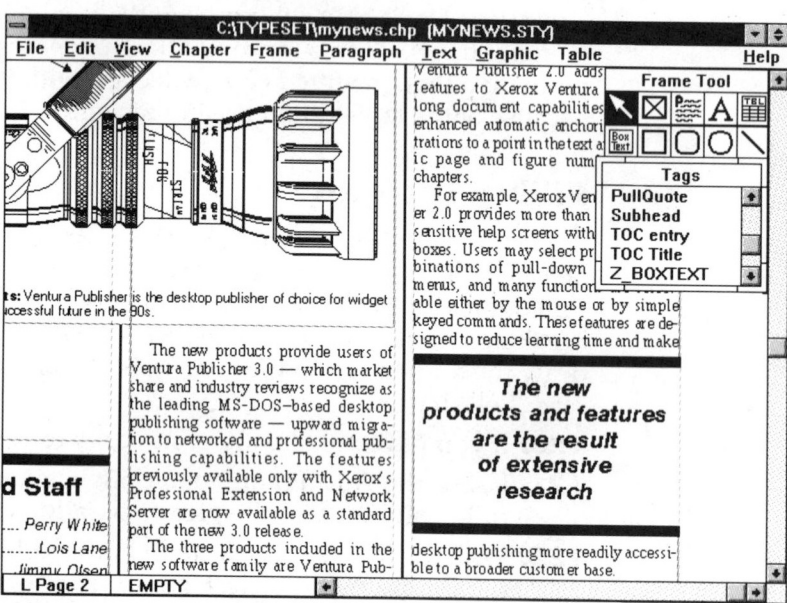

Figure 19-15. After adding the pull quote, your newsletter should similar to this.

Jumping the gun

Though not technically a part of copyfitting, knowing how to thread text from one page to another is an essential skill in piecing together the parts of a newsletter. Because your pull quote has now pushed the end of your story into oblivion, you need to continue this story on another page.

Ventura makes it a snap to thread stories from frame to frame. Just go to page three, select the text frame there with the Frame Tool, and click on the story name (MYNEWS2.TXT) in the File List Window. The end of the story appears in the frame.

Tip: You can thread text through as many different frames as you want. The first frame contains the beginning of the text, and the last frame holds the end. If text in frames appears out of sequence, fix it by cutting and pasting the frames (Delete then Insert) in the order you want the text to flow. Incidently, although you can get the frames out of sequence on a page, text cannot be made to flow backwards to a frame on a previous page.

Tip: You can always tell where your file ends by the end-of-file symbol, which looks like a small hollow box to the right of the last word in a file. To make this symbol visible, be sure Show Tabs & Returns is checked on the View menu.

Next, you need a jump line to tell the reader where the story continues to and originated from. We could do this with the Text Tool—but if you change the length of your story, you run the risk of forcing the jump line to the wrong page. To avoid this, create a separate frame for the jump line:

129. At the bottom of page two, use the Add Frame tool to create a small frame. It should fill the width of the right column and be only one or two lines high.

Tip: If your copy is running one or two lines short, a jump line that fills two lines is another sneaky solution.

130. Using the Text Tool, place the text cursor within the frame you just created. Type a jump line such as "Continued on page 3."

131. Using the Paragraph Tool, assign the jump line an appropriate tag (such as Z_CAPTION) or create a new tag to suit your tastes.

That's all there is to it.

132. Now use the same procedure to type a "Continued from" line on page three.

You may even decide to have another, perhaps abbreviated, headline at the top of this continuation. The second headline helps break up the type and makes it easier for a reader to spot the next part of the article. If a single page contains several continued articles, secondary headlines are a must.

Your newsletter looks great! But a quick glance over reveals a few more things you can touch up:

- If you decide to have no headline at the top of page three, give the frame a top margin so it doesn't run into the header rule.
- Resize the masthead frame so the bottom line of type aligns with the bottom of the article next to it.
- Use the Text Tool to adjust the line breaks (Ctrl-Enter) for headlines and pull quotes.
- Check all frames to be sure no type is "leaking" around the edges. If there is, fix it by adding a little horizontal padding (use the Sizing & Scaling dialog box from the Frame menu).
- Print out a copy for proofing.

Tip: Save your work a final time. Then save it again to another disk as a backup and as a template chapter.

Congratulations; let's toast your maiden issue. May your volume numbers and subscribers be many, and your work be little (when using the tips and tricks from this tutorial)!

Continuing on

In this chapter, you've gone through the steps of creating a newsletter. You've learned to use most of Ventura's functions to create the essential elements of a newsletter—from nameplate to pull quote. You've gotten some new tricks up your sleeve to solve common newsletter problems such as fitting copy and creating jump lines. You also know how to take advantage of Ventura's Graphic tools to create unique graphic effects such as creating shadowed text. We've given you a start. Now it's your turn to show your stuff.

Newsletters come in at least as many flavors as ice cream. Some of these are likely to become your favorites. For a taste of some tempting newsletter formats, see the next chapter, "Portfolio."

Easy Access

For more info on...	See chapter...
Creating, deleting, renaming, and modifying tags	3 — Building Basic Styles
Loading, creating, and editing text in Ventura	6 — Handling Text in Ventura
Creating pictures with Ventura's Graphic tools	9 — Creating Pictures in Ventura
Loading and placing picture files into Ventura	11 — Loading and Placing Pictures
Printing your newsletter	13 — Printing Ventura Documents

Part Seven:
Resources

20 Portfolio
A sampler of design ideas

In Chapters 18 and 19, we gave you hands-on instructions for creating a business proposal and a newsletter. In this chapter, we'll show you a range of documents created in Ventura by professional desktop publishers. We're not going to give you step-by-step instructions for each one (that would take hundreds of pages). Our goal in this chapter is to provide a sampler of ideas you can use to spark your imagination.

Ventura has the power to implement almost any idea. But don't let that power lure you into the trap of "overdesign." As you create a document, remember that its look should always be appropriate to the situation. Just because you *can* use 10 different fonts on a page doesn't mean you *should*. If discretion is the better part of valor, then restraint is the better part of graphic design. Your documents should use design to bring out the message, not to overwhelm it.

The samples in this chapter make our point admirably. As you look them over, notice that most of them are subdued and dignified. That's because most of them are business documents, where a loud, boisterous design would be unsuitable. These documents have a job to do, and they use graphic design to help them get it done. In these samples, design is a tool that helps readers find what they need. In the newsletters, for instance, headlines help readers find the story they want. Boxes and ruling lines separate stories from one another, allowing the designer to put a lot of information on one page without confusing the reader.

A full-scale course in graphic design is beyond the scope of this book. Perhaps the best advice we can give you is to consider the following three points before you settle on a design:

1. *The audience*. Who's going to read it? A technical manual for engineers should look very different from a brochure aimed at school age children.
2. *The purpose*. What is this document supposed to do for the audience? Inform? Instruct? Entertain? The design should help you accomplish the purpose.
3. *The image*. How do you want the audience to feel about the document and the people who created it? A brochure for a bank, for instance, should convey stability and conservatism.

A brochure for an art institute would probably want to stress excitement and creativity.

If you keep these three points in mind, you'll be able to create a design that is right for the audience, that emphasizes the essential information, and that projects the correct image.

So much for logic and practicality. But how do you achieve the creativity, inspiration, and excitement that are also a part of good design? How do you come up with fresh, new ideas? Most professional graphic artists collect good-looking documents. They are constantly on the lookout for new examples. When it's time for a new project, they pull out their example files and browse for ideas.

We suggest that you start a collection of your own. To get you started, we've gathered more than a dozen examples in the pages that follow.

Windows Watcher

Windows Watcher is a 8.5 x 11-inch newsletter designed by Scott Dunn for CompuThink, Incorporated (Figures 20-1 and 20-2). Its audience consists of the personal computing industry—software and hardware developers who track the Windows market, plus corporate power users and technology managers. Its purpose is to inform these busy professionals by packing a lot of information into a little space. Many industry newsletters still have a crude, typewriter look, but *Windows Watcher* seeks a high-end image. For this reason, it uses two colors and a contemporary, four-column design.

A four-column design creates a lot of design possibilities, but it also creates difficulties. Because the columns are so narrow, the type must be kept small (9.5-point Times Roman). And the layout operator must constantly be on the lookout for hyphenation problems and gaps caused when Ventura wasn't able to adequately justify the line. Still, the designer decided that these problems were offset by the fresh look of a four-column newsletter. With the advent of desktop publishing, two-column and three-column newsletters have become so common they no longer seem as interesting and unique.

The nameplate at the top was created with the Corel Draw drawing program and imported into Ventura as an EPS (Encapsulated Post-Script) file. The nameplate and the TOC panel in the lower right are in burgundy. The rest of the newsletter is in black.

Chapter 20: Portfolio

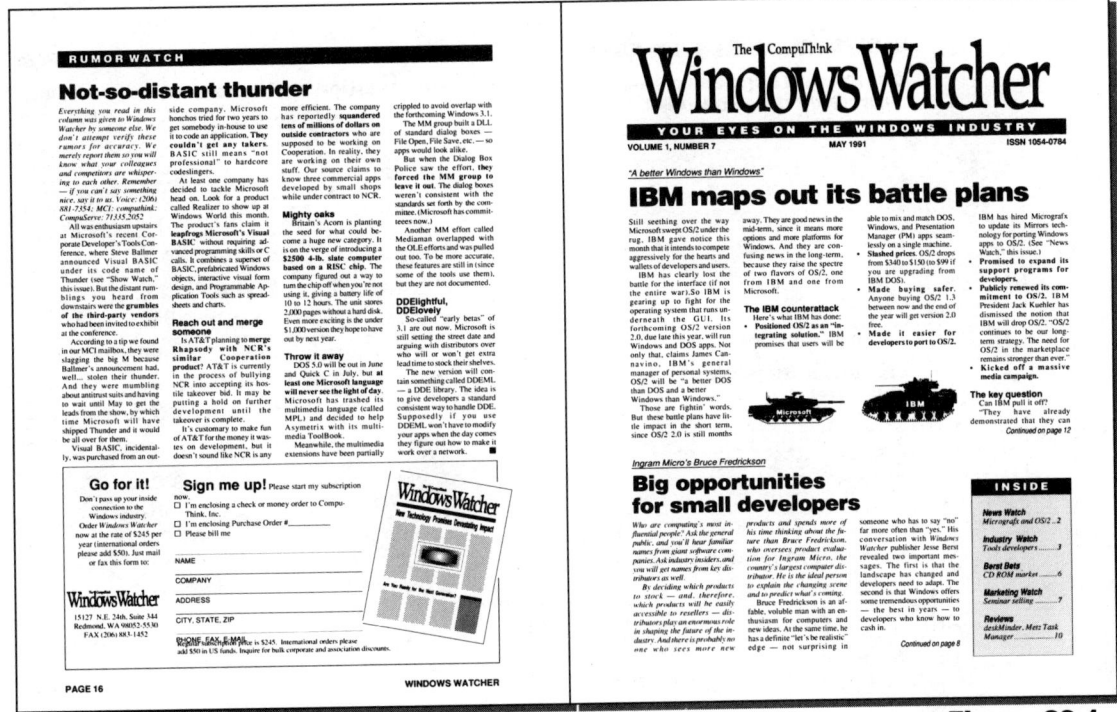

Figure 20-1.
Windows Watcher newsletter

The headlines are done with a member of the Helvetica family called Helvetica Black. It is wider and darker than the standard Helvetica you see on most laser printers, giving the headlines more weight and pulling power. Notice that the lead story at the top has a bigger headline than the secondary story below it. The hierarchy of sizes lets readers see at a glance which story is deemed most important.

Readers gets further help from the table of contents (TOC) panel at the lower right, which directs them to stories on the inside. This separate frame has a 10 percent tint to set it off from the rest of the text. Because Ventura's predefined patterns (from the Frame Background dialog box) are somewhat coarse, the designer created this tint with the Define Colors dialog box instead. He created a new color that had nothing in it except 10 percent gray. Then he applied this color to the frame background. The newsletter was taken to the print shop with instructions to print this box in the same burgundy color as the nameplate.

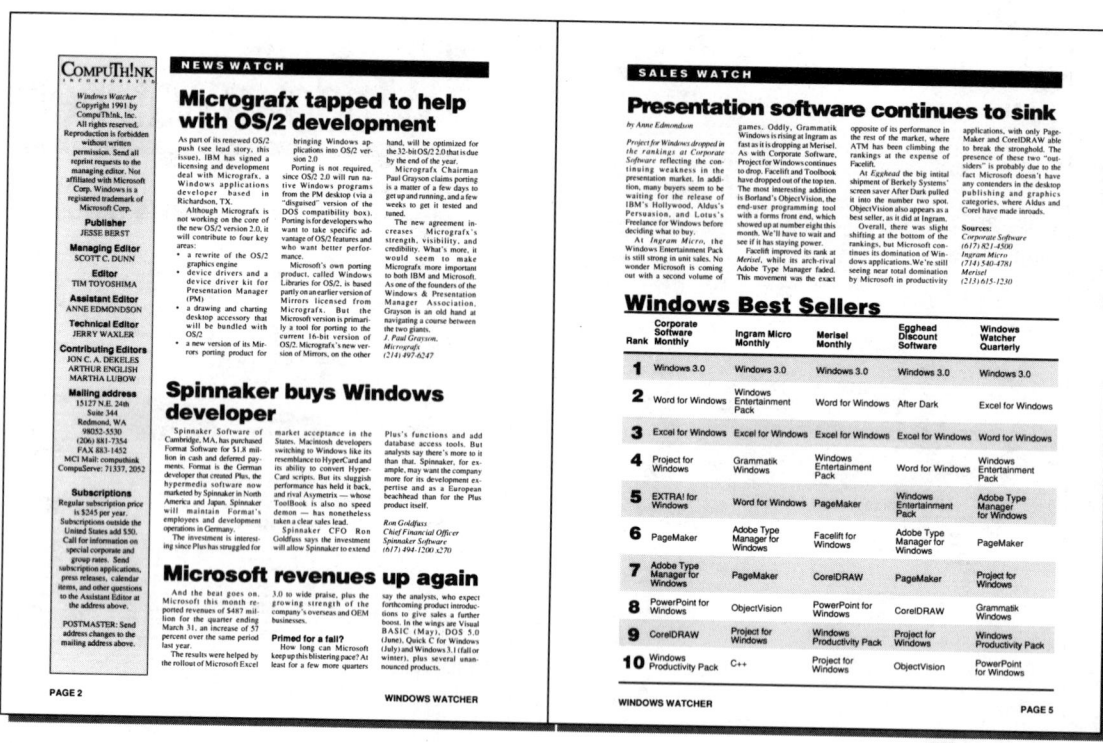

Figure 20-2.
Windows Watcher newsletter

To create a unifying element, the designer used a similar reverse type effect for the motto (beneath the nameplate), for the TOC title ("Inside"), and for the headings that mark the departments that appear each month. (Graphic artists often call these recurring headings "standing heads" as opposed to normal headlines, which change with each story.) The font (Helvetica Black again) has been given a color of white. A black ruling line has been placed on top of the type to create the effect of white type on a black background. The ruling lines were built with the Ruling Line Above dialog box, and have a negative Space Below Rule Three to move them down on top of the white type.

This particular newsletter does not use ruling lines between columns or between stories. Instead, it uses white space to separate different elements. Compare this approach to the next sample newsletter, which makes heavy use of ruling lines and boxes.

The Physician Insurer

The 8.5 x 11-inch *Physician Insurer* newsletter, designed by Maria Baseleon for Medit Associates, also has a lot of text packed onto the page (Figures 20-3 and 20-4). It is produced for members of the Physician Insurers Association. This audience already has a vested interest in the content, so the newsletter doesn't have to worry about being flashy or attracting attention. Its job is to create a professional image for the organization while delivering important information.

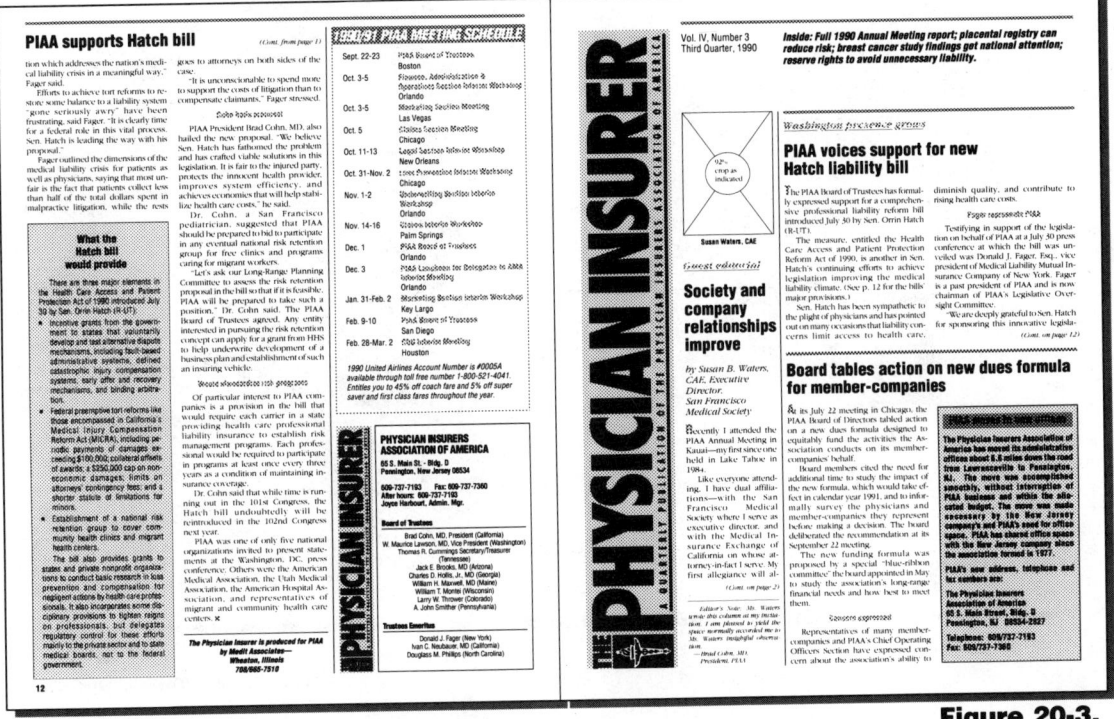

Figure 20-3.
The Physician Insurer newsletter

This newsletter uses the columns on the underlying page as a grid. The underlying page has five columns. However, no page in the newsletter contains five columns. Rather, these columns are used as a snap-to grid. Over this grid, the designer creates different columns of different widths. On the left side of the first page, the banner and the guest editorial each take up one column of the five. The other two articles are in frames that span three of the five columns, but the frames have a two-column format.

Who says the nameplate has to appear at the top of the newsletter. This example makes effective use of rotated text to create a vertical nameplate along the left side. This same logo is repeated in the small masthead box on the last page of the newsletter. And who says that a table of contents (TOC) has to be a vertical list with page numbers? This designer chose to run it paragraph style at the top of the page.

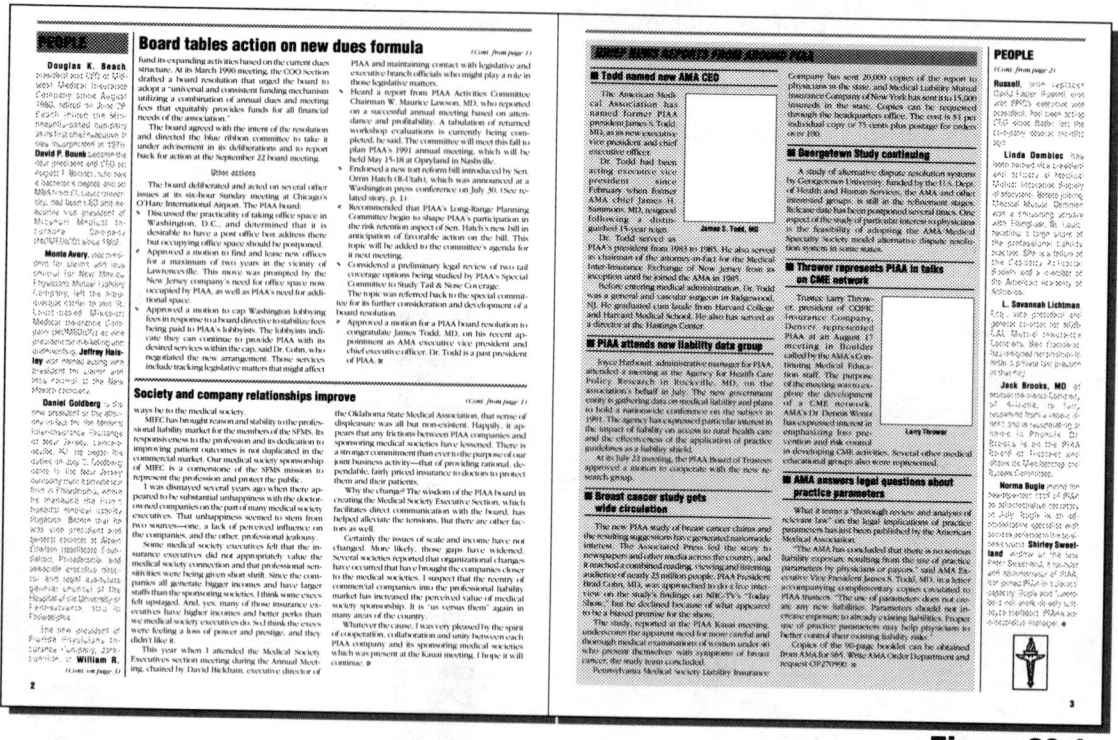

Figure 20-4.
The Physician Insurer newsletter

Instead of a lot of white space, Ms. Baseleon uses ruling lines and boxes to separate and group elements on the page. This can look cluttered if it's not done with caution. One reason this newsletter holds together is that except for the nameplate, the designer has used only two different typestyles (one serif and one sans serif).

But even though she is only working with two typestyles, look how many different looks she has achieved. You're sure to get some ideas by studying the way she has used different combinations of italics, bold, underline, reverse type, black type on a gray rule, centering, and left alignment.

Those of you who work with photographs should also note how the designer placed instructions to the printer inside the keyline frame at the upper left of the front page.

National Gypsum Corporate Communique

This 11 x 17-inch tabloid newsletter, designed by Deborah Dickson, is published for the employees and retirees of the National Gypsum Company (Figures 20-5 and 20-6). Again, this is a captive audience. In this case, however, the goal is not to pack as much onto the page as possible. Rather, this publication seeks to give employees a sense of community and knowledge of important company-wide happenings.

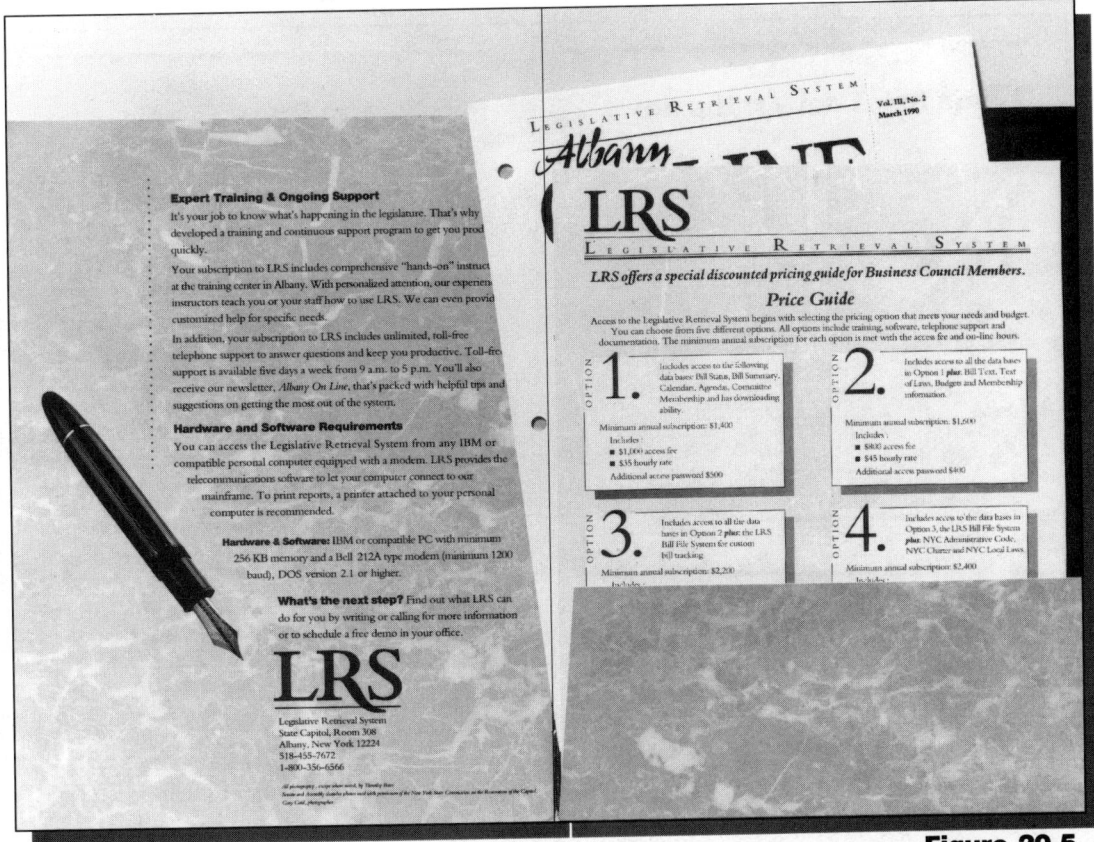

Figure 20-5.
National Gypsum Corporate Communique newsletter

Like the *Physician Insurer*, this newsletter uses the columns on the underlying page as a grid that allows variety (different column widths) and still retains consistency (all elements use the four columns for alignment). The designer draws frames on top of that grid and gives those frames their own internal margin and column settings, then flows the text inside.

The overall feeling of this newsletter is clean and spacious. The luxurious use of white space combines with the large page size, the heavy paper, and the use of two colors tells the readers that they are highly valued by the company. Another factor that contributes to the open feel is the left-aligned text. This causes Ventura to use a constant amount of space between words, avoiding excessively tight or loose lines.

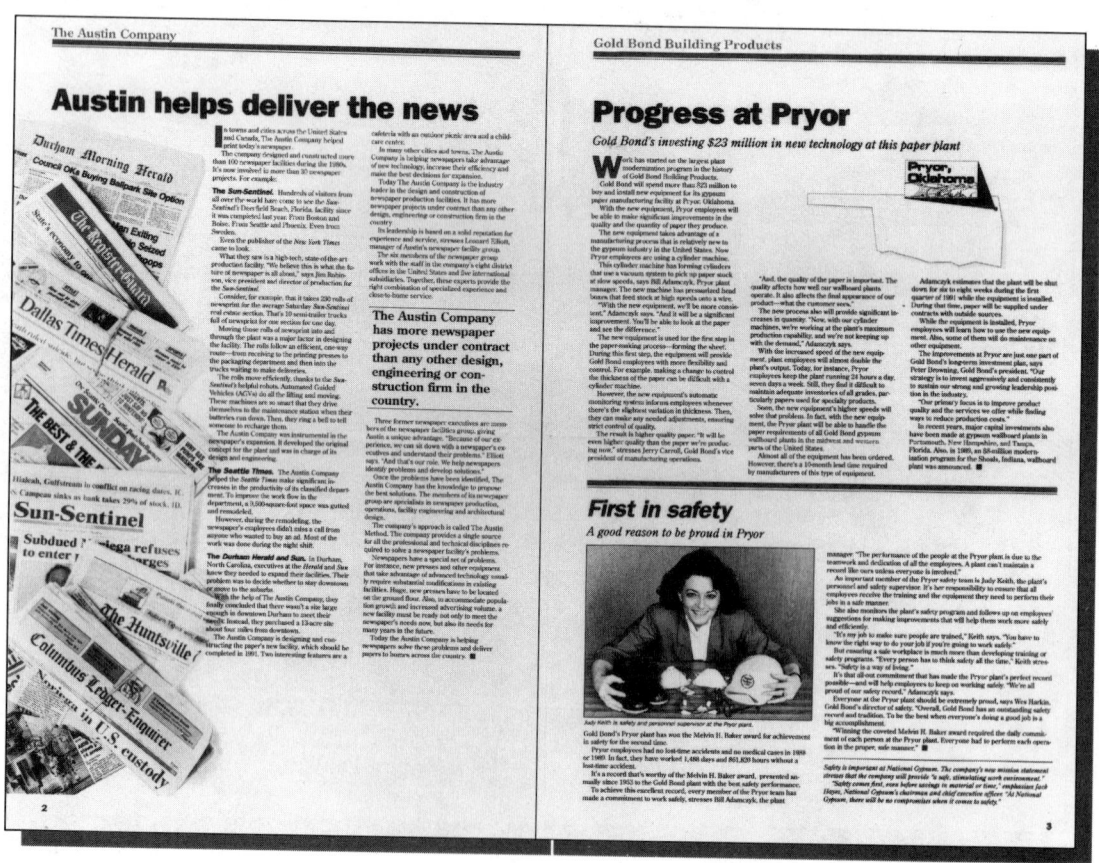

Figure 20-6.
National Gypsum Corporate Communique newsletter

The use of Franklin Gothic Heavy for headlines with Century Oldstyle for other copy also establishes a nice contrast. It's the old standby of sans serif headlines with serif body text. (The reason it's an old standby is that it works.) Notice the use of filled box characters (Insert Special Item, Text menu) as end of story markers.

Color is used in a low-key, restrained manner consistent with the overall image. On the front page, for instance, only the ruling lines and the big first character are in orange. The rest of the page elements are in black, except for the name "National Gypsum," which is set in gray type.

Despite its large size, the tabloid was made into a self-mailer by putting space for an address and a bulk mail indicia on the back page. The newsletter can be folded in half and mailed without an envelope.

Persuasive Technical Communications letterhead

Figure 20-7.
Persuasive Technical Communications letterhead

The main functions of a letterhead are to (1) make the name and address easy to find and (2) convey a powerful impression about the company.

This 8.5 x 11-inch letterhead, designed by Robbin Young, has a dynamic quality that suits this young company (Figure 20-7). The logo conveys a sense of motion; because its inverted triangle shape is like an arrow directing the reader's eye to the content of the letter and, ultimately, to the company name and address at the bottom. The company information echoes the shape of the logo. The design also uses symmetry (by centering all elements) to move the reader's eye decisively down the page.

The logo was created in Corel Draw and imported into Ventura as a GEM format file. The type at the bottom was created in Ventura.

Canfield Studios business cabinet

These business materials (letterhead, envelope, and invoice) were designed by Byron Canfield, co-author of this book (Figure 20-8). To advertise his proficiency with computerized publishing, Byron mimics the DOS environment. The monospaced font (Letter Gothic) in all uppercase resembles the fonts on a DOS screen. With the letters all uppercase, the small font size (6 point) is more legible. The logo cleverly connects the first letter of the company name with the DOS C> prompt. To produce a smaller picture file, the logo was created directly with the PostScript language rather than with a paint or draw program. It was then imported into Ventura as an EPS file.

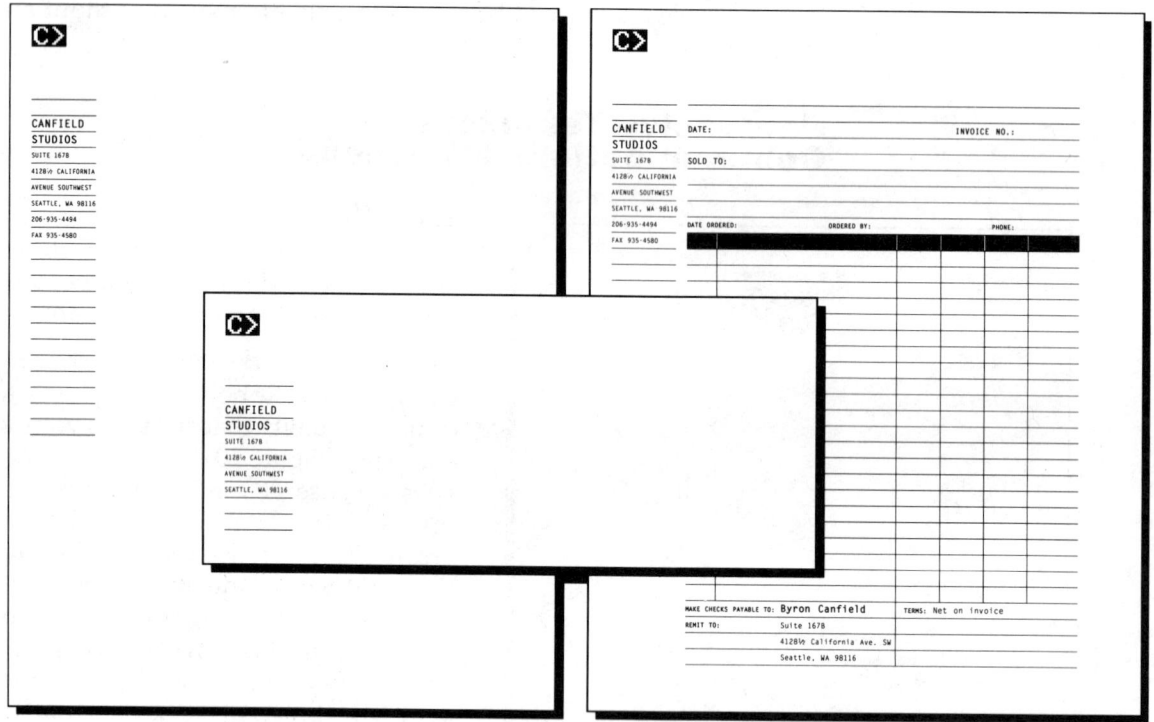

Figure 20-8.
Canfield Studios business cabinet

Leader dots separate each line of text. The alignment of these leader dot lines helps to consolidate the text into a single visual element.

Business proposal

This 8.5 x 11-inch, single-sided business proposal was designed by Martha Lubow (Figure 20-9). Its audience is prospective investors, and so needs to help them find key information while conveying the impression of an energetic, forward-thinking company.

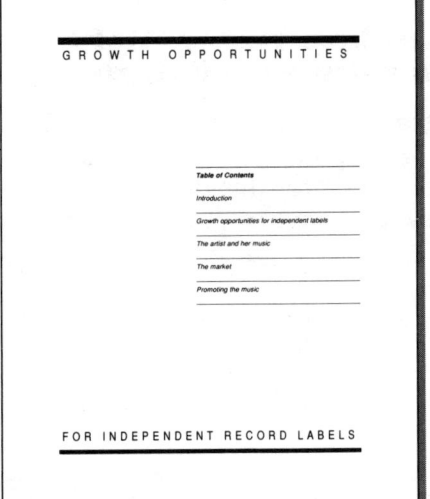
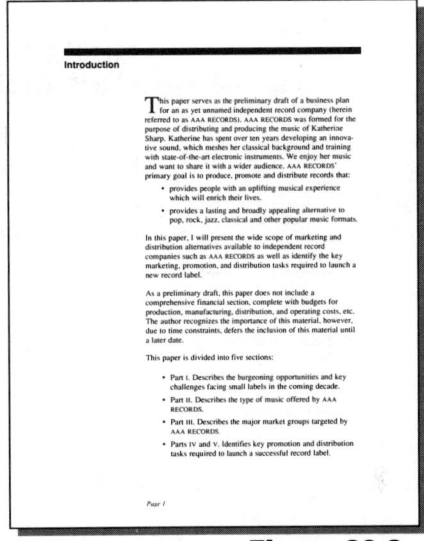

Figure 20-9.
Business plan

The title page is framed with ruling lines above and below. The designer used Ventura's tracking feature (Paragraph Typography, Paragraph menu) to spread out the type and give it a custom look.

By using ruling lines to set off main headings, the designer has made the interior of the proposal relate to the title page. The ruling lines also make it easy to spot the headings, so that readers can quickly refer to the information they need to make their decisions.

A single page-width column is hard to read. To make this document more accessible, the designer used In From Left spacing to create a wide companion column to the left of the body text. This technique gives the page a pleasing, spacious look while restricting the text to a more readable line length. The design is also practical for business people who may have to produce a proposal quickly at their own office or on a business trip. The document has no pictures and uses only typefaces found resident on PostScript printers: Times, Helvetica, and Helvetica Narrow.

Note how the designer aligned the page number at the bottom with the body text. Had it been aligned at the left edge, the page number would have dangled into the wide left margin. Instead, the designer created a footer with the Headers & Footers dialog box. Then she applied In From Left spacing to the Z_Footer tag, so that the page number aligns left with the body text.

Understanding Water Rights and Conflicts return mail card

This two-sided 8 x 9-inch return mail card was designed by Herbert C. Young, the author of the book being promoted (Figure 20-10). The audience for this document is prospective buyers. Its goal is to provide buying information plus an easy way to order.

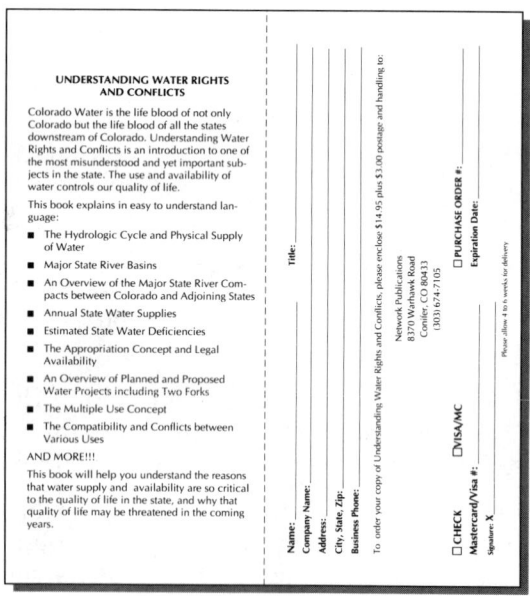

Figure 20-10.
Understanding Water Rights and Conflicts, return mail card

The document succeeds through understatement. The cover is simple with lots of white space. (The gray block indicates photograph placement for offset reproduction). Typefaces are Helvetica Light and Optima.

The return mail coupon was created with the Table Tool. The text in each cell was rotated 90 degrees. Auto-leaders (from the Tab Settings dialog box) create the information lines.

This designer decided to use a dotted line to indicate the fold mark. This can be difficult in Ventura, since neither the graphic lines nor the vertical rules permit a dotted line. There are several workarounds. One method is to create a frame-wide, dotted ruling line above a text element (even an invisible text element) and then to rotate that text so the ruling line is vertical rather than horizontal. A second method is to create a frame with a dashed ruling box around. Then you give the frame a width of zero, creating the effect of a dashed line. (A third method is illustrated in the Legislative Retrieval System sample later in this chatper.)

Legislative Retrieval System marketing materials

Figure 20-11.
Legislative Retrieval System, marketing materials

Ventura is best-known as a tool for creating technical manuals. But the program is equally adept at producing slick, glossy advertising materials, as this example attests. This self-contained, four-color promotional piece, designed by Elizabeth Wood, consists of an 8.5 x 11-inch pocket folder (Figure 20-11). "Pages" are created by a saddle-stitched 11 x 17-inch insert. The pocket of the folder holds additional 8.5 x 11-inch sheets (Figure 20-12).

The audience is comprised of lawyers, lobbyists, government agencies, and corporations that need to keep in touch with ongoing legislation. The goal is to convince them to purchase an expensive computerized database and retrieval system. The company wants to promote a high-end image of established success.

To lend a feeling of solidity and stability, the designer used architectural details and styles as decorative elements throughout the piece. For instance, many pages have a marbelized background. The generous use of white space, numerous full-color pictures, and thick, glossy paper all reinforce the high-end image.

The piece is full of quality touches. For instance, notice how the pen in Figure 20-12 effectively leads the reader's eye to the company name, address and phone. The pen is the same type of expensive fountain pen used to sign bills into law.

The dotted vertical line is similar to the dashed line from the Understanding Water Right mail card shown previously in this chapter. In this case, the designer used the Tab Settings dialog box to create the effect. First, she drew a tall, thin frame where she wanted the line. Then, she typed in a tab character. With the Tab Settings dialog box, she chose periods as leader characters. Next, the text was rotated (Alignment dialog box), so that the tab would run vertically instead of horizontally. With the Font dialog box, she controlled the size of the periods.

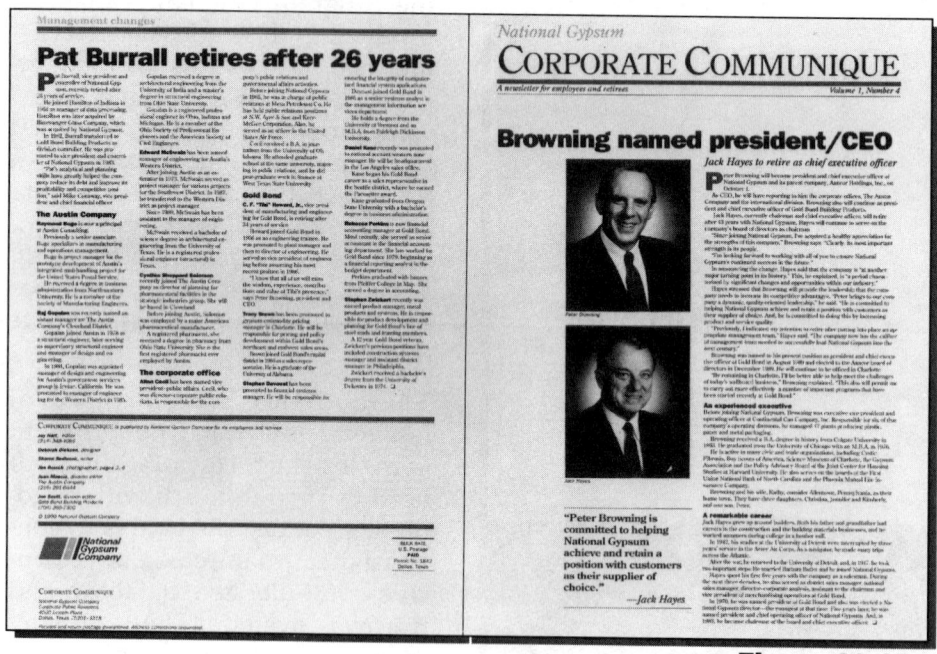

Figure 20-12.
Legislative Retrieval System, marketing materials

Rotated text also features in the Price Guide that appears inside the folder. Here the designer used frames with drop shadows and oversized numbers to help readers find and understand the five different pricing options for the service.

St. Peter's Hospital brochures

Marketing materials should reflect the intended audience. In the Legislative Retrieval System example earlier in this chapter, the audience was corporations and agencies, and the resulting pieces were slick, glossy, and expensive. The audience is very different for these two-color promotional pieces for St. Peter's Hospital, designed by Sister Barbara Roman (Figure 20-13). In this case, the documents are going to middle class mothers. The goal is to change the common belief that a hospital is a sterile, unfeeling environment while giving readers information on the hospital's programs.

Figure 20-13.
St. Peter's Hospital informational brochures

To accomplish this goal, the designer set out to create a fertile, friendly atmosphere. The flowers and hearts are shades of light red. All the other elements are dark green. To make the brochures less intimidating, a smaller page size was used (4.25 x 9.25 inches). Thick, textured paper with a beige color give the brochures a quality of softness. The designer used hearts as bullet symbols to set off paragraphs and to separate lines.

Notice how the designer created a theme by reusing the same elements in different ways throughout these related documents.

Directory: State Bar of Wisconsin

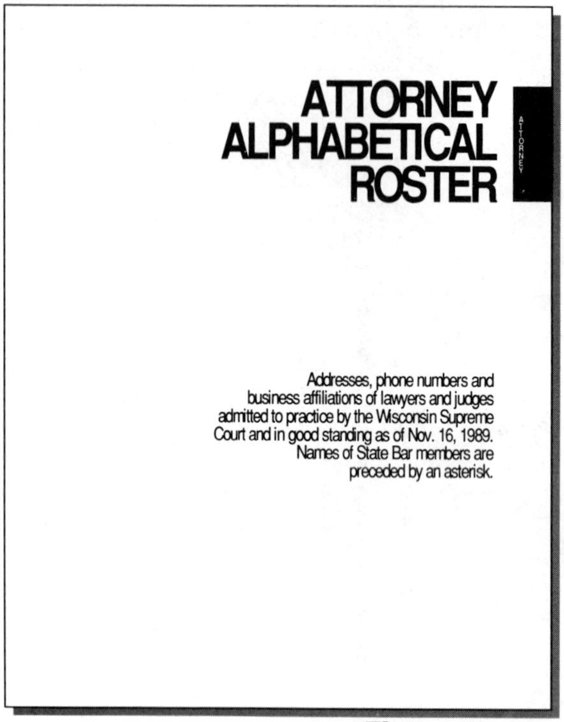
ATTORNEY
ALPHABETICAL
ROSTER

ATTORNEY

Addresses, phone numbers and business affiliations of lawyers and judges admitted to practice by the Wisconsin Supreme Court and in good standing as of Nov. 16, 1989. Names of State Bar members are preceded by an asterisk.

Figure 20-14.
Directory: State Bar of Wisconsin

By contrast, this 8.5 x 11-inch directory, designed by Art Saffran, is a utilitarian document (Figures 20-14 and 20-15). Produced for a professional association on a tight budget, its purpose is to put as much information as possible onto the page while still making that information easy to find.

The designer had the secondary goal of making production as easy and quick as possible. Because names and addresses are constantly changing, the only solution is to store association members in a database. Once they're in the database, why not let the database program do part of the formatting work? In this case, the database was used to store information, sort it (by last name in alphabetical order), and create a text file for Ventura. The database was also used to add tag codes to the text file. When the file was loaded into the chapter, the text flowed onto the page with formatting applied. Template chapters (with tags to match the tag codes created in the text file) were created for each section of the directory.

Ventura has several features that help make directories and listings more useful to readers. To help readers find the section that they need, the designer used section title pages with a large amount of white space. The title pages stand out from the other pages, which are filled with text. The section title and subtitle are right-aligned and placed on the the outside of the page so that ther reader can easily see them when thumbing quickly through the directory.

Equally important are the thumb tabs (Figure 20-14). These thumb tabs consist of white text inside a black repeating frame. Each section of the directory is a separate chapter, and each chapter has its thumb tab in a different location. Looking at the edge of the directory, the thumb tabs stair step down the page, making it easy to turn to any section.

The inside pages also provide help to the reader. At the top is a live header, which clearly shows the first and last items on that page. In addition, the designer made the names and phone numbers bold. Then he linked the name to the phone number with dotted leaders.

Figure 20-15.
Directory: State Bar of Wisconsin

Continuing on

In this chapter, we've given you a small taste of the many possible ways to use Ventura to create great-looking documents. We hope you will use this portfolio as the starting point for your own collection of design samples.

Easy Access

For more info on...	See chapter...
Setting up margins and columns on the underlying page	4 — Building the Underlying Page
Using advanced style sheet techniques, kerning, tracking, and setting tabs	5 — Building Advanced Styles
Using the Table Tool	8 — Creating Tables
Creating repeating frames	11 — Loading and Placing Pictures

For more info on...	See chapter...
Creating ruling lines and boxes for frames	**12** Enhancing and Editing Pictures
Creating a business proposal	**18** Building a Business Proposal
Creating a newsletter	**19** Building a Newsletter

21 Rapid Reference

Job aids and reference materials to speed up production

Table 21-1. *ASCII/ANSI character codes* 627

Use the number codes in Table 21-1 for generating characters. Use ASCII codes to create characters with bracket codes in your word processor and in Ventura's dialog boxes. Use ANSI codes to create them within Ventura. Note that you must change the font to create the Symbol and Zapf Dingbat characters. For the bracket codes for changing font, see Table 21-2, "Bracket codes: Text attributes," and Table 21-4, "Bracket codes: Font ID numbers."

Table 21-2. *Bracket codes: Text attributes* 631

Use the bracket codes in Table 21-2 to 21-9 for preformatting text in your word processor. Use the bracket codes in Table 21-2 to apply text attributes to your text files and to text in some dialog boxes. Use the "return to default" bracket code to return the text to the attributes of the paragraph tag.

Table 21-3. *Bracket codes: Colors* 632

Use the bracket codes in Table 21-3 to change the color of the text. Use the "return to default" bracket code to return the text to the color of the paragraph tag.

Table 21-4. *Bracket codes: Font ID numbers* 633

Use the font ID numbers in Table 21-4 for changing the font of text. See Table 21-2, "Bracket codes: Text attributes," for the syntax of the font change bracket code.

Table 21-5. *Bracket codes: Frame anchors* 638

Use these bracket codes to anchor frames. These bracket codes mark the place in the text where a frame with the specified anchor name should be anchored. However, you must give the frame its anchor name by using the Anchors & Captions dialog box.

Table 21-6. *Bracket codes: Index entries* 638

Use these bracket codes to insert index entries within text. These bracket codes mark the position of entries, contain the text of entry, and information about how the entry should be sorted. To compile all your entries, define your index format, and generate an index file, use the Make Index option in the Multi-Chapter dialog box from the File menu.

Table 21-7. *Bracket codes: Cross references* 639

Use these bracket codes for cross referencing. Use a marker bracket code to mark a position within the text. Table numbering, figure numbering, and frame anchors can also serve as markers (you don't need to mark them again with a marker). Use the reference bracket code to retrieve the type of information that you want from the marked position. Use the reference type codes within the reference bracket code to get specific information. Use the number format code to control the format of the reference information.

Table 21-8. *Bracket codes: Baseline jumps* 640

Use these bracket codes to shift text above or below the baseline. Use the following formulas to calculate custom shifts or simply use the bracket codes that we've already calculated for you.

Table 21-9. *Bracket codes: Non-keyboard characters* 641

Use these bracket codes in your text file to generate common characters that don't appear on the keyboard.

Table 21-10. *Bracket codes: Popular bullet characters* 641

Use these bracket codes in your text file to generate common bullet characters.

Table 21-11. *Ventura's generated tags* 642

Use this table to find the names of tags automatically generated by Ventura's functions. Some of these tags cannot be changed, others can be modified but not retagged, and a few can be replaced by your own tags.

Chapter 21: Rapid Reference **625**

Table 21-12. *Table formatting commands* 643

Use these tag codes to create and format tables in your word processor. These are also the codes that Ventura generates when you create a table with the Table Tool.

Table 21-13. *Equation commands: Functions* 645

Use the equation commands in Table 21-13 for generating equations and special symbols in Ventura's Equation Editor. Use these same commands in the equation bracket code (<$E*Equation commands*>) for preformatting equations in your word processor.

Table 21-14. *Equation commands: Text attributes* 647

Use these equation commands to apply text attributes to equation symbols and characters.

Table 21-15. *Equation commands: Characters/words* 648

Use these equation commands to generate special characters or words within equations.

Table 21-16. *Equation commands: Diacritical marks* 650

Use these equation commands to apply diacritical marks to equation text.

Table 21-17. *Shortcuts: Toolbox* 650

Use these keyboard shortcuts to select tools from the Toolbox.

Table 21-18. *Shortcuts: Key combinations* 651

Use these keyboard shortcuts to execute these common menu commands.

Table 21-19. *Shortcuts: Special characters* 652

Use these keyboard shortcuts to create special characters in Ventura.

Table 21-20. *Shortcuts: Essential keyboard functions* 653

Use these keyboard/mouse button combinations to handle text and graphic elements—as well as maneuver within Ventura.

Table 21-21. *File formats and extensions: Picture files* 655

Use this table to find Ventura's default file extensions for supported picture file formats.

Table 21-22. *File formats and extensions: Text files* 655

Use this table to find the default file extensions for supported text file formats. Use the recommended extensions to make each word processor format easier to distinguish.

Table 21-23. *File formats and extensions: Ventura files* 656

Use this table to find the extensions for Ventura's component files. This table also includes a short descrioption of the contents of each file type.

Table 21-24. *Ventura's fill patterns* 657

Use this table to see each pattern at different output resolutions.

Table 21-25. *Ventura's rule weights* 657

Use this table to see Ventura's standard line weights and end styles.

Table 21-1. *ASCII/ANSI character codes*

ASCII Decimal	ANSI	International	Symbol	Zapf Dingbats	ASCII Decimal	ANSI	International	Symbol	Zapf Dingbats
32	032	(space)	(space)	(space)	56	056	8	8	✘
33	033	!	!	✂	57	057	9	9	✚
34	034	"	⊇	⑩	58	058	:	:	✜
35	035	#	#	✄	59	059	;	;	✢
36	036	$	∃	✂	60	060	<	<	✣
37	037	%	%	☎	61	061	=	=	†
38	038	&	&	✆	62	062	>	>	✞
39	039	'	∋	✇	63	063	?	?	✟
40	040	(	(	✈	64	064	@	≅	✠
41	041	)	)	✉	65	065	A	A	✡
42	042	*	∗	☛	66	066	B	B	✢
43	043	+	+	☞	67	067	C	X	✣
44	044	,	,	✌	68	068	D	Δ	✤
45	045	-	−	✍	69	069	E	E	✥
46	046	.	.	✎	70	070	F	Φ	✦
47	047	/	/	✏	71	071	G	Γ	✧
48	048	0	0	✐	72	072	H	H	★
49	049	1	1	✑	73	073	I	I	☆
50	050	2	2	➔	74	074	J	ϑ	✪
51	051	3	3	✓	75	075	K	⋅ K	☆
52	052	4	4	✔	76	076	L	Λ	✫
53	053	5	5	✕	77	077	M	M	✬
54	054	6	6	✖	78	078	N	N	✭
55	055	7	7	✗	79	079	O	O	✮

Table 21-1. ASCII/ANSI character codes (continued)

ASCII Decimal	ANSI	International	Symbol	Zapf Dingbats	ASCII Decimal	ANSI	International	Symbol	Zapf Dingbats
80	080	P	Π	☆	104	0104	h	η	✳
81	081	Q	Θ	✱	105	0105	i	ι	✳
82	082	R	P	✲	106	0106	j	φ	✳
83	083	S	Σ	✳	107	0107	k	κ	✴
84	084	T	T	✴	108	0108	l	λ	●
85	085	U	Y	✵	109	0109	m	μ	○
86	086	V	ς	✶	110	0110	n	ν	■
87	087	W	Ω	✷	111	0111	o	ο	❑
88	088	X	Ξ	✸	112	0112	p	π	❐
89	089	Y	Ψ	✹	113	0113	q	θ	❒
90	090	Z	Z	✺	114	0114	r	ρ	❏
91	091	[	[	✻	115	0115	s	σ	▲
92	092	\	∴	✼	116	0116	t	τ	▼
93	093	]	]	✽	117	0117	u	υ	◆
94	094	^	⊥	✾	118	0118	v	ϖ	❖
95	095	_	_	✿	119	0119	w	ω	❘
96	096	'	―	❀	120	0120	x	ξ	❙
97	097	a	α	❁	121	0121	y	ψ	❚
98	098	b	β	❂	122	0122	z	ζ	❚
99	099	c	χ	❃	123	0123	{	{	'
100	0100	d	δ	❄	124	0124	|	|	'
101	0101	e	ε	❅	125	0125	}	}	"
102	0102	f	φ	❆	126	0126	~	~	"
103	0103	g	γ	❇	127	0127			

Table 21-1. ASCII/ANSI character codes (continued)

ASCII Decimal	ANSI	International	Symbol	Zapf Dingbats
128	0199	Ç		
129	0252	ü	ϒ	✿
130	0233	é	′	❖
131	0226	â	≤	❖
132	0228	ä	/	♥
133	0224	à	∞	♦
134	0229	å	f	✾
135	0231	ç	♣	✿
136	0234	ê	♦	♣
137	0235	ë	♥	♦
138	0232	è	♠	♥
139	0239	ï	↔	♠
140	0238	î	←	①
141	0236	ì	↑	②
142	0196	Ä	→	③
143	0197	Å	↓	④
144	0201	É	°	⑤
145	0230	æ	±	⑥
146	0198	Æ	″	⑦
147	0244	ô	≥	⑧
148	0246	ö	×	⑨
149	0242	ò	∝	⑩
150	0251	û	∂	❶
151	0249	ù	•	❷
152	0255	ÿ	÷	❸
153	0214	Ö	≠	❹
154	0220	Ü	≡	❺
155	0162	¢	≈	❻
156	0163	£	…	❼
157	0165	¥			❽
158	0164	¤	—	❾
159	0136	ƒ	↵	❿
160	0225	á	ℵ	①
161	0237	í	ℑ	②
162	0243	ó	ℜ	③
163	0250	ú	℘	④
164	0241	ñ	⊗	⑤
165	0209	Ñ	⊕	⑥
166	0170	ª	∅	⑦
167	0186	º	∩	⑧
168	0191	¿	∪	⑨
169	0147	"	⊃	⑩
170	0148	"	⊇	❶
171			•	⊄	❷
172			•	⊂	❸
173	0161	¡	⊆	❹
174	0171	«	∈	❺
175	0187	»	∉	❻

Table 21-1. ASCII/ANSI character codes (continued)

ASCII Decimal	ANSI	International	Symbol	Zapf Dingbats	ASCII Decimal	ANSI	International	Symbol	Zapf Dingbats
176	0227	ã	∠	❼	200	0194	Â	⎝	➡
177	0245	õ	∇	❽	201	0200	È	⎡	⇨
178	0216	Ø	®	❾	202	0202	Ê	⎢	⇨
179	0248	ø	©	❿	203	0203	Ë	⎣	⇨
180		•	™	→	204	0204	Ì	⎧	⇨
181		•	Π	→	205	0205	Í	⎨	⇨
182	0192	À	√	↔	206	0206	Î	⎩	⇨
183	0195	Ã	·	↕	207	0207	Ï	⎪	⇨
184	0213	Õ	¬	↘	208	0210	Ò		
185	0167	§	∧	➙	209	0211	Ó	〉	⇨
186		•	∨	↗	210	0212	Ô	∫	⊃
187		•	⇔	➤	211		•	⎛	➢
188	0182	¶	⇐	➡	212		•	⎜	➢
189	0169	©	⇑	→	213	0217	Ù	⎟	➢
190	0174	®	⇒	→	214	0218	Ú	〉	✒
191	0153	™	⇓	⇒	215	0219	Û	⎥	✏
192	0132	„	◊	⇒	216		•	⎦	➢
193	0133	…	〈	➡	217	0223	ß	⎤	✒
194		•	®	⩾	218			Ž	⎥	→
195		•	©	⩾	219			ž	⎦	➤
196	0150	–	™	➤	220			/	⎫	➤
197	0151	—	Σ	➡	221				⎬	➤
198	0176	°	⎛	➡	222				⎭	⇒
199	0193	Á	⎜	♦						

Table 21-2. *Bracket codes: Text attributes*

Attribute	Bracket code	
Normal (medium)	`<M>`	
Normal (medium) Italic	`<MI>`	
Bold	`<B>`	
Bold Italic	`<BI>`	
Underline	`<U>`	
Double Underline	`<=>`	
Overscore	`<O>`	
Strike-through	`<X>`	
Small	`<S>`	
Superscript	`<^>`	
Subscript	`<v>`	
Return to default	`<D>`	This code ends the effects of `<M>`, `<MI>`, `<B>`, `<BI>`, `<U>`, `<=>`, `<O>`, `<X>`, `<S>`, `<^>`, and `<v>`, then returns to defaults of the paragraph tag
Discretionary hyphen	`<->`	
Em Space	`<_>`	
En Space	`<~>`	
Non-breaking word space	`<N>`	
Figure space	`<+>`	
Thin space	`<|>`	
Hidden text	`<$!text>`	
Line break	`<R>`	
Color	`<Cn>`	n is a number from 0 to 7, representing the desired color (see "Bracket Codes: Color")
Font	`<Fn>`	n is the number, representing the desired font (see See "Bracket Codes: Font ID numbers")
Point size	`<Pn>`	n is the desired point size, from 1 to 254
Return to default	`<C255>` `<F255>` `<P255>`	This code ends the effect of `<Cn>`, `<Fn>`, and `<Pn>`, then returns to the defaults of the paragraph tag

Table 21-3. *Bracket codes: Colors*

Bracket code	Color
<C0>	White
<C1>	Black
<C2>	Red
<C3>	Green
<C4>	Blue
<C5>	Cyan
<C6>	Yellow
<C7>	Magenta
<C255>	Reset to tag's default color

Table 21-4. Bracket codes: Font ID numbers

Font type	Family name	Typeface	PostScript font filename	Face ID number
Serif	American Typewriter	American Typewriter-Medium	ATM_____	100
		American Typewriter-Bold	ATB_____	
	Benguiat	Benguiat-Book	BGW_____	26
		Benguiat-Bold	BGB_____	
	Bodoni	Bodoni	BDR_____	36
		Bodoni-Italic	BDI_____	
		Bodoni-Bold	BDB_____	
		Bodoni-Bold Italic	BDBI_____	
	Bookman	Bookman-Light	BKL_____	23
		Bookman-Light Italic	BKLI_____	
		Bookman-Demi	BKD_____	
		Bookman-Demi Italic	BKDI_____	
	Century Old Style	Century Old Style-Regular	CORG_____	38
		Century Old Style-Italic	COI_____	
		Century Old Style-Bold	COB_____	
	Cheltenham	Cheltenham-Book	CHW_____	39
		Cheltenham-Book Italic	CHWI_____	
		Cheltenham-Bold	CHB_____	
		Cheltenham-Bold Italic	CHBI_____	
	Courier	Courier	COURI	1
		Courier-Oblique	COURIO	102
		Courier-Bold	COURIB	1
		Courier-Bold Oblique	COURIBO	
	Friz Quadrata	Friz Quadrata	FQRG_____	28
		Friz Quadrata-Bold	FQB_____	

Table 21-4 Bracket codes: Font ID numbers *(continued)*

Font type	Family name	Typeface	PostScript font filename	Face ID number
Serif	Galliard	Galliard-Roman	GLR____	32
		Galliard-Italic	GLI____	
		Galliard-Bold	GLB____	
		Galliard-Bold Italic	GLBI____	
	Garamond	Garamond-Light	GAL____	22
		Garamond-Light Italic	GALI____	
		Garamond-Bold	GAB____	
		Garamond-Bold Italic	GABI____	
	Glypha	Glypha	GYR____	27
		Glypha-Oblique	GYO____	
		Glypha-Bold	GYB____	
		Glypha-Bold Oblique	GYBO____	
	Goudy	Goudy	GOR____	34
		Goudy-Italic	GOI____	
		Goudy-Bold	GOB____	
		Goudy-Bold Italic	GOBI____	
	Lubalin Graph	Lubalin Graph-Book	LUW____	24
		Lubalin Graph-Book Oblique	LUWO____	
		Lubalin Graph-Demi	LUD____	
		Lubalin Graph-Demi Oblique	LUDO____	
	Korinna	Korinna-Regular	KRRG____	53
		Korinna-Kursiv Regular	KRKX____	
		Korinna-Bold	KRB____	
		Korinna-Kursiv Bold	KRKB____	
	Melior	Melior	MER____	31
		Melior-Italic	MEI____	
		Melior-Bold	MEB____	
		Melior-Bold Italic	MEBI____	

Table 21-4 *Bracket codes: Font ID numbers* (continued)

Font type	Family name	Typeface	PostScript font filename	Face ID number
Serif	New Baskerville	New Baskerville-Roman	NBR_____	33
		New Baskerville-Italic	NBI_____	
		New Baskerville-Bold	NBB_____	
		New Baskerville-Bold Italic	NBBI_____	
	New Century Schoolbook	New Century Schlbk-Roman	NCR_____	20
		New Century Schlbk-Italic	NCI_____	
		New Century Schlbk-Bold	NCB_____	
		New Century Schlbk-Bold Italic	NCBI_____	
	Palatino	Palatino-Roman	POR_____	21
		Palatino-Italic	POI_____	
		Palatino-Bold	POB_____	
		Palatino-Bold Italic	POBI_____	
	Park Avenue	Park Avenue	PAM_____	35
	Souvenir	Souvenir-Light	SUL_____	25
		Souvenir-Light Italic	SULI_____	
		Souvenir-Demi	SUD_____	
		Souvenir-Demi Italic	SUDI_____	
	Times	Times-Roman	TIMESR_____	14
		Times-Italic	TIMESI_____	
		Times-Bold	TIMESB_____	
		Times-Bold Italic	TIMESBI_____	
	Trump Mediaeval	Trump Mediaeval-Roman	TMR_____	30
		Trump Mediaeval-Italic	TMI_____	
		Trump Mediaeval-Bold	TMB_____	
		Trump Mediaeval-Bold Italic	TMBI_____	
	Zapf Chancery	Zapf Chancery-Medium Italic	ZCMI_____	29

Table 21-4 Bracket codes: Font ID numbers (continued)

Font type	Family name	Typeface	PostScript font filename	Face ID number
Sans serif	Avant Garde	Avant Garde-Book	AGW____	51
		Avant Garde-Book Oblique	AGWO____	
		Avant Garde-Demi	AGD____	
		Avant Garde-Demi Oblique	AGDO____	
	Franklin Gothic	Franklin Gothic-Book	FRW____	56
		Franklin Gothic-Book Oblique	FRWO____	
		Franklin Gothic-Demi	FRD____	
		Franklin Gothic-Demi Oblique	FRDO____	
		Franklin Gothic-Heavy	FRH____	57
		Franklin Gothic-Heavy Oblique	FRHO____	
	Helvetica	Helvetica	HELVE	2
		Helvetica-Black	HVBL____	55
		Helvetica-Black Oblique	HVBLO____	
		Helvetica-Bold	HELVEB	2
		Helvetica-Bold Oblique	HELVEBO	
		Helvetica-Condensed	HVC____	59
		Helvetica-Condensed Oblique	HVCDO____	
		Helvetica-Condensed-Black	HVCBL____	60
		Helvetica-Condensed-Black Oblique	HVCO____	
		Helvetica-Condensed-Bold	HVCB____	59
		Helvetica-Condensed-Bold Oblique	HVCBO____	
		Helvetica-Condensed-Light	HVCL____	58
		Helvetica-Condensed-Light Oblique	HVCLO____	
		Helvetica-Light	HVL____	54
		Helvetica-Light Oblique	HVLO____	

Table 21-4 *Bracket codes: Font ID numbers* (continued)

Font type	Family name	Typeface	PostScript font filename	Face ID number
Sans serif	Helvetica	Helvetica-Narrow	HELVEN	50
		Helvetica-Narrow Oblique	HELVENO	
		Helvetica-Narrow-Bold	HELVENB	
		Helvetica-Narrow-Bold Oblique	HELVENBO	
		Helvetica-Oblique	HELVEO	2
	Machine	Machine	MAM	101
	Optima	Optima	OP	52
		Optima-Oblique	OPO	
		Optima-Bold	OPB	
		Optima-Bold Oblique	OPBO	
Other	Symbol	Symbol	SYMBOL	128
	Zapf Dingbats	Zapf Dingbats	ZDM	129
	Sonata	Sonata	MUSO	130
Mono-space	Letter Gothic	Letter Gothic	LGRG	105
		Letter Gothic-Slanted	LGSL	
		Letter Gothic-Bold	LGB	
		Letter Gothic-Bold Slanted	LGBSL	
	Orator	Orator	ORRG	104
		Orator-Slanted	ORSL	
	Prestige Elite	Prestige Elite	PERG	103
		Prestige Elite-Slanted	PESL	
		Prestige Elite-Bold	PEB	
		Prestige Elite-Bold Slanted	PEBSL	

Table 21-5. *Bracket codes: Frame anchors*

Bracket code syntax	Purpose
`<$&anchor name>`	Fixed, on same page as anchor (at whatever position it is placed manually)
`<$&anchor name[v]>`	Relative, below anchor line
`<$&anchor name[^]>`	Relative, above anchor line
`<$&anchor name[-]>`	Relative, automatically at anchor

Table 21-6. *Bracket codes: Index entries*

Function	Bracket code syntax	Example
Primary index entry	`<$IPrimary>`	`<$IPastries>`
Secondary index entry	`<$IPrimary;Secondary>`	`<$IPastries;donuts>`
See	`<$SPrimary;see entry>`	`<$SDoughnuts;donuts>`
See also	`<$APrimary;also entry>`	`<$ACake;Pastries>`
Alternate sort order, primary	`<$IPrimary[Primary sort]>`	`<$IThe Spike Theatre[Spike Theatre]>`
Alternate sort order, secondary	`<$IPrimary;Secondary[Secondary sort]>`	`<$ILights;3-way bulbs[Three-way]>`

Table 21-7. *Bracket codes: Cross references*

Type	Bracket code syntax			Example
Marker	`<$M[label]>`			`<$M[Widget]>`
Variable definition	`<$V[label]definition>`			`<$V[Company]MicroPublishing>`
				`<$V[product]Model 123-S>`
Reference	`<$R[type,label,format]string>`			("string" is an optional temporary value)
	Reference type	Chapter number	C#	`<$R[C#,Intro]>`
		Page number	P#	`<$R[P#,Mapinfo]>`
		Figure number	F#	`<$R[F#,Widget photo]>`
		Table number	T#	`<$R[T#,fiscal]>`
		Section number	S*	`<$R[S*,cash rule]>`
		Caption text	C*	`<$R[C*,Widget photo]>`
		Variable text	V*	`<$R[V*,Company]>`
	Number format	Arabic	1	`<$R[C#,Intro,1]>`
		Alpha, uppercase	A	`<$R[C#,Intro,A]>`
		Alpha, lowercase	a	`<$R[C#,Intro,a]>`
		Roman, uppercase	I	`<$R[C#,Intro,I]>`
		Roman, lowercase	i	`<$R[C#,Intro,i]>`
		Spell, uppercase	ONE	`<$R[C#,Intro,ONE]>`
		Spell, initial cap	One	`<$R[C#,Intro,One]>`
		Spell, lowercase	one	`<$R[C#,Intro,one]>`

Table 21-8. *Bracket codes: Baseline jumps*

Direction	Desired amount (points)	Bracket code (J*n*)	Actual amount	Result
	Calculate the number *n* for a jump *up* for the desired amount in points *p*, according to this formula: $n = 256 - \left(\dfrac{300}{72}\right) * (p)$			
Up	06.00	<J231>	06.00	Normal & Shifted Text
	05.00	<J235>	05.04	Normal & Shifted Text
	04.00	<J239>	04.08	Normal & Shifted Text
	03.00	<J244>	02.88	Normal & Shifted Text
	02.00	<J248>	01.92	Normal & Shifted Text
	01.00	<J252>	00.96	Normal & Shifted Text
	Calculate the number *n* for a jump *down* for the desired amount in points *p*, according to this formula: $n = \left(\dfrac{300}{72}\right) * (p)$			
Down	01.00	<J4>	00.96	Normal & Shifted Text
	02.00	<J8>	01.92	Normal & Shifted Text
	03.00	<J12>	02.88	Normal & Shifted Text
	04.00	<J17>	04.08	Normal & Shifted Text
	05.00	<J21>	05.04	Normal & Shifted Text
	06.00	<J25>	06.00	Normal & Shifted Text
Reset to original baseline		<J0>		

Table 21-9. Bracket codes: Common non-keyboard characters

Name	Character	Bracket code(s)
Open quote	"	<169>
Close quote	"	<170>
Copyright symbol	©	<189>
Registered trademark	®	<190>
Unregistered trademark	™	<191>
En dash	–	<196>
Em dash	—	<197>
Hollow box	□	<$B0>
Filled box	■	<$B1>
Multiplication sign	×	<F128><148><F255>
Ellipsis	…	<193>
Bullet (round)	•	<195>

Table 21-10. Bracket codes: Popular bullet characters

Typeface	Character	Bracket code
Standard round bullet	•	<195>
Hollow box	□	<$B0>
Filled box	■	<$B1>
Symbol round bullet	•	<F128><151><F255>
Zapf Dingbats	✓ and ✔	<F129><51><F255> and <F129><52><F255>
	●	<F129><108><F255>
	■	<F129><110><F255>
	▲	<F129><115><F255>
	▼	<F129><116><F255>
	❦	<F129><134><F255>
	❧	<F129><135><F255>
	♦	<F129><199><F255>

Table 21-11. *Ventura's generated tags*

Generated tag	Function	Purpose
Z_BOXTEXT	Box Text	Box Text
Z_CAPTION	Anchors & Captions, Frame menu	Caption when no numbering function buttons are used
Z_DOUBLE	Table mode, rules	Double lines in tables
Z_FNOT #	Footnote Settings, Chapter menu	Footnote numbers (or symbols)
Z_FNOT ENTRY	Footnote Settings, Chapter menu	Footnote entries (at bottom of page)
Z_FOOTER	Headers & Footers, Chapter menu	Page footer
Z_HEADER	Headers & Footers, Chapter menu	Page header
Z_HIDDEN	Table mode, rules	Invisible lines in tables
Z_INDEX LTR	Index, Manage Publication (Multi-Chapter), File menu	Letters used as separators in the generated index file
Z_INDEX MAIN	Index, Manage Publication (Multi-Chapter), File menu	Index entries
Z_INDEX TITLE	Index, Manage Publication (Multi-Chapter), File menu	Index title
Z_LABEL CAP	Anchors & Captions, Frame menu	Figure number in captions when Figure # button is used
Z_LABEL FIG	Anchors & Captions, Frame menu	Caption when either Figure # or Table # button is used
Z_LABEL TBL	Anchors & Captions, Frame menu	Table number when Table # button is used
Z_SECn	Auto-Numbering, Paragraph menu	Paragraph generated by Auto-Numbering; n is a number from 1 to 10 that specifies the numbering level
Z_SINGLE	Table mode, rules	Single lines in tables
Z_TBL_BEG	Table mode	Beginning of table
Z_TBL_BODY	Table mode	Assignment of tags used for each column in the main body of table
Z_TBL_END	Table mode	Ending of table
Z_TBL_HEAD	Table mode	Assignment of tags used for column headers in table
Z_THICK	Table mode, rules	Thick lines in tables
Z_TOC LVLn	Table of Contents, Manage Publication (Multi-Chapter), File menu	Table of contents entry; n is a number from 1 to 10 that specifies the TOC heading level
Z_TOC TITLE	Table of Contents, Manage Publication (Multi-Chapter), File menu	Table of contents title

Table 21-12. *Table formatting commands*

Code	Description R=Required; O=Optional	Example
@Z_TBL_BEG =	R — Beginning of table	@Z_TBL_BEG =
COLUMNS(*n*)	R — Number of columns (must immediately follow @Z_TBL_BEG =)	@Z_TBL_BEG = COLUMNS(3)
DIMENSION()	O — Unit of measure (inches, centimeters, picas, or points) used in table	DIMENSION(IN) DIMENSION(PT) DIMENSION(CM) DIMENSION(PI)
COLWIDTHS()	O — Width of columns in DIMENSION units, or in number of proportions. E*n* specifies *n* proportions	COLWIDTHS(.5,1,.5,2) COLWIDTHS(E2,E1,E1,E1) COLWIDTHS(1.25,E2,E1)
WIDTH()	O — Overall width of custom table (if not specified, width is current text column width)	WIDTH(4.5)
INDENT()	O — Indent of table from text column for custom table	INDENT(1.00) INDENT(2IN)
ABOVE()	O — Space above table	ABOVE(6.5) ABOVE(2PT)
BELOW()	O — Space below table	BELOW(1.0) BELOW(13PT)
VJTOP()	O — Vertical justification above table	VJTOP(2) VJTOP(15PT)
VJBOT()	O — Vertical justification below table	VJBOT(6)
HGUTTER()	O — Space between columns of table	HGUTTER(12) HGUTTER(1PI)
VGUTTER()	O — Space between rows of table	VGUTTER(7) VGUTTER(1PI)
BOX()	O — Tag name of rule around outside of table	BOX(Z_DOUBLE) BOX(Z_SINGLE) BOX(Z_USER_DEF)
HGRID()	O — Tag name of horizontal rules	HGRID(Z_SINGLE) HGRID(Z_DOUBLE) HGRID(Z_USER_DEF)
VGRID()	O — Tag name of vertical rules	VGRID(Z_SINGLE) VGRID(Z_THICK) VGRID(Z_USER_DEF)

Table 21-12. *Table formatting commands* (continued)

Code	Description R=Required; O=Optional		Example
KEEP()	O	Permits (off) or prevents (on) breaking of table to next column, frame, or page	KEEP(ON) KEEP(OFF)
RULE()	O	Rules (by tag name) for a specified range of cells	RULE(Z_THICK,R0C3..R2C5) RULE(Z_HIDDEN,R5C5..R5C6)
@Z_TBL_HEAD =	O	Tags for header row(s). This paragraph and its header rows must immediately follow the @Z_TBL_BEG paragraph, and precede the @Z_TBL_BODY paragraph	@Z_TBL_HEAD = HEAD2, HEAD3, HEAD3
@Z_TBL_BODY =	O	Tag names of cells within a row in main body of table	@Z_TBL_BODY = TABLELEFT, TABLECENTER, TABLECENTER, TABLERIGHT
C1, C2, C3, C4	R	Entries for a row of cells. Use a ^ character before the comma to join cell with the one above; use + to join cell with one to the right	1, Item, Description, 4, ^, 6, +,
<$!B$nm$>	O	Tint for cell (place at end of cell entry, just before comma; n is the color, and m is the pattern)	1, Item<$!B11>, Description<$!B12>, 4, ^, 6, +,
@Z_TBL_END =	R	End of table	@Z_TBL_END =

Table 21-13. *Equation commands: Functions*

Command	Example	Result
{ } (braces)	`text ~roman { text }`	*text* text
/ (fraction bar)	`1/2`	$\frac{1}{2}$
above	(see *pile*)	
back	`y back 120 x`	$x\,y$
ccol	`ccol{a above b}`	$\begin{array}{c}a\\b\end{array}$
cpile	`cpile{a above b above c}`	$\begin{array}{c}a\\b\\c\end{array}$
down	`y down 100 x`	$y \atop x$
from	(see *sum*)	
fwd	`y fwd 100 x`	$y\quad x$
int	`int sub 0 sup inf { ^1 over x ^dx }`	$\int_0^\infty \frac{1}{x}\,dx$
inter	`C~=~A inter B`	$C = A \cap B$
lcol	(see *matrix*)	
left	`left ( text`	$(\text{text}$
	`left { a sub b sup c`	$\{a_b^c$
lineup	(see *mark*)	
lpile	(see *pile*)	
mark	`y sub n + 1 ~mark = ~y sub n ^+^ 1`	$y_{n+1} = y_n + 1$
	`y sub 0 ~lineup = ~0`	$y_0 = 0$
	`y sub { last } ~lineup = ~inf`	$y_{last} = \infty$

Table 21-13. *Equation commands: Functions* (continued)

Command	Example	Result
matrix	`matrix { ccol { a above b } ~ccol { c above d } }`	$\begin{matrix} a & c \\ b & d \end{matrix}$
over	`a over { b ^+^ c }`	$\dfrac{a}{b+c}$
pile	`rpile { 0 above 2x above 0 } ~~lpile { x < 0 above 0 <= x <= 1 above 1 < x }`	$\begin{matrix} 0 & x<0 \\ 2x & 0 \le x \le 1 \\ 0 & 1<x \end{matrix}$
prod	`prod from { i ~=~ 1 } to inf X sub i`	$\prod_{i=1}^{\infty} X_i$
rcol	(see *matrix*)	
right	`left { rpile { { x ~+~ y } above x above x sup 2 } right }`	$\begin{Bmatrix} x+y \\ x \\ x^2 \end{Bmatrix}$
rpile	(see *pile*)	
sqrt	`sqrt { x sup 2 ^+^ y sup 2 }`	$\sqrt{x^2+y^2}$
sub	`a sub b`	a_b
	`a sub b sub c`	a_{b_c}
sum	`sum from { i ~=~ 1 } to inf x sub i`	$\sum_{i=1}^{\infty} x_i$
sup	`a sup b`	a^b
	`a sup b sup c`	a^{b^c}
	`a sub b sup c`	a_b^c
	`a sup b sub c`	a^b_c
to	(see *sum*)	

Table 21-13. *Equation commands: Functions* (continued)

Command	Example	Result
union	C ~=~ A union B	$C = A \cup B$
up	y up 100 x	$\begin{array}{c}x\\y\end{array}$

Table 21-14. *Equation commands: Text attributes*

Effect	Command	Example	Result
Color change	color *n*	These~words~ color 0 { are white } .	These words *are white*.
Different font	font *n*	Font~is~ font 55 { Helvetica~Black }	Font is **Helvetica Black**
Bold italic	fat	This~word~is~ fat BOLD .	This word is ***BOLD***.
Roman (normal)	roman	This~is~ roman NORMAL ~text.	This is NORMAL text.
Bold Roman	fat roman	This~is~ fat { roman { BOLD~NORMAL } } .	This is **BOLD NORMAL**.
Font size change	size *n*	These~are~ size 18 BIG ~and~ size 6 small .	These are BIG and small.
Symbol font	symbol *x*	symbol p ^r^ sup 2	πr^2

n = a number from 0 to 8 for color ID, from 1 to 255 for font ID, and of points for font size.
x = a character from the International character set that has the same ANSI code as a character in the Symbol font. See ASCII/ANSI character codes

Table 21-15. Equations commands: Characters/words

Special characters	Result
,...,	,...,
...	...
!=	≠
+-	±
->	→
<-	←
<<	<
<=	≤
==	≡
>=	≥
>>	>

Special characters	Result
approx	≈
cdot	·
ceiling	⌈
del	∂
floor	⌊
grad	∇
inf	∞
nothing	
partial	∂
prime	′
times	×

Spaces	Result
~	(space)

Spaces	Result
^	(thin space)

Greek character name	Greek character
DELTA	Δ
EPSILON	E
GAMMA	Γ
LAMBDA	Λ
OMEGA	Ω
PHI	Φ
PI	Π
PSI	Ψ
SIGMA	Σ
THETA	Θ

Greek character name	Greek character
delta	δ
epsilon	ε
gamma	γ
lambda	λ
omega	ω
phi	φ
pi	π
psi	ψ
sigma	σ
theta	θ

Table 21-15. *Equation commands: Characters/words* (continued)

Greek character name	Greek character	Greek character name	Greek character
UPSILON	Υ	upsilon	υ
XI	Ξ	xi	ξ
alpha	α	mu	μ
beta	β	nu	ν
chi	χ	omicron	o
eta	η	rho	ρ
iota	ι	tau	τ
kappa	κ	zeta	ζ

Romanized word command	Result	Romanized word command	Result
Im	Im	if	if
Re	Re	lim	lim
and	and	ln	ln
arc	arc	log	log
cos	cos	max	max
cosh	cosh	min	min
cot	cot	sin	sin
coth	coth	sinh	sinh
det	det	tan	tan
exp	exp	tanh	tanh
for	for		

Table 21-16. *Equation commands: Diacritical marks*

Diacritical mark command	Example	Result
bar	xyz bar	$\overline{xyz}$
dot	xyz dot	$x\dot{y}z$
dotdot	xyz dotdot	$x\ddot{y}z$
dyad	xyz dyad	$x\overleftrightarrow{y}z$
hat	xyz hat	$x\hat{y}z$
tilde	xyz tilde	$x\tilde{y}z$
under	xyz under	$\underline{xyz}$
vec	xyz vec	$x\vec{y}z$

Table 21-17. *Shortcuts: Toolbox*

Tool	Shortcut
Frame Tool	Ctrl-U
Paragraph Tool	Ctrl-I
Text Tool	Ctrl-O
Table Tool	Ctrl-P

Table 21-18. *Shortcuts: Key combinations*

Menu	Menu Item		Shortcut
File	Save		Ctrl-S
Edit	Cut	(Frame, Tag, Text, Graphic, or Row/Column)	Del
	Copy		Shift-Del
	Paste		Ins
	Renumber Chapter		Ctrl-B
View	Reduced View		Ctrl-R
	Normal View (1x)		Ctrl-N
	Enlarged view (2x)		Ctrl-E
	Show Tabs & Returns*		Ctrl-T
	Toolbox Window*		Ctrl-W
	Tag List Window*		Ctrl-V
	File List Window*		Ctrl-Y
Chapter	Go to Page...		Ctrl-G
Paragraph	Add New Tag...		Ctrl-2
	Update Tag List...		Ctrl-K
Text	Edit Special Item...		Ctrl-D
Graphic	Send to Back		Ctrl-Z
	Bring to Front		Ctrl-A
	Line Attributes...		Ctrl-L
	Fill Attributes...		Ctrl-F
	Select All		Ctrl-Q

*Toggle—Pressing the same combination again will reverse the status.

Table 21-19. *Shortcuts: Special characters*

Function	Key	Function	Key
Add frame, tag, or set font	Ctrl + 2	Line attributes (graphics)	Ctrl + L
Assign function keys	Ctrl + K	Line break	Ctrl + Enter
Bring to front	Ctrl + A	Non-breaking space	Ctrl-Spacebar
Copy	Shift + Del	Normal view	Ctrl + N
Copyright ©	Ctrl + Shift + C	Paragraph tool	Ctrl + I
Cut	Del	Paste	Ins
Delete to left of cursor	Backspace	Recall last dialog box	Ctrl + X
Delete to right of cursor	Del	Redraw screen	Esc
Discretionary hyphen	Ctrl + Hyphen	Reduced view	Ctrl + R
Double quote, closed	Ctrl + Shift +]	Registered trademark ®	Ctrl + Shift + R
Double quote, opened	Ctrl + Shift + [	Renumber chapter	Ctrl + B
Edit special item	Ctrl + D	Save	Ctrl + S
EM dash —	Ctrl +]	Select all (graphics)	Ctrl + Q
EM space	Ctrl + Shift + M	Selection tool	Ctrl + U
EN dash –	Ctrl + [	Send to back	Ctrl + Z
EN space	Ctrl + Shift + N	Show/hide File List window	Ctrl + Y
Enlarged view	Ctrl + E	Show/hide tabs & returns	Ctrl + T
Figure space	Ctrl + Shift + F	Show/hide Tag List window	Ctrl + V
Fill attributes (graphics)	Ctrl + F	Show/hide Toolbox	Ctrl + W
Go to first page	Home	Table tool	Ctrl + P
Go to last page	End	Text tool	Ctrl + O
Go to next page	PgDn	Thin space	Ctrl + Shift + T
Go to page	Ctrl + G	Trademark ™	Ctrl + Shift + 2
Go to previous page	PgUp	Update tag list	Ctrl + K

Table 21-20. *Essential keyboard functions*

Key		Function
Arrow keys	(↑ ← → ↓)	Control the movement of the text cursor, when using Text mode
Home	Home	Goes to first page of chapter (has no effect if already on first page)
End	End	Goes to the last page of the chapter (has no effect if already on last page)
Page Up	PgUp	Goes to the previous page (has no effect if already on first page)
Page Down	PgDn	Goes to the next page (has no effect if already on last page)
Delete	Del	1. Deletes the character to the right of the text cursor 2. Has same effect as choosing Cut from the Edit menu when a frame, graphic element, or a block of text is selected 3. When pressed simultaneously with the Shift key, same as choosing Copy from the Edit menu
Insert	Ins	Has same effect as choosing Paste from the Edit menu
Backspace	Backspace	Deletes the character to the left of the text cursor
Escape	Esc	1. Stops a Go To Page command 2. Has same effect as clicking on Cancel in a dialog box 3. Redraws the current page (screen refresh) if neither of the first two conditions exist

Table 21-20. *Essential keyboard functions* (continued)

Key	Function	
Shift	1	When used with the mouse, allows selection of multiple frames, graphic elements, and paragraphs: Hold down the Shift key and click on all the desired objects
	2	When using Text mode, allows selection of a range of text: Click text cursor at beginning or end of range, hold down the Shift key, and click again at other end of the range
	3	Allows creation of multiple frames and graphic elements: Select the New Frame tool or a Graphic tool, hold down the Shift key, draw all the element one after another
	4	When used with the arrow keys, allows interactive change of selected text: Use the left and right arrow keys to kern text (tighten and loosen text, respectively); use the up and down arrow keys to change the font size
Tab	1	Inserts horizontal tab characters
	2	When in a dialog box, moves from one option field to the next. When pressed simultaneously with the Shift key, moves backwards to the previous option
Function keys		F1 invokes the help index
		The other function keys are used to apply paragraph tags to selected text, either in Text or Paragraph mode (assign keys to tags with the Assign Function Keys option from the Update Tag List command)
Control	1	When pressed simultaneously with the Enter key, inserts a line break
	2	When pressed simultaneously with the hyphen, inserts a discretionary hyphen
	3	When held down while clicking on multiple graphic elements or frames, selects objects that are underneath
	4	When pressed simultaneously with the X key, recalls the last dialog box used or repeats a previous menu action such as a Save command
Alt	1	When used with the mouse, moves cropped pictures within frames
	2	When held down while drawing graphic elements, snaps lines at angles in 45-degree increments and makes perfect squares and circles
	3	When used with the numeric keypad, inserts non-keyboard characters

Table 21-21. *File formats and extensions: Picture files*

Type of file	Format	Extension
Line-art	Computer Graphics Metafile	CGM
	PostScript	EPS
	GEM	GEM
	HPGL	HPG
	MacPict	PCT
	Video Show	PIC
	AutoCAD Slide	SLD
	Windows Metafile	WMF
Image	GEM	IMG
	PC Paintbrush	PCX
	Macintosh Paint	PNT
	Tagged Image File Format (TIFF)	TIF

Table 21-22. *File formats and extensions: Text files*

Format	Filter name	Default extension	Recommended extension
ASCII	ASCII/8-bit ASCII	TXT	ASC
Displaywrite	DCA	RFT	RFT
Microsoft Word	MSWord	DOC	MSW
MultiMate	MultiMate	DOC	MTM
Wordstar 3.0	Wordstar 3	WS	WS3
Wordstar 4.0/5.0	WS4.0/5.0	WS	WS4/WS5
WordPerfect 4.2	WordPerfect	WP	WP4
WordPerfect 5.0	WordPerfect 5	WP	WP5
Xerox Writer	Writer	XWP	XWP
Xywrite	Xywrite	*(none)*	XY

Table 21-23. *File formats and extensions: Ventura files*

Category	Type	Contents	Extension	Typical name
Chapter files	Chapter file	Pointers to the other files plus formatting information	CHP	SAMPLE.CHP
	Style sheet	Formatting information	STY	SAMPLE.STY
	Chapter information file	Date of last save, last print, and other programming info	CIF	SAMPLE.CIF
	Ventura graphics file	Graphics created with Ventura's built-in drawing tools	VGR	SAMPLE.VGR
	Caption file	Captions, Box Text, and frame text	CAP	SAMPLE.CAP
Document files	Text file(s)	Text created with other programs	TXT, DOC, WP, etc.	SAMPLE.TXT
	Graphics file(s)	Pictures created with other programs	PCX, GEM, EPS, etc.	PICTURE.PCX
Multi-chapter files	Publication file	Pointers and information about the chapters that make up the publication	PUB	SAMPLE.PUB
	Generated files	Index and table of contents text and information generated by Ventura	GEN	SAMPLIDX.GEN (index) SAMPLTOC.GEN (table of contents)

Chapter 21: Rapid Reference

Table 21-24. *Fill patterns*

Pattern	Resolution (dots per inch)			
	300	600	1270	2540
Hollow				
1				
2				
3				
4				
5				
6				
7				
Solid				

Table 21-25. *Ventura's rule weights*

Line weight	Thin
	2
	3
	4
	Thick

End styles	Square
	Arrowhead (both ends)
	Round (both ends)

22 Glossary

anchor To attach a frame to a postion in the text. If the text moves, the anchored frame stays with it.

ascender The part of a lowercase letter that extends above the *x-height*, such as the long upper strokes of b, h, and d.

ASCII (American Standard Code for Information Interchange) A standard coding system that assigns numerical values to letters, numbers, and symbols. ASCII text files are the lowest common denominator for exchanging text between word processing and DTP programs.

aspect ratio The ratio of height to width. When you maintain aspect ratio, you keep the original proportions when resizing a graphic.

attribute A trait of a typeface. Common attributes include style (bold, italic), position (subscript, superscript), and color (black, blue).

banner A headline that stretches across more than one column.

baseline An imaginary horizontal line on which each character rests.

bit-mapped Type and images that are made up of patterns of dots (*pixels*), as opposed to line art, which is based on a mathematical description.

body text The main text in a document. When capitalized (Body Text), refers to Ventura's default *tag* for the main text.

box text One of Ventura's graphics tools. Draws a box that, like Ventura's other graphics, can be positioned anywhere on the page. But this box can contain text.

break The point where a line, column, or page begins or ends.

callout A small label that identifies one portion of a picture. Often accompanied by an arrow pointing to one part of the picture.

caption Text that accompanies and describes a picture.

cell An area that contains an entry in a table.

chapter The chapter is the central file that controls a Ventura document. It describes and controls the other files (style sheet files, text files, graphics files) that make up the document.

clipart Predrawn illustrations for later use. You "clip" the picture you want and put it into your publication.

clipboard An electronic storage area that temporarily holds text, graphics, or frames that have been cut or copied with the Edit menu. The cut or copied element can then be pasted elsewhere.

crop To cut out parts of a picture.

crop marks Alignment marks that indicate the outside edges of a printed page. Traditionally, designers also use the term for the marks on the corners of photographs that indicate which portion to keep and which to eliminate (crop).

dateline A line on the front page (in a newsletter) that identifies the date and volume number of the issue.

descender The part of a lowercase letter that falls below the baseline, such as the lower portions of g, p, and y.

dialog box A pop-up window used to choose among different options.

digitize To convert a picture into a *bit-mapped* image, usually with an electronic scanning device.

dingbats Ornamental characters used for emphasis or decoration, such as bullets and stars.

discretionary hyphen Indicates where to break a word if necessary to format a line. Does not take effect unless the word occurs at the end of a line and will not fit completely.

dither To use dot patterns to simulate shades of gray or other continuous tones.

drag To move, size, or select an object with the mouse. Point at an object, press and hold the left mouse button as you move the mouse, and release the button.

em A unit of measure equal to the point size of the font.

em dash A punctuation mark that is one *em* long and resembles a hyphen. To generate an em dash in Ventura, press Ctrl-].

en A unit of measure equal to half of an *em*.

en dash A punctuation mark that is one *en* long and ressembles a hyphen. To generate an en dash in Ventura, press Ctrl-[.

EPS (Encapsulated PostScript) A line-art file format for graphics. See *PostScript*.

family A group of related type designs, such as Times Roman, Helvetica, or Caslon. See *font*.

font A *typeface* in a particular size and style. Helvetica is a type *family*. Helvetica Bold is a typeface. Ten-point Helvetica Bold is a font.

footer Text (or graphics) that appears at the bottom of each page in the document.

footnote A comment or explanation at the bottom of a page that is referenced in the main text with a number or symbol.

format The size, style, and appearance of a document. Elements such as page size, margins, columns, spacing, and page layout are all part of a document's format.

frame A box-shaped container that holds text or graphics.

gray-scale Gray-scale images store the attribute of each *pixel* (each dot) as shades of gray rather than just black or white.

greeking Representing text with dummy type or lines.

grid The division of a page into regular rectangular areas to aid in arranging and aligning page elements.

gutter The space between two columns, or the margin between two facing pages.

halftone A picture that has gradation of tone (shades of gray), formed by dots of various sizes.

header Text (or graphics) that appear at the top of each page in the document.

image Text or graphics composed of a pattern of dots (*pixels*). See *bit-mapped*.

inter-line spacing The vertical spacing between lines of text. Also called *leading*.

jaggies The uneven, stair-step edges of characters and graphics on a low-resolution printer or screen.

jump line A shortphrase that directs readers to continue reading an article on another page.

justification The spacing of words and characters in a column so that the text aligns flush against both margins.

kerning In traditional typesetting, special spacing for certain letter pairs to make them fit together more tightly and, therefore, more attractively. In Ventura, this is called automatic pair kerning. The word kerning in Ventura means the process of adding or subtracting space between letters.

landscape The orientation of a page so that the width of the page is greater than its height. See *portrait*.

layout The arrangement of text and graphics on a page.

leaders Evenly spaced characters (such as dots) that fill the space between tab settings, helping to guide the reader's eye from one item to another.

leading The vertical spacing between lines of text. Also called *inter-line spacing*.

line art A graphic stored as a mathematical description that can be scaled without loss of quality.

logo A graphic that a company uses to provide a visual representation of itself or its products.

loose line A line of justified text that uses more than the *Maximum Space Width* setting.

macro A software feature that allows you to assign a sequence of commands to one key for playback.

margin The blank border along the edge of the page.

masthead Information about the publisher of a newsletter, magazine, or newspaper, usually placed inside a small box on one of the first few pages.

maximum space width In a line of justified text, the largest space between words that Ventura will allow, before the line is considered a "loose line."

minimum space width In a line of justified text, the smallest space between words that Ventura will allow.

moire Undesirable patterns in *halftones* or *bit-mapped* images.

monospaced font A *font* that has an equal amount of space allotted for each character.

Multi-Chapter The name of the dialog box called up by the Manage Publication command (File menu). It is used to copy, print, index, or create a table of contents for one or more chapters. When used as a verb, multi-chapter means using the Copy All option to move or copy a Ventura chapter.

nameplate The large title (as in a newsletter) that gives the publication its identity. Usually appears at the top of the first page.

non-breaking space Puts a space between two words but prevents them from being separated at the end of a line. To make a non-breaking space in Ventura, press Ctrl-Spacebar.

normal space width The optimum space between words in a line of text.

orphan A single line that occurs at the bottom of the page and is separated from the rest of its paragraph. See *widow*.

paragraph Any section of text that ends with a paragraph mark, which is created by pressing the Enter key.

paste To copy text or graphics from the *clipboard* to the page.

pica A unit of measure equal to 12 *points*, or approximately one sixth inch. Picas are used to specify page measurements such as size, line length, columns, and margins.

picture Any graphic (bit-mapped image or line art) that has been placed in a frame.

pixel The tiny dots that form the picture on a screen. Short for picture elements. See *bit-mapped*.

point A unit of measure equal to 1/12 of a pica, or approximately 1/72 of an inch. Points are used to specify type size, leading, and rule widths.

portrait The orientation of a page so that the height is greater than its width. See *landscape*.

PostScript A programming language that describes how an output device (such as a laser printer) should print a file on paper. This description is device independent. The same file can be sent to different output devices and the page will always be printed at the maximum resolution.

proportionally spaced font A *font* that has a different amounts of space allotted for each character, according to the size of the letter. For example, the letter *w* gets more space than the letter *i*, because the *w* is wider. See *monospaced font*.

publication In Ventura, a list of chapter files. Once you have put chapters into a publication, you can act on the whole group with a single command to print, copy, index, or build a table of contents.

pull quote An enlarged quotation from the body of an article, often set off by ruling lines or boxes. Also called a teaser or a lift out.

resolution The density of dots (or *pixels*) on a page screen, measured in dots per inch (dpi).

rules or ruling lines Vertical or horizontal lines used as a design element. The width of a rule is usually specified in *points*.

sans-serif A typeface that does not have *serifs*, small finishing strokes at the ends of letter strokes. Examples include Helvetica (Swiss) and Avant Garde. See *serif*.

scale To change the size of a picture without changing the size of the *frame* that contains it. See *size*.

Chapter 22: Glossary

scanned image A *bit-mapped* image created with a digitizing device such as a *scanner*.

scanner A digitizing device that converts a drawing into a *bit-mapped* image that can be loaded and manipulated by a software program.

serif Tiny finishing strokes at the ends of letters. Serifs typefaces are those whose letters have serifs, such as Times Roman (Dutch) and Palatino. See *sans-serif*.

sizing To change the size of a *frame*.

sizing handles The eight black boxes that appear around the outside of a *frame* when it is selected. Using a mouse, you can drag the sizing handles to change the dimensions of the frame.

snap to A feature that pulls a page element into alignment when placed near a guide or *grid* line.

style sheet A file that contains formatting information for a Ventura document.

tag A style sheet code that holds formatting information for text paragraphs. Tags specify attributes such as *font*, *inter-line spacing*, and *breaks*.

template A predesigned Ventura chapter that serves as a starting point for creating documents with a similar design.

thin space The width of a period.

Toolbox A retangular box on the workspace that holds Ventura's primary functions.

typeface A variation of a type *family*, including all sizes. Helvetica is a type family. Helvetica Bold is a typeface. Ten-point Helvetica Bold is a *font*.

underlying page A frame that contains elements repeated on every page of the document, including margins, columns, numbering, and repeating graphic elements. Every page in the document has a copy of the underlying page as a foundation.

vertical justification The arrangement of text and pictures so they completely fill the space from top to bottom.

white space Blank space as a backdrop or border for words or pictures.

widow A single line that occurs at the top of the page and is separated from the rest of its paragraph. See *orphan*.

width table A file that Ventura uses to control the spacing of characters on the screen and page.

WYSIWYG An acronym for What You See Is What You Get, which means that what you see on screen is very close to what you'll get on the printed page.

x-height The height of the center body of a lowercase letter, without ascenders and descenders. The bottom of the x-height is the *baseline*.

Index

A

Above paragraph spacing   62-64
Actual Frame Width   97
Add Box Text tool   78, 273, 278, 511
Add Frame tool   15, 29, 312-313
Add In Above   64
Add Line tool   278
Add New Tag command   71
Add Rectangle tool   278
Add Round Rect tool   278
Adobe Type Manager   377-378, 380-381, 502
alignment
    See also paragraph spacing
    baseline jumps   230
    big first characters   127
    bottom   56
    centered   55
    changing   71
    decimals   55
    footer text   102
    footnotes   459, 461, 467
    formatting   28, 54-56, 102, 154, 156, 158, 160, 214
    hanging numbers   142
    header text   102
    horizontal   55
    justified   55
    left   54
    middle   56
    right   55
    rotated   165-167
    tables   247
    tabs   134
    text   54-56, 71, 214, 230
    top   56
    vertical   56, 154, 156, 158, 160
Alignment command   27, 71, 215
Allow Within   72
anchors
    See frame anchors
Anchors & Captions command   234, 332
ANSI codes   195, 460-461
ASCII
    codes   195, 504
    defined   213
    file formats   212-213
Aspect Ratio   359-360
Attribute Overrides command   167-168, 466-467, 476
attributes
    See also graphic attributes
    defined   41
    Double Underline   53
    formatting   167-168
    generated tag attributes   49
    Line Width   167
    overriding attributes   167-168
    Overscore   53
    Overscore Height   168
    removing   199
    Shift Down By   168
    Shift Up By   168
    Small Cap Size   168
    Strike-Thru   53
    Strike-Thru Height   168
    Subscript Size   168
    Superscript Size   168
    text attributes   104-105, 167, 199, 202, 216, 224-225, 227, 251
    Underline   53
    Underline Height   168
Auto-Adjustments   61-62
Auto-Leader   136
auto-numbering
    auto-numbered paragraphs   151, 398
    chapter numbers   146
    creating unusual ruling lines   152
    deleting numbered paragraphs   146
    figure number in caption   345-346
    formatting   139-140, 142, 145-146, 148-149, 151-152, 347
    generated tags   142
    generating text with   149
    hanging numbers   142
    multi-level lists   142, 145
    renumbering   145, 491
    restarting   147-148
    simple lists   139-140
    starting at numbers other than one   146
    table number in caption   345-346

Auto-Numbering command 138-140, 142, 145-149, 151-152
AutoCAD picture file format
    See file format
Automatic Crop Marks 405
automatic figure numbering 344-346
automatic font downloading 391
automatic pair kerning 169-170
automatic table numbering 345-346
Automatically At Anchor
    See frame anchors

B

background
    See colors
    See Frame Background command
    See tables
ballot boxes
    See hollow boxes
Below paragraph spacing 62-64
big first characters
    alignment 127
    defined 125
    formatting 124, 127, 130
    reversed 128, 130
    shaded 128, 130
    using pictures 131
bitmaps
    See images
Bitstream Fontware 376
blended paragraphs
    See paragraphs
Bold text attribute 21, 200
bottom alignment
    See alignment
Box Char 197
Box Text
    creating 78, 273, 277-278, 284
    editing 278
    formatting 282
    formatting Box Text 284
    placing 78
    within frames 78
bracket codes
    adding spaces 230, 232
    baseline jumps 230
    caption text 346
    controlling breaks 230, 232
    cross-referencing 514
    defined 151
    discretionary hyphens 230, 232

equations 234, 478
font settings 228
footnotes 237, 470
formatting fonts 346
fractions 233
frame anchors 234-235
hidden text 233
index entries 235-236, 428-429
kerning 229
non-keyboard characters 232
return-to-normal 226
special rules for 225
tables 261-264
turning off 225
breaks
    Allow Within 72
    Column Break 66, 68-69
    column breaks 67, 71
    defined 66
    Line Break 66, 68-69, 71, 74
    line breaks 67, 71
    Next Y Position 71
    Page Break 66-69
    page breaks 67, 71
    special break tags 71
    using bracket codes 230-231
    within paragraphs 72
Breaks command 66-67, 70-71, 74
bullets
    characters 119-120
    defined 118
    formatting 118, 120, 122, 124
    using pictures 121-122
    using word processors 124
business proposals
    creating 541-542, 544, 548-549, 551, 553, 555, 557
    formatting titles and subtitles 552-555
    graphic design samples 613
    loading files 544, 546
    loading pictures 557
    loading style sheets 545
    planning 542
    printing 559
    refining style sheets 549, 551, 553, 555
    underlying pages 547-548
By Scale Factors 359-360

C

Calculated Frame Width 97

callouts
  See pictures
CAP files (Caption Files)   42, 483
Capitalize   200
capitalizing text   200
captions
  automatic figure numbering   344-346
  caption frames   341-342, 358, 558, 589
  caption labels   341-342, 344-346, 349-350
  caption samples   351
  caption text   341-342, 348, 590
  formatting   341-343, 345-346, 348, 350, 558, 589
  generated tags for   349-350
carding
  See vertical justification
centered alignment
  See alignment
CGM file format   302
Change Settings command   159, 249
Change Text To command   200
CHANGE.COM utility   504
Chapter menu
  Chapter Typography command   57, 156, 161, 163, 169, 248
  Footnote Settings command   455, 457-458, 460, 464
  Headers & Footers command   99, 103
  Insert/Remove Page command   88, 572
  Page Size & Layout command   89, 92, 382
Chapter Typography command   57, 156, 161, 163, 169, 248
chapters
  chapter files   18, 41
  chapter numbers   146
  chapter templates   506-507
  copying chapter files   482, 485, 505
  defined   18, 31, 41
  editing chapter files   530-534
  managing chapter files   481
  printing   391-399, 413
  renumbering   145, 490-491
  saving   30
  vertical justification within   156, 158
character sets
  See fonts
CHP extension   31, 41
CIF files (Chapter Information Files)   42, 483
clipboard   199, 300, 321

color overlays
  See printing
colors
  fonts   52, 202
  frame backgrounds   107
  pictures   281
  ruling lines   80
  ruling lines for frames   354
  tables   254-255
  Ventura graphics   281
column breaks   66-69, 71
  See also breaks
Column Snap command   315-316
columns
  See also Margins & Columns command
  balancing   163
  column breaks   66, 68-69, 71
  column guides   16
  column snap   315
  companion columns   108
  formatting   94-95, 97-98, 163, 246, 548
  gutters   94-95
  inter-column rules   96, 108
  margins   95
  number of   96
  table columns   246, 256-257
  widths   94-95, 97, 257
commands
  Add New Tag   71
  Alignment   27, 71, 215
  Anchors & Captions   234, 332
  Attribute Overrides   167-168, 466-467, 476
  Auto-Numbering   139
  Bold   21
  Breaks   66, 71, 74
  Change Settings   159, 249
  Change Text To   200
  Chapter Typography   57, 156, 169, 248
  Column Snap   315-316
  Copy   212
  Copy Frame   319-320
  Copy Row/Column   253
  Copy Tag   523
  Copy Text   199
  Custom Rules   259-260
  Cut   212
  Cut Frame   319-320
  Cut Row/Column   253
  Cut Text   199
  Define Colors   255, 407
  Edit Special Item   334, 427
  Enlarged View   205

Exit Equation Editing 472
File List Window 189
File Type/Rename 192-194
Fill Attributes 281-282, 287
Font 51-52
Footnote Settings 455, 457-458, 460, 464
Frame Background 107, 289
Frame Typography 57, 157
Grid Settings 275-276, 280
Headers & Footers 99, 103
Image Settings 306
Insert Column 249
Insert New Table 159, 243, 246
Insert Row 249
Insert Special Item 123, 197, 204, 242, 244, 333, 419, 463, 471-472
Insert/Remove Page 88, 572
Join Cells 255-256
Line Attributes 278, 280, 287-288
Line Snap 315-316
Load Diff. Style 23-24, 43-44, 190
Load Text/Picture 17, 30, 188-190, 324-326
Manage Publication 398-399, 436, 443, 482-483, 487-488, 491
Manage Width Table 386
Margins & Columns 97, 329-330
New 44
Normal 199
Normal View 21, 25
Page Size & Layout 89, 92, 382
Paragraph Typography 160, 170, 173-175, 235, 336
Paste 189
Paste ASCII Text 212
Paste Frame 320-321
Paste Row/Column 254
Paste Tag 523
Paste Text 199
Print 392-393
Printer Setup 379, 383, 388
Re-Anchor Frames 331, 335-336, 519
Reduced View 24, 29, 89, 313
Remove Text/File 191, 327-328
Renumber Chapter 140, 145-146
Revert To Saved 55
Ruling Box Around 78, 107, 260, 353, 355
Ruling Line Above 77-78, 84, 107, 260
Ruling Line Below 77-80, 83, 107, 260
Save 95, 343
Save As 30
Save Style As 44
Send To Back 289

Send To Front 289
Set Column Width 257
Set Font Attributes 172, 197, 201, 203, 230
Set Preferences 14, 44, 49, 103, 260, 350
Set Ruler 133
Set Tint 254-255
Show Column Guides 313
Show Loose Lines 177
Show On All Pages 288
Show On This Page 289
Show Rulers 318
Show Tabs & Returns 71, 182, 204, 425
Sizing & Scaling 92, 316-318, 358, 361-362, 365
Spacing 60, 66, 76, 80, 215
Special Effects 59, 119-120, 125
Split Cells 256
Tab Settings 133, 136, 215, 251
Update Counters 347, 491
Update Tag List 45, 48
Vertical Rules 107-108, 111, 113
converting files
  picture files 299
  text files 192, 211-212
Copy All option 483, 485, 489, 505
Copy command 212
Copy Frame command 319-320
Copy Row/Column command 253
Copy Tag command 523
Copy Text command 199
Copy To Facing Page 66, 98
copyright symbols 196, 232
creating
  Box Text 78
  column breaks 71
  line breaks 71
  page breaks 71
  ruling lines 78
  tags 71
  underlying pages 92
crop marks
  See printing
cropping pictures 363, 365-366
cross-referencing 514
Current Selection Box 16, 205
Custom Rules command 259-260
Cut command 212
Cut Frame command 319-320
Cut Row/Column command 253
Cut Text command 199

D

dashed lines 81
dashes
   See em dashes
   See en dashes
databases
   delimiters 219
   exporting data to Ventura 216-219
   saving data to text files 218
decimal alignment
   See alignment
DEFAULT.STY 50
Define Colors command 255, 407
deleting
   chapter files 485
   footers 107
   frames 319, 321
   headers 107
   index entries 428
   numbered paragraphs 146
   pictures 327
   tab stops 135
   table rows and columns 253
   tags 47
   text 199
   text attributes 199
   text files 191
delimiters
   See databases
design samples
   brochures 617
   business proposals 613
   directories 618
   letterhead 611
   mail cards 614
   marketing materials 615
   newsletters 604, 607, 609
diacritical marks
   See equations
dialog boxes
   defined 16
   features 16
   measurements button 27
discretionary hyphens 196, 231
Distorted Aspect Ratio 359-360
dithering 295
documents
   See chapters
Double Underline tag attribute 53
Double Underline text attribute 200

downloading
   See printing
draw programs
   See pictures
drawing
   See also Box Text
   Box Text 78
   crop marks 405-406
   frames 29, 311-316, 557
   multiple frames 313
   ruling lines 78
   shapes 273-275, 277, 279, 281, 287, 289
   tools 78
drawing tools
   See Graphic tools
drop cap
   See big first character

E

Edit menu
   Copy command 212
   Copy Frame command 320
   Copy Row/Column command 253
   Copy Tag command 523
   Copy Text command 199
   Cut command 212
   Cut Frame command 320
   Cut Row/Column command 253
   Cut Text command 199
   Paste ASCII Text command 212
   Paste command 189
   Paste Frame command 321
   Paste Row/Column command 254
   Paste Tag command 523
   Paste Text command 199
   Re-Anchor Frames command 331, 335-336, 519
   Renumber Chapter command 140, 145-146
   Set Preferences command 14, 44, 49, 103, 260, 350
   Show Tabs & Returns command 182
   Update Counters command 347, 491
Edit Special Item command 334, 427
editing
   chapter files 530-531
   index entries 427
   tables 252, 254
   text 21, 187, 198-199, 215
em dashes 232
em spaces 171-172, 202, 231
en dashes 232

en spaces   231
Encapsulated PostScript
    See file formats
End Styles   278
Enlarged View command   205
equations
    complex equations   473, 478
    creating in Ventura   455, 471, 473
    creating in word processors   478
    equation codes   473
    equation commands   473
    expressions   473
    formatting   476-477
    fractions   233, 472-473
    Grow Inter-Line To Fit   475
Exit Equation Editing command   472
expressions
    See equations

F

faces
    See typefaces
feathering
    See vertical justification
figure numbering
    See auto-numbering
figure spaces   196, 231
file extensions
    changing   531-533
    index files   431
    picture files   298
    tables of contents files   443
    text files   210
file formats
    ASCII text files   212-213
    AutoCAD SLD   301
    CGM   302
    converting   211
    Encapsulated PostScript   303
    GEM   300
    HPGL   304
    images   291, 294, 298, 304-306
    IMG   305
    line art   291, 298-301, 303-304
    Lotus PIC   301
    Mac PICT   302
    MacPaint   306
    PCX   305
    pictures   291, 294, 298-301, 303-304
    text files   209-211, 213
    TIFF   306
    VideoShow   302
    Windows Metafile   300
File List Window   16, 44, 189
File menu
    File Type/Rename command   192-193
    Load Diff. Style command   23-24, 43-44, 190
    Load Text/Picture command   17, 30, 188-190, 265, 324-326
    Manage Publication command   398-399, 436, 443, 482-483, 487-488, 491
    Manage Width Table command   386
    New command   44
    Print command   392-393
    Printer Setup command   379, 383, 388
    Revert To Saved command   55
    Save As command   30
    Save command   95, 343
    Save Style As command   44
File Type/Rename command   192-194
files
    See also file extensions
    changing file types   531-533
    changing publication file links   489
    chapter files   41
    converting text files   192
    copying chapter files   482, 485, 505
    copying publication files   489
    creating publication files   486-487
    creating text files in Ventura   193
    cross-referencing text files   514
    deleting chapter files   485
    editing chapter files   530-534
    file extensions   531-533
    File List Window   44
    filenames   513, 544
    Greek files   505
    index files   431, 435-436
    loading picture files   28, 30, 311, 324-325, 518-519, 544, 546, 557, 587, 589
    loading text files   17, 88, 188, 219, 544, 546, 577-578
    macro files   498
    managing chapter files   481
    moving text files   192
    opening publication files   488
    placing picture files   28, 30, 311, 326, 557
    placing text files   19-20, 188, 190
    printing to files   410-411, 413-414
    re-using filenames   512-513
    removing text files   191
    renaming text files   192
    renumbering chapter files   490-491

tables of contents files   443, 446
WIN.INI   371-377, 380-381, 388
fill attributes
   See pictures
Fill Attributes command   281-282, 287
filled boxes   197, 232
1st Match button   105
Fit In Frame   359-360
FIXCHP.EXE utility   505
fixed-position frames
   See frame
Font command   51-52
fonts
   Adobe Type Manager   377-378, 502
   Bitstream Fontware   376
   character sets   195
   character spacing   375
   character width   375
   colors   52, 202
   defined   50, 195
   downloading   374, 387-390
   font rasterizers   376-378, 502
   for LaserJet printers   51
   for PostScript printers   51
   formatting   52, 201, 203, 228, 346, 376-378, 384-390, 499
   printing   51, 372, 374-375, 377-378
   screen fonts   375-378
   sizes   52, 202
   soft fonts   374, 378, 387, 389-390
   special characters   195-197
   styles   52, 202
   typefaces   50, 202
   width tables   375, 384-386
footers
   See also headers
   defined   99
   deleting   107
   footer frames   99
   formatting   99-100, 103, 105, 107-108, 533-534, 548, 554, 582
   generated tags   49, 103, 108
   margins   107
   ruling boxes around   107
   ruling lines   107
   Z_footer tag   103
Footnote Settings command   455, 457-458, 460, 464
footnotes
   alignment   459, 461, 467
   creating in Ventura   455, 457-458, 460, 462, 464, 466, 468

creating in word processors   470
footnote frames   456, 463-464
footnote tags   467
footnote text   464, 468
formatting   466, 468
inserting references   462
margins   466
number reference marks   455, 457-458
separator lines   464
symbol reference marks   455, 457, 459-460
terminology   455
turning on footnote function   457
formatting
   See also alignment
   alignment   28, 102, 154, 156, 158, 160
   attributes   202
   auto-numbered paragraphs   151
   auto-numbering   139-140, 142, 145-146, 148-149, 151-152, 347
   big first characters   124, 127, 130
   blended paragraphs   72, 74
   Box Text   78, 282
   bullets   118, 120, 122, 124
   callouts   282, 284
   captions   341-343, 345-346, 348, 350, 558, 589
   chapter numbers   146
   column breaks   71
   columns   94-95, 97-98, 163, 246, 548
   equations   234, 476-477
   fonts   50, 52, 201, 203, 228, 346, 376-378, 384-390, 499
   footers   99-100, 103, 105, 107-108, 533-534, 548, 554, 582
   footnotes   237, 466, 468
   fractions   233, 472-473
   frame anchors   234, 331, 333-334, 336-337
   frame backgrounds   107, 289
   frames   29, 161, 311, 313-317, 319, 321, 328, 331, 333-334, 336-337, 351, 354-355, 357-358, 362, 519-520, 557, 573, 575-576
   gutters   94-95, 97
   header text   102-103, 105, 534
   headers   99-100, 103, 105, 107-108, 533-534, 571
   hidden text   233
   indenting   54, 57-59, 215
   indexes   436-437, 439
   inter-line spacing   60, 62
   kerning   169-170, 172, 202-203, 229
   leader characters   132, 135, 137, 447
   letter spacing   169-170, 172-173, 175, 202-203

Index

line breaks 71
line spacing 60, 62-65
loose lines 177
margins 94-95, 97-98, 107, 216, 328, 356, 466, 548
mirrored page designs 65, 98
outdenting 57-59
page breaks 71
rotating text 165, 167
ruling lines 152, 167
special characters 194-195, 197, 204, 232
standalone rules 112-113
style sheets 522-523, 549, 551, 553, 555
table graphics 254-255
tables 159, 241-242, 244, 246-247, 249-250, 258, 261-265
tables of contents 444-446, 448, 450
tabs 132-133, 215
tracking 172-173, 203
underlying pages 92, 547-548
vertical justification 154, 156, 158, 160
vertical rules 108
width of frames 56
width of text 56
with bracket codes 223, 225, 227
word spacing 175-176
fractions
   See equations
   See text
frame anchors
   anchor markers 331, 333
   anchor names 331-332
   re-anchoring frames 335
Frame Background command 107, 289
Frame menu
   Anchors & Captions command 234, 332
   File Type/Rename command 192, 194
   Frame Background command 107, 289
   Frame Typography command 57, 157
   Image Settings command 306
   Margins & Columns command 97, 329-330
   Remove Text/File command 191, 327-328
   Ruling Box Around command 107, 353, 355
   Ruling Line Above command 107
   Ruling Line Below command 107
   Sizing & Scaling command 92, 316-318, 358, 361-362, 365
   Vertical Rules command 107-108, 111, 113
Frame Tool 15, 19, 30, 87
Frame Typography command 57, 157
frames
   Add Frame tool 15, 29, 312-313

automatic figure numbering 344-346
Box Text within 78
caption frames 342, 558, 589
column snap 315-316
copying 319, 321, 575-576
creating text for 193-194
cropping pictures within 363, 365-366
cross-referencing 514
defined 19
deleting 319, 321
drawing 29, 557
dummy pictures 520
footer frames 99
footnote frames 456, 463-464
formatting 29, 161, 311, 313-317, 319, 321, 328, 331, 333-334, 336-337, 351, 354-355, 357-358, 362, 519-520, 557, 573, 575-576
frame anchors 234, 331, 333-334, 336-337, 517
frame backgrounds 107, 289
frame scrapbooks 515
Frame Tool 15, 19, 30, 87
Frame Typography 161
header frames 99-100, 107
line snap 315-316, 519
loading pictures into 324, 588-589
loading text into 189-190, 577-578
macros for fixing 499
margins within 328, 356
moving 317, 319-321
padding around 357-358
parent frames for graphics 274
picturemark paragraphs 517
positioning pictures 289
re-anchoring 519
repeating 322
ruling boxes around 351, 354-355
saving stock frames 511
scaling pictures 360-361
sizing frames 313, 316, 362, 574-575
stacking 289
versus underlying page 87
vertical justification 156, 158
vertical rules 109-110
width 56
function-key tagging 45-46

G

GEM file format 300

GEM/HALO DPE file format
    See IMG file format
GEN files (Generated files)   431, 443-444, 483
generated tags
    attributes   49
    captions   349-350
    footers   49, 108
    from auto-numbering   142
    headers   49, 103, 106, 108
    indexes   436-437
    showing in Tag List Window   49
    tables   49, 259, 262
    Z_ prefix   49
    Z_BOXTEXT   282
    Z_CAPTION   349-350
    Z_FOOTER   103
    Z_HEADER   103
    Z_HIDDEN   259
    Z_INDEX LTR   437
    Z_INDEX MAIN   437
    Z_INDEX TITLE   437
    Z_LABEL CAP   349-350
    Z_LABEL FIG   349-350
    Z_LABEL TBL   349-350
    Z_THICK   259
generating indexes   430-435
generating tables of contents   443-445
getting started
    guided tour   13
    recommended strategies   8
    starting Ventura   14
    system requirements   6
    using this book   5-8, 10
Graphic menu
    Fill Attributes command   281-282, 287
    Grid Settings command   275, 280
    Line Attributes command   278, 280, 287-288
    Send To Back command   289
    Send To Front command   289
    Show On All Pages command   288
    Show On This Page command   289
Graphic tools
    Add Box Text tool   273, 278, 282
    Add Line tool   278
    Add Rectangle tool   278
    Add Round Rect tool   278
    attaching shapes   274
    drawing crop marks   405-406
    drawing shapes   273, 277, 279, 281, 287, 289
    pros and cons   272
    repeating graphics   288
    using default settings   286-287
    using grids   275-276
graphics attributes
    fill attributes   281, 286-287
    line attributes   278, 286-287
graphics files
    See pictures
gray-scale images
    See pictures
Greek text
    See text
GREEKER.COM utility   505
Grid Settings command   275-276, 280
Grid Snap command   275
grids for graphics
    See Graphic tools
grouping paragraphs   72
Grow Inter-Line To Fit   178, 475
gutters
    defined   94
    formatting   94-95, 97

H

hanging numbers   142
hDC FirstApps utility   502
headers
    See also footers
    defined   99
    deleting   107
    formatting   99-100, 103, 105, 107-108, 533-534, 571
    generated tags   49, 103, 106, 108
    header frames   99-100, 107
    header text   102-103, 105, 107, 534
    live text within   104-105
    margins   107
    ruling boxes around   107
    ruling lines   107
    text attributes   104-105
Headers & Footers command   99, 103
headings
    keeping with text   72
Hewlett-Packard
    See LaserJet
hidden text
    See text
hollow boxes   197, 232
horizontal alignment
    See alignment
horizontal spacing
    See spacing
HPGL file format   304

hyphenation
    discretionary hyphens   178, 181, 196, 230-231
    formatting   178, 180-181, 215
    hyphenation dictionaries   178, 180-181
    ladders   180
    turning on or off   179

I

Image Settings command   306
images
    See pictures
IMG file format   305
In From Left   65
In From Right   65
indenting
    formatting   54, 215
    hanging indents   58-59, 65
    indexes   431-432, 437
    relative indents   59
    text   54, 57-59, 215
indexes
    copying index entries   428
    creating in Ventura   399, 417, 419, 422, 424-425, 427
    creating in word processors   235-236, 428-429
    defining index entries   419
    deleting index entries   428
    editing index entries   427
    formatting   436-439
    generated tags   436-437
    generating   429-430, 432-433, 435-436
    indenting   431-432, 437
    index files   431, 435-436
    inserting index entries   418-419, 422, 424-425
    letter group headings   431
    marking index references   419
    moving index entries   428
    page number appearance   433, 435
    planning   418
    primary and secondary entries   422, 437
    See and See Also entries   421, 423-424, 426, 435
    separating entries from page references   431-432
    separating page numbers   434
    sorting   423-424, 429
    tabs   437
    three-level   437, 439
    two-level   437

initial caps
    See Capitalize
Insert Column command   249
Insert New Table command   159, 243, 246
Insert Row command   249
Insert Special Item command   123, 197, 204, 242, 244, 419, 463, 471-472
Insert/Remove Page command   88, 572
inserting page and chapter numbers
    See auto-numbering
installing fonts on LaserJet   388-390
inter-column widths   110
inter-line spacing
    defined   60-61
    font size relationship   61
    formatting   60, 62
Inter-Paragraph spacing   62-64
interactive kerning
    See kerning
international character set
    See fonts
Italic text attribute   200

J

Join Cells command   255-256
justified alignment
    See alignment

K

Keep With Next   72
kerning
    automatic pair kerning   169-170
    defined   202
    em spaces   172, 202
    formatting   229
    interactive manual kerning   171-172, 203
    numeric manual kerning   171-172
    on-screen display   170
    with bracket codes   229
keyboard shortcuts   524

L

labeling captions
    See captions
Landscape   90

laser printers
    See LaserJet printers
    See PostScript printers
LaserJet printers
    downloading fonts   388-390
    fonts   51, 378
Last Match button   105
leader characters
    defined   132
    formatting   132, 135, 137, 447
    with tab stops   135
    without tab stops (Auto-Leader)   136
leading
    See inter-line spacing
left alignment
    See alignment
letter spacing
    See also kerning
    formatting   202-203
    kerning   202-203
    tracking   203
line art
    See pictures
Line Attributes command   278, 280, 287-288
line break bracket codes   231
line breaks   67
    creating   71
    defined   66, 68-69
    Line Break options   69, 71, 74
    Next Y Position   71
Line Snap command   315-316
line spacing
    formatting   60, 62-65
    inter-line   60, 62, 178, 475
Line Width attribute   167
lines
    See inter-line spacing
    See ruling lines
    See text
list of files
    See File List Window
live text   101, 104-105
Load Diff. Style command   23-24, 43-44, 190
Load Different Width Table   386
Load Text/Picture command   17, 30, 188-190, 324-326
loading
    picture files   28, 30, 324-325, 518-519, 557, 587, 589
    style sheets   23-24, 43, 49, 545
    tables of contents files   446
    text files   17, 88, 188, 219

loose lines   177
Lotus PIC file format   301
Lower Case command   200

M

Mac PICT file format   302
MacPaint file format   306
macros
    creating   495-496
    fixing frames   499
    macro files   498
    scaling pictures   500
    setting font attributes   499
    using in Ventura   497-500
Maintained Aspect Ratio   359-360
Make Equal Widths   95
Manage Publication command   398-399, 436, 443, 482-483, 487-488, 491
Manage Width Table command   386
manual kerning
    See kerning
margins
    defined   95
    footnotes   466
    formatting   94-95, 97-98, 107, 216, 328, 466, 548
    inside frames   328, 356
    Margins & Columns options   95
Margins & Columns command   95, 97
Maximum Rotated Height   166
measurements button   27
Microsoft Windows   4
middle alignment
    See alignment
mirrored page designs   65-66, 98
mouse
    cropping pictures   365
    moving frames   317
    sizing frames   314-316
    tagging with   45
    Whiskers utility   504
moving
    frames   317, 319, 321
    graphics   277
    index entries   428
    text   199
    text files   192
Multi-Chapter
    See Manage Publication

N

naming tags
    See tags
New command   44, 246
newsletters
    adding pages   572
    columns   570
    copyfitting   593-594, 596-597
    creating   563-564, 566-567, 570-571, 573, 575-576, 578-580, 582-583, 585, 587, 589, 591, 593
    credos   582-583
    design samples   604, 607, 609, 613
    footers   582
    frames   573, 575-576
    grids   570
    headers   571
    headline tags   579
    loading pictures   587, 589
    loading text files   577-578
    logos   592-593
    margins   570
    nameplates   584-585
    newsletter templates   506, 513, 565, 567
    planning   564
    re-using filenames   512-513
    refining style sheets   578-580, 582-583, 585
    ruling lines   570
    saving stock frames   511
    subhead tags   578
    tables of contents   580
    terminology   565
    threading text   596
    underlying pages   569-571
    vertical rules   573
Next Y Position   71
non-breaking spaces   196, 231
non-keyboard characters   195, 232
Normal command   199
Normal View command   21, 25
numbering
    See auto-numbering

O

on-screen kerning   170
    See also kerning
ornamental cap
    See big first character
orphans   162-163

outdenting
    formatting   57
    text   57-59
overall width
    frames   56
    tables   245, 247
    text   56
overriding text attributes   167-168, 466-467, 476
Overscore Height   168
Overscore tag attribute   53
Overscore text attribute   200

P

padding around frames   357
page breaks
    Allow Within   72
    creating   71
    defined   67-68
    Page Break options   67-68
    within paragraphs   72
page layout
    Landscape   90
    Portrait   90
page margins
    See Margins & Columns command
page numbers
    See auto-numbering
page orientation   90, 382
Page Size & Layout command   89, 92, 382
page sizes
    custom   92
    standard   90
paint programs
    See pictures
paper type   90, 382
Paragraph menu
    Add New Tag command   71, 260
    Alignment command   27, 71, 215
    Attribute Overrides command   167-168, 466-467, 476
    Auto-Numbering command   139
    Breaks command   66, 71, 74
    Define Colors command   255, 407
    Font command   51-52
    Paragraph Typography command   160, 170, 173-175, 235, 336
    Ruling Box Around command   78-81, 83-84, 260
    Ruling Line Above command   77-81, 83-84, 260

Ruling Line Below command 77-81, 83-84, 260
Spacing command 60, 66, 76, 80, 215
Special Effects command 59, 119-120, 125
Tab Settings command 133, 136, 215, 251
Update Tag List command 45, 48
paragraph spacing
    Above 62-64
    Add In Above 64
    Below 62-64
    defined 61
    In From Left 65
    In From Right 65
    Inter-Paragraph 62-64
Paragraph Tool 15, 24, 26, 28, 45, 71, 251, 260
Paragraph Typography command 160, 170, 173-175, 178, 235, 336
paragraphs
    auto-numbered paragraphs 151
    blended paragraphs 72, 74
    Box Text 78
    invisible paragraphs 450
    keeping together 72
    paragraph markers 204
    Paragraph Tool 15, 24, 26, 28, 45, 251, 260
    picturemark paragraphs 517
    rotating 165, 167
    ruling lines around 78
    side-by-side placement 71, 74-75
    spacing 60, 62-65, 71
    special break tags 71
    tagging 45-46, 220-221
    vertical justification 159-160
    widows and orphans 162
Paste ASCII Text command 212
Paste command 189
Paste Frame command 320-321
Paste Row/Column command 254
Paste Tag command 523
Paste Text command 199
PCX file format 305
pictures
    See also Graphic tools
    as big first characters 131
    as bullets 121-122
    automatic figure numbering 344-346
    callouts 282, 284, 591
    captions 341-343, 345-346, 348, 350, 589
    colors 281
    creating in Ventura 272, 274-275, 277, 279, 281, 284, 287, 289

    creating with other programs 291, 294, 298, 300-301, 303-306
    cropping 363-366
    deleting 327
    draw programs 292, 298
    dummy pictures 520
    figure lists 450
    file extensions 298
    file formats 291, 294, 298, 300-301, 303-306
    frame scrapbooks 515
    generated tags 282, 349-350
    Graphic tools 272, 277, 279, 281, 284, 287, 289
    gray-scale images 294
    images 291, 294, 298, 304-306, 362
    line art 291, 298, 300-301, 303-304
    loading 28, 30, 311, 324-325, 518-519, 544, 546, 557, 587, 589
    macros for scaling 500
    padding 357-358
    paint programs 292, 298
    parent frames for graphics 274
    picturemark paragraphs 517
    pixels 294, 376
    placing 28, 30, 289, 311, 326, 557
    printing resolution 292, 303
    repeating on every page 288
    ruling boxes around 351, 353-355
    ruling lines 351, 353-355
    scaling 358-362
    setting up grids 275
    stacking and combining 289
    two-color images 294
    Windows' Paintbrush 501
pixels
    See pictures
placing
    Box Text 78
    picture files 28, 30, 326, 557
    ruling lines 78
    text files 19-20, 188, 190
portfolio
    See graphic design samples
Portrait 90
positioning graphics 275, 277
positioning pictures
    See cropping pictures
PostScript file format
    See file formats
PostScript printers
    downloading fonts 390
    fonts 51, 374

prefixes
    generated   49
    Z_prefix   49
primary index entries
    See indexes
Print command   392-393
Print Manager
    See printing
Printer Setup command   379, 383, 388
printing
    activating printers   379
    adding crop marks   93
    adding printers   381
    Adobe Type Manager   377-378, 502
    Bitstream Fontware   376
    chapters   391-399, 413
    collated copies   394
    color overlays   406-409
    crop marks   403-406
    double-sided pages   402
    downloading fonts   374, 387, 389-390
    font rasterizers   376-378
    fonts   51, 372, 374-375, 377-378
    multiple copies   393
    page sides   90, 98, 402
    page sizes   91, 400-401
    paper sizes   90
    picture resolution   292, 303
    Print Manager   395-396
    printer drivers   374, 411, 413
    printing to files   410-414
    processes   371-414
    publications   398-399
    registration marks   408
    reversing print order   394
    ruling line resolution   83
    scaling down pages   400
    screen fonts   375, 377-378
    selected pages   392
    selecting printers   378-379
    setting up printers   382, 384
    soft fonts   374, 378, 387, 389-390
    stopping print jobs   397
    tiling pages   400-402
    Ventura's capabilities   4
    width tables   375, 384-386
    WIN.INI   371-377
PUB files (Publication Files)   483, 489
publications
    changing file links   489
    copying   489
    creating   486-487

defined   19, 398, 429
indexes   399, 417, 419, 422, 424-425,
    427-430, 432-433, 435-436
opening   488
printing   398-399
renumbering chapter files   490-491
tables of contents   417, 440, 443, 445-446,
    448, 450

Q

quotation marks   196, 232

R

Re-Anchor Frames command   331, 335-336, 519
Reduced View command   24, 29, 89, 313
registered trademark symbols   196, 232
registration marks   408
relative frame anchors
    See frame anchors
relative indent
    See indenting
Remove Text/File command   191, 327-328
removing tags
    See tags
renaming
    file extensions   193
    tags   47
    text files   192-193
Renumber Chapter command   140, 145-146
renumbering   145, 399, 490-491
repeating frames   322
repeating graphics   288
return-to-normal bracket code
    See also attributes
return-to-normal bracket codes   226
Revert To Saved command   55
right alignment
    See alignment
rotating text   165-166
Ruling Box Around command   78, 107, 260, 353,
    355
Ruling Line Above command   78, 107, 260
Ruling Line Below command   78, 107, 260
ruling lines
    colors   80
    creating   78
    footers   107
    for pictures   351, 354-355
    for tables   247, 258

formatting   76-77, 79-80, 82-83, 152, 167, 247, 258
headers   107
negative spacing   83
patterns   80
placing   78
printing resolution   83
Ruling Box Around   77
Ruling Line Above   77
Ruling Line Below   77
width   77, 79, 81-82, 167
running heads
   See headers

S

Save As command   30
Save command   95, 343
Save Style As command   44
saving
   chapters   30
   customized settings   526
scaling pictures   358-360, 362-363
scanners   295
screen basics
   column guides   16
   Current Selection Box   16
   File List Window   16
   menu bar   15
   Tag List Window   16
   title bar   15
   Toolbox Window   15
   workspace   16
screen captures   299, 308
secondary index entries
   See indexes
Send To Back command   289
Send To Front command   289
Set Column Width command   257
Set Font Attributes command   172, 197, 201, 203, 230
Set Preferences command   14, 44, 49, 103, 260, 350
Set Ruler command   133
Set Tint command   254-255
Settings For   65
setup strategies   525-526, 528
shareware utilities
   CHANGE.COM   504
   FIXCHP.EXE   505
   GREEKER.COM   505
   shareware programs   501

Shift Down By   168
Shift Up By   168
Show Column Guides command   313
Show Loose Lines command   177
Show On All Pages command   288
Show On This Page command   289
Show Rulers command   318
Show Tabs & Returns command   71, 182, 204, 425
Sizing & Scaling command   92, 316-318, 358, 361-362, 365
sizing frames   313, 316
sizing handles   20
Small Cap Size   168
Small text attribute   200
space widths   174-175
spacing
   Above paragraphs   62-64
   Add In Above   64
   Below paragraphs   62-64
   carding   155
   character spacing   375
   column breaks   71
   em spaces   172, 202
   feathering   155
   horizontal   65
   In From Left   65
   In From Right   65
   inter-line spacing   60, 62, 475
   kerning   169-170, 172, 202-203, 229
   letter spacing   169-170, 172-173, 175
   line breaks   71
   loose lines   177
   negative spacing   83, 130
   page breaks   71
   paragraphs   60, 62-65, 71
   separator lines   465
   Settings For   65
   special characters   204
   tables   248-249
   tracking   172-173, 203
   using bracket codes   230
   vertical justification   154, 156, 158, 160
   word spacing   175-176
Spacing command   60, 66, 76, 80, 215
special characters
   ANSI codes for   195, 460-461
   ASCII codes for   195
   breaks   204
   character sets   195
   creating with bracket codes   232
   defined   194
   filled boxes   197

    fonts   195-197
    footnote symbols   460-461
    formatting   204, 232
    hollow boxes   197
    non-keyboard   195
    paragraph markers   204
    spacing   204
    tabs   204
special effects
    big first characters   124, 127, 130
    bullets   118, 120, 122, 124
Special Effects command   59, 119-120, 125
spellchecking   215
Split Cells command   256
spreadsheets
    creating tables   264-265
    exporting data to Ventura   216, 218-219
    saving data to text files   218
starting Ventura   14
strategies
    getting started   8
    graphic design   603-604, 607, 609, 611,
       613-615, 617-618
    paragraph spacing   63
    production   510-511, 513-515, 517, 519-520
    recommended   32, 34, 117
    setup   525-526, 528
    style sheets   49, 522-524
Strike-Thru Height   168
Strike-Thru tag attribute   53
Strike-Thru text attribute   200
STY extension   43
style sheets
    building from default   50
    building from existing   49-50
    defined   15, 18, 41, 43-44
    file extension   43
    formatting   522-523, 549, 551, 553, 555
    loading   23-24, 43, 49, 545
    strategies   49, 522-524
    tables of contents   447
    tag scrapbooks   522-523
Subscript Size   168, 467
subscript text
    See text
Subscript text attribute   200
Superscript Size   168, 467
superscript text
    See text
Superscript text attribute   200
symbol characters   196, 232

T

Tab Settings command   133, 136, 215, 251
Table menu
    Change Settings command   159, 249
    Custom Rules command   259
    Insert Column command   249
    Insert New Table command   159, 243, 246
    Insert Row command   249
    Join Cells command   255-256
    Set Column Width command   257
    Set Tint command   254-255
    Split Cells command   256
table numbering
    See auto-numbering
Table Tool   15, 132, 159, 241-242, 246, 249,
    252-257, 259, 262
tables
    adding colors   254-255
    adding text   250
    alignment   247
    column widths   256-257
    copying rows and columns   253
    creating with spreadsheets   264-265
    creating with word processors   261-264
    deleting rows and columns   253
    editing   252, 254
    formatting   159, 241-242, 244, 246-247,
       249-250, 258, 261-265
    generated tags   49, 259, 262
    inserting   242
    joining cells   255
    overall width   245, 247
    pasting rows and columns   253-254
    ruling lines   247, 258
    selecting cells   252
    setting columns and rows   246
    spacing   248-249
    splitting cells   255
    table graphics   254-255
    table lists   450
    table tag codes   220, 261-264
    table text   251
    Table Tool   15, 132, 159, 241-242, 246, 249,
       252-257, 259, 262
    vertical justification   159, 249
    working with surrounding text   245
tables of contents
    chapter numbers   442, 448
    chapter titles   442, 448
    creating   417, 440, 443, 445, 448, 450
    figure lists   450

file extensions   443
formatting   444-446, 448, 450
generating   445
headings   442
invisible paragraphs   450
multi-level   448
page numbers   447
style sheets   447
table lists   450
tables of contents files   443, 446
tags   443, 447, 451, 580

tabs
   alignment   134
   defined   132
   formatting   132-133, 215
   indexes   437
   special characters   204

tag attributes
   Double Underline   53
   generated tags   49
   Overscore   53
   Strike Thru   53
   Subscript Size   467
   Superscript Size   467
   Underline   53

Tag List Window   16, 43-45, 52

tagging
   defined   22
   in other programs   220-221
   paragraphs   45-46, 220-221
   using function keys   45-46
   using the mouse   45

tags
   Add New Tag command   71
   adding   71
   applying   23-24, 45-46, 220-221
   attributes   41, 50, 52-53, 55-57, 59-63, 65-69, 71-72, 74-75, 77-81, 83-84, 108
   creating   71
   date tags   524
   defined   16, 22, 41, 44
   deleting   47
   footers   108
   footnotes   467
   generated   49, 103, 106, 108, 259, 262, 282, 349-350, 436
   headers   108
   headline tags   579
   new   47, 259
   Paragraph Tool   71
   renaming   47
   special break tags   71

subhead tags   578
table tag codes   261-262
tables of contents   443, 447, 451, 580
tag codes   220-221
Tag List Window   43-45, 52
tag names   221, 524
tag scrapbooks   522-523
Z_BOXTEXT   282
Z_CAPTION   349-350
Z_FOOTER   103
Z_HEADER   103, 106, 108
Z_HIDDEN   259
Z_LABEL CAP   349-350
Z_LABEL FIG   349-350
Z_LABEL TBL   349-350
Z_prefix   49
Z_THICK   259

templates
   chapter templates   506-507
   defined   34, 506
   newsletter templates   506, 511, 513, 565, 567

text
   See also Box Text
   Add Box Text tool   273
   alignment   54-56, 71, 214, 230
   applying attributes   225
   attributes   104-105, 167, 199, 202, 216, 224-225, 227, 251, 476-477
   baseline jumps   230
   Box Text   76, 78, 273, 282, 284
   caption text   342, 348, 590
   column breaks   66, 68-69, 71
   converting text files   192
   copying   199
   creating in Ventura   193
   creating with other programs   209-211, 213-216, 218, 220-221, 223, 225, 227, 229, 232, 234-237
   deleting   199
   editing   21, 187, 198-199, 215
   equations   234, 455, 471, 473, 478
   file extensions   210
   file formats   209-211, 213
   files   88
   footnote text   464, 468
   formatting fonts   50, 201, 203
   fractions   233
   generating with auto-numbering   149
   Greek text   505
   hanging indents   59
   header text   102-103, 105, 107, 534
   hidden text   233

Inside the Windows industry:

Controversy.
Breakthrough technologies.
Product blunders.
Secret developments.
Strategic alliances.
Political maneuvering.
Sneak previews.
Rumors.
Personalities.
And much, *much* more.

Find all the information you need about Windows…
now from a single source.
(Details on reverse side.)

WindowsWatcher — The CompuThink

FREE ISSUE RESERVATION CARD

Yes! Send me my first free issue of WINDOWS WATCHER today. I understand that I'll also receive one Special Report—**FREE**—for just trying WINDOWS WATCHER. If I subscribe, I'll get a full year (12 issues in all) <u>for just $245</u> (International orders, please add $50.) Plus I'll also get eight Special Reports—free with my paid subscription.

If I don't subscribe, I'll return your subscription bill marked "Cancel." The free issue and special report will be mine to keep and I will owe nothing.

Name:_____ Title:_____
Company: _____
Address: _____
City, State, Zip:_____
Tel: (   )_____ Fax:_____

The 1st Newsletter to See *Inside* the Windows Industry

WINDOWS WATCHER is written exclusively for industry executives who need to track the fast-paced Windows market. It's packed with news features, market research, sales tracking reports, product reviews, and surveys *unavailable anywhere else.* Plus one-on-one interviews with industry leaders *you can't afford to miss.* Each month you get in-depth coverage of key business issues, market trends, and fast-breaking technologies. You'll learn:

- What new developments are coming from Microsoft
- What tactics and strategies are behind the winning products
- Which tools will boost your productivity
- Rumors and reflections about alliances, conflicts, and behind-the-scenes politics.

And much, *much* more.

What Industry Leaders Are Saying About Windows Watcher:

"…the most complete coverage of the market…gets to the heart of the politics of Windows computing," Paul Grayson, Founder and CEO, Micrografx Corp.

"…an indispensable tool for developers," Brian Conte, President, hDC Computer Corp.

"…insightful reporting and commentary keeps us abreast of events in the changing marketplace," Rudy B. Batties, Product Marketing Manager, PC Market, Adobe Systems

"First-class! Up-to-date information I can really use," Arlen Bartsch, Sales & Marketing Manager, Corel Systems Corp.

There's no risk, because the first issue is FREE. To receive your free issue, just mail or fax this card today. For more information call: **(206) 881-7354, FAX (206) 883-1452.**

Mail or FAX this order form to:
The CompuThink Windows Watcher
**15127 NE 24TH STREET #344
REDMOND WA 98052-9936**

WINVENTBK

Bestselling References!

WINDOWS™ 3 COMPANION
The Cobb Group: Lori L. Lorenz and R. Michael O'Mara

"Excellent reference featuring dozens of live examples of how different functions work." **PC Magazine**

This comprehensive book shows you how to take advantage of the exciting features of Windows 3.0 to change the way you work with your computer—covering everything from installing Windows to using all its built-in applications and desktop accessories. Novices will value the book for its step-by-step tutorials and great examples; experienced users will turn to it for its expert advice, wealth of tips, and up-to-date information. Full-color section included.

544 pages $27.95   Order Code WI3CO

LASERJET® COMPANION, 2nd ed.
The Cobb Group: Mark W. Crane and Joseph R. Pierce with David A. Holzgang

This complete, comprehensive reference shows you how to get professional printing results from your LaserJet printer—no matter what model or what level of computer experience you have. This edition has been completely updated to feature the latest LaserJet II and III series machines and the newest software, font cartridges, and utilities. A special section covers printing from Windows as well as from the most popular software packages.

704 pages $27.95   Order Code LACO2

RUNNING MICROSOFT® WORD 5.5
Peter Rinearson

Updated to all the new features of Microsoft Word 5.5, this book is filled with insights and strategies; examples; and timesaving ideas, shortcuts, and tips to help Word users of all levels confidently organize, compose, format, index, and print any document. Includes an example-packed command reference and information on advanced features. RUNNING MICROSOFT WORD 5.5 is *the* book of choice for all Word 5.5 users.

704 pages $24.95   Order Code RUWO5

RUNNING MS-DOS,® 5th ed.
Van Wolverton

"Good one-book reference."   **Computer Book Review**

Now updated to include DOS 5, this is the classic, definitive guide to DOS for novice to experienced computer users. Throughout, the author addresses the exciting improvements in DOS 5 while providing in-depth coverage of every major version of DOS. Discover how to control your entire computer system—manage a hard disk, use the built-in text editor, increase your productivity with batch files, and more.

592 pages $24.95   Order Code RUMS5

Microsoft Press books are available wherever quality computer books are sold. Or call **1-800-MSPRESS** *for ordering information or placing credit card orders.* Please refer to* **BBK** *when placing your order.*

In Canada, contact Macmillan of Canada, Attn: Microsoft Press Dept., 164 Commander Blvd., Agincourt, Ontario, Canada M1S 3C7. ☎ 416-293-8141
In the U.K., contact Microsoft Press, 27 Wrights Lane, London W8 5TZ.

Great Resources for Your Desktop Publishing Library— from Microsoft Press!

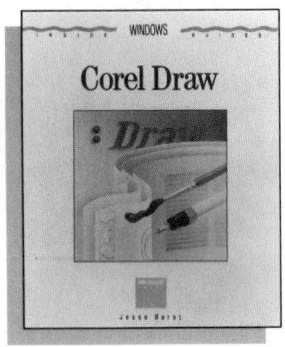

CorelDRAW!
Jesse Berst, Barbara Roll, and James Larkin

Whether you're new to electronic design or a pro, you'll find everything you need to create eye-catching, effective, and dramatic illustrations with CorelDraw version 2. Includes tips for installing Microsoft Windows and CorelDraw; hands-on tutorials; expert advice to help you create better illustrations, a toolkit of valuable, timesaving aids and techniques; and an inspiring portfolio of professionally created illustrations.

512 pages $29.95   Order Code CODR   *Available September*

POWERPOINT® PRESENTATIONS BY DESIGN
Roger C. Parker

A comprehensive reference and creative collection of project ideas for PowerPoint users at any level of experience. An overview of every PowerPoint tool and feature is accompanied by expert advice on designing and preparing slides and overheads. Includes ready-to-create templates and a full-color section of great slides. Covers both the Windows and the Apple Macintosh versions of PowerPoint.

400 pages $24.95   Order Code POPRDE

DESKTOP PUBLISHING BY DESIGN
Ventura Publisher® Edition
Ronnie Shushan, Don Wright, and Ricardo Birmele

Fact-filled, design-oriented resource that is packed with how-to information, layout ideas, and inspiration for anyone new to design, publishing, or computers. The authors offer a primer on the use of basic design elements—typeface, page layout, and graphics. Includes a series of hands-on projects to help you produce exciting, professional-looking printed pieces. The projects use Xerox Ventura Publisher version 2 for the IBM PC and compatibles.

368 pages $24.95   Order Code DEPUDV

DESKTOP PUBLISHING BY DESIGN, 2nd ed.
Aldus® PageMaker® Edition
Ronnie Shushan and Don Wright

"One of the most useful and attractive books we've seen on desktop publishing and design...Full of ideas and inspiration." **The New York Times**

You'll find inspiration as well as technical know-how in this bestselling resource to Aldus Pagemaker covering version 4 for the Apple Macintosh and Windows 3. With plenty of hands-on PageMaker projects, eight pages of color, and a portfolio of finished pieces, this is the book of choice for desktop publishers at all levels of expertise.

440 pages $29.95   Order Code DEPUD2

Colophon

The manuscript for this book was prepared in Microsoft Word. The pages were formatted with Ventura Publisher. The main text was set in Palatino, with display type in Helvetica Black. Output was via a Linotronic 300 laser imagesetter.

Interior design by Barbara Roll
Illustrations by Byron Canfield
Layout by Byron Canfield
Copyediting by Tim Toyoshima and Scott Dunn
Indexing by Anne Edmondson
Cover color separation by Color Control

Printed on recycled paper stock.

About the Authors

Jesse Berst is the founder and publisher of the *Windows Watcher* newsletter in Redmond, Washington. He has authored or co-authored more than a dozen computer books. He is a Contributing Editor of *PC World* magazine, where he produces the monthly Windows how-to column.

Byron Canfield is the founder of Canfield Studios in Seattle, Washington, a consulting and training firm specializing in Ventura Publisher applications. He is a founding member of the Northwest Ventura Publisher Users Group and a contributor to *Ventura Professional* magazine. This is his third collaborative book on Ventura Publisher.

Paul Henry is the president of Program House in Butler, New Jersey. He has written and produced educational audio/visual materials since 1978. He has contributed articles on computer, video, and business topics to magazines such as *Office Systems*, *Interactive Delivery Systems*, *Video Times*, and *A+ Magazine*.

Contributors:

Baseleon, Maria
PC PowerStation
2 Talcott Road Ste. 34
Park Ridge, IL 60068
(708) 825-4727
Services: Graphic Design

Dekeles, Jon C. A.
DMS
4595 E. Highland Drive
Post Falls, ID 83854
(208) 773-7605
(208) 773-2016 FAX
Services: Publishing

Dickson, Deborah W.
IconGraphics
P.O. Box 38265
Dallas, TX 75238
(214) 349-2655
Services: Graphic Design, User Group: DPublisher—The Association for Desktop Publishing

Dugan, Robert F.
Ficom Systems, Inc.
19237 181 Ave. NE
Woodinville, WA 98072
Services: Consulting

Dunn, Scott
CompuTh!nk, Inc.
15127 N.E. 24th
Suite 344
Redmond, WA 98052-5530
(206) 881-7354
(206) 883-1453 FAX
Services: Technical Writing, Consulting, Windows Watcher newsletter

Fermoyle, Ken
22250 Capulin Ct.
Woodland Hills, CA 98364
(818) 346-9384

Holt, Larry N. and Norma J. Curtis
Ventura Pagemaking Center
862 E. Main Street
Ventura, CA 93001
(805) 643-6828
(805) 643-0271 FAX
Services: Typesetting, Consulting

Lubow, Martha
PO Box 948
Quakertown, PA 18951
(215) 536-6743

McLeod, Pamela L.
HyperFormance, Inc.
4906 Fitzhugh Ave. #107
Richmond, VA 23230
(804) 355-0083
Services: Graphic Design, Software Development (VPDesigner)

Modly, Dora M.
1225 Spruce, #2R
Philadelphia, PA 19107
(215) 790-9763

Roman, Sister Barbara
Egeland, Wood, and Zuber
1003 Nott Street
Schenectady, NY 12308
(518) 374-3131
Services: Graphic Design

Ross, John
4222 Interlake Ave N.
Seattle, WA 98103
(206) 545-7900
Services: Consulting, Technical Writing

Saffran, Art
State Bar of Wisconsin
P.O Box 7158
Madison, WI 53707-7158
(608) 257-3838
(608) 257-5502 FAX

Stover, Theresa
Stover Writing Services
2928 Pt. Fosdick Drive
Gig Harbor, WA 98335
Services: Consulting, Technical Writing

Tobin, Randy
Theta Data Type and Design
1309 Riverside Drive
Burbank, CA 91506
(818) 955-5830

Tresman, Ian
Knowledge Computing
18 Fir Tree CT.
Elstree, Herts. WDG 3NF.
United Kingdom
001 4481 953-7722
Services: Consulting

Wickenburg, Greg
3010 Russet Road
Brier, WA 98036

Wood, Elizabeth
Egeland, Wood, and Zuber
1003 Nott Street
Schenectady, NY 12308
(518) 374-3131
Services: Graphic Design, Consulting

Worden, Mark
1530 NE Morris
Roseburg, OR 97470

Young, Herbert C.
Trans Mountain Consulting Co.
123 S. Paradise Road
Golden, CO 80401
(303) 526-9296
Services: Consulting

Young, Robin
Persuasive Technical Communications
18003 - 1st Avenue NW
Seattle, WA 98177
(206) 546-4809

V

Ventura Publisher
    elements of application window   15
    GEM vs Windows version   4
    starting   14
vertical alignment
    See alignment
vertical justification
    carding   155
    chapters   156, 158
    defined   154
    feathering   155
    formatting   154, 156, 158, 160
    frames   156, 158
    paragraphs   159-160
    tables   159, 249
vertical padding
    See padding frames
vertical rules
    between columns   96
    defined   108
    formatting   108
    frames   109-110
    standalone rules   112-113
    underlying pages   109-110
Vertical Rules command   107-108, 111, 113
VGR files (Ventura Graphics Files)   42, 483
VideoShow file format   302
View menu
    Column Snap command   315-316
    Enlarged View command   205
    File List Window command   189
    Line Snap command   315-316
    Normal View command   21, 25
    Reduced View command   24, 29, 89, 313
    Set Ruler command   133
    Show Column Guides command   313
    Show Loose Lines command   177
    Show Rulers command   318
    Show Tabs & Returns command   71, 204, 425

W

Whiskers utility   504
widows   162-163
width
    character width   375
    columns   95, 97
    frames   56
    inter-column widths   110
    ruling lines   77, 79, 81-82, 167
    separator lines   464
    space widths   174-175
    table columns   256-257
    text   56
width tables
    See printing
WIN.INI   371-377, 380-381, 388
    See files
Windows Metafile file format   300
Windows utilities
    Adobe Type Manager   377-378, 380-381, 502
    hDC FirstApps   502
    Whiskers   504
    Windows accessories   501
word processor files
    See file formats
word spacing
    See space width

Z

Z_ prefix   49
Z_BOXTEXT   282
Z_CAPTION   349-350
Z_FOOTER   103
Z_HEADER   103, 106, 108
Z_HIDDEN   259
Z_INDEX LTR   437
Z_INDEX MAIN   437
Z_INDEX TITLE   437
Z_LABEL CAP   349-350
Z_LABEL FIG   349-350
Z_LABEL TBL   349-350
Z_THICK   259

hyphenation   178, 180-181, 215, 230
indenting   54, 57-59, 215
inter-line spacing   60, 62
keeping headings together   72
keeping paragraphs together   72
kerning   169-170, 172, 229
line breaks   66, 68-69, 71, 74
live text   101, 104-105
loading   17, 88, 188, 219, 544, 546, 577-578
loose lines   177
moving   199
moving down to first baseline   163
moving text files   192
non-keyboard characters   195
outdenting   57-59
overall width   56
page breaks   66, 68-69, 71-72
pasting   199
placing   19-20, 188, 190
relative indents   59
removing attributes   199
removing text files   191
renaming text files   192
rotating text   165-167
ruling lines   76-77, 79-80, 82-83
ruling lines around   78
selecting   199
Small Cap Size attribute   168
spacing between letters   169-170, 172-173, 175
special characters   194-195, 197
spellchecking   215
subscript   168, 467
superscript   168, 467
table text   250
Text Tool   15, 21, 46, 199, 517
tracking   172-173
widows and orphans   162
word spacing   175-176
text attributes
   equations   476-477
   removing   200
   using macros to apply   499
Text menu
   Bold command   21
   Change Text To command   200
   Edit Special Item command   427
   Exit Equation Editing command   472
   Insert Special Item command   123, 197, 204, 242, 244, 333-334, 419, 463, 471-472
   Normal command   199
   Set Font Attributes command   172, 197, 201, 203, 230

Text Tool   15, 21, 46, 199, 517
thin spaces   196, 231
TIFF file format   306
Toolbox Window   15
tools
   Add Box Text   78, 273, 511
   Add Frame   15, 29, 280, 312-313
   Box Text   78
   Frame Tool   15, 19, 30, 87
   Graphic   78, 272, 277, 279, 281, 284, 287, 289, 405-406
   Paragraph Tool   15, 24, 26, 28, 45, 71
   Table Tool   15, 132, 159
   Text Tool   15, 21, 46, 199, 517
top alignment
   See alignment
tracking   172-173, 175, 203
trademark symbols   196, 232
trim size   92
type families
   See typefaces
typefaces   50, 52, 202

U

Underline Height   168
Underline tag attribute   53
underlying pages
   columns   94-95, 97-98
   creating text   193
   defined   34, 87
   footers   99-100, 103, 105, 107-108
   formatting   90, 92, 547-548, 569
   headers   99-100, 103, 105, 107-108
   loading text files   88
   margins   94-95, 97-98
   settings   87
   size and layout   89-90, 92
   standalone rules   112-113
   vertical rules   108, 110
units of measurement
   See measurements button
Update Counters command   347, 491
Update Tag List command   45, 48
Upper Case command   200
utilities
   shareware   501, 504-505
   Windows   501-502